What's in a Name

The Story Behind Saskatchewan Place Names

Third edition, with a new Foreword

E.T. RUSSELL

FIFTH
HOUSE
PUBLISHERS

Cover painting, *Coming Dusk, Prairie Village, 1935–c.1940,* by Alexander Musgrove. Reproduced courtesy of the Winnipeg Art Gallery and John P. Crabb.

Cover and front matter design by Brian Smith/Articulate Eye.

Printed and bound in Canada.

The publisher gratefully acknowledges the support of the Department of Canadian Heritage and the Canada Council for the Arts for our publishing program.

THE CANADA COUNCIL | LE CONSEIL DES ARTS
FOR THE ARTS | DU CANADA
SINCE 1957 | DEPUIS 1957

97 98 99 00 01 / 5 4 3 2 1

CANADIAN CATALOGUING IN PUBLICATION DATA

Russell, E.T. Pete (Edmund Thomas Pete), 1910–

What's in a name

3rd ed. / with new foreword by Dennis Gruending.

ISBN 1-895618-98-3

1. Names, Geographical — Saskatchewan.
2. Saskatchewan — History, Local,   I. Title.

FC3506.R87 1997   917.124'003   C97-920083-0
F1070.4.R87 1997

FIFTH HOUSE LTD.
#9–6125 11th Street S.E.
Calgary AB Canada T2H 2L6

Foreword

When I hosted CBC Radio's Morning Edition in the 1980s, we always said proudly that we covered all of Saskatchewan. In that task, part journalism and part history, we used two books as essential references: John Archer's *Saskatchewan: A History* and Peter Russell's *What's in a Name*.

The Archer book covered the broad sweep of history, from prehistoric times through the fur trade, agricultural settlement, and the provincial urbanization and diversification that followed.

Archer's history had a fine companion in Russell's book, which includes hundreds of community mini-histories, telling us how Bay Trail and Fortune, Kuroki and Neuhorst, Nipawin and Saskatoon received their names. The book is accessible—even folksy—dealing with history at a personal level, with all of the accompanying profundity and foible that you might expect.

For example, one might be tempted to believe that Shamrock was the namesake of a settlement in Ireland. But the town appears to have received its name from the emblem on a plug of chewing tobacco popular in 1912. Another community was to be called Botany, testament to a hill covered with brilliant orange tiger lilies in 1910, the year that the townsite was surveyed. But due to a mistake at some level of officialdom, the community name came back as Bounty.

Embedded in these wonderful names, we find our history and even our prehistory. Russell tells us, for example, that the community of Roche Percee near Estevan received its name from an outcropping of sandstone rock taking the form of giant lizards and dinosaurs. One of the rocks, much higher than the others and with a hole through it, was called Pierced Rock by Indians who roamed the Souris Valley. One assumes the later name was provided by French-speaking explorers or Métis traders. In years to come, the village became important for the soft, lignite coal that is strip-mined nearby. Roche Percee, then, contains in its very name a complex combination of histories: geological, aboriginal, exploration, fur trade and contemporary industrial. Many other place names in Russell's book contain a similar mother lode for those who want to understand Saskatchewan.

One must mention in this context what Russell calls "the spirit of optimism" that accompanied many of the people who came to live here, a spirit reflected in the names they chose for their communities: Fortune, Choiceland, Goodsoil, Paradise Hill, Pleasantdale, Plenty, Success, Superb and Supreme.

What's in a Name is a classic. That judgement has been made by more than a generation of people who buy it, read it, and treasure it. My own copy of the third edition, reprinted in 1981, was a Christmas gift from a friend who signed it with a warm inscription. The pages are by now smudged and well-thumbed—another sure sign of a classic. I have, at times, taken it along in the car, reading aloud about places as we drove through them. I have pulled the book from its shelf to add detail and zest to after-dinner conversations about this, that, or the other community. I've used it to settle minor arguments with friends about history and place.

The process of how this book came to be written contains a communal story of its own, one most fitting for Saskatchewan. Mr. Russell was the principal of Henry Kelsey Elementary, an historically named school, in Saskatoon. As he and his wife, Mabel, describe it, he suggested to his students that they search out the stories behind Saskatchewan place names. The fruit of their labor was published in booklet form in 1968.

But for the Russells it didn't end there. This research became both a hobby and a passion, and after Mr. Russell retired, they continued their investigation, traveling in summers to scores of communities, always seeking more information. It must have been a pleasingly social task. They had help from newspapers, which published their requests for information, from librarians, teachers, students and from citizens who, on hearing of the project, wrote letters containing their own recollections about communities that they may have left years earlier, but for which they retained a great fondness.

In their Preface, the Russells talk about the difficulty of updating information on places that no longer exist, except in name. Many small sidings, elevators and post offices have disappeared, even while larger towns and Saskatchewan's cities have grown and prospered. These losses, and this shifting of population, make the preservation of information about communities even more important.

Reynaud, for example, once a small, but thriving hamlet near my hometown of St. Benedict, is now nothing but a farmer's field, with only a stone cairn and a flag to commemorate its existence.

These places, like friends and relatives who have moved away or passed on, contain memories and personalities that we cherish. The Russells understood this, and it informs their work.

What's in a Name is a book that will be as interesting and useful next year as it was last. It's a book that remains on your shelf or in your cabinet, proudly surviving any urge to sacrifice it to garage or school book sales.

What's in a name? A lot as it turns out.

Dennis Gruending
June 1997

Preface

In the fall of 1996 the students and staff of Henry Kelsey Public School started gathering stories on how Saskatchewan places got their names. The findings were published in the booklet "What's In A Name?" on April 9, 1968.

That ended the students' participation in the project, but my wife and I had found the research very interesting, and realizing that we had only scratched the surface with the 679 place names published, we decided to keep on researching.

In order to gather material for the second edition, each summer we spent part of our holidays visiting different localities in the province, where we gathered information first hand.

Each winter *The Western Producer* ran a "Help Wanted" list of the places we didn't have. The resulting response from all across western Canada supplied us with valuable information.

Another source that helped us greatly was the official post office list provided to us by the Saskatoon postmaster, Ivor Flower. It included the "nixie list," which showed the post offices that had been closed and told us where the residents presently received their mail.

At one time these post offices/stores blanketed the prairies back from the railroads and were from seven to ten miles apart. In their day they served a little cluster of farms and were not only a source of mail and supplies but on "mail day" many families gathered there to socialize and get caught up on the news in their own district.

Most of these "inland post offices" have gone, but on the other hand, a few have stayed very much alive.

In preparing the third edition we once again faced the enormous task of attempting to update the information on locations that no longer exist, except in name. Many of these changes occurred in the 1960s and 1970s as a result of amalgamation and realignment of the grain services. Elevators have been closed, moved, and in some cases, torn down.

The third edition represents two years of research, resulting in over 250 new place names and updated information for many others.

As before, we have never claimed to be right; we simply print the different versions of how the places got their names. What we have tried to do is to save some of the facts and flavor of early Saskatchewan history. We hope you find some of that between the covers of this book.

The Russells

Introduction

The steel crept across Saskatchewan in the 1880s. The trains that followed brought settlers from near and far. They fanned out across the prairies and established centers of community life. In many instances the names given to these communities hold not only interesting stories, but help to make up the history of Saskatchewan.

Sometimes these names honored early settlers. For example, Vanscoy commemorated a single pioneer, while the village of Midale honored two of their early residents by combining parts of their names. The surnames of the Bremner, Taylor and Sayers families were joined to form Bresaylor, and at Vawn they honored four men by using an initial from each of their names.

Women played an important part in settling the new land, and some of their names remain: Junior, Beaubier, Lake Alma, Baljennie, Ruthilda and Milden.

It was a common practice of the times to name places for railroad officials; examples are: Melville, Biggar and Kerrobert.

Many settlements chose to commemorate ties with the "Old Land," and so we have a Stockholm, Amsterdam, Stonehenge, Bapaume, Odessa, Muenster, Shamrock and Orkney in Saskatchewan. Some names were just meant to describe the new geographical surroundings: Flat Valley, Bog End and Crooked River.

Names of people prominent in the political life of the times appear at Asquith, Baldwinton, Haultain, Dunning, Chamberlain, Clemenceau and Walpole. Sometimes the whole name was used: Earl Grey, D'Arcy McGee, Viscount Plunkett.

Many of the early settlers of Saskatchewan emigrated from the northern United States, and they named their new communities for their hometowns: Spiritwood, Cando and Cavalier.

Other patterns appear in the place names of Saskatchewan. Before the settlers arrived, the fur traders had stretched across the land, and some of their trading posts remain: Green Lake and Cumberland House.

Hundreds of years before the fur traders entered our province the Indians roamed the plains and forests, and they gave names to places of importance to them: Makwa, Wawota, Wapella, Sheho and Kinistino.

Meota, a village on Jackfish Lake, is a good example of an Indian name. The word Meota is a contraction of Me-Was-In-Ota, the Cree expression for "good place to camp" or "it is good here." This was evident to the Crees because at Meota they found water, wood and game in abundance. They made it a preferred, if not a permanent, place to camp. Today, on the hills that surround this lake, farm implements continue to turn up stone artifacts that date back thousands of years. In places, artifacts and "chips" are numerous. These were the camp sites of Stone Age people. Apparently they, too, found it a good place to camp.

If we were to pick one theme that runs through the letters we have received it would be this: "At one time we were a bustling little place, with stores, elevators, a station, a school, churches, a lumberyard, a livery stable, a hotel, a cafe, a bank, a butchershop, a barbershop and poolroom, a curling rink, etc., etc., and a community hall in which to hold our 'dos.' In short, all that went into the make-up of a typical prairie town. Now we are dwindling."

In some cases it is extremely difficult to locate anyone who remembers the reason for the place names. The face of Saskatchewan is changing; the bigger places are getting bigger, and the smaller places are getting smaller (or in many cases are now ghost towns). Here is a random listing of the major reasons for this trend. First, the consolidation of schools and the virtual disappearance of the one-room rural school. Any place that was chosen as an educational center has grown. Second, the curtailment of service, and sometimes the outright abandonment, of railroad lines. Third, the closing of many small post offices. Fourth, the closing of many small hospitals. Fifth, the conversion to direct dialing of telephones. Sixth, the disappearance of many rural homes. Seventh, the change in grain elevator service. This took place in five stages 1) The outright demolition of elevators—Arma and Indi. 2) The boarding up of elevators and usage of them only for storage—Strong and Swinbourne. 3) The sharing of elevator agents, where one man looks after two points—Fenton and Tiger Hills. He operates on a day basis or by appointment. 4) The moving of an elevator off its foundations and abutting it to another one close by. This enables one person to operate two elevators. 5) The most recent move has been that large elevator companies have bought out smaller ones and "traded off" grain points. Thus you have three "Federal" elevators at Meota handled by one person. At Vanscoy you have four "UGGs." At Revenue you have five "Pools" with one agent and a helper and so on. Much of this was made possible by the quota system of marketing of wheat. The net result was fewer people in the villages where it took place. Read the "Gibbs" story for a good example that illustrates this and one further point— all this curtailment of service despite an increase in wheat acreage in certain parts of the province.

Early in the century there was literally a family on every quarter section of land. The evolution of farm power saw the tractor replace the horse. It became uneconomical to operate a straight grain farm unless you had a large acreage and an outlay of thousands of dollars in machinery. Many small farmers sold out and moved to the towns and cities.

Eighth, and perhaps the most influential reason for the trend, has been the improvement in roads and cars. Not so long ago forty miles was a formidable trip with horses—now, it's forty minutes away. Merchants in small towns can't compete with merchants in the larger towns and cities.

This book completes our efforts in finding the derivation of place names in Saskatchewan. In these pages we have tried to preserve some of the history of a great and noble company of men and women who came to help tame a vast and pathless prairie land a century or more ago. It is to the people who have taken time out from busy lives to sit down and write to us that we are indebted. Without their co-operation we could not have assembled the information for our "What's in a Name" book.

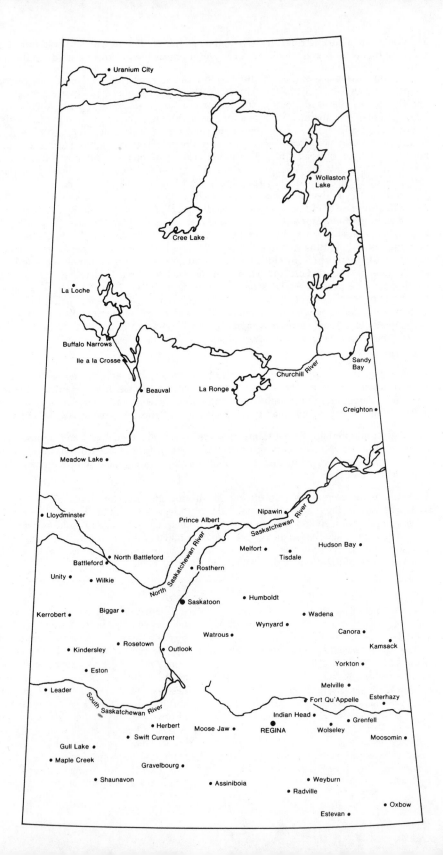

A

ABBEY

The first country post office used by the people of this area was Longworth, located at Cassie Baldwin's home. This post office commenced operations in 1910. In 1913 the CPR purchased a quarter section of land from Dennis Kennedy and established a siding which was named Abbey after a village of the same name in Ireland.

ABERDEEN

Aberdeen is 30 miles northeast of Saskatoon. One of the first settlers was P. W. Dueck. His house later became a store on the spot where Aberdeen now stands.

The name Aberdeen was selected to honor John Campbell Gordon, Marquis of Aberdeen and Temair (1847-1934) a British political leader who served as governor general of Canada from 1893 to 1898.

ABERFELDY

Aberfeldy is the first grain point south and east of Lloydminster on a Canadian Northern (now CNR) line that was built up from North Battleford in 1905.

The Barr Colonists were into this district ahead of the railway and although most of them were British there must have been at least one influential Scotsman either with the Colonists or the railway builders because Aberfeldy is likely named for Aberfeldy, in Perth County, Scotland.

ABERNETHY

The village of Abernethy is a few miles east of Hugonard on CPR line running northeast out of Regina.

The first settlers arrived there in the years 1882 and 1883 from Ontario, the United States and Europe.

The CPR had been extended as far as Brandon; and so they came, travelling by horse and ox drawn carts and wagons, or on foot. The CPR arrived in Abernethy in the year 1904.

W. R. Motherwell, J. R. Dinnin, James Morrison, Tom Rogers, the three Stueck brothers (Englehart, Conrad and John), H.

T. Smith, the Barnsleys and Teece's were some of the earliest settlers.

Tom Rogers was the first man to summerfallow the land in Saskatchewan. During the Riel Rebellion in 1885 Mr. Rogers hauled supplies for the army. He had tilled the soil for seeding and was unable to seed that year. The following year after harvest the crop yield was better than average.

W. R. Motherwell later became Minister of Agriculture and his homestead is presently in the process of restoration.

The first post office was located in James Morrison's house, where Hugh Stueck now farms. About 1905 it was set up in Gillespie and Williams Real Estate office. A few years later it was established in its present location.

The village was named by Reverend Alex Robson, after a town in Scotland from which he came. This enterprising pioneer, typical of the men who settled in the district many years ago, was a stone mason and did most of the masonry on the old stone church, still standing a few miles west of the village.

The Abernethy S.D. #300 was organized in 1890, and a school was built two miles southwest of the village site. In 1905 the first school was built in the village. Several buildings were moved in from Saltoun, including A. A. Hunt's Hardware Store, F. W. Anderson's General Store, Dave Ranson's residence and others. The hotel was built in 1904 and 1905, the old cement school was built in 1906 and the Presbyterian Church, now Knox United, was built in 1906 and 1907.

Abernethy is known as a "dry" town — no licensed premises. A story is told of a business man who had a barrel of whiskey on his premises. Someone reported him. Andrew Penny, justice of the peace at the time, was ordered by police to destroy the evidence. He had the barrel and its contents brought to the north end of town and dumped on the prairie grass. A bystander thought "What a pity some of it couldn't be saved at least for medicinal purposes."

In 1909 the hotel was destroyed by fire. The fire was stopped at the cement wall

1

of the Bank of Hamilton by a bucket brigade. There was no insurance. The business section on the west side of Main Street was destroyed by fire in October of 1932. The east side was destroyed by yet another fire about 1950 and the school in 1954.

A few buildings have been replaced on Main Street. A new school took the place of the old cement one. Since the installation of water and sewage in 1967 the village has been making a slow but steady comeback, and is now mostly residential.

This information was supplied by R. A. Penny of Abernethy in July of 1977.

ABOUND

Abound is at the top of a curve of the CPR that goes around the north side of Old Wives' Lake (for a while called Johnstone Lake). The line was started in 1929 and completed in 1931. When the first settlers came out to the treeless flat prairies of southern Saskatchewan it gave them a feeling that was expressed in many places we know today: Broadview, Broadacres, Longacre and Viewfield. Abound is one such name and Expanse less than twenty-five miles to the south is another.

The McBride ranch was the first settlement in the district. In 1907 Mr. Frank King took up a homestead and he was accompanied by his brother, Nelson, who opened a store and post office just west of what is now Abound. He brought the mail in by horse and buggy each day from Boharm, eight miles north on the main CPR line.

ADAIR

Adair is a short distance south of Wolseley. It was named by Mr. Garrick, the first postmaster, after his hometown in Scotland.

ADAMS

Adams is a short distance west of Regina. It is a shipping point for grain and until 1963 it had a post office. Mr. McNicol opened the first post office in 1910, and F. C. Tate hauled the mail from Grand Coulee until the GTP arrived in 1912. It was named for F. G. Adams, commercial agent for the GTP at the time.

The first elevator was the Security and Ray Smith was the first agent. John and Jim Howe delivered the first grain to Adams. The site of Adams was on the Jack Howe farm. Adams has had its share of sunny times and sad times. Alec Moore was one of the colorful characters of early days. He rode and drove many miles to call for dances and he was much in demand for his step-dancing. He and Sam Purse struck the first furrow west of Regina which is now Dewdney Ave. This was done with two horses and two oxen.

A triple tragedy occurred on the Alec Moore homestead in 1897. A well was being dug by hand and had reached a depth of 80 feet on July 1. When the digging was resumed after the holiday three men, Robert Moore, Charles Beatty, and Mr. Karl, went to the bottom of the well one at a time and never came up alive. They died of poison gas.

ADANAC

The CPR had three surveys in the area in 1905 and 1906. After the present line was decided upon, Adanac was to be Wilkie and the divisional point. Water was a railway problem and when plentiful supplies were found at the present site of Wilkie the two names were changed. CPR officials selected the name which when you spell it backwards comes out "Canada".

Adanac in its "heyday," 1908 to 1914, was a boom town. It had 20 places of business. It had the first Brass Band in the country. The band was formed by Forrest Snell and trained by J. L. "Jack" Martin. The band opened the first fair at Wilkie and at Unity and played at the various picnics and sports days in the area. The highlights of its existence came when W. C. "Billy" Wells, manager of the Galvin Walston Lumber Company, hired the band to open up the townsite of Luseland. They made the trip (30 miles) in Ford cars over country where there were no roads.

Mr. Martin did not confine his music to the band, on wintry evenings he'd hang a lighted lantern on a tall pole in his yard, other poles and lanterns went up around the country and a "dance was on!" How did people know where the dance was being held? The first dance of the year set the pattern to follow. At it the place of the next dance was declared. Often these dances lasted until morning and for a very good reason. It was easier to find your way home in daylight. This was no small problem on the prairies at times, particularly if a blizzard should blow up.

ADELSTEN

Adelsten post office opened September 1, 1937 and closed October 15, 1942. It was situated on NW 20-57-23 W3 near the Canadian-National railway grade between St. Walburg and Loon Lake. This grade was put in but no rails were ever laid. The grade was used in many ways for transportation. Most recently, it is used as a landing strip for aircraft near Loon Lake, so important a facility as our North opens up to tourists.

Fred Adler was the first postmaster and he had a store in connection with it. Both have been closed for years.

ADINE

Adine was a loading platform near Dodsland on a CNR line that runs southwest of Biggar. The railway officials named it and there is no record of why. It has been completely taken out now and the land is farmed. Some of the early settlers who hauled grain and loaded their own cars were: Jim Buckley, Harry Dougall, Bill Catherwood, Jim Bolton, Ole McLeod and Jack Crozier.

ADMIRAL

Admiral is between Scotsguard and Crichton on a CPR line in the southwest corner of the province. It was named for James Crichton (1560-1582), commonly called the "Admirable Crichton." Admiral is a corruption of the word Admirable. Crichton is also named for this man. The traditional account of Crichton's many-sided perfection owes much to the picture of him in Sir Thomas Urquhart's book, "Discovery of a Most Excellent Jewel (1652)."

A distinguished graduate of Admiral is Dr. Rod Wickstrom. He is currently employed by the Saskatoon Public Board of Education as superintendent of planning, development and research.

AIKINS

Aikins, a short distance north of Swift Current, is named for Sir James Aikins. At the time it was named he was solicitor for the CPR and later he became lieutenant-governor of Manitoba.

AITKOW

Aitkow is just south of Elbow and is named for a nearby creek of that name. It is an Indian word for the creek, or "river that turns," which flows from the height of land that divides the Qu'Appelle from the Saskatchewan river watershed.

AKOSANE

Akosane is on a CNR line that runs northeast from Yorkton to Hudson Bay. The name, Akosane, is of Indian origin. It is Cree for: "that is right, that is so, let it be" or "well done." For example, if someone hurt your feelings I might say to you Akosane Keyam. That means "so be it, let it go at that, and never mind."

ALAMEDA

The first post office was opened on December first of 1883 on section 20-3-2, west of the 2nd meridian. It was in a log building belonging to the Walsh brothers in which they had a store for the convenience of the early settlers. This was one of the earliest post offices in the Northwest Territories.

The name Alameda was suggested by Christian Toyor who had spent some time in Alameda, California. The meaning of Alameda in Spanish is an avenue of aspen trees. The only trees of any kind on the prairies at that time were in the Souris Valley at least two miles from the post office. The only other business was a blacksmith shop owned by Mr. Bishop. The mail was hauled from Moosomin once a week by Frank Stephenson. This was Old Alameda and nothing remains of it except a log building and a few bodies in the old cemetery. At a picnic held in Oxbow park in 1932, 31 of the original 82'ers registered in the guest book. These names iclude the following: Dunnigan, McKnight, Miller, Young, Galloway, Trumpour, Shepherd, Truscott, Walsh, Gibson, Deyell, Watson, Coffey, McDonald, McIllvenny, Anderson and McCaughey.

3

When the CPR line came through in 1892 a townsite was laid out on SE 1-43-2, three miles from the first post office and it took the name Alameda.

ALBATROSS

Albatross is the name for any one of several kinds of large sea birds. Albatrosses are found over nearly all oceans except the North Atlantic. The best known albatross is the wandering albatross of southern seas which has a white body and darker wings and tail. The spread of wings may measure up to eleven and a half feet from tip to tip.

The albatross sometimes follows a ship for days feeding on scraps from the kitchen. It seldom stops to rest. It lives ashore only while raising its young. It can easily be caught with a line and hook baited with meat. Sailors have long had strong beliefs about the albatross. It was commonly thought that killing the bird would bring bad luck. Coleridge describes some of these beliefs in his poem "The Rime of the Ancient Mariner."

Just whether the significance of the name Albatross meant good fortune to the early settlers or it meant bad luck we do not know. Perhaps, too, they mistook an eagle or broad-tailed hawk for an actual albatross. Both of these birds can sail endlessly at a great height.

Albatross is a siding a few miles north of Regina on the CPR line to Prince Albert.

ALBERTOWN

Albertown is a rural post office at 34-45-10-W3. It was named for the first postmaster Mr. J. Albert Fenderlet. It is near Hafford and Alticane.

ALBERTVILLE

Albertville is on a CPR branch line from Prince Albert to Nipawin. It was named in honor of Henry Albert Morin who was responsible for bringing 32 French settlers into the district in 1912.

Albertville has two unique features, the church (La Paroise St. Jacques) and the Credit Union. The original small church was built at Henribourg which is 4 miles to the west. After it was moved to its present site it was greatly enlarged and the high steeple is visible for miles

around. About 120 families are served by the parish.

When the railroad came through in 1932 the grain point (one Pool elevator) one mile north of the church took the name Albertville. It was never more than an elevator. In 1966 it was dismantled and the usable lumber was taken to Floral, Saskatchewan, to build an addition to an elevator there.

One building on the main street of the village stands out. Its sign reads:

La Caisse populaire
D'Albertville
Credit Union

Caisse Populaire is the French name for "people's bank". It was started in 1916 by the parish priest, M. l'abbé Albert Lebel. This was 20 years before there was a Credit Union Law! Father Lebel patterned this bank after the Desjardin's Caisse Populaire that he had watched grow in Lévis, Quebec. It was strictly a parish Credit Union at that time. As the early settlers had very little cash in those days, loan security was based on a man's good name. Father Lebel acted as secretary-treasurer until he left in 1926. His report of 1920 showed that $85,000 worth of business had been transacted.

In the 30s the Credit Union folded. In 1950 it was reactivated and its growth was steady. In 1960 it had 224 members, with assets of $213,000. The rented building that it had operated in was bought outright and remodelled into a fully modern bank with self-contained living quarters. Roman Brunwald became the full-time and salaried manager.

The new bank was officially opened on November 27, 1962. On this occasion a plaque was presented to Caisse D'Albertville by the Credit Union League of Saskatchewan. Two originals, Mr. Joseph Lavie and Mr. Alphonse Roberge, received honorary certificates.

Albertville oldtimers in 1968 included: Mrs. Victoria Beauchesne (who celebrated her 99th birthday on July 11, 1968), Mrs. Henri Pellerin, Mr. Joseph Lavoie, Mr. C. Brassard, Mr. Leandre Brassard and Mrs. Arthur Painchaud.

ALDINA

Aldina, an inland post office and store (now closed) was situated six miles west of Leask on the north shore of Paddling

Lake. Almost all of Paddling Lake is within the Muskeg Indian Reserve.

How it got its name is a mystery. However, there is no mystery about a remarkable man, Arthur Verreault, who lived near there for sixty-five years. Born in Salem, Massachusetts, Mr. Verreault spent his early years as a sailor. He came to Canada at the age of twenty-seven and farmed at Aldina. He sold his land in 1972 and retired to live in Saskatoon with his daughter, Mrs. Anne Barry. Mr. Verreault was a carpenter by trade, and over a long career worked on many public buildings, most notable of which were the Roman Catholic churches at Muskeg Lake, Bear Lake, Duck Lake and St. Laurent.

On February 12th, 1977 Arthur Verreault celebrated his 104th birthday.

ALFORD

The rural post office of Alford served a wide area in the early days. The nearest towns were Swift Current, sixty miles to the south and forty or more miles north to Zealandia.

It was operated by Mrs. Percy Alford, after whom the post office was named. Early settlers into the area were: the Coakwell brothers, and Harry and Archie Russell.

ALGROVE

Algrove is between Archerwill and Barford on a CPR line that runs north from Wadena to Nipawin. Back in 1931 when the line was put in, the people wanted it to be called Glenbush or Glenside. Neither was acceptable because both names had been used already.

A committee then suggested that it be named for Mr. Walter Allgrove who had been in before the railroad. He was an Englishman and a veteran of the First World War. The name came out as Algrove when someone dropped an "l".

Algrove at one time had a small train station, a Co-op store, a post office, a garage and a school. All this has disappeared and the few families left have their children bussed into Archerwill for school. Residents of Algrove now get their mail by a rural route. The ladies club of the community bought the schoolhouse from the Wadena School

Unit for fifty dollars. It is now used for card parties, dances, weddings and funerals.

ALIDA

In 1913 in the extreme southeastern corner of the province the CPR built a branch line from Manitoba to Saskatchewan that ended with Storthoaks, Nottingham and Alida. The president of the CPR named the townsite Alida after Lady Alida, the wife of Sir Harry Brittain an English author who had played a large part in the Imperial Press Conferences of the day. These had, in turn, worked for mutual understanding among the various parts of the British Empire.

ALINGLY

Seven miles straight west of Spruce Home is the inland post office and store of Alingly operated by Mrs. Mary McKay.

The first store in the district was a log cabin trading post about two miles northeast of the present store. It was opened in 1906 by Vic Belt. He traded furs for flour, tea, lard, bacon and other staples. In the winter he supplemented his income (as did many settlers) by freighting goods from Prince Albert to Montreal Lake, La Ronge, and Stanley Mission. They used two and four-horse outfits and travelled in groups in order to "double up" on the hills. This district was filled in (one family to a $10-quarter-section-homestead) by 1908. It was a predominately English settlement. Harold Longley was responsible for naming the district and he chose to honor his native village of Alingly, Sussex, England. In the early days the country was solid bush and, as Mr. Colin Belt put it, "You could get lost anywhere." Today good farms dot this picturesque part of Saskatchewan.

When war broke out in 1914 forty-eight men from the district answered the call to arms and the following fourteen lie buried in France: John Chisholm, Angus McLeod, Tom Long, John Belt, Harry Dennis, Monty Kemp, H. Elliott, Len Deveney, Fred Spratt, Frank Evans, Walter Hilton, S. Nickerson, E. Coppell and Yves Schoan. An imposing special shaft of granite in the centre of the local cemetery commemorates their sacrifice.

5

ALLAN

By coming overland from Rosthern with oxen and one tent nine families first set foot on what is now the townsite of Allan. The families were Heislers, Leiers, Boechlers, Garmans, Silbernagels, Krafts, Volks, Zacher and Bitz. They were mostly of a Russian-German heritage who through hardship and endurance saw the railway and townsite simultaneously put Allan on the map in 1908.

From 1903 to 1905 mail was addressed to Dundurn, District of Assiniboia, N.W.T. From 1905 until 1908 the mail came addressed to Kurzen P.O., Dundurn Assiniboia, N.W.T. But in 1908 the post office of Allan came into being. It was named for two reasons — first, a foreman on the railway was Allan and second, the towns were being named in alphabetical order on either side of them.

Wald and Diebert put up the first store which today has been replaced by Boechlers Store which stands on the same spot. In 1910 Mr. A. A. Fraser started printing the *Allan Tribune*. Four lumber yards served the area and by 1912 National Grain built the first grain elevator. The twenties were good to Allan and it rooted iself enough to survive the thirties despite a block destroyed by fire that levelled most of the commercial area.

During the forties fifty-seven from the area and village went off to war. None were lost in action but three returned having won the Distinguished Flying Cross.

The fifties centered on the advancement of education and the school increased to a teaching staff of eighteen teachers. This was good because in the mid sixties a potash shaft was sunk just north of town and an influx of people demanded more facilities.

The proximity to Saskatoon seemed to have curbed speculators, however, there are adequate businesses to serve the 800 or more people with good service.

ALLAN HILLS

Allan Hills was a rural post office about 20 miles south of Allan up in the gently rolling and sometimes rocky hills. It is from these hills that the Arm river rises to flow south parallel with Last Mountain lake and abruptly turns west to enter it at Regina Beach.

The first post office in Allan Hills 15-31-1-W3 was run by J. T. Holmes. Mr. F. R. Crook followed and then it was taken over by Mr. Tom Ellis and he ran it until it closed 35 years later. During that time they missed delivering the mail from Allan, twenty miles to the north, twice; both times they were forced to stay in Allan because of blizzards. The post office was closed in 1952.

Patrons of the Allan Hills post office included W. Holmes, Earl Steaffer, F. R. Crook, George Bowler, E. W. Ellis, Alec Bruce, P. B. Thomas, A. R. Atkinson, Harold Reeves, J. W. Barnes, Tom McCaul, Billy Ferguson, Harry Anderson, Bennie Todman and Moses Schwartz.

It was in Arm River while running as provincial leader that John Diefenbaker lost in 1938. It was in Lake Centre which takes in Arm River and the Allan Hills that he was invited to run federally in 1940. Although he was practicing law at Wakaw, outside the constituency at the time, he ran and was successful. He represented the Lake Centre constituency until 1953. In 1953 he ran successfully in Prince Albert and has been their member until the present.

ALSASK

Alsask is in west-central Saskatchewan right at the Alberta border. It takes its name from its location. The railway officials took the first two letters of Alberta and the first four letters of Saskatchewan to make "Alsask."

ALTAWAN

Altawan sits within six miles of the Alberta border in the extreme southwest corner of the province. The CPR officials named it and like Alsask, 150 miles to the north, the name is a combination of parts of the words, Alberta and Saskatchewan. Old timers relate how hard it was to get a good supply of water. Wells had to be dug by hand. This was hard work and until a good well could be found, snow in winter and slough water in summer was the best they could do. Slough water was hauled in barrels. Next the "wigglers" had to be strained out and the resulting chocolate mixture boiled before it was fit for use. As lemons did not grow on the northern prairies and were expensive to buy, the best way to deal with the water was to make it into coffee. This, in part, accounts for the heavy coffee drinking of the early settlers.

ALTICANE

Alticane is on a branch line between Speers and Mayfair. The first post office in the district was two miles southwest of the present town. It was run by Mr. McKye and he had named the post office Alticane, after his home town in Scotland.

When the Canadian National came through in 1928 the post office moved into the town and gave it its name.

AMAZON

Amazon is between Renown and Simpson on a CPR line. It was probably named for the Amazon river of South America, one of the really big rivers in the world. It contains more water than the Nile, the Mississippi and the Yangtze rivers together. It is 3,900 miles long and is exceeded in length by only one river, the Nile.

The first homesteaders settled in the Amazon district in 1904. They drove across the prairies from Davidson, the nearest railway, some 40 miles to the southwest. In 1910, the earthen grade for the CPR was built with horses and hand scrapers and the track then laid. A post office was established and the name Amazon chosen for the hamlet. The school was built in 1913 and opened with Miss Annie Reid as the first teacher. Some of the early settlers were J. Myhr, M. Kennedy, J. Badger, R. Douglas, J. Parry and J. Jorgenson.

AMBASSADOR

Ambassador is between Nokomis and Lockwood on a main CPR line that runs from Regina to Lanigan.

An ambassador is a person who represents the government of his country at the capital of another country. His headquarters are called an embassy. His duties are numerous and range from keeping the peace to promoting trade.

AMBLER

Ambler post office was twelve miles straight north of Annaheim. It opened in 1910 with Mr. Butler Ambler as postmaster. He hauled mail and supplies from St. Gregor. Later he hauled from Annaheim which is a rural post office. Butler and Ole Ambler came from Grand Forks, South Dakota. Mrs. Olga Lorenz (nee Ambler) remembers once of her father, Ole, accepting a ride with a bachelor to go the two miles to the store for supplies. The transportation consisted of a span of oxen and a stoneboat. It was rough going as the snow had hidden some of the stumps. On arriving home the groceries and mail were taken out of the flour sack only to find that the top had jarred off the syrup can and it was one sticky mess — mail, groceries and all.

In 1915 Mr. Butler Ambler took ill and returned to South Dakota where he passed away. Then the post office started a series of moves until, in 1918 when Mr. C. Saunders had it, the office closed.

AMELIA

Amelia was a country post office near Climax that opened in 1911 with Henry Huseby as postmaster. He named it after his wife, Emelia. Whether he accidentally substituted an A for an E or whether they made an error in reading his handwriting is not known but the name came back from postal officials Amelia. When this happens the post office frowns on any changes.

Mr. Huseby operated a store in connection with the post office and supplied the needs of life, saving the farmers many a trip to town to get a bag of flour or oatmeal.

AMIENS

Amiens is on a line between Shellbrook and Medstead. It is named for Amiens, a city and important rail centre on the Somme river in northern France.

Amiens, France, was the prime objective of the last great drive to the coast that the Germans started in March, 1918. They hoped to take this railhead and split the English forces in the north from the French and American forces in the south then roll the English to the Channel and the French back to Paris before the Americans could make their weight felt.

Amiens saw some of the most critical, sustained, and fiercest fighting of the war but it did not fall. The drive was blunted and finally stopped by the Canadian Cavalry Brigade. Marshal Foch, the Com-

7

mander-in-chief of the Western Front, said of this battle, "I shall never forget the heroism of the valiant Canadian Cavalry."

AMSTERDAM

Amsterdam is located 40 miles north of Yorkton. The CNR came through in 1912 and it was the beginning of the railway to Hudson Bay. The first homesteader was Joe Van Westernhouzen from Holland. Many of the settlers that followed were also from Holland and they named the townsite, Amsterdam, in honor of the largest city in their homeland.

AMULET

In 1910 a railway official picked up a trinket dropped by one of the workers, on the temporary platform of the station to be, and decided to name the site Amulet, which means charm.

On land that was part of the Jack Dicken homestead, Jack Harris built a large building in two parts; a restaurant and a poolroom. A large hall upstairs was used as a temporary school in 1910, with Gill Hulbert as the teacher of 15 pupils.

Amulet, always sportsminded, had their first sports day in 1912. There were baseball games and horse races. The Ogema band was in attendance and the Erickson Orchestra, consisting of Oscar, Pete, Gus, and John played for the big dance at night.

The station agent was removed from Amulet in 1933. One by one the business places were closed, the owners moving to larger centres or retiring. Today Amulet's once thriving L-shaped main street consists of many empty lots and vacant buildings.

Jack Thompson, who as a 13-year-old boy in knicker pants, climbed the stairs to attend school above the poolroom, runs the only business place in Amulet, with the exception of the Pool and Searle elevators. He owns and manages a combined garage, post office, and store.

ANCRUM

Ancrum is the second railway point north of Young on a CNR line that runs to Prince Albert. It was possibly named for the market town of Ancrum at the junction of the Ale and Teviot rivers in Roxburgh County, Scotland.

ANERLEY

In 1912 the CNR extended its line from Saskatoon via Macrorie to Anerley. The name had already been chosen, as O. J. Hopkins, who was the first postmaster and had the office in his home, had named it for the suburb of London, England, from which the Hopkins family came. The office was in his farm home until the railroad came, after which it moved into a local store in the new hamlet.

Anerley School No. 2277 was also there before the railway, having been built in 1909 five miles from the present townsite. In the late fall of 1915 it was moved to town. A huge steam engine, operated by Mr. Ramback, skidded the school in. It caused some excitement. Sparks from the steamer and from the skids hitting stones, set the tinder-dry prairie wool on fire and before it was finished most of the townsfolk, who had come to watch, ended up by pounding out the fires with wet gunny sacks.

In its day Anerley was a busy little town but now it's down to a population of 14 and the three Pool elevators are operated by Bill Cragg. He's an enthusiastic man and in 1969 he bought the only store in town and has converted it into one of the finest little museums you'll find in Saskatchewan.

The store was formerly operated for over forty years by Percy Higgitt, who in 1921 gave up his nearby homestead to move to town. At first he was the Imperial Oil agent and grain buyer for the Canadian Consolidated Grain Company and later he took over the store and post office. Mr. Higgitt spent many hours in public service to the community in various capacities covering a period of forty-six years. He retired in 1967 and he and Mrs. Higgitt now make their home in Outlook.

Their son, Leonard, is not only commissioner of the RCMP, but is the head of Interpol, the international police organization that has a communications and an intelligence network which links 114 countries. He will occupy that office for four years. What an honor to Canada, to the RCMP and to a Saskatchewan boy, born and raised at Anerley!

8

ANEROID

This Saskatchewan town, situated in the southern part of the province on a CPR line that runs from Weyburn west to the border, owes its name to a lost article. Aneroid marks the spot near which a survey partly lost an aneroid barometer.

One of the best known persons to come out of Aneroid was Cecil "Ace" Corbin. After a very successful baseball career of 27 years he took up umpiring where he was colorful and played no favorites. Ace, now 64, is still active as an umpire. On Sunday, July 23, 1972, the Saskatoon Baseball Council and the Saskatoon Commodore Booster Club, staged an "Ace Corbin night" just prior to a game with the Yorkton Cardinals. Ace remarked after it was over that it was the only time in his life that both the crowd and BOTH teams stood up and cheered him at the same time.

ANGLIA

Anglia is between Herschel and Rosetown on a CPR line. It was named by British settlers for their old hometown in England. Anglia at one time was the name for England.

ANNAHEIM

Annaheim is a short distance northeast of Humboldt. It is named for St. Ann's parish there. The parish was established on July 26, 1903, and since that day was the feast of St. Ann, the mother of the Blessed Virgin, the new parish was called St. Ann. Later the post office was changed to Annaheim, "the home of Ann."

ANTELOPE

Antelope is between Webb and Gull Lake in the southwest corner of the Great Sand Hills. It was named for that inquisitive, sleek speedster, the prong-horned antelope of the plains. (You can see one on the side of any STC bus.)

Wild animals were abundant on the prairies in the early days and we find many towns and villages named directly for them. In fact, two are named for antelope, the other being Cabri, also on the edge of the Great Sand Hills a little to the north. Cabri is an Indian word meaning antelope. Others are Waskesiu, named for red deer; Red Deer Hill and Deer Ridge. Possibly the best known of

the animals in the early days was the buffalo and we find his name from north to south: Buffalo Narrows, Buffalo Gap, Buffalo Horn, and Buffalo Head. Bears, particularly the silver-tipped grizzly, preyed on the buffalo herds and we have a White Bear and Bear Creek. Foxes were everywhere: at Fox Valley, Fox Hill, Foxdale, White Fox and Foxford. If you want a real fox story read Sintaluta

Saskatchewan produced its share of beaver in the fur-trading days and this peerless engineer created meadows on many a prairie creek and so we have a Beaverdale and Big Beaver, the latter almost at the international boundary!

There were rabbits all over, not just at Rabbit Lake. Moose Range was named for what is today one of the few "trophy" animals left. This does not exhaust the place names of the province derived from animals. Their great numbers made such a deep imprint on the minds of early settlers that many places in Saskatchewan bear names with animal connotations.

The first winter after the Antelope area was declared open for homesteading was 1906-1907. It was a terrible winter which lasted from October until May. There were many ranches in the district prior to this with the "76" the largest. Their losses were in the thousands that year. Settlers' fences did not help the cause. In the spring they were invariably heaped with frozen cattle that had drifted with the storm.

Some of the first to take up land were the following: Frank Appleyard, Dick Steele, Tom Keatley, and John Small. The latter with five other homesteaders survived the winter of '06-'07 in a 12 by 14-foot frame shack.

ANTLER

The village of Antler is the first stop of a CPR line just inside the Saskatchewan border in the southeastern corner of the province. It got its name from Antler creek which flows from northwest to southeast three miles west of the village. Early settlers arrived in 1894 and many of their descendants still live in the district: George, Corbet, Sylvester, Dellet, Ramsay, Delaite, Harris, and Steele.

The railroad arrived at Antler in 1900 and the first load of grain was delivered by Walter Churcher.

AQUADELL

The first post office opened in this district in 1912 in a little valley (dell) near a small lake (aqua). It moved several times and when the CNR branch line was put in from Mawer to Main Centre in 1930 the post office moved to the townsite, less than four miles from the site of the original post office. The CNR has now applied for abandonment of this line.

AQUADEO

Aquadeo, on the north shore of Jackfish lake, was incorporated as a hamlet in 1970. Prior to that it was known for years as Delaney's Beach.

In the 1940's Mr. and Mrs. Clarence Delaney acquired farmland which fronted on the lake. They decided to develop a tourist resort on their lake frontage and they worked hard at it.

Their first major promotion was a rodeo. It was successful and to this they added water (aqua) sports. The Delaneys then named the resort Aquadeo by combining water "Aqua with Rodeo".

The rodeo closed out in the late 1950's and was replaced by a nine-hole golf course. This, too, proved successful and many people began to build cabins by the lake.

The Delaney family worked in the short summer season to make theirs one of the cleanest beaches on the lake.

In 1971 Mr. Delaney was able to purchase the convent building at Jackfish and he had it moved to Aquadeo. He renovated it into a two-story Aquadeo Beach Golf Club House, complete with licenced premises for members.

The hamlet continued to expand and by 1976 the store, coffee shop and marina were catering to a summer population of 150 cabins and 111 trailer court spaces with power.

Mr. Delaney's son, Pat, is now in partnership with his Dad and including family and friends, a staff of twenty take care of summer residents.

In winter it's another story, everything closes down and the population drops to the Delaney family.

ARABELLA

Arabella is an inland post office south of Swan Plain. It is located at 34-35-1-W2. The first postmaster, Donald Currie, named it for his wife, Arabella.

ARBORFIELD

Arborfield is the end of the steel on a branch line north of Crooked River. The first settlers arrived on June 8, 1908. It was to be 20 years before they were serviced by a railroad. Aubrey, George and William Miller, along with Jim Pickering and Frank Cummings were the first to push on to the new settlement after leaving their wives at Tisdale where they had arrived by train from Ontario. A large group of settlers, under the guidance of Father Berube, arrived from New Bedford, Mass. in the spring of 1910. This was also the year in which a post office was granted for the new area. The name suggested to postal authorities was Fairfield. But there was already a community by that name in Saskatchewan. The letter carrying the suggested name arrived at postal headquarters on Arbor Day so postal authorities came up with the substitute name of Arborfield and it was accepted.

ARBUTHNOT

Philip Stapleton and William O'Dell filed on homesteads in the district at Moose Jaw in the spring of 1909. They bought a load of lumber in Rouleau and started on the way to their land 150 miles to the southwest. There were no roads and even trails were poor. After they arrived in the general vicinity it took them two days to find the stakes for their particular section. While Mr. Stapleton stayed to build the shack and "prove up", his partner, Mr. O'Dell, went 24 miles north to work for a farmer. (Mr. Stapleton still lives on his original farm and part of his present house is built from some of the lumber he brought in with him in 1909.)

At first they got their mail from the post office at Morse which was 50 miles away. When the CPR came through it was first decided to name the district Stapleton, for Philip Stapleton, but the CPR later decided on the name Arbuthnot in honor of Sir Robert Keith Arbuthnot (1864-1916), English rear-admiral in command of the first cruiser squadron at the battle of Jutland (May 31, 1916), who sank with his cruiser, Defence, when it was destroyed by German fire.

ARCHERWILL

Archerwill is about halfway between Nipawin and Wadena on a CPR line. Mr. William Pierce was secretary-treasurer of the R.M. of Barrier Valley No. 397 from January 1, 1918 to March, 1938. When the CPR railway was constructed from Wadena to Tisdale in 1924, a name was needed for the new townsite and members of the R.M. met in Mr. Pierce's home, which served as municipal office. He and two council members, Archie Campbell and Ernie Hanson, worked out the name of Archerwill by using the first letters of each of their names — ARCHie, ERnie, and WILLiam.

ARCHIVE

On a CPR line south of Moose Jaw to Mossbank you have Archive, Buttress, Crestwynd, Dunkirk and Expanse. There was little significance to these names because the railway just went about getting them in alphabetical order.

ARCHYDAL

Archydal is a hamlet of 11 people on a line that runs northwest from Moose Jaw to Riverhurst. Archy Dalrymple and the Getty brothers arrived in 1882. When the CNR went through in 1914 it crossed the land Mr. Dalrymple lived on. The Railway officials named it for him by taking his first name and combining it with the first three letters of his second name.

George Dalrymple, a son, and his two brothers still farm in the district.

ARCOLA

Arcola is a town 113 miles southeast of Regina on the CPR Regina-Souris line. Peter McLellan, the first postmaster in the district, selected the name Arcola. Arcola is a small place in Northern Italy where in 1800, Napoleon defeated the Austrians. Because of this battle, Arcola, like other small places where important battles have been fought — Waterloo, Lundy's Lane and Hastings — became famous. That is why Mr. McLellan chose it for the name of the new town.

ARDATH

In 1909 T. H. Vincent started a general store and post office in his home three miles north of the present village site. The names for the post office that he sent in were turned down and so he asked Bruce Girvan for a suggestion. The name he picked was Ardath from the book by the same name by Marie Corelli.

In the spring of 1911 the CNR built south from Delisle to Conquest. Mr. Todd started a store in the new village that sprang up by the tracks and he wanted a post office. Mr. Vincent did not wish to keep his any longer so it was moved from his home into the village and this country post office gave its name to Ardath.

ARDILL

This is from the Pion-Era Press of 1965:

"The story goes that Ardill was named because of a cockney Englishman who claimed that the road up from the river to the settlement was a 'damned 'ard 'ill' for his team to climb."

ARDWICK

In Saskatchewan Ardwick is between Stonehenge and Lakenheath on a CPR branch line that wanders west out of Assiniboia and ends at Mankota. Many of the earliest settlers came from Scotland and they wanted to call their town Ardwell. Postal officials declined and so they settled for Ardwick.

In Scotland, Ardwell is between Sandhead and Drummore on the east coast of Luce Bay. It is one of the most southern towns in Scotland.

ARELEE

Arelee is between Environ and Struan on a branch line of the CPR built north from Urban Junction in 1927. It was headed for Battleford but ended short of it at Baljennie.

Two of the first settlers into this area were Fred Fertuck and Harry Smith. They came in the early 1900's and by 1903 a sizeable community was established. Mrs. Stewart Currie had the first post office in her farm home two miles north of the present town. There are two versions as to how it was named. The first story is that Arlee, submitted by W. J. Forsyth Jr., in honor of the school hockey team on which he played in Lake Whitewater, Manitoba was chosen. However, when the stamp for the post office arrived a mistake had been made in spelling and the name came out Arelee.

The second story comes from Mrs. Spinks, wife of Dr. Spinks, former president of the University of Saskatchewan. She was raised in Arelee. Her version is that in the early years immigrants to Saskatchewan tended to settle in ethnic blocks and many of the early settlers near Arelee were from Russia. In former years eagles were plentiful in the area and in the Russian language Arelee means eagles.

So, take your pick. In "What's In A Name?" we have never claimed to be right; we simply print the different versions of how places got their names. What we have tried to do is save some of the facts and flavor of early Saskatchewan history.

Of one thing we are certain — when the CPR arrived in 1927, Mrs. Currie's Arelee post office moved two miles south to the townsite and gave it its name.

ARGO

In 1911 the Grand Trunk Railway built southwest of Biggar through Ruthilda. It crossed the meridian at Alsask and was headed for Hannah, Alberta. It stopped short at Hemaruka; but that's another story. The steel was laid through Argo, the first stop out of Biggar, in 1912. Mr. Charles Keeley, who still resides in the district, was a mule skinner on the work crew that built the grade. Teams of mules or horses hitched to a big two-handled scoop called a scraper were used to move the dirt. These scrapers came in two sizes, the smaller one could be loaded and dumped by the driver but on the larger model the "grade foreman" took one handle while the driver took the other and they flipped the bucket to empty the earth where desired.

Two elevators, the Scottish Co-op and the Saskatchewan Co-op, were built and soon all the usual buildings of a small prairie town popped up: the railway station, the section house, the store and post office, the cafe, the blacksmith shop, the lumberyard and the pool hall.

By 1968 it was all gone except one Pool elevator and the house where Mr. R. K. Jones, the agent, lived. Where the town used to be is all farmland.

ARMA

The Saskatchewan *Valley News* of Tuesday, July 13, 1972, carried the final story on Arma. It was entitled "End of an Era." "The modern trend of centralization of facilities has witnessed the demise of many old establishments, not the last of which are the sentinels of the prairies, as the grain elevators are often referred to. Small grain points give way to larger and more modern facilities in larger centers. The Saskatchewan Wheat Pool Elevator No. 909 at Arma, four miles south of Rosthern, is a case in point. Built in the summer of 1928 this elevator served the community for four decades, and was closed down three years ago. Saskatchewan Wheat Pool demolition crews moved in Monday morning. All salvageable dimensional lumber and equipment will be offered for sale. An estimated three weeks will be needed to dismantle the building."

No building of any kind grew up around the elevator except the agent's house. The last agent was D. J. Lueke who moved there on April 30, 1968, and was there when the point closed on July 31, 1968.

Henry Markwart lives within a stone's throw of Arma on SW¼-10-42-3-W3. His grandfather, Adolf, homesteaded there in 1898. Adolf's brother, Otto, farmed a half mile southwest. It was the center of a German-Lutheran community.

In 1900 the railway erected a flag station and suggested that it be called Markwart because it was on land adjoining both homesteads. The Markwart brothers declined and instead selected the letters A R M A from their name and that's what the station was called. When the Pool built an elevator in 1928 it adoped the same name.

Between highway 11 and the railway, on land donated by Otto Markwart, is a well-kept little cemetery. There are fifty-two graves — 25 marked and 27 unmarked. In the 25 marked graves there is one Breadlaw, two Pauls, two Rotenburgers, nine Knuths, and eleven Markwarts.

When interviewed at his home Mr. Markwart told the story of his interesting house. It looks like something out of seventeenth-century Germany. The two entrances, six dormers and bay windows are beautifully decorated with tiny wooden pillars, spikes and scrolls. When it was built by Gustav Furst in 1907 to house a family of ten, it was the talk of the country.

Today (1972) Mr. Markwart has visitors after visitors who come to see and photograph this unique building. One feature which Mr. Markwart is proud to show his guests is the surveyor's stake which is imbedded in the northwest corner of the fieldstone and cement foundation. From it many places were located and many arguments settled as homesteads were being laid out in the early days.

Asked about a story of the pioneering days he recalled one that concerned the railroad. It was in the days before the snowplow and trains had great difficulty in bucking the heavy drifts. After a big blow farmrs were hired at $1.50 a day and "all found" (i.e. food and lodging included), to accompany the train in to Saskatoon or Prince Albert. When the train got stuck they shovelled it out. Farmers welcomed this cash, always a scarce item with homesteaders, and besides, they got a free roundtrip into the city!

ARMIT

Armit is the last stop in Saskatchewan on a Canadian National Railway line that runs east from Hudson Bay to Swan River, Manitoba. It was named for the Armit River which rises north of the village and flows south and east into Manitoba, where it empties into Armit Lake.

When the line went in first the main industry was pulpwood, and although Armit was never the site of a mill, there were many nearby.

At its height, the village consisted of a school, a combined post office and store operated by Mr. and Mrs. Skilleter, a Department of Natural Resources house, a station, section crew and several residences.

This information came from Leslie Hoffus of Prince Albert, who as a girl lived there for a time.

ARMLEY

Armley is on a CPR line about twenty miles south of Nipawin. The first settlers into this area came from England and Ontario in 1909.

The railway didn't arrive until 1924. Those laying the track wanted to call the place Pickthall. However, there was a Pickthall south of Assiniboia. Early residents, particularly the Nicklens and the Berrys, suggested that the name be Armley.

Armley was a large jail in England near which many of the early residents had lived and in which some of them had worked.

Armley, in the late 1920's, was a thriving little town. It had a lumberyard, bank, two stores and a small hospital. Later a community hall was built and a United Church. Services had been held in the school previous to this.

Over the years Armley dwindled. The school closed and the students were bussed to Ridgedale or Tisdale. The station closed. The post office closed. The two elevators closed. All that is left is the United Church, the hotel, the community hall and a few residents.

This information came from Mrs. Thelma Van Blaricum of Ridgedale who taught in the Manluis Rural School near Armley.

ARMOUR SIDING

A Parrish and Heimbecker and a Pool elevator now sitting side by side with Interprovincial Steel and Pipe, R. J. Fife Road Machinery, and Saw Pipe Construction, on the northern outsirts of Regina, commemorates the name of Philip Danford Armour, one of the most famous names in the meat-packing industry in North America.

At Regina he was, for a time, associated with Pat Burns, whose name became a household word for meats in Western Canada. Mr. Armour became head of Armour and Co. in 1875 and he was responsible for methods of utilizing waste products, introduction of refrigeration, preparation of canned meats and the establishment of the Armour Institute of Technology (1893). He had built his industrial empire on the foundation of a pork-packing plant established by his brother, Herman, and he expanded it into fields other than meat-processing. Following his death in 1901, his son, Jonathon, carried on the business.

13

ARPIERS

Arpiers is a grain point between Colonsay and Viscount. It was named for ARthur PIERS.

ARRAN

Arran is the first stop on a CNR line that comes into the east-central part of the province and branches at Sturgis. It was named after a township in Bruce Country, Ontario, formed in 1850, which in turn was named after the island of Arran in the Firth of Clyde, from which early settlers emigrated.

ARRAT

Arrat was an inland post office east of Frankslake which is situated near the present hamlet of Zehner just north of Regina. Established in the early years of the province, it gave way when Frankslake came into being with the arrival of the railway in 1911.

ARTLAND

Artland is the last station on the old Grand Trunk Pacific Railway before it leaves northwestern Saskatchewan for Alberta. This is rough, sandy, hilly country with numerous lakes. Wildlife abounds. It reminded the Indians of Noah's Ark because it seemed to them that every animal and bird could be found there. They 'called it Ark Land. When the railway came in they changed the name to Artland.

ASHLEY

In 1907 Percy Ashley came to Canada from London, England. Rev. G. E. Lloyd had received instructions that he would be given funds to take 50 college students across the Atlantic to assist as catechists of the Church of England in Western Canada. By the time Percy applied, the 50 applications had been filled but Rev. Lloyd promised to try and find a place for Ashley if he would finance his own passage, which he did.

Ashley was sent into the district northeast of Lloydminster known as Hewitt's Landing, where a new church (St. Michael's) had been built. However, Percy soon decided to take a homestead. A few years later he was joined by his parents from England. They ran the first post office which they named Ashley. It was located on their farm about eight miles north and east of Greenstreet. It opened on the 1st of June, 1919, and closed on January 31st, 1956.

ASOR

Mr. Joe Hufnagel opened a post office and store on his farm four miles north and two miles east of Salvador in 1908. The mail was hauled from Unity twenty-seven miles to the northeast. When the CPR built in to Salvador in 1911, Mr. William Fry brought the mail in from there.

The post office was in the center of a German, Norwegian and English settlement. The Boser families, the Nelsons, and the Uptons were some who used the post office and store. The latter saved a lot of freighting.

Mr. Hufnagel passed away in 1915 and his widow closed out the business. This information came from Mr. Joe Ell, now retired and living in Unity.

ASQUITH

The first settlers began coming into the district in 1902. The CPR came through in 1908 and named the town for the Earl of Asquith, who was prime minister of Britain at the time. In 1922 the Earl of Asquith donated a cup to the school for annual competition. On the cup is the inscription: "To the children of Asquith, Saskatchewan, from H. H. Asquith 1st July, 1922."

Verla Jean Forsyth, music consultant in the Saskatoon Public Schools (1971), is a graduate of Asquith school and she won the cup when she was in grade 8, grade 10 and grade 12.

ASSINIBOIA

The town is named after the old district of Assiniboia that was formed in the Northwest Territories in 1882. When Saskatchewan was formed into a province in 1905 it absorbed most of Assiniboia. Alberta got the rest. The name "Assiniboia" came from the Assiniboine Indians and "Assiniboine" is an Ojibwa word meaning "one who cooks with stones," that is why they are sometims known as "Stonies."

ASTUM

Astum is about fifteen miles southeast of Kerrobert on a CPR line that runs to Rosetown. It is an Indian word meaning "come here."

ATTICA

Attica is the first grain point north of Lanigan on a CPR line that runs to Prince Albert. It received its name from a school district that was in operation before the railway arrived.

The first settlers in the Attica district were the Frank Hawk and John Underdown families. Others that came later were: Dr. J. H. P. Armitage, Flint Cramer, Edward Rankin, Edward Armitage and O. W. Armitage.

Mrs. L. McK. Robinson of 702 Tower Gardens, 1100 Broadway Avenue, Regina, describes one of the hardships that all pioneers faced. Here is a direct quote from her letter: "Our family moved to the homestead in the spring of 1907 and my mother died shortly after the birth of a child that did not live. It was buried beside a small child of the Underdown family on a corner of their land and a pile of stones was put on the top of both graves."

Attica is a common name. The states of Indiana, Kansas, Michigan and New York have an Attica. Likely early American settlers brought the name in. The name Attica goes far back in history. It was one of the many early Greek city states or "polis." Much more famous than the state itself was the city on which it centered — Athens. With its port Piralus, Athens became the center of a great trading empire in the ancient world.

ATWATER

Atwater was another place along the GTP main line where they named stations alphabetically. Atwater, following Zeneta, started a new series and was named after Mr. A. B. Atwater, the engineer on the first train to come over the track. This was in 1907.

The first settlers had arrived in 1903: the McNiels, the Warners, the Russells, the Jepsons, the Andersons, and the Foshagers. Their first homes were often inverted wagon boxes while sod shacks could be built. Diet was restricted to rolled oats, game for meat, salt pork, and wild duck eggs.

AUBURNTON

Auburnton is a rural post office on Auburnton creek fifteen miles straight south of Manor. The post office took its name from the creek. The office is closed now. The name Auburn comes from Ireland and they just tacked on the town. There are many, many places in the U.S.A. named Auburn.

AUTO ROAD

Auto Road is very close to Leacross. In fact there was an Auto Road post office in the district by 1910. It was named by Mrs. J. D. McNair and no one seems to know why because there were no autos and no roads in the district at that time. Three other people who kept this post office are as follows: Mrs. L. R. Ennest, Mrs. R. Wilkinson and Mr. P. Sims.

When the CPR line from Tisdale came through in 1924 the railway officials named it Leacross to signify the crossing of the Leather river. The Auto Road post office moved in to the townsite and took the name Leacross.

AVA

Ava is on a CNR line that runs south and west from Biggar to Dodsland. It was named after an inlet in Hudson Strait, Franklin District, which in turn had been named after Lord Ava, son of Lord Dufferin, who was killed in the South African War (1899-1902).

AVERY

Avery is a railway junction only one-half mile east of Glenbush where two CNR lines from North Battleford merge. The line through Iffley to Avery junction and on to other points west and north has CPR "running rights".

The Avery School, from which the junction took its name, was built in 1912 and it was named after George Avery on whose homestead it was located. This was two miles south of Glenbush.

During the late 1920's, approximately sixty students attended the one room school on half day shifts under the tutelage of Mr. Fish. After a school district meeting it was decided to divide the area, and a school was built in Glenbush in 1930. Around 1949 a new Avery School was built one-half mile south and one-half mile east. This school closed in 1958 for centralization. The school house was moved to Minnehaha where it is used today as a Co-op Hall.

This information came from Mrs. W. J. Oster of Medstead.

AVEBURY

Avebury is near Leask. It was named in honor of Lord Avebury, an English titled gentleman.

AVONLEA

It was on August 24, 1911, that the first Canadian Northern official train whistled long and loud and stopped at the end of the newly laid rails in Sunshine Valley, for that was the first name for the district which surrounded what was to become Avonlea.

The late Thaddeus Babcock, accompanied by his wife and two children, Vera and Leslie, Mrs. James Bovie, John Johnson and daughter Shirley, Margaret Muir, Mrs. Frost and many others formed the welcoming committee.

Avonlea just came into being at the time the book "Anne of Avonlea" was popular and the name was selected because the author, Lucy Montgomery, had relatives in the district.

AXFORD

Axford is about twenty-five miles west of Weyburn on a CPR line. It was named for Mr. Axford who was a member of the board of railway commissioners in 1913.

AYLESBURY

Aylesbury is on number 11 highway between Craik and Chamberlain. This follows fairly closely one of the first railroads in Saskatchewan. It was fin-anced by British capital and built in 1889-1890. It ran from Regina to Saskatoon and then on to Prince Albert. Many of the places along the line have British connotations and Aylesbury, named for a market town in Buckinghamshire twenty-five miles north of London, England, is one of them.

Dave Matthews homesteaded the quarter section on which the village stands and other early settlers included the Jones, the Eppards, the Dreschlers, the Coldwells, the Elliotts, the Wilds, the Clearwaters and the Pratts. One of these original settlers, Mrs. Joseph Amundrud (nee Pratt) still resides in the district.

AYLESFORD

Aylesford was named by the Department of Education. It was probably named for Aylesford, a market town on the Medway river, in southeastern England. There is also an Aylesford in Nova Scotia.

AYLSHAM

Aylsham is the second last stop on a CNR line that runs northeast from Melfort to the end of the steel at Carrot River. Many of the early settlers — the Thirkettles, the Flowerdays and the Clarks — came from England and one of them, Dick Laxton, named it for Aylsham, England. Aylsham in England is a market town just north of the city of Norwich, in Norfolk, England.

B

BADGERVILLE

Badgerville is one of the largest and most modern Indian villages in Saskatchewan. It is located on the Cote Indian Reserve north of Kamsack. The village was named in honor of the reserve's chief, Hector Badger.

BAGLEY

Bagley is a rural post office southwest of Gronlid at 12-47-19-W2. The first postmaster was Mr. Henry O. Hanson. It was named for William Chandler Bagley (1874-1946), who was an American writer and educator. He was president of the National Council of Education from 1931 to 1937. The post ofice has been closed for several years and the people of the district get their mail from Fairy Glen.

BAILDON

This is taken directly from a letter from E. H. Kaiser of 1340 Algoma Street, Moose Jaw. "I have taken some interest in the history of our area, and am only too pleased to give you a rough outline of events leading up to the establishment of our hamlet; its short years of glory, and its eventual demise — or near demise."

The area around Baildon began to be

settled in the early 1880s. The first settler has never been actually named since there is (as there usually is) some disagreement as to who was first. However, here are a few: Lind, Stewart, Lewis, Bennie, McMillan and Pearce. These settlers took up homesteads along the Moose Jaw creek which is three miles east of the townsite of Baildon. About the same time a settlement began to grow south and west of Baildon near a small coulee. This group came from England and consisted of: the Nettletons, the Milnes, the Lowes, the Urtons, the Campbells and the Scotts. They established a school, Cataraqui, before 1900.

My father, Andrew Kaiser, came as a young man to the district in 1900 and eventually settled on the NE quarter of 25-15-26-2. By 1911 the district was completely filled and people were hoping for a railroad. Baildon was surveyed by J. Waldon of Moose Jaw and approved by the province on the 30th day of April, 1912.

The settlers of the Cataraqui area had established a strong local government and had considerable influence, so that when it came time to name the new town they petitioned the railway requesting the name of Baildon. Most of the settlers (or at least the most influential ones) had come from the village of Baildon in Yorkshire, England. Their request was granted.

Baildon grew rapidly and once had two general stores, a church, a lumber yard, a school, a blacksmith shop, a carpenter's shop, a municipal hall, a station, a large section crew, and two elevators — one of them owned by a local family, the Lowe Brothers.

Improved roads and faster cars have made it but a short run in to Moose Jaw, less than 12 miles away. Baildon is now down to two families who live permanently in the hamlet. The elevator agent, the municipal secretary and many farmers of the district (like myself) live in Moose Jaw."

BAHDONVKA

In 1899 the Russian author Leo Tolstoy and others helped more than 7,000 Doukhobors to emigrate to Western Canada, where they established communal farms. Who were these Doukhobors? They were an 18th century Russian Christian Sect that were having troubles with their government. They refused to bear arms. Emperor Nicholas I during the Russo-Turkish War of 1828-29 forced them to freight military supplies from Tbiilsi to Baku on the Caspian Sea.

When the infant Dominion of Canada completed the CPR transcontinental railway, she had a problem on her hands. Great stretches of track lay through the sparsely settled prairies. Canada went out into the world and invited immigrants to come and take up land at 160 acres for ten dollars. Canada needed goods to carry on her railway and the Doukhobors had an excellent record as farmers.

One of the communal farms established by the Doukhobors was Bahdonvka, located just north of CeePee on the banks of the North Saskatchewan River.

First settlers included the following: Bill Shukin, John Tarasoff, Bill Kaskhoff, John Boykin, and William Perehudoff. The latter's son, Bill, is an artist whose work is acclaimed Canada-wide.

BAIN

Bain was a siding near Bredenbury on the CPR Winnipeg-Saskatoon line. It was named for James Bain, Section Foreman of Bredenbury. He won the Distinguished Conduct Medal and the Military Medal in the First Great War.

BAIRD

Baird is just a small point a few miles north of Swift Current on a CPR line that ran west from Moose Jaw. It was named for J. Baird, former Bridge and Building foreman, Moose Jaw.

This information came from CPR files supplied from the Superintendent's office in Moose Jaw.

BALCARRES

The east-central Saskatchewan town of Balcarres owes its name to the first postmaster of Indian Head, Balcarres Crawford. The name actually found its way north from the nearby Qu'Appelle Valley via the pioneer mail route which once linked Katepwa, Blackwood, Kenlis and the "Morrisons" to the northern end at the "Johnsons", just east of the present townsite. The history of Balcarres dates back to the 1880s when the pioneers arrived by ox and horse team from the rail head at Brandon.

Thomas Cavanaugh and Thomas Kelly, two U.S. Civil War veterans came from Fort Tallon, Devil's lake, N.D. by pony and squatted on land in the Balcarres district. These first two settlers were soon followed by numerous others, all of whom had to haul their grain to Indian Head before the railroad came to the district.

The growth of the town and district took a big leap in 1903 when the CPR reached the townsite.

Balcarres citizens saw little action in the Riel Rebellion as the Indians living on nearby reserves refused to join the rebels. They did, however, provide transportation for many of General Middleton's troops, making the trip from Troy, via Fort Qu'Appelle and Touchwood to Batoche.

BALDWINTON

Baldwinton, a small village on a branch line from Cut Knife to Lloydminster, was named to honor Stanley Baldwin (1867-1947) who served as prime minister of Great Britain three times.

Early settlers in the district included the following: Fairley, Petovella, Paron, Castellan, Tesolin, Stephenson, Stonehouse, Grant, Martin, Quast, Herbert, Elmore, Chisan, Ernest, Mantiefell, Sprague, McCrea, Kortright, Crunkhorn, Stewart and Franklin J. Bullerwell.

In the Second World War, 1939-1945, the following young men of the district gave their lives for their country: Flt. Sgt. Beaudry, E. J; Flt. Sgt. Niven, C.M.; Flt. Sgt. Riggs, L.E.; and Lance Sgt. Paradis, M.S.

BALGONIE

Balgonie is between Pilot Butte and McLean on the main line of the CPR just east of Regina. It was named by early Scottish settlers for "Balgonie Castle" in Scotland.

BALIOL

Baliol is on a CPR line halfway between Luseland and Kerrobert. It was named for Baliol Castle in Scotland.

In a letter received from Mr. J. B. MacGregor on March 20, 1977, I received this information. Mr. MacGregor once lived near Baliol for several summers during the 1920's. On a trip back to Saskatchewan with his wife in 1972 he visited around the country and found nothing remained of the station house, loading platform, elevator, section house and nearby school, that once made up the little community. He concludes "there is nothing between Kerrobert and Luseland".

BALJENNIE

The CPR built a branch line north of Asquith through Environ, Arelee, Struan, Sonningdale, Spinney Hill, terminating at Baljennie.

The little hamlet that developd was named for the first two baby girls born in the district, Belle and Jennie Warden. This name had been applied to a post office which was opened in 1891.

At its height Baljennie had two general stores. One was operated by Mrs. Parkinson and the other by Mr. Mitchell. It had two elevators and a dozen or so residences.

However, with railway abandonment, this was one of the first lines to go.

Today, after the closure of the Pool elevator in 1975, all that remains is a boarded up town. The only place of business is a small garage operated by Robert Fullerton, a retired farmer of the district.

BALLINORA

Ballinora was never more than a flag station on the CPR line which ran west from Cut Knife to Lloydminster. At one time they were promised an elevator if the residents of the district built a road but by the time the road was completed there was no longer any necessity for the elevator so it never materialized. Even the flag station was jacked up and moved away. At one time there was a Ballinora Grain Growers store in Carruthers to the north.

The Ballinora post office was located at 23-44-24-W3 with George Newton as the first postmaster. Early residents of the district were: Rodgers, Loveday, Wilfred, Chrisholm, Schmidt, Goulett, Duff, Ferguson and Ryan.

BANGOR

"We have found a better land
In the far South,
It is Patagonia.
We will live there in peace,
Without fear of the treachery or war,
And a Welshman on the throne
Praise be to God.

The singers' voices rose, strong and buoyantly, on a Liverpool wharf on a late day in May, 1865, as 153 Welsh folk made ready to board a small chartered sailing vessel, the "Mimosa," with the Welsh dragon flag at her masthead which was to carry them to a no-man's-land across the Atlantic under the tenuous and remote control of the Republic of Argentina. The emigrants, the hoped-for vanguard of a movement of thousands, were the actors in a drama which had been stage-managed by a few ardent Welsh nationalists, bent on creating a Welsh state where their language, cultural achievements, customs and non-conformist religious traditions would be preserved free of the compulsions of the British political and religious establishment and the blandishments of the assimilative nationalism which had absorbed so many Welsh migrants to the United States earlier in the century."
(Lewis H. Thomas, *Saskatchewan History*, Winter, 1971)

To make a long story short it didn't work out. After surviving the terrible hardships of the early years they had some success with irrigation on the Chubut river. However floods in 1899 and again in 1901 coupled with the new policies of the Argentine government led many colonists to migrate to South Africa and Canada.

The group that came to Canada settled in the Bangor district in 1902. The Grand Truck Railway arrived six years later and named the townsite Basco. The settlers resented this and, led by Thomas Owen, asked that the name be changed to honor Bangor, Wales, the birthplace of many of them. Since Bangor started with a "B" this did not disrupt the railway's pattern of naming towns in alphabetical order so permission was granted.

BANKEND

Bankend is between West Bend and Wishart and got its name from being right on the last "railway cut" through the hills to the plains which stretch to Wishart. From there on there are no more banks or hills, hence the name, Bankend.

BANNOCK

The principal foods of the early settlers, explorers, and traders were bacon, bannock and tea and the game afforded by the country. Bannock is made from flour and water, kneaded into a thick pancake or "scone" and roasted before the fire in a frying pan. Bannock is named in honour of this pioneer food.

It is located between Mistatim and Prairie River on a CNR line built from Crooked River to Hudson Bay in northeastern Saskatchewan. It began as a sawmill town in the 1920's, as did most of the towns along that line.

BAPAUME

Don and Bill MacDonald were the first settlers in the district and they operated a ranch north of the present village site. Their stock brand was OXO. When a school district was formed it took this brand as its name.

When the CNR came through from Shellbrook to Medstead in 1929 a large group of French settlers came and homesteaded south of the village. They were responsible for naming it Bapaume after their hometown in France. The most prominent of these settlers were: Chenier, Lavasseur, Doucette, Renaud, Caffett, Fournier, Morin and Neveu.

BARBOUR

Barbour is ten miles east of Yorkton on a CNR line. It was named for Robert Barbour, who was the mayor of Yorkton when the line was built.

BARFORD

Barford is about halfway between Nipawin and Wadena on a CPR line. The name is made up of the first part of the name Barrier with the addition of the word Ford. This was chosen because it is close to one of the main fords in the Barrier river.

BARING

Baring is nine miles northwest of Glenavon and was named after a noted English gentleman, Lord Baring.

BARNES CROSSING

Barnes Crossing is where highway 4 crosses the Beaver river. It was named for Mr. R. T. Barnes.

BARRIER LAKE

The early post office at Barrier Lake situated at 4-39-15-W2 took its name from Barrier lake which is northeast of Little Quill lake at 41-12-13-W2. The first postmaster was John Armstrong. The rural post office has been closed for some time and the residents of the district get their mail at Saint Front.

BARTHEL

Barthel is about 20 miles north of St. Walburg and an equal distance southwest of Meadow Lake. These are railheads. The community was named after Mr. Lawrence Barthel, a pioneer who came to the district in 1927.

BARVAS

Barvas is close to Yorkton. A school district was formed in 1914 and named Barvas by the Morrison family, after their native village in Lewis, Scotland. This also became the name of the village on the CNR close to the school.

BATEMAN

Bateman is a short distance northwest of Gravelbourg. It was named for Jim Bateman who came from Ontario with his family in 1908 and filed on his quarter section on the bank of crooked Notukeu creek, section 6-12-6. He opened the first post office in his home on the flat in August of 1911. His daughter, Lydia, was sworn in as assistant postmistress and drove with her father to St. Boswells to pick up the first Bateman mailbag. Mr. Bateman kept the post office for over 20 years, for nine years on the flat, and then he moved to the townsite of Bateman in 1920 when the railroad came through.

BATOCHE

Batoche is a post office at the site of a former Metis village on the South Saskatchewan river about 60 miles northeast of Saskatoon. Batoche is named for Xavier Letendre, a trader, whom everyone called Batoche.

In 1871, he established the first ferry in the Northwest Territories. This was the centre of the Metis settlement that had moved westward after the Red River Rebellion. Batoche prospered. Then came the Saskatchewan Rebellion of 1885 and Louis Riel selected Batoche as his headquarters.

During the seige of Batoche the rectory was a virtual prison for five priests of the surrounding Metis missions and several nuns from the Order of the Faithful Companions of Jesus who had fled from the St. Laurent district early in April. Despite an agreement of neutrality between the priests and General Middleton the rectory was at least once sprayed with gatling gun slugs and the marks are still there today. No one was hurt.

It was there on May 11, 1885, that the decisive battle was fought between Metis forces under Gabriel Dumont and the militia under General Middleton. It was near Batoche that Louis Riel was captured.

In 1886 Father Julien Moulin made application for a post office and it was granted. The space set up for it was upstairs in the rectory that still stands beside the church, St. Antoine de Padoue, built in 1884. The chapel was upstairs, too. The downstairs was used as a school.

The first move of the post office was from the rectory to a house one mile south along the river road. It was operated for years by the late Raphael Boyer. The Caron family presently live in the house.

In 1942 it made its second move a half mile further south to the general store of Bob Chevier. At present, it serves not only the farms surrounding it but does an excellent business with the families of the One Arrow Reserve, four miles to the west.

In the 1950s the rectory was converted to a museum, and in the 60s great advances were made in restoring and marking this historic site.

BATTLE CREEK

Battle Creek is a rural post office on Middle Creek south of Fort Walsh. It takes its name from famous Battle creek a short distance to the east. It was on a Sunday in early May of 1873 near Abel Farwell's trading post on Battle creek that a fight between a party of hunters and traders from Fort Benton, Montana, and a band of North Assiniboines touched off an international incident that speeded up the formation of the NWMP. Conflicting evidence surrounds the incident which took the life of Ed Grace and an undetermined number of Indians. It is known in history as the Cypress Hills Massacre.

BATTLEFORD

Historic Battleford takes its name from being on a ford of the Battle river. The Battle river rises in the Battle and Pigeon lakes south of Edmonton and flows east to join the North Saskatchewan river at Battleford. The river derived its name from the fact that its course lay through the disputed ground of the Crees and the Blackfoot tribes. It was therefore the scene of many battles. The Indian name for it was "fighting water."

After the Northwest Territories Act of 1875 provided for a resident lieutenant-governor and administrative services, Battleford was chosen as the capital. This was only natural because it had been frequented by the Nor'Westers and Hudson's Bay Company traders from the late 18th century. The Dominion Telegraph line was completed to Battleford in 1876. Battleford was on the original route planned for the CPR. The NWMP established a post there in 1876. In 1878 the *Saskatchewan Herald*, first newspaper west of Winnipeg, started publication. Battleford was the centre for land registration, a judicial district, and the site of the office of Indian Affairs branch. In the early 1900s it looked as though Battleford would become one of the largest cities in western Canada. It was incorporated as a village in 1899 and as a town in 1910. There it stayed. Why?

First, the CPR came in across the southern part of the province. Second, in 1882 the capital was moved to a point on this line named Pile o'Bones, later Regina. Third, when the Canadian Northern Railway was built in 1905, it came north of the river and the little siding of North Battleford (that wanted at first, to be called Riverview) became the vital trading point in the area.

Battleford did secure rail connections in 1912 but they came in the back door. Two stations were built but one soon stood empty and the other was little used. Battleford was not on a "main line."

In recent years the federal government has restored and preserved part of Battleford's glory in "Fort Battleford," a museum centered on part of the former NWMP barracks.

BATTRUM

Battrum was named for William Battrum who donated the land for the townsite. He is now retired and lives in Calgary. Battrum has developd into an important light oil field in southwestern Saskatchewan.

BAVELAW

Bavelaw was an early rural post office placed at 22-19-30-WPM. The first postmaster was Mr. M. O. Barker. The post office has been closed for some time and the people of the district get their mail from Millwood, Manitoba. The word Bavelaw is of English origin.

BAY TRAIL

Bay Trail is the first station south of Humboldt on a line to Lanigan. It was called Bay Trail because it was on the old freighting trail from (Fort Garry) Winnipeg to Edmonton that linked the Hudson's Bay Company posts along the Saskatchewan. This came to be known throughout much of its length as the Carlton Trail. In many parts it was called Bay Trail.

Settlement in the district started in 1904 and some of the first families to arrive were: Hiebert, Schedlosky and Larroff.

BAZENTIN

In 1928 the CNR flag station of Bazentin was put in between Medstead and Belbutte. It was named by railway officials for a town in France. There used to be a loading platform, stockyards, and a small building on the site. On one end of the building Bazentin was posted and on the other Bazentine. These were all dismantled and taken away in 1961. Mail used to be dropped at Bazentin and transported three and one-half miles south and east to the inland post office of Little Buffalo which was in the farm home of the postmaster, William Stuart Simpson. Before 1928 the mail used to be brought out by buckboard or cutter from Medstead or Glenbush.

BEACON HILL

During the threat of the Spanish Armada every hill in southern England from Plymouth to Portsmouth was a "beacon hill" with its tower and tinder ready to flash the warning to London. Saskatchewan has a Beacon Hill located 60 miles north and west of St. Walburg. It didn't get its name from England. It could more properly be called an Indian place name. It happened this way:

In the early days an independent trader established a little post at the foot of this hill and carried on business with the Indians. One of his most popular trade items was bacon. Although the Indians were very fond of it they couldn't quite say it and it came out "beacon" in English.

The post prospered and the district became known as Beacon Hill. When a post office was established on top of the hill it took the current name for the district. A railroad grade was pushed through this country in 1929-30 but no rails were ever laid. The proposed rail line that came up from St. Walburg was to join up with a line in Alberta.

In spite of the lack of a railroad, settlers filled up the country and the freighting is all done now by trucks over gravel highways.

BEADLE

Beadle is the first station east of Kindersley. The CNR officials named it in honor of Lady Beadle, the wife of Lord Kindersley. The roadbed was laid through Beadle in 1909 but it was not until August of 1910 that the first all-passenger train arrived.

The early settlers came in by oxen-drawn covered wagons over the Saskatoon route a distance of 150 miles. These homesteaders had to cut and haul their wood for cooking and heating from the South Saskatchewan river banks which were forty miles away.

Some of the first pioneers of the Beadle district were: Mr. and Mrs. Robert Hayes who kept a boarding house which served meals and provided lodging to people passing through; Fred James who was the first storekeeper and postmaster;

S. McDonald who was blacksmith; Russel Gordon who was sheriff of the district; Charles Scott who built the first Beadle school in 1911 and the Mellor brothers who built and operated the livery barn and draying business.

One of the incidents that people of Beadle recall when speaking of the early days concerns Bill Crocker, a young settler who managed to buy four horses and a plow. One afternoon, while he was busy breaking up some raw prairie on his homestead, an electrical storm came up and a bolt of lightning killed his four horses. Luckily Bill was unhurt.

Merv Johnson of Kindersley likes to tell this story about Beadle: "In the early years Mr. Bob Woods, the typical green Englishman, was called upon by neighbors to help butcher a pig. They had the pig in a pen and were prepared to shoot it when Mr. Woods arrived. He considered this to be very poor sportsmanship and insisted that they turn the pig loose to give it a 'sporting chance.' They gave in and let the pig go, it ran over the prairie for two hours before they finally got it captured and ready to butcher."

BEAR CREEK

Bear creek is a small branch of the Qu'Appelle river just before it leaves the province. Mrs. M. C. Wilson who moved to Moosomin to live in 1953 wrote as follows:

"My home was at the top of Bear Creek Hill about three quarters of a mile from the elevator. One of the first settlers, David Hogg, took up a homestead and pre-emption here on 18-17-32 in 1883. In 1884 he built a log house with thatched roof and two log stables on the north bank of the creek. In 1885 his wife and three sons came and made their home in the district. After seeing bears in the creek he called it Bear Creek."

BEATTY

Beatty, just west of Melfort, was named for Reginald Beatty, one time employee of Hudson's Bay Company, who was the first settler in what is now the Melfort district. In the summer of 1884, with the help of Indian friends, he built a log house and established a farm on the banks of Stony creek. Here he was joined by his brother, Fred. For nine years

"Stony Creek House" was the lone home in a huge wilderness and early travellers all knew and appreciated the fine hospitality of the Beatty residence.

BEAUBIER

Beaubier is 50 miles west of Estevan. It is named in honor of Miss H. Beaubier, a young school teacher who sacrificed her life in caring for the sick during the flu epidemic in 1918.

Well-kept Beaubier Park, within the town, is a rewarding memorial to a fine young person. Every year it is a riot of color with its flowering shrubs.

BEAUCHAMP

Mr. J. Beauchamp cleared some land and started a store and post office around 1902. He gave his name to the post office.

BEAUFIELD

Beaufield is the next station north of Coleville. The first settlers arrived by wagon and ox team (very few had horses) in 1906-07. The first winter Fred Harvey did the freight hauling from Battleford which was the nearest town, 100 miles north. One of the early settlers was Carl Jellenick who originally came from Bohemia. He was nicknamed "The Bo" and the town that eventually grew up when the railroad came in 1913 was named Beaufield in his honor.

Other early settlers and their families to arrive besides Carl Jellenick and Fred Harvey were: Harry Turner, John Harvey, Barney Needham, Joe Dailey, Abe Gaylord, Herb Bingham, George Wilson, Joe Little, Eddy Elder, Wally Muntz, Ira Hobbs, Fred Burke, Fred Bran, Howard Nelson, George Whittley, George Jackson, George Cummins, Teddy Adams, Percy Smith, Bill Close, John Webb, George Bott, Hector Close, Archie Elliott, Ira Holmes, George Merideth, Ross McClentick, Angus Morrison, Barney Beamish, Dan O'Neil, and the Gowan family.

BEAUVAL

Beauval is in a picturesque setting in the beautiful Beaver river valley. The town is on the west bank and it overlooks the four bridges necessary to cross the Beaver and LaPlonge rivers which merge

a few miles north and flow on through Lac Ile a la Crosse to join the Churchill watershed.

High on the east bank stands the imposing Roman Catholic mission which was establaished there in the early 1900s. Beauval is well named, it means Beautiful Valley. Before highway 155 was put through to Ile a la Crosse in 1957 all their freight came through Beauval, up the west side of the Beaver river to Fort Black and then it was transported by barge in summer and over the ice in winter, the seven miles west to the Roman Catholic mission site.

BEAUVAL FORKS

At Mile 63 north of Green Lake where you either turn off northeast to Beauval and Lac la Plonge, or you follow highway 155 to Ile a la Crosse, is Beauval Forks. It is named for Beauval which is five miles to the east.

Mr. Burnouf is building a good garage, oil and restaurant business there and he has a four unit motel under construction. There is also another service station and a Department of Highways depot.

BEAVER DALE

The original name was Beaver Dale but the railway has since coupled it to read Beaverdale.

Long before the railroad came through there was a post office about two miles north of the present siding. The mail was brought in from Theodore. Charles Dunning, an outstanding politician, provincially and federally, came from Beaver Dale.

The first settlers to come into the district were the Andersons in 1895 and the Wilsons and Duffs in 1896. The Duffs still live on the original homestead. The Canadian National didn't get to Beaver Dale until 1928 when they built a stub line northwest from Yorkton that ends at Parkerview. This information came from Susan Duff, a grade eight student at Silver Willow school.

BEAVER FLAT

Beaver Flat is a country store and post office. Mr. Willard Schriock, the mailman, brings the mail by truck twice a week from Waldeck fifteen miles to the south.

In the days of the HBC and the Nor'Westers this area was a flooded flat and beaver were plentiful. The beaver were trapped out; the flat dried up, and it was turned into grain fields. In the South Saskatchewan river four miles to the north there is an island called Beaver Flat Island. The very first settlers were ranchers along the Swift Current creek to the west: Ed Hogg, Ed Tully and the McNee brothers. They had established ranches by 1902.

The greatest influx of homesteaders came in 1906-07 when a group of Mennonites settled in what is called the "Friesen" district. Klass Friesen and Dave Klassen were two of the first in 1905 and then came C. B. Wohlgemuth. Walter Smith and Jack Armstrong arrived in 1905 from Ontario with their "effects" and settled east of Beaver Flat. To the north a group of Norwegians led by Pete Thodeson and John Austring settled in to start the Hovdestad district.

Many of the first homes were mere shells. A lot of houses had no floors, just the dirt which swept off hard and clean. One of the many hardships suffered by the early settlers was extreme cold. On January 3, 1907 the mercury dropped to 65 degrees below and stayed there for three weeks. Pete Thodeson sat up all night, with his four coat, fur cap and mittens on, to keep the fire burning so that he wouldn't freeze to death. In those days the "Mounties" made a periodic patrol among new settlers to check on this sort of thing. Sudden sickness could lay a man out so that he couldn't get help, too. Many are the tales told of lonely happenings in the "batch halls" that dotted the pairies and not all of them were funny.

BEAVER PLAINS

Beaver Plains was an inland post office and trading post less than twenty miles northeast of Kamsack. The Cote Indian Reserve lay to the west and Duck Mountain Provincial Park to the east.

The fur trade led to the opening of the West and the number one fur was the beaver.

Many places in Saskatchewan commemorate this animal and Beaver Plain is one. Beaver Park would have been more appropriate because it is in parkland on a tributary of the Whitesand River which flows in from the west, turns south and east near Kamsack, and eventually joins the Assiniboine.

BEAVER VALLEY

This rural community near Cadillac received a post office in 1915 and called it Conflict. A few years after World War I it changed its name to Beaver Valley. They didn't say why. Now, the post office is closed.

BECHARD

Bechard is a hamlet twenty-eight miles southeast of Regina on the old GTR to Northgate. The earliest residents drove into the district from the rail head at Milestone. Many of them were Americans. One of the few remaining people of that era is Mr. G. W. Stewart of Regina.

When the railway arrived in 1912 they had the name of "Linley" all ready for the community. The residents objected and since the land used for the townsite belonged to Mr. A. Bechard they carried considerable weight. At length the railroad consented and the name of Bechard was placed on the station.

BECKENHAM

Beckenham post office (now closed) was called after its namesake in Kent, England, which was the home of Mr. Garts, the first postmaster.

BEDFORDVILLE

This formerly was a rural post office. Mail was brought in twice a week from Ituna which was about fifteen miles away on the CNR. Its name was derived from the original homesteader upon whose land it was first located about 1906. He was Fred Bedford who came from Nottingham, England, where he was a gamekeeper on the estate of the noted Miller Mundy, a wealthy industrialist.

After Bedford's death in 1918, Bedfordville post office was carried on by the Yates family at their farm until it was closed and the service discontinued a few years ago.

BEECHY

Back in 1919 Beechy was part of the farm of Neil Oliver. The need for a railway was great and in 1919 CNR surveyors staked a line to follow the plains of the Missouri Couteau range of hills south from Dunblane. In the spring of 1920 work commenced and by the spring of 1922 the first train puffed into the station at the end of the steel deep in the Matador country. The CNR gave Beechy its name after a northern explorer, Lieutenant Beechy of the British Navy, who had done outstanding expeditional work in the Arctic and North-West Passage, thus giving the townsite an honored name. The most recent development in this district has been the establishment of the Beechy Co-operative Farm. This was set up in 1949 by a group of veterans of the Second World War.

After over twenty years of successful operations the Beechy Co-operative Farm dissolved. The land is now farmed on a private enterprise basis.

BELANGER

Harry Belanger, a surveyor in the early years of the opening of Northern Saskatchewan, is commemorated not once, twice, but three times in Saskatchewan place names:

1) Belanger Creek which flows southeast into Frenchman River in southeastern Saskatchewan.

2) Belanger Lake which is southeast of Cumberland Lake.

3) Belanger River which flows into Pinehouse Lake in Northern Saskatchewan.

BELBECK

Belbeck is on a branch of the CPR running northwesterly from Moose Jaw. It is named for Mr. Belbeck who, about 1907, was CPR superintendent at Moose Jaw. He retired from the railway service in 1908 and engaged in business in Victoria, B.C.

BELBUTTE

Belbutte is twenty-two miles east of Glaslyn. John Bellamey started the first post office on his farm three miles northeast of the present village site in 1912. He submitted the name of his wife, Belle, and to it added Butte because of a large, wooded hill on his land which can be seen for miles around.

When the CNR was extended north from Medstead in 1928 the post office moved to the town taking the name Belbutte with it.

BELLEGARDE

Bellegarde is a country post office six miles south of Antler. It was called the "Fourth Coulee" by the first settlers: Alphonse Copet, Cyrille and Joseph Dlaitre, and Cyrille Libert, who came into the district in 1891. In 1892 Cyrille Sylvestre came from Lavoie, France with his four sons and it was he who named the district Bellegarde after a stream which flowed by his birthplace in France. It was likely the Gainsborough creek which flows through the district that gave him the idea.

BELLE PLAINE

Belle Plaine was named by early settlers after Belle Plaine, Iowa. The name is appropriate to the locality. Belle Plaine (beautiful plain) is between Regina and Moose Jaw, and is just one of a series of names that told how people felt about this great wide province of ours. Others include Beauval (beautiful valley), Belvue (beautiful view), and Belbutte (beautiful butte). At Belle Plaine is located one of the many producing potash mines in Saskatchewan. It was not the first mine to come into production (Esterhazy was) but it was the first to use the solution method.

Potash is one of the three major plant foods necessary for life and, along with nitrogen and phosphorous, constitutes a primary component of plant food fertilizers. Hundreds of years ago, man discovered that the ashes from his fire promoted plant growth. Subsequently the first potash production was attained by burning hard wood in iron "pots," adding lime, leaching with water and evaporating the solution to dryness. The remaining "pot ashes" were potash.

Space does not permit telling how our present potash beds were laid down millions of years ago. However, it is a very important industry in Saskatchewan and one which everyone should know something about.

BEMERSYDE

Bemersyde is on a branch line south of Peebles that ends at Handsworth. The first settlers came into the district in 1900. Among them was W. R. MacPherson of Selkirk, Scotland, who was responsible for the naming of the hamlet. he had it named in honor of Bemersyde Castle, Scotland, which is located between St. Boswells and Earlston. It belonged to the famous Haig family of Scotland and the last to live in it was James Haig. He died in 1851 and is buried in a stone vault in the cellar.

Sam A. Dzioba tells it this way:

"This town consists of a hall, a repair shop, gasoline service, small general store and a post office. I am the owner of all of it but the hall, and I have been postmaster here since 1927. Our population at the present is six persons. Sometimes we are bigger depending on the size of the families of the two elevator agents."

BENBECULA

Benbecula was the name given to a settlement in the Wapella district, by some Hebridean Islanders who had settled in there. It takes its name from a small island off the west coast of Scotland.

BENDER

Bender is near Kipling in the southeast corner of the province. It was named for Mr. E. N. Bender, general purchasing agent for the CPR. The line has been taken up but such places as Kennedy, Welby, Windthorst, Dumas and Wawota still hang on.

BENGOUGH

Bengough is a village south of Moose Jaw on the Radville-Willow Bunch line of the CNR. The steel was laid in 1911 and some of the settlers who were already in the district were Henry Kjelson, Ed and Martin Dahl, John Dersch, Hiram Finch and William Staple.

Bengough was named after John Wilson Bengough (1851-1923), one of Canada's most prolific and brilliant cartoonists.

BENSON

Benson is the third stop out of Lampman on a CNR line to Regina. It was incorporated as a village in 1928 and named after a former post office of the district. We believe at the time this name was given there were a number of people in the district who were former residents of Benson, Montana, and they wished to have it named for their hometown.

BENTS

Bents is on a branch line of the CPR between Perdue and Rosetown. The community was settled some years before the railroad was built and farmers had to haul their grain to Harris about 20 miles away.

The first post office was called Piche after one of the early settlers but when the rail line was built in 1928 the people wanted a new name. A number of the residents held a meeting and sent in a list of names. James Elder, who had been appointed secretary, wrote the letter to the railway officials and at the bottom he added a postscript saying that he had emigrated from Bents, Scotland. A reply came back from the authorities saying that as most of the suggested names were duplicates they had chosen Mr. Elder's postscript of Bents for a name.

Bents was never a very large place. It had two elevators. Its only store and a dance hall were both built and operated by M. A. Longworth. As well as running the store and post office, Mr. Longworth was well known in the pure-bred cattle business. Once a year he held a beef barbecue and people attended for miles around. This became an annual event and is still carried on by his sons.

BERNARD

In 1908 the Bernard country post office was established in a farm home, situated on the north side of the Saskatchewan river, near the town of Morse.

Alex Heggie was the first postmaster and he was responsible for having it named for one of the early pioneers of the district, Bernard Grant.

BERTWELL

Bertwell is in the far northeast of the province on a CNR line to Hudson Bay. The first name given to it was Kakawa. This was an Indian name and no one seems to know what it meant. The name stood for four years and a considerable mix-up in mail was caused by another place in Saskatchewan having the name of Makawa. The name was changed to Bertwell and this honored the first storekeeper, Bert Webb, and a gas well that was found here in the early days. The Etomami river runs through the village. There are miles of spruce trees and good roads and the lakes in the district afford good fishing.

BETALOCK

Betalock is on the west bank of the South Saskatchewan river at Outlook. There's nothing there but the elevators and agents. It was named after Beta Lock, a friend of Mr. Coleman, a CPR official

BETHUNE

Bethune on number 11 highway just a little northwest of Regina was named for C. B. Bethune, the locomotive engineer on the first train to travel this line. The year was 1887. This information was received from W. C. McLean, present overseer of the village of Bethune.

BEVERLEY

Beverley is a short distance west of Swift Current. The first homesteaders came into the district in 1904 and most of them came from the United States. Among these were three who have retired and now live in Swift Current: C. A. Qualle, J. C. Swanzey and W. Lunan. The original name of the community was Levine but when the CPR came through in 1882 the name chosen was Beverley, to honor Beverley Seward Webb, an influential railway official of that time.

BEXHILL

Bexhill is the first grain point south of Assiniboia on a branch line of the C.P.R. It was named by early settlers for Bexhill, a port on the Strait of Dover in East Sussex, England.

BICKLEIGH

Bickleigh and Totnes are on a branch line of the CPR south of Rosetown that ends at McMorran. From Audrey Ridalls comes this story:

"In June of 1910, John Ridalls, my great-grandfather, and his eldest son, John Henry, my grandfather, along with two Watson families, Thomas Watson and George Eland arrived in the district. When a post office was opened in the home of John Ridalls in 1912 the name selected was Bickleigh. He had suggested it because as a boy he had lived near the village of Bickleigh in the county of Devonshire, England. At that time the mail was brought in by buggy from Fiske.

In 1923 the CPR came through and the road boss asked my great-grandmother, Mrs. John Ridalls, what she would like to name the station. She suggested Bickleigh or Totnes which is another village in Devonshire, England. The road boss was very gracious. He named our village Bickleigh and the next town six miles west Totnes. My great-grandmother was delighted.

"Mail day was an eventful one in those days as the settlers for miles around would be on hand hoping to receive letters from home, as well as getting newspapers and magazines to keep in touch with the world happenings and also as a means of passing many a pleasant evening reading, especially in winter."

BIENFAIT

Bienfait is a town nine miles east of Estevan. It is served by both the CNR and CPR. The CPR reached Bienfait as early as 1895 but regular train service did not begin until 1905. The CNR started about 1909. The name, Bienfait, which in English means "well done" is obviously a French name and it is said that it was given to the settlement by two French railway workers. Ranching and mixed farming were carried on by the early settlers. When lignite coal was discovered the CPR opened a mine, later known as the Bienfait Mines Ltd. and operated by R. J. (Bob) Hassard and W. J. (Bill) Hamilton. Today, the Bienfait district produces most of Saskatchewan's coal. This comes from an open-pit mine where the dirt or "waste" is stripped off by modern machinery and then it is quarried by giant power shovels which gobble up the ore and dump it into trucks to be hauled to the loading ramp ready for shipment.

The village of Bienfait was incorporated in 1912 and the first overseer was A. E. Watt, the first secretary-treasurer was A. J. Milligan, the first councillors were G. J. Oliver and V. F. Doerr. Some other firsts were: post office — 1903, hotel —1905, blacksmith shop — 1905, barber shop — 1907, drugstore — 1907, bank — 1914, bakery — 1920, and the first garage in 1920!

Bienfait was incorporated as a town in 1958 when water and sewer were in-

27

stalled. The population is fairly stable at around 1000 people.

BIG BEAVER

Big Beaver is at the end of steel on a line south from Assiniboia. It is almost at the international boundary. When the CPR went in there they had to build around a very large beaver pond. In it were exceptionally large beavers and so they named the townsite Big Beaver.

BIG BUSH

Big Bush is halfway between St. Walburg and Loon Lake. At one time it had a store and post office. It was named for a stand of poplars in the area. This was unusual in a country that had huge stands of spruce all about.

BIGGAR

The Grand Trunk Pacific started northwest from Saskatoon in the early 1900's in a neck-and-neck race with the CPR for Edmonton.

The first divisional point out (sixty miles the shortest in Western Canada) was named for William Hodgins Biggar, an official of the company.

It and North Biggar, on the CPR, served a large farming community. At Oban Junction, first stop west, a branch line was put in north to Battleford. In 1911 the GTP built another branch line southwest to Loverna. Making up and servicing these trains kept the roundhouse busy.

With the conversion from steam power to diesel in the 1960's the shops and maintenance crews were withdrawn and the roundhouse closed. Wainwright, Alberta became the "turn-around".

Biggar's population and payroll declined. However they held on and then in the seventies two events happened that brought on a manufacturing and building boom.

In 1971 Ken Esler, a local man turned a hobby into a business and Univision Industries was born. Today he employs forty-five workers manufacturing trailers of many kinds: drill and swath, gooseneck, industrial and farm. Sales of the product extend beyond Saskatchewan into Manitoba and Alberta.

The second big boost to Biggar's economy came in 1975 when SEDCO and Saskatchewan Wheat Pool combined

with Henninger International of Frankfurt, Germany in the building of a malting barley plant. It will use approximately three and three-quarter million bushels of barley annually.

Because of these two events, and other small ones, building in the west end of Biggar has mushroomed with a fine new hospital, a senior citizens home, one of the best working museums in Saskatchewan and many fine residences. It's a proud and booming town.

This information came from Mr. and Mrs. Roy Paul, long time residents of the district who now, in retirement, make their home in Biggar.

BIG MUDDY

Big Muddy, 9-1-22-W2, was an inland post office close to the lake from which it gots its name. It has been closed for some time now. Big Muddy was one of a chain of typically shallow prairie lakes that started at Old Wives to the northwest and drained through Lake of Rivers, Willow Bunch lake, Big Muddy lake, and on over the boundary to join the Missouri system. It was part of the great central flyway for migratory water birds. There is another Muddy lake in Saskatchewan and it is 12 miles south of Unity. It was at this lake that the first strikes of oil and gas were made by Imperial Oil in the 20s.

BIG RIVER

Big River is at the end of the steel on a line north of Shellbrook. The name was derived from the Indians who called the long narrow lake on which the village is located "Oklemow Cee Pee" which means Big River.

In 1909, just as the railroad came in, William Cowan began cutting timber in the area for the Ladder Lake Milling Company. Big River was incorporated as a village in 1921.

BILLIMUN

Billimun is an inland post office less than ten miles west of Mankota. It was named by a group of Russian immigrants for a town in their homeland.

BIRCH HILLS

Birch Hills is just a little southeast of Prince Albert. It is named for ranges of hills east and west of the town on which there are groves of birch trees.

BIRCH LAKE

Art Roske opened a post office at the south end of Birch Lake in 1912. After the post office closed and when the CPR ran a line north from Medstead to Meadow Lake in 1927 they took the name Birch Lake for the new siding.

BIRDVIEW

In the fall of 1911, when the Canadian National built a railway through the area, the hamlet of Birdview was started. The building site was laid out on SW quarter of 6-33-8-W3 on land homesteaded by W. E. Bell, and located nine miles south of Delisle.

The Goose Lake Grain Co. built the first elevator in the fall of 1911 with P. Metcalf as agent. The Security Lumber Co. opened up a yard with Harry Weldon in charge. The first residence was built by A. F. Mielke.

In the spring of 1912, Thomas E. Hahn of Hanover, Ontario, arrived and built a general store with living quarters attached. He also took over the post office which previously had been established at the farm home of Mr. and Mrs. W. D. Pattison about three and one-half miles to the southwest. The post office had been named "Birdview" in honor of Mrs. Pattison whose nickname was "Birdie".

Within a few years postal officials suggested a change of name since mail was getting mixed up with Broadview. Of the several names suggested, that of "Donavon" was chosen by postal officials, being the names of two rivers "Don" and "Avon" in Stratford, Ontario, where Mr. Hahn had attended a business college.

The last date used by the Birdview post office was June 8, 1914. The railway station retained the name Birdview. However, when box cars rather than mail began landing up at Birdview instead of Broadview, the Grain Growers Association made petition for change of name and Birdview station became Donavon.

BIRMINGHAM

Birmingham is a small hamlet six miles west of Melville on the main line of the CNR to Saskatoon. The original settlement was predominately English and they named it for Birmingham, England. At one time it was a thriving town with a hotel, four stores, a garage, a hall, and street lights.

BIRSAY

Birsay is on a CNR line that runs down from Dunblane to Beechy. It is named for the town of Birsay on the Mainland Island of the Orkney Islands.

In the 30s when money was scarce and coyotes were plentiful, more than one farmer augmented his income by hunting coyotes in the winter months. There were a variety of ways to do this successfully and here is how Jack Kent did it. Take the front bobs of a sleigh and build a square dog house on it — 5x5x4. The top is where you will carry your rifle carefully cushioned in a blanket. The back has a narrow platform to stand on and you are protected from being pitched off by a substantial railing along the back of it.

When a coyote is flushed he usually heads for the open because he is confident of his speed. First, two of the five or so hounds in the kennel are let out and the coyote easily outdistances them and particularly the team pulling the dog house.

However when the team closes in and two fresh dogs are loosed it is another story. They close ground on the coyote and as this happens he finally stops and turns. There are two ways to take him, either with the gun or with one dog you have saved who is a fearless killer. Jack used to prefer to have a man on horseback along to make the kill with a .22 rather than trusting it to dogs who sometimes in their excitement damaged the pelt.

Today the coyote literally has no chance when chased with a ski-doo. Even before this time cyanide bombs down his hole had thinned his numbers. Now people are busy trying to enact legislation to prevent his complete destruction. It is dangerous to upset the balance of nature. Over-kill on coyotes and foxes had led to an abundance of mice and gophers who do far more damage than the coyote with his occasional chicken-snatching. The west may lose something distinctly its own if the coyote is allowed to die out — or haven't you heard his peculiar howl echo over the hills at sunset?

BISHOPRIC

Bishopric is near Expanse and close to the south shore of Old Wives' lake. It was named for the founder of the sodium sulphate industry there, the Bishopric and Lent Company.

BJORKDALE

Bjorkdale is on a CNR line that runs south and east of Crooked River to end at Reserve. Sid Coppendale was the first into the district. He chose to build his cabin near the springs at the head of Crooked river. The site, when later surveyed, was the southeast quarter of section 22, township 43, range 12, west of the third meridian.

A few years later, about 1904, Charlie Bjork, a former railroad contractor arrived. He started south from the Peesane area with a team of oxen, a wagon and a plow. He hewed bush and trees to get through and he squatted on what was later the southwest quarter of section 18, township 43, range 2, west of the third meridian. This was approximately a mile from Sid Coppendale.

In the next few years many settlers came in and when it was time for the post office they took part of each man's name. There is a Bjork Lake not far from the townsite.

Bjorkdale had is name changed to Speddington when Mr. William Speddington took over as postmaster. However when he passed on the named reverted to Bjorkdale.

BLACK LAKE

Black lake is directly east of Lake Athabasca and drains into it through Fond du Lac river. The post office of the same name is some six miles northeasterly from Black Lake (settlement), on the west side of Black lake. The name is derived from the name of the lake.

The water route between Wollaston lake and Lake Athabasca was explored in 1796 by David Thompson. There is no doubt that Thompson was influenced in giving this name from the high prominent hills of norite which rise along the northwestern shore of the lake.

BLACKWOOD

Blackwood is an inland post office less than ten miles north of Sintaluta. It was named after one of the early pioneers of the area, Harry Blackwood. The post office is now closed.

BLADWORTH

Bladworth is between Davidson and Kenaston on a CNR line from Saskatoon to Regina. It was named after Mr. Bladworth, an official of the railway.

BLAINE LAKE

In 1885 a small settlement was started at what is now the junction of Highways Nos. 12 and 40. A rush of settlement began in 1899 when large numbers of Doukhobors arrived from Russia. They arrived at Petrofka, south of town, in August and at once began preparations to survive through the winter, digging dugouts in the hillsides and river banks. Some French settlers came in 1902 from Brittany and this group took up land close to where the town stands.

The town is located on land formerly known as the William Johnston homestead. When the railway came through in 1911 the settlement was named Blaine Lake after a lake three miles west which, in turn, had been named after a land surveyor, Mr. Blaine, who had drowned in it.

BLEWETT

Blewett is the end of a branch line of the CNR that runs west from Lampman. It is quite common for towns on this line clear to Brandon to be named for famous writers.

This point was named for Mrs. Jean Blewett (nee McKishnie) 1862-1934. She was born in Scotia, Harwich township, Kent County, Ontario. For many years she was a contributor to the Toronto *Globe*, and later she joined the staff there. She was the author of one novel "Out of the Depths" (1890) and she published several volumes of poetry: Heart Songs, The Cornflower, and Poems.

BLOOMING

Blooming was originally a Norwegian settlement a few miles north of the boundary and just south of Radville.

At one time they had a post office and a school. The name came from the profusion of wild flowers that grew there, especially the wild rose.

No railway ever reached Blooming and these farmers had to haul their grain to Radville.

BLUCHER

Blucher is a hamlet 25 miles east of Saskatoon. It was named for Gebhard Leberecht von Blucher (1742-1819) a Prussian field marshal. He had a long, exciting, and distinguished career which reached its climax when he aided Wellington in victory at Waterloo. He was nicknamed by his troops "Marschall Vorwarts" which means Marshall Forward.

BLUE BELL

Blue Bell is an inland post office forty miles north of St. Walburg. It was so named because of the many bluebell flowers (sometimes called hairbells). Settlers came into the district in the early 30s, many of them from the dried-up prairies to the south. Some of the first to come were: Sitter, Colfuss, Kramer and Dyck.

BLUE HERRON

Blue Heron is south of Prince Albert National Park. The school is closed now and the children are bussed fourteen miles to Canwood, the nearest town. School, store and post office are situated on the shore of Fish lake. In fact, Fish Lake was one of the two names submitted to the postal authorities in 1939. The other was Blue Heron named for the beautiful stately birds that nest on the lake. Ed Thompson of Congress, Saskatchewan, built the first store and was instrumental in getting the post office. Pete Peterson was the first settler in the district and he came in 1919. The first wheat was grown on his land, too, in 1922 — a crop of Marquis on ten acres of land that went forty bushels to the acre and graded number three.

At that time Blue Herron was solid bush and clearing ten acres was considered a good year's work. Homesteaders had a hard time clearing land which had to be done with axe and grubhoe — in some cases when they could afford it they used dynamite.

At one time there was a spur in from the main railroad to haul out logs but the line was taken up years ago. Part of the old roadbed has been converted to a road

and is known locally as the railroad track.

BLUE HILL

In 1892, Mr. and Mrs. Robert Gracy and family moved into the Blue Hill district 25 miles south of Moose Jaw. In 1904, the J. B. Glover family followed and then settlers came thick and fast. In 1907 Mr. Glover opened a post office in his home and called it Blue Hill because of a clay hill south of his house which showed up blue for miles. Mr. Glover hauled the mail by horse and buggy two days a week from Moose Jaw and received $2.50 a trip.

Religious services were held in the various homes until 1907 when a church was built. It was the first church built south of the Soo line to the American border and it is still open for services.

BLUMENHEIM

Blumenheim is a small Mennonite community seven miles west of Hague. The name is German and means Flower Home. Living as they did in a close-knit community some of the work was done by "bees." These people built with wood which was reasonably cheap. When the walls of a house or barn were ready to go up, a group of neighbors would gather at the place, and with an altogether "Heaveho" an entire wall would be lifted up and nailed into place. The families were then left to finish the doors, windows and partitions. Women, besides preparing the huge meals, worked right alongside the men in hammering and sawing. Some families built the barn adjoining the house, others left a space.

Precaution told these people to plough furrows around the entire settlement's buildings as a fireguard. These had to be cultivated regularly and kept clean.

BLUMENHOF

Blumenhof is a Mennonite village 18 miles south and 4 miles east of Swift Current. In English Blumenhof means "a yard full of flowers" and each Mennonite home has that plus a good vegetable garden. The post office is still listed as open and so is the store operated by Frank and John Ens. Other families in the village include the following: Fred Wernicke, Isaac, Peter and John Hildebrand,

Miss Penner, Jake Heibert, Jake and Pete Ens, Walter Friesen, Jake Knelson and Roy Deobald.

BLUMENORT

This Mennonite village northwest of Hague started in 1899. The name translated from German to English comes out "blooming village" (ort is village in German). This is typical of Mennonite villages. Their homes are surrounded by flowers. Their spacious gardens and yards appear literally to be "manicured." They're beautiful.

BLUMENORT

Blumenort is twenty miles straight south of Swift Current on highway number 4. It has 14 houses and a population of 70. It is a Mennonite village and its name means "flower village" (ort in German means village).

Students in grades 1 to 8 are bussed south to Neville; all other grades go to Swift Current.

We are indebted to Mrs. Pete Weiler and her family for information, not only about Blumenort, but about many other villages in the vicinity. Pete Weiler was born in Durango Province, Mexico, where many "Old Colony" Mennonites moved from Canada after 1917 when they felt that the School Act, asking them to teach some English in their schools, was too strict. Pete came back to the Osler-Hague district northeast of Saskatoon and later moved to the Swift Current area.

The Weilers gave the name of every person in the village but what is of more interest was their explanation of why so many Mennonites are called Jake, Pete, Abe, etc. These are nicknames for Jacob, Peter and Abraham. Mennonites live very close to the Bible in word and deed.

BLUMENTHAL

Blumenthal is a small Mennonite settlement six miles south and east of Hague. The name is German and means Pleasant Dale. There are very few people living there now and the school is used as a church.

BODMIN

In 1910 McKenzie and Mann built the Canadian North Railway northwest from Shellbrook to Big River to bring out timber. The second last stop was Bodmin and at first it had a regular station, section men, stores, a post office and all. Today, only the store is left and it is operated by Joseph James Harvey, a long-time storekeeper in the district. Many of the stops on this line from Shellbrook north — Polwarth, Debden, Wrixon and Dumble — were given names by the CNR officials which had no significance to the communities.

Mr. J. J. Harvey was working in the store at Eldred when Bodmin was started and knew nothing of the name until years later when he bought the store and post office. It was while he was postmaster that he received a letter addressed to the "Mayor of Bodmin" from a man in Bodmin, England, inquiring as to how the place got its name. It would seem reasonable to assume that it was named by someone connected with the CNR who was acquainted with Bodmin, England, which is in Cornwall.

BODO JUNCTION

At the railway crossing west of Unity there is a black and white sign which reads "Bodo Junction". In the late 1920's a branch line of the CNR started southwest of Unity headed for Castor, Alberta.

It continued through End Lake, Sunny Glen, Reward, Donegal, Heart's Hill, Cactus Lake and Cosine, but stopped abruptly at Bodo just inside the Alberta border. The deep depression of the 1930's had struck.

The line was never completed, but over the years some substantial towns developed. Maintenance, always a big expense item on railways, necessitated the conversion of the wooden bridge over the "valley" to an earth-filled one. The line struggled along until 1966 when railway abandonment was first talked about.

In the Thursday, March 14th, 1976 edition of *The Western Producer* on page ten, the headline read "CN wants to drop the Unity-Bodo line". The railway made its recommendation March 4th to a local hearing of the Hall Commission on grain handling and transportation.

Abandoning the rail line would affect 316 producers delivering to fourteen elevators on the line in the Saskatchewan communities of Reward, Heart's Hill, Cactus Lake and Cosine, and Bodo in

Alberta. According to Saskatchewan Wheat Pool figures, there are 2.6 million bushels of grain on the line.

The community of Bodo, represented by local merchant Alf Hauck, said producers would face hauls to Hayter, sixteen miles away, or Provost, twenty-two miles away.

Bernard Weidenhammer, general storekeeper at Cactus Lake, criticized declining rail service and said rather apologetically that although it probably mattered little to anyone else, he would lose a business that has occupied his life and that of his father.

The Unity-Bodo line is only one of many in Saskatchewan up for abandonment. It is sad to see them go, but progress has its price.

BOGGY CREEK

Boggy Creek is between Regina and Condie, the first grain point. H. M. Purdy, Box 238, Balcarres, Saskatchewan, writes as follows:

"I don't know who the first postmaster was, nor any dates, except this is the address on my birth certificate — Boggy Creek PO, NWT, May 7, 1899. The first homesteaders came into the area in 1882 and my grandfather, Thomas Purdy, was one of them. The first school, S.D. No. 64, was opened in 1885 with him as one of the trustees."

BOHARM

Boharm is the first grain point west of Moose Jaw on the main line of the CPR. It was named for Lord Strathcona's home in Scotland. Boharm is the English of the Gaelic "Bothsheirm." 'Both' means residence and 'sheirm' means sound.

BOLDENHURST

Boldenhurst was an early rural post office near the present town of Riverhurst. Its first mail came from Davidson and later from Elbow when the C.P.R. built a line through there in 1908.

When the G.T.P. built northwest from Moose Jaw in 1916 and established Riverhurst, Boldenhurst post office was closed and gave up part of its name to the new town. This also closed another post office in the area, Riverview, and it, too, gave up part of its name to Riverhurst.

BOLNEY

Bolney is the first grain point on a CNR line that runs from Bolney Junction to Frenchman Butte. It is named for Bolney, England. It was quite a busy little place in 1930. It had a school, a cafe, an elevator, a store, a post office, a hall, a filling station and a dozen houses. By 1970, most of the business places had been boarded up. The houses are now disintegrating and many people have moved to Paradise Hill, the first stop west.

BOLNEY JUNCTION

Bolney Junction is between Spruce Lake and St. Walburg where a branch line of the CNR runs west to Frenchman Butte. There have never been any buildings there. It is named for Bolney, the first stop west, which in turn was named for Bolney, England.

BONNE MADONE

Bonne Madone is about half way along a CNR line that runs from Saskatoon to Melfort. The post office was opened in 1901 and the school was built in 1905. Post office, school and siding were all named after an old earlier church in the district which was built by a French Catholic Missionary. Bonne Madone means "Good Lady".

BONNINGTON

In the very early 1900's on the Canadian Pacific Railway built north from Regina the village of Bonnington was established where the town of Kenaston is today. The first settlers came from the northern United States and chose the name Bonneville, a common name in Wyoming, Idaho and Utah. However, postal officials turned it down because there was a Bonnyville in Alberta. They compromised by using Bonnington.

This is not an isolated incident — in the early years Robin in Saskatchewan became confused with Roblin, Manitoba and mail and freight were frequently mixed up. Robin was asked to change its name so added Hood to become Robinhood. Similarly Eaton became Eatonia to avoid confusion with Eston.

In 1905 Bonnington was asked to change its name entirely. It was renamed Kenaston to honor F. E. Kenaston, wealthy implement manufacturer of Minneapolis. He was the vice-president of the Saskatchewan Land Valley Company which developed much of the area between Davidson and Dundurn. He was instrumental in bringing in many settlers from the United States.

BOOTH SIDING
The GTP came through in 1908 and established the points of Raymore and Semans. G. W. Booth, reeve, at that time, of the R M of Mount Hope No. 279, was instrumental in circulating a petition to have a siding established between Raymore and Semans and to have a grain elevator built there. This was aimed at serving the farmers directly north and south of the line because in those days there was a family on every quarter section and grain was hauled by horses and wagon.

Within a short time a loading platform was put in but it was not until 1920 that an elevator went up. Some of the early settlers who were served by this elevator were: Henry Roe, W. J. Schouten, Malcolm Nicolson, Henry Greenshields, George Felton, Fred White, Louis Young, Roger McIntosh, and Tom and Jacob Benson.

The siding was named in honor of Mr. Booth who had worked very hard to get it.

BORDEN
Borden is located on highway 5, 40 miles northwest of Saskatoon. It was originally called Baltimore but was renamed by the Canadian Northern Railway after Sir Frederick Borden, minister of militia in Sir Wilfrid Laurier's cabinet.

The railway reached Borden in 1906 and a village was incorporated three years later. The first council consisted of Thomas Graviston, William Tallis and Norman Smith. Mr. Smith served on the council for 35 years.

BORDERLAND
Borderland is an inland post office about fifty miles straight south of Quantock. It is less than ten miles from the international boundary or "border," from which it takes its name.

The post office is closed now and the people get their mail from Killdeer to the west.

BOUNTY
The district was fairly well settled by 1909. In 1910 Guy Hanna and his nephew, George Greenstreet, built the first store on a hill west of where Miles Rogers now lives. When the townsite was surveyed in the summer of 1910, the prairie was covered with the most beautiful tiger lilies, so "Botany" was the name chosen for the new town. Due to a mistake in the blue prints, it became "Bounty" instead of "Botany".

BOURNEMOUTH
In 1909 Austin Zeller, Albert Walker and Harry Johnson homesteaded in the Bournemouth district. The CNR railroad came through in 1927 and a farmer, W. W. Taylor, started a store and post office at Bournemouth siding. When it came time to name the post office, the names of Albertville and Walkertown were suggested but it was the name Mr. Taylor's wife suggested, Bournemouth, that was accepted. She chose it because she had been a First World War bride and her home had been in Bournemouth, England.

BRABANT LAKE
Brabant Lake is a settlement situated on a lake of the same name located about fifty miles southwest of Southend in Northern Saskatchewan.

Brabant Lake was named for a service man who lost his life in World War II.

BRACKEN
Bracken is down in the southeast corner of the province, on a branch line from Consul to Val Marie and is named for John Bracken, premier of Manitoba, 1922-43, and leader of the Progressive Conservative Party from 1943-48. Mr. Bracken earlier had served with the Saskatchewan Department of Agriculture and University of Saskatchewan.

BRADA
Arthur Thorpe, took up a homestead half a mile east of Brada in 1903. The Canadian Northern arrived in 1905 and gave the townsite its name, believed by some to commemorate a town in Ireland.

The first passenger to ride from Brada to North Battleford was Mrs. Bessie Thorpe.

BRADDOCK

Braddock is on a branch line of the CPR between Tyson and Hak. It commemorates the name of Edward Braddock (1695-1755), an English general, who became commander of the British forces in America in 1754. In the French and Indian Wars of that time he led an ill-fated expedition against the French Fort of Duquesne which is the present site of Pittsburgh. George Washington was on his staff and warned him of his method of attack. He paid no attention and his force of 1200 men was trapped on July 9, 1755, by 900 French and Indians with a loss of half of his troops and three-fourths of his officers. Braddock showed great personal bravery and fell mortally wounded after four horses had been shot from under him. He died of his wounds on July 13.

BRADWELL

"When the Grand Truck Pacific was built from Winnipeg to Edmonton in the early 1900s, the names of places, wherever possible, were kept in alphabetical order. Long stretches of these occur in Saskatchewan and Bradwell is in the middle of one — eg. Undora, Venn, Watrous, Xena, Young, Allan, Bradwell, Clavet, Duro (now just an unused station) then Earl, which was later called South Saskatoon.

Originally Bradwell was called Sunny Plain, after a school that opened there in 1906. When the railway came through in 1907 the name was changed to Bradwell. It is named after a place in England, Bradwell-on-Sea."

BRASS

Brass is a station southwest of Battleford, 6-39-19-W3. The CPR named the place after Mr. J. A. Brass, their chief clerk at Moose Jaw.

BRATTON

In 1906 Aubrey George Sealy came from Bratton in Wiltshire, which is about thirty miles west of London, England, and filed on homestead section 2, township 28, range 9, west of 3rd. He and Jack Sealy came to Hanley where they hired two teamsters with sleighs which they loaded with lumber, and started looking for their homestead following corner stakes. Although it was December the weather was good and the snow not too deep. When they reached their destination they unloaded the sleighs and lived in a tent banked with snow while they erected a ten by twelve shack of two ply one-half inch board with tar paper between to keep out the winds. They finished the house in two days. They melted snow for water; for fuel they walked across the river to get wood which they pulled home with a rope. When they went for fuel they took their Winchester, which friends had given to them when they left England to ward off Indians, and were able to shoot rabbits for meat.

Not long after they finished their shack, A. D. Adkins, Harry Johnston, Fred Nicholson, Jack Salmon and Oscar Cleveland arrived to start homesteads in the district. While they were building their abodes all of them slept on the floor of the Sealy home.

With the growing of the districts the Sealys applied for a post office to be kept in their house and asked that it be called Bratton in memory of their hometown in England.

The CNR built a branch line from Elrose to Macrorie in 1911-1912 and when a hamlet formed near Sealy's, the post office moved in and gave the name Bratton to it. Soon there was a school, a store and two elevators.

By 1973 only one elevator was left, the store was gone, the school closed and the building was used for a community hall.

In December of 1975 the 50,000 bushel Pool elevator was trucked by road to Delisle.

BREDENBURY

Bredenbury is a town 26 miles southeast of Yorkton on the CPR Winnipeg-Saskatoon line. It was named after A. E. Breden, a railway land inspector.

BREDIN

Bredin siding is situated on land owned by the Bredin brothers. The siding was named after their farther, Mr. A. Bredin. It is a grain point on a CNR line running from Regina to Saskatoon.

BREMEN

Bremen is between Totzke and Cudworth just off the northeast end of Muskiki lake. The first three settlers arrived in 1903, they were Joe Kleiter, Joe Thiel and John Blasig. Those who followed included Frank Hamm, George Hoffman, August Blasig and Frank and Joe Walerius. This was a predominately German settlement and when the railroad came through in 1911-1912 Pete Boxlers's suggestion, that it be called Bremen in honor of a large city in their homeland, was accepted.

The first elevator to go up was the Beaver. It was built in 1913 and painted green. Bill Duerker was the first agent. Before the elevator was built the farmers had to load over the platform; in order to get a place they stacked their grain in sacks and then when cars were moved in a man threw one of his sacks into a car to "stake his claim." Most farmers couldn't fill a car (1000 bushels to the old wooden cars) with any one variety and so he would either go in with a neighbor or build a partition to separate his grain. Wheat, oats, rye, barley and flax were the main crops grown in this area in the early years. Where homesteaders settled in distinct ethnic blocks it was not uncommon for them to name their towns after a large city in their homeland and so we have in Saskatchewan the following: Amsterdam, Stockholm, Aberdeen, Leipzig, Odessa, Madrid and Bournemouth, besides a Bremen.

BRESAYLOR

Mr. and Mrs. Joseph Sayers married January 6, 1890, spent almost their entire lives in Bresaylor, 30 miles west of Battleford.

The first settlers to enter Bresaylor came there in the early 1880s from Headingly and White Horse Plains in Manitoba. Early arrivals among the pioneers were three families after whose names the village of Bresaylor would be named: The Bremners, the Sayers and the Taylors.

Joseph Sayers, then only 12 years old, arrived with his family. Mrs. Sayers, the former Mary Rose Pritchard, was the daughter of John Pritchard, a hero of the Frog Lake Massacre in 1885. Her father rescued two women whose husbands had been murdered by the Indians at Frog Lake and for two months Mrs. Sayers was held prisoner, along with about 30 others, in the war camp of Big Bear as he roamed

down the North Saskatchewan pillaging Fort Pitt, standing briefly to fight at Frenchman Butte, and eventually being routed at Steele Narrows at Loon Lake. Chief Poundmaker whose reserve was a short distance from Bresaylor held 16-year-old Joseph Sayers captive for more than two months which ended when Poundmake surrendered to General Middleton at Battleford on May 12, 1885.

BRIARLEA

Fifteen miles southeast of Shellbrook is the community of Briarlea. It once had a store, post office, school and church. All that is left is the name and the church. The church is St. Martin's Anglican and it is located on a high hill in well-kept surroundings. The church inside is like new. The name Briarlea was given to the post office by William Brewer and it was named in memory of his hometown in England.

Other oldtimers who lived in the district include: Henry Nelson, Arthur and William Beaven, William, Fred and Charles Roberts, Brian Greenwood, Samuel Soles, William Grahame, Calvin McKay, Frank Anderson, Colonel P. W. Pennefather, Albert Brunsdon and Annie and Charlie Quayle.

Possibly the best-known settler of Briarlea was Horace Hackett (1880-1953) who moved to Crutwell ten miles to the south on the railroad and there he operated a store and post office. In addition he built a pentagon-shaped building of rough-hewn logs — 18 foot to the side — that hasn't sagged an inch in fifty years. It was known far and wide as Horace's Dance Hall and some of the dances he put on are still talked about. He drew people from as far away as Prince Albert, 18 miles to the east — no small feat for those days!

BRIDGEFORD

Bridgeford is on the Moose Jaw-Outlook line a little southeast of "the Elbow." Like many other places in Saskatchewan it took its name from an early country post office in the district. This post office was opened in 1904 by Alfred Bryan and named "West Bridgeford" for his hometown in the north of England. When the CPR came through in the fall of

1908 a few miles to the north, the post office moved to the tracks and gave the new town part of its name, Bridgeford. At the railway officials request the West was dropped from the name.

BRIERCREST

Briercrest is less than 20 miles southeast of Moose Jaw. From Edna Jaques comes the following:

"On a day in the summer of 1902 my father and mother, two little sisters and myself were riding along the east edge of our farm 22-14-24. My father and mother were riding on the spring seat of the wagon, we three little girls were bouncing around in the wagon box. There is a hill just before you get to the house which used to be simply covered with brier roses and my mother said, 'That is what we will call our farm, Dad . . . Briercrest, because the crest of the hill is covered with roses,' and so it was named."

The mother, Mrs. Captain Jaques, later started a post office in her home. It was Briercrest, too. And when on July 24, 1911, J. A. Sheppard wrote to the railway officials he started his letter thus: 'It is the wish of many settlers living here that you give the name "Briercrest" to this town. Briercrest is the name of the present post office and the oldest name they have in the settlement.' The wish was granted.

Edna Jaques liked to tell the following story and it merits a place here:

"Back in 1902, my parents decided to sell out and come west. We brought very few things with us. One thing I vividly remember was a huge red book with gold letters on it which said 'Remedies for Man or Beast.'

"As we lived 25 prairie miles from a doctor, that book was cherished and kept in a safe place on the top shelf on the pantry for over 50 years.

"If a horse got sick down came the BOOK. Dad would turn to the page where it said 'cure for colic in horses' and my mother would start to haul down bottles and a cup for measuring.

"If a person got sick the procedure was about the same. I remember once I had neuralgia or some awful pain in my head so Dad read out loud, 'If there is extreme pain in a child's head, give it two Stern's headache wafers'. About five minutes after I got the medicine down I started to

get sleepy, my head got fuzzy and I went down in a heap. Everyone in the family was scared to death. I could hear my mother's voice from far away screaming 'Make her walk . . . make her walk', so they heaved and pulled on me and got me moving and for four hours by the clock the family took turns walking me. I can remember it distinctly. Every time I threatened to fold up and go to sleep, someone would yell, 'Make her walk, keep her going' and from some unknown inner strength I'd walk.

"Then after making me drink about a quart of water, they decided I was cured and let me sleep and I never came to until noon the next day. The pain was gone and I never mentioned it again, I can tell you, if I had a pain I kept it to myself."

BRIGHTHOLME

Brightholme is a rural post office fifteen miles south of Shellbrook. It is located at 30-47-3-W3, and the first postmaster was Mr. F. Buckle. There is a German touch to this name, "holme" being home in English.

BRIGHTMORE

Brightmore is less than ten miles northwest of Weyburn on a CPR line to Moose Jaw. It was named for Mr. Brightmore, a roadmaster on the CPR.

BRIGHT SAND

Bright Sand is a country post office and store situated 15 miles northeast of St. Walburg. It took its name from Bright Sand lake six miles to the southeast. The Indians named the lake. The first settlers arrived in 1911 and they included J. P. Peterson, Olaf Magnuson, Nels Hanson, Anton Johnson, and A. Gunderson and his two sons, Fred and Elmer.

"Old Mary Ann" was the name given to the first threshing outfit in the district. It was powered by a 10-horse sweep and was hand-fed by one man who had the help of two band cutters. There was no straw blower and one man had to be "straw monkey." This job consisted of forking the straw away from the back of the machine. It was a dusty, dirty job. Threshing time required good cooks who could provide plenty of filling food, as these men were really hungry for every meal.

BRIGHTMORE

Brightmore is between Yellow Grass and McTaggart on a CPR line that runs southeast of Moose Jaw to North Portal on the old "Soo Line" built in 1893. It was named for J. T. Brightmore, Roadmaster, when the line was built.

BRISBIN SIDING

Brisbin Siding is between Harris and Zealandia on the old Goose Lake Line that runs from Saskatoon southwest to Rosetown. It consists of one elevator and a loading platform which allowed grain to be "scooped" directly into the cars.

Mrs. Ethel Brisbin of Three Hills, Alberta, writes as follows: "My late husband, W. C. Brisbin, was secretary-treasurer of the local Grain Growers Club at the time a loading platform was needed. It was in his name that an application was sent in. The Brisbin Siding was used a lot in the early days, as wheat and livestock went out and coal, cordwood, and coal oil by the barrel, came in."

The following are some of those who used the siding: Cliff C. Clark, S. J. Wagner, A. M. Dunlop, Harry Dunlop, Harry Hill, Newton Gill and W. H. King. Russell Brisbin, a grandson of W. C. Brisbin, still farms the original homestead.

BROADACRES

Many of the early settlers of Saskatchewan came from homelands where they had forest. Many had put in considerable time at the backbreaking job of "clearing the land." The prairies looked like heaven to them and the names of several towns of the province reflect this feeling: Broadview, Expanse, Horizon, Victoria Plains, Belle Plaine, Grainland, Laniwci, and La Plaine to name a few. Broadacres is the second stop north of Kerrobert on a CPR branch line to Wilkie.

BROADVIEW

Broadview is an important divisional point on the main line of the CPR 92 miles east of Regina. The name was given to it in 1882 when it was the west end of the railway and nothing could be seen to the west but a great expanse of prairies. It had one of the earliest railway yards in Saskatchewan and was for many years known by travellers as a place where the time changed.

A highway picnic park is located at the west side of the town. Within the park, markers have been placed to point out the original grade of the railway constructed in 1882, and later abandoned in favor of a better grade, and the ruts of the early trail from Fort Ellice to Fort Qu'Appelle, one of the storied links in the system which knit together the scattered trading centres from the Red to the Rockies. Along this trail passed such important visitors as the members of the Palliser and Hind exploratory expeditions and the Earl of Southesk. The route was probably known and used by Indians centuries before it was developed by the fur trade.

A distinguished graduate of the schools of Broadview is Director of Education for Saskatoon Board of Education, Dr. F. J. "Fred" Gathercole. Fred started teaching at Clifton, a nearby one-room country school. He stayed there a year and then returned to Normal School in Regina to complete his teaching certificate. His next school was at Ketchen which is between Sturgis and Hazel Dell that runs northwest from Sturgis to Kelvington. He entered the Regina school system in 1929 and after serving as vice-principal and principal in Regina, Dr. Gathercole taught in both Regina and Saskatoon Teacher's Colleges.

In 1950, he was appointed superintendent of public schools in Saskatoon, and in 1966, when the Saskatoon public school and collegiate boards decided to work together towards the establishment of a single board of education, Dr. Gathercole was named as director of education for the two systems.

On Friday, June 16, 1972, the Saskatoon Board of Education held a special program to pay tribute to their director of education by naming their office building "The Dr. F. J. Gathercole Education Centre."

BROCK

The railroad builders always had a name ready for a new townsite just in case the settlers from the surrounding districts hadn't been thinking about it. No place went unnamed for long. When the CNR put in the famous Goose Lake Line southwest from Saskatoon to Rosetown they tried to give the name of Brock to Zealandia. The settlers disputed this and even though they didn't have a name ready they didn't want Brock. They suggested that the old timers of the district should be given a chance' to submit names. Many did so and Mr. Inglebrett's suggestion of Zealandia was chosen.

After the track passed Rosetown and neared Kindersley the railroad officials tried Brock again. This time they were successful. Brock perpetuates the name of General Sir Isaac Brock, a British soldier, who dramatically lost his life at the battle of Queenston Heights. A momument was erected on this famous battle field to this hero of Upper Canada.

BROCKINGTON

Brockington is a rural post office seven miles northeast of Fairy Glen. Its exact location is 28-47-19-W2, and its first postmaster was Martin Lofthus. It is named for a village in England.

BRODERICK

Broderick is very close to Outlook. When the CPR arrived it suggested the name of St. Aldwyn, but it was prevailed upon by the settlers to call the townsite Broderick to honor Dr. Broderick, the dentist.

Broderick is one place in Saskatchewan which is due to grow when the effects of the South Saskatchewan River Project begin to be felt.

Miss Marion Graham is one of the outstanding graduates of this town. She became a teacher and after a series of country schools she came on the Saskatoon public school staff in 1928 under the superintendency of the late Dr. Oulton. She was one of the first teachers used in experiments with teaching the gifted and the slow learners. In 1950, she went on loan for one year to the Saskatoon secondary school system. At the Technical Collegiate she taught a class of boys who needed extra help to learn to work to the top of their capacity. She never returned to the public schools. In 1942 she joined the Air Force and was discharged in 1945 with the rank of squadron leader. She then returned to "Tech." She officially retired in 1965 but "retired" is not in Miss Graham's vocabulary and she was elected to the Saskatoon School Board in 1966.

Her persistent, and so far fruitful, aim is to develop in every school a Learning Resource Centre, the heart of the modern school. In 1972, Miss Graham was named Citizen of the Year by CFQC television.

BROMBURY

Brombury was an early post office at 24-28-12-W2, and the first postmaster was Mr. Robert Dalrymple. He named it for a village in England. The post office has been closed for some time and the people of the district get their mail at Winthorpe, a hamlet northwest of Yorkton at 24-28-11-W2.

BROMHEAD

Bromhead is on a branch line of the CPR that runs west from Estevan to Minton. Early settlers came into the district in 1904 and included the Vaughans, Freemans, Morleys and Bechitts. The railroad arrived in 1913 and with it Mr. C. Berg (the first postmaster), J. and W. Mingle, J. Mathison, C. Webbe, C. Vestu, J. Sampson and A. Torgunrud. The village was named for Dr. Jim Bromhead.

BRONCHO

Broncho is an inland post office less than fifteen miles west of Mankota, the end of the CPR steel. It is a Spanish word which means rough or wild. Cowboys also use the word to describe the Mustang, the small wild horses of the American West.

Easterners sometimes call any horse shipped from the West a broncho or bronco. These wild horses are descended from the horses that early Spanish explorers brought to America. Today, bronchos are used on ranches to herd cattle and for roughriding exhibitions and contests in rodeos.

BROOKING

Brooking is the first stop west of Radville on a CNR branch line that runs to Willow Bunch. Many of the first settlers were from the United States and the first settlement was called "Strowe" for Harriet Beecher Stowe, the author of the antislavery novel, "Uncle Tom's Cabin." However, another group of Americans wished to call it Brookings for Brookings, South Dakota. The latter group won out and somewhere in the shuffle an S was dropped.

Building started to boom in Brooking in 1910 and soon it had two stores (one run by the Lewerton brothers), a butcher shop, a cafe, three elevators, a lumber-yard, a livery stable, a hotel, a machine dealer, a poolroom, a dance hall and a school. The latter came before the town and was called Buffalo Valley. The village also had a blacksmith shop run by Bill Leonard, a Negro from Ontario. All in all it was a typical prairie town. Today, all is gone except the elevators, and wheat fields grow over the old site.

BROOKSBY

The name in itself tells a story. Brook Partridge, a pioneer, owned a shack where the Canadian Northern Railway right-of-way was to be built. In order for it to get "by" he had to move his shack, and so they called the new hamlet which grew up on his land Brooks-by!

BRORA

Brora is halfway between Regina and Craven on a CPR line that runs up to Lanigan. It was named for a town in Sutherlandshire, Scotland.

BROWNING

Browning was named by railway offi-cials for one of England's most distin-guished poets, Robert Browning (1812-1889). Before the railroad arrived in 1911, as a branch line from Lampman to Estevan, Nellie McCurdy came as one of a group of settlers and she writes as fol-lows:

"In May of 1904 my husband and I drove in with a team and wagon from Alameda 30 miles to the southeast. The prairie was a sight to behold! The grass was so green and rolled ahead as far as you could see. There were very few trees and these were small and clustered around the sloughs. My husband died that year and I was left alone with a four-month-old baby. I was 19 years of age. I stayed on the homestead and proved up and got it in the fall of 1906."

BROWNLEE

Thirty-seven miles northwest of Moose Jaw on a C.P.R. line that runs to Elbow is Brownlee. The village was incorporated in 1908 and was named for a superin-tendent of the Moose Jaw division of the C.P.R., J. Brownlee.

Surrounded by good land, Brownlee prospered and soon had several general stores, a bank, a doctor, a restaurant, a butcher shop, a hall, churches, a harness shop, a hotel and even a bowling alley.

Declining rail service coupled with improved roads and cars, have en-couraged people to shop further afield with the result that many places of business on main street of Brownlee have now closed up. The actual population of the village has dropped to well below one hundred and many of the residents are pensioners.

BRUNO

Bruno is named in honor of Rev. Bruno Doerfler, O.S.B. In August, 1902, Father Bruno and three other men from St. John University, Collegeville, Minnesota in-spected sites in Saskatchewan, Alberta and Manitoba for the starting of a new colony.

Their choice was the site of Hoodoo Mail Station in the vicinity of what is now St. Benedict, Leofeld and Cudworth. A German American Land Company was organized which bought 100,000 acres of railway land in this area. Both the land company and the settlement society ad-vertised widely in German language newspapers in the United States. By December, 1902, 1000 German Ameri-cans had applied for homesteads. This was the start of the town of Bruno and others in the surrounding district.

BRYANT

A short CNR spur line runs west of Lampman through Cullen, Bryant, and ends at Blewett. Bryant is named for William Cullen Bryant (1794-1878). He was a distinguished lawyer who retired in 1825 to devote his time to writing. His early works included a poem still includ-ed in the grade 8 curriculum, "To a Waterfowl." He became co-owner and co-editor of the New York *Evening Post* and held that position from 1829 to 1878. Some of his lines have become household quotations, as: "Truth, crushed to earth, shall rise again," from "The Battlefield", "The melancholy days are come, the saddest of the year," from "The Death of the Flowers". On a branch line southwest from Maryfield that ends at Blewett you'll find stations named for the following authors: Ryerson, Parkman, Service, Cowper, Carlyle, Wordsworth, Browning, Lampman and Bryant. Bryant, as far as we know, is the only writer to have two points named for him. The other point being Cullen.

B-SAY-TAH

B-Say-Tah is a summer resort near Fort Qu'Appelle. It is an Indian name, said to mean "stay here." It was incorpoated as a village in 1915.

BUCCLEUGH

In 1907 about twenty miles west of Unity the CPR put in the grainloading platform of Buccleugh. A section house went up. A flag station was built and soon cream cans lined its platform.

Settlers were slow in coming into the "sand hills" of the "valley." However, when the good land to the west filled up they came and one of the first was Lewis St. Germain. He was soon followed by Avery Ghent, Bill Trout, Ira Sinkey, Bill Conley, Harold Watson, Jim Crowell, Bill Brown, Jim Cook, Harry Briggs, Frank Boskill and Harry Dancer. Every quarter had its family. Buccleugh School was built on the side of the valley and took its name from the railway point. The point was named Buccleugh for an old Scottish ducal family tracing descent from Sir Richard le Scott (1249-85) but taking origin in grants of land by James II of Scotland to Sir Walter Scott of Kirurd and Buccleuch.

By 1968, with the exception of Walter St. Germain (Lewis' son) and Bill Boskill (Frank's son), the settlers of the valley were gone. The school burned down in 1940 and was temporarily held in the Smith home for the few children left until it came time to bus them to Unity.

The section house and section men have gone from Buccleugh Siding. A faint trail, overgrown with trees, winds down from the top of the "valley hill." No more grain is shipped from this point. Pasture land has taken over and Dr. Doyle and Dr. McIsaac of Unity run cattle over much of this quiet land.

BUCHANAN

Buchanan is a village between Canora and Humboldt. It was named after R. Buchanan, a pioneer rancher.

BUCK LAKE

The Buck Lake community had its beginning in 1883 when Walter Buck arrived to homestead. The Kirby's and Mr. Chapman located six miles northwest of Mr. Buck the same year. A small lake nearby was named after Mr. Buck, who soon abandoned his homestead.

The real founding of the community did not take place until 1889 when the Bratt and Carrothers families arrived. They located on the former Buck homestead and the surrounding area became known as the Buck Lake community.

Families to arrive shortly after were: W. E. Jones, George McGillivray, Strettens and the E. C. Jones. In 1903 the Jasper family arrived, followed by the Helstroms, Rodgers, Howletts and Statons in 1905 and 1906.

Others who played an important part in the early life of the community were Bernard and Estley Moats.

The first religious services were in the form of a Sunday school in the Bratt and Carrother's homes, followed by church services. The Buck Lake Methodist Church was built in 1893. It was the only church between Regina and the United States border until after the turn of the century.

The land for the church and cemetery was donated by Jesse Bratt and the building supervisor was George McGillivray, a millwright by trade. The lumber was hauled from Regina, the work was voluntary, and the church was completed in time for fall services. This was the social center for miles around and thrived as such until the Grand Trunk Pacific Railway came through and the village of Gray was built in 1912. Two of the early student ministers were Mr. Bennie and Mr. Robertson. Reverend Hancock, who served in 1918 and 1919, was the last minister. Shortly after the church was closed, a violent storm twisted it diagonally on its foundation and destroyed the barn. The church was sold and is still in good repair as a Masonic Hall in Gray. Alfred Howlett was secretary of the Buck Lake Church for several years and was also in charge of the burial permits for the cemetery.

John Carrothers was appointed justice of the peace in 1896. About that time a post office was established in the Jesse Bratt home and was called the Buck Lake post office. The first mail, which was picked up in Regina, was delivered by J. N. Beattie. Later it was delivered to Milestone, after the C.P.R. extension, and was picked up there by J. N. Beattie and delivered to Buck Lake. This post office closed in 1912 after the Grand Trunk Pacific came through and the town of Gray was established.

Jesse Bratt was the first chairman of the Local Improvement District and he became the first Reeve of the Rural Municipality of Bratt's Lake, #129, when it was formed. It was named after him.

The small lake known as Buck Lake was renamed Bratt's Lake by the Department of Natural Resources in 1971. It is located about eighteen miles south of Regina and four miles west of Gray.

A cairn in memory of these pioneers was erected and dedicated on September 27, 1970. A stone mason was commissioned to construct it in the cemetery. A plaque was supplied by the Historic Sites Branch of the Department of Natural Resouces.

Mrs. Marjorie Bell of Regina sent in the above information.

BUCKLAND

In 1911 the railway built west from Prince Albert and headed for Shellbrook. Today, go three and one-half miles west on number 3 and you come to Wilf Callahan's Buckland Service. Proceed along the highway to the historic marker and picnic area at the cement bridge over the Shell river. A Saskatchewan Historic Marker there reads as follows:

GOLD DREDGING
ON THE
NORTH SASKATCHEWAN
RIVER

"From 1905 until 1909 a gold dredge operated on the river in this vicinity. Owned by the partnership of Dr. W. H. Roughsedge and the Hon. C. M. Ramsay, later incorporated as the International Gold Dredging Company Ltd., the dredge was 100 feet long and 80 feet wide in the beam. The machinery powered by its two 100 horsepower boilers could put through 1000 cubic yards of the gold-bearing river gravel each day.

The operation failed because of technical difficulties which made too costly the process of separating the minute particles of gold and platinum from its matrix of rock and sand."

Now proceed four miles west to the Buckland sign and turn south. You're in historic territory! Markers on the old highway will lead you into a Federal Historic Marker on the very edge of the river and it reads as follows:

PETER POND
EXPLORER AND FUR TRADER

"Built the first trading post on this site, 1776. One of the founders of the North West Company, in which he served until 1790. He opened the North Saskatchewan river and the Athabaskan District, kept a journal, and made the first general survey of the area.

"Born and died in Milford, Connecticut, 1740-1807."

You're just four miles west of Buckland siding. At one time it had a flag station, a loading platform, and buildings nearby housed the section men. Over this platform McKenzie and Ellis, timber contractors, loaded cars of cordwood for the prairies, the cheapest fuel at the turn of the century. North of the tracks is the huge overgrown gravel pit from which all the gravel came to do the grade to Shellbrook.

John McLeod lives within sight of this. He pioneered the district along with Jim Soles and Clarence Neff. He worked on the track. Later he tried farming at Traynor in the late twenties but he shortly returned to the North. When the gold dredge was dismantled he acquired the anvil from Bill Piper, the carpenter. Part of his present house was built from the timbers of the dredge.

After the complete break-up of the dredge Bill Piper stayed to homestead. Times were hard and cash was scarce. He dug seneca root and sold it in Prince Albert to get by.

Buckland is named for the many fine deer that abounded in the early days. Yes, you're on historic ground when you're at Buckland. It's well marked provincially and federally to remind us of our heritage.

BUFFALO GAP

Buffalo Gap is a station on the CPR extension southeast from Assiniboia. The country is somewhat rugged and there is a gap in the hills through which the great buffalo herds used to pass on their way to water at the East Poplar river.

BUFFALO HEAD

Buffalo Head was an inland post office near Horsham in the southwest part of the province. It is now closed (1969). Buffalo Head was only one of many places named for the buffalo. We have a Buffalo Horn, Little Buffalo, Buffalo Narrows and Buffalo Gap.

When the bones of these great beasts whitened the prairie the most prominent part was the head and many people made collections of them. Others gathered all the bones and sold them at $8.00 per ton to be shippd East to make bone meal.

BUFFALO HORN

Buffalo Horn is an inland post office south and west of Aneroid. The following is a complete letter sent in by Mrs. Myrtle M. Moorhouse of Aneroid.

"Dear Sir,

I am very interested in your project of names. I see you have Buffalo Horn on your list, and I was there before it was. People settled here in 1910-11, bringing wife and children. Only three families had children. There was need of a school. The bachelors voted it down because it would raise their taxes.

Mr. Pleas Isaacs, one with a large family, studied law before coming West. He suggested waiting until winter when the bachelors would be away working in the towns or lumber yards. It worked. The school district was formed. Suggesting names one man, Mr. S. Dixon, picked up a horn of a buffalo on the site and holding it up he said, "Buffalo Horn," which it was. A few years later a post office was opened in Mr. Charlie Condie's home and it inherited the same name. Mr. Condie kept the post office for thirty-eight years."

For clarity this letter is hard to beat.

BUFFALO NARROWS

The buffalo in his natural state ranged from Texas to the far north. In the opening of the West a myth developed about him being a creature of the plain, just as Saskatchewan is referred to as a "prairie province." The center of Saskatchewan (north to south) is one hundred miles north of Prince Albert and there's not much prairie up there! When, in the 1940s, a large captive herd of buffalo was moved from Wainwright, Alberta (to make way for an army camp) to Wood Mountain National Park in the N.W.T., it prospered and multiplied until today the herd has to be culled periodically to fit it to its range. In their natural state buffalo did a limited amount of migrating and one of the places where Indians used to lie in wait for them was Buffalo Narrows. There, a natural funnel was provided by Peter Pond lake and Churchill lake.

Buffalo Narrows is a town of well over 1000 people. Compared to Ile-a-le-Crosse to the south and La Loche to the north it is a relatively new settlement. However, it is growing rapidly and its strategic location takes advantage of our expanding tourist trade.

BULYEA

Bulyea is forty-three miles north of Regina on a CPR line. It was incorporated as a village in 1909 and named by the railway officials for G. H. Y. Bulyea, former lieutenant-governor of Alberta. Some of the first settlers in this district were Gustane Walter, Angus McDonald, William Connell, Benjamin Greenfield, Walter Munro, John Mackay, Byron Meyers, Harold Morton, William Haslett, Campbell Livingstone, William Renwick, Carl Carlson, James McMillan and John Malcolm.

BUNGLASS

Here is a complete letter written on May 6, 1976 and sent in by Mrs. M. Bellavance of Lake Lenore.

"When my grandparents came from Europe in 1909 they bought land in the already flourishing district of St. Joseph's School, eight miles southwest of Ituna.

The name of their inland post office was Bunglass. It was run by the Watson family for years."

BURES

Bures is the first stop past the junction of a CPR branch line that runs from Wallace to Cardross. It was named for Bures, England.

BURNHAM

The first settlement of the Burnham district centered around the years of 1905 and 1906, pioneered by such men as Wm. James Malone, who came from Ireland and was the first settler to file a homestead; Albert Lightfoot, Arthur Ward, Thomas Wilson and Ralph Bettany from England; W. A. Dafoe and T. K. Linklater from Manitoba; Thomas Norris from Scotland. During the first few years these homesteaders had to go to Waldeck, a booming town fourteen miles to the northwest for their supplies.

The CNR surveyed a right-of-way in 1911 but the grade was not built or steel laid until 1930-31, though the post office of Burnham was opened in the home of T. K. Linklater in the fall of 1908. It was named for a village in England.

BURROWS

Burrows is between Whitewood and Wapella. It was named for Acton Burrows, one time deputy minister of agriculture for Manitoba.

BURSTALL

Burstall is the last station in Saskatchewan on a CPR line from Leader running southwest into Alberta. The steel was laid on the site in 1920. When it was incorporated into a village the following year it was named Burstall in honor of General Burstall who lost his life while commanding the Second Canadian Division in World War I. The first settler into the district was A. K. Walker. By 1910 most of the land was taken up and farmers hauled their grain 30 miles north to Estuary.

The Pacific Petroleum Company has a plant six miles west of Burstall and the men they employ have given the town a boost.

BURTON LAKE

In 1904 John Burton homesteaded at the south side of a little lake north of Humboldt that was later to bear his name. In 1913 Mr. Burton became the first reeve of Humboldt municipality.

In 1930 when the CPR was completed on to Prince Albert the first siding north of Humboldt was called Burton Lake. A Pool elevator was built there but it has been closed for the past 10 years.

BUSHELL

The Honorable J. H. Brockelbank, when he was minister of the Department of Natural Resources in 1951 recommended the name Bushell Inlet (59° 31'-108°45'. At the same time the department proposed to subdivide a small townsite near the inlet to serve as the transhipping center to Uranium City. It was proposed to call the settlement "Bushell" on survey.

The name was approved by the Canadian Permanent Committee On Geographical Names on January 17, 1952. It is named after Squadron Leader Christopher (Kit) Bushell of Fort Qu'Appelle, who was killed in action during World War II.

On the Canadian Forces Base at Moose Jaw (50°20'-105°33', an RCAF station before the unification of the armed forces) the post office and the married quarters area have been named Bushell Park in memory of Mr. Bushell.

BUTTE ST. PIERRE

Butte St. Pierre is a small place with a store, post office, church and school. The nearest railway is 10 miles away at Paradise Hill.

Sondall, named for the farmer in whose house it operated, was the first post office in the district. When this post office closed and moved to its present location beside St. Pierre Church, it took the name of St. Pierre.

The location of this church is on high ground and later another change in the name was made by adding butte, the French word for hill, to make the name, Butte St. Pierre.

BUTTRESS

Buttress is the second grain point south of Moose Jaw on the C.P.R. The significance of the name has not yet been determined. Other points south, Crestwynd, Dunkirk, and Expanse have been identified, but Buttress is a puzzle.

CPR records simply state Buttress was named from the nature of the countryside.

BUZZARD

The earliest settlers in this area were the Barr Colonists who spread south from Lloydminster. There is no post office at

Buzzard now as it is just a small siding on the CPR which came through in 1927. The name was chosen by the railway officials from a name of a large coulee on the Battle river nearby.

The Buzzard Coulee was named from the great number of buzzards circling around it in the early days.

Strictly speaking the birds were American eagles. They have made a comeback in Saskatchewan and have been sighted and reliably recorded at Baljennie, Empress and, of course, in the Eagle Hills southwest of Battleford.

C

CABANA

Cabana is twelve miles southeast of Meadow Lake. At one time it had a school, store and post office and a large Roman Catholic church, nicely grouped and laid out. It was named for Father Cabana and in the early days it was a predominately French settlement with the following families prominent in community affairs: Prudat, Beaubien, Lussier, Shartier, Martin, Biraud, Lehaux, Roger, Plouzin, Millon, Moran and Legace.

The school is now used as a dwelling and the children are bussed into Meadow Lake. The church provides a limited service. The store and post office have closed — a victim of good grid-roads. The spacious school grounds are still used for sports which shows that a community spirit is still alive.

CABRI

The town of Cabri is 41 miles N.W. of Swift Current on the CPR. It is close to the Fosterton oil wells and also serves a large farming community. Cabri is the Indian word for antelope, and the town was so named because of the presence of great herds of these animals in the district.

Cabri has enjoyed some fabulous times in the past, as in the fall of 1915 when the district harvested 1,000,000 bushels of grain.

CACTUS LAKE

The first settlers came to the "Battlefords" by train in 1906 and then travelled 100 miles southwest by team and ox cart to what is now Cactus Lake. The district took its name from a lake three quarters of a mile wide and seven miles long upon whose banks an abundance of wild cactus plants grew.

Prior to the arrival of the white settlers Indians used the lake as a meeting place in summer because of the ducks and geese which abounded there. This settlement was a long way from a railroad. In 1910 the CPR built from Moose Jaw to Macklin and this still put the people of Cactus Lake 20 miles from a store or elevator — quite a drive with horses.

Then in 1931 the CNR started a line from Unity, Sask. to Castor, Alberta. It came to the south edge of the lake and the village of Cactus Lake came into being and was named for the Cactus lake by the CNR officials. The railway brought a boom with three stores, three elevators, a RM office, a blacksmith's shop, a pool hall, a dance hall and a school.

CADILLAC

Cadillac, a town in southwestern Saskatchewan, is named for Antoine de Lamothe Cadillac (1658-1725) famous fur-trader and governor of New France.

On July 24, 1710, with 100 soldiers and habitants, he arrived at the site of what is now Detroit and there founded Fort Pontchartrain. Despite the turbulence of his rule and his unpopularity with colonists and Indians alike, he remained commandant of the fort until 1710, when he was appointed governor of Louisiana. He was equally unsuccessful in his new post and was recalled and imprisoned in the Bastille for a time in 1717. He was released the following year and for the last seven years of his life was governor of Castlesarrasin.

Besides the town of Cadillac, Sask., there is a Cadillac, Michigan, but perhaps the best known of all is the well known General Motors product of Detroit that is named for him — the Cadillac car.

CALDER

The Canadian Northern Railway track arrived at Calder on Oct. 26, 1909. Calder was then known as the third siding west of Shellmouth, Man. Calder received its official name on January 1, 1911.

It was named after the Honorable J. A. Calder, member for Saltcoats in the provincial legislation and minister of education.

The first settlers in the village were Icelandic, German and Ukrainian.

CALDERBANK

"The first homesteaders arrived in Calderbank district in 1909. R. W. Clelland opened the first post office on his farm in 1911 and called it Calderbank in memory of a large house in mid Calder, Scotland, which had been his homeland. He hauled the mail from Ernfold for more than 20 years. The following are some of the early settlers: Elliott, Lafferty, Brownlee, Birtwistle, Rourke, Biggs, Pinch, McLean, Kerr, Plumtree, and Barton.

All settlers were delighted when the CNR branch line from Mawer to Main Centre was pushed through in 1930. Les Bradley was the first agent."

CALDWELL

The first village was started in the summer of 1903 on Sec. 22-9-9 W2 on the farm of Hamilton Caldwell. It was christened Caldwell by William Russell and Lost Williamson, two homesteaders who lived nearby.

When the CPR came through they selected a site on the west of Mr. Caldwell's farm so all the merchants moved their buildings to the new site and the name remained the same, Caldwell.

CAMEO

The first point west of Shellbrook on a line that runs to Medstead is Cameo. Settlers came into this area as early as 1896. However, those with definite records of arrival are the Groves in 1900 and the Buckinghams and Willoughbys in 1914. The first buildings were a store and post office and the first mail carrier was Isaac Belfry who brought it out all the way from Prince Albert. The district was called Jackpine. In 1909 a school was built and named Cameo. In 1929 when the railroad came through the school gave its name to the townsite.

CAMHOLTZ

Camholtz was a rural post office near the present site of Zelma. It was operated in the home of T. A. S. "Tom" Campbell. The post office took parts of the name T. A. S. CAMpbell and Frank ImHOLTZ, pioneer residents of the district. When the GTP came through they were naming their townsites in strict alphabetical order and the post office moved to the railroad and took the name of Zelma.

CAMSELL PORTAGE SETTLEMENT

Camsell Portage is twenty miles northwest of Uranium City, on the north shore of Lake Athabasca. Trapping in winter and commercial fishing in the summer is the occupation of the hundred people who live there. Some of the largest lake trout (up to 100 pounds) in the world are caught in Lake Athabasca.

The portage is named for a very famous man, Dr. Charles Camsell (1876-1958) a geologist and explorer. He was a civil servant and a member of survey and exploration trips to Great Bear lake and the "Coppermine Country." He was in turn deputy minister of the Department of Mines 1920-1935; commissioner of the Northwest Territories 1936-1946; member of the National Research Council 1921-1930; founder of the Canadian Geographical Society and its president (1929-1941).

CANA

Cana is the first stop east of Melville on the CNR. Cana was first known as Wakefield. The first families consisted of: the Gyugs, the Puhls, the Benedicts, the Reves, the Korpanys, the Millers and the Humphries. This was in 1905. In 1907 and 1908 a large settlement of Hungarians moved in. They were very religious and in deference to them the name of the district was changed to Cana.

This commemorates the marriage feast at Cana of Galilee at which Jesus performed one of his first miracles, the changing of water into wine. Cana is one of four Saskatchewan place names directly associated with the Bible. The other three are Galilee, Mont Nebo and Ebenezer.

CANDIAC

Candiac is between Montmartre and Glenavon on a CNR line. It is named for Mr. Candiac, a Canadian Northern Railroad official.

CANDLE LAKE

This beautiful evergreen surrounded lake lies just east of Prince Albert National Park and is drained by the Torch river into the Saskatchewan river.

Indians gave the lake its name. On the east side of the lake there are two islands and on some evenings a great light shone between them in the shape of a candle. The Indians believed the lake to be haunted and called it Candle Lake.

In 1912 Mr. Con Hanson settled at the lake and he was told this story. Besides Con Hanson and his wife, Curly, Mr. Fred Cole of the area has also seen the strange lights.

The post office at Candle Lake was put in during the 1930s.

CANDO

Cando is on a CNR line built in 1912 and 1913 that ran north from Oban Junction (ten miles west of Biggar) to Battleford.

Settlers moved into this area as early as 1907, many of them coming from Cando, North Dakota.

Mr. and Mrs. Charlie Edwards opened the first post office in their homestead home on Section 18, Township 39, Range 16, west of the 3rd, in the early 1900's. The name Cando was applied for and accepted by postal authorities. Mr. Edwards hauled the mail from Traynor.

The railway grade was built in 1912 and the first train arrived in 1913. Mr. Edward's country post office moved into town and gave it its name.

Some Cando firsts were: 1) Elevator — Brooks with John Munro as agent. This is now the Wheat Pool "A" elevator.

2) Store — Mr. Heagle's General store. He later sold out to Guidinger and Murray.

3) Church — Congregational. It was built in 1913 with Reverend George Hindley as minister. Congregational church services were also held in Norwich, Ibstone and Naseby schools, with all three points being served by a student minister. Leslie Sanders was one of these students, and after his ordination he was minister of Cando for three years before moving on to Biggar.

This information came from Etha Munro, a long-time resident of the Cando district. It is interesting to note in her letter a story of how Cando, North Dakota got its name from a country school. The school was named as a result of a dispute between two groups over where it should be located. One group said it couldn't be built in a certain place, and the other group said, "We *can do* it." They did and the school was named Cando!

CANOE NARROWS

Canoe Narrows is a settlement on the west shore of Canoe Lake from which it takes its name. Highway 101 was built in from Beauval in the 1970's and the tourists that followed it in have found the summer fishing good and the hunting in winter, the same. The result is that Canoe Narrows is booming.

Canoe Lake got its name in an interesting way. Two men who were doing a geological survey started out to cross the lake and were caught by a summer squall and their canoe overturned. They held fast to it and were washed ashore. Thankful for their deliverance they named the lake Canoe.

CANOPUS

Canopus is on a branch line of the CPR that runs south of Assiniboia and ends at Killdeer. It is also on the main branch of the Poplar river which empties into the Missouri river at Poplar, Montana.

Canopus is a star of the first magnitude in the constellation Argo, not visible north of 37 latitude. Although very many times as far from the earth as Sirius, yet next to the latter it is the brightest fixed star.

The name was given to the town by Reverend Morris. His daughter, Mrs. Reah Solverson still lives on the original homestead at Canopus. The first postmistress was Mrs. Lovica Urquhart who now lives in the Pioneer Lodge in Assiniboia. Walter Hoffman of Wood Mountain was one of the earliest settlers in the district. The Canopus post office closed in 1969.

CANORA

Canora was named after the CAnadian NOrthern RAilway. It was incorporated as a village in 1905. Growth was steady and by 1910, the community had achieved town status, and now has a population of 2600.

CANTAL

Cantal is a settlement northwest of Carnduff 36-5-34-WPM. The first postmaster was Mr. C. Bertholet. It was named for "Plomb du Cantal" a little southeast of St. Julien, France.

CANTUAR

Cantuar is between Success and the junction at Java on a CPR line that runs from Swift Current northwest around the "Great Sand Hills." It is the signature of the Archbishop of Canterbury.

CANUCK

Canuck is on a branch line of the CPR that runs east from Notukeu to Val Marie. In places this line is less than 12 miles from the U.S.A. border. Canuck took its name from a country post office that was operated in a private home two miles south of the present townsite. This post office was established in 1911 — 14 years before the railway arrived.

Canuck is a nickname for a Canadian and they tell this story as to how Johnny became attached to it. The United Empire Loyalists, as individuals, were derisively called "Johnathon" by their American compatriots. This name followed them into their new lives in Canada, just as the "Oakies" of Oklahoma carried theirs into California in the '30s. Over the years it became simply John and was absorbed by other elements of the pioneer population. It reached its final form when an American whisky pedlar was apprehended by the North West Mounted Police in present day Alberta — with an American's gift for coining slang words he shouted, "No . . . Johnny Canuck ain't gonna arrest me!" But they did!

CANWOOD

Canwood is on a branch line of the CNR that runs north out of Shellbrook through heavy timber to Big River. The line was built in the early 1900s, to bring lumber out of the north. This led directly to the name Canwood which is a contraction of CANadian WOODs.

The first settlers in the district were mostly Scandinavians with a few Irish mixed in.

CAPASIN

Capasin, an Indian corruption of "camp soon," was one of the favorite camping sites on the old Green Lake Trail. Edward Landry, Pete Warkentin and Pete Peppner were some of the earliest settlers. The CPR built a branch line north from Debden to Panton in 1931 and the Indian word "Capasin" was given to the townsite.

CARDELL

Cardell is the first stop east of a CPR line that runs to Swift Current. It was named for Mr. John Cardell, former master mechanic with the CPR at Calgary.

CARDROSS

Cardross is the end of a branch line of the CPR that runs northwest from the junction at Amulet. It is named after a place in Scotland located in Dunbartonshire on the Firth of Clyde. The Reverend John Macauley was at one time the minister of Cardross in Scotland, and it was at Cardross manse that Zachery Macauley, the well-known emancipator and father of Lord Macauley was born.

CARIBOU CREEK

The Hanson Lake Road or Highway 106 was started in 1957 at Smeaton and completed to Flin Flon, Manitoba in 1962. The total distance is 240 miles and as it winds its way through bush and muskeg country it skirts many fine fishing lakes. It was named for Olaf Hanson, a long-time prospector in that area of the province.

At Smeaton (once named Dorrit) the road starts at Mile 0. From there up to Flin Flon places are designated by the distance from the starting point, Mile 0.

Caribou Creek is Mile 46. This name was established by the Indians long before any white men came to the district. The name of the creek was chosen because of the abundance of Woodland Caribou in the area. These animals, next to the moose, are the most sought after game in the district.

Caribou Creek now has a lodge. From it tourists may fish in any one of five lakes in the vicinity. In winter, the lodge caters to big game hunters.

The only communication with the outside world is by two-way radio because there are no towns or telephones between Smeaton and Flin Flon.

CARIEVALE

John Young, who arrived in the district in 1886, suggested the name for the post office which opened in 1891. It is of Scottish origin and is said to mean "lovely valley".

CARLEA

Carlea is near the junction of the Carrot river and the Leather river. It was named by taking the first three letters of Carrot river and the first three letters of Leather river.

CARLTON

Carlton is a small village at the end of the steel of a branch line 60 miles north of Saskatoon. It takes its name from Carlton House, one of three Hudson's Bay Company posts of the same name, this one built in 1810 on the North Saskatchewan river west of Duck Lake. Carlton House was consiered a halfway house on the long trail from Red River to Edmonton and it also gave its name to this route, "The Carlton Trail".

Carlton House was an important transportation centre in the days of the Red River cart. This post was also known at times as Fort Carlton. After the disastrous skirmish at Duck Lake which started the Northwest Rebellion in 1885, it was abandoned and burned when the troops withdrew to Prince Albert. In May of 1965 work was started on the restoration of this historic site.

CARLYLE

There are two versions of the naming of Carlyle. Canadian Pacific Railway sources contend that it was named for the famous Scottish writer Thomas Carlyle (1795-1881). A local informant maintains it was named for a couple named Carlyle, early settlers who kept a store, and were buried in West Carlyle cemetery.

CARLYLE LAKE RESORT

The following is a complete letter received from H. V. Stent, of Summerland, B.C.

"This name was chosen by my mother, Mrs. F. J. Stent, in 1910 or thereabouts. She won a contest for the best suggestion for a name for the then new resort, and as a prize she received a lot on "Sandy Beach" at the lake. A cottage was built on this lot in partnership with Mr. Bruce Forsyth and our families took holidays in it in turn for many happy summers."

CARMEL

Carmel is the first station east of Bruno. It is named for Mount Carmel, three and one-half miles to the north. The original name of this high hill was "Big Butte." Then in 1878 an event happened which led to its being called "The Hill of the Cross." Here is the story:

Henrietta MacKay of Fish Creek was ordered by her parents to marry a man she did not want. In order to escape the marriage she fled from home. Either inadvertently or otherwise she took poison and died. She was buried northeast of the Big Butte by Isidor Dumas and Alexander Ablois. In her memory a wooden cross was erected on the hill. People began to call it "The Hill of the Cross".

When the district was surveyed in 1886 by Lestock Reid, he named the Hill of the Cross, Mount Carmel.

In 1921 officials from St. Peter's Abbey at Muenster visited Mr. John Bunko, on whose land the Mount is located, and arrangements were made to make it a place of pilgrimage. The work (The Chapel — the Statue of Our Lady — the Stations of the Cross) has progressed steadily ever since. Each year the annual pilgrimage draws thousands of people from all over Saskatchewan.

CARMICHAEL

Carmichael is on a CPR line that runs southwest of Swift Current to Maple Creek. It was named for Mr. Carmichael who was a civil engineer on the line when it was being built.

CARNAGH

Carnagh is an inland post office about halfway between Piapot and Eastend.

Mail for the settlers in the early 1900s in what was later known as the Carnagh district, came from Maple Creek to Skull Creek post office which meant patrons had to travel some distance for their mail.

Then in 1913 the Cypress Hill post office was opened with A. J. F. Lambert as postmaster. The post office was in his home and the mail was delivered once a week from Piapot. Due to the fact that other post offices had Cypress in their name, Mrs. Lambert changed the name to Carnagh in 1915 in memory of a town in Ireland. Mr. and Mrs. Lambert retired from the farm in September, 1929, and Mr. A. G. Dakin acted as postmaster until Donald Neely was appointed postmaster in December 1929 and the post office moved to his home. On June 28, 1968, Carnagh post office closed and a rural route was opened from Eastend to bring the mail to the district.

CARNDUFF

Carnduff is a town in the extreme southeast of the province. It was named for John Carnduff; the first postmaster, in whose home the first post office was opened September 1, 1884.

CARON

Caron is the second station west of Moose Jaw on the CPR.

Mr. John Hans came to Caron in 1889 and his family joined him in 1890. Their first Christmas together was spent fighting a prairie fire.

Grandmother Thompson and Grandmother Getty of the Summerside district used to get together to rock, and chat, and to smoke their clay pipes, filled with cuttings from "McDonald Plug."

Before the first elevator at Caron the wheat was hauled in two-bushel bags, and stacked by the thousand waiting for the arrival of a grain car.

One of the very few sources of money in those days was the sale of buffalo bones. They brought $8 per wagon load.

The first church services were held in the section house. All denominations attended.

Mr. English introduced power farming, consisting of two independent units, "Buck" and "Bright." They were good oxen except on hot days when they disregarded all advice, either by word or prod, and would bolt off and lay down in the nearest slough.

The first train came into Moose Jaw in December of 1882. The CPR was built from Calgary to meet it and the road came through Caron early in 1883 and the townsite was named at that time in honor of Sir Adolphe Caron then minister of militia and defence, who served in the Canadian cabinet from 1880 to 1896.

CARONPORT

Just west of Moose Jaw on the main line of the CP is the town of Caron. Near Caron is an abandoned airport, one of many that were used during World War II to train British Commonwealth airmen. Here is how it got its name.

In 1934 Sinclair Whittaker, who has retired and is living in Moose Jaw now, started a Bible and High School in an old house. His enrolment was eleven. The next year it jumped to thirty. By 1946 they just had to have more facilities and so they were able to arrange to take over the abandoned airport near Caron and hence the name Caronport.

CARPENTER

Carpenter is between Wakaw and Alvena on a CNR line that runs from Saskatoon to Melfort. It was named after Mr. H. S. Carpenter, deputy minister of highways in the province of Saskatchewan at the time the line was being built.

CARRAGANA

The village of Carragana is between Porcupine Plain and Somme but the original rural post office from which it received its name was ten miles to the north.

In the year 1921 Mr. Pegg had just been appointed postmaster and was wondering what to suggest as a name. Mrs. Pegg, sitting at the kitchen table looking through a seed catalogue, suggested the name Caragana. Mr. Pegg was intrigued with her suggestion and submitted it. It was accepted.

When the railroad came through the post office moved south and gave its name to the village. However, the authorities, or someone, made a mistake in the spelling and that is why the village of Carragana came up with an extra "R".

CARROT RIVER

The first post office in this district was named for the Carrot river as it was just two miles from the river.

Carrot River is the English translation for the Cree Indian name for the river which is "Oska Task Se Pe." Wild carrots grow on the banks of the river and the Indians call them Oska Task. They use the same word for our garden variety of carrot, too. So the Indians named the river Oska Task Se Pe. It is a very nice sounding name when it is pronounced properly in Cree.

CARRUTHERS

The Grand Trunk Pacific built west from Battleford on its way to Lloydminster. It stopped at Carruthers in 1913 and never went any farther. Being the end of the line Carruthers served a large territory and this was not challenged until the CPR built west from Cut Knife in 1922 and went on to "Lloyd."

During its boom days Carruthers had the following: one bank, one post office, four stores, two livery barns, one hotel, one lumberyard, four churches, one blacksmith shop, one pool hall and barbershop, two elevators (one burned down, the Scottish Co-op), and one cafe operated by George Bozak who cooked for Wells' Construction gangs for years. By 1971 Carruthers was literally boarded up with one elevator open a few days of the week (Pool agent, Dave Crittall served Tatsfield, too) and a small general store.

Early residents include the following: George Reuben, John Thomson, Hans H. Thompson, Clarence Kolwalsky, Leonard Creelman, Douglas and George Marling, John Grant, Robert Goodall, Philip Lee Bird, James Mackie, Herbert Greenwood, Robert Oxland, John Wright, Thomas and Clifford Bullerwell, Englwold Brothen, Will Burge, Henry Kornder, John and William Cross.

Ray McInnes, principal of North Battleford Composite School, likes to tell this Hallowe'en story that took place in Carruthers. A carefully prepared little party had been arranged. George Bozak closed his cafe doors at 6:00 p.m. and opened them again at 12:00 midnight for the entertainment of his selected friends. It was a real spread with your choice of turkey, goose, duck or chicken. These fowl had all been "lifted and partially prepared" well in advance. Pete Picard was one of the unsuspecting guests. He chose chicken. When asked how he was enjoying his meal he said, "Fine!" When informed that he was eating one of his own chickens he laughed and replied, "Well, all I can say is 'Pete Picard, he raise damn fine chicken!'"

CARSDALE

Carsdale was formerly a post office at the junction of the Wascana and the Qu'Appelle rivers. It took its name from Edward Carss, the very first settler within the region known as the "Regina Plains."

CARVALE

Carvale was opened as a sub-post office east of Winside on August 1, 1909, by the Carr brothers, Jim and Bill. Because of a similarity with the name Carievale, mail became mixed up and the smaller place was asked to change names. On May 1, 1910, Carvale changed to Maxton. We do not know the significance of the name, Maxton. The post office was short-lived and closed on April 30, 1912. A railway, better roads and cars made it unnecessary.

CASTLEWOOD

Castlewood is between North Biggar and Oban on a CPR line. At one time it had an elevator and a section gang. Mr. Joe Gallucci now retired in Biggar was the section foreman. The elevator has been torn down and even the loading platform has been removed.

In the 1930s the CPR built south from Perdue to Rosetown and the first grain point was called Catherwood. There was considerable controversy over the naming because it was contended that the name was too much like Castlewood and there would be mix-ups. However, both names stood.

CATER

Twelve miles east of Glaslyn, where highway No. 3 intersects the CPR line from Medstead to Meadow Lake, is the little hamlet of Cater. Less than a mile east lives Mrs. Austin Thompson whose mother, Mrs. George Starling, submitted her maiden name, Cater, when a post office was started there in 1914. It was accepted.

Mrs. Starling's brother, Harry Cater, of Brandon, Manitoba, was the man who invented, manufactured and sold the famous Cater wooden pump of early days. One of these pumps is still in use on the farm of Robert Orr of Cater.

CATHERWOOD

On a branch line of the Canadian Pacific Railway from Perdue to Rosetown, built in the "30s", is an elevator called Catherwood. There used to be a store there too. It is named in honor of Ethel Catherwood.

Ethel was born in Hannah, North Dakota, U.S.A. on April 28, 1908, the sixth child of a family of nine, all of whom were athletic. Her high jumping started as a game in the yard of her home at Scott, Saskatchewan, with the neighborhood youngsters participating. Her father encouraged and coached her along with the rest of the family until they moved to Saskatoon in 1925.

Ethel attended Bedford Road Collegiate and continued to win the high jump at the various athletic meets. At this point Joe Griffiths of the University of Saskatchewan became interested and played an important part in her training until she went to Toronto in 1928, under the sponsorship of the Elks Club of Saskatoon, to receive special training under the famous Walter Knox.

At the Olympic Games in Amsterdam, Holland, in August of 1928 Ethel won a gold medal when she set a new world record for high jump with a jump of 5 feet 3 inches. From then on she was called the "Saskatoon Lily."

She now resides in San Francisco, California.

CATHKIN

When the CPR built a branch line south of Wilkie to Kelfield the first grain point was named Cathkin. A settlement nearby already had a name Pascal, named for St. Pascal's Parish. There was a store there run by Mr. Deilaney and also a post office.

However, one of the railway officials was responsible for the name Cathkin which commemorates a series of hills which surround the city of Glasgow, Scotland. People were so glad to see the railroad they didn't argue over the name.

Johnny Anderson, 241 Railway Avenue, Unity, remembers buying grain for the Pool at Cathkin in 1946-47. Local farmers who drew grain to him were: John and Louie Kaufmann, Louie Schmidt, Wilbert Wismer, Forest Jansen and Mr. Vanden Banbell.

CAVALIER

Cavalier is named for Cavalier County, North Dakota, the home of many of the first settlers in the district. The advance party arrived in 1902 and included Alphonse Waterer and his two sons Fred and Bert, John Russell, Jim and Frank Coney, and Bill Schaefer.

CAVELL

Cavell is the first stop west of Landis. It is named for Edith Louisa Cavell (1865-1915), an English nurse whose tragic death made her a martyr of the First World War. She was in charge of a hospital in Brussels, Belgium, when the German troops occupied the city in 1915. For several months she assisted Allied soldiers, about 200 in all, to escape to the Dutch border. Arrested by the Germans, she admitted her activities, and was shot.

Feeling ran very high about this and the little hamlet of Coblenz in Saskatchewan changed its name to Cavell.

Cavell was started in 1908 when the main line of the CNR arrived. Early immigrants to Canada tended to settle in ethnic groups and Cavell was largely German. It grew rapidly and at its height in the early twenties had three elevators, three lumber yards, two general stores, a hotel, a school, a municipal office, an Anglican church and many fine residences.

In 1924 the Wilkie-Kelfield branch line of the CPR was completed and Leipzig, a few miles west of Cavell became the large trading centre.

Cavell steadily dwindled until today there are no services available. Two families — that of Otto "Mike" Krump and Jake Frey live there only in summer but spend the winter in towns nearby.

There is one other activity in summer. A Pentecostal church known as the "Beulah Mission" holds services at 10:00 a.m.

One further note of interest is that on a large faded and boarded up store front you can see in large black letters "J. Kaufmann". The J. was for Jack and he was the father of Jake and Lawrence, founders of the famous Kaufmann stores you find throughout Saskatchewan today.

CAZALET

Cazalet is a few miles east of Biggar. When the GTP and CPR left Saskatoon for Edmonton they ran very close together in places and nowhere were they closer than at Cazalet. In fact, the early local residents named the point "Double Crossing." Some of these were Buxtons, Palmers, Lowrys, Fauvers, and Brickies who came in covered wagons from Washington State.

In the 1930s after the CNR had taken over, the station at Neola, the next stop to the west, was moved to Double Crossing and the name was changed to Cazalet. It is possible that this was done to honor Victor Cazalet, M.C., M.P., born 1896. He was a prominent British politician in the 1920s and 30s and a colleague and close friend of John Buchan.

CEDOUX

Cedoux is a short distance north of Weyburn. It is named for a former rural post office in the area. It is interesting how the Cedoux post office got its name. Mr. Maronczuk, an early settler, suggested Ledoux in memory of his hometown of Ledoux, North Dakota. It was accepted but because of a spelling or writing mistake it came out officially as Cedoux.

The first settler in the district was Mr. Lucyk who arrived with his family in 1902. Mr. Lucyk still lives at Cedoux.

CEEPEE

Ceepee sits by the side of the North Saskatchewan river east of the Borden Bridge on the way from Saskatoon to North Battleford. Ceepee is an Indian word meaning "river".

CELTIC

Celtic post office opened on September 1st 1914 and closed April 4th 1945. The first postmaster was W. J. Stewart and the office was on N.W. 2-52-23 W3. The name given the post office came from the British Isles.

The first Celts were a mixture of people. They tended to be fair-haired and light-skinned, but some had dark colored hair and complexion. They were taller than many of their neighbors but not so tall as the Norsemen.

CENTRAL BUTTE

In the early days this country was devoted entirely to ranching. There are three big hills in the district which were called "The Buttes." One was on the north side of the South Saskatchewan river towards Demaine, one was to the west just north of Eyebrow, and the one where it was the most convenient for all to converge at round-up time was the one in the centre or the central butte. Central Butte takes its name from being close to this hill

CEYLON

Ceylon is the second stop out of Radville on a CNR line that runs west to Willow Bunch. The first homesteader into the district was J. S. McPhee in 1905 and he was closely followed by George Balius and Joe Malonson. A considerable community had grown up before the railroad arrived and it was called Aldred after the post office located in the log cabin home of Mr. and Mrs. John Aldred. When the railway arrived they wished to call the townsite Aldred but Mr. Aldred declined and requested that the station should be called Ceylon. We do not know the significance of the name.

CHAGONESS

Chagoness is an inland post office north of Kinistino. It gets its mail from Silver Park. The district was named in the early days after Chagoness Nippi (Nikwas Naa Nip), a former chief on the reserve. In the Sioux dialect the name means "Bobcat."

CHAMBERLAIN

Chamberlain is on a CNR line between Saskatoon and Regina. It's a healthy little town far enough from the cities to have a life of its own.

In 1903 Alfred Cuthbert came to Chamberlain at the age of eleven with his five brothers and parents, Mr. and Mrs.

John William Cuthbert, from Durham County, England. Other early settlers in the district were Arnold and Fred Mallinson, Walter Greenwood, John Ball, George Destree and George Barton.

William Elkerton was the first station agent and Jack Prentice was the first section foreman. The first railroad from Regina to Prince Albert was built with English capital and leased to the CPR.

Geraldine Shatkowski of Chamberlain wrote to tell us that the town was named for Mr. Joseph Chamberlain (1863-1937), noted British politican. The CNR provided information that it was named after Mr. F. A. Chamberlain, a banker of Minneapolis. Many United States businessmen financed their countrymen in a move to Canada in the early 1900s. The Saskatchewan Land Valley Company was one such organization and it sold thousands of acres of land along the line in the vicinity of Chamberlain.

CHAMBERS

Chambers is a single Pool elevator between Delisle and Donavon. Recently the elevator was closed, boarded up and used for storage. It was named for Mark and Beverly Chambers who homesteaded the land on which the grain point was located. Lloyd and Howard Shoemaker farm the land at the present time. Some of the men who drew grain to this elevator in the early years were: James, William and John Thomson; James and Frances Harburn; James and Nels Anderson; Simon, Albert and Frank Walper; Robert Larmour; James Wilkie; George Gwilliam; John Adams and Menno Souder.

CHAMBERY

Chambery post office first opened July, 1911, on the SW section 31-5-18-W3. Mrs. Hugh Forrest was the first postmistress. Mr. and Mrs. Forrest came from a place called Chambery in Scotland and suggested the new post office be named after their old home town and so it was named Chambery. The mail was first hauled from Gull Lake (which is about 55 miles north on the main line of the CPR) by team and buggy or light wagon once a week.

The mail went from Gull Lake to Cloverly post office which was about 15 miles northwest and then someone had to take it over to Chambery. When Shaunavon came into being October, 1913, the mail was brought from there every day and for places south of the river: Bracken, Climax and Frontier. Mrs. Hugh Forrest was the first postmistress and was followed by Mrs. J. Waldorf, Mrs. W. McMurray and Mrs. A. Dynna. The post ofice closed in 1959.

By 1908 the land was being taken up for homesteaders and by 1911 it was pretty well all taken up. Here is a list of the names of the real old-timers of the Chambery district: Edward Dokken, Hugh Patterson, Paul Bloom and family, Arran McIntyre, Wm. McIntyre, Gunder Jacobson, Jacob Aadland and family, Edward Moolin and family, Miss Ida Lange, Henry Lange, Mrs. Duggan and family, Geo. Johnson, Wm. Halley, Hans Roholt and family, Jack Ferguson, John Waldorf, Duncan Waldorf, Victor Pigeon, Mr. Van Allen and son William, Mrs. Vera Latego, Wm. Loftus, Wesley Quennell, Roy Quennell, Ingerberg Dynna, Miss Elizabeth Sanderson, Miss Bessie Quennell, Earl Smart, Bud Smart, Miles Smart, Henry Nelson, Geo. Fisher, Harold Fisher, Thomas Truper, Olif Olson, Adolph Olson, Peter Hornslein and family, and Mrs. Jennie Hunter and family.

Mr. Roy Quennell composed this list in 1971, at which time he was 82 years old and the only one left of the original homesteaders still living in the district. He had retired from farming twelve years before and gone to live in Shaunavon.

CHAPLIN

Chaplin is a village on the north shore of Lake Chaplin. It takes its name from the lake. The lake was named in 1861 by Sir John Rae who hunted in the area with two companions, Viscount Chaplin and Sir Frederick John W. Johnstone.

CHAPPELL JUNCTION

Chappell Junction is on the western outskirts of Saskatoon where the C.N.R. used to come in from the west and then circle north of the city before coming in to the downtown station. It consisted of one small building for railway use.

In the 1960's the C.N.R. moved their station out west of the junction. The building is gone but there is a Canadian Transport Commission power switch there to control traffic going into northern Saskatchewan.

Chappell Junction was named for a Saskatoon district farmer, Joseph Chappell, who homesteaded the land on which the present CNR station stands.

CHARLOTTE

Charlotte post office opened on the first of December 1910 on the N.W. of 22-53-23 W3 and was run by Pierre Adolph Bertrand. He named it for his daughter Charlotte, who had died at an early age from tuberculosis.

In 1918 Joseph H. Marshall took over the post office and moved it to N.E. 26-53-23 W3 and added a store. When the rails reached St. Walburg in 1921, Mr. Marshall moved into town where he started a general store. It is still carried on today by his son, Ken.

CHARLTON

Charlton is on a CNR line a short distance southwest of Battleford. It was named for Mr. H. R. Charlton, the manager of the Advertising Bureau of the CNR at the time.

CHARMIAN

Charmian is a flag station south of Burstall. There are several stories as to where the name came from. 1) It was the Christian name of Dr. C. M. MacArthur, a superintendent on the CPR. 2) It was named by Mrs. Hamilton Schild meaning "great day in the morning." 3) It was named for Cleopatra's faithful servant, Charmian, who committed suicide rather than live without her mistress. 4) It is the name of a city in Pennsylvania. And for some places we can't even get one story!

CHELAN

Chelan is between Porcupine Plain and Bjorkdale. It is an Indian name meaning "By the side of the Beautiful Waters" and was chosen by Mrs. Peter Bell.

The CNR constructed their railroad to Chelan and through the Porcupine Solier Settlement during 1929. The first grain elevator was located at Bjorkdale and the next one was built in Chelan, both owned by Saskatchewan Wheat Pool. The first elevator agent in Chelan was Paul Mabry. The hotel, to begin with, started as a store owned by Bill Clouse. Another store

which started up was owned and operated by Pete Sorochuk.

The first school was at the junction of Highway 23 and the present Greenwater Highway. The teacher was Miss Trembly. Later on the school house was moved into Chelan where it now stands with additions.

The first post office was run by Joe Toifer and was located two and a half miles west of Chelan. Chelan had the first curling rink in the area. It was described by one of the residents as "not too fancy, but people had fun".

CHEMONG

Chemong is on a CNR line running northeast from Hudson Bay, Saskatchewan, to The Pas, Manitoba. Chemong is a Cree word meaning canoe.

CHESTERFIELD HOUSE

Chesterfield House, a Hudson's Bay Trading Post, was built at the mouth of the Red Deer River in 1800. Its first factor was Peter Fidler and it is thought he named it for the market town of Chesterfield in his native Derbyshire, England.

Colin Watson, of the Historic Sites Branch of the Department of Natural Resources, did a preliminary search for the exact site and later one was done by Hugh T. Mackie, but neither could find the actual location and to date it has not been found.

However, in 1968 a cairn was erected near the original site and it reads:

"In 1800 Peter Fidler of the Hudson's Bay Company established Chesterfield House at the mouth of the Red Deer River. The North-West and X.Y. Company built nearby. Hostility of the Indians and poor returns led to the abandonment of these posts in 1802. The site was reoccupied by the Hudson's Bay and North West Company in 1804-05 and by Donald Mackenzie in 1822-23".

The cairn is on ranch land owned by Mr. and Mrs. Barry Cocks who, although they live in Saskatchewan, get their mail at Empress, Alberta, just across the border.

CHEVIOT

Cheviot is a grain point on the CPR eighteen miles southeast of Saskatoon. The first settlers came into this district in

1903 and by the time the steel came through from Lanigan in 1907 the country was pretty well filled up. Names of elevators before the present Pool took over were: North Star, Maple Leaf Milling Company and Western Elevator Company.

At its peak in 1915 there were six passenger trains a day through Cheviot. For some years now, passenger service has been discontinued. Miss Marion Goodale, who was 91 years old in 1969, could remember "school fairs" at the Lone Star School near Cheviot. Children would bring their calves, pigs, lambs, vegetables, chickens, ducks and geese. The ladies would bring their fancy sewing, bread, buns, pies, canned fruit, butter and eggs. The Peidts, McKays, Horans, Petersons, Mundles and Allens were some of the people who took part in these activities. They can remember, too, when most schools had a garden.

Many of the early settlers in the district were English and Scottish and it is from them that the name Cheviot came, possibly to commemorate their memories of the Cheviot Hills that form a natural physical barrier between England and Scotland.

CHICKNEY

Chickney was named by Mr. S. Chipperfield, the first postmaster who opened the post office in his farm home. He chose the name in remembrance of the locality he came from in England.

CHIPPERFIELD

Chipperfield was an inland post office (now closed) close to Wartime. It was named for Harry Chipperfield, an original homesteader who was killed in World War I. The post office was located on his farm.

CHITEK LAKE AND CHITEK SIDING

Long before the white man arrived the Indians named this beautiful pine-encicled deepwater lake Chitek. In Cree "chitek" means pelican and many of these birds still nest on Big Island in the lake. The hamlet of Chitek Lake has over 100 permanent residents and this swells to many hundreds of cottagers and campers in the summer who have simply followed the pelicans to a good fishing ground.

Chitek Siding, five miles north on the CPR, knew stirring days in the 1930s when the Ferguson and Horner Lumber Company cut and shipped out train loads of cord wood. In the winter the population rose to the 200 mark. When other fuels replaced cord wood the camp closed. Over the years the remaining residents moved to the hamlet of Chitek Lake and the siding is now a ghost town.

CHOICELAND

The history of Choiceland dates back to the 20s when Murray McTaggert, George Cann, Peter Rotz, W. W. Steves and T. W. Robertson moved into the district.

It wasn't until the spring of 1927 that a meeting was called for the purpose of establishing a post office. It was Pete Rotz who suggested Choiceland because there was choice land and lots to choose from in the district.

When the CPR arrived in 1931 they accepted the name of the post office for the townsite.

CHORTITZ

Chortitz is a small Mennonite village between Hague and Rosthern. The first settlers arrived in 1897 and included the following families: Friesens, Gerbrandts, Doells and Brauns. All these families are represented in the village today. See the story of Chortitz southeast of Swift Current for the significance of the name.

CHORTITZ

Chortitz is a Mennonite village 15 miles south and about five miles east of Swift Current. The name came from a province in the Ukraine of Russia. A large group of Mennonite villages north of the city of Zaporozhye were called Chortitz and the village names went by numbers — Chortitz number 1, Chortitz number 2, etc. This information came from Mr. and Mrs. Zigmund Reichert of 5 Valens Drive, Saskatoon. The city of Zaporozhye is two hundred miles north of the Crimea and is built on the Dnieper river.

CHRISTOPHER LAKE

This district was surveyed in 1912 by a man named Monier. He named Christopher Lake after his brother, Christopher, and Emma Lake after his wife, Emma. Christopher Lake hamlet is situated a mile southwest of Christopher lake on Number 2 highway and takes its name from the lake. There is no railroad. The first post office was opened there in 1922 by Mrs. Rice and two years later she added a store. The hamlet grew slowly and the population is now 250.

CHRYSLER

Chrysler is within six miles of Yorkton and so it has never consisted of any more than an elevator and a loading platform. Its history is tied closely with Yorkton. The first settlers came in 1882. Many of them were brought by a colonization company organized in Toronto and known as the York Farmer's Colonization Company Ltd. Most of the settlers came from York County, Ontario, and hence the name.

The CPR arrived in 1890 and by that time the following homesteaders were settled: Wm. P. Hopkins, C. J. McFarlane, W. H. Meridith, Thos. H. Garry, Robert Bull, J. J. Smith, W. T. Smith, Charles Langstaff, Wesley Jackson, Edward Hopkins, Levi Beck and others.

The name Chrysler was given to the grain point because it was from Mr. W. J. Chrysler that the CPR bought the land.

CHURCHBRIDGE

Churchbridge is located 35 miles southeast of Yorkton. With the arrival of the Manitoba and North-Western Railway in 1886 settlement began under the leadership of a Church Colonization Land Society, which was under the auspices of the Anglican Church. One of the prominent directors was the Reverend John Bridges. They combined the name "Church" from the society with the "Bridge" from Bridges to form Churchbridge.

One of the largest potash mines in the world is located at Yarbo 12 miles to the south. A second shaft and processing mill are under construction at Gerald, five miles away. This puts Churchbridge very close to an important potash development area.

CLAGGETT

Claggett is the second point southwest of Melfort on a CNR line to Saskatoon. It was named for Jim Claggett, a very prosperous rancher-farmer of the Melfort area.

Here is an excerpt from "Voices of the Past," a booklet of the history of Melfort and district written on the occasion of Saskatchewan's golden jubilee in 1955:

"In 1903 Mr. D. Hammond of Ottawa began construction of the $20,000 Melfort hotel. The first ball was held in the unfinished building the following New Year organized by Jim Claggett and William McMaster."

CLAIR

Clair is on a CNR line a few miles north of Little Quill lake. Mr. J. H. Yerex sent in the following information which he got from Mr. Kenneth Riese, who homesteaded in the district ahead of the railway. Clair is named for Clair Heller, the first white child born in the district.

The Canadian Northern came through in 1908 and Mr. J. A. Leary was appointed agent in 1920. He was followed by Mr. Heaps, Mr. Harry Yerex took over in 1929 and continued until August of 1964 — surely a record for a stay in one place!

At one time Clair served a large district that stretched as far north as Dahlton. That was before the CPR built their line north from Wadena to Nipawin.

Clair was one of the heaviest stock shipping points along the line and it also ranked high as a raw fur shipping point. Muskrats from the Ponas lake area to the north were especially high in demand on the fur market, being of a type rarely found elsewhere. Hundreds of bags of raw fur were shipped each season.

Clair remained a busy little place until after World War II. Since then population has dwindled and only a few businesses are left — a hotel, a cafe, the post office, grain elevators and little else. The march of progress has taken its toll.

CLANSMAN

Clansman was an inland post office which opened on the N.E. 8-54-22 W3 about 1914 and closed when the railroad reached St. Walburg in 1921. Andrew Willy was its only postmaster.

CLARK'S CROSSING AND CLARKBORO

These places, a dozen miles north of Saskatoon on the river, are named for Mr.

and Mrs. J. F. Clark, pioneers of Clark's Crossing who came before the Temperance Colony.

This is historic ground. James W. Whillans in his book, "First In The West," traces Henry Kelsey's route to Clarkboro:

"Kelsey travelled by the river, likely close to water, and left it, perhaps not far from Clarkboro."

In later times the first telegraph line that connected Fort Garry to Edmonton crossed the river at Clark's Crossing. It knew stirring times during the Rebellion of 1885 as General Middleton's column marched to the attack of the Metis at Batoche. The following is from the book, The Carlton Trail by R. C. Russell:

"Though only 63 miles from Batoche, the rebels had not disturbed the Humboldt settlement. There the trail forks; one path continuing almost due north to Batoche, the other leading west along the telegraph line to Clark's Crossing on the South Saskatchewan river. The trail to Clark's Crossing was followed, and the advance force camped for the night at Muskiki lake. Fire signals blazed on the hills to the north and west, showing that the troops had reached the enemy's country. At Clark's Crossing there were a couple of ferry scows. It was thought that the rebels would seize it, destroy the scows and attempt to prevent the troops from crossing. Middletown sent a special detachment of French's Scouts to seize the Crossing. They made the 38 miles in eight hours and Clark's Crossing was safe. To this point the Midland Battalion came down the South Saskatchewan river from Saskatchewan Landing on the steamer Northcote. Part of the battalion was left to guard the stores at Clark's Crossing while the remainder pushed on and joined the Middleton's forces at Fish Creek."

CLASHMOOR

In 1929 the CNR built north from Crooked River to Arborfield and the first grain point on the line was Clashmoor. The name came from the nearby rural school of Clashmoor which had been in operation since the early 1920's. It had been named by Tom Wilkinson, a local farmer, after a place near his home in England.

Jack Saunders opened the first store and post office in the little village. It grew and at its height had three stores, a blacksmith shop, a garage and, of course, the elevator.

The Pool closed out its elevator in the early 1960's. Stores began to close and the last one burned down in the late 1960's. The post office was closed out in 1969. Nothing much is left of Clashmoor except one house.

This information came from Ivan Earl, a graduate of Clashmoor school who now is branch manager of the Teacher's Credit Union at Saskatoon.

CLAVET

Clavet is about twenty miles southeast of Saskatoon. It was incorporated as a village in 1908 and was called French. In 1909 when the Grand Trunk station was being built they were naming the stations alphabetically and the name was changed to Clavet to fit this run of names: Allan, Bradwell, Clavet, Duro and Earl. Then Saskatoon broke the chain.

CLAYBANK

Claybank is the first stop west of Avonlea on a CNR line that runs to Moosbank. It was named for the large clay deposits where the Dominion Brick and Clay Products plant now stands.

CLAYDON

Claydon is on a branch line of the CPR in the southwest corner of the province that runs east of Notukeu to Val Marie. In 1910 Mr. Howard Husband located a homestead on 4-4-22-W3. In 1911, his family moved in and several families followed. They soon began to think of applying for a post office. Mr. Husband offered to be postmaster and everyone began thinking of a suitable name.

The Husband sons, Wilfred and George, went north to the river about eighteen miles away to get a load of poles for fence posts. They stayed overnight at the Potter ranch and told the Potters about the new post office and how they had not yet selected a name. Mrs. Potter said their estate in England had been called Claydon. The boys liked that name and it was sent in and subsequently it was accepted.

Mr. Howard Husband kept the post office for several years and then it was taken over by Mr. Vandruffs. Later Mr. A. P. Husband took it over and when the CPR built through 9-3-22-W3 in 1923 Mr. Husband moved his house to the townsite and the CPR accepted the name of Claydon.

CLAYTONVILLE

Claytonville is an inland post office on the north side of the North Saskatchewan river about twenty miles northwest of Prince Albert. It was named for the late Clayton Smith, the first postmaster.

A school was built in the district in 1917. The first teacher was Miss Stella Macdougald. She taught 34 pupils for a salary of $55 a month. The next year there were about 70 schools in Saskatchewan looking for a teacher and her salary was raised to $70 a month. The school was called Husiatyn S.D. No. 791.

In 1918 the municipality that was formed was called the Rural Municipality of Russia. This name was changed to Garden River in 1928. The school later changed its name to Claytonville.

In 1931 W. J. "Bill" Berezowski, later an NDP MLA, taught in this school. Names common in the district are Bradley, Scraggs, Channons and Smith.

The original log building which housed the post office for many years still stands. Mail now comes on a rural route out of Prince Albert.

CLEARFIELD

Clearfield is halfway between Weyburn and Radville on a CNR branch line. It consists of a Pool elevator. No one lives there. Larry Talbot is the agent and he resides in Weyburn and comes down on certain days when a quota is set.

Clearfield is one of a number of places like Broadview, Broadacres, Longacre, and Laniwci which express the feeling of virgin land ready for the plow. It's a place, too, like Tiger Hills, where no one actually lives and the elevator is opened on certain days.

CLEARSITE

Clearsite is in the Maple Creek area. The post office has been closed for several years but the name lives on in the community. Clearsite was a welcome sight to homesteaders, many of whom had arrived from lands where they had to get rid of trees before they could farm.

There were few roots and rocks to get rid of on the prairies around Maple Creek. It is classed with names like: Clearfield, Broadview, Longacre and Laniwci.

CLEEVES

Cleeves is between Spruce Lake and Turtleford on a CNR line that runs north from North Battleford to St. Walburg. It was named for one of the early settlers in the district, Manford Cleeves.

At one time in the 20s, Cleeves was the end of the steel. All fish brought out of the north were shipped from Cleeves. It had a few boom years.

Then the railway moved on to St. Walburg and branched to Frenchman Butte.

For a time Cleeves hung on and then a decline set in that leaves it today (1972) a ghost town. Elevator, school, post office, stores are all gone, boarded up or stand with gaping open windows. Not a place of business remains. The most unique feature left is a relatively small two-storey faded-green building with a simple inscription between two top windows, HOTEL.

CLEMENCEAU

Cleamenceau is a small village in the northeast of Saskatchewan on a line that runs from Reserve to Hudson Bay. It was named for George S. Clemenceau (1841-1929) a French statesman who led his country triumphantly through the last and most difficult period of the First World War.

CLEMENS

Clemens is the first stop south of Melfort on a CPR line that runs to Watson, Lanigan and on to Regina. The line was built in 1924. The point was named for C. O. Clemens of Melfort.

CLIFTONVILLE

Cliftonville is a rural post office near Maple Creek 19-15-27-W3, and the first postmaster was Mr. D. H. Kendall. They simply took the name of a prominent early settler, Clifton Wright, and made up the name.

CLIMAX

Climax is about halfway between Notokeu and Val Marie on a CPR branch line that runs almost parallel with the border from Divide to Masefield.

Small ranchers from south of the border were the first to settle in the district and most of them were along Boulanger creek. The first big ranch was the Turkey Track outfit whose cattle ranged from north of Wood Mountain to Val Marie. After the killing winter of 1906 and 1907 the Turkey Track sold out to the "76" Ranch with Harry Otterson as manager.

From 1908 to 1910 a few ranchers settled long the banks of the White Mud river, some of them being the Corbett brothers, G. L. Greenlay, Bill Kyle, Bill Moore, McGuires, McNaught Brothers, and Angus Dalgleish.

Land south of the White Mud was opened for homesteading in 1909, the nearest land office being Moose Jaw. Among the first to file were John Kluzak, his son George, and Tom Holm. John and George Kluzak were the first to take up residence, building their shacks in the spring of 1910.

Grading for the railroad started in 1922. Steel reached Climax in 1923 and was extended to Val Marie in 1924. The original Climax post office was located three miles southeast of the present townsite. The first postmaster was Charlie Truswell. The name Climax was chosen by Fred and Christ "Chris" Fuglestad who, along with many other Scandinavian settlers, had come to the district from Climax, North Dakota. With the coming of the railroad the post office moved into town and gave it its name.

In 1925 Mr. A. H. Stevens opened a printing business and founded the *Climax Weekly Newspaper*. Climax became quite a little town. Not just a boom town but a solid little town. Even though it never passed the 250 point in population it became a natural local center for a large trading area. It had several general stores, three lumberyards, two doctors, a hospital, two dentists, a jeweller, law office, two poolrooms, several restaurants, a hotel, the Union Bank, a barbershop, a gents' ready-to-wear, a station, section houses, a drayman, garage and auto dealers, a butcher, a bakeshop, several implement agencies, and several elevators (one burned down early, the Lake of Woods). The Silver Dollar Pool Hall operated by Clark Walters and R. E. Robinson was a center of continuous action. A 24-hour service supplied steaks, onions, bacon and eggs all fried behind the counter by Dick Patterson right in front of the customer's eyes. A few card tables, pool tables and a refreshment counter completed the picture. Here, when there was no other place available, a Chautauqua program (3 days) was held, planks being placed over pool tables to provide a platform. It is rumored that at a tense and still moment when one of the plays was being enacted, a voice came from behind the stage, "I'll raise you ten," accompanied by the jingle of poker chips being dropped into the pot.

The first Sports Day in Climax was on August 5th, 1924. Any Saskatchewan town settled predominantly by Americans, as Climax was, had a good baseball club. Climax Advertisers (later Cardinals) was one of the best. They built a big boxcover on a truck and, in the interests of frugality, all travelled in it. They were hard to beat. The battery of Comartin (catcher and coach) and Gordon Ramsay is still remembered. They toured the sports days in southern Saskatchewan and southeastern Alberta and made it pay — no mean feat with the money they put up for tournaments in the 30s.

The Climax Board of Trade was very active from the day it was inaugurated in 1923. The big event of the year is the Board of Trade sponsored "Fall Carnival." Over the years it has built up to a two-day affair. It's a money raiser pure and simple. Queen Contests are climaxed then, dances are held every night but the money in this free-wheeling town is "Crown and Anchor," no limit. Open air stands all over the place accommodate the customers and at some wheels you can see two or three hundred dollars change hands on a single roll. Many of the "first" facilities of the town have been built from the "take" of this two-day affair: a warehouse, erected by one of the early merchants, was purchased and remodelled into a community hall where dances and "dos" were held regularly. An outdoor skating rink was built and maintained — skating or any other use of the rink was free; later a fine covered rink was built; if a person's house or barn burned down some of the help to restore it came from this fund. There was tremendous community consciousness and spirit in Climax.

CLOAN

In 1911 the CPR started building a line from Wilkie northwest to Lloydminster. The first grain point out was Thackeray and the second was Cloan. It was named for an official of the railway.

The first elevator built was the Co-op with Percy Wright as agent. Russell Reid opened the first post office and store. The Bruce brothers, Charlie and Alec, opened a garage. There was a station, a school, and several residences.

Over the years Cloan went through many changes. The store and post office closed. The school closed and the children are bussed to Wilkie. The station closed and when visited in July of 1976 Cloan was down to one business — wheat.

The Federal elevators closed in 1975 and the remaining 63,000-bushel Pool elevator, run by Dennis Dumont, handles over a quarter of a million bushels of grain a year. Rail service is good and Cloan will be on the map for some time to come.

CLONFERT

Clonfert is the first grain point north of Shellbrook on a CNR line that runs to Big River. Some of the early settlers were Irish and they were instrumental in having it named for Clonfert, Galway, Ireland. Being so close to the sizeable town of Shellbrook, Clonfert never amounted to much.

CLOUSTON

Clouston is the first stop south of Prince Albert on a CNR line that runs to Saskatoon. It is reputed to have been named after one of the members of the Clouston family which originated in the Orkney Islands and was distinguished in the service of the Hudson's Bay Company. The family has long had "country" standing in Orkney, and one of the members of the Canadian branch was the late Sir Edward Clouston, the general manager of the Bank of Montreal. Dr. Clouston was also of this kinship, as is also J. Storer Clouston, the well-known author.

CLUFF LAKE

Cluff Lake is south of Lake Athabasca in northwestern Saskatchewan. Amok Limited of Saskatoon had decided to proceed with plans for development there of an open-pit uranium mine with production to commence in 1979.

Amok will invest $133 million dollars in the project and at full production the mine will turn out four million pounds of uranium oxide (yellow cake) a year.

Cluff Lake, like so many places in the far north, was named for an early prospector.

COALFIELDS

Ten miles south of Estevan on highway 39 and three miles east to the mine buildings put you in the center of Coalfields. There is not a more descriptive place name in Saskatchewan. High, even man-made hills radiate off in every direction as huge strip mining machinery chews its way into the prairies. Lignite coal deposits in the Souris Valley were first noted by American railroad surveyors in 1853 and by the Palliser expedition in 1857. The North-West Mounted Police burned coal in their 1874 camp at Short Creek. In 1880, George and Sydney Pocock, immigrants cruising for homesteads, selected two fine lumps of coal from visible seams and took them to Winnipeg in a buckboard. There they stimulated such interest that an expedition organized by Hugh Sutherland mined the first coal in the district and barged it to Winnipeg via the Souris and Assiniboine rivers.

The first of the undergound mining companies was organized in the 1890s. Many of them operated for years. Then strip mining started and was firmly established by 1930. Amalgamation of operations took place and by 1970 according to Mr. R. S. "Kelly" Glaspey, superintendent of operations, it was down to two—M. and S. (for Manitoba and Saskatchewan) and Western Dominion. Char and briquets are moved out and the market for these is the United States.

Art Cote, long-time employee, and now watchman, has seen some remarkable changes in the last few years. At the mine site there used to be a company-sponsored town with accommodation for fifty families. This was complete with store and post office. They even had a high school. The company phased all this out by selling buildings to its employees for one dollar providing they were moved out. Many of them wound up in Estevan and now men commute to work from Estevan, Bienfait, and even as far as Hitchcock.

COCHIN

Cochin is named in honor of Rev. Father Louis Cochin, O.M.I. Father Cochin belongs to that class of pioneer missionaries who came West when times were hard, suffered for the sake of religion and have been instrumental in helping the Indians. Society owes these men of God a debt of gratitude.

Rev. Father Cochin lived and worked on Poundmaker's Reserve (Cut Knife), at the Thunderchild Reserve (Delmas), at Meadow Lake and finally at Cochin. He was present at Poundmaker's camp at Cut Knife Hill when Colonel Otter attacked it. He buried the dead left on the battlefield by Otter. He acted as courier between Chief Poundmaker and General Middleton in the correspondence that led to Poundmaker's surrender. He was at Battleford on November 27, 1885 when the eight Indians paid the supreme price for their share in the rebellion — in fact he was on the scaffold with them.

CODERRE

Coderre is on a CPR line that runs very close to the north shore of Old Wives lake. It was incorporated as a village in 1925 and named Coderre for one of the first settlers in the district, Mr. E. B. Coderre.

CODETTE

The first point south of Nipawin on a CPR line running to Wadena is Codette. Before the railway reached the district there had been an established name, Codette Rapids, four miles west on the Saskatchewan river. The rapids had been so named to honor a Metis, Jean-Baptiste Codette, who was a partner of the elder Alexander Henry. Codette was incorporated as a village in 1929.

COLE BAY

Cole Bay is at the south end of Canoe Lake in Northern Saskatchewan. Three Indian Reserves are nearby. In the early years there was only a twisting wagon trail to Meadow Lake, far to the south.

The start of the present thriving community came when a Frenchman began building log tourist cabins at the present site. Then in the 1960's, the Department of Highways began to build all-weather roads into the lakeland to tap the tremendous tourist potential and No. 104 reached Cole Bay.

The growth that followed was rapid and today Cole Bay has a population of 200, a three-room school, a church, two stores, a post office, and a fine recreation hall. The school is of special interest. There are three teachers and two teacher-aides for 60 children in grades K-1-9.

There is no telephone service but contact with the south is maintained by radio.

The town caters to tourists year round and has ample accommodation.

COLEVILLE

The first post office was situated on the southwest quarter of section 22, range 23, west of the third meridian. Malcolm Cole was the first postmaster. That is where Coleville got its name.

When the Grand Trunk came in 1913 the post office moved to the townsite. The town took its name from the post office.

In 1951 oil was discovered on the farm of A. M. Cole, a nephew of Malcolm Cole. A huge oil and natural gas field developed. Four miles south of Coleville is a Saskatchewan Power Gas Plant. Much of the gas now used in Saskatoon comes from this field.

In 1952 an oil refinery was opened in Coleville but it was shut down in 1958. During this oil and gas boom the hamlet of Coleville rose to a town of 650. The population has now levelled off at 500 or so.

COLFAX

B. A. Brown and Mr. Sharp of Colfax, Iowa, came here in 1904 with James Porter, who at that time was conducting prospective land buyers to the Colfax area. They bought two sections of land. In 1911 the GTR built through one of these sections (33-11-15) and Mr. Brown was given the privilege of naming the townsite. He named it after his hometown,

Colfax, Iowa. Other early settlers in the district included the Thomases, the Hiltons, the Smiths, the Muirs, the Campbells and the Leaches.

COLLINS

Collins was an inland post office ten miles southwest of the present town of Beechy. The first mail was hauled from Herbert across the river.

John Riley Collins was the postmaster and he named it for himself. This post office closed in 1922 when the CNR reached Beechy.

COLONSAY

Colonsay is forty miles east of Saskatoon on a CPR line built in 1906. At one time eight passenger trains a day passed through it. All passenger trains were discontinued in 1960.

Most of the early homesteaders came from Scotland. John Chesley had the honor of naming the town. Colonsay is one of the many islands off the northwest coast of Scotland that make up The Inner Hebrides. Streets and avenues of the town in Saskatchewan are also named for islands in this group: Tiree, Jura, Islay, Oronsay, Butte and Kintyre.

COLWYN

Colwyn is a small place on a CPR line in southern Saskatchewan. It was named by early Welsh settlers for their home town of Colwyn Bay, a port on the south shore of the Irish Sea next to Rhyl. Rhyl is a siding in Saskatchewan less than thirty miles west of Saskatoon on the main line of the CPR.

COMINCO

Cominco is an important Saskatchewan place name. It's a potash mine near Vanscoy and Delisle. In the early years Saskatchewan was known far and wide for one product, wheat. In the 1960's this changed and it became known as the "POW Province". P for potash, O for oil and the W, of course, for wheat.

The name, Cominco, is a contraction of Consolidated Mining Company. The company is a subsidiary of Canadian Pacific. Testing for a desirable potash ore body in the Vanscoy-Delisle area began in 1964. By March, 1969, the mine and associated refinery were in production.

Along with other potash mines developed at Allan, Lanigan, Colonsay, Saskatoon, Esterhazy, Belle Plaine, Patience Lake and Rocanville, Saskatchewan has become one of the major producers of potash. It is one of the three major plant foods necessary for life and, along with nitrogen and phosphorous, constitutes a principal primary component of plant food fertilizers.

COMPASS

Compass is a rural community twenty miles northwest of Meadow Lake. The coming of the settlers began in 1929 when homesteads in the area were opened up. Among the first were E. Martin, H. Bachman and N. Stein. Others that followed soon after were the Howards, Petersons, Gells, Wiens, Dycks and Esaus.

A post office and store was opened in 1936 by Gus Rankel and named Compass because the community centered around four roads that came from every part of the compass. Prior to this the mail had come in from Meadow Lake to Loon Forks and the settlers took turns going in for the mail.

The first regular mail carrier to Compass was Jake Esau and he was followed by Harry McRae. Mail service was twice a week until 1966 when both the post office and store closed.

CONDIE

The first settlers to arrive in this area in the spring of 1882 came by CPR to Brandon. From there they travelled with ox carts to their homesteads. Some of the names of these original settlers were: Robert Condie (for whom the town was named); John Dougan; George Burns; W. C. E., Michael, and Thomas Cullum; Adam Traynor; Jos., G. W., and Thomas Brown; Thomas Bredin; Russell and Len Purdy; Sylvester Conn.

The CPR had built as far as Regina by the fall of 1882. In 1885 a private firm, the Qu'Appelle — Long Lake Saskatchewan Railway and Steamboat Company, built north from Regina as far as Craven. They had plans to load the trains onto barges there and go up Last Mountain lake to the north end. From Last Mountain lake they would continue north by rail. However, the company soon ran into financial difficulties and had to lease the line to the

CPR, who dropped the barge idea and built through from Regina to Lumsden and on up to Saskatoon. Condie was the first point on this line.

In the first days a railroad would only build a main line; if the farmers wanted a siding they got together and put in the grade for it themselves. Later the CPR built loading platforms up which the farmers could drive wagon loads of wheat (it was all bagged in those days) and unload it into the box cars. No wonder the farmers were glad to see the first small squat elevators! They might have been crude affairs but they were certainly an improvement over loading grain by the bagful.

During the decade and a half from 1895 to 1910, Condie attained its peak as a commercial and grain shipping point. There were four elevators, a station, a lumberyard, a general store, a restaurant, a church, a skating rink and a sports field.

Practically all the virgin prairie was brought under the plow during this period with the advent of large steam and oil-pull tractors drawing anywhere from 8 to 21 bottoms. During one year over one million bushels of grain were shipped from Condie — only Indian Head surpassed them in production in the province.

About 1908 automobiles began to make their appearance with Model T Fords, Reos, Cases, McLaughlin-Buicks and chain drive International auto buggies being a few of the different makes. Practically every farmer in the district became the owner of one of these contraptions and though their top speed was 20 to 25 miles per hour they were still twice as fast as the horse. The automobile sounded the death knell for many of the small hamlets and villages because the farmers could go further afield to the larger centres where they had a more varied choice of goods and supplies.

As Regina grows it is spreading out until now the Flowing Springs Golf Course is on the banks of Boggy creek to the north of Condie. Who knows, perhaps in the next hundred years Condie Heights will be only a district in Regina or maybe there will be a Condie Crescent. Perhaps then some person will say, "Wherever did they get that name?"

CONGRESS

Congress is 10 miles north of Assiniboia. The first settlers into the district came from North Dakota in 1910, many of them under the leadership of G. P. Mollberg, a lay preacher. Their first school was called Progress Hill and the first post office was called Dew Drop. When the CPR came through in 1917 Mr. Mollberg tried to get them to adopt the name of Dew Drop for the town. At first it seemed that they would accede to his request but finally word was received from their office in Calgary that the plans for the townsite had already been drawn up and it had been given the American-sounding name of Congress in the hopes of attracting more American settlers. The streets and roads of the townsite followed this pattern and in Congress, Saskatchewan, you have such names as Washington Ave., East Roosevelt Ave.; Taft Road and Hughes Streets, and North Lincoln Road.

CONKLIN

S. A. Conklin gathered signatures and applied for a post office which was opened at his home at 14-33-6 on June 25, 1908. It was called Conklin. That year Gledhow post office was moved to 6-33-3 and Mr. Conklin became postmaster at both locations.

Other people to have the post office were: Fred W. McKay — 1910, Mrs. A. Simmons — 1910, Mrs. W. H. Bond — 1916 and finally Fred Bond, who looked after it until the post office closed on August 16, 1963.

CONNELL CREEK

Connell Creek, a rural post office 15 miles east of Arborfield, took its name from Connell Creek, one of the many tributaries of the Carrot river. They were both named to honor A. B. Connell, a land surveyor. His name was submitted to postal officials by a group of settlers under the leadership of Harry Nicholson, the local forest ranger at that time.

It was at Connell Creek on February 23, 1948, that the first cougar to be captured in Saskatchewan was taken by L. J. Fournier and his father. It was presented to the Saskatchewan Provincial Museum.

CONQUEST

The early settlers came into this district, Fertile Valley, in the spring of 1904. They travelled in wagons, with horses and oxen. The name "Conquest" originated when these settlers found ways and means of getting themselves and belongings across the South Saskatchewan river at Outlook. For years farmers around Conquest have planted trees around their farms as others planted shelter belts around their buildings. A drive through this district is a strange but pleasant sight as you see so many trees on the Prairies.

CONSTANCE

Constance is a hamlet situated about forty miles south and east of Assiniboia. Before the CPR arrived in 1926 the farmers had to haul their grain south to Scobey, Montana, or north to Verwood, both a considerable distance away. When the railway did arrive J. B. Dangerfield was the first to load a car of grain. Constance was named for the wife of the local minister at the time. Our information does not give her last name but she must have made a considerable contribution to the community before the railroad arrived to be accorded the honor of having the hamlet named for her.

CONSUL

Consul is on a CPR line in the extreme southwest corner of the province. The school was built before the railway came in and it was called Kelvinhurst for a place in Scotland. The post office took the same name. However, when the railroad arrived it named the townsite Consul in spite of the wishes of many of the citizens.

COOKSON

Cookson is a country post office midway along the south side of Prince Albert National Park. It gets its mail by truck three times a week from the nearest railway which is at Shellbrook, 25 miles to the south. The hamlet took its name from the school district which was formed in 1931. The school in turn took its name from a combination of the names of two members of the first school board, Mr. Cook and Mr. Hudson.

COOT HILL

Coot Hill is not a town; it is a community four miles east of the town of Wapella on the Trans-Canada Highway. The first settlers to arrive in the district came in 1883 and included Don Black, Angus Ferguson, Fred Rossen and Harvey McGinnis.

Railway officials gave the place its name. The tracks ran between two hills and coots were often seen crossing these hills from one slough to another.

The coot is a plump, dark gray bird about the size of a barnyard hen. It is a member of the grebe family and therefore has scalloped, or lobed toes, which enable it to walk over mud or mushy ground without sinking. It is sometimes called a marsh hen or mud hen. Although it is listed as a game bird it's not very exciting to hunt and even less exciting to eat.

COPEAU

Copeau was a rural post office established in 1921 and was served by the railhead at Prairie River. Mail was the medium by which most of the early settlers kept in touch with the outside world. It was at the post office where both pleasure and, sometimes disappointment, were handed out.

The first mail carrier was Knobby Clarke who used everything but a boat to get the mail out to the various post offices twice a week. Mr. Clarke's successors were Black Jack McLean, Jack Wilton and Garth Johnstone. These carrirs deserve a lot of credit for the way in which they kept the mail moving over so-called roads. It was a long, and often quite rugged trip, no matter what the season or weather happened to be.

The first postmaster at Copeau was J. Stevens (1921-22). He was followed by J. Pilson (1922-26); J. J. Wilton (1926-42); Margaret Wilton (1942-46) and finally J. J. Wilton (1946-47), when the post office was closed out.

The district took its name from the Copeau River which was named long before the settlers arrived and no one seems to know the significance of the name.

COPPEN

Coppen is the first stop northwest of Gravelbourg. It was named for Corporal

Coppen who had a distinguished record in the First World War.

CORINNE

Corinne is between Wilcox and Milestone on a CPR line from Regina to Weyburn.

This is a complete letter from Homer Shetterly: "It was not too far off 1905 when my father, Oran Shetterly, built a store at what is now Corinne. It was a two-story building with a Chinese operating a cafe upstairs. My father got the post office and the officials sent him a list of suggested names. But my father, being a single man at the time, suggested the name Corinne to honour Corinne DuVal."

CORNING

Corning is the second last stop on a short stub C.N.R. line running south of Peebles to Hansworth.

Quite a little settlement had grown up before the railway arrived and it was called St. Kilda for one of the islands of the Outer Hebrides, west of Scotland, from which some of the early residents had come to Canada.

When enough people arrived they got a post office and they called it Glenada. This, too, had a Scottish ring. However, when the railway arrived the name settled on was Corning.

Despite considerable research it has not been possible to determine the significance of the name. It is a common name with seven Cornings listed in the U.S.A.: Arkansas, California, Iowa, Kansas, New York, Ohio and Wisconsin.

CORONACH

Not many places in Saskatchewan can claim to be named for a horse! Coronach is a village 86 miles south of Moose Jaw on highway 36, a part of the old Powder River Trail. It was named by early English settlers for an Epsom Derby winner, Coronach.

CORY

Up until five years ago the first grain delivery point on the CPR west of Saskatoon was Cory. Being so close to Saskatoon it never developed beyond an elevator. Five years ago they moved the elevator towards Saskatoon and now it is very close to the government elevators on eleventh street. Cory is the rural municipality that surrounds Saskatoon. Both the municipality and the grain point took their name from W. W. Cory, who was deputy minister of the interior in the early 1900s.

Cory developed a good community spirit and in the late 20s "Cory Colts" were a baseball team to be reckoned with at Saskatoon Exhibition time. Of course, it was not uncommon to find them bolstered by such Saskatoon stars as Ossie Jones, Hobb Wilson and Ray Watkins.

COSINE

If you were to trace your finger along the Saskatchewan-Alberta boundary from south to north and stop after you have travelled 220 miles, you would then be in township 37, range 28, west of the third meridian. Three miles east from that point is the hamlet of Cosine which received its name from a mistake — the mistake of a surveyor when using the trigonometric function of cosine from his logarithm table.

COTE

Cote in the Fort Pelly district is named after an Indian chief whose reserve was in the vicinity. This chief was of the Saulteaux tribe and he was of considerable influence in arranging the signing of the Qu'Appelle Treaty in 1874. His name, Gabriel Cote, was attached to the treaty.

COTHAM

Cotham is an English settlement north of the Qu'Appelle Valley at a place called Crooked Lakes. The original settlers came out to Canada in association with the late Wm. Trant, an English journalist, who had a remarkable and chequered career. It was named after a village in Bristol, England, from which some of the colonists originated.

COTTON

The CPR built west from Lemberg to Lipton in 1904. The head surveyor on the line was Miles Patrick Cotton. Two miles west of Balcarres they put in a water tower and called it Cotton. They got Patrick in at the next point but the residents around Lipton would not hear of Miles for a name. At the time they didn't have a name but they didn't want Miles. Read the story of Lipton to see how the argument was resolved.

COURT

Court is the last stop on the Saskatchewan side of a CPR line built from Kerrobert, Saskatchewan, to Coronation, Alberta, in 1911.

The year during which the line was being built coincided with the coronation of King George V and many names of towns along the line reflected a strong British sentiment for the Royal family.

Coronation, Throne, Veteran, Consort are in Alberta and Court, Fusilier and Major are in Saskatchewan.

One of the first settlers into the Court area, ahead of the railway, was Thomas Albert Hill and his son, Milton. They came out from Guelph, Ontario, and homesteaded north of the townsite in 1910. Other early settlers included the following: Farrel, Broste, Hjalte, Beniot, West and Cooper.

At its height besides the Pool elevator, Court had a general store with post office, a cafe and several dwellings. Today, not a single soul lives in the place. In the 1940's the cafe went, in the 1950's the store closed and Harold Dahl its last owner, moved to Compeer, first stop over the Alberta line.

In 1973 the elevator closed and was offered for sale. Jake Miller was the last agent. The elevator and the store buildings are still on the site but it is sad to see these once active community centres becoming ghost towns.

COURVAL

Courval, Saskatchewan, is a hamlet southwest of Moose Jaw at 18-14-2-W3. It was named in honor of Courville near the Chartres, southwest of Paris, France. The first settlers, predominately French, wanted to call their town Courville but they had to settle for Courval because of a conflict of name. This occurred many times in Saskatchewan. Whenever it happened, the smaller point had to change or alter its name.

Eaton conflicted with Eston and changed to Eatonia. Broadview and Birdview conflicted and Birdview became

Donavon. Robin even conflicted with Roblin, Manitoba and so changed its name to Robinhood — a popular flour of the time.

COVINGTON

Covington was a rural post office a dozen miles south of Webb. It was first established in the home of Mrs. Walter Simpson in the early 1900's. She named it for her birthplace, Covington, Michigan, in the United States. The first mail carrier was Charlie Hastings. He brought it from Webb by buckboard to Covington and also to Maeshowe, five miles further on to the southwest.

When Mrs. Simpson retired her son, Stanley, took over. When he went into registered cattle and had to name his farm, he called it Covington. So, although the post office is gone, the name Covington is still printed in large letters on the end of his barn.

This information came from Miss Grace Nelson of Swift Current.

COWPER

Cowper is named for William Cowper (1731-1800), a famous English poet. He started out as a lawyer and after serving as clerk in the House of Lords he took up writings full time. "The Progress of Error", "Truth", "Home and Charity" are but a few of his works.

Start at Maryfield and take the CNR southwest to Blewett and you'll pass through eight other railway points named for English authors. In fact, two, Cullen and Bryant, are named for one man — William Cullen Bryant.

COXBY

Coxby is a rural post office over twenty miles southeast of Prince Albert, 12-48-23-W2. It's on a bend of the South Saskatchewan river very close to the junction of the North and South Saskatchewan rivers. The first postmaster was Mr. R. Ballandine. It was named for Palmer Cox (1840-1924), illustrator and author, born in Grandby, Canada. He wrote and illustrated a series of "Brownie" books for children. The people would have preferred Cox but the name had been used in Canada and so they took the "by" from the name of his birthplace and formed the name Coxby.

COZY NOOK

This was an early inland post office which was 12 miles north of Freemont. The first mail carrier was Mr. Gates who was appointed in 1910. His mail route was from Cozy Nook to Deals' home, on to the Elsie post office, into Maidstone, and then back again over the same trail. This trip of 60 miles was made one day a week, summer and winter regardless of weather.

When the railway finally reached Carruthers in 1913 this district benefited by having less distance to haul their produce. The post office closed in 1923 when the railroad was built through from Cut Knife to Lloydminster and Freemont became the closest grain and mail point.

The Cozy Nook School continued until the advent of the composite schools; now the children are bussed to Neilburg and only the district name remains.

CRAIGAVON

Craigavon is on a CPR line less than fifteen miles northeast of North Battleford. It was named after Viscount Craig, one time premier of Northern Ireland.

CRAIGIE

In 1917 Billy Robertson opened the Craigie post office two miles east of Lightwoods. He named it for Craigie, Scotland near his hometown. Jim Andrews hauled the mail from Craigie via Lightwoods to Chagoness.

Leonard Murton opened the first grocery and hardware store and he served the area for many years. All of his goods had to be hauled by team and wagon or sleigh, from Tisdale or Valparaiso.

CRAIK

Craik came into being 78 miles N.W. of Regina when the railway line was built in 1889-1890. This line was built by British capital, leased to the CPR until 1906, and then it was taken over by the Canadian Northern. A station was erected in 1902 and named Craik after an engineer with the railway construction party. The line later became part of the Canadian National system.

CRAMERSBURG

Cramersburg is a post office northwest of Swift Current, 30-22-20-W3. The first postmistress was Miss S. E. Cragg. The name was taken from an early settler, Mr. Cramer, and the "burg," which in German means town, was added. Burg and ville are common endings for place names in Saskatchewan, ville is French for village or town.

CRANE LAKE

Crane Lake is on a CPR line in the southwestern part of the province near Maple Creek. It is situated very close to the south shore of Crane lake from which it takes its name.

This is in the central flyway and many migrating waterbirds besides the sandhill crane are seen in great numbers during the spring and fall.

CRANE VALLEY

Crane Valley is 50 miles south of Moose Jaw. It's in line with a chain of lakes that include Old Wives, Lake of the Rivers, and Big Muddy. This is a favorite flyway for migrating waterfowl. Crane Valley is named for the thousands of sandhill cranes that use the district for a resting place spring and fall.

The first post office in the district was called Crane Valley. When the CPR came through in 1925 they adopted the name of the post office for the townsite. A trading centre had been established before the railway arrived and when a proper survey was made many squatters had to move their buildings. Crane Valley grew rapidly to include three stores, a doctor, a lawyer, a drug store, a hotel, a poolroom, a bowling alley, two lumber yards, two garages, and three elevators.

CRAVEN

Craven is close to the south end of Last Mountain lake. The Hudson's Bay Company had a store there in the early years and its first name was "La Fourche" or "The Forks." It was here that the old trading trail north out of Regina branched to one side or the other of Last Mountain lake; it went northwest to the Elbow or straight north to link up with the Carlton Trail at Humboldt.

When the homesteaders moved in they petitioned that the post office be called Sussex. This was refused because there was already a Sussex in the Maritimes. The postal officials sent a list of names to the people and they chose an equally "British" name, Craven, which honors William Craven (1606-1697), Earl of Craven, an ardent English Royalist.

CRAYLAND

In 1908 Mrs. William Moffatt started the Crayland post office in her home on the southeast quarter of 16-34-11-W3. Some of the early settlers who used the office were: Mr. G. H. Pratt, Alfred Fetherstone, Edward, Oliver and George Major, the Coben brothers and George Montgomery.

Roy and Jim Worthington of Perdue had the contract for hauling the mail and Bill King was the man who actually delivered it. He had an old white horse and buggy and slept most of the way while the horse poked along. Harry Pratt often related the following little story. One day when he had a letter to mail he ran out the door of his shack when he saw the old horse and buggy coming. The horse saw him come out on the run and it got frightened and started off at a gallop. By the time Mr. King got wakened enough to gather up the reins, get the horse back on the trail and look around to see what had frightened his horse, Mr. Pratt had gone back into his shack and there was no one in sight. Mr. Pratt often wondered if Mr. King ever did figure out what had scared his horse that time!

CRECY

Crecy, a small place on a CPR line in southern Saskatchewan commemorates one of the turning points in history — the battle of Crecy which took place in France in 1346. Edward, king of England, at war with France, advanced to the very gates of Paris. He pillaged as he went and the sky was livid with the flames of burning villages. Yet his army was soon worn out and he was obliged to retreat. At Crecy, a little north of Amiens, he turned to face his foes. There the English archers with their long bows proved more than a match for the French armored knights. That battle tipped the balance of power and England went on to be a very powerful nation both at home and abroad.

CREEKFIELD

Creekfield was a rural post office eight and one-half miles west and one mile south of the present town of Delisle. It was so named by John Darnborough, its first and only postmaster, for its proximity to Eagle creek. It opened in 1904 and got its mail from Loganton, ten miles to the northeast. Creekfield was closed out when the Canadian Northern Railway came through Delisle with the Goose Lake Line in 1909.

Some of the early settlers who used the Creekfield post office were: John Winder, Tom Douglas, Jack and Alf Harding, W. G. Morris, A. W. Miller, George and Cecil Carr, Mr. Stoll, Mr. Best, George Binch, Jim Mrack, Bill Boomhower and Tom Pollock.

CREE LAKE SETTLEMENT

The settlement of Cree Lake is on an island on the south shore of the lake from which it takes its name. The name was submitted by Mr. J. C. Sproule, a geologist with the Department of Mines and Resources in Ottawa. A private trading post was established there over 100 years ago. It has been operated by the Hudson's Bay Company for the past twenty-eight years. Reports indicate that the lake, the river and the settlement were named after the Cree Indians.

CREELMAN

The first to arrive here were the Andrews brothers, who had travelled north by covered wagon from Kansas, U.S.A. They filed their homesteads on 18-10-10, west of the second meridian on June 1, 1900. The main reason why they chose this location was that it had some bluffs growing on it. These had escaped the ravages of prairie fires because they were protected by sloughs. This was also an indication that possibly water would be found in the vicinity. This country at that time was devoid of trees because of the recurring prairie fires.

The nearest railroad points were Arcola, Wolseley and Weyburn, each one at a distance of about 40 miles. The nearest post office was New Hope, located near where Stoughton is today. Mail came addressed New Hope, Assiniboia, Northwest Terrories, Canada.

In the year 1903 a meeting was held in a tent on the present site of Creelman. Its purpose was the naming of the district, because the railway was soon to be built.

Three names were proposed by those present, Garnet, Melrose, and Hazel, each one having some connection with the settlers in the district. The name of Hazel was selected.

In 1904 the CPR completed the line from Arcola to Regina and the first train ran on it in the fall of that year. The Canadian Pacific then proceeded to change some of the names that had been given to towns and the name Hazel was changed to Creelman after A. R. Creelman, a solicitor for the CPR at that time.

Creelman today is an average prairie town giving good service to the district surrounding it.

CREE RIVER SETTLEMENT

Cree River Settlement is on the north shore of Cree lake where the Cree river drains north into Black lake. It was named after the Cree Indians.

CREIGHTON

Incorporated as a village in 1952, the community had been officially named in 1948 in honor of Tom Creighton, one of the original prospectors who in 1915 staked the claims which eventually became the large base metal mine of the Hudson Bay Mining and Smelting Company, straddling the Manitoba-Saskatchewan border at Flin Flon. Mr. Creighton died in 1952 and at the age of 75 years.

CRESCENT CITY

Crescent City is twenty-one miles south of Yorkton on highway number 9. In the same year, 1882, that York Colony (later Yorkton) was being settled, similar activity was taking place at Crescent City. Mr. Moore, a colonization agent, was bringing pioneers into the land area near Crescent lake.

Like the York Colony pioneers, many of these other adventurers came from Toronto. Frank Baines is witness to the fact that the destination marked upon the settler's effects read: Crescent City, Assiniboia, Northwest Territories. One can well imagine the feeling of depression that must have affected these people when their transportation agent deposited them in front of one log hut and five scattered tents and informed them that they were now at Crescent City.

In those days, as the sun fell towards the west, there was one reception committee that turned out "en masse" to welcome blue blood from the east, and that was the mosquitoes. About the only relief from the vicious attack of these pests was to become as well smoked as kippered herring. There were also large numbers of fireflies in those days, which prompted one settler to write home to his friends that, "the mosquitoes attacked you by day, and at night searched you out with a lantern."

Crescent City was just a high-sounding name like Green Acres or Forest Lawn to attract settlers.

Mr. J. I. Moore was the leader of the first group to settle at Crescent City. With him were William Eakim, W. S. Eckhart, George McBean, J. G. Phelps, George Thompson, W. C. Middleton, Edward Outhwaite, T. Evans, William Cross, Alex McDougal, G. Partridge, Homer, Willie and Horace Middleton, Richard Metcalf and George Addison.

CRESSDAY

Cressday on the CPR in southern Saskatchewan was named for W. Cresswell and Tony Day, large-scale ranchers in that district when the line came through.

CREST

Crest was a country post office about eighteen miles northeast of Nipawin. It was opened in 1931 and was named by George Bilbrough, who became the first postmaster. No one knows where he got the name Crest.

In 1929 a partnership was formed by Pete Matthew, his wife, Shirley, and her parents, Mr. and Mrs. Robert Booth, to open a general store on Pete Matthew's homestead on the Torch River. The country on both sides of the river had filled up with homesteaders, mostly from the drought stricken prairie. They were particularly glad to have the Crest post office open. Previously they had to go to Ridgeview post office, some distance away, for their mail.

Mrs. Bilbrough did all the post office work until she passed away in 1940. George looked after it until his death in 1941 and then his brother-in-law, S. R. Newman, became acting postmaster. He did not want the job and so a petition was sent to the post office headquarters in Saskatoon requesting that the Crest post office be installed in the store. This was finally granted and it opened there in October, 1941, with Shirley Matthew as postmistress. It remained there until March, 1952 when the store closed and the post office moved to the Don Voysey home. He was postmaster until Crest post office officially closed. By this time the town of White Fox had grown to a good size with elevators and a variety of stores. It was only ten miles away and with the improvements in roads shopping was done there.

This information was send in by Mrs. Shirley N. Matthew, of Langley, B.C.

CRESTWYND

Crestwynd is a hamlet seven miles east of Old Wives' lake on a CPR line running south of Moose Jaw. The first settlers were ranchers: W. D. Harrison, Fred Bevitt, Joshia Annabel, Thomas McRae, Joseph Bratten and William Howes. The railway came through in 1911 and with it enough settlers to fill up the district.

Crestwynd gets its name from the way the railroad winds up and over the top of the hills. From the little station it is downhill each way whether you go to Assiniboia or Moose Jaw. Crestwynd is well named, being on the crest of a row of hills.

CRICHTON

Crichton is between Admiral and Cadillac on a CPR line in the southwest corner of Saskatchewan. It was named for James Crichton (1560-1582), commonly called the Admirable Crichton. Crichton was a wonder in his day. He made a wide acquaintance among philosophers. His memory was astounding and he had a knack for learning languages. He deserved the adjective "admirable," applied to him early in life.

Admiral is also named for this man, Admiral being a corruption of the world admirable.

CROCUS

In 1905 Russell and Jim Palmer homesteaded the land adjoining the present elevator site at Wolfe, which is on a CPR line about halfway between North Biggar and Wilkie. The first post office in the district was named Crocus for the feathery, soft purple, lilac or white prairie flower which is the true harbinger of spring, often being in full bloom before the last snow bank in the nearby bluff has melted.

The first postmaster of Crocus was Ruby Cushing and the first mail was hauled from Battleford by team and democrat.

With the coming of the railway in 1908 the townsite of Wolfe was established and named. Now the mail came by train and soon the Crocus post office moved into the village and took its name, Wolfe.

CROCUS VALE

Crocus Vale was a post office established in the early 1920's in the home of Wes Cowell and operated by Ruth, their daughter, who later married Henry Dreyer.

Crocus Vale was just a few miles north of the present town of Perdue. It was named for Crocus which grows in abundance across the prairies. It blooms in the spring so early that it sometimes has to peep through the snow.

Unlike many other districts in Saskatchewan, this community still has many descendents of the early settlers working the land.

When the school was named it was called Dreyer to honor one of the pioneering families and today Crocus Vale only shows up in one place in the district — it is the name of the cemetery.

CROOKED RIVER

Crooked River is 13 miles east of Tisdale. It was the site of the lumber mill in 1905 when its surrounding district was for the most part heavily wooded. The shutdown of the lumbering operations in 1947 reduced the population, but this has been offset by the rise in importance of the district as a farming area. With most of the timber cut out over the long years of lumbering, settlers started stumping and clearing the fertile land.

In the 1930s the Crooked River Lumber Jacks were a powerhouse in Saskatchewan baseball circles.

The community is named for a twisting little river which was dammed to create a millpond at the site of the hamlet.

CROSS

Cross is five miles east of Piapot. In 1884 the main line of the CPR was built through Piapot and on to Maple Creek. In 1906 the CPR made a new right-of-way. At the intersection of the two roadbeds a town grew up by the name of Cross, named for William Cross, a CPR vice-president. At one time it had three elevators, a general store, a hardware and a post office. In 1919 a fire levelled the townsite and it was never rebuilt. Today no habitation remains, but you can see where the old right-of-way crosses the present one.

CROWTHERVIEW

Crowtherview was at the end of a branch line of the CNR that runs northwest of Yorkton. The first construction occurred in 1920. At that time, people had to travel eighteen miles to the nearest town. There were no cars and the roads were very rough.

One of the local farmers, Frank Crowther, built a country store. In 1922, a second store was built by Paul Coates. When the post office was obtained it was called Crowtherview.

The railway arrived in 1928 and with it a change of name to Parkerview. This was done to honor the Honorable James Mason Parker (1882-1960). He served as councillor and later reeve of the R.M. No. 247 (Kelliher) for a number of years. In 1917 he was elected as an M.L.A. for the Touchwood riding and held that post until 1938. From 1934 to 1938 he was the Speaker of the House.

CRUICKSHANK

Cruickshank was an inland post office in the hills between Tuberose and Beechy to the east.

It was operated by Mr. Cruickshank who had a large ranch where he ran cattle and horses.

CRUTWELL

Crutwell is a hamlet eighteen miles west of Prince Albert. It started as a logging camp in 1910 and it was a big one. The gravel for all the railway grade to Shellbrook came from Crutwell as well. A store opened and is in business today because a large colony of Metis have settled at the hamlet site. There are two elevators, a Pool and a Searle.

The best-known early settler was Horace Hackett (1880-1953) who came from Briarlea to open the post office and store. It was named for Mr. Crutwell, a CNR official at the time the line was built. There is a small Presbyterian church in Crutwell. However, the most notable building is a pentagon-shaped dance hall. It is built of rough-hewn logs 18 feet to the side, and it hasn't sagged an inch in fifty years. It was known far and wide as Horace's Dance Hall and some of the dances he put on are still talked about. He drew people from as far away as Prince Albert — no small feat in those days.

CRYSTAL BEACH

Four miles southwest of Harris there used to be a little lake, not much over a mile long and three-quarters of a mile wide. It has had an interesting history.

On May 24, 1910, Harris residents established a picnic ground at the northwest end and on July 12, held a celebration there. From then on activities proceeded briskly. George Dawson, who owned the land, cleaned up the shore and built a pavilion. He named it Crystal Beach. it became a very popular summer resort.

In rapid succession recreation areas were built, including a golf course, tennis courts and baseball diamonds. The touring House of David, Ruthilda, Saskatoon Gems, Neilburg All Stars and other prominent teams played there. A dining hall and liquor outlet were opened and did a good business. A small launch took people for rides on the lake. Cottages lined the shore. The resort got its own station on the railway opposite the lake! Special excursion trains came from Saskatoon.

In 1918, Dominion Day at Crystal Beach drew a crowd of 4000 while the Orange Day celebrations had a gathering of 5000. At this gathering the Red Cross booth cleared $700.00.

Almost all this has gone. The playing fields are now overgrown. The cottages have been moved away. In 1944, disaster struck Crystal Beach and many of the beautiful buildings were completely destroyed by fire. The station was moved into Harris and remodelled into a teacherage. The resort closed completely in the 50s.

Only two things remain as mute testimony to once happy times, the depression where once there was a lake, and a large concrete swimming pool built above ground. The names of the contractors, Hamilton and Patrick, and the date the pool was built, 1939, can still be seen inscribed in the walls. The lake has gone completely dry and only early spring runoff brings it back briefly to slough proportions.

There is a stretch of sandy hilly wasteland about six miles by eight miles straddling the highway between Harris and Zealandia. This has been established as a game preserve and approximately 400 deer live there. If you visit it you'll go through the farm yard of Mr. and Mrs. Fred Selsey and family. You can't miss the entrance because it's right beside the old cement swimming pool which Mr. Selsey now uses to store grain.

CRYSTAL HILL

Crystal Hill is an inland post office 35 miles southwest of Rouleau. Mr. and Mrs. Wesley Hyslop and their family of six homesteaded there in 1910. The site they chose for their home was on a small knoll or hill. One day Mrs. Hyslop found some beautiful crystal stones just behind their home and she christened their farm Crystal Hill. In 1912 a school was built a mile east of the Hyslop home and it was named Crystal Hill. In 1914 a country post office was opened in the Hyslop home and it, too, was named Crystal Hill. Subsequently a CNR line went in north of them and a CPR line went south. The latter proved to be the closer and mail came up from Kayville, fifteen miles away, to Crystal Hill.

The post office is closed now.

Other early settlers besides the Hyslop family were the Petrescus, the Fluters, the Donisons and the Aleanders.

CRYSTAL LAKE

The Canadian Northern Railroad was built through Stenen, six miles southwest of Crystal Lake in 1912. Mrs. Ida M. Black, a widow, homesteaded on the lake shore in 1904. She and her family began to develop Black's Beach in 1936. The lake was given its name for the fact that the water is exceptionally clean and pure.

The following are a few of the early settlers: Alex Belau, Harry Simes, Angel Stenen, Adolph Busch, John Hallick, Frank Morgan, Metro Keller, Robert Wilson, Victor Gogal, John Martin, Petro Bazansky, Kost Krotenko and Frank Tanton.

CRYSTAL SPRINGS

Surveyors working in this area between 1882 and 1895 camped beside a small lake and found the water clear and free of alkali. The company, apparently French, named it Lake Bon Eau. Early settlers in the district called their first community Bon Eau.

Later, when English settlers moved in they changed the name to Crystal Springs. When the CPR came through in 1930 Crystal Springs was the name selected for the village site.

Crystal Springs is between Waitville and Tway on a CPR line that runs north from Humboldt to Prince Albert.

CUDWORTH

In 1911 the Grand Trunk Pacific constructed a new line south of Prince Albert to Watrous. Fifty-seven miles out of Prince Albert the town of Cudworth was born. The name of the town perpetuates the memory of Ralph Cudworth (1617-1688) a distinguished philosopher who was a strong opponent of the atheistic tendencies of the 17th century.

CUFFLEY

Cuffley was an inland post office twenty-five miles northeast of Spruce Lake. It received its mail from Emmaville. The postmaster, Mr. Miller, named it for Joe Cuffley, one of the first homesteaders in the area.

CULLEN

Cullen is the first stop on a CNR spur line from Lampman west to Blewett. The second stop is Bryant and here we have another in the pattern of two place names giving honor to the one man such as Viscount and Plunkett, D'Arcy and McGee, Albert and Henribourg, Patrick and Cotton. Cullen, like Bryant, next stop on the line, commemorates William Cullen Bryant (1794-1878). Mr. Bryant was a lawyer who turned to writing and was an editor in his later years. some of his best known poems are: "The Battlefield," "The Death of the Flowers" and "To A Waterfowl". The latter is on the Saskatchewan literature course for grade eight.

Along this CNR line that runs from Maryfield southwest to Blewett many writers are honored by having a grain point named for them: Ryerson, Parkman, Service, Cowper, Carlyle, Wordsworth, Browning and Lampman. Then we have Cullen and Bryant side by side.

CUMBERLAND HOUSE

Cumberland House, the oldest permanent settlement in Saskatchewan, is a trading post of the Hudson's Bay Company, founded in 1774 by Samuel Hearne on Cumberland lake just north of the Saskatchewan river, into which it drains.

It was named after Prince Rupert, Duke of Cumberland. This was the first post built far inland by the company. It represented a fundamental change in policy and was intended to meet the competition from the Montreal "pedlars" who for several years had been intercepting furs in the vicinity.

Cumberland House is still a working Hudson's Bay Company post. It is a group of pleasant looking white painted buildings. Furs traded locally are mostly muskrat. These animals breed freely in the Saskatchewan marshes nearby.

CUPAR

Cupar is a village N.E. of Regina on the CPR line north of the Qu'Appelle Valley. It was named for the town of Cupar in Fifeshire, Scotland.

CUPID

Cupid post office was located on the N.E. quarter of 10-35-7, midway between Vanscoy and Pike Lake. The postmistress was Mrs. George Knight. The mail was picked up at Vanscoy by Frank Dowling who dropped it off at Cupid and then proceeded to Pike Lake post office.

Cupid opened in the early 1900's and closed out about 1910. The following are some who used this facility: Alfred Lewis and Reg Lewis, J. Ravenburg, Clifford Pearson and Straton Gwyn.

CURIE

Curie is very close to Moose Jaw. It is on a CPR line and it was named for W. H. Currie of Montreal, who was general solicitor for the CPR at the time the line was built.

CURZON

Curzon was an inland post office near Allan. The first post office was on the homestead of Mr. Rodwell who came from England. He named it Curzon in honor of the great British statesman and author, George Nathaniel, Marquis Curzon of Kedleston (1859-1925).

When the GTP railway came through in 1909 the town of Allan was given its name by the railway officials to start a new sequence of alphabetical names and the name Curzon disappeared. Allan was named for Hugh Allan, a director of the GTP railway.

CUTARM

The Grand Trunk Pacific came through from Manitoba in 1907 and the fourth site chosen inside the Saskatchewan border was Cutarm. It was just a siding and it was named for Cutarm creek which flows nearby. Cutarm creek got its name from an incident that happened in the early days. An Indian boy galloping his pony along the banks toppled off and broke his arm which led to the creek being called Cutarm.

CUTBANK

On July 25, 1958, the Government of Canada signed an agreement, previously approved by the Government of Saskatchewan, authorizing the commencement of construction on the South Saskatchewan River Project, a large-scale multi-purpose water conservation complex proposed for development in south-central Saskatchewan.

Control of the South Saskatchewan river was to be achieved by two dams, the major one on the river itself at a point approximately halfway between the towns of Outlook and Elbow, the other at the divide between the valleys of the South Saskatchewan and the Qu'Appelle rivers.

On September 5, 1959, Victor Hunter, successful applicant for postmaster, opened the Cutbank post office in his general store at the main dam site. He had been asked to submit three names and the two not chosen by the postal officials were: Saskatchewan Point and Hydro. All of his names had a local significance and the successful one, Cutbank commemorates the steep water-eroded banks immediately north of the present dam. At its peak this post office served over 3000 people.

The town has become much smaller now since the construction crews have finished their work and left. However, much of the face and future of Saskatchewan has been changed by the water from Diefenbaker Lake as it is evenly spread over the land by the Gardiner Dam and its system of canals. The electricity that is generated by the flow of this water will, if necessary, serve any point in Saskatchewan.

CUTHBERT

Cuthbert is on the Alberta border west of Eatonia. It was named for Cuthbert Harnett, the youngest son of an Ontario family who were pioneers in the district.

CUT KNIFE

There is a hill just a few miles north of the present site of Cut Knife. Dr. James Hector of the Palliser expedition, 1857, was told the name was "Broken Knife Hill".

A story is told that in the early 19th century a small hunting party of Sarcees from the Blackfoot confederacy in Alberta found themselves surveying the countryside for buffalo from this very same hill. They were surprised and surrounded by a large band of Crees. The Crees, finding they had the hated Sarcees trapped, took their time and sent word for their women and children to come and see the fight. The Cree Chief, when he found out the leader of the Sarcee party was the famous fighting Chief, Cut Knife,

gave orders that no firearms were to be used. the Sarcees were to be exterminated by hand-to-hand combat.

Many are the stories of individual fights that took place that day — particularly of the strength and skill of the Sarcee Chief, Cut Knife. The Crees made much of this victory and ever afterwards referred to the place as Cut Knife Hill.

When the CPR line out of Battleford reached the district in the early 1900s the name of Cut Knife was chosen for the town.

CYMRIC

Cymric is between Govan and Duval on a CPR line that parallels the east shore of Long Lake. It is a Welsh name that means "St. Mary's".

CYPRESS HILLS PARK

Cypress Hills Park post office is twenty miles south of Maple Creek. It is named for the Cypress Hills. The hills were first named by the Cree Indians Mun-a-tuh-gow meaning beautiful highlands. A British expedition led by Capt. John Palliser explored the area in 1859, reporting it to be well watered, with excellent grass, abundant game and fine timber. Pine, spruce and poplar trees are plentiful. One of these, the lodgepole pine, gave the area its name by mistake. French fur traders, thinking the lodgepole pine to be the same as the cypress of eastern Canada, called it Montagne de Cypres — which means mountains of cypress but somehow it came out Cypress Hills. In these hills or mountains is found the highest point above sea level in Saskatchewan — 4500 feet.

In 1931 eighteen square miles of this area were set aside as the Cypress Hills Provincial Park and it has been well developed since then.

D

DACER

In the early 1900's the GTP built a branch line north from Oban Junction to Battleford. Dacer was the last grain point on the line. It had one elevator which has long since closed and the whole rail line has been abandoned.

The point was named for Harry Dacer, an official of the railway company.

DAFOE

Dafoe is named in honor of John Wesley Dafoe (1866-1944), one of the prominent and certainly one of the most influential Canadian journalists of his age. He made his greatest mark while working for the *Winnipeg Free Press*. He was a champion of western issues in particular and Dominion status in general.

DAHINDA

Dahinda is between Edgeworth and Kayville on a branch line that runs west from Weyburn and ends at Cardross.

There are two versions as to how it got its name. The first came from private correspondence in 1971 and went like this:

'Dahinda is a very small place, probably not known to many people. It has a population of twenty-five. The Sioux Indians named Dahinda after a slough which was shaped like a bullfrog. Dahinda is the Sioux way of saying "bullfrog".'

A search of the CPR files in 1976 produced this:

'Dahinda — Derived from a low-German word meaning "Back there". An old gent had settled in the district and when other settlers met him and asked him where he lived, the old Dutchman, not being able to speak English, pointed toward a hill and said, "Dahinda" (Back there).

DAHLTON

Dahlton is a country post office 13 miles west of Archerwill and 16 miles east of Naicam. The district was first settled in 1908. The post office was opened in 1913 and the first postmaster was Justin Slund. The first mail carrier was Walter King of Quill Lake who delivered mail weekly. Quill Lake, thirty miles to the south, was the closest town at the time.

Dahlton is named for Dalton, Minnesota. It is not known why the letter "H" was included in the spelling. The name Dahlton was favoured by the Scandinavian settlers as it included the Norwegian "dal," which in Norwegian means valley or ravine. This seemed appropriate as the original post office site was near a deep ravine. The post office is still in operation, serving approximately 30 families.

DALBY

Dalby was an inland post office that opened in 1909 eight miles northwest of

Beechy. It was named for Dalby, a town on the island of Fyn just off the east coast of Denmark.

Dalby, in Saskatchewan, was the centre of a Scandinavian settlement. The post office closed out in 1922 when the Canadian Northern Railway reached Beechy.

DALMENY

Jacob Lepp and John Buhler came to the district in 1901 and were closely followed by Jacob Warkentine in 1903. The Canadian Northern missed the little settlement of Saskatoon (20 miles to the southeast) when it built into Dalmeny in 1905. Jacob Giesbrecht built the first elevator the following year. Williams and Sons opened the first store. A large Mennonite settlement moved in and built a Mennonite Brethren church five miles north of town. Rev. Jacob Lepp, who farmed in the district, served as its unsalaried minister until his retirement in the 40s.

Dalmeny by its proximity to Saskatoon has developed into a dairying district. Some of the bulk shippers are: David Lepp, Claus Thiessen, Sam, Edwin and Dan Buhler, Orlando Schultz, John Wiens, Elmer Peters, John Friesen and Abe Kruger.

Clarence Giesbrecht, whose father built the first elevator, visited Dalmeny, Scotland, recently and there is reason to believe that Dalmeny, Saskatchewan, was named for it.

DALZELL

Samuel Glydon came to Dalzell in 1903 from Prince Edward Island. The place was then called Neelby, NWT, and the nearest railroad was twenty miles away at Broadview. When the Canadian Northern came through in 1907, Dalzell was to be a divisional point. However, the people who owned the land around the townsite held out for a stiff price so the railway officials just backed up one stop and made the divisional point at Kipling. The railway gave Dalzell its name, probably for some official. In 1909 the CPR built a railroad in competition to the CNR; at Kipling and Dalzell the lines were only four miles apart. Windthorst on this new line became the large town. However, in 1962 the Reston to Wolseley line was taken up and Dalzell began to grow again.

DANA

Dana is on the CNR Humboldt line 50 miles northeast of Saskatoon. It is named for James Dwight Dana (1813-1895) an American geologist who published widely. He was for a time editor of the *American Journal of Science* and one of his best known reports which appeared in 1865 was on the "Origin of Prairies."

In more recent years Dana has given its name to a nearby RCAF radar station.

DANBURY

The first Danbury post office was established in 1914 five miles south of Glen Elder. The first postmaster was Mr. Moore and he named it for Danbury, England. There was also a Danbury School. Danbury post office is now located in Danbury hamlet twelve miles north of Hyas, Saskatchewan.

DANKIN

Dankin was a grain point on a CNR line between Glidden and Eatonia. It had two elevators, a Pool and a United Grain Growers. The Pool opened in 1954 with Lynn Jensen as agent. He bought grain there until the elevator closed in 1967.

Prior to 1967, the United Grain Growers was taken over by the Pool. Shortly after 1967 the elevators were sold to a local farmer, Frances Craney, who now uses them for grain storage.

Lorne Smith, long-time resident of Dankin, now living in Kindersley, sent in the following information on how the name of Dankin was formed: parts of the surnames of Bob Daniels and Bill King, two of the early settlers were used to form Dankin.

D'ARCY

D'Arcy and McGee are named for Thomas D'Arcy McGee, one of the most brilliant orators in Canadian parliamentary history. He was also an accomplished writer, poet, and administrator. His birthplace was Ireland and he came to Canada by way of the United States in the mid 1800s. He entered politics as an Independent and represented Montreal West from 1858 until his death. He was a delegate to the Charlottetown and Quebec conferences and was an eloquent advocate of Canadian union. He was in a very real sense a Father of Confederation.

After coming to Canada, McGee loyally supported the Imperial connection. He became increasingly critical of Irish extremists and in 1866 incurred the enmity of the Fenian Brotherhood by his denunciation of its activities. Early on the morning of April 7, 1868, just after he had made a speech in Parliament, he was shot at the door of his boarding house on Sparks Street in downtown Ottawa. Patrick James Whalen, a young Fenian, was convicted of the crime and executed. This was one of the very few political murders in Canada's history.

D'Arcy and McGee are on a line between Rosetown and Kindersley with the town of Fiske between them.

DAPHNE

Daphne is the first grain point north of Watson on a CPR line that runs to Melfort. It was named by James Duff, townsite Department, Calgary. He states his sole reason for choosing the name was its dissimilarity to any other then in use.

This information comes from CPR files.

DARMODY

Darmody is between Mawer and Eskbank on a CNR line that runs from Moose Jaw to Riverhurst. it was named after Mr. J. J. Darmody, who farmed in the district when it was first settled. Darmody was incorporated as a village in 1923.

DAVIDSON

Davidson was named for Colonel A. D. Davidson of Minnesota, one of the two organizers of the Saskatchewan Valley Land Company. In 1902 he brought in a special excursion train for American capitalists and toured the Saskatoon area. He eventually sold 5,000,000 acres in the Davidson area.

In order to make this site more attractive to Americans some of the streets in the new town were named for former presidents of the USA — Lincoln, Washington, Grant and Garfield.

DAVIN

Davin is named in honor of Nicholas Flood Davin, lawyer, journalist, and politician. He was born in Ireland in 1843 and was educated at Queen's College, Cork.

In 1872 he came to Canada and worked as a newspaperman in Toronto until called to the Ontario Bar in 1874. In 1883 he moved to Regina and published the *Regina Leader,* the first newspaper in the territorial district of Assiniboia.

DAVIS

Ten miles southeast of Prince Albert on a railroad that runs to Regina is the little village of Davis, named for Senator T. O. Davis, a merchant of Prince Albert. If you go in by grid road, a mile out you'll come to an imposing United Church built on a hill. The past record told by the headstones in the adjoining graveyard will give you some idea of the nature of the early community: Henry Graves of Sheffield, England and his son, F. T. Graves (F. T. stands for Francis Thomas but nobody ever called him that, just F. T.); the MacKenzies — J. C., Daniel, Alexander and Norman; William James Evans; William Coomes; John A. Scott; John and Thomas Atkinson; Richard Miller; Ole Newhouse; Richard Smith; Walter and John Fraser; Thomas Lamb; John Riddell.

As you drive further east the elaborate little community hall sits in a hollow on the left and the square red-brick Island Lake School sits on a hill at the right, complete with a belfry. Next comes the William Edward Dannatt Store and post office in a hollow to the left, operated by Miss Noelle Dannatt and her sister, Mrs. Marjorie McKay. Their father, Captain Edward Dannatt, came from England and farmed at Macdowall to the west from 1927 to 1937 before taking over the store from F. T. Graves. To put it in Mrs. McKay's own words: "Davis was quite a little town once upon a time."

Besides being one of the first homesteaders in the district Mr. Graves built the first store and did a thriving business with the Indians from the John Smith Reserve eight miles to the east. John Smith was a chief and a full-blooded Indian. They traded wood and hay for groceries. Robert Bear, a later chief, was a good customer at the Graves' store, too. Mr. Graves built his own elevator a quarter of a mile down the track from the present Pool elevator. There was a broom factory on the hill behind the store. It burned down and it was replaced by a hotel which after a few years of business likewise burned down and was not re-

built. In those days Davis had three stores and the usual number of other businesses.

Today, the store previously mentioned and a lone Pool elevator operated by Paul Beauchene are about all that is left of a once thriving little town.

DAVYROYD

The Davyroyd district is sixteen miles north and east of Assiniboia. It was settled mainly from Moose Jaw by English and Scotsmen. The name Davyroyd came from Bill Davy who ran the first post office. He used davy and to this added royd, a Yorkshire word meaning district. The first post office was opened in 1908 and the mail was hauled from Moose Jaw by the Gaudrys of Willow Bunch. The Davyroyd post office continued until 1953.

Some of the first settlers included the following: Gordon Spicer, Lyle McDonald, Mike Bocuo, B. C. Padfield and Claud Smith.

DAYLESFORD

Daylesford is a grain point on the CNR line that runs from Humboldt to Melfort. It is close to the middle of the east side of Lake Lenore. The first settler in the district was Calveston Folden who came in 1909; he became the first postmaster also. When it came time for a name several suggestions were sent in. The one chosen, Daylesford, had been submitted by the two Francis brothers who had come from Daylesford, England.

Jack Kisgen hauled mail and supplies from Humboldt. The Foldens had the post office in their home and they retained it until the CNR completed the track in the early 30s. The next to have it was Mrs. Clease. The town started to grow and Mr. and Mrs. Martin opened a new store. Albert Phanueff had the post office for awhile; the last one to have it was Mrs. Bob Folden.

With better cars and roads Daylesford began to dry up and in 1962 the post office closed. Today Daylesford is a ghost town.

DAYSVILLE

The Day brothers were the first into this area seven miles north and east of Edam. They ranched. When a post office and store opened in the early 1900s it was given the name Daysville and was operated in the homestead home of Mr. Wilson.

DEANTON

Deanton was a townsite between Verwood and Willows on a CPR line in southcentral Saskatchewan. It was named Deanton after the first postmaster L. S. Dean and his brother Roy M.

Established on March 3, 1908, it changed its name to Readlyn on May 1, 1913. See Readlyn for the rest of the story.

DEBDEN

Debden is on a CNR line that runs north and west of Shellbrook and ends at Big River. It is also the terminus of a CPR line to Meadow Lake. It is a growing town in its own right, being the center of a prosperous farming area. It is a predominately French community. However, it was the railway officials who named it in the early days for Debden, a small country village in North Sussex, England. Debden, England, is famous for having within its precincts the Molehall farm. When this was built in the 1600s it had a complete moat with a drawbridge. Now, part of the moat has been filled in and the drawbridge is gone.

Some of the early French settlers in the district were: Octave Cyr, Joe Latiers, Monseigneur J. E. Joyal P.P., Alphonse Demers, John Lajeunesse, Pierre Larose, Paul Voisin, Lucien Leclarc, George Gauthier, Leo and Rene Groteau, Arthur Chretien and Willie Sevigny.

DEBORAH

Deborah is on a CNR line in the extreme southeast corner of the province near Estevan. It was named after the wife of a Jewish farmer who homesteaded in the district.

DEER CREEK

Deer Creek took its name from Deer Creek Ranch, which was operated in the area in the early days by Mr. McCallum. The first homesteader in the district was Alvin Moore. Two of his sons still farm near Deer Creek. The first postmaster was Mr. Rutherford. The CNR built a branch line from just north of Spruce Lake through to Frenchman Butte in 1928,

and Deer Creek is the second stop on the line.

The latest development at Deer Creek is that a bridge has been put across the North Saskatchewan River. The old ferry at Frenchman Butte, a few miles upstream has been closed.

This information came from R. B. Calder, secretary-treasurer of the RM of Frenchman Butte, Paradise Hill, Sask.

DEER RIDGE

Deer Ridge is seven miles north of Sturgeon lake. It is a combined store and inland post office operated by Eddie Nelson to serve a small farming community and some of the residents of the nearby Sturgeon Lake Indian Reserve.

The site is on a ridge and was given the name Deer Ridge for the following reason. There are many, many ridges in the district and there are many, many deer. In the morning the deer like to come out of the thick forest in the valley and get up to a "spot of sun" on a ridge. Hunters knowing this patrol these ridges — in season — for many reasons. One, they get a good view of the feeding meadows below. Two, if they can work into the wind they may come across a dozing deer. Three — and possibly most important of all — landmarks are easier to keep straight and there is less likelihood of "misplacing your camp."

DELISLE

Twenty-two miles west of Saskatoon is the town of Delisle. In 1907-1908 the Goose Lake Line was built through land owned by four brothers, Amos, Eddie, Eugene and Fred Delisle. The town was named in their honor.

The most exciting thing about Delisle has been the honor brought to it by "The Bentleys" in hockey and baseball, but particularly hockey. Mr. and Mrs. William Bentley had a large family, six boys and seven girls. The six boys: Max, Doug, Reg, Wyatt (Scoop), Jack and Roy all played for the Drumheller Miners in he late 30s when that team won the Western Canada Senior Championship.

Max and Doug went on to carve out hockey careers with the Chicago Black Hawks. Reg joined them briefly, and all three played on one line. Max was eventually traded to Toronto where he helped the Maple Leafs win the Stanley Cup. Both Max and Doug are in Hockey's Hall of Fame.

DELMAS

Delmas is the second stop on a CNR line out of North Battleford to Lloydminster. The Canadian Northern built the railway in the early 1900s and much of the gravel needed for the roadbed was taken from a pit just south of the town. The huge scar on the countryside is still plainly visible.

The name Delmas was to honor Rev. H. Delmas who was the local priest when the railway went through; later he served at Duck Lake.

DEMAINE

Demaine is named for the late E. J. Demaine who in 1910 started a post office located on his homestead, one-half mile west of the present town. He brought the mail in from Lucky Lake, and it had been hauled there from the steel at Elbow. The railway arrived in the early summer of 1921 and on their survey map railway officials had already named the site "Scappa." Immediately the residents took steps in the form of a petition to have the name changed to "Demaine." It was granted and so Demaine honors one of the earliest pioneers in the district.

DENARE BEACH

Denare Beach is a summer resort on the northeast shore of Amisk (Beaver) Lake. It serves as a summer resort for Creighton, Saskatchewan, and Flin Flon, Manitoba.

The first white people to settle there were Gisli Norman and John Anderson. They came in 1920 and still live there.

The name Denare was formed by taking the first two letters of the words DEpartment of NAtural REsources.

In 1958 some startling archaeological findings, some dating back to 1000 BC, were made in the area and these have been housed in a splendid new log cabin. The men who unearthed these artifacts were Dr. "Scotty" McNeish, of the National Museum of Canada; Harry Moody, long time resident of the area; and Professor W. Mayer-Oakes, University of Toronto. Included in their findings were spearheads, arrowheads, pottery and human skeletons.

DENDRON

Dendron is between Vogel and Hallonquist in south-central Saskatchewan. It was named by an early settler after his school in England.

DENHOLM

Denholm is on the CNR line that runs from Saskatoon to North Battleford. It is just 12 miles southeast of North Battleford. There are many stories of the fur trade when it was at its height along the North Saskatchewan. Some of them are tragic and perhaps one of the most tragic took place at the Eagle Hills House, near Denholm. In 1778 Peter Pangman, working for the Pedlar's group of fur traders (who were soon afterwards called the Nor-Westers) built a trading post on the north side of the Saskatchewan river (E2-42-15-W3) about ten miles east of the junction of the Battle river. Behind the fort site the outer bank of the river rises by a steep incline to the prairie level on which the town of Denholm now stands.

In charge of this trading post was John Cole and helping him were Charles McCormick, an Irish trader, and another man, Gebosh. An incident that followed the Indians trading their furs for liquid refreshments led to the death of their chief. He wasn't shot, he just died right at the fort. The Indians took him home and buried him; however, they grew very resentful of the traders after this incident. They bided their time and when they were ready they deliberately stole a horse which provoked a shooting quarrel. The first shot killed McCormick's interpreter; the next shot killed a trader. After a short skirmish John Cole raised a flag of truce. In the parley that followed it was agreed that the Pedlars would give the Indians forty gallons of rum (5 kegs). The next day they gave them one more keg, and offered to surrender all their goods. The Indians refused the offer saying that they would kill the lot and get all their goods anyway.

Finally, taking advantage of the cover of darkness and the drunkenness of the Indians, the traders loaded two canoes with furs and men and escaped down river. That was the end of the Eagle Hills post. It was never rebuilt.

DENNY

Denny, a single Pool elevator, is the first stop south of Conquest. It used to have a water tower and a flag station. The stop was named for Denny Johnstone who farmed extensively in the district. West of the river at Outlook and running south from Denny to Bratton is a Scandinavian settlement. These are some of the men who deliverd their grain to Denny: Art Torvik, Andrew Olson, Andrew Sjovold, Ole Odegard, Olav Skaalid, Elgin Amy, John Emerson, Ole and Endre Odegard, and Charles, Peter, Marit, John, Ole, Albert and Karl Farden.

DENZIL

Denzil is on a CPR branch line from Kerrobert to Macklin. A. F. Olson, an early settler in the district, had a lumberyard on his homestead near the townsite before the track was laid. When the CPR officials came along they called on Mr. Olson. He asked the gentlemen in to dinner and in appreciation for the courteous service they received, the representatives said they would name the townsite after Mr. Olson's oldest son, Ansel. However, the CPR men either misunderstood Mr. Olson's Scandinavian accent or there was a mix up in spelling at their office, because when the name officially came out it was Denzil.

DERMINGTON

Kisbey is about halfway between Stoughton and Carlyle. Percy Kisbey, a young Irishman from Dublin, hauled mail from Alameda and Moosomin and his customers thought so much of his services that they named the Kisbey post office after him. Mr. Kisbey had a post office of his own less than ten miles north of Kisbey. He named it Dermington for his only son, Percy Dermington Kisbey. The son was a casualty in World War I.

DESCHAMBAULT LAKE SETTLEMENT

Deschambault Lake Settlement is about the centre of the eastern shore of this very irregular lake (54°55' — 103°22'.) The lake, river and settlement were named by A. S. Cochrane, surveyor in 1880, after Mr. Deschambault, a Hudson's Bay Company postmaster at the time, who was stationed at Reindeer Lake.

DEVERON

Deveron is less than twenty miles southeast of Wolsely. At one time it was served by a railroad but that has since been taken up. It was named by the CPR officials for a river in Aberdeenshire, Scotland.

DEWAR LAKE

Donald M. Dewar moved into this district in 1907. He located on the shore of a small lake that came to bear his name and besides farming and ranching he opened a post office one and one-half miles from the present village site. The first mail came in from Coleville by way of Battleford. When the GTP came through in 1913 the townsite took the name Dewar Lake from the post office.

Don Dewar, a grandson of Donald, won the North American Championship for steer decorating in 1950 and followed it a year later with the World's Championship for bulldogging at Boston. Two sisters, Clare and Lois, were very famous trick and fancy riders. Another son of Mr. Dewar, Murray, was killed overseas in the Second World War and there is a second Dewar Lake in the far north of Saskatchewan named for him.

DIANA

Diana is between Rouleau and Wilcox on a CPR line that runs southeast of Moose Jaw down to North Portal. Some Saskatchewan place names are puzzlers and Diana is one of them.

CPR files simply say: 'Diana — "Temple at Ephesus".' Diana was the Roman goddess of hunting. She also looked after maidens and helped women in childbirth. Her temple at Ephesus in Asia Minor was one of the most splendid in the ancient world.

DILKE

The rural area of Dilke was partly settled as early as 1904. The site of the village was established in 1909, surveyed in 1910 and incorporated into a village in 1912. A great many of the first settlers were from England, so it is fitting that they named the village for Sir Charles Wentworth Dilke (1843-1911) who was a noted author, imperialist and a member of the Gladstone ministry.

The first train came through in 1911, much to the relief of the farmers. Up to this time they had to haul their grain with horses or oxen to Lumsden or Bethune.

In 1913 a little stone Anglican church was built. Some of the oldtimers still talk about a team of driverless oxen bringing in loads of stone to the church from the farm of Hugh Naldrett. Ben Brewer was the stone mason. He is retired now and lives in Regina.

DILLABOUGH

Dillabough is the first stop on a CNR branch line from Reserve to Arborfield. It was named for Mr. J. V. Dillabough, a civil engineer who located and supervised the building of the line.

DILLON

Dillon is a post office in a Hudson's Bay store at the mouth of a river system that drains Vermette lake and Dillon lake to Peter Pond lake. It is a northern fishing village with a Roman Catholic mission and a school that teaches up to grade four.

Originally it was called Buffalo River by the Indians and this was the name of the first post office. However, there were just too many buffalo post offices in Saskatchewan—Buffalo Gap, Buffalo Head and Buffalo Horn. They are all closed now but Buffalo Narrows on the same lake remains open. This led to considerable confusion in the mails and post office officials changed the name Buffalo River to Dillon to tie in with Dillon Lake to the southeast. An army map produced in 1961 shows the whole district (55 degrees to 56 degrees latitude and 108 degrees to 111 degrees longtitude) as Dillon.

DINSMORE

Dinsmore is 99 miles southwest of Saskatoon. In 1907 on the N.E. quarter of section 36, township 27, range 12, west of the 3rd, James Mason opened the first post office in the district. It was named for Mr. Dinsmore who lived two miles west of Mason's.

When the Canadian Northern came in April of 1913 the post office was moved to the new townsite and placed in the back of Tom Cowan's store. The town took its name from the post office.

DIRT HILLS

Dirt Hills is part of the Missouri Coteau that stretches up into Saskat-

chewan. Both the Dirt Hills northeast of Assiniboia and the Cactus Hills to the north are at an elevation of 2700 feet.

Besides being hills they are sandy and sparse of vegetation.

A post office was opened to serve the homesteaders of the district on September 1, 1912, with Allan H. Buchanan as postmaster. The office stayed open until October 31, 1926, when the CPR built west from Weyburn and with better roads and cars the post office became obsolete. One other factor was at work in cutting down post office patrons. Many settlers soon discovered that much of their land was too light and sandy to be really good farming land. In 1937 the Federal Government passed the Prairie Farm Rehabilitation Act, by which much of this light, poor farming land was bought by the government and made into community pasture, where farmers could pasture livstock at a nominal cost during the spring, summer and early fall. This was a real help to these farmes for they were paid a reasonable price for their land, which was unsuitable for grain growing anyway, and they were at the same time provided with good pasture and water for their stock. These community pastures became known as PFRA pastures or land. There are many of them dotted throughout southern Saskatchewan.

DISLEY

Disley is very close to the southern tip of Last Mountain lake. It was incorporated as a village in 1907. Disley was named by Mr. T. W. Ashe, an early homesteader, for the place from which he came in England.

DITTON PARK

Ditton Park post office opened in 1910 in the home of Mr. H. G. Winterbourne. It was located on the SW¼-S3-T48-R13-W2. It was named for Ditton Place, England.

The first settlers included the following: Bob and Bert Cole, John Hunter, Mr. E. Fawcett, Fleet and West Cragg, Mr. F. Williams, the Clisbys, the Wrigleys and the Clewes.

Mr. Winterbourne was postmaster until 1955. In that year he received the Queen's Jubilee medal for his long years of faithful service both as postmaster and a mail carrier. The post office is now closed.

DIVIDE

Divide is between Arena and Katherine on a branch line of the CPR that runs east from Notukeu, parallel with the International Boundary, and ends at Val Marie.

CPR files say that this point is a local height of land. One other version of the name is that since it is twelve miles north of the International Boundary it marked the "dividing" line between Canada and the USA.

DIXON

Dixon is the first grain point east of Humboldt on the CNR. The first settlers came in 1903 and included the Koetts, the Mycocks, the Blairs, the Schaeffers, the Hellmans, the Michaels, the Friburgs, the Ehls, the Feltons and the Fauls. The area was not surveyed until 1904. Mr. Dixon, the surveyor, allowed these early settlers squatter's rights and their duties counted from the time they arrived. He was well thought of and the settlers named the site for him.

In 1905 the steel came through and the G. Schaeffers built a store, a Roman Catholic church was built and then a school No. 1872 was erected and named Dixon. All that was left by 1967 was the siding and the last living member of the first settlers, Harry Ford.

DNIEPER

Dnieper is an inland post office northeast of Yorkton. Many of the first settlers in the district came from the Ukraine and they were responsible for having the district named in honor of the Dnieper river of their homeland.

DOBROWODY

Dobrowody was an inland post office that developed eleven miles south and two miles east of Hazel Dell in the early 1900's. Many of the early settlers came from Poland and they named their post office Dobrowody for the village many of them came from in their homeland. Dobrowody in Polish means "good water".

Mr. Bugiera was the first postmaster. Two churches, Roman Catholic and Greek Orthodox came next and eventual-

ly a school made of logs which is no longer in use. When the Canadian Northern Railway built through to the south and the town of Rama developed, the Dobrowody post office held on for several years before it was closed out. However, the two churches are in operation today.

Besides Mr. Bugiera, two other early settlers were Frank Matsalla and John Polach. Heavy bush made travel difficult and earliest settlers journeyed by ox cart to Yorkton to shop once or twice a year. It took two days or longer to make the round trip.

Pioneers in that country didn't eat the cows who produced milk, cream and butter, they ate moose, deer or elk and the ruffed grouse's white meat was tastier than any pheasant-under-glass.

We are indeed indebted to three men for this information: Jim Little and Steve Matsella of Okla and John Bugiera of Rama.

DODSLAND

The townsite of Dodsland on the Biggar-Loverna branch of the Grand Trunk Pacific Railway was opened in August of 1913. It was incorporated into a village the same month and year. It was named in honor of Doctor Dodds who came from Nebraska. At one time he had an equity in 2000 acres of land in the surrounding district.

DOLLARD

Dollard is situated in the southwestern corner of the province near Shaunavon. It has always been a predominately French community. It was named for Adam Dollard des Ormeaux, soldier of New France. In 1660 Montreal, indeed all of New France, was being threatened with a gigantic Indian attack. With 16 other Frenchmen and a band of four Algonquins and 40 Hurons, he encamped on May 1 at the foot of the Long Sault, below the present town of Hawkesbury, Ont. He planned to surprise these invading war parties. He moved his men into a disused Indian palisade and waited. First 300 Onondagas came bounding down the rapids. The French and their Indian allies opened fire. The Onondagas attacked the palisade but were beaten off day after day. A numerous band of Iroquois joined the Onondagas and the Hurons inside the palisade deserted to the enemy. The Frenchmen's position was hopeless but they fought gallantly to the end. Their unflinching stand saved New France from a wholesale invasion that had been planned by the Five Nations.

DOMREMY

In 1895 a group of settlers newly arrived in Canada from France reached Duck Lake by train and then pushed on with horses through St. Louis to their land 35 miles south of Prince Albert. They expected to find an established community around which they could take up homesteads. This was the information they were given by the immigration officials. They found only prairie and bushland!

Disappointed but undaunted, they determined to make their own village; and they named it after their home community in Old France, Domremy.

Among the original group were Pierre M. Marsollier, A. Godin, A. Joubert, the Blondeau family, P.M. Agaesse, Peter Rabut, Courteaus, and Revoy Anse.

The Anse family operated the first post office in their home. Mail was brought in once a week from Duck Lake by horses and buckboard.

The original settlement was two miles north of the present site of the village. Buildings were moved to the new site when the railroad came through in 1918.

Today this bit of Old France on the Prairies has a population of over 300.

DONAVON

The CNR built south from Delisle in 1912 and the first town, nine miles out, was Donavon. The naming of Donavon was of considerable complexity. Prior to the coming of the railroad Mrs. W. D. "Birdie" Pattison operated a post office and small store in her home three miles southwest of the present townsite. It was called Birdview. When the railroad arrived the post office moved into the store of Thomas Edward Hahn and gave its name to the town. Things didn't go well because Birdview is very close to Broadview in name. The mail kept getting mixed up, so a change in names was needed. Broadview, the big divisional point to the south, was allowed to keep its

name and Birdview was changed to Donavon. The suggestion for this name came from Mr. T. E. Hahn, who chose it for sentimental reasons. He had formerly lived in Hanover, Ontario, where the Don river and the Avon river were close by. His original suggestion of Don Avon was contracted by the postal officials to Donavon. Glen Hahn, the present postmaster, has in his possession the last stamp used in the old post office and it reads "Birdview, Sask., June 8, 1914."

Troubles, however, were not over. Mr. Hahn would get things assigned to Donavon Post Office, Birdview, Saskatchewan. Now a mix-up in letters is one thing but when box cars intended for Broadview arrived in Birdview it didn't take the railway long to change the name of their station to Donavon.

Some of the early settlers in the district besides those already mentioned were: Rutherford, French, Shaw, Faulhaber, Cairns, Norrie, Wood and Christie.

DONCREST

Doncrest is a closed rural post office near Dillabough in the northeast of the province. It is situated on Shand creek which used to be called McDonald creek. Because the townsite was on the crest of a hill overlooking McDonald creek, the name given to it was Doncrest.

DONEGAL

Donegal is a single Searle elevator (closed since 1965) southeast of Reward. The name Donegal was first applied to the country school three miles northeast of the elevator. The school was built in 1911 and Andrew Buchanan, one of the three trustees, suggested Donegal in memory of his home town of Donegal, Ontario. The other two trustees were Art Mumford (chairman) and Joe Schloser. The first teacher was Mr. W. W. Warnock who now lives at 121 - 4th Avenue East in Unity. At that time he was teaching school and homesteading in the Amaranth school district six miles to the east of Donegal.

The first post office in the district was opened in 1909 at Asor (two miles to the east) in the general store of Joe Hufnagel. Mr. Hufnagel hauled the mail from Unity twenty-seven miles to the northeast. Mr. William Fry took over the business and when the CPR line came up through

Salvador, nine miles away, in 1911, he hauled the mail from there.

In 1930 the CNR put in the Unity to Bodo, Alberta, line and when it reached the present site the name of the country school, Donegal, was applied to the elevator and the store and post office which moved in. The name Asor disappeared. Old-timers of the district include: Ben, Henry, Mike, Adam, and Joe Ell; Pete Usselman; John Manning; Louis Vetter; Peter Herbs; Jim Alexander; James Danbrook; William Watson Warnock. The latter's son, Bill, still farms Warnock's Arbor Homestead. Arbor was added to commemorate 1500 tiny trees planted around the buildings as a windbreak. Today (1968) they form a solid green barrier around one of the best-kept farms in the district.

DONWELL

In 1911 the CNR built south from Canora and north from Hamton and when the two gangs met and the track was finished one of them said, "Now it's finished and done well!" It was exactly at the place where Donwell is now. Mr. Ernest Schenkoth donated the land for the townsite. The first postmaster was Emil Ochitwa and the first store was opened by Bruce and Bros Phillippi. Originally there were two schools, Bogudz, three miles to the east, and Bridok, three miles to the south. In 1935 a new school was built right in Donwell. The first elevator was the Bawlf which was built in 1915. Many people had settled in the district as long before the railway as 1898. Some of them were: Wasyl Malenovich, Theodor Anaka, Philip Kopelchuk, Tony Olinyk, John Chocholik, Alex Warcholik, Wasyl Heshka Kuzaik, Paul Ochitwa. The first Ukrainian Hall was built in 1914 and became the place where many community gatherings were held. It also housed a big library. The hall is still standing, having been renovated and enlarged quite recently.

The Hon. A. J. Kusiak, former MLA and cabinet minister, came from the Donwell district.

Donwell was only a hamlet of 41 people in 1964 but it won a Provincial Certificate for Cleanliness and as the postmaster, Mr. P. W. Procyshen, put it "everything is well done in Donwell."

DOONSIDE

Twenty-three settlers in all came into this district in 1882—the first three being Robert Everett, Murdock Campbell and Charles Callender. The first post office to serve the community of Moosomin, Assiniboia, Northwest Terrories, opened on Nov. 1, 1882 with Joseph Daniels as postmaster and it was housed in the C. Moulson and Company's tent store. This was 20 miles from Doonside and the fastest mode of travel was by horses.

The CNR did not come until 1906. The name Doonside was selected in memory of a town in Scotland. Thomas Miller, son of James Miller, one of the pioneers of 1882, became lieutenant-governor of Saskatchewan in 1945. He died in office shortly after his appointment.

DORÉ LAKE

Doré Lake is a small settlement of fifty-five people or so on the south bay of Doré lake. The name is derived from the French word "d'or," which means gilt or golden. It was chosen by the early settlers because of the golden reflection of fish as they cleared water in the evening sun.

The lake itself is large — covering an area of approximately 150 square miles. Industry in the area consists of commercial fishing and mink ranching. There is excellent sport fishing and the area has a large supply of wild game. This leads to many visitors. There are four tourist camps to supply this need.

The early settlers were a tough and courageous lot. They lived off the land and had very little communication with the outside world since in the early 1900s the only means of transportation was by dog and horse teams and all supplies came in by way of Big River fifty-five miles to the south. The oldtimers still often sit around the wood stove telling stories about the olden days. They had their way of life and enjoyed it.

DORINTOSH

When Dorintosh was incorporated as a hamlet in 1939 a name was chosen to honor two people, Doris Neilson and C. R. McIntosh, who were active in politics. They took part of the name "Doris" and part of the name "McIntosh" and made it into Dorintosh.

Mr. Cameron McIntosh was a member of Parliament for the area, 1925-1940.

On July 1, 1972, Mr. Bill Halpenny, a longtime resident of the district, gave a different version of the naming of Dorintosh when being interviewed for CJNB North Battleford by Harry Decker. According to Mr. Halpenny, Mr. McIntosh picked the name for the town. The "Dorin" came from a village in his homeland, Scotland, and the "tosh" came from his name.

DOUGLASTON

In 1902 the country post office of Douglaston was opened fourteen miles northwest of Alameda. It was named for Senator James Moffat Douglas who at that time was MP for Assiniboia East, 1896-1904, and later a Senator, 1906-1920.

DOWD HILL

This was an inland post office which was located in Fred Dowd's sod house just southwest of Dodsland. The post office was named in his honor. Although there was some controversy for a while as to whether it should be called Campbellville, Dowd Hill won out.

The first settlers to move into what was to become the Dowd Hill district arrived in 1906. The famous "Bone Trail" had already left its mark on the virgin soil when Albert and Fred Dowd, Tommy Middleton, Harry Castle, Walter Underhill, Jimmy Skane, Harry Boyce and Tommy Boddy trekked west on their optimistic trip to prosperity and adventure.

The "Campbell Clan" arrived in 1907 and included Archie, James, Colin, Duncan and William S. Campbell along with their mother, "Grandma Bandy," as she was called. The latter lived to spend almost ten years out in the prairie west and was always ready to lend a helping hand to anyone in trouble or need.

Another pioneer woman, Mrs. Foran, aptly summed up the pioneer spirit of the district when she said, "I never regretted my move west as I loved the prairies and had hopes in it. I was lucky in the district we came to, for though they were of nearly every race and creed, they were the most wonderful people I ever met. I think I can truly say every one of them was my friend as well as my neighbor."

DOWNE

Downe is six miles west of Ruthilda on the edge of a valley. The Grand Trunk Pacific built the original line in here in 1911-1912. The first settlers around Downe were Myles McMillan, George McIntosh and John McLeod. They came in 1905, others followed — many from Glengarry County, Ontario. The community was called Glengarry Plains and the school was called Glengarry School. However, when the railroad came in they named the village site Downe, probably for a railway official.

DRACUP

Dracup is very close to Yorkton and it was named for an oldtime citizen of that city, Mike Draycup.

DRAKE

Drake was named by the CPR officials for Sir Francis Drake (1540-1596), the first Englishman to sail around the world. He was the most famous of the Elizabethan sea captains.

Drake is also the center of a good duck hunting district. It is a sportsman's paradise. This theme is carried on in the local hockey and baseball teams with the name of "Mallards."

DRINKWATER

Drinkwater is a short distance southeast of Moose Jaw on the mainline of the CPR that runs to Weyburn. It was named for Charles Drinkwater, secretary of the CPR Company at the time.

DRISCOL LAKE

The Driscol Lake post office located at 13-7-14-W3, south and east of Shaunavon, had Engebret Olsen as the first postmaster. He suggested the name as he came from Driscoll, North Dakota. Either a mistake was made in spelling or in reading his handwriting and one "l" was lost.

DRIVER

Driver is on the edge of Buffalo Coulee halfway between Coleville and Smiley. The first post office in the district was established in 1908 by George Loney and it was called Glenloney.

When the GTP line was put through in June of 1913 the Glenloney post office moved to the townsite and would have given it that name except for the following chain of events.

When the railroad was being built through Buffalo Coulee on the way to Smiley, Milt Culham, Alex McKilligan and Vern Hambly, young farmers and businessmen of the district, used to take their racing horses or drivers hitched to sulkies or carts out on the new grade and race, just as young folks now like to take their cars out and "drag." This so intrigued the railroad officials that they named the townsite, Driver.

DROBOT

Drobot was an inland post office 12 miles northeast of Theodore. It was located on 28-29-6-W2, and was named for the first postmaster, Thomas Drobot. It is now closed.

DRUID

Druid is on a CPR line that came through from Rosetown on October 20, 1910. Dodsland, just a mile to the west, is on the Biggar-Loverna line that came through in 1913. These two lines cross and the "diamond" is between the towns.

The first buildings in Druid were the CPR station, the Netherhill Trading Co. general store, the Neil Stewart lumberyard, and Mrs. Cowden's restaurant and boarding house. The Druid school, built in 1912, served as a church and community center during the early years. A blacksmith shop was built in 1912 and the Saskatchewan Co-op elevator was built the same year. The Alexander Hotel, built in 1913 on the south side of Railway Avenue on the corner facing the railroad station, was a large three-storey building. This hotel, with its bar, run by Mr. Dion and Mr. Beauchemin, did a thriving business until prohibition was introduced in 1917. After it closed, the upper floors were turned into suites while the ground floor was at various times, the high school, the telephone office and a Chinese restaurant. The village of Druid reached its peak in the 1920s. After that, as Dodsland grew larger there was a gradual decline until it was finally reduced to a hamlet and its present state of quiet inactivity.

The railway gave the station its name of Druid, meaning a Celtic priest; there was no significance attached to the name as far as any of the present inhabitants can recollect.

DUBUC

Dubuc is the second stop west of Esterhazy. It was incorporated as a village in 1905 and named for Joseph Dubuc, a member of the first legally constituted Northwest Council in 1873.

DUCK LAKE

Duck Lake is a town on the CNR, 36 miles southwest of Prince Albert on the line from Saskatoon. The first settlers in the vicinity, in 1870, were Metis from the Red river. The original site was at the edge of Duck lake a few miles west of the present town. Duck Lake took its name from the little lake.

On March 26, 1885, the first shots in the Saskatchewan Rebellion were fired near here. Major Crozier with 100 mounted police and volunteers from Prince Albert, set out from Fort Carlton to seize supplies at Mitchell's store in Duck Lake before they fell into the rebels' hands.

Four miles west of Duck Lake they were met by an armed force of rebels under Gabriel Dumont. Crozier and his interpreter William McKay, went out to parlay with an Indian chief and Isador Dumont, Gabriel's brother. They talked briefly. William McKay thought the Indian was going to seize his gun. He shot him. Next Isador was killed and then general firing broke out on both sides. Gabriel Dumont fell, his scalp creased by a bullet. The skirmish lasted 40 minutes. The rebels lost five men and the mounted police 12. The mounted police were caught in a trap and all might have been slaughtered on their retreat to Fort Carlton had not Riel, who had now taken command, begged for the love of God that no more should be slain, saying that already there had been too much blood spilt. However, the rebellion had just begun. If you should visit Duck Lake today, you would find the old two-storey red brick school house being converted into a remarkable museum under the direction of Fred Anderson.

DUDLEY

Dudley is the third last stop on a CNR branch line that runs south and west from Dunblane to Beechy. It was probably named after the town of Dudley in Worcestershire, England. This town possesses the ruins of a historic castle said to be erected in the 8th century by Dudo, a Saxon chief, hence the name.

DUFF

Duff is on a branch line of the CNR that connects Melville and Balcarres. It was named for a mountain 7,170 feet high on the international boundary between British Columbia and Alaska. The mountain had been named for the Right Honourable Mr. Justice Duff, of the Supreme Court of Canada, junior counsel before the Alaska Boundary Tribunal, 1903.

Duff is a small place and like many similar small towns and villages it has not grown; in fact, it is hardly holding its own with Melville to the northeast and Neudorf and Lemburg to the south.

DULWICH

Dulwich is on a line running from North Battleford to St. Walburg. The original community was predominately English and Jack Truss selected the name of Longstaff to commemorate a town in England. This was refused because there was already a post office by that name in Saskatchewan. The next name chosen was Dulwich and this also was taken from a town in England.

Dulwich today is hard to find. All that remains are a few dilapidated unpainted buildings that could pass for granaries. The elevators were dismantled in the late 60s and all salvageable lumber was used to help building a new, large (70,000 bushel) "flat top" Pool elevator at Edam, the next grain point south.

DUMAS

Dumas is a predominately French community that took its name from Alexandre Dumas, 1824-1895, famous French playwright and novelist.

The railway arrived in 1906 and this led to the growth of a fair-sized village. The railway line was abandoned completely in 1961 and not much more than a post office remains.

DUMMER

Dummer is between Truax and ↓ on a CNR line than runs from Moose Ja. to Radville. It is named for a township in Peterborough County, Ontario, organized in 1821. This in turn was named for the Hon. William Dummer Powell, chief justice of Upper Canada in the early 1800s.

The railway arrived at Dummer in 1911. Early settlers from Ontario brought the name with them. Among their number were the following: Tom Tullock, W. J. Patterson, James Scott, the Brecken brothers, C. V. Henderson, J. S. Park, Alex Nesbitt and Edward Devins.

DUNBLANE

Dunblane was named by a railway engineer after his home in Scotland. It developed into a typical prairie town. Today it is a ghost town. Here is an account of its history taken from the Saskatoon *Star-Phoenix* of December 17, 1969:

"Dunblane is a ghost town not quite abandoned by the living. Those few who remain, showing little nostalgia for better days, have resigned themselves and quietly bear witness to an abrupt death of a Saskatchewan small town.

Perhaps there is consolation for them in knowing that Dunblane is only a more startling example of a fate forecast for many rural towns in the province.

'Actually, all the small towns are failing — but not so quickly,' said one Dunblane resident. Small towns fade away; Dunblane closed up.

Three years ago, Dunblane was among the living. Dunblane had three cafes, a high number for a town its size. There were two grocery stores, one with self-serving shopping carts and a checkout counter. There was a hotel without a beverage room, a TV-Electric shop, service stations, a Liquor Board store, a covered curling rink, a skating rink, and a solidly built brick school that had served the community since 1928.

Today there is hardly anything except a post office, a CNR station soon-to-be-closed, and three grain elevators.

A deserted, nameless, main street lies between the silent rows of empty buildings, some boarded up and others open, their windows shattered. On a windy day, with thistle tumbling along and the hotel door, held by one hinge, banging on the boarded window, Dunblane's main street would look as if it had been lifted from the set of a Grade B Western.

But Dunblane, six miles west of Gardiner Dam, had lived. Not as a short-term boom town but as an integral part of the province, a province no older than Dunblane.

Leonard Bartzen, the grain elevator agent and a town councillor, has spent all his 36 years in Dunblane. It was a railroad town, he said, and until 1918 was the end of the steel. 'In the early 20s there were three lumber yards, no end of boarding houses, cafes and livery barns.'

Somewhat of a boom town, Dunblane was invaded by about 300 construction workers around 1926 when the railroad built a roundhouse, its cement walls still standing on the outskirts. Besides a source of economic activity, the roundhouse provided the town with electrical power until finally closing down operations in 1939.

But even then, explained Mr. Bartzen, the town had a lease on life, because the railroad, busy hauling oil used Dunblane as a divisional point.

Throughout this period the population held at about 300 and it was not until the pipeline was stretched across Canada to carry oil that Dunblane felt its first major decline.

Instead of two or three trains a day, one lonely train a week began visiting Dunblane as it still does today. But there was still a community. In part because there were still many farmers but also due to preliminary work on the Gardiner Dam.

'In the early 1940s, they were drilling at the dam site and making surveys. It affected life here because a lot had families and lived right in town,' said Mr. Bartzen.

The population held at between 200 and 250 during these years and then began the gradual decline as fewer farmers began farming larger acreages.

This was Dunblane's second decline, one similar to other prairie towns, but full scale construction on Gardiner Dam kept the town's gradual fading in check. Beginning in 1959 with the invasion of construction crews, Dunblane had a modest boom with the houses full, as

many as 65 trailers packed into the court, and a population nudging 500. It lasted until the end of construction and the town collapsed. Now there are 20 houses occupied, only seven school-age children and a population under 50, the majority pensioners.

The force gradually emptying other prairie towns, namely fewer farmers, had been working at Dunblane as well but was camouflaged by dam-site acitivity. In addition, the dam geographically cut off a supply of even more farmers who now find it more convenient to frequent other centers.

When Dunblane fell, it fell with a vengeance of 10 years. Other doomed prairie towns were picked away gradually but Dunblane had a ten year respite and then died quickly. Perhaps for that reasons there is no regret in Dunblane.

Outside Dunblane and its boarded buildings, a sign reading 'This Dam Town Thanks You' lies half buried in the weeds.

DUNCAIRN

Duncairn is the second stop south of Swift Current on a CPR line that runs to Simmie. The name was the title given to Sir Henry Carson, prominent politician and former member of the Privy Council. It is also the name of an electoral division of Belfast, Northern Ireland, which he represented for many years.

DUNDURN

There are two schools of thought on how Dundurn got its name. The first is: A pioneer and his family journeyed by Red River cart west from Winnipeg in search of land. They travelled for weeks and weeks until at last they came to a place that suited them. There was lots of water, good soil and pasture. Winter was approaching. As the father stood and looked about the spot he had selected he said to his family, "I think we have dundurn well."

Here is the other story. When the old GTP came through they named townsites alphabetically. When they came to this site the letter was "D" and there happened to be a Scotsman on the railway crew who had been born near Dundurn Castle in Scotland. It was his birthday and so he asked if the new town could be named Dundurn and his wish was granted.

Dundurn is a 24 mile drive south of Saskatoon. The first settler in the district was John Mawson, a rancher who came in 1886. The big rush of settlement came in 1902 by Americans under the leadership of E. J. Meilicke. It is the centre for a wheat growing and ranching area and for a large army camp.

Mr. Edgar Sullivan of Dundurn tells this story of the early days. "In the early June of 1909 I rode horseback from Regina to Hanley and then 20 miles west to my homestead. When I was coming up the hill north of Lumsden a passenger train passed me. At 3:00 p.m. that afternoon I passed the train. In those days we used to say 'CNR for comfort but oxen for speed'."

DUNDURN CAMP

Drive south from Saskatoon to Regina and 20 miles out of Saskatoon you'll see a sign reading Dundurn Military Camp. Four miles west and you're at the camp. The first thing that will impress you is the water tower. All the buildings are modern. There is always a PMQ (permanent married quarters) staff on hand. There are enough buildings to house 3000.

Training camps vary during the year and may be scheduled at any time. In the winter of 1971 a complete winter camp was held, with the men living in tents outdoors. This gave a good test of both equipment and men.

J. C. (Joe) Stretch of 1424 — 8th Avenue North, Saskatoon, now retired from the reserve army, when asked what was his greatest experience while on maneuvers, didn't hesitate a bit: he recalled a few years back when they were testing 25 pounders they set fire to the surrounding bush and 'had a hell of a time putting it out.'

DUNELM

Dunelm is the first stop south of Swift Current on a CPR line that runs southeast of Meyronne. The name is said to be a signature of the Bishop of Durham.

DUNFERMLINE

Dunfermline is seventeen miles west of Saskatoon on the main line of the CPR to Edmonton. In the early 1900s when the line was built that represented quite a distance from Saskatoon and so a little town grew up; a station (for milk and cream), a section house, a blacksmith shop, a school, a water tower, a livery barn, a pool hall and two stores (one run by Solomon Isaac and the other by George Spence, who later sold out to Bill Tripp). There were a few Scots in the district — the Tripp brothers, George Spence and Milton Watson — and they were instrumental in having the village named for Dunfermline, Fifeshire, Scotland.

In the last 20 years the village has gone the way of many places close to a large center. It has dwindled. The Grain Growers elevator sold out to the Searle and when it burnt down it was not rebuilt. The Spence store sold out and Milt Watson tore it down and used it for farm buildings. By 1969 all that was left was a railway shelter bearing the name Dunfermline and part of an old store.

However, Saskatoon as one of the fastest growing cities in Canada has been reaching out in all directions and Dunfermline has been affected. The 13 lots that comprised the original village site have been put up for sale. Ralph Young's Esso Service on highway 14, a mile to the west, has a few houses built around it and some trailers have been parked. The Vanscoy Municipality has passed a bylaw that anyone building in the area must have at least 40 acres. In time Dunfermline will be part of Saskatoon.

DUNKIRK

Dunkirk is close to the east shore of Old Wives' lake. It is forced into an alphabetical pattern that goes Archive, Buttress, Crestwynd, Dunkirk and Expanse. These are all on a CPR line south of Moose Jaw.

Dunkirk is a town in Scotland. It is also a sea port in France on the English Channel made famous in World War II. Dunkirk in Scottish means "church among the sand dunes." Many of the first settlers in the district were of Scottish descent and it was their suggestion that Dunkirk be used for a name.

DUNLEATH

The country post office of Dunleath was opened in 1894. The name was suggested by Colin Mackay, a pioneer school teacher. The name suggested was

Dunlea, a combination of two Gaelic words, but it was changed in Ottawa by adding two letters, making Dunleath. After the country post office was closed in 1928 the name was taken for a station on the Yorkton branch of the CPR.

DUNNING

Dunning is on a short branch line of the CNR east of Radville that ends at Goodwater. It commemorates one of the best known Saskatchewan success stories. Charles Avery Dunning, an immigrant farmhand, arrived on the Prairies from his native England in 1902. He was 17 years old. At 27 he was elected to the provincial government of Saskatchewan. At 31 he was made a cabinet minister and elected to the provincial legislature. At 37, he was the premier of the province. At 41 he was minister of railways and canals in the federal government and later became minister of finance.

Failing health ended his political rise and in 1939 he left Parliament Hill and moved to Montreal where he confined his activities to the business world.

DUPEROW

Duperow is the second stop west of Biggar on the CNR. There was a post office there long before the railway came through. It was called Lydden for Lydia Dirks, the daughter of the first settler. When the railway came through in 1908 the townsite took its name from the post office. However, considerable confusion in freight deliveries came about because there is a town called "Glidden" in Saskatchewan, so the CNR requested that the name be changed to Duperow, for W. E. Duperow, general passenger agent, Winnipeg.

The post office retained the name, Lydden, until four years ago when they changed to Duperow.

DURO

The main line of the GTP came to Saskatoon in the early 1900s. Finishing the alphabet at Zelma to the east they started over with Allan, Bradwell, Clavet, Duro and Earl (which was within the city limits). No significance to the name has been ascertained. It was just a grain siding and it remains that today.

DUVAL

Go north from Regina on highway 40 and you'll come to Duval about halfway up the east side of Last Mountain lake. It's a well-kept town. In the community hall hangs a picture of the man for whom the town was named. The inscription below the picture reads: Edward W. DuVal, lieutenant, P.P.C.L.I., killed in action, July 2, 1918, at Arras.

Dr. Ernest R. Myers, his commanding officer, wrote of him: "Edward died gloriously, enshrined in the hearts of his friends, having touched with the magic of his spirit, for their ever lasting good, everyone with whom he came in contact."

We are indebted to Mr. Mervyn Essery and his son James, pioneer merchants, and to Mrs. Bert Mann, the postmaster's assistant, for this information.

DYSART

Dysart is a village northeast of Regina on the CPR line north of the Qu'Appelle Valley. It is named for Mr. Dysart, and here is the story of why:

In 1907 when the Canadian Pacific was building the railroad through from Brandon, Manitoba, to Bulyea, Saskatchewan, a camp was made on the homestead of Mr. Bishop, the father of the First World War flying ace, Billy Bishop. One night at a party, Mr. Bishop found himself in conversation with the chief surveyor of the project, Mr. Dysart. In a generous mood, Mr. Bishop agreed to name the site for the surveyor if he would agree to run the line through Bishop's land, and that's how Dysart got its name.

William Avery (Billy) Bishop (1894-1956), airman and author, was born in Owen Sound, Ontario, and was educated at the Royal Military College, Kingston. He went overseas in the First World War with the Canadian cavalry. In 1915, he transferred to the Royal Flying Corps, and after a period of training went to France in 1917. He proved to be one of the most successful "fighting airmen" in the Allied forces; and was awarded, in rapid succession, the V.C., the D.S.O. and bar, and the D.F.C. He shot down a total of seventy-two enemy aircraft. After the war he was a successful businessman in commercial aviation and also became the author of "Winged Warfare" (New York 1918) and "Winged Peace" (Toronto 1944).

E

EAGLE CREEK

It was 1902 when Mr. Jim Forsyth came out from Ontario to take up a homestead on the banks of the Eagle Creek, where the Old Battleford Trail crossed it, four miles north and four miles east of the present site of Arelee. He became the first postmaster when the mail was hauled by team and wagon from Saskatoon. Naturally, the post office took the name Eagle Creek. Around the post office there sprung up a store (also operated by Mr. Forsyth) and a blacksmith shop run by Ned Huxtable who had come to the area from Scotland.

By 1907 Mr. Forsyth had left the district and the post office was taken over by Sylvester Currie and during his term of office the rail line went through Asquith. This meant that the mail now came that far on the train and then Tom Bowes, the Asquith livery stable operator, delivered it the twelve miles north to Eagle Creek.

This information was received from Mr. and Mrs. Forrest Currie of Delisle. They were both born and raised in the vicinity of Eagle Creek. Mr. Currie told us that his father, George Currie, helped many of the first Doukhobors who came to the district to homestead with the filing of their claims. At that time it required a trip to Battleford to fill out the necessary papers. Since most of these people could speak little English and write none at all, Mr. Currie did the paper work. Many of the names he could not spell so he would say, "We'll call you Joe Smith" and so the deed would be filled out. Even today there are many families of Smiths, etc. in the district who have a bit of a foreign accent.

EARL

Earl does not appear on many present day maps. The original survey of the Grand Trunk Pacific went through Hanley. By exerting considerable pressure, Saskatoon businessmen were able to have it changed to come through Saskatoon but instead of entering the town, the survey skirted the southern edge of Nutana. GTP officials purchased a section and a half of land south of Nutana; presumably they hoped to pull the growing city southward toward their station,

Earl. There was no significance in the naming of Earl, it was just another name that the GTP was able to place in alphabetical order. On the way into Saskatoon they had come to the end of the alphabet with Zelma. They started over with Allan, Bradwell, Clavet, Duro, and then Earl. John Lake had already changed Minnetonka to Saskatoon, but happy as the city fathers were to have the Grand Trunk Pacific, no one suggested that the name Saskatoon should be dropped in favor of Earl.

EARL GREY

This town was named for Earl Grey, a governor general of Canada, who took office on December 10, 1904, and was so popular that his term of office was twice extended, until October 13, 1911. At his suggestion, the battlefield of the Plains of Abraham was preserved as a national park.

He presented the now famous "Grey Cup" for rugby football.

EASTEND

Eastend takes its name from the old North-West Mounted Police post that was established there in 1877. It was called Eastend because it was at the eastern extremity of the Cypress Hills.

EASTLEIGH

Eastleigh is an inland post office sixteen miles south of Mortlach. Early settlers in this district included: Love, Smith, Day, Savage, Bull, Hillar, Dew, Downtown and Osman. They were predominately English and they named their post office, community and school, Eastleigh, in memory of the hometown of many of them in Eastleigh, England.

EAST POPLAR

East Poplar is a customs point on the east bank of the East Poplar river where it crosses the international boundary. It takes its name from the river, which is the east branch of the Poplar river. East Poplar is also a village 4 miles north of the customs office. It is on a CPR line that comes down from Assiniboia and ends at Big Beaver, and takes it name from the customs point.

EASTURLEA

Easturlea, a rural post office now closed, was near Vanscoy. It was named for three men in the district, Mr. W. W. EASTman, Mr. Sam TURbott, and Mr. Ernie LEAch.

EATONIA

Eatonia was one of the last areas of central Saskatchewan to be settled. The CNR was built through the townsite at the end of the First World War and Eatonia became a divisional point and remained so until the early 1930s.

The CNR named the townsite Eaton in honor of Timothy Eaton, the mail-order-house tycoon. The original school district here was called Eaton, too, and the high school is still officially known as Eaton High.

Some years ago the post office officials changed the name to Eatonia to avoid confusion in the mails with the nearby town of Eston.

EBENEZER

Thomas Goulden and his brother William, pioneered in this district in 1900. The GTP built north from Yorkton in 1909 and when they got to the village they called it Anoka. It was a settlement of German Baptists and they didn't like the name. A committee consisting of S. Deckert, J. D. Runman and L. Zimmer met with the railway officials and strongly suggested a change of names. The committee suggested the name Ebenezer and the railway officials accepted it.

ECKNER

Eckner is the first stop south of Meadow Lake on a CPR line that comes up from Medstead. It was named for Charlie Eckner, an early settler in the area.

EDAM

Edam was first settled in 1907 and the railway came through in 1911. It was named for Edam, Holland, from whence the first settlers came and which, of course, was famous for its cheese.

EDENBRIDGE

In 1905, 56 Hebrew families left South Africa to seek independence in Canada. They chose the Carrot River Valley as their new home. Soon after, this group was joined by others from all parts of the world. Settlers arrived from Latvia, South Africa, Russia, Poland and England.

When word was received that a post office was being granted, the name Edenbridge was agreed upon. The word "Eden" is derived from the Hebrew translation, meaning Jewish, and since the bridge across the river had just been erected at this point the words "Eden" and "bridge" were combined. The first post office was established in 1907 one-quarter mile north of the Carrot River and five miles north of Brooksby.

EDENWOLD

Edenwold is just a little northeast of Regina. The first settlers: the Mangs, the Frombachs, the Kochs and the Bredts came from Austria. They spoke German. They were greatly impressed with all the trees and wild fruits that grew in the district. They named their district Edenwald. The Eden was for the Garden of Eden and wald in German means forest. In ensuing years the "a" got changed to an "o".

EDFIELD

Edfield is just north of Foam Lake. It was named for Edward Field, one of the earliest pioneers in the district.

EDGELEY

The first settlers arrived in the district in the early 1880s. Although they were chiefly from Ontario there was a family who came from England by the name of Sykes. Since they came from Edgeley, England, they called their farm Edgeley Farm. It was a big farm employing between 25 and 30 men. Huge machinery was imported from England — the only machinery of its kind to be brought to this country. They had a 10-furrow plow and it was pulled by a steel cable half a mile long from one engine at one end of the field to another engine at the other end of the field. The engines had large boilers like locomotives and they kept a team busy hauling coal from Qu'Appelle. Due to the heavy expense of the steam engines, the farm soon reverted to horse power.

The Sykes sold out before the railroad arrived in 1911 but the name of their farm was given to the new town.

93

EDMORE

Edmore is the first grain point south of Foam Lake on the CPR. This line continues south to West Bend and then turns west to end at Wishart.

The first settlers into this area came from the United States and they were responsible for naming the new town Edmore for Edmore, North Dakota. This information came from the CPR files.

EIGENHEIM

Eigenheim is a rural school and church community six miles west of Rosthern. The first settlers came to the district in 1892 and included the following: Friesens, Regiers, Duecks, Epps, Wilers, and Klassens. They named it Eigenheim which means "your own home".

In 1896 these true pioneers built a log church and named it Rosenort which means "place of the rose". It was the first Mennonite church built in the Northwest Territories.

In the early 1960's the school was closed and the students were bussed to Rosthern.

A fine new church was built and still serves the community. The present pastor is Reverend Irwin Schmidt and some of his parishioners include descendants of the originals and others like Letkeman, Riekman, Unger, Heinricks, Thornton, Adrian, Roth and Janzen.

ELBOW

Elbow was named because of a configuration of the South Saskatchewan river. While the town of Elbow dates only from early years of this century, the general location had been so designated for more than 100 years. The earliest journal in which reference is made to it is that of John McDonald of Garth who led a North-West Company party upstream in 1804 to Chesterfield House. McDonald wrote, "There is an elbow in the river parallel to that of the north branch, a most beautiful place. I crossed the neck of land, perhaps two miles, with my interpreter, while the canoes, always in sight, had to go around 10 miles at least."

ELDERSLEY

Eldersley is between Tisdale and Peesane on a CNR line east of Melfort that runs to Hudson Bay. The railroad first called it New Osgoode Siding. When the CNR built north from Crooked River the second point was called New Osgoode at the request of the settlers. (See New Osgoode.) This led to a confusion in names and New Osgoode Siding changed its name to Eldersley, named for a village in Scotland. The original name requested by the settlers was Elderslie but a spelling mix up made it Eldersley. Theodore Will has a small store there and there is a Pool elevator but that's about all.

ELDORADO

Eldorado is a uranium mining community of 700 people a few miles east of Uranium City, on Lake Athabasca. It is named for the Eldorado Mining and Refining Company Limited, a Crown corporation which was a pioneer developer in the area.

ELDRED

Eldred is the first stop northwest of Debden on the Shellbrook to Big River line. Eldred was quite a little trading centre before Debden expanded as an agricultural and religious centre. Eldred had one of the finest stores around — a two-storey structure complete with post office. It had a good community hall, a church, a school, a station, a section gang, a water tower and all. It even had tennis courts! The store was operated by Philip Eldred and the place was named for him. (Refer to the story of Neeb.) Another long-time operator of the store was Victor Harvey and his clerk was his young brother, Joseph, the present proprietor of the store at Bodmin. He well remembers playing tennis on the courts and attending the gay dances held in the nearby hall.

ELFROS

Although less than twenty miles west of Foam Lake, the village of Elfros got its start much later. it wasn't until the early 1900's that the first settlers came in. At that time an Icelandic colony settled and these were followed by a group from Sweden.

The village was established in 1910 and the name Elfros was chosen by Mr. Lund. In Icelandic Elfros means "Garden of Roses".

ELK HILL

Take the CNR northeast from Melfort to Carrot River and the second last stop is Moose Range. Ten miles west is the inland post office (now closed) of Elk Hill. Here within a few miles two of the most sought after big game animals in Saskatchewan are honored, the elk and the moose.

The bull elk stands about five feet high at the shoulder, and many weigh from 700 to 1000 pounds. Its rounded antlers may spread as much as five feet and have as many as twelve points. It is a stately and beautiful animal.

ELLISBORO

Ellisboro is near Wolseley. It is named for the Ellis family who were prominent pioneers of the district.

ELM SPRINGS

Elm Springs was an inland post office eight miles west of Scout Lake in the south-central part of the province. It was named for fresh water springs and a heavy growth of trees. Its exact location was 34-4-2-W3. The Elm Springs post office opened on August 8, 1898, with Mr. Conrad Linden as postmaster. After a succession of seven postmasters it closed on June 12, 1954. Mr. Daniel Lawrick was the last postmaster.

ELROSE

In 1885 when General Otter and his troops were hastening to Battleford during the Saskatchewan Rebellion, the Militia camped at what is still known as Otter Springs, 10 miles southwest of Elrose on the old Battleford Trail and on the farm presently occupied by Mr. and Mrs. Earl Kleutsh.

The first settlers took up land east of Elrose and when the present townsite was selected by the CNR a spectacular race ensued to obtain the better locations — a race which is still talked about by townsfolk today.

Originally, around 1909 and 1912 when settlement was at its height, the town was known as Laberge, one of the pioneers of the district being so honored, but at a mass meeting of the residents in the fall of 1913, Louis Chirhart, a contractor, suggested the name of Elrose and this was favored by the majority of those present.

Just why he proposed that name is not known today, although it has been suggested that it was after a place in the United States.

ELSTOW

Elstow is between Blucher and Colonsay on the CPR just out of Saskatoon on a line to Lanigan. Three homesteaders filed in 1902: J. W. Lewis, Abraham Buck and Mr. A. E. Black. Those who came in '03 were: P. Brown, H. Daless, C. Mycroft, J. Ross, W. Taylor, William McConnell, Mr. McKenzie and Mr. Preston. The village of Elstow is situated on the homestead of James Harvie and it was named for Elstow, England, near Bedford in Bedfordshire. It is the birthplace of John Bunyan, the author of "Pilgrim's Progress." Some people say it was named by a railway official who was reading "Pilgrim's Progress" at the time the line went through. The first train came through in 1907. Some freight service was supplied then. The first passenger train came through Elstow on June 3, 1908. Until then mail was brought out from Saskatoon by buggy. Mr. W. S. Taylor was the first postmaster.

ELSWICK

Elswick was an early inland post office located at 3-5-12-W2. Mr. J. Huff was the first postmaster and he named it in memory of his hometown, Elswick, England.

EMERALD

Emerald was a rural post office north of Prince Albert. It is now closed. It was named by G. M. Atkinson, MLA, who came to Round Plain in 1886. He suggested the name because the grass always stayed green (emerald) longer here than in any other district.

EMMAVILLE

Emmaville is a small rural community southwest of Spruce lake. This community played a great part in the early history of Spruce lake. The school district (Emma) and post office finally died out following the coming of the railway. The name, Emmaville, was derived from the name of Mrs. Emma Roussel, who with her husband, Etienne, came to the district as a newly married couple in 1896. The first post office was set up in 1902 and the first mail contract was let to Mr. Slater of Fort Pitt. He drove a team and democrat and picked up the mail in Saskatoon and delivered it to Onion Lake, with stops at Battleford, Jackfish, Emmaville and Fort Pitt. For thirteen years the people of Emmaville received their mail through this post office. Some of the homesteaders who were likely to be "in town" on "mail day" were: Hugh Lockart, George Marchant, Bert Preston, Christopher Jackson, Isaac and Walter Wooff, William Davis, James and Dave Mason, Ted Morgan, the Atkinson brothers, and Robert Buck.

When the railway came into Spruce Lake in 1920 the post office soon closed and the business places moved into Spruce Lake. This information came from Mr. Robert H. Wooff, MLA for the district in 1966.

ENDEAVOUR

Endeavour is on a branch line of the CNR running north from Sturgis. When the railway went through the area in 1928 a hamlet sprang up. The railway company decided to call it Endeavour after the airplane which made the first overseas flight that carried passengers from England to America. The settlement had previously been called Annette after a Ukrainian settler.

END LAKE

On the CNR line from Unity southwest to Bodo, Alberta, built in 1930, the first grain delivery point was End Lake, a siding with a loading platform. It's right on the edge of the valley overlooking End lake.

It was at End lake in the 30s that exploratory drilling discovered natural gas in commercial quantities. There are four wells right in the middle of the lake and five others around the perimeter. Unity got its first gas from this field. By 1968 the field had been closed and was being used as a storage site. Pipe lines come into it from Coleville and other parts of the provicne and the gas is forced back into the ground to be held in reserve.

No more grain is shipped from this siding but some of the people who used it when it was first put in use were: Charlie and Tom Carson, Carson Atchinson, Charlie Gibbons, Jack Brownlee, Simon Schell and Isaac Wrightson.

Edgar Sherwood's fine farm is the closest dwelling to it today.

ENFIN

Enfin is the first stop south on a CNR line from Yorkton to Melville. York lake was the name given to a small lake south of Yorkton. Enfin was the name given by the GTP railway to the stopping place on the bank of York lake where they had a water tower and flag station for picnickers out from Yorkton or Melville.

ENGELFELD

Engelfeld is between Watson and Muenster. It takes its name from the local parish of the Holy Guardian Angels of Engelfeld. Engelfeld is a German name meaning "Angel's Field." This name was chosen to honor the man who aided the Canadian Benedictines so much in the pioneer days, Abbot Peter Engel of St. John's Abbey, Collegeville, Minnesota.

ENGEN

Engen is the first siding east of Saskatoon on the main line of the CPR. It was named for Fred Engen, a member of the Saskatoon real estate firm of Sutherland, Engen, and Hanson. This agency was involved in memorable real estate deals of the early days. In the fall of 1905 it purchased 100,000 acres from the Saskatchewan Valley Land Company. Within three months it had sold three-quarters of its purchase. The headline news of July 15, 1906, was the purchase by the CPR of land for right-of-way and station in the center of the town. Through the agency of Sutherland, Engen, and Hanson, the CPR company purchased 180 lots for $78,000.

Even though the little town of Saskatoon was booming in the early 1900s everything was not rosy, financially, as the following incident will testify:

"On September 18, 1907, the power plant — today the water works plant — was officially opened in a ceremony in which Lieutenant-governor Forget turned on the city lights.

"The Allis-Chalmers Bullock Company had supplied the electrical machinery for the plant, accepting a short term note from the city. All winter the city's finances were slim, and twice the company renewed the note. When, in the spring of 1908, the note came up for renewal the third time, the representative of the company walked into the mayor's office and informed him that, on orders from the head office, he was about to seize the plant and operate it until the revenue had paid for the machinery.

"Mayor Wilson had until noon to raise $12,000. With Fred Engen he canvassed the business men of the city, and in two hours had the money to pay the city's debt."

ENID

Enid is a rural post office near Leross. it was named after Enid, Olklahoma, by George Frey, a farmer in the district.

ENS

Between Domremy and Wakaw is the grain point of Ens. Mrs. George Luciuk runs the combined store and post office. The latter is small serving only 17 patrons. The GTP built the grade in 1910 and laid the steel in 1912. Car load after car load of cordwood was shipped over the loading platform and when wood gave way to other fuels the railway was ready for the grain.

The Reliance and Federal companies put up elevators in 1924. Joe Hegedus and his sister hauled water for the cement that went into the foundations of these buildings. Joe, who had been born in a log house on his father's farm just a stone's throw away from the elevators, was a twelve-year-old boy at that time. By 1934 he was farming three quarters of land adjoining the townsite; he also became a grain buyer for the Reliance Grain Company. Nine years later the Federal bought out the Reliance and he began to run both elevators. In August of 1968 the Federal bought out the Pool elevator that had been built in 1936 and Mr. Hegedus now runs all the elevators in town. That's quite a tribute to a man. How many others can say that they have spent all their lives in one small community serving the public and obviously getting along well with everyone?

Mr. Hegedus remembers how Ens got its name. It was named after Gerhard Ens, one of the pioneers of the Rosthern district. He was at one time connected with the Immigration Department and was instrumental in settling a great many Mennonites in the district. He was a member of the first provincial legislature and was a strong advocate of Saskatoon as the site of the capital of the new province.

ENVIRON

The CPR built west from Saskatoon and in 1908 reached Asquith. A spur line was run north to Environ and gravel for the line was hauled from there. At that time Environ was known as "The Pit." The railway did a limited amount of grain hauling from the site as farmers loaded cars over the platform.

In 1927 the CPR started to build north from Environ to Battleford. They got as far as Baljennie and quit. The depression had struck; furthermore, North Battleford was the booming town, not Battleford.

The railway officials gave the site its name and it had no connection with anything locally.

One of the first settlers, Alex Demoskoff, came into the district in 1899 and settled eleven miles north and east of Environ. Other early settlers included the following: J. Turner, J. MacSorley, the Larsons, Dodds, Petersons, Atkinsons, Johnsons, Lundys and George Shea.

John A. Demoskoff, general merchant at Environ writes in to say that the latest improvement in the district is the establishment of the Eagle Creek Regional Park, three miles west and one south of Environ.

EPPING

Epping is twenty miles south of Lloydminster and very close to the Alberta border. it was possibly named by a settlement of Barr Colonists. These people were very "British" in their thinking and they probably named it either for Epping, a town northeast of London, England, or the famous Epping forest nearby.

ERINFERRY

Erinferry is an inland post office and store between Eldred and Bodmin on highway no. 55. It is operated by Jerome Lafreniere who has been there for four years. It was during the tenure of the previous owner, Leonce April, that a change in location and of name took place. The point on the railway was Wrixon, a mile to the south of the present site. Considerable confusion in mail handling had occurred between Wrixon and Wroxton and the postal officials asked for the change of name. The men responsible for the suggestion of the name were: Robert O'Connell, his nephew, Sam McKee, and Robert Banks, oldtimers of the community. They chose Erinferry in memory of a place in their homeland of Ireland.

ERMINE

Ermine used to be a grain point on the CPR between Druid and Kerrobert; "used to be" because it's all gone now. The last to go was the Pool elevator.

At its height in the 1920s the village had the following: two lumberyards, a shoe and harness shop, a general store, two churches, one livery barn, one poolroom and barbershop, one Spencer elevator, and a hotel that was later moved to Millerdale.

A disastrous fire in 1929 levelled most of the village and since it was well into the depression the buildings were not rebuilt. Some of the oldtimers in the district were the following: George, John and Jake Neumeier, Henry Draves, Henry Danneker, John Fridgen, Joe Funke, Walter Ellis, Ben and Bert Doll, Robert Reoch, Joseph Bermel and Vic Culham.

Albert Jacob (Jake) Neumeier, who was one of the best-known settlers in the district, did a great deal of trapping to supplement his income. Weasels were abundant and it was Jake who suggested the name. However, the postal officials persuaded him to change it to Ermine.

Take a weasel's skin and make it up into the trim for a ladies' coat and it becomes ermine. This fur decorates the robes worn by judges of many countries. When used as an emblem of royalty it takes on another name, miniver. At one time noblemen wore different arrangements of the black tail tips as signs of rank.

Jake not only caught a lot of weasels but in the winter of 1921 when coyote hides brought from $10 to $15 and badgers were worth $45 he shot and skinned 721 rabbits. They brought from 4 cents to 14 cents depending on the condition of the fur.

ERNFOLD

Ernfold is between Morse and Uren on the main line of the CPR from Moose Jaw to Swift Current. Railway officials gave the village its name.

Here are some firsts: settler — John McGough (1904); woman — Mrs. Fred Robertson; car — Model T owned by Joe McDonald; elevator — Beaver, agent Wes. Moore; church — Methodist; Bonspiel — 1929.

The 1969 population was 109. In the fall of 1969 Premier Ross Thatcher officially opened the water works which had been completed late in 1968.

ERWOOD

Erwood is the first station east of Hudson Bay. It is not known who was the first to establish a residence on the site where Erwood now stands; or indeed anywhere in this locality. Old-timers tell that as the railway construction crews moved west, their progress was retarded by the Red Deer river. For a time, Erwood was the end of the steel and until the original wooden bridge was built across the river, this was as far as anyone could travel by railroad.

Thus Erwood developed into a thriving community before the turn of the century and during the early 1900s. The railway built a "Y" off the main line, so that turning around would be possible for its trains. Great quantities of supplies were shipped here to replenish the building crews and the shipments were addressed to E. R. Wood, a railway official. When the flag station was built, it was identified as Erwood.

ESK

Esk, the first stop east of Lanigan, was named by CPR officials for the Esk river in Scotland, made famous by the Poem "Young Lochinvar."

ESKBANK

Eskbank southeast of the "Elbow" is named for the Earl of Southesk who came West in the spring of 1859 for his health and to enjoy the sport of big game hunting. During much of his travels he followed the Carlton Trail. However, he made a side trip from the Trail and hunted buffalo at the Elbow. He shot a grizzly bear near Stranraer and hunted as close to Saskatoon as Goose lake.

ESME

Esme is on a CPR line in southwestern Saskatchewan between Glen Bain and Vanguard. It was named for Miss Esme Gooding, postmistress.

ESTERHAZY

Esterhazy got its name from Count Paul Esterhazy, a benevolent native of Hungary, who lived in New York in 1885. At that time a number of his countrymen who had been peasants and had previously migrated from Hungary to the United States were working in the coal mines in Pennsylvania under very trying conditions. Count Esterhazy acquired a tract of land between what is now the site of the town of Esterhazy and the Qu'Appelle Valley. In 1886 a number of these people migrated from Pennsylvania to the Esterhazy district and began farming. In 1888 quite a number of peasants came directly from Hungary to the same district.

At present the population of Esterhazy is between 3000 and 4000 people and it is one of the fastest growing towns in Saskatchewan due to the potash developments in the area.

ESTEVAN

Arthur Kelly homesteaded the original townsite. The railroad survey was made in 1892. The Soo Line was completed from Moose Jaw to North Portal in 1893 and a flurry of activity went into the start of Estevan. Like many communities of Saskatchewan the settlement was a child of the railroad and the railroad gave it its name. Estevan is derived from a combination of the names of George Stephen, first president of the CPR and William C. van Horne, the company's second president.

ESTLIN

The hamlet of Estlin originated in 1912 when the Grand Trunk Pacific Railway (now CNR) laid the steel through this farming community. It was named "Estlin" by the railway company to perpetuate the name of one of their prominent officials.

While the hamlet of Estlin did not appear until 1912, the community was very much alive years before that time. During the 1885-1890 period members of the Bratt family settled beside the only prairie lake of the region. It is known as Buck lake and in six miles south of the present site of Estlin.

The Bratts were ranchers and made good use of the marshes and hay flats, while the lake was a certain source of water and mosquitoes. The Bratt brothers became well known ranchers and farmers and today the local rural municipality bears their name.

Early-day Estlin was geared to a horse-and-buggy economy and reached its peak in the 1920s. At that time it had a church and school. It also had the excitement and color provided by the blacksmith from Switzerland, the tinsmith from Ireland, and the old fashioned crackerbarrel general store and post office. Then there were places and things that today's youngsters have never even heard about — the livery barn, the stock yards, the slaughter house and the loading platform. Rounding out its amenities and necessities were the lumber yard, the pool room, cafe, station agent, section foreman, machinery warehouse, and of course, the grain elevators — its main reason for existence. During the boom years the total population was never more than 50.

This little prairie town had its share of excitement — some of it rather tragic. The general store burned, was replaced, and burned again. Then there was great excitement among the children and dismay among the taxpayers when the new two-roomed school burned. Over the years spectacular blazes took an elevator, a house — then in a tremendous holocaust the villagers lost their store, lumber yard, community hall, poolroom, and garage.

The hamlet more or less recovered from these fires. The school of course, was replaced immediately, but some of the other buildings never were.

Two different families tried at different times to set up a general store business, but neither could compete with Regina merchants only 15 miles away. The gravel gridroad and the auto had changed the rural way of life.

The store is closed, the station agent is gone, so is the blacksmith shop, the tinsmith shop, the livery barn, the stockyards, slaughter house, and the cafe.

But Estlin is still there — three huge modern grain elevators and annexes with nearly half a million bushels capacity represent big business in the little grain farming community. The church remains, educational standards rise steadily and Estlin lives on, serving its community well.

ESTON

Eston is 160 miles southwest of Saskatoon. It was named for the English home of A. J. Harris' family, Eston, in the West Riding of Yorkshire. It is one of the best wheat growing districts in Saskatchewan.

ESTUARY

Estuary is a town just inside the Saskatchewan border where the Red Deer river empties into the South Saskatchewan. It takes its name from this geographic fact, even though an estuary is really the tidal mouth of a river.

ETHELTON

Ethelton is the second grain point east of Meskanaw on a CNR line that runs from Saskatoon to Melfort. In 1901 Miss Ethel Traill, eldest daughter of William Edward Traill, was married to Frederick Johnstone Bigg. The late Rev. Thomas Clark of Melfort performed the ceremony. He suggested that the new district being formed to the east be named Ethelton for the first bride in the area. This name was accepted by the new post office that was set up.

When the CPR built northeast of Sasktoon to Melfort in the 20s the grain point took the name already established in the district, Ethelton.

This information came from Mrs. Phyllis West of Meota, who is the eldest daughter of the above mentioned couple, Mr. and Mrs. F. J. "Jack" Bigg.

ETTINGTON

Ettington is on a CNR line directly south of Old Wives' lake. There is a story that Ettington got its name this way:

Someone found an empty tin can by the right-of-way and on picking it up found that the label read "Ettington Plums." Some of the first homesteaders were: Emil Magnuson, John Sellers and E. O. Thomas. The first section foreman was Mr. Riley and the second was Peter Eppy. Here are some more firsts: storekeeper - L. J. Nicholson; baby - Harvey Nicholson; resident minister - Mr. McLaughlin; teacher - Miss Edna Wade, who was from Eastern Canada and whose salary in 1916 was $70 a month. The first school was held in the old butcher shop.

Ettington was incorporated as a village in 1914 and at its peak it had the following: 2 general stores, butcher shop, bank, poolroom, cafe, 2 implement dealers, blacksmith shop, livery stable, lumber yard, 13 houses, station agent and two elevators. All in all it had a population of 200.

By 1969 it was down to one Pool elevator and a population of two, Mr. and Mrs. Len Coomber. We are indebted to Mrs. Coomber for the above information.

The second story of how Ettington got its name goes like this: Mr. R. Henderson, a homesteader in the district in 1909, who also ran the first post office, which was located in his home, was given the chance to name the townsite when the Canadian Northern built the grade in 1911 and he chose Ettington to commemorate Ettington, England. Ettington, England, is a Warwickshire village along the famous Roman Fosseway.

EUSTON

Euston is a junction of the CPR at the south end of Last Mountain lake. One line goes up the west side of the lake and the other goes up the east side. There are no habitable buildings at Euston, just a small signal house. It was named for Euston station in London, England.

EVANSVILLE

Evansville was named for the oldest oldtimer, John Evans, who settled there in 1895. He conducted Sunday School in the school and led the singing, his wife taught, and she was for many years secretary of the school district. Later John Evans became MP for the district.

EVESHAM

Evesham, Senlac, and Rutland, are adjoining towns on the CPR west of Unity towards the Alberta border. The names suggest that it was a predominately British settlement. Evesham commemorates one of the most famous battles in early English history. It was in the Valley of Evesham in 1265 that Henry III, who was not known for keeping his promises, defeated the forces of Simon de Montford and set back the establishment of a true parliament for several years.

EXPANSE
Expanse is a settlement northeast of Assiniboia at 12-12-29-W2. It's on a CPR line very close to the south shore of Old Wives' lake. The name is just another way of expressing what the first settlers felt when they could see for miles and miles in every direction. A Texan expressed it this way, "Our country is so flat you can see ahead for two days." Being modest, early Saskatchewan settlers came up with names like Expanse, Broadview, Abound and Longacre.

EYEBROW
Eyebrow is named for Eyebrow lake nine miles from the village. It is southeast of the Elbow and the center of one of Saskatchewan's better hunting and fishing districts. Bucks are plentiful on Eyebrow lake, while deer are bagged regularly in the Qu'Appelle Valley, 15 miles away. At Long Lake, 60 miles to the northeast, there is excellent fishing.

EYRE
Eyre is at the junction of two CNR lines, in southwestern Saskatchewan. It was possibly named for Eyre, in Haliburton district, Ontario, formed in 1872. This in turn was named for Brigadier-General Sir William Eyre, 1805-1859. He distinguished himself in the Crimean War, 1854-1856. In June, 1856, he became commander-in-chief of the military forces in Canada.

F

FAIRHOLME
Mr. Alfred Brand on whose quarter the townsite was located was a bachelor and a wonderful cook. He boarded the engineers who constructed the railway and when it came time for a name he suggested Fairholme after his hometown in Ontario. It was accepted.

In the 30s and 40s Fairholme had three general stores, a butcher shop, a drug store, a radio shop, a bakery, a pool hall, a hotel, two schools and all the rest that goes with a bustling little town. However, due to centralization brought about by better roads and faster cars it has dwindled to a population of sixty.

FAIRLIGHT
Fairlight is in the southeastern part of the province between Maryfield and Doonside on a CNR line to Regina. In the early 1860s Mr. Hyde came from Fairlight in the Old Country to homestead. A few years later he got the post office which was named Fairlight. It was six miles from the present townsite. Years later the railway built into this point and took the name Fairlight Station but the homestead post office retained its identity. In fact,

the school in this old district bears the name Fairlight although the school district in the town is called Novra.

FAIRMOUNT
Fairmount is eight miles west of Kindersley on the Goose Lake Line that was built in the early 1900s.

The track ran along the edge of a deep coulee that had considerable water in it all year round and particularly in the spring. Ranchers to the south often had to swim their stock across to the railway.

In the town there were stock loading facilities, a station, 4 elevators, a general store, a post office, a blacksmith shop run by Mr. Peterson and Mr. McKenzie, a lumber yard run by Mr. Holmes, and many residences.

The first store and post office was run by the McCormick brothers, Mack and Collie, who had come from Ontario along with most of the other early settlers.

Mr. Rasmuson homesteaded near Fairmount in 1908 and his family grew up in a sod house on the edge of the coulee. They swam and boated on the water and searched for teepee rings on the hills. Then in the 1930s the coulee went dry for good and on windy days the alkali blew off it in a huge white cloud you could see for miles.

With the coming of better roads the businesses went to Kindersley and Fairmount all but disappeared when the store burned down in the 1940s.

This information came from Mrs. Dorothy E. Sutton (nee Rasmuson) of Aldergrove, British Columbia.

FARWELL

In the southwestern part of the province many small creeks run down to join the Missouri system. Farwell, on one of these creeks commemorates the name of Abe Farwell, an early trader with a checkered career. It was near Abe's trading post in 1873 that a group of American trappers searching for their stolen horses came in contact with a band of Assinboine Indians. Fighting broke out in what later became known as the Cypress Hills massacre. This hastened the formation of the North-West Mounted Police.

FAIRY GLEN

Fairy Glen is the second last stop on a CPR line running from Melfort to Gronlid.

Before the railway arrived Charles Chapman carried the mail to his home for distribution. Later the post office was situated at the home of Mr. N. Backstrom, then Mr. K. Holmes took it over. With the arrival of the railway in 1928 the mail service moved into the hamlet of Fairy Glen named by Mr. Markley, a long time resident of the district, for his hometown in England.

FAIRY HILL

The Pheasant Hills branch line of the CPR enters Saskatchewan at Welwyn and runs northwesterly to Southey, the closest town to Fairy Hill, a rural neighborhood beautifully situated in the Qu'Appelle Valley. The post office was named by Mr. H. C. Lawson who came from Fairy Hill, Isle of Wight.

The first settlers came as ranchers in 1882. The CPR rails reached Southey in 1905 and many homesteaders from Central Europe came to the district to join the Lawsons, the Stewarts, the McDougalls and the Thollards. The school, Cornwall S.D. No. 698, opened in 1903 with six pupils, the minimum allowed. After the influx of the Europeans the attendance soared to 40.

FALCON

Falcon is a siding between Summerberry and Wolseley. Many places in Saskatchewan are named for birds: Killdeer, Makwa (loon), Buzzard, Albatross, Chitek (pelican), and Sheho (prairie chicken). Falcon is named for a hawklike bird. They differ from true hawks in having long pointed tails, and a different kind of flight. Their wing strokes are rapid and they do not soar. The commonest falcon in Saskatchewan is the sparrow hawk, the smallest American falcon and one of the most handsome birds of prey. Another common one is the duck hawk.

FARLEY

Farley is just out of Saskatoon on the mainline of the CNR. The name has no significance since it was proposed by the railroad to get things in alphabetical order Farley, Grandora, Hawoods, Iwona, (now changed to North Asquith), Kinley, Leney, Mead, Neola and then Biggar which broke the chain.

Farley had only a small station where cream cans were picked up. It was a whistlestop.

The following farmers lived there in the early days: John Soden, the Hope Brothers, Mr. Cherry and George Finan.

FARMINGDALE

Farmingdale is a post office northeast of Little Quill lake, 12-39-11-W2. The first postmaster was Mr. E. Fletcher. The name is descriptive, farming in a small valley. It compares with such names as Clearsite, Clearfield and Broadacres.

FARRERDALE

Bruce Farrer of Qu'Appelle, Saskatchewan, writes as follows: "My grandfather, Harry Farrer, came west in 1909 and worked on a farm near Strasbourg for four years. On April 1, 1913, he moved to a homestead twenty-some miles west of Simpson. My father remembers driving directly across Last Mountain lake, despite the water that had already formed on top of the ice. it was April Fool Day and as they passed a homestead, children yelled out to them that the cow, which they had tied on behind the sleigh, was loose. When they arrived at their 'quarter' they found a few families in the area, but it had not been settled very long.

In 1915 the residents decided to build a school. Two names were sent in to the Department of Education and were turned down. A third choice, Farrerdale, was accepted. At the time my grandfather's family consisted of eight children and so about half of the school enrolment was made up of Farrers. Later, three more children were born and then my grandfather's brother and his four children moved into the district, so the name Farrerdale, seemed appropriate.

Today, not a single relative lives in the area. The school was built on land owned by Douglas Brown. The "dale" part of the name was definitely appropriate as the whole area is called "The Hills." There is hardly a level piece of land anywhere.

The post office was established in the late 30s and was named for the school. The local school closed in 1965.

Although the highway now runs right through the district, until it was built the area was rather isolated, the school being about twenty miles from Simpson, the nearest town. Now, store, filling station, and post office sit beside the highway and serve the little community."

FAUNA

Fauna is on a CPR line a few miles northeast of Swift Current. The abundance of wildlife (fauna) on the prairies, from gophers to prairie chickens, impressed the early settlers. Indeed, many of them depended on rabbits for part of their winter meat.

The reasoning behind the naming of Fauna is similar to that behind the naming of another Saskatchewan place name, Bounty. The residents of that area requested Botany as their name because of the surrounding flora of the plains. However, a mix-up in spelling by government officials resulted in the designation of the town as Bounty, and the officials then refused to change the name.

FELLS

Fells was a post office and store situated twenty miles south and two miles west of Unity. It was started in the early 30s by Harold Fell in one room of his house using a twelve by twelve plank for a counter. He was a wheeler-dealer and he took anything in on trade: eggs, butter, hides etc. Actually most of his business was with relief orders.

In 1945 Charles Harrigan and David Sutherland bought the store and started the post office in 1947. For $200 a year Charles had to haul the mail from Unity twice a week.

The store and post office burned down in 1953 and was never rebuilt.

FENTON

Bert Leask of 470-22nd Street East in Prince Albert worked with the Canadian Northern Railway as it came up from Dauphin, Manitoba, to Hudson Bay Junction and west through Melfort. He helped to build the bridge (1905) where it crossed the South Saskatchewan river at Fenton. Prior to this many settlers had moved into this district following the Rebellion of 1885. Some of those settlers who took part in the Rebellion were: Bert Brewster (captain of Company 4); Harold and William Loucks, J. Small and W. G. Cromartie (scouts); George Taite, Bob and Jim Mack and Charlie Adams (guides). In 1896 a ferry (Fenton) was installed. It was operated by Charlie Adams, who also opened the first post office. The first elevator was built and operated by Mr. Leadbetter. The first store was owned by A. W. Brewster and when he left in 1902, Bob Sutherland took over. The first church to be built in the community was St. Andrews, founded in 1868 with Reverend James Nisbet coming out from Prince Albert to take the services.

By 1905 the bridge across the South Saskatchewan river at Fenton was completed. On New Year's Day, 1906, the steel was being laid at Senator siding; soon after, it passed through Davis and reached Prince Albert.

As late as 1955 Fenton consisted of a garage, a school, a community hall, two general stores, a post office, a station house, a water tower, a curling rink and two elevators. By 1968 it was down to one store, one elevator and a post office. The store was being operated by Mrs. Alexandrine Lavigne whose father, Ashill Godim, was a carpenter on the "Northcote". He was present at the bluff northeast of Duck Lake when Almighty Voice and his two companions were taken. Mrs. Robert Lavigne had the post office in her home, serving 25 families. The Pool elevator was managed by Glen McCullman who bought grain three days a week at Fenton and two days a week at Tiger Hills, two stations to the south.

Fenton is named for one of the presidents of the Chicago and Great Western Railways. Mrs. Ernest Wait (nee Orton) taught for years at Fenton's Heatherdale School and in 1955 her students compiled an illustrated booklet of the history of the district from which much of this information has been taken.

FENWOOD

Fenwood is the second stop northwest on the CNR line out of Melville on its way to Saskatoon. The GTP officials gave the town its name and there was no significance to it other than that it fitted into an alphabetical pattern: Fenwood, Goodeve, Hubbard, Ituna, Jasmin, Kelliher and Leross. Some of Fenwood's firsts are as follows: settler — Houser; lumberyard — Pete Sandbeck; store — Outamby and Sandbeck; postmaster — S. Good; church — Lutheran; hotel — John Boyle; bank — Bank of Montreal; station agent — Oscar Deshay.

FERLAND

Settlement in the district, which is predominately French, started in 1910. In July of that year Edmond Chabot petitioned the postmaster general to open a post office in the community under the name of St. Claire des Prairies.

This name was modified to "The Prairies" because there was a post office with a similar name in the Cadillac district. The name did not please the settlers and they asked the authorities for the name of St. Edmond. This could not be accepted since there existed in the province a post office under that name. The next name suggested was Ferland and this was done to honor Jean Baptiste Antoine Ferland (1805-1865), a Roman Catholic priest of eastern Canada, who had distinguished himself in the field of Canadian historical writing.

FERTILE

Fertile is in the extreme southeastern part of the province between Storthoaks and the Manitoba border. The district was first called Council but after the railway came in a mix-up in mail developed with Consul. The railway officials suggested the name Fertile because of the heavy growth of prairie wool which was the main feed for livestock and made excellent hay. The settlers accepted. In those days many settlers were so glad to see the railway arrive that they never thought of disputing any of its decisions.

FEUDAL

Feudal is on a CPR branch line running from Perdue to Rosetown. It was first settled about 1905 and some of the early pioneers were: J. A. Miller, J. D. Miller, Bob Gibson, John and Jim Taylor, and J. F. Gamble. Mr. and Mrs. Gamble had the first post office in their home and for the men of the district going for the mail was a special treat as Mrs. Gamble's cooking was quite a change from batching.

When the survey for the railroad was made in 1927 the settlers met to decide on a name. They submitted Fertile but as there was already a place by that name in Saskatchewan the officials asked them to accept Feudal. It is not known whether or not there was any significance in the name.

At one time Feudal was quite a thriving place with three elevators, a store and post office, a hotel, a cafe, a blacksmith shop and a dance hall. Today only the store, post office, one elevator and the dance hall remain.

FIELDING

The following information was received from Mr. M. McLaughton, overseer of the town of Fielding:

"The quarter section where Fielding is now was homesteaded by Peter Shack in 1903. A settlement grew around this spot which was known as Shack Town. When the railway went through and a station was built in 1904 they named it Fielding in honor of William Stevens Fielding, the minister of finance in the Laurier Cabinet of the day. Prior to that Mr. Fielding had been in provincial politics in Nova Scotia and had been premier of that province. The present population of Fielding is 50 people."

FIFE LAKE

Fife Lake is straight south of Moose Jaw on a CPR line that sometimes runs less than six miles from the border. Fife Lake was incorporated as a village in 1928 and takes its name from a nearby lake. In 1937 this lake completely dried up. Wes Grant, who in the early days had lost his gun in the middle of the lake while hunting, remembered it and went to the spot where it had fallen out of the boat — there was the gun.

FILLMORE

There was a settlement at Fillmore before the railway arrived. They came in from the railhead at Wolseley to the north and from Weyburn to the southwest. These were the Williams, the Sleightholms, the Lanes and the Trebles. When the CPR built through from Carlyle to Regina one of the first to unload a car of settler's effects — horses, cattle and machinery — was Frank Wiggins. The station was named for the man from whom the land was secured.

Quoting directly from the minutes of the Fillmore Baseball Club of February 13, 1906:

"On February 13 a meeting was called in Morrison and McLeod's Hardware Store to re-organize the Fillmore Baseball Club. The chair was taken by the president. In the absence of the secretary, the president read the minutes of the last meeting and they were adopted. The officers for the ensuing year were then elected. Hon. Pres. — C. W. Fillmore, Pres. — T. G. McGarvey, Vice-Pres. — H. Biden, Sec. Treas. — R. G. Cook."

The minutes run on but you can see how Fillmore got its name. In those days it was a bustling little town and it had one of the best Sports Days in the surrounding country — Weyburn included! Fillmore had one of the best baseball teams for miles around. It was made up of four sets of brothers: Cliff and Buzz Boll, George and Walt Pringle, Ray and George Piper, and Gordon and Goldie Wiggins. The ninth man varied.

Later on, Buzz Boll played junior hockey with Regina Pats and then came back to Weyburn for senior hockey. In the 30s he made it to the NHL and played for the Toronto Maple Leafs.

Bruce Wiggins, a younger brother of Gordon and Goldie, was a good player a decade later. After a successful teaching career he joined the STF in 1958 as an executive assistant and on September 1, 1967, he became assistant secretary.

Sargent McGowan of the Fillmore district, who now lives at Northside, tells an interesting tale of the first car in Fillmore, an Overland. It was owned by Frank Boll who operated a garage in town. Mr. McGowan recalls that one day, as his mother, his brother and he were returning from town in the buckboard the Overland came up behind them. His mother was driving and she pulled out onto the prairie to let the car pass. The spirited ponies she was handling became alarmed and "lit out" keeping parallel with the road. Mother tried to hold them in but with the boys in the back yelling. "Let 'em go, Ma!" and the racket of the car over a rutted road, she had little choice. She had little trouble, too, in outdistancing the Overland, so she swung back up on the road and disappeared in a cloud of dust. The arm-weary mother and the happy boys made it home safely and if Sargent McGowan were telling the story in today's language, of course, he'd say: "We out-dragged 'em!"

FINDLATER

There are a number of disputed or alernative versions of the origins of place names. Findlater has its share of these. Findlater is said by some to have been named when either railway surveyors or construction men lost some equipment, eventually gave up the search, still hoping to find it later. There is another story that a homesteader lost some cattle, approached the construction party in search of them and was assured that he would find them later. There is still another story which may be the correct one. It is that the town was named for the Scotch piper, George Findlater, who was awarded the Victoria Cross for his heroism during the attack on Dargai Heights (India) in 1898.

FINNIE

Henry Q. Stilborn arrived in 1872 by wagon train from Brandon, Manitoba, which was the end of the steel at that time. He was the forerunner of a Methodist Colony that settled in the area.

The GTP railway ran a branch line west from Melville to Balcarres in 1909 and named the townsite Finnie, after Jim Finnie, the foreman of the construction crew.

Finnie grew to have a store, a post office, a school, and one grain elevator. Then gradually it shrank until by 1966 it had been reduced to the one elevator — even the station had been moved away! By 1970 the elevator was gone, too.

FIR MOUNTAIN

Fir Mountain is a hamlet southwest of Assiniboia at 13-5-5-W3. It's on a branch line of the CPR that runs north and then west of Rockglen and ends at Mankota. The name is misleading — there's no mountain and no fir. It's just a high bare hill. There are no natural mountains in Saskatchewan.

Fir Mountain is just a fancy name meant to attract settlers. It's on a par with the following Saskatchewan place names: Goldburg, Fortune, and the most misleading of all, Crescent City.

FIR RIDGE

Fir Ridge is an inland post office about twenty miles west of Prince Albert on the north side of the South Saskatchewan river. It was first called Birson for George Robins (they got the name Birson by scrambling the name Robins). He came to the area in 1890 from Fenton, bringing a herd of 150 cattle with him into this unsettled area so that he could pasture them.

After the post office was named Birson, the school and local ferry took the same name. In 1968 the ferry was renamed Birch Hills. The school is abandoned and has been used as a community hall.

The more recent change in name came because mail was getting mixed up with Bryson, Saskatchewan. Mr. Lester Miller, the postmaster, called it Fir Ridge.

This is a fitting name because it is situated on a ridge on the edge of a forest reserve which runs west between the branches of the North and South Saskatchewan rivers and there are an abundance of clumps of fir trees.

FISH CREEK

Fish Creek is an inland post office about 40 miles downstream from Saska-toon. A steep ravine cuts back from the river for many miles. It is called Fish Creek because of the water that rushes down it in the spring run-off and the spawning fish that ascend it from the Saskatchewan river.

On April 23, 1885, General Middleton started the march to Batoche from Clark's Crossing and that evening a party of Metis and Indians led by Dumont set an ambush at the ravine. Behind bluffs and boulders or lying in rutted game trails hidden in the brush, Dumont's force of probably 160 men waited for Middleton's men on the morning of April 24. The ambush was upset by lack of discipline among Dumont's troops. Some of the high-spirited youths of the Metis cavalry ignored Dumont's orders to remain under cover. They rode out of the ravine and had fun chasing stray cattle along the trail leading from Fish Creek to Clark's Crossing. They even built a fire to roast the flesh of an animal they slaughtered. Middleton's scouts were alerted.

In the day-long battle that followed in the drizzling rain Middleton lost 10 men and had 40 wounded. Dumont lost 11 and 18 wounded. The battle was a draw. Middleton didn't move on to Batoche for two weeks and Dumont returned to Batoche to wait for him.

Today, the battlefield of Fish Creek looks much as it did in 1885. It is a lonely place, standing high on the banks of the Saskatchewan river. The creek still winds sluggishly through the narrow ravine, and the old buffalo trails in which the Metis sharpshooters crouched and shot at the troops on the skyline are still clearly visible.

In a clearing in the poplars a short distance from the creek stands a head-stone marking the graves of three gunners who were killed in action. Overshadowing the simple headstone is a cairn commemorating the Battle of Fish Creek.

FISHING LAKE

An Icelandic colony came to the area in 1890 and 1891, settling around the south shore of Fishing lake where they raised cattle and horses. When the CPR linked Tuffnell and Wadena the village site on the south shore of the lake took the name Fishing Lake.

FISKE

Fiske is between D'Arcy and McGee. Some of the first settlers into the district were: McNeill, Cross, Arnold, Ronald, Dechin, Richmond, and Pierce. The CNR came through in 1909 and gave them their name, Fiske. It honored one of the financial backers of the line. Mr. Fiske's family later became connected with a well-known rubber company in the United States.

FITZMAURICE

The Fitzmaurice post office was originally named Gladwin and was operated by James Guy in his home up to 1934. It was then closed and opened up again in the hamlet of Fitzmaurice where there was a Searle grain elevator, a general store and a few houses. Mrs. Katherine Lasch was the postmistress. The store closed in 1964 and the elevator was torn down in 1967. The mail is brought in by truck from Yorkton. The name, Fitzmaurice, was given the hamlet in memory of a pilot in the RAF in World War I.

FLAT LAKE

The inland post office of Flat Lake was four miles north of Freemont. The first mail carrier was Mr. Gates who made the trip from Maidstone once a week.

The first settlers into the district in 1907 were Mr. and Mrs. Elmer Bassett and their two sons, Ben and Dick. Other homesteaders soon arrived: Cranes, Leggs, Gates, Milnes, the Brown brothers, and Cecil Smith.

An incident that people remember which caused great concern happened one evening late in November of 1914. Little Emily Crane wandered away from her home and was not missed until dusk set in. That night was spent looking down wells, in bluffs, and every conceivable place they could think of where she might be found. There were no telephones so messengers had to ride out to other homes to spread the alarm and organize search parties. Those that didn't go out in wagons or on horseback, walked. The search continued all day, the men not stopping to eat or rest. Late in the evening Guy Cayford and Billy Graham were walking together when Guy noticed something moving in the tall grass. Upon closer inspection they found it to be the little girl, cold and frightened. It certainly came as a relief to everyone to have little Emily returned home, for 24 hours during a cold November is a long, long time for a small 3-year old girl to be lost on the prairie with only a dress and a small jacket for protection.

People also recall happy times in the district as spent at picnics around Flat lake in summer and skating on the lake in winter. Walter Rogers remembers some ingenious person sinking a "sleeve" in a hole in the ice, a pole was stood up inside this sleeve and a crossbar was fastened about 4 feet up the pole. Then ropes were attached to the crossbar and skaters whirled the crossbar around and around playing a form of crack the whip. If you fell you sure had to have your eye on the crossbar when you got up or you got a crack on the head!

FLATS

Homesteading was hard and sometimes dreary work but the people never lost their sense of humor as the naming of the Flats post office shows. Oldtimers claim that one of the first women to come there wore a pair of silk stockings. They called the district Silk Stocking Flats. The post office wouldn't go for the full name and they settled for Flats.

FLAT VALLEY

At a settlers' meeting in July of 1929 held at a homesteader's house it was proposed to name the settlement Flat Valley. This was accepted by the twelve persons present and later ratified by the Postal Department.

The settlement was so named because it is a nice valley surrounded by gently sloping hills. It starts just north of the Beaver river and extends six miles north on highway 26 and roughly eight miles east and ten miles west.

It is a mixed farming community with ranches established along the Beaver river flats. The first settlers were the Livingstone brothers who came in 1919. Mr. Schroeder came in 1926 and opened a store and post office which was still in business in 1970.

With the building of a bridge over the Beaver river in 1929, new land was opened and an influx of settlers came in 1930 and 1931. In the fall of 1939 a number of Sudetan Germans arrived from Czechoslovakia.

In the summer of 1942, people north of the Beaver river were isolated for three months when ice took out the bridge and many of the hay flats were flooded. Everything had to be hauled across with boats which was quite a chore.

FLAXCOMBE

The village of Flaxcombe started in 1909 when Mr. Buswell opened a store one-half mile east of where the village is today. In 1910 the CNR came through and the village was named Harwell, using part of the names of Mr. Harvey and Mr. Buswell, two of the earliest settlers in the district. Mr. Harvey was later MLA for Kindersley constituency.

Confusion in the delivery of mail followed when Harwell was found to have a name similar to another place in Saskatchewan. The village council called a meeting to change the name. Flaxcombe was suggested by George Languish, a homesteader and also CNR pumpman. He made this suggestion because at that time thousands of acres of flax were being grown on new breaking in the district. The combe, meaning valley, was added because the village was in a valley. Flaxcombe is 19 miles west of Kindersley.

FLEMING

Fleming is named after Sir Sanford Fleming. This man had a remarkable career that started when he studied engineering and surveying in Scotland. He came to Canada in 1845. His rise was rapid. In 1871 he was appointed engineer-in-chief of the CPR. He surveyed the Yellowhead Pass route now followed by the CNR, and was the first to demonstrate the practicability of the route through the Rogers Pass. He designed the first Canadian stamp, the three-penny beaver, issued April 23, 1851. The main street of Fleming is also named in his honor and is called "Sanford."

FLETT'S SPRINGS

The Fletts, Selkirk settlers, came west in 1875 with their five children, John Junior, William the eldest, Jim, Anne and Christine, and settled for a short time at Prince Albert. They moved to Wil-

loughby (now MacDowell) in 1876. For eleven years they homesteaded in this area, and during the Rebellion all were called into the comparative shelter of the fort at Prince Albert. Rifles were scarce and some of the volunteers were armed with barrel staves.

In 1887, the Fletts homesteaded NW¼-10-44-20 west of Melfort by the large springs which today still bear their name. The post office was at John's home. His wife, who operated it, was the daughter of John Bannerman.

Rancher, farmer, thresherman and lumberman in the Carrot River Valley — that was John Flett, Junior, one of the best known and respected of the oldtime pioneers. His friends were legion throughout northeastern Saskatchewan. At one time he was the first and only thresherman east of Prince Albert.

The two big events of the year for children in those days were the community picnic in the summer and the coming of the threshers in the fall. How they loved threshing time! Even the small children were kept busy — there were open gates to be watched to keep the cows out of the fields; tables to be set where every dish in the house was used; and many errands to be run.

The sound of the whistle at suppertime warning the busy cooks that the crews were finishing for the night and the rattle of the racks coming in, are sounds that will not readily be forgotten.

FLIN FLON

The town of Flin Flon is in Manitoba, as is the entrance to the mine, but most of the ore comes from the Saskatchewan side of the boundary. Flin Flon was named by the discoverers of the extensive deposits of gold, copper, zinc and silver at the site, after Professor Josiah Flintabbatey Flonatin — the hero of a novel, The Sunless City, by J. E. Preston-Muddock, which had been found on a portage near the Churchill river.

This information came from the book, *Saskatchewan*, by D. C. McLeod.

FLINTOFT

Flintoft is between Wood Mountain and Lakenheath on a CPR line in the south of the province. It was named for Mr. E. P. Flintoft who was the general solicitor for the Canadian Pacific Railway from 1929 to 1936.

Flintoft post office opened on November 15, 1927. The first postmistress was Mrs. George Stefan. She was followed by Mrs. Lena Nicholson and the following people had it in turn: Mr. Victor Staseson, Mary S. Radu and Mr. Johnnie Yorga handled the post office until it closed out on September 23, 1951.

FLORAL

Thomas Plunkett moved into the Floral district in 1901. When it came time to form a school district he suggested the name Floral because that was the name of the school he had attended at Pilot Mound, Man. It was accepted. When the railroad came through Mr. Plunkett also suggested that the siding be called Floral. The officials agreed. Floral is just a little place outside of Saskatoon and is best known as the birthplace of Gordie Howe, famous hockey player.

FLOWING WELL

Flowing Well was an inland post office near Morse. It closed in 1966. It was named by Mr. Reichenberg in 1908 after he dug a well on his homestead that overflowed — and is still doing it today. A store and post office located on the opposite corner of his land took the same name at the request of the residents.

FOAM LAKE

The town of Foam Lake has a history dating back to 1882 when Joshua Milligan first settled in the district, 16 miles west of where Foam Lake is now located. The Milligan family was the first into the district by nine years, and they earned a living by operating a trading post for the Indians and carrying on a ranch. The Milligans originated the name for Foam Lake, a large shallow body of water which always shows foam along its shores.

It was in 1909 that the village of Foam Lake was incorporated, three and one-half miles south-east of the lake from which it takes its name. The first store was built by Robert Cain. Foam Lake became a town in 1924 with Dr. R. H. Chant, a dentist, as its first Mayor.

FOND-DU-LAC

Fond-du-lac (59°19'-107°12') is a Hudson's Bay Company fortified post at the east end of Lake Athabasca, situated on a low point of sand and rock on the north shore where the lake is only two miles wide. It's on the Fond-du-lac river which drains Black lake into Lake Athabasca. It consists of a number of well-built log houses surrounded by palisades of stout poles. This post is on a principal line of travel of the Barren Ground caribou. It was first built by Jose Mercredi, a French half-breed, in 1851, who in 1892 was 75 years old and had been in charge of the post for 41 years. In the early part of the century, about 1820, the Hudson's Bay Company had a post on a point on the south shore. The three employees were killed by Chippewyan Indians and the post was looted.

At the same time the North-West Company had a post on a point on the north shore a short distance farther east. After the murder of the HBC traders they moved to the south shore. The post was abandoned by both companies until it was rebuilt on the original site by the HBC, in 1851. Since then, the post has been in constant operation.

According to Ottawa records the name Fond-du-Lac is a descriptive term for "the river entering Lake Athabasca at the bottom of the lake."

FONEHILL

This is the first stop west of Yorkton on a CNR branch line running west and north to end at Parkerview. The name was suggested from a local name of a siding — Phone Hill — but the spelling was changed by the railway.

FOREST FARM

Forest Farm is an inland post office near Whitewood. It was established in 1882. The first settlers into the district were Thomas Reid and Robert Munn. It was customary in those days to name your farm. Mr. Munn named his Forrest Farm for his mother's maiden name which was Forrest. However, when a post office was granted the word came out Forest and later the same thing happened to the school district. It seemed that government officials did not think the settlers could spell.

FOREST GATE

In 1918 Mr. and Mrs. Street and their family came from England to pioneer in the district eight miles east of Christopher lake. They started a store and post office in their log cabin and named it Forest Gate after their hometown in England.

As the settlement grew, an Anglican church was built 2 miles south of the store and was called St. Columba. Across the road from the church a school was erected in 1918 and the people decided on a unique method of choosing a name for it. The names of all the girls enrolled at the school were placed in a hat and Dorothy England's name was drawn so it was called Dorothy School. The church is closed but its doors are still open to all. The school has been moved away and the children of the district are bussed to Paddockwood. The post office still serves 30 families and Mrs. George Scaife, the present storekeeper and postmistress, says that they still get the odd letter addressed to Forest Gate, England.

FOREST HALL

Forest Hall was an inland post office which opened in 1905 in the home of William Lamb. It was 2 miles north and 11 miles east of North Battleford. The name Forest Hall, which came from a village in England, was first given to the district school and then to the post office.

Mrs. Doris Nesom was the last postmistress and she ran it from 1925 until it closed out in 1929 to become a rural route out of North Battleford.

First families in the district included the following: Bob Waterhouse, John Deegan, George and Jim Paul, William Strain, Charlie and Frank Gale, Sam Eccles, John and William Garland, Walter and James Sidebottom, John Acaster, Frank and George Dobbs, Mr. Boyes and the Nesom brothers, Fred and Ben.

Settlers in those days made their own fun. Fred Nesom likes to recall how a real surprise party was put over on him. John Garland called on him one winter evening and said, "Let's get up a surprise party for Frank Dobbs." Fred was game and so was his wife and they piled into the sleigh box. Next they called on Mr. and Mrs. James Sidebottom and so on halfway around the district. When the sleigh was

full Garland drove into Fred's yard. "Why are we stopping here?" asked Fred. Garland replied, "This is where we're having the surprise party — pile out." And they did!

FORGAN

"The Canadian National came to Forgan in 1913. Shortly before this the municipality of 'Monet' had been formed. Bill Forgie was the fist reeve and the first councillor for our division was J. Keegan. The first part of Forgie was combined with the last part of Keegan to make Forgan. And so the little hamlet was named. Settlers started arriving in the district in 1905 and began proving up their homesteads. To get "title" a homesteader had to build a shack on the quarter section he had chosen. One group of relatives: E. M. Sweet, Fred Sweet, Tom Sweet and William Bell, took land on the same section. Then they went to the very middle of the section and built a four room house with one room on each quarter section."

FORGET

Forget, on a CPR line in the southwest of the province between Stoughton and Kisbey, was named to honor A. E. Forget who was the last lieutenant-governor of the North-West Territories and the first lieutenant-governor of the province of Saskatchewan when it was formed in 1905.

FORMBY

Formby was a rural post office northwest of Tatsfield and near the present site of Carruthers. Isaac Thomson was the first postmaster; he named it for his hometown, Formby, England. The post office opened in the early 1900s. The mail was brought in from Paynton by Mr. Ray who also delivered to Wardenville, Carruthers and Ballinora. The post office closed when the GTR reached Carruthers in 1913.

FORREST BANK

The Canadian Northern Railway ran a line from Battleford to Lloydminster in 1906. Sixteen miles north of the village of Waseca a community developed called Forrest Bank. It was named after the first two permanent settlers, Richard Forrest, who had arrived from Lancashire, England in 1903, and Barr Colonist William Banks, also from Lancashire.

In 1906 William Pike, an early resident, was granted the right to open the Forrest Bank post office in his house. He hauled the mail from Lashburn. He was its first and only postmaster until it closed out in 1920. Residents of Forrest Bank now get their mail from Waseca, Maidstone or Lashburn.

Forrest Bank was a very progressive community. The following are some of their "firsts": school — 1907, church — 1909, soccer club — 1908, and telephone company — 1916.

One of the most notable people of Forrest Bank was John H. Wesson, Commander of the British Empire. Mr. Wesson was president of the Saskatchewan Wheat Pool from 1937 to 1960 at which time he retired. He is buried in the Forrest Bank church yard.

Like most rural districts, the closing of Forrest Bank rural school No. 1659 in 1962 started to bring about the end of an era. The students were bussed to Maidstone. This, coupled with enlarged farms, inflated land and machinery prices, which prevented many young men from becoming future farmers and future community neighbors, caused a once fine district to find it increasingly difficult to keep its integrity, its former culture, and, indeed, its very population.

This information came from Christine Pike, Waseca, Saskatchewan. She is the granddaughter of William Pike and the niece of J. H. Wesson.

FORSLUND

Forslund is between Young and Colonsay on a CPR line that runs to Saskatoon. It was named for Mr. J. E. Forslund, former immigration agent for the CPR.

FORT A LA CORNE

Fort à la Corne is the location of a French fur trading post built by Chevalier de la Corne in 1753 on the south bank of the South Saskatchewan river about twenty miles east of the forks and twenty miles northeast of the town of Kinistino. The fort was moved a couple of times but not more than a few miles.

It changed hands, too, and eventually became a Hudson's Bay trading post which operated until 1932. Now it is an inland post office. A marker has been placed in Kinistino to commemorate this post. The French post established by La Corne is celebrated as being the site of the first attempt at agriculture within the boundaries of this province. Visitors at the fort recorded their pleasure at being served food grown on the spot.

FORT BLACK

Fort Black is directly east across the lake from the settlement of Ile-à-la-Crosse. Before highway 152 was put through, all supplies went from Beauval north along the Beaver river to Fort Black and then by barge over to Ile-à-la-Crosse.

Plans of Ile-à-la-Crosse (settlement), Department of Interior 1920, compiled from official surveys by G. A. Bayne, D.L.S., 17 July 1899 and G. H. Blanchet, D.L.S., July 1919, show Fort Black to be a "N.W. Co. post." Fort Black was adopted as an established name in June of 1951. No information could be found as to its origin.

FORT PITT

Fort Pitt was named in honor of William Pitt (1759-1806) a statesman who became one of England's greatest prime ministers.

Founded in 1829, Fort Pitt was one of the great houses of the Hudson's Bay Company for over half a century. It was the only major post on the North Saskatchewan between Carlton House and Edmonton.

In 1885, following the massacre at Frog Lake, it was besieged by Indians of Big Bear's Band. The NWMP abandoned it and it was sacked by the Indians. Partially rebuilt the following year, the fort was finally closed out in 1890.

Robert H. Hougham bought the land from the Hudson's Bay Company and started a ranch. One day as he was preparing some hay land his plow ripped open the unmarked graveyard of the old fort. He drew in four large stones to mark the area and then erected a field-stone cairn and on the plaque he wrote:

"As the shadows lengthen into a purple wave I gently close this lonely grave at Old Fort Pitt and here resolve that these first-comers shall have title to this scarce half-acre of sod, for I deed it back to God."

Mr. Hougham had a dream of rebuilding the fort but in spite of his considerable efforts very little was accomplished. When he passed on in 1960 he had his body cremated and his ashes lie beneath that lonely cairn.

Today, on the site of the fort is a ranch operated by a syndicate in California headed by Mr. Hougham's son. A rural post office 12 miles north of the original site and a rural school nearby commemorates the famous name.

The closest railway is Frenchman Butte 11 miles to the east.

FORT QU'APPELLE

Fort Qu'Appelle is on the Qu'Appelle river 20 miles north of the town of Qu'Appelle. The valley, the fort, and the town, all take their name from the river. The first historical note is that of Daniel Harmon, an employee of the North-West Company who makes reference to the "Calling" river in his journal of 1804. He wrote that the river was so named by the superstitious natives who imagine that a spirit is constantly going up and down it — they say they often hear a voice which resembles the cry of a human being.

Peter Hourie was the man who actually named Fort Qu'Appelle. Born in 1827, he grew up in the Red River Settlement and joined the Hudson's Bay Company as a young man. In 1864 he chose the site of the present Fort Qu'Appelle and erected the first establishment there. Camped in the "Valley" one day Peter Hourie and his companions watched with astonishment as a herd of shaggy black bison waded into a ford and crossed the slow winding stream, and climbed the opposite hillside. The watchers' vigil lasted a full 24 hours. The number of animals in that herd was estimated at one million. When Hourie died in Regina in 1910 at the age of 83, the surviving bison in all of North America numbered less than one thousand.

FORT SAN

Fort San is a post office north of Fort Qu'Appelle at 19-21-13-W2. It takes its name from the local sanitorium. There used to be three sanitoria in Saskatchewan but because of the wonderful

work done by doctors and the Associated Commercial Travellers, tuberculosis is no longer the scourge it was even 30 years ago. The sanitorium at Prince Albert has been closed for TB patients and is now used for treating the "mentally retarded." At Saskatoon there are 150 beds but 64 of them treat geriatric patients, the rest treat TB. Fort San is used 100 percent for the treatment of TB patients.

The railroad came to Fort San in 1911 and it was then possible for picnickers to come out from Regina and enjoy the Qu'Appelle lakes. Before this the condition of the roads and the steep hills, added to the type of cars of those days, made it quite a venture "to go to the lake."

FORTUNE

Fortune is on a CPR line that runs from North Rosetown southeast to Milden. The name is accounted for by the fact that the majority of homesteaders were filled with a spirit of optimism as they broke the land and built their shacks. This attitude was manifested in other place-names in Saskatchewan: Abound, Choiceland, Expanse, Forward, Goodsoil, Grainland, Onward, Paradise Hill, Pleasantdale, Plenty, Success, Superb and Supreme.

FORT WALSH

Fort Walsh was a post established in 1875 by the NWMP in the Cypress Hills. It was named for Major James Morrow Walsh, superintendent of the North-West Mounted Police. It was abandoned in 1882 when the barracks of "A" Division were moved to the railroad at Maple Creek. The buildings of the historic fort were reconstructed in the 1950s.

FORWARD

The following description of Forward is taken from an article by Larry Guina which appeared in an October 1969 issue of the Regina *Leader-Post*.

There are a few scattered poplar trees and lilac bushes and a road overgrown with weeds, the remains of pioneers' dreams of a town that would never die.

Today there is no one at Forward. The last residence was moved from the community in August, 1966. The town of

Foward sprang up at the end of the steel on the Canadian Pacific Railway, 28 miles west of Weyburn, in 1911. It grew in population to approximately 1,200 people. As the railway progressed westward, the Canadian Northern Railway was also laying rails on the Moose Jaw-Radville line. The CNR crossed the CP tracks three miles southwest of the original Forward townsite. The crossing raised visions of a better townsite in the minds of some of the businessmen and moving the town was suggested. Arthur Davidson is a name often mentioned as one of the agitators of this move. In 1912 and 1913, the town of Forward moved almost en masse from the original site, which was renamed Axford, to the junction of the two railways.

The great visions the men had of a thriving town came true for a few years. Businesses that seemed to be built overnight included: a coal and feed store, a hardware store, a department store, a printing and publishing shop, a drugstore, an implement agency, a real estate office, a blacksmith shop, a bakeshop, a lumberyard, a hotel, a livery barn, a telephone office, a church and an Orange Hall. They had a fire hall where the bell was run by a pulling a rope. There was even a small jail building which has an interesting story. It is said that a bachelor, Ole Rude, became so irate at the idea of his pal, a certain man usually referred to as "Whiskey Smith," being locked up overnight that he hitched a team of horses to the building and hauled it out of town during the night, and in the comparative safety there set about freeing his friend.

With the CPR station being three miles by road from Forward, there was a large dray and livery business between the two places. Travellers changing trains would require transportation in the winter by sleigh. Salesmen in those days had as many as five or six trunks with them making it impossible to carry all of them.

For a few years business was good with settlers coming in from the north and south to shop and trade, but other towns were born along the line and business tapered off. The CPR refused to move its station from Axford. There were also three grain elevators at Axford, while there were none at Forward.

Fires took their toll and once businesses burned down they were never rebuilt. The school closed in 1949. The last store and post office closed in 1950 and so a little town has gradually died.

The longest continuous resident of Forward was Tom Lyons, who came when the town was new and ran the diamond. This operated the switches, which let the CN trains cross the CP tracks. He, Mrs. Lyons and their son, Tom, lived in a converted boxcar placed by the track and close to the diamond. Young Tom became a station agent and ran the CN station until 1933. While he was agent he also operated the diamond and his parents moved to a small farm at the edge of town. The diamond was torn down in the summer of 1969 and replaced with an electrical device.

There are still depressions, the remains of cellars or basements, beside the faint traces of what were once the streets — the streets that were never quite as busy as the forefathers of the town had hoped they would be. The last gasp of life was taken from Forward when the last house was moved to Radville. There are a few run-down buildings left, an old garage, an old storage shed and nearby there are some old railway buildings, but there is no life.

The town at the junction of the tracks is history and will soon be forgotten.

FOSSTON
Fosston is on a CPR line that runs south from Nipawin to Wadena. When the steel came in they took the name of a nearby post office which, in turn, had been named by settlers for their hometown of Fosston, Minnesota.

FOSTERTON
Fosterton is on a short branch line of the CPR from Pennant to Verlo. The elevator, the post office and the school are all named Fosterton for Mr. William Foster, a homesteader in the district.

The nearby junction of highways No. 22 and No. 10 is also called Fosterton.

FOUR CORNERS
Four Corners is at the intersection of two main market roads less than ten miles northwest of Meadow Lake.

FOXDALE

Mr. H. D. Laidlaw came to the district in 1911. He was closely followed by Mr. Orman, George Watson, and Albert Pugh and his son, Norman. In 1914 more land was thrown open and the following families arrived: Strube, Coles, Stead, Gunn and Henderson. In the early years their nearest post office was Wild Rose (now closed). Many of the settlers lived miles apart and a welcome visitor was the "Mountie" on patrol.

Mr. Albert Pugh was responsible for getting the post office at Foxdale and he was the man who named it.

FOXFORD

Foxford is between Weirdale and Shipman of the CPR line that runs north and east of Prince Albert to Nipawin. Homesteaders came into the district in 1914 and the name Foxford was adopted because the main road in the settlement crossed the White Fox creek at the "ford" beside Bill Gear's farm.

The post office operated by Jack Gear took the name Foxford. In 1924 the first school was built with lumber hauled in by oxen from Henriboug, the nearest rail point at that time. Suggested by Dad Thirkell, it took the name of Foxford, too. It was only natural then that when the railway came through in the early thirties, almost three miles to the north, it took the same name and the original settlement was referred to as Old Foxford.

Foxford was a busy cordwood town in the thirties, a thriving grain delivery point for a score of years. But that's all gone now, no school, no CPR depot, no elevator — just a country store and post office with about two dozen inhabitants.

FOX HILLS

Fox Hills was an inland post office near Cupar. It is closed now. The first homesteaders reached this site in 1905; most of them came from Europe. The area got its name from the hills and the great numbers of red foxes that were about. Steve Macan, a homesteader, placed out a lot of poison bait and that reduced the fox population considerably.

FOX VALLEY

A village grew up on the present site in 1908. Some of the first settlers were: Frank Yeast, Chris Mustachler, Wendeline Mater, Ben Grant, John Massong, Kelian Ibach and Kenneth Myrol. This village was in a valley, in which there were many red foxes. Mr. Strong, who ran a stopping place, dug out fox pups and kept them as pets. When the CPR came in from Alberta in 1924-25 they took the name of Fox Valley for their terminal.

FRANCIS

Francis is named for Mr. J. Francis, the man who donated the land for the town site. Mr. Francis now lives in Indian Head.

FRANKSLAKE

Frankslake is the second stop northeast of Regina. Settlers came into the district in 1892.

In 1911 the railway arrived and the settlement was named. The first request was that it be called Franksberg to honor Frank Keirl an old Scotsman, one of the oldest men in the district. Railway officials advised against it since there was already a Franksberg in the province and they feared a mix up in mail.

A compromise was reached in the name Frankslake, there being a large slough nearby. It covered a quarter section and in the early years many people came on weekends to have picnics on its shore and sail boats. The slough is still there and the land around it is owned by Mr. Harris.

FREEMONT

Freemont is seven miles east of Neilburg. In the early years it had a doctor, a municipal office, two stores, a butchershop, a cafe, two elevators (the National burned down in '58 and was not replaced). The post office was never combined with either of the stores. Freemont never had a school, the children attended Flat Lake school, five miles to the north.

By 1971 the town was literally boarded up. The post office closed in 1970 but the last postmistress, Miss Donna Goodall, lives on in the building. There was a long succession of storekeepers and the last one was Alec Foster. He closed out in the early 60s.

Freemont was named by early American homesteaders for Freemont, Nebraska. This follows a pattern like Cando, Cavalier, Spiritwood, etc. In 1956 a cyclone hit Freemont, Nebraska, causing much damage. An appeal for aid from all places in the world named Freemont revealed that there was only one Freemont in Canada. Freemont, Saskatchewan, residents, with the help of nearby Neilburg, staged a variety concert and sent a consierable sum of money to aid the stricken families.

FREMANTLE

Fremantle is between Arcola and Carlyle on a CPR line. It was named for a town in New Zealand. Eyre and Zealandia were named for places in New Zealand, too.

FRENCHMAN BUTTE

The naming of Frenchman Butte is interesting. It was so called after a Frenchman who was killed there by Indians about 1800. Who he was we cannot be certain. How or why he met his death on this hill, which in after time was near the scene of a battle between General Strange's army and Big Bear during the Saskatchewan Rebellion of 1885, we do not know. Probably he was a winterer out from Fort Vermilion living with the Indians.

FRENCHVILLE

Frenchville is a post office southwest of Swift Current at 12-7-15-W3. The name of the first postmaster was Filiatrault and he had the post office in his home. The name was changed in World War II to Frenchville to honor John Denton Pinkstone French (1852-1925), first Earl of Ypres. He commanded the first British soldiers sent to France in World War I. French returned to Britain in December 1915, to lead the home forces. He served as chief of Great Britain's general staff from 1912 to 1914. After World War I, he was lord lieutenant, and British governor of Ireland, from 1918 to 1921. French became a navy midshipman when he was 14 years old, but joined the army four years later.

FRIEND

Friend is less than ten miles east of Swift Current. It is named after C. E. Friend, assistant construction comptroller of the CNR. He lived in Montreal.

FROBISHER

The village of Frobisher is in the extreme southeastern corner of Saskatchewan. The CPR named it for Sir Martin Frobisher (1535-1594), the first English navigator to search for a Northwest Passage to India and the East. He became known as one of the greatest seamen in the reign of Queen Elizabeth I. He fought against the Spanish Armada and was knighted for his services.

In the early days Frobisher was a lively place and one of its outstanding sports accomplishments occurred in 1908 when Frobisher soccer club won the southern Saskatchewan cup and a stirling member of the team was a youthful "Jimmy Gardiner."

FRON

From 1902 to 1905 a group of almost twenty Norwegian families from Minnesota, U.S.A. came to Saskatoon by rail and then settled in a solid block on the west shore of Rice Lake.

In 1907 Nelson rural school was built in their midst and named for Andrew Nelson, one of the first homesteaders. At first they got their mail at Loganton to the west and then from Asquith when the CPR reached there in 1908. Later it came from Delisle ten miles to the south.

They were Lutherans and at first church services were held at Nelson School. In the 1920's a new Nelson school was built further west and the old school was purchased by the community and moved to the front of the cemetery which had been in existence for some time.

Families represented besides those mentioned are: Afseth, Olson, Gilbertson, Myhren, Roaldseth, Malmin, Stenson, Hamre, Brandvoldt, Erland, Mogenson and Munro.

Today the church is a shell and all boarded up. The altar, pews, organ and all the furnishings were moved years ago to Zion Lutheran church in Saskatoon.

The name Fron was suggested for the new church by John M. Afseth, a hardworking and influential member of the community. It was in memory of his hometown in Norway.

FRONTIER

In 1913 a municipal organization, meeting in the district, submitted three names to the Department of Municipal Affairs. They chose Frontier. It was an appropriate name, because at that time this district was a sort of "last frontier", with the United States border just a few miles to the south and nothing much to the west.

The CPR built a branch line east from Notukew to Val Marie in 1923. The townsite which developed between Loomis and Climax on that line took the name Frontier from the municipality.

Five elevators and a coal chute rose beside the tracks. Ole Heggestad, Louis Anderson and the Gilbertson brothers started general stores. Next followed a restaurant, garage, hardware, an implement agency, hotel, pool room and barber shop, livery barn and dray, butcher shop, school, blacksmith shop and a United Church. Frontier was on its way.

Early settlers of the district who kept it humming were largely Scandinavian.

Climax, the next station east, was a lively town and because it had the hospital, was always one jump ahead of Frontier. However, on May 2nd, 1930, Dr. M. C. O'Brien came to Frontier and was the resident doctor for ten years. In 1954 Frontier was picked as the locale for the celebrations honoring Dr. O'Brien, pioneer medical man of the Southwest.

When the depression hit in the 1930s Frontier, like many other Saskatchewan points, went downhill. It was not until quite recently that it made a most dramatic recovery revolving around the enterprise and initiative of the Olaf Friggstad family.

Olaf Friggstad, fifty-seven, has spent his entire life on the homestead his Norwegian-born father filed on after coming from Minnesota. When his father died in 1941, Olaf took over the farm.

Mr. Friggstad and his two sons, Terry and Dale, started their manufacturing enterprise in 1970. The project wasn't launched as a spur-of-the moment haphazard scheme. The trio carefully considered every foreseeable eventuality before embarking on their venture. They had plenty of experience building their own machines in a well-equipped farm workshop. That's really how Friggstad Manufacturing Limited came into being. Friggstads, the farmers, had built a deep

tillage cultivator (chisel plow) and a stone picker for their own use.

Could they build these units for others? The challenge of the idea lured them on ... as Mr. Friggstad said, "each person lives only once and we enjoy working with steel".

The Friggstads employ an average of eighty men all year round and although some live in Loomis to the west and Climax to the east, the vast majority live in Frontier. This has had a dramatic effect on the once struggling little community.

A municipal report prepared on March 10, 1978 by Ray Dube, Secretary-Treasurer, showed the following facts: population — 493; business enterprises — 24; recreation — a golf course, a heated swimming pool, an arena and curling rink both with artifical ice; churches — 3; elevators — 6. Frontier is humming!

FROUDE

Froude is the first stop west of Stoughton on a CPR line that runs to Weyburn. It was named for James Anthony Froude, English historian.

FRYS

The original Frys post office is closed now and the people get their mail at Redvers. The post office and town were so named by Mr. James Fry who, in 1915, kept a store and post office there, and was a good Liberal.

FUKUSHIAMA

During the Russo-Japanese War (1904-1905) many Japanese officials passed through Saskatchewan on the way to New York for the purpose of negotiating financial assistance. Baron Yasumasa Fukushiama (1835-1919) who was vice-chief of the general staff in 1905 stopped his special train just east of Regina to view the prairies. The siding where he stopped was named Fukushiama.

FULDA

Fulda is on the CPR line directly north of Humboldt. The name is derived from the old high German word Fultaha, meaning water-land. A famous Abbey, founded in 744 by Abbott Sturmius the disciple of St. Boniface, Apostle of Germany, was named Fulda. To commemorate this great Abbey, the name of Fulda was given to the town and district. With its many lakes and creeks this name well describes the surrounding country.

FUSILIER

Fusilier is between Court and Major on a CPR line that runs from Kerrobert, Saskatchewan, to Coronation, Alberta. This railway was built in 1911 at the time of the Coronation of King George V, and many towns along the route commemorate the event: Coronation, Throne, Veteran and Consort in Alberta, and Court, Fusilier and Major in Saskatchewan.

FURNESS

Furness is on the Saskatchewan-Alberta boundary line a short distance south of Lloydminster. The Slater family was one of the first to settle in the district. They came from Furness, England. When a post office was opened in 1912 they were instrumental in seeing that it was given the name of Furness. When the railway came through it adopted the name of the post office.

G

GAINES

Mr. J. O. Snustead of Fairview Court, a Pool grain buyer at Gaines before his retirement, tells this story. Gaines was named for Gaines Cameron who homesteaded in this district. Gaines is the first grain point south and west of Milden on a CPR branch line that ends at McMorran. Other early settlers in the district were as follows: William Isley, Jim Turner, Johnny Weir, Grant Greer, Bernie Saunders, Bob Turner and Jim Elliott.

GAINSBOROUGH

In the extreme southeastern corner of the province is the pretty town of Gainsborough. The original inhabitants planted as they planned, so that early in the century beautiful trees surrounded many homes. As trees are removed for safety reasons, the later-planted ones are showing up to good advantage. The concrete sidewalks laid in 1921 gave the town a permanent appearance.

J. Sadler had suggested the name of Gainsborough after his hometown in England. On May 23, 1894, Gainsborough was registered as the first incorporated village in the province. The stone buildings are well-preserved, the frame ones painted and the new houses are the equal of those found in modern cities.

A well-known pioneer of the district was Ed Burke who came to the area in 1894. Farming 8000 acres of land he harvested a crop of 240,000 bushels of wheat in 1910. On more than one occasion Mr. Burke shipped an entire trainload of wheat from Gainsborough.

There is a second story as to the naming of Gainsborough. Some people claim it was named in honor of Thomas Gainsborough (1727-1788), who was one of England's greatest portrait painters. Among his most notable canvases are The Blue Boy, Duchess of Devonshire and George III.

GALILEE

Galilee is halfway between Mossbank and Avonlea on a branch line of the CNR. George Kitchen, ninety years old in 1969, sent us the following information. The railway came through in 1913 and the settlers followed. This was contrary to the general pattern of settlement on the plains. The early settlers were: George Kitchen, John Gommersall, Mr. Rue, Mr. Klippert and Ed Nicholson. Galilee was never anything but a grain point and now even this is gone, as the elevator was torn down years ago. The name remains in the community and there is an active Ladies Aid to the church there.

There used to be a small lake nearby, given the name Galilee by Mr. Hughes, a travelling minister of the early days, who built a tabernacle by the lake and held services there. When the railroad came they took the name from the lake for their townsite. There are three other Saskatchewan place names with a religious connotation — Cana, Mont Nebo and Ebenezer.

On a strip of unbroken land on the Kitchen farm there are still tepee rings and deep buffalo trails visible.

Two of the early settlers of Galilee whose families still live in the district are the Garners and the Swansons.

GALLIVAN

"Gallivan is 20 miles west of Battleford. On May 20 in 1903 my father and two other men came from working in the bush near Prince Albert and filed on homesteads in the area now known as Gallivan. In 1912 the Grand Trunk started building a line from Battleford west to Wainwright, Alta. The present site of Gallivan was to be a divisional point. However, the CPR headed them off with their line to Lloydminster and ours became a branch line that ended at Carruthers, 25 miles to the west. My father had sold his entire homestead to the railroad for a townsite but later purchased it back.

The naming of the town took place during the surveys that went on. My oldest brother, Wilbert, was a baby at this time and his proud father wanted the town called Wilbert, but the CPR had a townsite planned and named Wilbert just 12 miles due west on their line. My father settled for his last name "Gallivan."

The above information was given to us by Mr. Thomas Gallivan of Onion Lake, Saskatchewan.

GAP VIEW

Gap View was an inland post office that was served from Forget on a Regina to Winnipeg CPR line. Mr. R. Rayney was the first mail carrier.

The post office got its name because the location gave a view through the Moose Mountain Range to the north.

In 1925 the railroad came to Handsworth and the Gap View post office closed in 1926. The people from the district went south to Handsworth for their mail.

GARDEN HEAD

Garden Head is an inland post office southwest of Gull Lake. It is located at 23-10-20-W3. Mr. William Houston was the first postmaster and as his wife liked to garden he named the post office after her hobby.

GARDENIA

The first Gardenia post office located seven and one-half miles north and four and one half miles east of Quill Lake opened in 1907 in the home of Andrew Cutler. It took its name from the local school which had been built the year before. The school had actually been called Rogers School for the Hon. Robert Rogers, minister of public works in the Manitoba Conservative government. Since he was a controversial figure in this province, as far as Liberal supporters were concerned, because of his intervention in Saskatchewan politics, the Department of Education objected to the name and sent out three for the residents to choose from. They picked Gardenia. The name has no significance to the district.

Mail came down the old 38 Trail from Barrier Lake to the north, and then on south to Quill Lake. Mr. Wraith was the mail carrier and when roads were really bad in the winter he used a dog and sled.

First settlers to arrive were the following: Robert Rogers, Frank and Walter Vickers, James Holt, R. H. Brown and son Harry, George and Frank Towle, Clayton and Bill Block, Andrew Cutler, Henry Walsh, W. N. Penfold, Percy Bayne, Charlie Meyers, Joe Freeman, Harvey Beck, Tom Walsh and Mrs. Jones — the last mentioned lived alone and always carried a gun.

Homesteaders were always short of cash. Some went to extreme lengths to get it. Billy Block rendered skunk fat into oil. He sold it at the drug store for a good price because it was considered helpful for relief of rheumatism. It was applied externally.

GARNOCK

Garnock was a country post office started in the home of Robert Nairn in 1906. It was nine miles northeast of Headlands and the first mail carrier was Mr. G. T. North.

The mail came out from Lipton to Headlands and there Mr. North picked it up.

The post office was named for Mr. Nairn's hometown in Scotland and was closed out in the 1940's.

GARRICK

Garrick is between Love and Choiceland on a CPR line that runs from Prince Albert to Nipawin. It was named in honor of Corporal Garrick who lost his life in World War I. Among the early settlers were: Ken McBain, William Rudolph, Hugh Cathcart and Mrs. Pearson. Here are Garrick firsts: post office — 1929; railroad — 1931; school — 1934; Legion Hall — 1937; curling rink — 1940.

Today, Garrick continues to be a nice little village, far enough away from large centers to hold its own.

The CPR list indicates that Garrick was named for David Garrick (1717-1787), a well-known English writer.

GARSON LAKE SETTLEMENT

Garson Lake Settlement (56°19'-109°58') is on the west shore of the lake from which it takes its name. Garson lake is half in Saskatchewan and half in Alberta. The river, lake and settlement were named for Mr. C. N. Garson, manager of the Hudson's Bay Company post at Onion Lake. The lake was previously called Whitefish. The name was changed to Garson lake in 1911.

GASCOIGNE

Gascoigne is between Burstall and Mendham on a CPR line that runs down from Leader. It was named for Lieutenant Colonel F. A. de Long Gascoigne, superintendent of transportation on the CPR. He won the D.S.O. during World War I and he returnd to civilian life and rose to be secretary-treasurer of the Canadian Pacific Steamships from 1918 to 1934.

GERALD

Gerald was named for a GTP railway official when the line was put through in 1907. The earliest settlers included: William Redpath, Sam Thompson, John Salkeld, Art Tebb, Everett Bligh, Moses Besharoh and the Burnell brothers. Gerald is close to one of Saskatchewan's large deposits of potash.

GERROND

Gerrond is on a CNR line a short distance north of St. Louis. It was named after Mr. Gerrond, one of the early settlers of that district.

GETTYSBURG

In May of 1907, Mr. John Sigel Graham and family came from Lowell, Michigan, to Battleford and then journeyed south and west to the southeast end of Tramping lake. Among the early settlers there was another American family, namely Mr. Herman Getty. He opened a small store in his home and applied for a post office. Mr. Graham was the one who suggested the name, Gettysburg, thus doing honor to Mr. Getty and preserving, in name, their association with the United States. This post office was in existence until, in 1913, the CPR ran a line south from Wilkie to Kelfield. Gettysburg then disappeared as a post office and the settlers got their mail at Kelfield, nine miles away.

GIBBS

The CPR being built north from Regina got as far as Gibbs by 1911. Mr. W. H. Gibbs, a Qu'Appelle land company agent, gave his name to the town. The Qu'Appelle Land Company, a colonization company, was alloted land in this area in 1882.

A school district had been set up before the railway arrived. It was named Sprayville in honor of John and George Spray. It retained that name when it was moved into Gibbs.

At one time Gibbs was a bustling place with about 130 residents. It had a flag station, a hardware store, a poolroom, two grocery stores, a big hall and two elevators.

Mr. Phil Myers, the present Pool agent, says that in the early days there were about 19,000 acres under cultivation and that most of the grain was bought during a three-month period. It took two grain buyers and two assistants to handle the job — buying all day and loading all night. Now, almost 31,000 acres are being farmed, but there is only one buyer because with the establishment of the quota system, grain buying is spread over the whole year.

The school was closed and the children are bussed to Bulyea. All places of business have closed. They drew one elevator over and abutted it to the other and now Mr. Meyers runs both for the Pool. Boarded-up houses stand empty and the once lively little village has dwindled to a population of 12.

GILLESPIE

Gillespie is next to Balcarres. The CNR officials named it for Mr. J. B. Gillespie, resident manager for the Dominion Lands Colonization Company.

GILROY

For a time Gilroy was the end of the steel on a line that was built northwest out of Moose Jaw in 1913. It was first called St. Louis by the residents but the name was unacceptable to authorities because there was already another St. Louis in Saskatchewan. Gilroy was just a snap name taken from one of the many carpenters busy in the booming little town. Here are a few statistics:

Dr. J. E. Kitely opened an office in town. The Cannaught Club was formed and held regular dances with Mitchell's Orchestra from Moose Jaw supplying the music. A Toronto male quartet presented a concert in 1915. Excursion trains ran periodically. In 1915 eight coaches were filled to the doors with country residents taking advantage of a day in the city before Christmas. One and a quarter million bushels of wheat were billed out of Gilroy elevators in a good year.

In 1916 the line was built on to Riverhurst. In 1917 the first blow came to Gilroy when the bank moved to the new terminus. The implement men followed and the gradual exodus to Riverhurst was on. By 1966 this once thriving little town was down to two families — seven persons in all.

GIRVIN

There are two stories of how Girvin got its name. First J. A. Andrew, Thomas Ross and Ron McCosh filed on land in 1902 and brought their families out in 1903. Mr. John Girvin homesteaded the actual townsite and the town was named after him.

Second, the CNR list of sources of the place names along its line indicates that the town was named after John Girvin, a well-known contractor of Winnipeg who built a great many of the stations from Winnipeg west when the line was controlled by the Grand Trunk Pacific.

A few years ago when number 11 highway was being built somewhere between Aylesbury and Chamberlain the construction machinery unearthed a number of skeletons. After considerable research it was established that these were the remains of railway workers who had been struck down with typhoid fever and who had been buried along the right-of-way.

GLADMAR

Gladmar is on the CPR's Minton-Estevan line in south-central Saskatchewan. The names of two children of the community's first postmaster. Gladstone and Margaret, were combined to give the hamlet its name.

The settlement sprang up originally in 1910 following the opening of a now inoperative coal mine in the district. Something of the community's early day atmosphere is maintained today with the Sybouts Sodium Sulphate Company's salt mines located eight miles to the south and employing 20 to 35 men full time.

GLAMIS

Glamis is halfway between Gunnworth and Milden on a CPR branch line that was built in 1923. A settlement was established before the railway came and it was called Douai. The majority of the early settlers were English and Scottish and included the following: Thomas Anderson, William Whyte, Wes Billetts, Edward Sparks, Harry Maxwell, William Leith, William Orth, Frank Lynch and Henry Curry. These were the people who came in 1905 and 1906. They objected to the name of the district and had it changed to Glamis in memory of Glamis Castle in Scotland.

GLASLYN

First settled in 1908, the village of Glaslyn was named by the Welsh pioneers who first made it a frontier community. The name Glaslyn, which is Welsh for "clear water" was inspired by the small lake on the homestead of Edwin Hoskins who, with his wife and eight children, was the first to arrive. The Hoskins and J. E. Taylor families made the journey from Battleford to the district by oxen. John Lofts and his son, William arrived from South Africa later in the same year. William Lofts, who still resides in Glaslyn, is a former MLA for "The Battlefords."

The CNR extended a branch line from Turtleford to Medstead in 1929 and brought service to Glaslyn. The name Glaslyn was originally applied to the rural post office run by the pioneer settler, Hoskins. It was taken over by the new village when it was incorporated in 1929.

GLASNEVIN

Glasnevin is the first stop east of Ogema. When the CPR reached there in 1911 the village was built on land belonging to Grace Clark. Glasnevin was named by Robert Anderson for a small village in Ireland which was really a suburb of Dublin. Parnell is buried there and a very famous botanical garden was founded there in 1790.

Mrs. Owen, the first bride of Glasnevin, is the only resident left of the early days.

GLEDHOW

Gledhow is eight miles south of Pike Lake; the turnoff is marked on highway 60, just before you come to the Park gates. The name was given to it by Mr. Bumby, who came from Yorkshire, England. There is a village named Gledhow, near Leeds in Yorkshire. Mr. Summers had the first post office, then William Bond and finally Fred Bond, his son. The office was closed in 1963.

Most of the original settlers in the Gledhow district were of English origin. Some of the surnames of the families that lived there in 1919 were as follows: Bumby, Kimberley, Campbell, Fisher, Earl, Hawkins, Priest, Miller, Ham, Lennox, Wrightson, Buckle, Whitaker, Henson and Faulhaber.

In 1919 there was a family on almost each quarter and it was a well-populated district. The farms are bigger now; there are fewer people; the school and post office have been closed; there is a good highway to Saskatoon — so life has changed considerably. One of the residents put it this way:

"We were sorry when the Gledhow post office closed — we seemed to lose our identity when we became just a number on the many miles of Rural Route 3!"

GLENAVON

Glenavon is about halfway between Regina and the Manitoba border on a CNR line that leaves Saskatchewan at Maryfield. Early settlers into the district included the Kindreds, the Bruces, the McGinnises and the Evanses. The place was originally called Kendal. However, when the railroad came through and it was incorporated as a village in 1910, Mrs. John Hay from Scotland and Mr. R. T. Young, a justice of the peace, suggested Glenavon after Glenavon in Scotland.

GLEN BAIN

One of the first settlers in the area was Richard B. McBain who came via Langdon, N.D. from Glengarry County in Ontario. When there were enough settlers it was decided to form a municipality and it was named Glen Bain for Mr. McBain — who became its first reeve — and Glengarry. The municipal offices were kept at Vanguard, then the end of the steel of a line coming from Meyronne. In 1930 the CPR finished this line and where it passes through the municipality of Glen Bain it was given the name of Glen Bain.

GLENBOGIE

Glenbogie was an inland post office which opened on January 18, 1912 and closed on March 31, 1925. It was situated on SE 21-54-23 W3 and the postmaster was Alex Wilson. It was named for a town in Scotland.

GLENBUSH

Glenbush is on a CNR line northeast of North Battleford. Homesteaders poured into the district from 1907 to 1912 and filled it up. Some of the earliest to arrive were: G. Gordon, R. Henderson, H. Thompson, H. Michaels, G. Walker, J. Gilchrist, J. Smith, M. Weldon, J. Johnson, C. Bartholomew, Pete and John Grant, G. Reynolds, A. Duncan, H. Newman, A. McGuiness, H. W. Dixon, the Vine brothers, and G. Avery. The school was named for the latter.

Glenwood was the name favored by the local residents but the postal authorities persuaded them to change it to Glenbush. Glenwood would have been a more appropriate name for the district at the time because you'd have had a hard time convincing the oldtimers that they were just removing bushes to clear their land. They were trees — big poplar trees! Of course, now, it's no problem with the power machinery and brush-breakers we have, but in those days it was a back-breaking job with a cross-cut saw, axe, grub hoe and horses.

For the first four years the mail service was a sporadic affair because the settlers hauled their own and this occurred only when someone was making a trip into North Battleford. Today, however, fine grain farms stretch out where solid bush used to stand. Here and there tucked away in the trees is a beautiful country home with "power."

GLEN ELDER

Glen Elder post office came into being in 1917 and was located on the SW section 12-36-2-W2, this is just northwest of Norquay. The first postmaster was a Mr. Curry. A group of American settlers named the post office after Glen Elder in Kansas. A school which was built in the same district was also called Glen Elder; this school was closed in 1959. The post office, which had two later locations, was closed in 1967 after fifty years of service.

GLENELLEN

Glenellen is near Herschel. It was an inland post office which is now closed. Its location was 12-33-17-W3, and Mrs. A. Henwood was the first postmistress. A glen is a secluded narrow valley and the word comes from the Scottish language. Many Scottish homesteaders were influential in having this name repeated in Saskatchewan places: Glen Kerr, Glen Ewen, Glen Payne, Glenside, Glenbogie, and Glenbush to name a few.

GLEN ELM PARK

Glen Elm Park was an early post office close to Regina. It is closed now but the name lives on in the district. A glen is a secluded narrow valley and in this one someone had planted an elm tree. Glen is a simple Scottish name and is used over and over again in Saskatchewan place names: Glenburn, Glenside, Glenellen, Glen Payne and Glen Mary.

GLEN EWEN

Glen Ewen is between Oxbow and Alameda in the southeastern part of Saskatchewan. It was named for the first postmaster, Thomas Ewen. Thomas and Sandy Ewen homesteaded on section 16-3-1-W1, in 1882.

At first they got their mail at Alameda west of Moose creek and the settlers south of the Souris got theirs at Boscurvis. When more people came in and took land north of the river they decided they needed a post office of their own. They were short of names when they took up their petition and, as the Ewens had three growing boys, Tom suggested that they sign. When a name was talked about several were suggested. It was James Maitland who suggested the name should be Ewen. When the CPR came through in the 1880s they accepted the name Ewen for the village site and put a Glen in front of it.

The only descendant of the Ewens left in the district is David Watson of Alida, a great-grandson of Tom.

The village of Glen Ewen is going downhill, losing out to Oxbow and Carn-duff. However there is some thing they can not take from Glen Ewen. It has the only known burial mound in Saskatchewan; this prehistoric monument consists of a central conical mound fifty feet in diameter and one and one-half feet high, plus four linear mounds extending out from the central mound to conical terminal mounds. The central mound covered a burial pit three and one-half feet in diameter and nearly seven feet deep.

The original significance of the burial mound is not known, but similar mounds were being built by Assiniboine Indians when they were first visited by explorers in the eighteenth century. Many occur in former Assiniboine territories in southern Manitoba. The plan of the mound is also similar to the stone cairns with radiating lines of stones built by Indians in early historic times as monuments to deceased war leaders.

GLEN KERR

The Glen Kerr post office was opened in the fall of 1915. The first postmaster was John Wilkinson Kerr and the office was called after him. When the CNR built a branch line from Mawer to Main Centre in 1930 it came close to Glen Kerr. The post office was then moved from the farm of Mr. Kerr to the hamlet which took over the name, Glen Kerr.

GLEN MARY

Glen Mary was an inland post office fifteen miles north of Kinistino. It was named for its first postmistress, Mary Glen. The post office opened in the early 1900s and closed in 1956. This information came from Shirley Svenkeson of Kinistino.

GLEN McPHERSON

Glen McPherson (now closed) was an inland post office located 31-T5-R11-W3, just west of the present Mankota. It was named for the McPherson family, early settlers in the district.

GLEN PAYNE

Glen Payne is very close to Rosetown on a branch line of the CPR that runs south and then west to McMorran. A glen is a narrow secluded valley and the word comes from the Scottish language. Payne came from one of the early settlers, Mr. R. Payne.

GLENSIDE

Glenside is a grain point on a CPR line that runs west and then south to Hawarden and Elbow. A glen is a secluded narrow valley. Glen is a simple Scottish name and we find it used over and over again in place names of Saskatchewan: Glenburn, Glen Elm Park, Glenellen, Glen Payne and Glenbogie to name a few.

GLENTWORTH

Glentworth is between Fir Mountain and McCord on a CPR line in southern Saskatchewan. The first name suggested was Waverley but it was turned down. The railway came through in 1928 and they were instrumental in selecting the name.

GLIDDEN

Glidden is 20 miles west of Eston. The building of the original town started in the spring of 1916, a year before the railway arrived. Two stores, two cafes, and a livery barn went up. During that summer the rains came and the immediate area went under water. Rafts were used to get from store to store.

It was decided to relocate a mile east on higher ground. The spot selected belonged to Mr. Glidden. Mr. Glidden was a man of note. He had taken part in the Klondike gold rush and had recently turned land locator and farmer. He had extensive holdings in the district. Before this he had interests in a barbed wire and paint company that bore his name. When the railway arrived in 1917 it was not surprising that the hamlet was named for him.

GOLBURN

In 1924 the CPR built north from Wadena through Tisdale and on to Nipawin. The first stop south of Tisdale was Golburn, named for a valley nearby.

At its height the village had two elevators, a store, post office, a station, a school and several residences.

As a lad of eight years, Carl Sorge came with his family from Sparta, New York State in 1916. He grew up in the district and eventually became a teacher. When World War II broke out, he enlisted and was wounded in action.

On his return to Canada he found employment with the North Battleford Fire Department and officially retired from it in 1971. However, Mr. Sorge's vocabulary does not include the word "retired". He took his savings and went into private business.

Earlier in his life Mr. Sorge became interested in bees and always kept a hive or two for the family's use. Now he went into bees in earnest. He purchased the vacant Prince school, had bees shipped in from California, set out hives, and began producing honey on a large scale under the name of Aunt Lil's Honey Ltd.

When interviewed in July of 1978 Mr. Sorge had 2,000 hives set out as far south as North Battleford, north to Glaslyn, west to the Turtle River and east to Scentgrass. He employs from four to six workers and averages 150 pounds of honey to the hive.

Bears cause him concern from time to time and over the years it has been necessary to shoot several of them.

GOLDBURG

Goldburg post office was opened in the home of George Moore 1-34-16-W3, eighteen miles south of Biggar, in the early 1900s. Mr. Moore gave it the fancy name with tongue-in-cheek since it was never hoped that anyone would get rich there or even that there would be a town. We find other fancy names in Saskatchewan — for example, Fortune, Success, Crescent City and, by 1971, White City eleven miles east of Regina. It's not a new idea. Like Kingsland to the south Goldburg was never more than a rural post office — not even a store was included.

Mr. Bill Craig, long-time resident in the district, says the most exciting event that took place in the district was in 1932. Henry Tremblay who had a large farm and an even larger family — 11 or 12 — took sick one spring and the neighbors all pitched in to put in his crop. In the fall, the Randall Studio of Biggar was on hand to photograph the old-fashioned "community bee" that cut and stooked 200 acres of wheat in one day. The picture shows 14 binders, 20 men, 14 women and 10 children.

In 1910 the post office moved to the home of Mr. Edwards, 24-33-16-W3, and soon after it closed down. Here are a few of the early settlers of the Goldburg district: Harve Dubreuil; Arthur, Joe, Leo and Rudolph Boisvert; Henry Tremblay; William Lane; William Windslow; Milton Porter; Munro Clark; Harry Sharp; William Morley; James Robinson; George and Sam Pollick.

GOLDEN PRAIRIE

Golden Prairie is the end of a very short CPR branch line that runs north of Hatton in the southwest corner of the province.

Mrs. William F. May, a resident of Golden Prairie, has this to say: "A post office called Golden Prairie preceded the railroad; it was called Golden Prairie for the beautiful fields of ripened wheat. When the railway came in they accepted the name of the rural post office. Fifteen years ago (1955) it was a going concern but like many little towns it has steadily gone downhill. It still has 4 elevators, a general store with a liquor outlet, a modern school (teaching all grades with only 6½ teachers), one garage, a curling rink with artificial ice, and an assortment of houses. The hotel burned down 12 years ago and was never rebuilt. The population is 130.

Here are some of the oldtimers' surnames: Gardner, Swaok, Schuster, Murray, Luker, Oster, Innis, Arndt, Sulz, Herter and Gieser."

GOLDEN RIDGE

Golden Ridge is forty miles northwest of Meadow Lake, the nearest railhead. It is served by Number 55 highway. Homesteaders did not arrive is this locality until 1929 and 1930. Many of them came from the "dust bowl" of the prairies with all their household belongings on a canvas-covered bundle rack and their stock straggling along behind.

Mr. Lay acquired the post office in 1934 and it was he who named the district Golden Ridge. A ridge runs between the Waterhen River to the north and the Beaver River to the south of the area.

GOLDFIELDS

Golfields is a ghost town close to Uranium City on Lake Athabasca. Settlement began with the discovery of gold in 1934 and the development of the property by the Consolidated Mining and Smelting Company. Labor shortages and a run of low-grade ore led to the abandonment of mining operations in 1950. Most of the buildings have been moved to Uranium City.

GOLIER

Golier is a rural post office less than five miles east of Flintoft. It opened on December 1, 1913, with Mr. Clyde Johnson as postmaster. He was followed by Mr. John Edward Everatt and under John Tonita, the next postmaster, it closed out on October 1, 1948.

GOODEVE

Northwest out of Melville, Fenwood starts another of the alphabetical series so favored by the Grand Trunk Railway. Then in order comes Goodeve, Hubbard, Ituna and so on.

Although it cannot be positively proved, research in the Saskatchewan Archives indicates that the GTP named the town for Arthur Samuel Goodeve, MP, a member of the Dominion Railway Commission at the time the line was built.

In 1974, Thomas Battersly, the last surviving son of a family which came from Great Britain and settled in the Goodeve district in 1892, donated 320 acres of beautiful countryside land to the provincial government to ensure its protection as a wildlife and historic area.

The government purchased another section, added it to the Battersly property, and made it a haven for wildlife. The full-time manager of the site is David Ivanochko.

At the entrance to the Battersly wildlife protected area is the old station house, moved there from Goodeve. It has been refurbished but many of the original items have been retained, such as the pot belly stove, coal scuttle, clock, scales, morse code equipment, mail bag, dispatcher's hoop, iron stamp, typewriter and files.

GOODHUE

The Goodhue post office about 15 miles northeast of Stenen opened in 1915 in the home of Matt Hanson on section 9, township 35, range 3 west of the second meridian. Mr. Hanson named it in memory of his home in Goodhue, Minnesota. It lasted only six years.

GOODSOIL

Goodsoil lies between the Beaver and Waterhen rivers on Highway 26 in northwestern Saskatchewan. The first families, mainly of German descent, arrived in the area in the 1920s. This makes the village a relative newcomer to Saskatchewan history.

When it came time for a name, officials submitted Goodsoil because they felt "good soil" aptly described the farmland of the district. The land has lived up to its name and the thriving village of today contains 25 businesses, a bank, a doctor, a hospital, a hotel, a 13-room school, and three tourist camps.

GOODWATER

Goodwater is the end of a short branch line southeast of Radville. Mrs. Colin Belt of Alingly was born in the hospital there in 1916 and its name at that time was Jewell. This had been done to honor the Jewell family of the district.

When the railways pushed across the prairies in the early 1900s the surveyors were always on the alert for a plentiful supply of water. The great puffing steam engines of the day had to replenish their supply at regular intervals from huge water towers. When the CNR was approaching Jewell they had considerable difficulty in locating water; when they did find it they struck it at 12 feet — good water and in abundance. Most of the wells are sand points. The surveyors were so pleased to locate this water that they changed the name of the townsite to Goodwater.

GORKENDON

Gorkendon is the name of a rural post office southwest of Limerick. It opened at the turn of the century in the farm home of Mr. and Mrs. James Fraser. The post office got its name from the Fraser's three sons, Gordon, Kenneth and Donald. They took the first three letters of each name to form Gorkendon. The post office closed in 1914. Donald lost his life in World War I.

GORLITZ

Gorlitz is north of Yorkton on a CNR line that runs to Canora. The Grand Trunk Pacific originally built the line.

J. F. Paul Barschel born in Langeneau, Germany, in 1875, took his public school education there and later attended the state agricultural college in Gorlitz before coming to Canada in 1893 as an 18-year-old boy. He is credited with giving the name to the town. The following were some of the prominent Ukrainian families that moved into the district after 1897; E. Schnider, Gustane Gabert, J. Reiman, Gottlich Welk, C. Schmalz, John Andrusiak, Alec, John and Charley Wiwchar, Recko Homeniuk, and one who was always a leader, Alec Chabun.

GOUDIE

Goudie is on a CPR line that runs from Yorkton to Wadena. At Goudie a branch line runs south and west to Wishart. It was named for Mr. W. C. Goudie, the late city treasurer of Moose Jaw.

GOULDTOWN

Gouldtown is the second last stop on a short CNR branch line south and west from Mawer which ends at Main Centre. It is named to honor an old pioneer of the district, Mr. Gould.

GOUVERNEUR

Gouverneur is between Cadillac and Ponteix in the southwestern part of the province. It was named for Mr. I. Gouverneur Ogden, financial vice-president of the CPR.

GOVAN

Govan is on the east side of the north end of Last Mountain lake. Just after the turn of the century the Pearson Land Company started to bring settlers up the lake and into the district. Oscar Landstrom built the first house. The first post office in the area was Bucclough, five miles east of the present town site.

In 1907, the Kirkella branch of the CPR arrived via Balcarres and Bulyea, and the town site was officially named Govan after Walter Govan, an early homesteader in the district.

One name which stands out among these pioneers is Samuel J. Latta. He homesteaded in the district in 1905. In 1907 he established the Govan *Prairie News* and then he took a turn at teaching. He was also a farmer, writer, and artist of note. In 1912 he entered provincial politics and in the Martin administration he was minister of highways and later minister of education. He served also in the Dunning and Gardiner administrations and took on several more portfolios, continuing until 1929.

GOVENLOCK

Govenlock is between Altawan and Senate on a CPR line running from Ravenscrag south and west into Alberta. It was named for an early rancher in the district.

GRACE

Grace started as a rural post office in the Cardross area on June 1, 1910, with Mr. J. R. Brown as postmaster. He named it for his wife, Grace. Samuel Walker and then Mrs. Walker followed as postmasters.

When William J. Amies took over on April 1, 1916, he had the name changed to Cardross. See the story of Cardross for further details.

GRAINLAND

Grainland is a settlement southwest of Craik at 5-23-4-W3. It's on a CNR line a short distance south of the "Elbow". You couldn't find a more descriptive word to describe, not only Grainland, but almost all of southern Saskatchewan.

Grainland had a good start. First, the elevator, post office and store at Aitkow on the CPR line a few miles to the east relocated when it became evident Grainland was the trading centre.

With the development of Elbow, Grainland faded. Today only one small shack remains.

GRAND COULEE

Grand Coulee is just west of Regina. It was originally called Cotton Wood Coulee but as it was the largest coulee in the vicinity it obtained the named Grand. Actually it is a small valley where the railway used to store water. It was incorporated as a village in 1907 but returned to its original status in 1919. Improved roads and cars put it too close to Regina to develop on its own.

GRANDORA

Fifteen miles west of Saskatoon stands a station, a few homes, a post office, service station, and elevators. It is Grandora. This is the story of how it got its name.

A newly married settler drove out west of Saskatoon with his bride to locate a homestead. Eventually they came to a place where he exclaimed, "Isn't this grand, Dora!" and Grandora it is to this day.

GRASSDALE

Grassdale is on a short CNR branch line that runs southwest from Weyburn to Radville. It is a name the settlers used to describe their new home. Others like it are Grasswood, Yellow Grass and Pleasantdale.

GRASSWOOD

Grasswood is a natural as a name because it expresses just what the early settlers found, ample grass and wood. It's not a unique way of naming a new home as is borne out by the following: Grassdale, Yellow Grass, Greenbush and Wood Mountain.

There's a lot of history tied up in Grasswood, next-door-neighbor to Saskatoon. In the early years Saskatoon suffered greatly for want of a railway. Finally, in August of 1889, after prolonged negotiations that took in the infant colony, the Dominion Government of Sir John A. Macdonald and a hard selling job to the Old Country firm of Morton Rose and Company, enough capital was raised to start work on a railway north of Regina to Saskatoon and on through to Prince Albert. The contractors were James Ross, H. S. Holt, William Mackenzie and Donald Mann.

On the evening of Wednesday, May 14, 1890, the gleam of a headlight of a work train — still six miles distant — was the signal for a celebration in the village of Saskatoon. A torchlight parade was staged and just about where the Pool elevator at Grasswood now stands, an impromptu get-together was held.

The following is a look at Grasswood as it is remembered by one man, Walter (Harry) Henry Brown of Suite 103 Park Plaza, Saskatoon, retired caretaker from the Saskatoon Public School Board.

Harry's dad, also Walter Henry Brown, was employed by a stationer's firm in London, England, when he felt the call of Canada, land of opportunity. Mr. and Mrs. Brown were ready to sail with the Barr Colonists when it became necessary to "wait for Harry." He was born in Liverpool and the newly increased family took the next boat to Canada.

Mr. Brown senior and later Harry, farmed off and on in the Grasswood district. Harry remembers the Herman Richard family arriving in 1909 from Wisconsin with several cars of settler's effects that included six Holstein heifers and up-to-date farming equipment. Son, Walter Richard, is still on the original homestead in Grasswood.

Other early settlers included the following: Barney and Paul Sommerfeldt, Walter Gray, Hastings Baker, John Fahl, Mr. Schmidt, Frank Owen, Hembro Smith, Martin and Morris Harris, Charlie Taylor, Henry (Hank) Rose and William Watson.

Mr. Brown's land faced the river and he called his farm "The Woodlands." It was eight miles south of Saskatoon, which has now grown until its city limits are four miles from Grasswood.

Grasswood never had a store or a post office. A school was built in 1923 and this doubled as an Anglican church. Mr. Brown, senior, was one of the original organizers and each Sunday he drove the minister out from Saskatoon for services at Grasswood. One man who served the parish well was the Rev. Sampson, now retired and living at Victoria.

As mentioned before Harry farmed off and on. When he was off he was, in turn, a Canadian Northern express driver, an express clerk in the office, an express man on the old Goose Lake Line out as far as Eatonia — Eaton then. Next came a spell of batching which ended when he met Alma Letrud at his sister Vera's home at Young in 1929. The Saskatoon Fire Department came next and Harry served overseas with the London Firefighters in the Second World War. On his return to Saskatoon he was employed as a caretaker by the Public School Board until his retirement in 1967.

An elevator was built at Grasswood in 1928 and the first agent was John Manson. Its present agent is Mr. "Jack" Briggs. His daughter, Beverley, is one of the best women golfers in Saskatchewan.

In the past few years many prominent professional people have built beautiful homes in the district and these incude the following: Dr. Dick, Dr. Kunkel, and Dr. Stephen Worobetz, former lieutenant-governor of Saskatchewan.

GRAVELBOURG

Gravelbourg is named in honor of Father Louis Pierre Gravel and his two brothers, Dr. Henri and Emile. In 1906 they arrived overland in wagons from Moose Jaw and carried out an amazing colonization scheme which made Gravelbourg a flourishing religious and cultural centre. The "bourg" part of the name comes from the French which means "town". Hence, Gravelbourg means Gravel's town.

GRAY

Gray is 25 miles southeast of Regina on the CNR (which succeeded the old GTP railroad) Regina to Northgate line. In 1902 settlers began to move into this area. Among them were many Americans, particularly from the state of Iowa. When, in 1904, an application for a post office was approved, a name for it was discussed. Sam Spillar, secretary-treasurer of the newly formed Iowa School district, suggested "Gray" after the town of Gray in Audubon County, Iowa, an area from which a number of settlers had come. The name was accepted.

John Beatty, a settler on S.W. 16-14-18-W2, was appointed postmaster and the post office was installed in his home. Mr. Beatty transported the mail 16 miles to Milestone and back once a week. When a townsite for the new railroad was surveyed, just two miles west of the Gray post office, Mr. Beatty asked the officials to name the new town Gray, a request which was readily granted.

With the completion of the steel in 1912 the Gray post office was moved into Walter Greer's grocery store in the new town.

GRAYBURN

Grayburn is a short distance northwest of Moose Jaw. The first settlers into the district were the McBrides, the Fergusons, the Peevers, and Joe English. The town was named for a family by the name of Gray who came in somewhat later but who owned the land on which the town was built. The "burn" part came from a small creek which flows nearby. Grayburn was never very large but at one time it had a store, a post office, a railway station, and two elevators. Now, because of its proximity to Moose Jaw it is down to a post office and the two elevators.

GRAYSON

Grayson is a village of 350 people 25 miles south of Melville. Settlers from Austria, Poland, and Germany began to enter this region in 1896. The community was first called "Nieven" and nobody seems to know why. In 1903 the CPR came through and renamed it Grayson, for Harry Grayson, a construction contractor.

GRAYTOWN

Graytown was an early post office in the homestead home of Mr. Gray near the present town of Grenfell. It has long since closed out and his son now lives in Edmonton, Alberta.

GREAT BEND

In 1905 the inland post office of Great Bend was established by J. S. Goodrich at S.W. 20-40-10 W3rd. This is about 20 miles north of the present town of Borden, Saskatchewan.

The post office and general store were operated by J. S. Goodrich. It was named for a sharp bend in the North Saskatchewan River.

Great Bend was located on the "Battleford Trail" which ran from Saskatoon to Battleford. The mail was first carried by stage coach from Saskatoon.

GREAT DEER

Great Deer is an inland post office fifteen miles north and east of Borden. It is named for the abundance of red deer or jumpers in the vicinity. As farms get larger and settlers get fewer per square mile, the red deer is fast making a comeback.

GREENAN

Greenan is situated on the SE ¼-9-26-17-W3. Settlers from England, Scotland, Ireland, Eastern Canada and the U.S.A. began filling up the district in 1910. The CNR grade was built in 1914. The same year a building was moved in for a general store by the late John Bone of University Drive, Saskatoon, who was a pioneer of the Rosetown district in 1907. The local residents petitioned the postal department to have the Bisley post office moved to Greenan. This was done. Mr. Bone and his brother, Matthew, hauled the mail by buggy from Elrose to Wartime, Greenan and Plato.

The name Greenan had been submitted to the post office officials by Mr. Bone in memory of Greenan Castle, a ruin still standing on a high cliff on the Ayrshire coast of Scotland. It was built in 1500 A.D. and is kept in repair as an historic site.

Early settlers in the Greenan district included the following: Tom Hallahan, Harry Collins, Ernest and Stewart Thompson, Mike Hudson, William and George Fraser, Donald McLeod, Harold Smyth, Alex MacDonald, George Adams, Jack Webb, William Smith, William Kelsey, Robert Melrose, Gordon White, John Fish, Alfred McWatters, Norman and William Sedgewick, John McDonald, George Caverhill, Murdo McIver, George and Jack Gibbs, George Braid, John Ripley, Nels Markold, Otto Larson, Peter Topp and Jack McCartney.

GREEN BRIER

Green Brier (now closed) was a rural post office S 18-T23-R7-W3, just south of the present Lucky Lake. It was named after creeping cedar and rose bushes on the original post office site.

GREENBUSH

In 1903 the Canadian Northern Railway began construction of a Swan River, Manitoba, branch line west to Prince Albert. Along the line logging centers grew up and Greenbush was selected as a Forestry Branch headquarters. The town became an important and active place. In the first year of its existence the Great West Lumber Company, alone, employed over 200 men in logging operations. The Forestry Headquarters carried on intensive survey operations in checking timber quotas. Sixteen Ranger Fire Stations were connected by telephone to Greenbush.

Stores and other town facilities opened up: a poolroom and barber shop, a large roller skating rink and dance hall, a station and a railway foreman's home — bunk houses were supplied for the crew. Two restaurants and a hotel opened. It had everything and business was good. On July fourth the annual baseball tournament drew entries from as far away as Melfort, Preeceville and Kinistino, a tremendous distance for those times!

Today, nothing remains. When the logging operations closed down it was a blow. In 1930 the Forestry Headquarters were moved to Hudson Bay. Next came the depression and buildings were gradually torn down. The last to go was the section foreman's house in 1965.

Mrs. Catherine Dobrowski who now resides in Hudson Bay lived through all this and she reflects that it is sad to see such an active place as Greenbush die.

GREEN CANYON

Green Canyon is a station on the CPR northwest of Redberry lake. It is located on the side of a deep ravine on a farm owned by Mr. Green.

GREEN LAKE

Green Lake is a settlement at the north end of a lake of the same name. It is 108 miles northwest of Prince Albert and 30 miles from Meadow Lake, the nearest town. A government-sponsored program for the rehabilitation of the Metis has been undertaken here and a farm has been established for them.

Over the years they have raised livestock with considerable success.

The town became an educational centre. It was the first to inaugurate bus tours of whole classes to southern Saskatchewan points. Their example was followed by other schools of the north, particularly Ile-a-la-Crosse.

On January 10, 1977 at exactly 8:00 p.m. Green Lake achieved another first. Residents were able to tune in their FM radio sets to CHGL Megahertz to listen to its first broadcast.

The station offered two hours of music and news on week day evenings and four hours of programming each Saturday and Sunday. The station has received technical assistance from the CBC and financing from the department of northern Saskatchewan (DNS). The most important development of this facility is that students from the Green Lake School will take part regularly in the actual broadcast.

Katie Mapes, co-odinator, and Keith Spencer, a teacher at Green Lake School, deserve a lot of credit. They have worked over two years to achieve this accomplishment.

GREENE

In the early 1900's the Grand Trunk Pacific built southwest from Biggar to Loverna and on into Alberta. Six miles east of the Saskatchewan-Alberta border the grain point of Greene developed. The town was named for a railway official.

Some of the first settlers were: John Nisbet, William and Sam Bolingbroke, Carl Firth and the Tisdale brothers.

The first postmaster was Bill Bolingbroke who had the office in his home located a mile from where Greene eventually developed. He received fifty dollars a year for his services plus fifty cents per trip for meeting the mail train three times a week. He was fined two dollars if he missed a trip.

Later the post office was moved to the site of Greene and housed in a small store run by Hugh Rogers and subsequently by Merle Fagan.

Nothing remains at the site now; even the elevators have disappeared.

This information came from Mrs. A. L. Ewing of Alsask, Saskatchewan, who lived near Greene for several years.

GREENSTREET

Greenstreet is a hamlet directly north of Lloydminster and eight miles east of the 4th meridian. It is in the municipality of Britannia, the original name of Lloydminster.

Greenstreet was named for an early postmaster, Mr. Greenstreet, who lived there in 1912. The CPR ran a line north from Lloydminster to Hillmond in 1928 and Greenstreet is the second last stop on this line.

GREENTHAL

Greenthal is a Mennonite village six miles west of Hague. In English the name mans Green Valley. Most of the early settlers came from Russia.

GRENFELL

Grenfell is half way between Regina and the Manitoba border on the main line of the CPR. It was named for Pascoe du Pres Grenfell, a director of the CPR in 1883. Grenfell was incorporated as a village in 1884 and as a town in 1911.

The first settlers arrived in the community with ox teams and wagons as early as 1881. Some were from Eastern Canada and some were from Great Britain.

William John Patterson, son of a railwayman, grew up and got his first education in Grenfell. He herded cows at $5.00 a month to supplement the family income. He was employed in the Dominion Bank at the age of 16 and became the manager at the age of 21. He became Premier of Saskatchewan in 1935 and Lieutenant Governor in 1951, the only Saskatchewan born man up to that time to hold both of these positions.

"Billy" Patterson, as he was known to so many, was quite a man.

Grenfell in the early years was a thriving community. A. Switzer operated a brick yard and a large portion of the bricks were used in the construction of the Parliament Buildings in Regina.

In those early years Grenfell also had a pop factory, a creamery and a cheese factory.

Grenfell has the oldest continuing Agricultural Society in Saskatchewan. In 1905 they held a two-day fair. It drew an attendance of 2000 visitors and 400 horses were judged!

Grenfell produced people who shaped the affairs of not only their community, but the province. The early town planners were people of vision and foresight. Fine stone and brick buildings were erected which still continue to wear an air of venerability and permanence. The streets are wide with tree-lined boulevards. Lilacs bloom profusely in the spring.

Grenfell is a solid beautiful little town today. I am indebted to two ladies for much of this information: Lois Argue of Edmonton, Alberta and Mrs. Annie Yule of Grenfell.

GRIFFIN

The CPR ran a branch line west from Stoughton to Weyburn in 1908. When the GTP built between the CPR lines it intersected this branch line at Griffin. The village was named for Mr. Fredrick T. Griffin, a land commissioner for the CPR from 1901 to 1911. Some of the early settlers were: Jack Campbell, James Sullivan, Nelson Clough, Jim Chipman, and Robert and John Charlton.

GRONLID

On August 25, 1912, under the leadership of Pastor H. O. Gronlid, a number of settlers gathered on the farm of Mr. and Mrs. Ben Broste, and the Beaver Creek Lutheran congregation was formed with 11 members, one family counting as a member. It became a branch of the Norwegian Lutheran Church of America. Gronlid is named in honor of Pastor H. O. Gronlid.

GROSWERDER

Groswerder was an early inland post office five miles southeast of Primate. The first postmaster was Alex Schactel. The earliest settlers were German Roman Catholics but we have not been able to establish where the name came from.

GRUENFELD

Gruenfeld is a small Mennonite village north of Osler. It is a German name meaning Green Field. Early settlers on the plains, that were barren of trees, learned to use buffalo chips as their first fuel. Mennonites used the same product but carried it a step further by processing it and storing it for winter use. The overnight cattle pen provided the raw product — cattle were penned at night, let out to graze in the daytime. They would be looked after by a herdsman and brought home in the evening. In late fall horses were used to trample down the entire pen to an even surface, which was then left to dry to spading consistency. With spades men then squared off "ten by ten" or similar squares of about a foot deep layer of manure. This was again left to dry and bake in the hot fall sun until it would be gathered up and taken out of the pen and stacked. This work was often done by women and children. These stacks of dried-up squares were then carried into the "sheen", a building adjoining the barn, and used in a specially built "brick-oven" built between two rooms in the home. The plastered oven would be capable of holding heat for a considerable length of time. Thus homes were kept warm. Sometimes, too, the oven was constructed in such a way that sleeping space was provided on the top of it.

GRUENTHAL

Gruenthal is a small Mennonite community consisting of 12 to 14 families, seven miles south and west of Hague. The name is German and means Green Dale. Peter Klassen had the first store and his son carried on the family business until it closed in the 1960s.

This little village was odd in one respect. In the early days it had no church or school. Now, 1972, it has two churches, The Gruenthal Pentecostal and a regular Mennonite church.

GUERNSEY

Guernsey is the first stop west of Lanigan on the main line of the CPR. It is very close to one of the recent potash mines that has opened in Saskatchewan. This may bring some growth to the little town which was named in honor of one of the Channel Islands that lie between England and France.

The following streets in Guernsey, Saskatchewan: Hanois Avenue, St. Peter Street, St. Samson Street and St. Martin Street are named after places in Guernsey, Channel Islands, England.

GULL LAKE

Gull Lake is a translation of the Indian name "Kiaskus" so named by Professor John Macoun, the Dominion botanist who, during 1879, was studying flora and fauna of the southern prairie region. He was impressed by the number and variety of gulls frequenting the place. Gull Lake was incorporated as a town in 1911.

GUNDERSON

The present town and railway station of Kyle derived its name from a couple of oldtimers from Ontario — Jerry and Ann Kyle. The post office, which was in the home of "Old Jerry and Old Lady Kyle" as they were affectionately called, was called Kyleville. Later on as settlement increased the people received a closer post office called Gunderson, named after the postmaster, Mr. Ole Gunderson.

GUNNAR

Gunnar is a self-contained uranium mining community on the extreme tip of Crackingstone Peninsula which extends into the centre of Lake Athabasca. It is named for Gunnar Mining Limited, the company which commenced production there in September, 1955.

GUNWORTH

Gunworth is twenty miles south of Rosetown of a CPR line out of Milden. It was named for Mr. Gunn, an early settler in the district.

GYE

Gye is seven miles southeast of Willow Bunch on a CNR branch line. At its height it consisted of three elevators and a small station. The buildings were on Frank Bellefleur's land. Amie Proulx homesteaded right next to the elevator and his little family had a busy time. Mrs. Armand Lautier (nee Proulx) remembers that as a girl, she and her sister cooked for 27 men while they were building the Pool elevator. Her father and mother were away on a custom threshing outfit at the time.

The Grain Growers elevator burned down in 1929 and it was not rebuilt. The other two elevators have been boarded up for the last ten years. There is no significance to the name Gye, it was just given to the grain point by the CNR officials.

H

HAFFORD

There are several versions to the origin of the name of Hafford. One version stems from the business deal between the railway agent and Henry Hudek upon whose land is the townsite of Hafford. The agent was offering Henry Hudek $20 an acre for the site and Mr. Hudek said he could not afford to sell for the price offered. In the course of this conversation they used the world "afford" several times. When they agreed on the purchase price, the agent suggested that the letter "h" from Hudek's name be taken and placed in front of the word "afford." Some people say the word "afford" was mispronounced to sound as beginning with the letter "h."

Another version is that there was civil engineer, Hafford, who surveyed the railway line here, and who lost his life in an accident in B.C., and so Hafford got its name in his memory.

HAGEN

Joseph L. Hagen contributed the following" My father, Andrew C. Hagen, came to this district in the fall of 1902 and filed on a homestead for my four brothers and himself. I was only six then so I didn't get a homestead.

The CPR (Regina-Lanigan) came through to us in 1930. A meeting of local residents in the schoolhouse decided that the hamlet should be named for my father. The railway officials accepted the suggestion."

HAGUE

A letterhead from Jacob E. Friesen of Box 225, Hague, shows an outline of the town in 1912. Besides showing the general store of John A. Friesen and Son, it names a few of the places of business: Windsor Hotel; North Star elevator; Klassen's Stationery; Dyck's Jewellery; G. Klassen's Linoleums, Carpets and Suit Cases; Imperial Bank; Mahnke's Barber Shop; G. McCann — wood by the cord or carlot.

Hague started to fill up in 1883 when George Lovell took out the first homestead. The railway came in 1890 when a line was built through from Regina to Prince Albert. Until 1937 the actual naming of Hague had been in doubt. Now, due to the personal search of Jacob Friesen, local merchant, it has been established that it was named for Mr. Jenkins Harry Hague, an early bridge and railroad engineer who was never a resident of the town. He was working on the stretch of line to Prince Albert when it was casually suggested in a business meeting of bridge and rural engineers which was held in Saskatoon, that the as yet unnamed siding north of Osler be named for him. It stuck. In later years Mr. Hague owned and operated the Windsor Hotel in Vancouver and died there in 1962 at the age of 83.

Mr. J. E. Friesen of Hague has been doing research on the history of the town as a hobby. A visit to his store and private museum will take you back in time. It was thought for a time that Hague was a derivative of The Hague, Holland, since some of the ancestors of the present settlers did migrate from there in the late 1700s. However, Mr. Friesen cleared this up in 1937 when on a visit to Victoria, B.C., he met Mr. Jenkins Harry Hague.

One of the outstanding men to come out of Hague was John Michael Uhrich. Born in Formosa, Bruce County, Ontario, in 1877, Dr. Uhrich was in turn, a Saskatchewan teacher, county doctor at Hague and an MLA. He was elected as Liberal for the constituency of Rosthern in 1921. In 1923 he was appointed to the cabinet as minister of the Department of Public Health. He served for 16 years in the Dunning, Gardiner and Patterson administration. He retired from politics in 1944. On March 23, 1948, he was sworn in as lieutenant governor of Saskatchewan and held that position until his death, in office, on June 15, 1951.

HAK

A CPR line runs south of Swift Current and branches at Hak. One line goes to Tyson and the other line goes to Meyronne. This is the only place in Saskatchewan that we know of that is named for the initials of a man — H. A. K. Drury, who was an engineer with the Board of Railway Commissioners when this line was being built.

HALBRITE
Halbrite is about halfway between Weyburn and Estevan on the CPR. It got its name from the last names of three civil engineers who built the railroad, Hall, Bruce and White.

Halbrite was incorporated as a village in 1904.

HALBSTADT
Halbstadt is a Mennonite village five miles southeast of Hague. The German name means Half Town when translated into English. It was homesteaded in 1899 by the following families: John and Peter Ens, William Fehr and John Peter.

HALFWAY HOUSE
In the late 1880's, one of Saskatchewan's trails ran north from Swift Current to Battleford. About halfway along this route was a carter-stop which included a stable, a log house and a store. Eventually, about 1905, a church and a Northwest Mounted Police station were built and several dwellings added.

There is hardly a vestige of this site left fifteen miles southwest of Biggar. It's on private land and foundations are reasonably preserved.

The town of Biggar, for its size, has a splendid working museum. Under the direction of its curator, Agnes Wilson, it has a project underway now to built a miniature replica of Halfway House as it was in 1885.

The police had a special name for their station, 60-Mile-Bush, because it centred on a bush that actually ran for sixty miles.

Other individuals had still another name for it "Frenchman's Retreat". I have not been able to find the significance of the last name.

HALKETT
Halkett is very close to Estevan. It was named for Mr. A. Halkett, a CPR superintendent.

HALLONQUIST
Hallonquist is on a branch line of the CPR from Tyson to Hak. In the summer of 1902, the Turkey Track cattle were in motion, 25,000 of them, and 600 horses, moving north and west. It was the last of the major cattle drives. The route led out of South Dakota, to Billings, Montana, and then north to cross the boundary. At the border, Tony Day paid $40,000 to meet the duty demands of the Canadian Customs. The Turkey Track was now a Canadian brand and one of the administrative centres of this famous ranch was near Hallonquist.

Cattle grazed from Hallonquist to the American border, west past Maple Creek and east as far as the settlers would let them. When the CPR came to the district in 1923, they named it Hallonquist in honor of J. E. Hallonquist, a CPR employee of Moose Jaw who had been decorated for bravery in the First World War.

HAMLIN
The Canadian Northern Railway built north from North Battleford in 1909. The first stop was Hamlin. This name was taken from John Hamilton on whose homestead the hamlet was situated and Joe Nolin the first settler in the district in 1890 and moved north of Jackfish lake in 1905. At one time he was MLA for the Meadow Lake area. Nolin No. 903, a country school, close to Hamlin and right on the highway to Meadow Lake was named for Joe Nolin.

HAMTON
This information was taken from a booklet of the R.M. of Sliding Hills which was put out to commemorate Canora's centennial. The hamlet of Hamton, about 15 miles southeast of Canora, is on the Russell, Manitoba, branch of the CNR that runs northwest and joins the main line at Ross Junction, a short distance east of Canora.

Place names came about in many unique ways. Hamton was named for one of the earliest residents of the district, a rancher by the name of Charlie Hammond. Mr. Hammond put up tons and tons of hay to winter his stock, hence the name Hamton. We are indebted to Mr. Merlin M. Roske of R.R. 2, Canora, a grandson of Mr. Hammond, for this information.

Today (1972) Hamton has three elevators, one general store and service station, a community hall and seven dwellings. The population is 17.

HANDEL

Handel, a predominately German settlement is named in honor of George Fredrick Handel (1685-1759), and outstanding German composer. He is best known for his oratorios, especially the immortal Messiah.

Three of the streets in the village bear the names of other famous German musicians: Wagner, Schuman and Mozart.

HANDSWORTH

In 1923 grading started on a CNR spur line south from Peebles to Handsworth, a distance of 22 miles. It was completed and the rails laid by the fall of 1924. The United Grain Growers and Co-operative Elevator Co. built elevators there to take in the 1924 crop.

In the spring of 1926 the land was surveyed into lots across the tracks from the elevators and the little village of Handsworth came into being on the northeast quarter of 25-10-8. The name Handsworth was given as there had been a country post office by that name nearby for a number of years. The name for it had been suggested by Mrs. Clara Wilson, whose former home was in Handsworth, England.

HANLEY

This information is from the booklet on Hanley compiled by the high school students in 1955: "Just how the name was chosen, we can only speculate. A map of the Northwest Territories copyrighted in 1891 bore the name of 'Hanley,' thus eliminating the possibility of its having been selected by early settlers. Attempts to connect it with Hanley, Staffordshire, England, have hinted at the possibility that the name was chosen in honor of that town by some individual associated with the construction of the Qu'Appelle, Long Lake and Saskatchewan Railway."

Also, from Mr. J. A. "Dewey" Nystuen, long-time merchant of Hanley, came the following information:

On April 30, 1889, the government of Canada granted $80,000 annually to the Qu'Appelle, Long Lake and Saskatchewan Railway and Steamboat Company in exchange for free transportation for government officials. In addition, the railway received a land subsidy of 6400 acres per mile to construct a railway linking Prince Albert with Regina crossing the South Saskatchewan river at Saskatoon. Within a year the line was a reality and Hanley, 40 miles south of Saskatoon, was an important point on this line. In 1905 the Canadian Northern built seventeen miles north of Saskatoon at Warman. The GTP survey at that time showed it crossing the south-north railway at Hanley and for a short while it looked as though Saskatoon was to be just an ordinary town and Warman and Hanley would become cities.

Hanley had high hopes and one item that entered into them was the construction of an "opera house." It's long since closed but it should be preserved as a museum. Just consider these two excerpts from the *Hanley Herald* of 1909:

"Tom Marks and his company will appear in the Hanley Opera House on Friday and Saturday, April 9th and 10th. Tonight (Friday) they will present the play called "The Irish Immigrant" and on Saturday evening "The Hypocrite." There will also be a matinee performance on Saturday Afternoon."

Another reads:

"E. De Alva Sutherland, the Hindoo healer, is at the Hanley Opera House this week, advertising his great Hindoo remedies, and many claim to have benefited greatly by them. Mr. Sutherland is not a Hindoo; he was born in Galt, Ontario." etc. etc.

The booklet referred to at the start of the Hanley story was compiled by the high school students under the guidance of Mr. George Chase, the principal. Today (1972) Dr. George Chase is a professor at the University of Toronto.

On August 5, 1972, another story came to light on the naming of Hanley. It came from Jack Cotton who arrived in Hanley at the age of four in 1911. He tells of hearing a story from T. O. Hamre, longtime storekeeper in the town, that the name came from early American settlers in the district who came from Hanley Falls, Minnesota. Ole Nelson, another oldtimer in Hanley backs up this story. It's possible, too, since other places like Cavalier, Cando and Spiritwood are place names that came in with settlers from the United States.

HARDY

Hardy is named for Thomas Hardy (1840-1928), one of Britain's greatest novelists. He was also a distinguished poet. He concerned himself particularly with the part that fate plays in the lives of men and women. Many other authors have been honored by having towns and villages in Saskatchewan named for them: Wordsworth, Carlyle, Service, Cowper, Lampman, and Ryerson.

Archie Kelly, a pioneer storekeeper of the district who sold everything from needles to threshing machines, wrote of some of his experiences with the railroad in the early days. Here they are in his own words:

"I rode up from Radville to Richie in May of 1912, a distance of 40 miles and some of the box cars jumped the tracks 13 times. Sometimes if a car was too hard to put back on the track they would push it into the ditch. In 1916 the train got stuck in the snow west of Roe and we had no service for six weeks. For three weeks I did not have a fire in the store. My mother and two sisters lived with me in rooms behind the store and we did our cooking on a coal heater. We had more coal than most people, some burned oats and some used flax straw."

HARFIELD

Harfield is made up of the first three letters of the name of A. E. Harshaw and the last five letters of the name of C. E. Mansfield, both chief dispatchers for the CPR.

HARLAN

Harlan is a country post office on the North Saskatchewan. The mail comes by truck twice a week from Frenchman Butte, just down the river a little.

Mr. Lewis and Mr. Gibbs and their families were the first into the district in 1909. They came from Harlan, Iowa, U.S.A. and the name Harlan was given in honor of the birthplace.

That same year Sam Woods and Ed Oxby came by boat down the river from Edmonton and located homesteads for their families which they moved onto in 1910.

HARPTREE

This was ranching country before the settlers began to arrive in 1905. William Halwell, the first settler, and a large number of his followers, came from Harptree, England. When the post office was opened in 1911 by William Start they named it Harptree. When the CNR extended a line west from Bengough to Willow Bunch in the fall of 1926 the country post office of Harptree, halfway between these points, gave its name to the new townsite.

HARRIS

In 1904, Richard Harris, a farmer of Huron County, Ontario, came west. He located halfway between Goose lake and Crystal Beach, or Devil's lake as it was called and they found the Harris home a good place to stop for a rest.

As more settlers arrived there became a need for a post office and one was established in the Harris home for which it was named. When the railroad came through as far as Zealandia in 1908 it missed the "Harris Stopping Place" by two miles. The post office and the little hamlet that had grown up around it then moved south to the railroad and gave its name to the town.

HART

Hart is between Fife Lake and Coronach on a CPR line in south-central Saskatchewan. It's only twelve miles from the international boundary. It took its name from an early post office in the district which was operated by Mr. Hart.

HARTWELL

Hartwell if the first stop east of Turtleford on a line of the CNR to Glaslyn that was built in the 1920s. It was named for Fraser Hartwell on whose land the village site was located.

HATFIELD

Hatfield is on the CPR six miles east of the north tip of Last Mountain lake. All that's left is the name since they moved the elevator in 1969. It was named for a town in Hartfordshire, England, seat of the Marquis of Salisbury.

HATHERLEIGH

Hatherleigh is on a CNR line that jogs north and west of Medstead. The name possibly came from Hatherleigh in Devon, England. The English market town is straight north and a considerable distance from Plymouth. The most historic building in the town is a church that is 500 years old. Hatherleigh Moor is close by and it is an area of high rainfall and badly drained land known as culm measures. This moor is of some 430 acres and was given to the inhabitants for grazing their cattle and cutting furze (or gorse) for fuel. One writer refers to this market town as resembling Abilene on market day and the owners of one of the pubs there has renamed it the Rodeo Inn and decorated it like a saloon of 1890 Texas!

HATTON

Hatton is in the extreme southwest corner of the province near Maple Creek. It was named for Mr. A. Hatton, general superintendent of transportation of the CPR in Montreal.

This is a place that changed its name. It started out as Forres and was incorporated into a village in 1912 under that name. However, in 1920 railway officials made the switch in name to Hatton. This was a Scottish name given, no doubt, by the directors of the company.

HAULTAIN

Haultain, an elevator a few miles south of Saskatoon, is named in honor of Sir Frederick William Gordon Haultain (1857-1942). Canadian jurist and provincial government official; premier, attorney general, and commissioner of education, Northwest Territories (1891-1905); member of legislative assembly, Saskatchewan (1905-1912); chief justice of supreme court, Saskatchewan (1912-1938).

HAWARDEN

Hawarden is on a CPR line about half way between Outlook and Elbow. It got its name from Sir William E. Gladtone's estate, Hawarden, in Wales. William Ewart Gladstone was the most famous political leader of England during the reign of Queen Victoria. He served as prime minister of Britain four times. He was the first prime minister to take up the fight for Irish Home Rule.

The streets of Hawarden are named for him and his family. Main street is Gladstone and two on either side of it are named William and Ewart.

HAWKER

Easton was a grain loading platform about seven miles out on the main line from Saskatoon to Calgary. It was named for John Van Eaton who farmed extensively in the area.

Later the name was changed by the railway officials to Hawker to honor Captain George Hawker who flew the North Atlantic to Europe in the early years of the century.

Hawker never had an elevator, just a small station (used mostly for picking up cream cans) and the loading platform for grain. All that is left today is a passing track.

HAWKEYE

Hawkeye siding has been closed, Hawkeye post office has been closed, but the name lives on in the school district for which they were all named.

Many of the early settlers in this district came from Iowa. The first group consisted of the families of Mr. Stewart, Mr. McRory, Mr. Bear, and Mr. Nicholl. Later the Aylesworths, Knights, and Wymans arrived.

Iowa is called the Hawkeye state. This honors Black Hawk, a chief of the Sauk Indians, who fought bravely to keep their hunting grounds. Settlers from that state were often nicknamed Hawkeyes. They were proud of it and that's how we have a Hawkeye in Saskatchewan.

In 1915 the early settlers named their school district Hawkeye. In 1917 the first post office got the name and finally when the CNR arrived in 1929 the siding got the name, Hawkeye.

HAWOODS

Hawoods is just a little west of Saskatoon. Before the railway came the area was known as Bridgeford. With the coming of the railroad a townsite was purchased which consisted of huge hay flats, stretching south towards the bluffs, or woods, which surrounded Rice lake, at that time called Couleau's lake for a Metis who ranched there. It was called Haywoods but later the "y" was dropped.

HAZEL BANK

Hazel Bank was an inland post office (now closed) eight miles northeast of Handsworth. Both the post office and school district were named by Mrs. T. Harkness in 1912 for her birthplace in Scotland.

HAZELCLIFFE

Hazelcliffe is between Esterhazy and Tantallon. It had a post office in 1892 and a school in 1893. Mr. William Delmage, the first postmaster, named it Hazelcliffe because of the abundance of hazel nuts growing on the banks of the Little Cut Arm creek which flowed near his farm.

HAZEL DELL

Hazel Dell is on a branch line of the CNR that runs from Sturgis northwest to Kelvington. This district was opened in 1906 and the first group of settlers came from Hazel Dell, Minnesota. That accounts for the name.

The railway grade was laid in 1913 but it was used as a highway until the steel arrived in 1919.

HAZELWOOD

A post office was opened in 1899 and given this name because of a grove of hazel nut bushes in the area. The post office is closed and the residents now get their mail at Kipling. The municipality still carries on the name Hazelwood.

HAZENMORE

R. W. Jewitt came to this district in 1909. He opened a post office and store five miles north and three miles east of the present site of Hazenmore. The name of the post office was Stellena, named for his wife Stella.

Before the railway came through he made 67 trips to Morse, 50 miles to the north, with team and wagon. In the fall of 1910 he took his wife and family of five by wagon to Swift Current for the winter. It was 65 miles away and it took two-and-a-half days to get there.

When the CPR came in 1913 the post office was moved into the townsite which had been named Hazenmore in honor of

Sir John Hazen, at the time minister of fisheries in the Borden cabinet and formerly a premier of News Brunswick. The post office then took the name of Hazenmore.

HAZLET

In 1928 the CPR built a branch line south from Wickett to Verlo. Hazlet is the second last stop on that line. It is a small town of 220 people but it has a large consolidated school of 300 children. The town was named for one of the first settlers in the district, Ike Hazlet, who came in 1911, long before the railway.

HEADLANDS

Mr. Archie Lochhead started Headlands post office in his home on the S.E. quarter of 34-24-14-W2 in 1905. He named the office for a place in Scotland. Mr. Kelsey brought the mail out from Lipton and Mr. G. T. North picked up the Garnock mail and took it to the Garnock post office which was in the home of Robert Nairn nine miles to the northeast.

The Headlands post office moved about. Mr. Gilliston took over in 1914 and had it until 1917 when John Leslie moved it to his home and kept it until 1938. John Fleming then took over until the post office closed in the mid 1940's. Mr. Leslie was an obliging man and brought out supplies for his neighbors — coal oil, binder twine, groceries and the like. He would also shop for needles and thread for the ladies.

HEARNE

Hearne is between Avonlea and Briercrest. Hugh Patterson and his son, Joseph, were the first settlers. They arrived in 1901 and lived in an overturned wagon box for several months until they could get their sod shack built. They broke their land with oxen. It wasn't long before they had plenty of neighbors, the Rogers, Baldwins, Mintos, Peacheys, Thompsons, Websters, McCreas, Clarkes, Daniels, and Moores to name just a few.

The village of Hearne came into being in 1912 when the CNR built a line from Moose Jaw through to Radville. The name was taken from one of the men who worked on the construction gang. Like countless other prairie villages Hearne knew booming times with a store, a blacksmith shop, a garage, a lumber yard, a post office, a pool room, and three elevators. All that are left are the post office, store, and the elevators.

HEARTS HILL

In 1912, Hearts Hill R.M. 352 was formed with Messrs. Weybrecht, Rhodes, Harrow (reeve), Stetser, Currins, Mosentine, Saunders and Moscup as councillors. It was this municipality that gave its name, first to the local school, and then to the grain point located on the CNR Unity to Brodo, Alberta, line, that came through in 1930. The name Hearts Hill itself was taken from a range of hills in the municipality whose configuration at the top looked, from a distance, like hearts. The Indians called Hearts Hill, "Ha-ou-ta-at-tim-ak."

There is much good land in the municipality as a whole but in the immediate vicinity of the hills it is rolly, bluffy and sandy. Many of the people who homesteaded there in the early days let their land go for taxes. Mr. Body, a rancher, bought up quite a tract — in fact, at one time, he knew how many acres he had but not how many cattle. His son, Tom, still operates "Body's Ranch."

There is a Pool elevator at Hearts Hill, and general store and post office operated by Ray Bronsensky.

HEDNESFORD

The post office and district were named by a family of Bartons who came from Hednesford in Straffordshire, England.

HENDON

Hendon is the second stop from Wadena on a CPR line running north to Nipawin. It was named for Hendon, a town in England.

HENRIBOURG

Henry Albert Morin was a very influential early settler in the district. Residents suggested that the village be called Morrinville in his honor but there was already a place by that name in Saskatchewan. They settled for Henribourg. When the district next to Henribourg opened up they named it Albertville in honor of Mr. Morin.

HEPBURN

Hepburn is one of those pioneer villages in Saskatchewan whose beginning was prompted by the need of a central trading point. When the railway came through, Gordon Hepburn donated 40 acres for a town site. The town was named in his honor.

Today the railway is seldom used and some day soon transport trucks may do all the hauling.

HERBERT

Herbert is located on No. 1 Trans-Canada highway thirty miles east of Swift Current. Two of the earliest settlers were Abram Goertzen and Diedrich Schultz. They arrived in the early 1900s. Growth was rapid and in 1912 Herbert was incorporated as a town with well over 1000 of a population. It was named for an English diplomat, Sir Michael Henry Herbert, who had a distinguished career in the British Foreign Service.

HERSCHEL

Herschel is on a CPR line that runs northwest from Rosetown to Macklin. It is named for John Frederick William Herschel (1792-1871), an English astronomer. He continued his famous father's studies on double stars and nebulae. He contributed to further knowledge of the Milky Way, brightness and color or stars, variable stars, and Magellanic Clouds. He also made important discoveries in the field of photography.

Herschel sits in the valley of an old river bed through which the Eagle creek now runs. Some of the earliest settlers were: Michael Hollick; Henry Cargill; Ernest and Alfred Beckett; William Heatherington; Donald McCallum; William and Henry Seymour; Robert Craig; Henry Todd; David Clarke; William Thompson; Eugene Crowe; Andrew Lawson; Wesley, Rodney, and William Walker; John Elgren.

HEWARD

Heward is on a CPR line in the southeastern corner of the province between Stoughton and Creelman. In the summer of 1900 Ham Caldwell homesteaded on sec. 22-9-9-W2. Another to arrive at that time was Bill Irwin. The first village did not start where Heward now stands but was on Ham Caldwell's land a quarter of a mile northeast. This village was called Caldwell. Here, a store was set up by Phil Munroe in a tent until a frame building was erected. A lumberyard and livery stable were added. This was in 1903.

In the spring of 1904 the CPR surveyed a site nearby. Mr. Munroe packed his goods in boxes and put them out on the snow. Tom Henderson picked them up and unloaded them at the new railway site. The railway did not accept the name of Caldwell as suggested by the settlers. Instead they called the village Heward to honor A. R. G. Heward, former assistant secretary of the CPR in Montreal.

The settlers did not object very strenuously because they were glad not to have to haul their wheat 35 miles to Arcola or Weyburn. Also, coal could now be shipped in and this saved a 40-mile trek to Estevan.

HEWITT LANDING

Hewitt Landing was the first post office north of Lloydminster. It opened on December 1, 1905, in the Hewitt home located at 1-53-27-W3. This was situated at the ferry that crossed the North Saskatchewan river between the Hudson's Bay post at Onion Lake and Lloydminster.

Louis William Hewitt emigrated from England to South Edmonton in 1897. He was employed in the lumber industry. In 1903 the Barr Colonists came to make their home in what is known as the Lloydminster district. There was no railroad between Saskatoon and Edmonton. Louis Hewitt was asked to be the agent to sell lumber to the colonists. He accepted the offer and decided to build a new home on the site. He came down the North Saskatchewan river from Edmonton on a raft loaded with lumber and necessary supplies. He landed on the south shore three miles from old Fort Pitt, unloaded the cargo and set up temporary quarters. The next year he built a house and other buildings just above where he landed.

His venture proved to be very rewarding, for many Barr Colonists who had been living in tents made haste to make the twenty-five mile trip to the "Landing"

for this lumber in order to get a house of some kind built before winter set in.

Louis Hewitt owned the first ferry at Hewitt Landing. It was built by Walter's Mill in 1904. After Saskatchewan became a province in 1905 he was the first government ferryman for the Fort Pitt Ferry.

HIGHGATE

Highgate is on the CNR line 11 miles west of Battleford and half a mile off number five highway. It is a very small hamlet now, that at one time was a good sized village. The railway came in 1905 and the name Highgate Siding was given to it by the first train coductor, Harry Cameron, who had emigrated from Highgate, England.

HIGH POINT

High Point was an inland post office south and east of Sanctuary. It was located on 15-23-14-W3. The first postmaster was Lester Alexander. The post office closed in 1969 and in that year the population was listed as 12. There is no significance to the name, it is just a geographic description of the locality. This follows a pattern of giving place names, as elsewhere in Saskatchewan we have Flat Valley, Bog End and Hillside.

HIGH TOR

High Tor is a rural post office (now closed) near Porcupine Plain. High Tor is Scottish for high hill. It was named by Mrs. George Rhodes after a district near her home in England.

Harold Baldwin of Swift Current is one of the two male survivors of a handful of men who pushed their way into the wilderness north of the beginning of Kelvington in the fall of 1920. They came to hack soldiers' settlement farms out of the dense bushland. Mr. Baldwin pays tribute to the womenfolk of the settlement this way: "Twas a case of the isolated band to 'root, hog or die', and most of them rooted successfully, aided and abetted by their womenfolk. And among these brave ladies was Mary (Molly) Herbert, recently deceased.

Mrs. Herbert was the mother of Jack Herbert, well known in Saskatchewan for his academic career and for his historical research which led to the establishment of a number of museums.

Most of the children born in the remote wilderness settlement came into this world with the assistance of Mrs. Herbert and Mrs. Jim Forbes. One wonders if the children of today can ever conceive of what pioneer women like the High Tor volunteer midwives endured in their journeys to women in labor. It often seemed that babies insisted on being born while blizzards raged or cascading rains made trails just thin avenues of mud and water.

Molly Herbert was involved in every community affair that was organized to try to make pioneer living a little more bearable. At dances and concerts, to which people came many miles through the bush by sleigh or on horseback, she would be extracting music from a wheezy old organ. Programs were usually the result of her work or her supervision. No activity was complete without her participation. Perhaps her greatest contribution of all was to the morale of the people who lived largely on hope and the produce wrung out of the wild bush country."

HILLANDALE

Hillandale is near Val Marie which is the terminal of a CPR branch line out of Notukeu. This region, because of its hills and valleys, was appropriately so called by Mrs. Robert Southcombe, a pioneer lady.

HILLBURN

Hillburn was an inland post office (it closed in 1905) at S25-T15-R32-W1, about halfway between Wapella and Welwyn.

Mr. Hill, one of the first settlers in the district, operated the post office. Being of Scottish descent he just added burn to his name. A "burn" is Scottish for small creek.

It was an appealing and descriptive name and even though the post office is gone the name lingers in the district. This information was sent to us by Miss H. McMullen, 125 Pioneer Lodge, Moose Jaw, Saskatchewan.

HILLMOND

The CPR ran a short branch line northeast of Lloydminster in 1928 and it ended at Hillmond. The village was named for two men who lost their lives in the First World War, Raymond Hill and Mr. Desmond. Mr. Hill had homesteaded in the district in 1912.

HILLSIDE

Hillside post office is just east of Jackfish lake. It is located at 23-47-15-W3. E. J. Carr was the first postmaster. The post office took its name from a description of its geographical location on the side of a hill. Other places in Saskatchewan which were named in the same manner are Hillandale, High Hill, Lone Spruce and Poplar Bluff.

HINCHCLIFFE

Hinchcliffe is on a CNR line which runs north from Canora to Hudson Bay. Originally it was called Etomami but when the first overseas flight to carry passengers from England to America was made in 1930 — the same year the railway was being built — it was decided to change the name to Hinchcliffe to honor the pilot of the plane.

HIRSCH

Hirsch, 15 miles east of Estevan is named in honor of Baron de Hirsch, who founded a Jewish Colonization Association. In 1890 he was able to authorize disbursements of $500 loans per family for settlement of 60 families on farms in western Canada. In the spring of 1892 47 families were selected and sent to the Hirsch Colony site.

HITCHCOCK

Hitchcock is 9 miles northwest of Estevan and has never exceeded the size of a hamlet. There is only one place of business left in the hamlet, and that's the Pool elevator operated by Harold Bettridge.

The first settler was Peter McDonald who homesteaded on the Souris river four miles to the south, in 1888. The first building was a store built in 1903 by Mr. Deuchesneru of Bottineau, North Dakota. Next a hotel went up with Mr. Forcier running it, then a lumberyard with Mr. Sindahl in charge. Over the years these were all closed as it was found that Estevan to the south became a shorter trip with improved roads and cars.

The name came about in an odd way. In the boom days of the early 1900s two men from Moose Jaw visited the hamlet with the thought of opening a branch of the Royal Bank. It did not materialize but one of them, Mr. Arthur Hitchcock, left his name.

The post office closed in 1957 but after years of decline Hitchcock has recently had a face-lifting. Many of the old vacant homes have been taken over by young couples who commute to Estevan and south to Coalfields to work.

HOCHFELD

Hochfeld is one of a cluster of Mennonite villages northwest of Hague. The German translation into English is High Field. The first settlers came into this area of 1899 and first families included the following: Peter and John Wall, Jacob and Gerhard Bartsch, Gerhard Janzen, Johann Harms and Jacob Klassen.

It would be well to describe the Old Colony custom of handling cattle: About seven o'clock in the morning the village herdsman would start his daily drive — a walk from one end of the street to the other — all gates were opened and the cattle would be driven to the "fence". The fence was a commonly owned community pasture. The herdsman would drive all cows, heifers, calves and one bull to the fence for pasture. In the evening the herdsman drove the cattle back down the street and each animal knew its own home. Summer milking was done outside in the cow pen and one of the cow's hind legs was peg-tied to prevent it "kicking the bucket." Each owner contributed a small amount of goods or money to the herdsman. It was oftentimes customary that the herdsman be the schoolteacher for six to eight months of the winter season when the cattle were being housed and stall fed.

HOCHSTADT

Hochstadt is a Mennonite village two miles southwest of Hague. It's a high-sounding name and means Big City. This is not unknown to other place names of Saskatchewan with its White City, a small building development eleven miles east of Regina, and Uranium City in our northland.

HODGEVILLE

Hodgeville is about thirty miles southeast of Swift Current on a CNR line. The first settler was Mr. Tom Walsh and he ran the T. W. ranch. Many settlers came in around 1908 and a post office was established in 1910. Mr. Hodges was postmaster and it was he who named the community Hodgeville.

When the CNR arrived in 1921 they accepted the name. Hodgeville was incorporated as a village in the same year, 1921.

HOEY

Hoey was named after the first homesteader in the district, Captain Hoey. He was of Scottish descent and settled here in 1885. Oliva Baribeau, a retired postmaster of Hoey, gave this information and he in turn learned it from his uncle, Joe Baribeau. Some of the early settlers in the district were Joubert, Autet, Guillet, Marsollier and Blondeau. Hoey is predominately a French community.

HOFFER

It was April 1, 1926, when the CPR unloaded horses, machinery, men, tents, cabooses and boxcars in Bromhead to start a branch line east to Minton. Oungre was the first townsite; Hoffer was the second. It was named in honor of Israel and Mayer Hoffer who did so much to promote the line.

Determined farmers, many of Jewish extraction, got the blessing of Mr. Motherwell and the astute advice of Sir Henry Thornton and parlayed it into a bluff which caused the CPR to build.

HOFFNUNGSORT

Hoffnungsort is a small Mennonite village (ort in English means village) close to Hague. The whole name means Village of Hope. It was settled between 1900 and 1905. First families included: John Quiring, Abe Buhler, Henry Funk and Jacob Andres. In visiting cemeteries in the area you find them well kept. Some graves show a mound of grass but no headstone. These graves for the most part are those of "Old Colony" Mennonites. This practice was not dictated by lack of money; it was part of their belief — God knew where they were and that was enough.

HOLBEIN

Holbein is 20 miles northeast of Prince Albert. A local homesteader J. N. Miller suggested the name for the post office in honor of a painter, Holbein, whose work he admired greatly.

HOLDFAST

Holdfast is north of Regina on the west side of Long lake. The first settlers came in 1904 and were of Russian-German descent. The CPR came in 1910 and proposed to build on the east side of the existing village. John A. Fahlman who owned the land couldn't come to terms with the railroad officials and so the rails went west of the village. The farmer who was so determined to "hold fast" to his land gave the name to the town of Holdfast.

HOLLGARTH

Hollgarth was named for a town in England. In Saskatchewan it opened an inland post office January 18, 1913 and closed September 30, 1924.

An incident which people still remember happening in the district occurred when Saskatchewan went "dry" in the 30's. Bootlegging had flourished and the local bootlegger was caught and convicted. The fine was $100 or a term in jail. He went to his regular customers and collected ten dollars from each on the promise that when everything blew over he would deliver a gallon of brew. So he was able to pay his fine and stay out of jail. All of which proves where there's a will there's a way!

HOLLOWAY

Holloway is between Halbrite and Midale on a CPR line in the southeast corner of the province. It was named for Edward Holloway, a locomotive foreman who worked out of Estevan.

HOLMES

Holmes, a small railway (Canadian National) point south of Prince Albert was named after a former mayor of Prince Albert, Andrew Holmes who came over to Canada from Scotland in 1881, four years before the Riel Rebellion, and worked his way up from being an apprentice carpenter to being a large contractor who built many of the buildings

and fine homes now to be seen in Prince Albert. He became mayor before the First World War. It is interesting how he arrived at Prince Albert.

He worked for a time in Winnipeg, then went up Lake Winnipeg to Grand Rapids by Hudson's Bay Company boat. At the Rapids he and a group of other immigrants from England and Scotland hired several Indians and their canoes as guides to take them upstream to Prince Albert. They paddled against the current many days before arriving at Prince Albert.

Oddly enough, while Mr. Holmes came to Prince Albert against the current, the young red-headed Irish girl he married came by barge downstream from Medicine Hat in 1884, to where the north and south Saskatchewan rivers fork, then from the forks to Prince Albert by wagon.

HONEYMOON

Honeymoon is an inland post office about twenty miles northeast of Prince Albert and very close to the Garden river. The community opened up in 1914 with the arrival of 18 Ukrainian families. Prominent among these were the following: Zbaraschuk, Palidvar, Chreschovetz and Rusnitsky.

One of the first things the settlers did was build a school which they named Podole in memory of the district they came from in the Ukraine. Next came a church and then they applied for a post office. Postal officials gave them the name Honeymoon, perhaps to make it easier for the people to endure their hardships.

Michael John (Mike) Kindrachuk, area superintendent of Saskatoon public schools in 1970, was one of the teachers who taught in the district.

HOOD

Hood is a grain point between Druid and Plenty on a CPR line. It was likely named for L. E. Hood. Lew was born in Indiana, and moved to North Dakota after his marriage. He moved to Saskatoon in 1909 and filed on a homestead a quarter of a mile from Anglia. Lew knew less than nothing about homesteading and he moved back to Saskatoon, where he worked in a hotel. His wife and her children, Gladdie, Sid and Glee stayed and "proved up."

In 1912 Mr. Hood teamed up with Dave Shields and they went into the construction business at Rosetown. For the next four years the family lived in Rosetown during the school year and moved out to Anglia in the summer where Mrs. Hood ran a small general store.

In the spring of 1919 a telephone exchange was built at Plenty. Mrs. Hood applied for the job as agent and got it. Six weeks later she died. Mr. Hood then took his family to Plenty where he bought a livery stable and operated a dray for the next twenty years. After that he lived in retirement at Plenty and passed away in 1949.

HOODOO

Hoodoo is one of the most intriguing place names in Saskatchewan. A natural formation of a column of rock, often in fantastic form because of wind erosion, is called a hoodoo. These are common in the Badlands east of Drumheller, Alberta. But there was not the slightest similarity between the wonder of nature and the reason for naming a school 8 to 10 miles straight east of Cudworth, Hoodoo. Here is how it happened.

Mrs. Olivia, an old French grandmother who homesteaded in that district, was responsible for the name. She spoke no English and in greeting people instead of saying, "How do you do?" said, "Hoodoo!" This unusual salutation captured the imagination of the residents and before long everyone was using it. Eventually the entire district fell heir to this aberration. The school, the post office, the church and finally the municipality were all named Hoodoo.

Many of the first settlers into this district came from Minnesota, U.S.A., as far as Rosthern by train and then trekked east to their homesteads. A few of the first ones were: Ben Billisberger, Mattie DeMond, Mike Renneberg, Jake Eul, John Duerr, Henry Grending, John and Paul Wilde, Tony Serfect, Tony Croll, "Poppa" Benny, along with the Baders and Gyorericks. Coming from the States as they did their first love in sports was baseball and their team was noted far and wide both for their playing ability and their name, "The Stubble Jumpers."

HOOSIER

There were already several settlers in the Hoosier district when an advance group of Americans arrived from Indiana in 1909. They had come by GTP to Scott and then drove south by democrat in search of land. They located between Loverna and Smiley in a settlement that became known as Hoosier Valley. Just as inhabitants of our Maritimes came to be known as "Bluenoses" the early residents from Indiana were known as "Hoosiers". This came about by their habit of calling out "Hoosier?" (Meaning who's there?) when someone knocked at their door.

A post office was opened in the Valley in 1912 in the home of Mr. J. Yoos, one of the Americans, and he named it Hoosier Valley. When the Grand Trunk Pacific arrived in 1913, two and one-half miles south of Mr. Yoos' post office they proposed to call the townsite "Fee". The residents, now augmented by more American arrivals urged that the name be changed to Hoosier Valley. The officials settled for Hoosier.

HORIZON

The CPR built west from Pangman in 1912 and arrived at Horizon the same year. The name Horizon came indirectly from one of the survey crew. As the crew reached the spot that is now the town of Horizon they found themselves on a plateau between small lakes and looking south they could see the clouds over the Big Muddy Hills 25 miles away. One member exclaimed, "Well, for once, I can see over the horizon!"

The first settlers came to Horizon and district in 1907. They came by the old wagon trail that stretched from Winnipeg to Willow Bunch. This trail, still visible in parts, passed 300 yards south of where the village now stands. Among the first settlers to enter the district were Mike, Frank, Max and Peter Kisslering, John Nagy, Charlie Voight, Aubrey Parmenter, Oscar and Hugo Hesterman, Norman Brisbin and Charles Malone.

HORSE BUTTE

Horse Butte was the name of an inland post office (now closed) and a rural school on the north side of the South Saskatchewan river S25-T20-R16-W3,

143

close to the present Saskatchewan Landing.

The name come from Indians who used it to describe a range of hills in the vicinity.

HORSE CREEK

Horse Creek is an inland post office fourteen miles south of McCord. It was named for Horse creek nearby which flows north into Wood river and on to Old Wives' lake. The post office was opened in 1916 by Harold and Ed Smith. They had a small store in conjunction with the post office.

When Harold went into the service in World War I the post office and store was turned over to the Chalettes family. They had it only a short while when they turned it over to Emery Tetreau who kept it for forty years. On his retirement Emery was commended as having served in that capacity the longest in any country post office in Saskatchewan. Emery turned the post office over to Alex Tetreau and he was postmaster until the post office closed in 1968. Horse Creek people now get their mail in McCord and the children are bussed in to school there, too.

HORSE HEAD

"Horse Head is 35 miles from a railway. It is equal distance from St. Walburg and Meadow Lake. The district was opened in 1928 by a trapper named Austin. The first homesteaders: Long, McDonald, Blythe, Graham and Moncrief, came in the late 20s. Mr. Austin and his brother kept a stopping house at Horse Head Crossing on Dead Horse creek which flows into the Horse Head river.

The river circles the district and whether it is shaped like a horse's head or whether a horse's head was found near it can only be guessed, but the post office got its name from settlers going into St. Walburg, the earliest supply centre, and asking for the Horse Head settler's mail.

HORSE LAKE

Horse Lake, an inland post office now closed, was located at S6-T28-R12-W2. This is just east of the Touchwood Hills. The post office tooks its name from a small lake eight miles to the east which was roughly shaped like a horse.

HORSHAM

Horsham is a little hamlet located approximately fifty-five miles northwest of Maple Creek and five miles east of the Alberta border on a CPR line that comes from Alberta and ends at Fox Valley. The present population is nineteen.

Mixed farming and cattle ranching are the main sources of livelihood. The hamlet was incorporated in 1924 when the CPR built in to the site. It was named by railroad officials after a city by the same name in Sussex, England.

The first family to arrive was that of Mr. and Mrs. Frederick C. Haskell. Mr. Haskell built a general store in 1929 and it stayed in the family until it was sold seven years ago to Mr. and Mrs. Elmer Lang.

HUBBARD

Hubbard is between Ituna and Goodeve on the main line of the CNR. The name was chosen by GTP officials to fit into an alphabetical pattern: As the line came out of Melville they started at Fenwood and kept the order almost intact to Zelma and then started over with Allan. It was reputed that Mr. Hubbard was a GTP official.

In 1907, the steel reached Hubbard and a new village was born on the prairies. The first store was opened by Mr. S. E. Riggs of Abernethy. The nearest post office was at the farm home of Alec Longmore a few miles south of the Hubbard townsite. It was named Drumague. The citizens of Hubbard applied to the federal government for a post office and it was granted in April of 1909 with Mr. S. Chipperfield as the first postmaster. The Drumague post office closed up. Mr. Robert Longmore was the first justice of the peace. Mr. Black opened an implement business.

In 1910, the village of Hubbard was incorporated with Mr. W. H. Black, Mr. Thomas Burns and Mr. S. Chipperfield as the first council. Mr. Burns was appointed the first overseer. Mr. Burns operated the first livery stable and kept some fine horses.

Some of the highlights of the early Hubbard days were the Ukrainian weddings. They were very well attended, lively and full of songs, with dancing that sometimes lasted for days.

HUDSON BAY

Originally Hudson Bay was called Eto-mami, an Indian word meaning "three rivers join together." This name dates back more than 160 years to the fur trading days in the 18th century.

In 1909 the settlement was renamed Hudson Bay Junction. The "Junction" part was officially dropped when the village was incorporated as a town in 1947.

HUGHTON

The first group of settlers arrived in the district in 1905. Some came from Davidson, others came by way of Saskatoon, Mr. Reed, Mr. Ritchie, Mr. Gorgie, Louis and Harry Hintze and A. E. Cooney were among the first. When the railroad arrived in 1913, Mr. Winter, who had worked so hard to get the townsite, named it in honor of his two sons, Hugh and Milton.

HUGONARD

Hugonard is the next station to Lebret and was named for Father Hugonard who served for many years in missionary work at Lebret and later became the principal of the Indian residential school there.

HUMBOLDT

Humboldt was named after the German scientist and geographer, Baron Von Humboldt, at the time of the original survey of the Pacific Railway in the 1870s. Humboldt was a station on the government telegraph line from Winnipeg to Edmonton and knew exciting times during the Saskatchewan Rebellion of 1885. Settlement began in 1902 with German-American immigrants from Minnesota.

HUME

Hume is eleven miles east of Weyburn on a CPR branch line to Stoughton. It consists of half a dozen houses and a Pool elevator operated by Ray Chessall. He buys at Hume on Thursdays and Fridays and at Ralph the first part of the week.

Being so close to Weyburn, Hume never developed into a town. It stayed as a hamlet and over the years businesses closed up and houses emptied. In the late 60s it staged a recovery as young couples rented the houses and commuted to Weyburn for work.

Harold Jacobsen, long time resident of the district, thinks that Hume was named for David Hume (1711-1776) a Scottish philosopher and historian. Certainly there is logic in this because in southeastern Saskatchewan there are many place names that commemorate famous writers.

HUNTOON

The hamlet of Huntoon came into existence in July, 1908, with the arrival of the Grand Trunk Railway. It was named after a foreman who supervised the construction of that section of track.

Huntoon was six miles southeast of Innes and six miles northwest of Viewfield. The big trading centre was Weyburn, thirty-five miles to the northwest.

Dick Allen had originally homesteaded the quarter section that the railway bought and on which the townsite was built. His shack stood for many years after he left the area.

In the beginning, Huntoon consisted of a railway station, the Saskatchewan Co-operative elevator, and coal sheds built beside the track from which Mr. R. M. Kruger sold coal and wood.

Here are some other Huntoon firsts: elevator agent — Herbert Evans, store — Charles Evans, farm machinery dealership — Arthur Hanson, lumber yard and hardware — Weyburn Security Company. It was operated by Arthur Hanson until 1934, when he left to open his own hardware business in Fort Qu'Appelle.

Other businesses included a butcher shop operated by Cecil Tart and a garage owned and operated by Fred Richard.

A number of railway men lived in Huntoon in the early years. The first station agent was Mr. Patterson and the first section foreman was Belton Foster.

Other buildings included a curling rink and an outdoor skating rink.

Social life consisted of house parties, dances and box socials in winter. In summer there were picnics and an annual sports day.

The latter became so popular that people came from seventy-five miles away to attend it. The main attraction was horse racing. Horsemen such as Jack Dashney and Jack Campbell, as well as others from Stoughton participated in sulky racing, while young people raced their horses and ponies. There was always a baseball tournament held in conjunction with the event and a big wind-up dance completed the day.

The Mona School District No. 2310 was organized in 1908. It was named by Jim Bagnel for an area in Ontario from which he came. The school was built on the northeast quarter Section 2, Township 7, Range 10, West of the Second Meridian. The first teacher was Miss Kate Bayless from Morden, Manitoba. At that time, fourteen students were enrolled in the school.

In 1923 a new brick school was built and the old one used as a community centre until 1958. Then Mervin Knibbs bought the building and moved it to his farm where it is still used as a granary.

The brick school closed in 1957 and Huntoon children are now bussed to Griffin or Stoughton.

In the 1960's and 1970's Huntoon prospered, but with fast cars and good roads people shopped in the larger centres and stores and dwellings began to close.

All that remains of the once lively little hamlet of Huntoon is the family of Mr. Hoff, the elevator agent.

I am indebted to Mrs. Fern Knibbs of Weyburn, a longtime resident of Huntoon, for the above information.

HURDMAN LODGE

Hurdman Lodge was a post office twelve miles northwest of Asquith. It opened in 1904 in Mr. Hurdman's home and closed in the early 40's. Residents who used this office include: Len Moore; Jim, Mat and Ray Stack; Jim Cleghorn; Bob Burwell; Harold McTavish.

HURONVILLE

In the years 1902 and 1903, people in search of land on which to build new homes filed on homesteads twelve miles northeast of Fillmore in an area which later was named Huronville. Many of the pioneer settlers came from Huron County, Ontario, and this accounts for the name.

The Huronville post office was opened in 1905. Mr. Treble was the first postmaster and it was located on his home-

stead. Mail was brought from Fillmore on Tuesday and Friday of each week in all kinds of weather by Mr. Frank Wiggins, the first mail carrier.

Frank Wiggins came to Huronville district from Virden, Manitoba, in 1902 and took up his homestead. He returned the next summer and broke some land and in 1904 he and his wife, formerly Mary Treble, and small son Golding (Goldie), took up permanent residence there. Theirs was the first carload of settler's effects to arrive by rail at Fillmore. It was a cold 40-below-zero day in December of 1904, when they moved into the small shack built previously. Mr. Wiggins resided on this homestead until his death in 1943.

Mrs. Wiggins later made her home with one of her daughters, May (Mrs. Dan Smith) of Creelman. Stella (Lackey) now resides in Weyburn; Mary (Holliday) is at Herschel; Goldie is employed at Landis; Charles lives in Fillmore; Gordon is on the home farm and Bruce, after an outstanding teaching career, became assistant general secretary of the Saskatchewan Teachers' Federation in Saskatoon.

HYAS

Hyas is on a CNR line between Stenen and Norquay. Back in 1910 the CNR came through and Hyas was named. It is a great wonder to strangers how the place got its unique name. It was like this:

The late Tim Morgotch was driving his oxen along the trail and they did as oxen are often wont to do headed for a slough to cool off. Tim yelled, "Haaz! Haaz! Haaz!", telling them in the Austrian tongue to make a left turn. One railway official turned to another standing on the right-of-way and said, "Hays, that would be a good name for this berg." But alas, Hays was short lived as there was confusion with another post office of that name. After some consideration the letters were put in a hat and drawn out, resulting in the name Hyas — very pleasing when one shudders to think of the words some ox drivers might have used under the circumstances.

HYDE

In 1883 Norman McLeod, a worker with the CPR, took out a homestead about nine miles south of the present town of Neudorf, and eighteen miles north of Grenfell.

Just north of his homestead, an Englishmen named Hyde, who had some capital established an English style estate with hotel, store, church, blacksmith shop and stables for his numerous riding horses. He was primarily a sportsman and had several friends with whom he rode after foxes and coyotes behind their hounds in true English fashion.

Mr. Hyde also ran the post office which was named for him.

I

IBSEN

Ibsen is between Lang and Yellow Grass on a CPR line that runs south and east of Moose Jaw to Estevan. In southeastern Saskatchewan there are many places named for writers and Ibsen is one of these.

Henrik Ibsen (1828-1906), was a Norwegian dramatist. He is considered the father of the modern drama, because he promoted realism in the theatre. His importance was so great that he became known as "The Colossus of the North."

Ibsen's plays have been translated into many languages and have been staged in almost every country.

IBSTONE

Ibstone is on a CNR branch line that was built in 1911 north from the main line at Oban Junction (which is west of Biggar) to Battleford. The railway officials called the original siding Charlton but English settlers, who had been in the district since the early 1900s, were instrumental in having it changed to commemorate Ibstone, England.

IDALEEN

Idaleen is a rural district near Rosetown. The post office was in Dr. Raynor's home in the early years. It took its name from the district which was named Idaleen after Mrs. Harry Collins whose first name was Ida. She was a real pioneer, having ridden with two small children the 100 miles from Saskatoon behind a yoke of oxen in a lumber wagon. This was in 1906. With the coming of the railway the post office moved into Rosetown but the district of Idaleen remains.

IDYLWILD

Idylwild is a community northwest of Spiritwood close to Witchekan Lake. When a post office was obtained, the name submitted by Richard Shano was Idelwylde. Postal officials changed it to the present name and the first mail was hauled by Charles Hare.

The post office has long since closed out but the name, Idylwild, lives on in the district.

IFFLEY

The district just north of North Battleford was first known as Round Hill but the post office could not be called that because another place in Saskatchewan had that name. Iffley was suggested by Mr. Lambert to honor a famous church in England. It was accepted.

The first post office operated in somewhat primitive fashion. A local carpenter, Peter Omelchenko built a desk for stamps and postal supplies and when the mail arrived by team from the nearest rail point, Prince, it was laid out on the kitchen floor.

Dan Finlayson was the first settler in the distict and he came in 1892. He later became MLA for North Battleford in 1908-1917 and for Jackfish Lake, 1917-1934.

One other early settler of note was Michael Policha who arrived in 1911. He raised a family of eight daughters and one son. The son is J. M. Policha, a judge in North Battleford.

ILE-A-LA-CROSSE

Ile-a-la-Crosse is one of the oldest Roman Catholic missions in Saskatchewan. The first priest arrived in 1845, and a mission was established the following year by Father Tache — later Bishop Tache.

Prior to that time, Chipewyan Indians lived at what is now Ile-a-la-Crosse. For some obscure reason, Cree Indians moved in to do battle with Chipewyans, and consequently drove them north to what is now La Loche and Patuanak.

Lac Ile-a-la-Crosse is literally, "lake of the crosier, or stick." The lake itself is shaped like a Bishop's staff. The Cree word for Ile-a-la-Crosse is "Sakittawak" (the k is silent), meaning, literally, "the place where the rivers meet." The actual name, La Crosse, is derived from the game lacrosse, which was played by the Chipewyan Indians on the sandy shores of big Island before white people settled on the peninsula. Some authorities suggest that the game was introduced by Iroquois voyageurs accompanying the early North-west fur traders.

There are two headstones of particular interest in the sandy windswept graveyard on the "Point" at Ile-a-la-Crosse. The mission was established in 1845 and the Grey Nuns opened a hospital in connection with it. One of the first Grey Nuns was Rev. Soeur Marguerite Marie (Riel) who died there on 27th of December, 1883, at the age of 34. She was a sister of Louis Riel.

Another headstone reads: Rev. Pere Marius Rossignol O.M.I.—17 of March 1961—at the age of 86 years. The present school which is on the mission grounds is named for him.

ILLERBRUN

In 1907 Mr. Illerbrun of North Dakota homesteaded in the district. In 1909 he opened a post office and suggested the name, Maitland. Whether it was a mistake or not we do not know, but the post office wound up being called Illerbrun. Mr. Illerbrun was postmaster until 1940 and then turned it over to his son, Charles, who kept the office until it closed in 1964. The Illerburn mail is now handled in Gull Lake.

IMPERIAL

Imperial is a town 84 miles north of Regina on the CPR line to Saskatoon. It is close to Long lake. Many of the early settles were British. After an examination of the name of the town and the names of the streets it would seem that one of these very British settlers had a hand in, not only naming the town, but laying out the townsite. The main street is Royal. On either side is King Street and Queen Street. The next two to the outside are Prince and Princess and on the outside of the town on either side are Duke Street and Duchess Street.

Certainly, some loyal subject of her "Imperial" majesty named this town.

INCHKEITH

Inchkeith was first known as Hawthorn. Because there was a Hawthorn in Ontario, the people were asked to change the name of their village. As Mr. Keith was the first settler, the name of Keith was suggested, but postal authorities said this name was also used elsewhere. Someone suggested then that they call it Inchkeith. This would include the Keith and since at the mouth of the Firth of Forth, there is a huge rock formation called Inchkeith Rock, it would denote the Scottish ancestry of many of the residents of the district. The name Inchkeith was accepted.

INDI

The hamlet of Indi was established five miles west of Dundurn soon after the turn of the century by two pioneer families, Shults and Baumack, who came from Indiana, USA. They shortened the name to Indi. Others who came to the district soon afterward were: the Meilicke, Guderian, Just, Libke, Hass, Peters, Wilson, and Torguson families, who took up land within a mile and a half of the siding.

At one time Indi boasted two elevators, the CNR station, two cottages for elevator agents and a school named Hoosier. Never large, Indi dwindled away until in early August of 1969 the last of the hamlet disappeared when a Wheat Pool construction crew dismantled the one elevator that remained.

INDIAN HEAD

Indian Head is an old, old name. Hillyer, a missionary, records on his return journey from Qu'Appelle Lakes on August 30, 1854, that he "reached the Indian Head (ustiquanuci)." This was the Indian name for a range of hills southeast of the town. The westerly peak of the hills is called either "The Head" or "The Indian Head."

INGLENOOK

Inglenook is south of Kindersley on a short CNR branch line running to Glidden. It's one of the quaint place names in Saskatchewan — like Nestledown.

A lone Pool elevator stands halfway down a gently curving slope sheltered from northerly and westerly winds. The dictionary defines inglenook as a sheltered place by the fire. I have been unable to get anyone to say how the place came to be named. It never was very big, but now the elevator is closed and the only sign of life around are the cars whizzing by on nearby highway 21.

INNES

The earliest settlers in the Innes area wrote their address as Assiniboia District. George Innes, an American, arrived in 1910 and acquired a large tract of land and formed the Innes Land Company. When the Grand Trunk Railway arrived in 1912 they bought a townsite from him and named it Innes. It was situated on the N.W. corner of 31-7-10-W2.

Innes had a railway water tower used by the steam engines for their refill of water. A large dugout by the track was the source of supply. On hot days crowds of young people used it as a swimming hole. They even gave it a name, Lake Auldabina.

The first post office was opened in the home of Mr. and Mrs. Axel Lund in 1908. That same year there were enough children to start a school and it was called Dunreath.

Early years saw some tragic events — eight-year-old Jimmy Brown lost his life at a railway crossing in a severe blizzard in the winter of 1916; in the summer of that year a cyclone levelled nearly every barn in the disrict and killed livestock; in 1918 every home in the area was struck with the influenza epidemic. The school was closed for six months.

In 1924 an American, George Prall, came to farm at Innes. He was an inventor and built a stooker. George Innes became interested, bought the rights, had it patented and built a "factory" to assemble the parts. The machine was sold until 1927 when combines made it obsolete. the factory still stands in Innes.

The 1940's, 1950's and 1960's saw great changes. New families moved in and farms expanded to the point where a quarter or even a section no longer made an adequate farm. Farming methods and machinery improved with knowledge through P.F.R.A. research. Every farm had a dugout and trees were planted.

There is now a flourishing farming district around Innes; the country is beautiful, like parkland, trees having grown up in the nearly eighty years since the first settlers came. The hamlet of Innes is not now marked on the map, the elevator is not used, the store and post office are gone. With the return of prosperity, fast cars and good highways, life has passed it by, but it is there, about thirty miles east of Weyburn, next to Griffin on the Canadian National Railway line that runs from Regina to Northgate at the United States border. Two small homestead shacks still stand — the McWhinnie's and the Grey's.

INSINGER

Insinger is the fifth stop northwest on a CPR line out of Yorkton. It was named after Mr. F. R. Insinger, a member of the Territorial Government and a supporter of Sir Fredrick Haultain. In private life Mr. Insinger was a rancher.

INSTOW

Instow is the first station east of Shaunavon. Ed Barton took out a homestead in 1908 on land two miles east of the present townsite. He had come from a small town in England called Instow.

When Ed James opened the first post office in 1910 the name of Instow was given to it. When the CPR came through in 1913, the name of Instow was adopted for the town. Work on this line was done by Japanese laborers as well as local settlers. Mr. Mooney bought grain "over the tracks" before the following elevators were built: "The State," "The Alberta Pacific," "The Saskatchewan Co-op," and "The Pioneer."

INVERGORDON

Invergordon was an inland post office about fifteen miles south of Kinistino that opened in the early 1900's. It was named for Invergordon, a seaside town in northern Scotland on Cromarty Firth.

The post office has long since closed and residents now get their mail by rural route.

149

INVERMAY

Invermay is 65 miles west of Yorkton. The first settler into the district was a rancher, Mr. Walter Tullock, who came in 1903. He had the post office, named Tullock, at his ranch which was three miles southeast of the present village of Invermay. He was soon joined by Mr. Rattray, the Abbott brothers and the Christopherson families.

The main line of the Canadian Northern Railway laid the grade through the district in 1903 and the steel came through in 1904. Mr. Alfred Cook, a lad at the time, remembers the fascination of them actually laying the steel ahead of the engine. He particularly recalls the flagman who rode on the front car and directed the steel gang on the laying of the rail on the ties. At his signal the rail was raised and carried into position. If it fitted correctly he would yell "End O." If it needed to be lifted to the left or right he would indicate the direction with his flag and yell "Little Mucher."

After the steel was down and the location of the townsite was settled the Tullock post office moved into town and became Invermay. The first choice of name by the residents was actually Inverness but the post office department turned it down because there was already one Inverness in Canada. They suggested Invermay and it was accepted.

IRVINTON

Irvinton post office is ten miles north of Star City. It was named after the first postmaster, Bill Irvin. The post office has been closed for a number of years and the school is gone but the name still lingers in the district.

ISHAM

In 1925 the CNR built a short stub line from Eston, southeast to White Bear. The hamlet of Isham, fourteen miles out, was the second grain point. In 1926 three elevators were built. The Pool was run by Lester How, the Federal by Mr. McIntyre and the Pioneer by Mr. Micks.

However, settlers moved into the district long before the railroad. Gilbert and Arthur Miller were the first. They homesteaded a mile west of the present site of Isham. The townsite was on the land of Mr. Walker but his suggestion of Wal-kerville for a name was turned down because there was already a Walkerville in Canada. Mr. Shuttleworth, the postmaster, was an Englishman and it was he who suggested Isham to commemorate the name of James Isham, former English governor of the Hudson's Bay Company who wrote extensively. In fact, he was one who wrote some very uncomplimentary things about the Indians.

ISLAND FALLS

Island Falls is the site of the Churchill River Power Plant which supplies electricity to Flin Flon and the Hudson Bay Mining and Smelting Company there. It is on an island in the river where there is a natural waterfall, hence the name Island Falls.

ISLAND HILL

Island Hill was an inland post office on an island in the Beaver river northwest of Meadow Lake. It is closed now but while in operation it got its mail from St. Cyr lake.

ITUNA

Ituna is a town on the CNR main line 35 miles west of Melville. In 1956 H. M. Rayner, then secretary-treasurer of the village, made a thorough study of the origin of the name. He believes it was selected by a railway official familiar with the Celtic name, Ituna, for the Solway Firth which Kipling used in one of his books.

IVOR

Mr. Davidson established a country store in the Hughton-Elrose area in the early 1900's. In 1910 he got a post office and named it for his eldest son, Ivor.

This was located on the homestead of Andrew Reid N.E.-12-27-15-W3. Frank and John T. Lynn hauled the mail from Zealandia to Bonnyview, Teyerton and Ivor post offices.

Some of the people served by it were: John Curtiss Lynn, Stanley Thurston, Joe Dietz, George Bigelow and Harry Holler.

IWONA

For the most part the railways and post offices avoided duplication of names. In fact, in many cases, where the names were even similar, the smaller point was asked to change its name. Lydden, west of Biggar, clashed with Glidden and became Duperow. Rainton, next to Weyburn, clashed with Paynton and became Worcester. Eaton clashed with Eston and became Eatonia. Robin, Saskatchewan, even clashed with Roblin, Manitoba, and it changed to Robinhood. Birdview clashed with Broadview and became Donavon. But the old main line of the CPR and GTP from Saskatoon to Unity where the tracks are very close together, the reverse took place. Iwona, twenty-five miles west of Saskatoon was changed to South Asquith, right out of the alphabetical order: Hawoods, Iwona, Juniata, Kinley, Leney, Mead, Neola, and then Biggar broke the sequence. At Kinley, it was Kinley and North Kinley. At Biggar it was Biggar and North Biggar and the same happened at Unity.

At all these places the old-time dray—wagon in summer and sleigh in winter—met all trains and made the necessary deliveries without any apparent mix-up in freight or mail. In view of this fact it is hard to reconcile the two systems of naming places.

J

JACKFISH LAKE

"Jack Fish" is a nickname for the Great Northern Pike, a fighting fish plentiful in Jackfish lake which is 20 miles north of North Battleford. Perched on one of the gently rolling hills northwest of the lake is the rural post office of Jackfish Lake. This is a predominately French settlement. The closest railway is at the village of Meota six miles away on the south shore.

One store operated by Beulah and Roland Corbeil serves the community which includes an imposing church, a school, and a dozen dwellings. The school and convent have now closed and the students are bussed to Vawn.

JAN LAKE

Jan Lake settlement is on the southeast corner of the lake from which it got its name. The lake was surveyed in 1924 by J. S. Delury. The name was adopted on Apr. 18, 1933 after a Mr. A. J. Jan of Pelican Narrows.

JANOW CORNERS

Janow Corners is three miles southeast of Meath Park. In fact is was the original Meath Park. When the railway came in 1929 it missed Meath Park by three miles. Most of the merchants moved to the new townsite which was called New Meath Park.

With an Old Meath Park and a New Meath Park it is understandable that there were postal difficulties and the smaller place was asked to change its name. Janow was chosen from among the many Polish and Ukrainian settlers of the district. The store, operated by Mr. Bearse, hung on for a while but eventually everything closed up.

By 1971 all that was left was a boarded-up school, a Polish Roman Catholic church, a few deserted homes and the foundations of the first store.

JANSEN

Jansen is very close to the west shore of Big Quill lake. It was named after John Jansen, the first settler in the district. Other old-timers include Perry Holland Dawson, who was the first postmaster, and the Loeppky brothers who built a hotel and started an implement agency in 1908.

JASMIN

Jasmin is between Kelliher and Ituna on a CNR line. It was incorporated as a village in 1909. The name was just put in to keep things in alphabetical order — as we come northwest out of Melville: Fenwood, Goodeve, Hubbard, Ituna, and then Jasmin.

Jasmin is a tropical or sub-tropical shrub of the olive family, with fragrant flowers of yellow, red or white.

JAVA

Java is the junction west of Swift Current where the CPR sends one track northwest around the Great Sand Hills and another line around the southwest side. It is named for one of the East Indian Islands, Java. The word java entered our language in the early 1900s as a slang term for coffee. It is rarely heard now; an example of how language changes.

JAYS

Jays is between Glenside and Hawarden on a CPR line. It was named after Jays' lake nearby which in turn was named for Mr. Jays, one of the first settlers in the district.

JEDBURGH

The wild tribes of the Gad and Gadeni that roamed the Cheviot Hills at the time of the coming of the Romans gave the River Jed and the city of Jedburgh in Roxburgh County, Scotland, its present name. As one of the "Border" towns, and standing at the geographic centre of Britain, it has an old and rich history.

Jedburgh in Saskatchewan is on a branch line of the CNR that runs northwest of Yorkton and ends at Parkerview. With the rapid influx of settlers in the early 1900s and the building of a school, the demand for mail service grew. Finally, in 1910 Mr. Peter Hoy was hired to drive the mail in twice a week from Theodore. With a democrat and team of horses he serviced Gladwin, Jedburgh and Beaverdale.

Faced with the necessity of finding a name for the new district, Mr. Joe Clark, the postmaster at Yorkton, and Mr. William Barber went into conference. From these two men came the suggestion that the district be named after the birthplace of the first mailman, Mr. Peter Hoy—Jedburgh, Scotland.

Jedburgh is an important grain delivery point; in 1970 it still supported four elevators. Here they are with their agents: Wheat Pool—Bert Pearce; Grain Growers—Tony Bogdasavich; Federal—John Popowich; Searle—Joe Lasco.

JONESVILLE

Jonesville was an inland post office three miles south of the present town of Beechy. Dave Santy was the postmaster and he had a country store in connection with it. The post office was named for a prominent family (Jones) in the district.

The first mail was brought in from Herbert across the river by Mr. Tuplin. The post office closed out when the CNR reached Beechy in 1922.

JORDAN RIVER

Jordan River is an inland post office on the Jordan river a short distance east of Arborfield in the Carrot River Valley. It's interesting to know how the Jordan river got its name. Settlers moving north from the drought-stricken prairies of the 1930s were so impressed with the verdant growth of the land that as they crossed the little river they jokingly remarked that they had crossed the "Jordan river into the promised land." Henceforth they called it the Jordan river and when it came time for a post office, Bob England and Albert Hirsch, two of the earliest settlers, sent that name to the postal officials at Ottawa. The name was granted.

JUNIATA

Fourteen miles west of Saskatoon the GTR resumed their practice of naming stations in alphabetical order with Grandora, Hawoods, Iwona (now South Asquith), and in 1906 they reached and named Juniata.

One of the first homesteaders in the district was Albert Warren who filed in 1902. Before the railway came he hauled his grain to Saskatoon with one horse and one ox. This "team" was also used in the haying season and proved very frustrating at times when the ox would take the horse, mower, AND man into the middle of a slough to cool off.

With the coming of the railway three elevators were built at Juniata—The Atlas, the Standard, and the Co-op. J. B. King operated the first store. At one time there was an implement business, a lumberyard, and a blacksmith shop. In 1933 an attempt was made to start a co-op farm but it never got beyond the planning stage.

Albert Warren's son, Norman, bought the store in 1945 and when he closed it in 1967 there was only the Pool elevator left and it also closed in July of 1968. So officially there is no more Juniata. However, when people hear the noted pianist,

Boyd McDonald, play, perhaps some will remember that he grew up in Juniata.

JUNIPER

Juniper is a railroad siding one stop south of Dinsmore. The Canadian Northern reached there in 1913 and gave the railroad siding its name. This is how it happened.

As the grade for the railroad was being built in June it extended along the side of a long narrow lake where a lot of bushes were loaded with saskatoon berries. Some of the workmen thought they were juniper berries and made a request to the Head Office in Winnipeg to call the place Juniper. The request was granted.

JUNOR

Mrs. Donald Junor operated a post office named Junor in her home four miles north of Robinhood. When the steel came to Medstead in 1927 her office was closed and she moved into town as the first postmistress. When the CPR built north Mr. Cook, the chief engineer on the line, named a townsite in her honor.

Junor is 25 miles north of Medstead on the line to Meadow Lake.

K

KALYNA

Kalyna is near Prince Albert on the Garden river. The district is predominately Ukrainian and they named their post office, Kalyna, which in their language is a cranberry-like fruit. This they found in abundance around their new home.

KALIUM

Kalium is on the CPR just west of Regina. After years of research and experimentation, Kalium Chemicals has been successful in developing a process for the solution mining of potash.

In 1964, near Belle Plaine, it brought its refinery into production. The rail site was named Kalium. Kalium is the Latinized form of the Arabic word for potash.

KAMSACK

The following information is taken directly from Encyclopedia Canadiana. "Kamsack, Sask., town on the Assiniboine River, 14 miles from the Manitoba border; divisional point 278 miles N.W. of Winnipeg on the CNR line through Dauphin to Saskatoon. Its name was that of a post office established about 1888, which was named after a well-known Indian. The general area was fur-trading territory for many years. Grant's House was established by the North West Co., in 1791, a few miles S.E. on the river. Later posts were established by the same company, the Hudson's Bay Co., the XY Co.

and free traders, mainly N.W. of the present town. The best-known of these was Fort Pelly, 10 miles N.W."

KANDAHAR

Kandahar is on the south shore of Big Quill lake. The first settlers arrived from Norway in July of 1904. The group included Odin Granhus, Henry Skjerven, Bert Lorenson, Amund Hagen, and Gilbert Sather. At that time the railway reached only as far as Sheho. This left the settlers with a 50 mile trek with horses or oxen over winding prairie trails whenever they needed supplies. They usually confined their trips to twice a year.

In 1909 the CPR extended its line to Kandahar and named the station in memory of the site of a famous battle won by the British army under Roberts during the Afghanistan War.

KAPOSVAR

Kaposvar was a rural post office (now closed) near Esterhazy. It opened in 1891. Several names were suggested by post office officials but no agreement could be reached. Many of the earliest settlers were from Hungary, the same as was the case of Esterhazy. The officials in an attempt to settle the question of a name asked for a map of Hungary and one placed his finger on the map and asked the name of the place nearest to it. It happened to be Kaposvar. The name was adopted although none of the residents came from there.

There is a second version of how the post office got its name. A travelling entertainer is supposed to have made his appearance in the district about the time of the naming of the post office. His name was Kaposvar.

KATEPWA

There are many lakes in the Qu'Appelle Valley. A string of four: Pasqua, Echo, Mission and Katepwa are known as the "Fishing Lakes." Katepwa is a summer resort on the lake with the same name. It got its name this way:

Robert Balcarres Crawford, a Hudson's Bay man, later a postmaster at Indian Head, was visiting his friend, J. B. Lauder in the '80s, when they heard someone repeatedly calling, and suggested the place be called Katepwa which is "Who calls?" in Cree.

KAYVILLE

Kayville is a hamlet on a CPR branch line northwest from Wallace to Cardross. Billy McKay and Julius Martin, ranchers, were the first to settle the area, arriving in 1903. Between 1908 and 1911 many homesteaders of English and Scottish descent entered the district and these were followed in 1912 by a group of settlers from Rumania.

The post office at Kayville was built in 1912 and Billy McKay was the first postmaster. When the railway arrived in 1924, a hamlet was formed but was not organized as such until 1949. The name Kayville was formed by taking the last part of the name McKay and adding ville (village) to it. This was done to honor Billy McKay.

KEALEY SPRINGS

Kealey Springs is an inland post office 20 miles south of Piapot. It is located at 4-9-23-W3. It was named by Mr. P. Kealey who was the first postmaster. Fresh water springs nearby made it a good camping ground in the early years.

KEARNEY

Kearney is a locality at 26-17-19 W2 on the CPR near Belbeck, which is near Moose Jaw. It was named for the late Mr. T. Kearney, former Chief Clerk to the General Superintendent, Moose Jaw.

KEATLEY

In 1904 James Keatley homesteaded in what is now the Keatley area. At that time there were no railways through the district and Mr. Keatley's home was the first country post office with Mr. Keatley as postmaster, so the post office was named Keatley.

A year or two later another homesteader, Sigard Brevik, took up a homestead four miles east of Mr. Keatley. In 1928 when the CNR was built through the area, a townsite was started close to Mr. Brevik's home and on land donated by Mr. Brevik.

Mr. Brevik wanted the new town named Breviksville since it was on land that formerly belonged to him. Mr. Keatley wanted the town named after him and the post office which he had run for more than 20 years. Feelings between Mr. Brevik and Mr. Keatley ran high, and some feared a feud would be started. The CNR officials decided to disregard both men and officially named the town "Peacedale"—indicating that peace should come between Keatley and Brevik. But peace was not for long—a little over a year later Mr. Keatley got some of his cronies to take around a petition to have the town of Peacedale renamed Keatley. He managed to get enough signers to have this done.

In the North Battleford and district telephone directory "Peacedale" is still listed there.

KEDDY JUNCTION

This is just east of the town of Melfort where the CPR joins the CNR tracks going past the Union Station. It was named for a pioneer auctioneer, H. E. Keddy, who came from Exeter, Ontario.

KEDLESTON AND
KEDLESTON BEACH

The CPR line from Valeport to Colonsay was built in 1912. The line winds along the southwest shore of Last Mountain lake from Valeport to Kedleston Beach. It then leaves the lake and the first station north is Kedleston about one and one-half miles from the lake.

Kedleston was named for George Nathaniel, Marquis Curzon of Kedleston (1859-1925), British stateman and author, who had an interest in the CPR.

The oldest settlers were the Bushby and Bunker families who came in 1900. Mr. Angus Wilkie came to the district shortly after. These people took to ranching and raised horses and sold them to the homesteaders. Kedleston, like a lot of other communities, has suffered from changing times. The Pool elevator is the only business left and its days appear to be numbered. Mr. and Mrs. Ferraby were the only residents living there in 1969.

Years ago there used to be four passenger trains a day. In the 30s it was reduced to two. Today, there are none. In the spring of 1956 melting snow and a heavy April rain raised the waters of the lake to a height never before seen. The water ran over the track at Valeport. The train went across the grade but it did not return that night. That was the last passenger train on the Colonsay line, after that it was freight trains only.

Kedleston Beach, one of many on Last Mountain lake, has many fine cottages. During the summer months of the 20s and 30s large excursion trains of up to 10 coaches would bring passengers from Regina out to the beach for a day. A "Y" was put in at Kedleston for the engines to turn around. The track incline from Regina Beach to Kedleston is quite steep and it used to be quite a sight to see the giant steamers pulling up to Kedleston. They would usually stop there and the "header" would uncouple and head back to Craven to help the next train.

This is almost all from a letter sent by J. C. Bull of Box 264, Bethune, who in 1927, as a twelve-year-old boy, hauled his first load of wheat to Kedleston for his dad. Mr. Bull was still hauling to Kedleston as late as 1969.

KEELER

The village of Keeler inherited its name from the first settler to arrive, Mr. Joseph P. Keeler. He was an Oxford, Englishman, who had lived in Winnipeg for 20 years.

In 1902, at the age of 40, he came into the area to search out a homestead. In 1903 he and his family took up permanent residence here and also persuaded the families of John Snow, Jim Geofferies and John Morgan to settle in the district.

KEGWORTH

The first post office here before the CNR came through was Beeston, the name of the hometown of the first postmaster. Each Friday mail was brought in from Grenfell 20 miles away.

The railroad came through in 1908 and the post office was moved to Lovat station the nearest point on the railroad. This name was chosen by the CNR after a regiment called Lovat's Scouts in Scotland. This served for a few years and then it was found it clashed with a similar name in Alberta. Being the smaller place, Lovat, Sask., had to yield. The post office department then sent a selected list of names and the people of Lovat chose Kegworth. It may bear some relationship to Kegworth, England.

KELFIELD

Kelfield gots its name from David H. Kelly, commonly known as Father Kelly. An airplane landed on his field so they got the name Kelfield or Kelly's field. He ran the first post office out on his farm, in 1910 before the village was started. Father Kelly lived on section 20-34-19-W3, which was his homestead. Some of the first settlers were: Harvey McGowan, Tom Moore, Oliver Penfound, Switzers, Jack Bielby, Bill Penley, P. R. Carter and George Weese.

KELLIHER

Kelliher is between Jasmin and Leross on the main line of the CNR. The line was built by the Grand Trunk Pacific and Kelliher was fitted into the alphabetical sequence. It was incorporated into a village in 1909—a rapid growth, since the steel had only gone through in 1908.

The village was named for Mr. B. B. Kelliher, chief engineer on the GTP railway at the time.

KELSO

Kelso is between Vandura and Doonside on a Canadian Northern line built by McKenzie and Mann in the southeast corner of the province. Before the Province of Saskatchewan was formed a post office named Riga, Northwest Territories, served the community. The first settlers arrived in the 80s. A partial list follows: Levi Havens, John Greenbank, John and William Henry, Robert Steele, William Moffatt, James Porter and Robert Randal. The closest town at that time was Moosomin. The settlers had to sell their products and buy their supplies. Farmers hauling to Moosomin would go in groups of 10 or 15. In this way the lead team on the sleigh would change every mile or so, making it easier to "break trail." There were regular stopping places along the way. When the railway arrived in 1908 the officials named the townsite for the town of Kelso, Scotland, which is the extreme southeast corner of the country very close to Flodden.

KELSTERN
Kelstern is between Vogel and Shamrock on a CPR line. The village of Kelstern started in 1922 and was named after a returned soldier named Stern who lived nearby.

KELVINGTON
Kelvington is the end of a branch line of the CNR that runs northwest from Sturgis. The first post office in the district was established in 1905 in the home of Mr. and Mrs. John McQuarrie. Mrs. McQuarrie was given the privilege of naming it and she chose to name it in honor of Lord Kelvin who had a large estate near where her parents lived in Scotland.

Lord Kelvin (1824-1907) was William Thomson, a British mathematician and physicist, who was a professor at Glasgow University.

During the centennial year citizens recalled many of the hard times in the district in the "thirties," but many memories were happy too! One of the highlights in those days, before hockey or curling had become a way-of-life in the long winter, was the Annual Dog Derby on New Year's Day which was begun by Carl Stever. The first race had only about four dogs, but in later years as many as 10 took part. This, of course, resulted in a great many dog fights, so men had to be placed at strategic intervals to help straighten these out and keep the dogs running.

Some of the early contestants were Earl Taylor with his dog Bud; Scholfields with Sport; Bill Wishart with Nick; and Johnny Zeufle with Barry. Gladys McDonald was the only female contestant.

KENASTON
This village was first known as Bonnington, Northwest Territories, and it was not until 1905 that it was given its present name. This was done to honor F. E. Kenaston, wealthy implement manufacturer of Minneapolis, who was vice-president of the Saskatchewan Land Valley Company, which developed so much of the area between Davidson and Dundurn.

He was instrumental in bringing in many settlers from the United States. Worth recording is the fact that one of the first homesteaders, Mr. Zeman, ploughed a furrow with oxen to Outlook 40 miles away, roughly paralleling the present No. 15 highway as a directive for incoming immigrants.

KENDAL
Kendal is between Odessa and Montmartre on a CNR line. It was named after a Russian town, Kendal, which is situated near Odessa.

There is another story that it may have been named for Kendal, Westmoreland, in the Lake District of northwest England.

KENLIS
Kenlis was a rural post office (now closed) located at S26-T19-R11-W2. This is about halfway between Abernethy and Sintaluta. Mr. Ferguson, an early settler in the district, named it for this birthplace, Kenlis, Scotland.

KENNEDY
From the late 1800s until 1907 the mail was driven by horses from the town of Whitewood on the main line of the CPR to a little rural post office at Fletewode. This was a distance of 35 miles south. On this route mail was dropped off at other country postal points: St. Huberts, Montgomery, Reid's Farm, and finally Fletewode. Reid's Farm was the point which later became Kennedy. The man who had the contract to drive the mail over this route was Findlay Kennedy.

In 1907 the CPR branch line between Reston, Manitoba, and Wolseley, Saskatchewan was completed and the mail then started to come by train. With the coming of the railroad a town built up about one mile from Reid's Farm and it was named in honor of Findlay Kennedy, the first mail driver in the area.

Mr. Kennedy presented the new town with its first flag, a Union Jack. While

Canada was celebrating its centennial, Kennedy was celebrating its 60th birthday.

KENSMITH

Kensmith was an inland post office about 20 miles northeast of Biggar. Tom D'Arcy was the first postmaster when it opened in his home in 1910. There were quite a few English settlers in the district and it is believed the name was chosen to commemorate a place in England. In 1915 a school was built in the district and it took its name from the post office.

Some of the early settlers besides Mr. D'Arcy were: Mr. Ray Whitcomb, Fred and William Mountford, and the Cox brothers. Mrs. William Mountford says she remembers dressing up in her "best costume" to walk the five miles across the prairies to pick up her mail from the log house post office.

KEPPEL

Keppel is situated on the CPR although the CNR happens to run only a few yards to the south. Both railways were built in the same years with the roadbed coming in 1906-07 and the steel following in 1908.

It was named after Sir Henry Keppel, who started out as a British sailor and rose to hold the chief navel command at the Cape, Brazil and China. He became admiral of the fleet in 1877 and died January 17, 1904.

Mrs. Les Nimmo was the first postmistress and kept the office in her home. The Jackson brothers: Clare, Jim, Harry and Steve and their cousins: Fred and Arnold, were among the first to take up land in the district in 1906. Fred Jackson, who is now retired and living in Perdue, passed on much of this information.

KERELOWKI

This district was named after a Russian village. The area was called the "First Village" and was located where Pete Rebalkin (R.R. Langham, Sask) now lives.

KERMRIA

If you make a triangle of Dalesford, Lac Vert and Naicam, at its centre will be Kermria. It was a French Roman Catholic community that centered on a beautiful church established by early residents long before the railway came. Some of these were Briton, Crozon, Quequen and Tezekel.

In recent years attendance at the church has dropped to the point where services are held intemittently by a Father who comes down from St. Brieux.

This information came from Joseph Cousin of Hoey, Saskatchewan.

KERROBERT

Kerrobert is named for Robert Kerr, a traffic manager of the CPR. It is a large town and a divisional point from which branch lines go to Wilkie, Sask. and Coronation, Alta. First settled in 1906, it was incorporated as a village in 1910 and as a town in 1911.

Pioneer folk worked hard and played hard. It became the custom in the short season between seeding and harvesting for small communities to hold a sports day. People came from miles around. The baseball diamond was always a major attraction and usually cars encircled the playing field.

One particularly lovely summer day, Angus McTavish carefully parked his car, being a canny Scot he put it where he thought it would be safe from foul balls. However, that day he was unlucky and a ball went through his windshield—as if that wasn't bad enough an English spectator cracked, "I think that lit in Scotland—I'm sure I heard Glasgow!"

KESSOCK

Kessock was named after the McKessock family, one of the early settlers in the district. The district began to build up in the early 1900s and the railroad came through in 1911.

Arthur Kempan of nearby Wroxton wrote this about Kessock: "I'd like to tell you about what Kessock is like today. It is not even a town, only a grain elevator and three houses (one empty) and has a population of two people. It's a little place, and thus only a little story."

KETCHEN

Ketchen is on a branch line of the CNR that runs from Sturgis northwest to Kelvington. It was named for Brigadier-General Huntly Douglas Brodie Ketchen who commanded the Winnipeg military district for a number of years. He served for a time with the NWMP and the Canadian Mounted Rifles and distinguished himself during World War I.

KETTLEHUT

Kettlehut is a little place on a branch line from Mawer to Halvorgate in the south of the province. The first settlers: Frank Rebbein, John and William Wendle and Martin Horkle came in 1906. The CNR did not arrive until 1928. Kettlehut was named for John Kettlehut who homesteaded a mile from the present settlement.

KEYSTOWN

Keystown is about halfway between Regina and Moose Jaw on the main line of the CNR. It was named for the first settlers who took up land there, about six miles north of Pense (1883, 1884). There were six Keys brothers and they all homesteaded near the townsite, the land for the town being bought from Adam Keys. The first settlers included the following: Keys, McGillivarys, McLarens, Bowies and Wilkies. The first general store was operated by John Walton, first blacksmith was Bill Ducker, the first hardware was run by Archie McCarroll, the first pool hall and barbershop was owned by Harry Lovell who still lives in the village and has a mink ranch.

The first elevator was built by the Security Grain Company in 1913 and later was sold to the National. The second elevator, built a year later, was the Co-operative Grain Company which later became the Pool.

The old homestead of the father of the six Keys' boys was known far and wide as "36." He died at Saskatchewan Landing where he and his sons were transporting out from Swift Current in 1885.

KEY WEST

Key West is six miles straight south of Dahinda. This rural post office was established on October 1, 1908, with Mr. R. F. Heron as postmaster. When the CPR built through from Weyburn to Cardross in 1925-1926 this post office was no longer necessary and it closed on October 31, 1926.

The name, a very fancy one for the bald-headed prairie, came from Key West, Florida.

KEYRELIVKA

A communal farm established by the Doukhobors following their immigration in 1899, Keyrelivka was just four miles west of present day Langham.

John Rebalkin and Fred Strelioff were two of a dozen families that made up the farm. Their land stretched down to Cee-Pee by the River. Some of their buildings still stand and modern day machinery works around them.

The children of these early immigrants have moved out into the world and have done well.

KHEDIVE

Khedive is on the CPR between Pangman and the "diamond" made with the CNR a few miles to the east. It was incorporated as a village in 1916. The name was selected by railway officials and has little significance to the village. Khedive is the title of Viceroy or Governor of Egypt.

KILLALY

During the year 1902 the portion of the CPR from McAuley to Neudorf was being surveyed and in 1904 the line was completed. It was while this portion of railway was being constructed that an engineer of the construction by the name of "Killaly" was working here. It was from this man that the village acquired its name.

During the early years Killaly was a flag station and not until 1910 was a permanent station agent, E. R. O'Hara, employed. John Ruff was the first resident of Killaly. He was the grain agent for the Federal elevator. Mr. Ruff built the first house in Killaly, which still stands and is presently occupied by George Exner.

Because of lack of outside entertainment, the early pioneers provided their own. They gathered in groups in homes and joined in singing songs and playing cards. These affairs lasted well into the morning and took the monotony out of life. A wedding was always a great occasion with everyone in the district joining in the celebrations. Marriages took place in the homes in early days and after the ceremonies, which usually took place in the morning, the celebration began and often lasted until noon the next day. The music was usually provided by a violin. Outside of the newly married couple, the musician was the happiest person present for he received money for special requests.

KILLDEER

Killdeer is at the end of a branch line of the CPR south of Assiniboia and within ten miles of the international boundary. It is named for the killdeer, a common plover with black breastband, named for its plaintive and penetrating cry.

In 1931 the railway reached Killdeer. By the end of 1932 both the Pool and UGG had erected elevators. Other firsts include the following: cafe—run by Charlie Weed; barber—Lloyd Morrison; general store—E. H. Van Ripley; lumberyard—Bert Colbo; drayman—Jack Hindle. The Killdeer post office opened on April 1, 1919, with Charlie S. Root as postmaster. Mrs. Mabel McGowan is the present postmistress.

KILRONAN

The following is a complete letter we received from Mrs. K. W. Hougham (nee Guy) of Frenchman Butte.

"In 1911, my mother, Mrs. H. E. Guy, thought a post office would be beneficial to our district thirty-five miles north and west of Turtleford. She applied for and was granted the post office which was named Kilronan after her father, Paul Kingston's home in Ireland. My grandfather was the Earl of Kilronan, an estate near Cork, Ireland.

The post office was on the NW ¼-6-54-23-W3 and Mrs. Guy was the postmistress until 1920. She sold out that year and moved to Lloydminster. The post office carried on for a few years in the farm home of a neighbor two miles farther north. The post office is closed now and does not show on modern maps."

KILWINNING

Kilwinning is between Leask and Parkside on a CNR line that runs northeast of Denholm to Shellbrook. It was named for Kilwinning Castle, southeast of Glasgow, Scotland.

The first family into the area was the Dunlops who arrived in 1902. The grade for the railway went through in 1910 and the steel arrived in 1911. A little hamlet grew up with a post office, two stores, a section crew and an elevator agent.

Over the years, Kilwinning faded and now it has only one store, and the mail comes from Leask. However, the name lives on in the district. This information came from Mrs. West Smith of Leask.

KINCAID

Kincaid is between Hazenmore and Meyronne on a CPR line that runs from Assiniboia west to Notukeu in southwestern Saskatchewan. It was named for Charlie Kincaid, an early and prominent settler in the district.

The railroad reached Kincaid in the summer of 1913. That year, on August 18th, the first village council was formed with Bill Maxwell as mayor, Dan Downie and Teddy Rodbard as councillors and George Pomeroy as secretary-treasurer.

When visited in the summer of 1978, Kincaid was found to be a friendly village of over 300. One of the most colorful individuals in Kincaid's history was Teddy Rodbard. He was English and came to Kincaid following service in the Boer War. Teddy was a bachelor all his life and following some astute real estate deals he was able to retire to town early and indulge himself. He served on the village council for years and was very community-minded.

Mr. Rodbard was health conscious. He walked ten miles a day accompanied by his Great Dane, Chester. Summer and winter he sunbathed in his backyard on every possible day — wearing the least possible clothing — sometimes causing acute embarrassment to his neighbors!

KINCORTH

Kincorth is a rail point between Hatton and Maple Creek on a CPR line in the southwest corner of the province. Its exact location is S5-T12-R28-W3. It is a Scottish name given, no doubt, by the directors of the CPR.

KINDERSLEY

Kindersley is on a CPR line running west from Rosetown to Alsask.

In 1907 W. R. Tindall, the first settler in the district, erected a sod house and began to break the virgin prairie with oxen. In 1909 the Canadian Northern

Railway laid the steel through the townsite, which was named in honor of Sir Robert Kindersley, a heavy stockholder in the CNR at the time the town was born. He later became governor of the Hudson's Bay Company. Shortly before his death, which occurred in 1954, he gave the town a portrait of himself done in oils. You can see it by visiting the mayor of the town.

KINGSLAND

Kingsland is a little over twenty miles south of Biggar. It was only a rural post office in the home of Herb McGlaughlin. It closed out in the early sixties. A mile west of Mr. McGlaughlin's home is the Kingsland country school. The children of the district from grades on to six are bussed to Howard Powell school out on highway number 4 and if they are above grade six they are bussed to Rosetown. The Kingsland school is used as a community hall. Right beside is a one-sheet curling rink; it and the adjoining ball fields are in excellent shape and the community is an active one — far enough away from any big center to have a life of its own.

Kingsland school was built in 1909 by Allan Ireland and when it came time for a name, Mr. Goodyear, Bishop Briggs and L. J. Pepper suggested the name Kingsland because they knew of a place by that name in England. The post office took its name from the school. A few of the residents of Kingsland district not mentioned before would include: Wilfred, John and Dick Rawson; Chris Rasmussen (a stone mason in the old country who built his lovely Saskatchewan home largely out of stone, too); Alvin Monks; Clarence Hobson; Stan Slocombe; William Simpson; Jack, Jimmy and George Ireland; George Ogg; Roger Ronson; Arthur Bartlett; Andy Shannon; Andy McCullough; Howard Powell; David Baldwin.

KINGSVIEW

The district surrounding Tako was settled in 1904. Mrs. Roy King operated the first post office in her home on a rise of land two miles east of the present site of Tako. Because of the wonderful view she had from her kitchen window she named the post office Kingsview. Some of the early settlers were: Jimmy Dickson, Alec Taylor, Frank Krips, Johnny Grant, Bill Dempster, Tom Gauley, Joe Savard and Tommy Lloyd. See the story of Tako for a detailed account of how the GTP chose the name Tako over Kingsview for their grain point.

KINHOP

Kinhop, a siding halfway between Tessier and Harris, was named for William Hopkins. Mr. Hopkins owned a large farm five miles west of Tessier and in 1914 he put pressure on the railway company to put in a loading platform which was a mile from the corner of his farm so that he could load his grain directly into box cars. The CN consented.

The R. B. McLean Grain Company built an elevator at the siding and in 1915 it handled 300,000 bushels of grain. When it came to naming the siding the name of Hopkins was suggested but there was a place by that name in Saskatchewan so they just juggled the letters, dropped an "S," and came up with Kinhop. The name was accepted.

Mr. Hopkins was mayor of Saskatoon in 1909 and 1910.

KINISTINO

Kinistino is one of the variations of the original tribal name of the Cree Indians who became predominant in this area by 1800. There is a local tradition that a Saulteaux chief was known by this name. Founded in the late 1870s as the Carrot River Settlement, a post office named "Kinisteno" was opened in January 1, 1883, with the spelling officially changed to "Kinistino" in 1887.

KINLEY

Kinley on the CNR just west of Saskatoon was named in honor of the Reverend H. J. Kinley, a Methodist minister who had taken up a half section of land two miles directly west of the present townsite.

It grew into a fine little town and being on the main line of the CNR it has held on. It's not a big place but it's alive. Bill Dunbar, one of the finest all-around athletes of the 30s, farmed just a few miles southwest of the town.

KINLEY

Kinley on the CPR just west of Saskatoon never grew to be anything but two elevators (now boarded up) and a station (which has now disappeared).

The CPR and the CNR were very particular about NOT duplicating names within the province — sometimes even going outside the province as happened with Roblin, Manitoba, and Robin, Saskatchewan. This policy was followed to lessen confusion in handling mail and freight. However, this certainly never happened at Kinley and if things were shipped to the wrong Kinley it was only a matter of a one-mile drive to get things straightened out.

KINOOSAO

Kinoosao 57°05'-102°01' is right on the Saskatchewan-Manitoba border halfway down the east shore of Reindeer lake. Kinoosao is the Cree word for "fish." The name for the settlement was approved on October 2, 1952, when a fish-filleting plant was established there. Regular mail service started on the first of November 1954 and they received mail twice monthly by aircraft from La Ronge.

KIPLING

Kipling is between Dalzell and Inchkeith on a main line of the CNR. It was named to honor Rudyard Kipling, the renowned British poet and storyteller. He was also known as a leading supporter of the British Empire. He received the 1907 Nobel prize for literature.

His most famous poem, "Recessional," was written in 1897 in honor of Queen Victoria's Diamond Jubilee and contains a strong warning to the British not to exploit other races. However, you should read "If" occasionally just for your own good!

KISBEY

Kisbey was the choice of name settlers sent in to call the village in honor of a pioneer mail carrier, Percy Kisbey, who came by sleigh or buggy to the Percy district post office, no matter what the weather and roads were like. He hauled the mail from Moosomin and Alameda. He was a young Irishman from Dublin. He named his own post office Dermington for his only son, Percy Dermington

Kisbey. The son was killed in World War I.

The CPR was built to Arcola from the east in late 1900 and to Stoughton from Regina in 1904 and the link through Kisbey from Arcola to Stoughton was completed in 1905, the year Kisbey was incorporated as a village.

KLAMATH

Klamath post office opened in 1920 in the farm home of Mr. C. Lorenston. It was situated 16 miles south and 3 miles east of Marriott Corners. It was not a paying proposition and was closed so long ago it does not even appear on the post office "nixie" list which shows the post offices that have been closed and also tells you where to send printed matter to the people who still live in the district. Mr. Lorenston suggested the name Klamath as a remembrance of where he came from in Oregon. Many people homesteaded twice. Actually Mr. Lorenston came from Sweden to Oregon, and then up to Saskatchewan. Cando, Cavalier and Spiritwood were named in much the same way.

KLECZKOWSKI

Kleczkowski was an inland post office at 32-45-9-W3, and Mr. W. A. Bellamy was the first postmaster. The district gets its mail from Oscar Lake now. The first settlers to the district were predominately Polish and they named their new home for a famous Polish general. There is a Kleczkowski lake in Quebec.

KLINTONEL

Klintonel is near Eastend. The first post office was on the ranch of C. L. Lewis and originally they wanted to call it Clinton or Lewis but the post office officials would not approve. Since Mr. Lewis always signed his name Clinton L. Lewis the combination was made into Klintonel.

KNOLLYS

Knollys is on a CPR line between Eastend and Ravenscrag in the southwest corner of the province. It was named for Mr. Knollys, a close advisor to the late King Edward VII of England.

KOHLSVILLE

Kohlsville, one of the newest (1967) place names in Saskatchewan, honors

Rene Kohls, former Indian agent at Duck Lake. It is on the combined Indian reserves of Beardy and Okemasis six miles west of Duck Lake.

The actual location is on the Beardy reserve and consists of a well-laid-out village site with a good school; a fine Roman Catholic church where Father Gauthier holds services; an outdoor rink, boarded and well lit; and the most eye-catching of all, "the shop."

Doug McDonald is the project supervisor, and in a large complex of new buildings with the most up-to-date machinery, houses are prefabricated for the Beardy-Okemasis and other reserves in the agency: One Arrow, James Smith and Moose Woods. Jacob Mike is the timekeeper and his worksheets show that from 32 to 44 men (depending on the season of the year) are employed. Here are some of their names: Harold and Joseph Seesequasis, Edwin Thomas, Ronald Gardypie, Walter Cameron, Ray Smallchild, Frank Eyahpaise, Miles Spencer and Ernest Mike. The Chief of the combined reserves is Albert Seesequasis who is just starting his second term. He works in the shop alongside the others.

The project at Kohlsville is not an isolated one, it is repeated at Sweet Grass, Punnichy and other points in the province.

KROMSTAL

Kromstal is a Mennonite village in the Osler-Warman area less than thirty miles northeast of Saskatoon. It is a German word that, when literally translated, comes out "a place full of gadgets." It is named for Kromstal, Germany, the former home of many of the residents of the district. They immigrated to Canada in the late 1890s.

KRONAU

Kronau is the second stop south of Regina on a CPR line that runs to Carlyle. It was incorporated as a village in 1907 and was named, by early settlers who came into the district in the 1890s, from a place in southern Russia. These settlers, although former residents of Russia, were of German extraction and had retained the original language and customs. The

village was reorganized on November 15, 1917, and someday may very well be just a suburb of Regina.

KRUPP

Krupp was a rural post office at 1-29-27-W3 near Fox Valley. Its first postmaster was Mr. P. E. Hamel. The office is closed now and the residents of the district get their mail at Fox Valley.

The first homesteaders into the district were German and they gave it a proud German name, Krupp. Krupp is the name of one of the leading German industrial families. The Krupp firm became one of the greatest in the world producing munitions, steel and machinery.

Friedrich Krupp (1787-1826) founded the Krupp works at Essen in 1811. His son, Alfred Krupp (1812-1887), later took over and developed the firm from one with 4 workmen to one employing 20,000. He invented the seamless railway tire, an important development for railroads throughout the world. He also perfected a method of casting steel cannon which helped Prussia defeat Austria in 1866 and France in 1870, and gave the Krupps control of Germany's arms industry.

Friedrich Alfred Krupp (1854-1902), the son of Alfred Krupp, expanded the company's shipbuilding activities. He had one child, Bertha, for whom the "Big Bertha" long-range guns of World War I were named. She married Gustav von Bohlen und Halbach (1870-1950), whom the Kaiser permitted to bear the name Krupp. He became head of the firm.

After World War I, the allies reduced the firm's steel capacity and forbade it to make munitions. Concentrating on peacetime goods, Gustav Krupp rebuilt the company. But under Adolf Hitler, the Krupps produced arms again. After World War II, Gustav Krupp escaped trail as a war criminal because of illness. But his son, Alfred (1907-   ) was sentenced to 12 years in prison. The company was confiscated after World War II. But in 1951 Krupp was freed.

Krupp purchased equipment and rebuilt the firm. Much of it had been destroyed in World War II. The firm now makes only industrial machinery.

The Krupps have had a social security program for 100 years, and the workers have never struck.

KRYDOR

Krydor is on a CNR line than runs from North Battleford to Prince Albert and is just north of Redberry lake. The name is a combination of the first letters of Krysak and the last letters of Teador. These letters were taken from the names of Peter Krysak and Teodor Lucyk, prominent Ukrainian pioneers of the community.

Dr. Stephen Worobetz was Prime Minister Trudeau's choice as Saskatchewan's new lieutenant-governor to succeed R. L. Hanbidge in February of 1970. Dr. Worobetz is one of three children raised by Ukrainian parents who moved to Krydor in 1906. When asked if he felt Ukrainians were increasing their contributions to Saskatchewan life he said, "A lot of credit must go to the original pioneers who come here with nothing, having only the land and some basics. As things improved, instead of buying luxuries, they educated their children. And for the youngsters who benefited from that opportunity, it was much easier."

Dr. Worobetz is married to a slim, attractive wife he calls Mick. She is one of ten children. Her parents are also Ukrainian, having come to Canada and settled in Cudworth in 1907.

Dr. Worobetz, who was awarded the Military Cross in 1944 while serving with the Princess Patricia's Canadian Light Infantry in Italy, says anything to do with people interests him. The couple live at 405 Lake Crescent, Saskatoon.

KUROKI

During the Russo-Japanese war of 1904-1905, headlines in the press appeared when General Kuroki passed through Saskatchewan enroute to New York for the purpose of negotiating financial assistance for the Japanese.

It was at this time that the CNR was building in the district. The railroad officials suggested Kuroki as the name and since there was a strong sympathetic feeling for the Japanese it was accepted.

KUTAWA

In 1883 Mr. A. V. Lindeburg built a new telegraph station approximately 8 miles north of the present town of Punnichy. He chose a spot where there was an opening or clearing and there he built a log house which is still standing. Donald A. Lindeburg, a grandson, lived in it until October, 1966, when he moved into Punnichy. While Donald's grandfather was building the house some Cree Indians visited him and asked him what he was doing. He told them and they informed him that the clearing in which he was building was called, in Cree, a kutawa. This was the name he gave to the new telegraph station on the old historic line that ran from Qu'Appelle to Prince Albert. This telegraph station in turn gave its name to the post office, the local municipality and the school.

At its height, which was shortly after the Rebellion of '85, Kutawa was the headquarters of the Indian Agency that included the following reserves: Poor Man, Day Star, Gordon and Moscowequan. Mr. Keith was the first agent. W. A. Heubach opened a store three miles to the west and later another store opened right at Kutawa, owned and operated by Henry Foster. A police detachment was sent to Kutawa and their barracks were erected a mile to the east. A great annual event at Kutawa (May 24th) was the horse races, conducted by the "Touchwood Turf Association." A most ardent supporter and promoter of this association was Joseph Holis, a rancher. He was a familiar figure mounted on horseback with a long string of hounds following behind. When he "rode to the hounds" the hunted animal was not a fox but the coyote, of which he caught many.

When the Grand Trunk Pacific built through in 1908 it missed Kutawa, and Punnichy, eight miles to the south, grew into the town. The telegraph and post office have long since been closed, and the old line has been dismantled but here and there on virgin pasture lands you can see the remnants of the cart ruts that followed along the old historic telegraph line — the main line of its time.

KYLE

Kyle is the second last stop on a branch line south from Rosetown to Matador. Before the steel came in 1923, the district was known as Kyleville, as that was the name of the local post office, named for Jerry Kyle, an early settler in the district. When the CPR arrived in 1923 they shortened the name to Kyle for their townsite.

KYLEMORE

Kylemore is the first station east of Wadena and within sight of Fishing lake just to the south. As the CNR tracks were being laid in 1904 one of the crew, a Scotsman, looked south toward Fishing lake and saw a large island. He exclaimed, "Kylemore!" This is the Gaelic word for "big island" and this became the name of the townsite.

Mr. Menzo van Patten became the first postmaster and in 47 years never missed a train.

L

LACADENA

This account of how Lacadena got its name was taken from the Elrose Review of May 12, 1966.

The Lacadena municipality was formed in the fall of 1910 and the first meeting was held in January, 1911, with Henry Bailey as reeve. The name Lacadena was suggested by Mr. Kellogg. It is said to be a Spanish word, meaning "chain" or a linking together. In Spanish it's written "La Cadena."

LAC PELLETIER

The village of Lac Pelletier is five miles from Lake Pelletier, southwest of Swift Current 11-14-W3. The whole district was named for Mr. Pelletier, an early resident. Originally the lake was called "Lac la Plume" which in English would be Quill Lake.

The first white man in the district to take up land was Alphonse Metivier, who came in April of 1906. His wife and four children came on May 15th. There was quite an influx of people—mostly bachelors—A. Deschamps, O. Couture, H. Sylvain, A. Charron, N. Roy, four Perron brothers, F. Lacroix, L. Letourneau, J. Arcand, N. Monette and E. Dumisnil. Many Metis families moved in and lived along the lake. They were all French-speaking.

A most tragic thing happened on January 11, 1917, when a fierce blizzard arose while the children were at school. They were attending Congress country school which was a school in the district. Four girls had to go to the outhouse so they left the school to go outside. The school yard was not fenced and visibility was nil. They never found their way back. They were found a day later frozen to death, the oldest girl with her back to the wind and the other three girls in a circle in front of her with their heads on her lap. Three of them (aged 14, 12 and 10) were daughters of Mr. and Mrs. Ovila Deschamps.

The other was a daughter of Mr. and Mrs. Wetherstrand, aged 9. They were found a quarter of a mile from the school. The teacher and a small girl also went out and became lost and finally bumped into a bachelor's home. The teacher was so badly frozen that she spent six months in the hospital. The little girl suffered only from shock. Blizzards took a terrible toll of homesteaders lives. It was not uncommon for a man to string a rope between his house and barn during the winter. It was also common to leave a lamp burning in the window to guide people to safety.

LAC VERT

Lac Vert is on a CPR line than runs from Watson to Melfort. The hamlet is named for 'the nearby lake of the same name. Lac Vert is French for Green lake and this gives us two Green lakes in Saskatchewan.

The first settlers came in 1905 and they had a thirty-mile haul with their grain either north to Melfort or south to Watson. They were very glad to welcome the CPR in 1923 and railway officials just took the local name for the townsite.

LADDER VALLEY

Ladder Valley is less than ten miles east of Bodmin and to the south of Ladder lake from which it takes its name. The creek and the lake gave their name to the post office and to a very famous logging company of the 30s, the "Ladder Lake Lumber Company."

LADY LAKE

Lady Lake is on a CNR line north of Sturgis on the way to Hudson's Bay. Originally it was called Astwood, however, the first overseas flight from England to America to carry passengers led to the changing of the name. Lady Lake honors a titled lady from England who was one of the passengers.

LAFLECHE

In French Lafleche literally means "the arrow." Lafleche is named in honor of Louis Francois Richer Lafleche who, as a youth, was a missionary among the Metis hunters of the plains and who later rose to be the bishop of Trois Rivieres, Que.

LAIRD

Laird is a village on the Carlton branch of the CNR, 50 miles north of Saskatoon. When the Northwest Territories were organized in 1876 as a separate administrative unit, with the capital at Battleford, David Laird was appointed the first resident Lieutenant-Governor and superintendent of Indian Affairs. In 1877 he negotiated Treaty Seven with the Indians of Southern Alberta. Laird is named for him.

LAJORD

Lajord is less than twenty miles southeast of Regina on the famous eighty-mile straight stretch of CPR track to Stoughton. Many of the early settlers were Norwegian. The quarter section for the townsite was owned by Mr. P. E. Thompson of Bannville, Minnesota. He wished to name it Lajordwas, for his mountain home in Norway. The railway officials shortened it to Lajord.

LAKE ALMA

Lake Alma has a sad story connected with its name. It is named for nearby Lake Alma which in turn was named for Alma Johnson, a daughter of early pioneers in the district, who lost her life in a boating accident on the lake.

LAKE FOUR

Lake Four got its name from Camp #4, one of five lumber camps operated by the Prince Albert Lumber Company on the west side of Amyot Lake.

Victor Hodgins was one of the first settlers along with Mr. and Mrs. John Reimer and his brother, Pete.

LAKE LENORE

Lake Lenore is just south of Melfort on the shores of Lake Lenore from which it takes its name. Mr. George Gerwing, pioneer postmaster tells the following story of how Lake Lenore got its name:

"The government official who surveyed this part of Saskatchewan had a daughter by the name of Lenora. When he came to the lake which extended from township 39 almost to township 43, and nearly 18 miles long, he named it Lenora Lake. When this community received its first post office in 1904, it was changed to Lake Lenore, as it was then commonly called."

LAKENHEATH

Lakenheath took its name from Twelve Mile Lake nearby. This plus the fact that there was some rough country between the lake and Lakenheath village accounted for the name.

Charlie Silzer was one of the first settlers in the area and he still lives there. Lakenheath used to be a fair sized village but now it is down to two houses, an elevator and a bulk gas station.

LA LOCHE

The settlement of La Loche was named by the Chipewyan Indians on this area, probably in the early 1800s. The name La Loche is French for a fish which is found in Methy lake, a species called mariah. I have not been able to find out anything further about these fish, except that I saw several, and they resemble a tadpole.

Peter Pond was the first person to explore this area. He travelled over Methy lake (now often called Lac La Loche) in 1778, and in the same year reached the Arctic Watershed via Methy Portage. At this time La Loche was known as Methy Portage — named for the famous 12½ mile portage that separates the water routes of the Athabasca, Mackenzie and Churchill river systems.

The North-West Company had a fort here as early as 1808, but this establishment was closed when that company amalgamated with the Hudson's Bay Company in 1812. The Hudson's Bay company established a post at Portage La

Loche (La Loche is sometimes called Portage La Loche) in 1853 and it has been in continuous operation since that date. In the 19th century, the York boats left lower Fort Garry on the Red river and travelled by the Saskatchewan river, Amisk lake, Frog Portage and Churchill river system, to reach Methy Portage some two months later. Here the men from the south met the men from the Mackenzie river and trade goods were exchanged for furs.

The present population of La Loche is approximately 1400 and Chipewyan and English are spoken. Fur trapping is the main industry and squirrel, mink, beaver, muskrat, ermine, otter, lynx, fox and bears are trapped. Methy lake is also fished on a commercial basis. Many of the people still depend on hunting and fishing to supply food for their families.

La Loche can rightfully be referred to as the Squirrel Capital of Saskatchewan as its trappers are among the world's most proficient in the taking of squirrel.

The Royal Canadian Mounted Police opened their detachment here in 1967, and presently there are two members posted at La Loche. The settlement of Turnor lake is policed from La Loche.

This information came from Cpl. F. T. Martin and Cst. G. D. Rees of the RCMP.

LAMPARD

Lampard is a rural post office twenty miles north of Dafoe on the west side of Quill lake. In 1906 a young Scottish lad, Bob Lampard, homesteaded there. He was killed in World War I and when it came time to establish the rural post office in 1920 his name was used. In 1923 a rural school was also named for him. The school closed in the 50s and the post office in 1970.

LAMPMAN

The village of Lampman is on the CNR 67 miles S.W. of Maryfield and on two short branch lines to the south (to Northgate and Estevan).

It was named for Archibald Lampman. 1861-1899, Canadian poet; author of "Among the Millet" and "Lyrics of Earth."

The first settlers came into this district in 1890 and the railway arrived in 1909.

Whoever was in charge of naming the stations on the line had considerable influence and a deep appreciation of the written word. Start at Lampman and work northwest and you'll find the following stations named for authors: Browning, Wordsworth, Carlyle, Cowper, Service, Parkman,and Ryerson.

LANCER

The CPR came to Lancer in 1913 and gave it its name. No one knows why the name was chosen but it was worked out by someone who had a knowledge of the Crimean War (1854-1856). The men who led the famous cavalry charge there were called Lancers even though they were using sabres. Here are the names of the streets in Lancer: Balaclava, Plume, Sabre, Spur and Pennon. The avenues bear the following names: Hussar, Flag, and, of course, every village has a Railway Avenue.

LANDIS

Landis is on the main line of the CNR about halfway between Biggar and Unity. The rails were laid by the GTP in 1908 and among the first passengers to get off the first train was Miss Fanny Wilson of Elm Creek, Manitoba. She had come to live with her sister, Mrs. Alex Porter.

Here are some other Landis firsts: building—Bob Butler; livery man — Jack Tinant; storekeeper — E. E. Bent; pumpman for the railway — Mr. Atkinson; butcher — Frank Bingham; doctor — Dr. N. L. Phoenix; druggist — Mr. Sam Martin; editor of the Landis Record — Mr. A. M. Brock.

Landis was named by the railway officials for Judge Kenesaw Mountain Landis (1866-1944). He was an American Jurist who became district judge of the Northern District of Illinois (1905-22). In later years he became baseball commissioner for the American and National Leagues of Professional Baseball Clubs (1920-1944).

Landis is a progressive town in a good farming district.

LANDSCAPE

Landscape is between Verwood and Viceroy. It was a humming little hamlet in 1912 with the arrival of the CPR. In 1912 the Co-op erected an elevator, and in

1913, Mr. W. D. Gunson built an elevator of his own. The drayman was Nels Robstad. The Wenaus brothers, Axel and John, started a store and a machine agency. Alfred and Ted Wenaus had a feed barn. The post office was in the back of the Wenaus store and was run by Mr. Mackin. The pioneer venture of the Wenaus brothers continued about two years. After the store closed the post office was moved to the Mackin farm, just south of Landscape, and the Mackins along with their daughter, Marjorie, kept the office in their home until 1917. It passed on to Alex McMillan and then Mr. J. Heroux took it over until it closed on March 3, 1925.

The CPR built a section house and water tank which obtained its water supply from a heavy spring on the Mackin farm. In 1960 the CPR closed the section and the house and water tank were sold. They also took out the railroad switches and Landscape came to a quiet end. It had provided the people of the district with a market for grain, a place to purchase coal, wood and groceries, and ship the odd can of cream.

There is no special significance to the name, Landscape. The former name of Wenaus apparently caused confusion with another place and the smaller point was asked to change. Their answer, Landscape, is a very general word and not very imaginative.

LANG

Lang is on a CPR line between Milestone and Ibsen. It was named after Mr. Lang, a resident engineer who lived in Moose Jaw in the early days. It was incorporated as a village in 1906.

LANGBANK

Langbank is between Inchkeith and Vandura in the southeast corner of the province. It was given its name by McKenzie and Mann who built the railroad through there in 1907. Langbank is named for a small town just out of Glasgow, Scotland.

LANGENBURG

Langenburg is 40 miles S.E. of Yorkton. It was settled in the late 1880s by German immigrants and named after Prince Hohenlohe Langenburg.

LANGHAM

The town of Langham was given its name in 1905 by Canadian Northern officials to honor E. Langham, who was purchasing agent for the line at that time.

LANGMEADE

The first to arrive in the Langmeade district, south and west of Vawn, about forty miles from North Battleford, were James and Andrew Spence and their eldest sister, Letitia Ann (Annie), in June, 1906.

The brothers cut and stacked hay for their nearly 200 head of cattle and their sister cooked and kept house in their log shack.

There was no ferry, so they crossed the North Saskatchewan river by boat to shop for supplies in Bresaylor, visiting with their cousins at the same time.

By October they were joined by the rest of the Spence family. Their parents, George C. and Maria (Adams) Spence were homesteading for the second time. In 1880 they travelled from Manitoba over the old Carlton Trail to the Lindsay district, south of Prince Albert. One son, Andrew, was born in the Prince Albert barracks during the Riel Rebellion.

In 1907, other families moved in and a school, called Spenceville, was erected. In 1908 All-Saints Anglican church was built and stands today in a beautifully tended churchyard.

The post office was in the Spence home. Application was made to call the settlement Long Meadow, but as there was a place by that name, postal authorities suggested Langmeade, which in old English means long meadow.

Other familiar names in the district are Foulds, Head, Jones, Gunson, Boggust, Swain, some in the third and fourth generation.

The post office and school have long since closed at Langmeade, but church services go on. Reverend Duncan McLean of Battleford holds services regularly at his home church, Meota and Langmeade in the summer. In winter, Langmeade residents meet in private homes for service.

This information came from Mrs. J. A. Struble of Calgary, Albert and Mrs. Rodney Fitch of Meota.

LANIGAN

Lanigan is a fast-growing town in east-central Saskatchewan. No less than five CPR rail lines radiate out from this junction point and in addition the community is served by No. 4 and No. 20 highways.

With the discovery of potash nearby it won't be long until Lanigan is a little "Hub City."

It was named for W. B. Lanigan, a freight traffic manager of the CPR.

LANIWCI

Whether our early settlers came from Europe, eastern Canada, or the United States they tended to settle in blocks and the names they chose for their communities reflected their native language.

Laniwci, a rural post office, 50 miles N.E. of Saskatoon is typical of the Ukrainian centers that dot our province. One-eighth of the population of Saskatchewan is Ukrainian! Laniwci is named after the world "Prairies" which in Ukrainian is "Lani."

Near Prince Albert where they settled on the Garden river they called their post office Kalyna which is the Ukrainian name for a cranberry-like fruit. This they found in abundance around their new home.

They named their settlements for the towns and cities of their Ukrainian homeland: Whitkow, near North Battleford; Gorlitz, near Yorkton; Tarnopol, near Melfort; Odessa S.E. of Regina; and Dnieper, an inland post office N.E. of Yorkton, named for the largest river in the Ukraine.

LA PLAINE

Leckford, Bonne Plaine and now La Plaine are all the same place. It consists of two Pool elevators with Albert Bonneau as agent and a huge potato storage and processing shed situated six miles south of Duck Lake.

Taking the names in order this is how it happened. The railway built north from Saskatoon to Prince Albert and arrived at La Plaine in the 1890s. The first settlers in the district were American and when the Western Elevator Company built on the site it was named Leckford.

Gradually the Americans proved up and moved out and the district became predominately French. As this happened the influential farmers began to think of a French name. However, two factions began to develop: those who sided with Emiti Cecillion favoured Bonne Plaine and those who supported Ferdinand Lanovaz thought La Plaine would be better. The one thing they agreed on was "Plaine"; it was apparently settled when, with Ed Schmidt as agent, Bonne Plaine was painted on the elevator. It didn't last six months!

A new petition which was circulated in the district showed that the majority of the people preferred La Plaine and so the sign was changed forthwith.

Some of the settlers who were deeply involved in this besides the two previously mentioned were: Albert Perret, Ernest Doucette, Joe, Ernest and Marcel Lanovaz, Henry Gauthier and Pete Como.

The $100,000 potato storage and processing plant known as La Plaine Processors Ltd. was built in 1966 by owners Terry La Borash and the Benarchuk brothers, Alec, Terry, Pete and Walter. The plant has storage space for 160,000 bushels of poatoes besides the processing equipment which converts them into fresh-frozen chips.

LAPORTE

West of Eston and south of what is now Laporte was the farm of the Martin Land Company, which purchased a large tract of CNR land. Most of the employees of this farm came from Laporte, Indiana, hence the name Laporte was given to a post office which opened in the district in 1914. When the railroad arrived the post office gave its name to the townsite.

LA RONGE

The quest for beaver led to the westward thrust of exploration in pre-settlement times and many of the place names reflect this preoccupation.

La Ronge, a growing northern settlement that thrives on the tourists that come to catch the prize lake trout, is situated on the west shore of the lake in far northern Saskatchewan from which it took its name.

Two theories exist regarding the name La Ronge and the beaver figures in both of these. The first is that the name is derived from the French verb "to gnaw"

— thus it has been maintained by some that the name was given the lake by voyageurs who discovered evidences of beaver cuttings in the La Ronge area.

The alternative suggestion is that the lake's numerous deep-cut inlets and bays appeared to have been gnawed into the shoreline by some gigantic animal, perhaps a "Kitchi-Amik" or "Great Beaver."

LASHBURN

In 1903 a number of the Barr Colonists settled around Lashburn. In 1904 they were joined by a group from eastern Canada. A post office and store were opened by A. B. Klombie which he called Wirral after Wirral of Cheshire, England. The first school No. 1406 was also named Wirral.

The Canadian Northern arrived in 1905 and their chosen townsite was three miles east of Wirral. The railway officials named it Lashburn — the Lash was for Z. A. Lash, Canadian Northern Railway solicitor, and the burn came from a small creek nearby (in Scottish a burn is a small creek).

Wirral post office and store moved into the townsite and became Lashburn. Mr. Klombie remained postmaster until 1926 when he and his family moved to the United States.

LAST MOUNTAIN

References to Last Mountain Lake appear as early as Daniel Harmon's journal, 1804, and it is so-named on the map of the Palliser expedition, 1857.

In 1869, the Hudson's Bay Company established a post on the west shore and near the south end of Last Mountain Lake. Here, Isaac Cowie carried on a booming trade in provisions and robes gleaned from the buffalo herds still to be seen in the area. By 1872, the rapidly dwindling herds had retreated so far to the west and south that the post was closed.

There were no rail lines north of Regina and so the Pearson Land Company operated two small sternwheelers, the "Qu'Appelle" and the "Lady of the Lake" on a shuttle service. They were kept busy carrying supplies and settler's effects to the new settlement areas along the shores of the lake and carrying grain and other produce on their return trip.

In the early 1900s, about ten miles west of the present day Duval an inland post office developed called Last Mountain. Improved transportation by road and car have caused it to be closed.

LAURA

Mrs. Lillie McCurdy and the CNR arrived at Laura in 1908. Her family opened a boarding house. Her son, Jim, until his death in 1969, operated a confectionery, cafe and post office in the same building.

Besides handling the mail, Mrs. McCurdy is a long-time agent for the Star-Phoenix. Her first papers were delivered from Saskatoon each morning by Bill's Taxi. She writes that this was a great surprise and boon to early settlers.

Two of the first settlers in the district were Andrew Boomhower and William Darnborough. In the 1920s Mr. Darnborough won a Canadian Wheat Championship, was recognized Canada-wide for his sheep and developed the "Homesteader" strain of peas used today. He also was quite artistically inclined and made many signs out of seeds. One of these hung in the offices of the Saskatoon Exhibition for years.

Mr. Fred Ingran, a CNR surveyor, named the town in honor of his wife, Laura.

LAVENTURE

Halfway between Spiritwood and Leoville on Highway No. 24 is the country post office and store of Laventure. Across the road is the imposing St. Bonaventure Church. Aime Turgeon, postmaster and storekeeper at Laventure for over 30 years told this story. His father, Alfred Turgeon, and Napoleon Laventure came to the district in 1911. The Laventures were a large family and they all homesteaded in the vicinity. It is from this family that Laventure takes its name.

LAWRIE

Robert Lawrie came from Scotland to Ipswich, South Dakota in the middle 1880's. He farmed there before homesteading in Saskatchewan in 1892 between Theodore and Insinger. He established a post office in his home and named it Lawrie. This was carried on by his son, Robert, until the office closed out about 1920.

Annie M. Krill, Robert's daughter, of Calgary, Alberta, sent in this information.

LAWSON

Lawson is near the end of a branch line northwest from Moose Jaw to Riverhurst, and named for the pioneer settler, Joseph Lawson. Angus H. MacLean, a Presbyterian student-minister, was stationed at Lawson during the summer of 1911 and the following is taken from his book, "The Galloping Gospel."

"I began by spending a night with the Lawsons of Lawson, the founders of the community. They were the oldest settlers and were among the most prosperous, yet they lived in a sod house. It was no more beautiful than a heap of earth from the outside, but within it was roomy and one of the cosiest homes I was ever privileged to share. The walls, which were made of plowed furrows a yard thick, were whitewashed so that they caught and reflected the light from the few small and deeply-set windows. The dirt floors were as hard and shiny as tile. As for warmth it was the most efficient kind of dwelling that could have been devised."

LAYCO

Layco is on the CPR near Foam Lake. It was named for a small lake nearby of the same name.

LEACH SIDING

Leach Siding is between Dinsmore and Wiseton on a CNR line. Walter Leach of 1227 Avenue E North, Saskatoon, clearly remembers his dad, Walter Leach, driving the 200 miles with horses from Regina to the homestead in 1906.

Although the railroad came through in 1913 it was not until 1925 that they were able to persuade the CNR officials to build the siding. It was on Mr. Walter Leach's land, hence the name. Two elevators were built, the Pool and the UGG. Two elevators and two elevator agents — that's all there ever was to Leach Siding.

They had their good times and their bad times. This is the account of a sad time. In the early 1900s Eugene Milicke of Dundurn and his hired man were boring a well on John Cowden's farm with a horse-powered bit. They struck a rock and set off a dynamite charge to break it up so they could take it out in pieces. Soon, too soon, after, Mr. Melicke stepped on the hook, grabbed the cable and was lowered into the 2-foot-wide hole. He was overcome with gas and died. The people who came to the rescue used a long rope with a blanket attached. This they alternately lowered and raised, much the same way you'd swab out a gun barrel. After it was safe they recovered Mr. Melicke's body.

LEACROSS

The information on Leacross, Silver Stream, Waterfield and Carlea was received from Mr. H. S. Sims, secretary-treasurer of Leacross.

The earliest settlers in this immediate district came in 1905. The original name was Auto Road. The name was quite misleading because at that time there were no autos and there were no roads. The CPR from Tisdale came through the district in 1924 and it crossed the Leather river here. The settlers changed the name Auto Road to Leacross to signify the crossing of the river.

LEADER

Leader is on a CPR line 84 miles northwest of Swift Current. It was originally called Prussia, a name selected by the predominately German settlement which surrounded the town. During the First World War (1914-1918) feeling ran very high, particularly after the execution of nurse Edith Cavell as a spy.

Residents had the name of their town changed to Leader. At Coblenz they had their named changed to Cavell. These were not the only changes of place names in Saskatchewan. Many others took place and here is a list furnished by Dr. A. Becker, M.D. of 102 Canada Bldg. Saskatoon.

First is the name of the town as it is known today and this is followed by the original name: Peebles — Kaiser; Mazenoid — Deckerville; Young — Eigenheim; Kronau — Katharinenthal; Scottsguard — Kramer; Springside — Lekmann; Killaly — Mareahilf; Sedley — New Holstein; Burstall — Schmidt; Prelate — Schulz; Langenburg — Hokenloke; Raymore — Wolfsheim; Bethune — Waldorf; Rheine

— Rhine; Strasbourg — New Elsace; Edenwald — New Tulcea; Vibank — Alsace and Simmie — Maeskow.

LEAKVILLE

Leakville was a country post office seventeen miles south of Moose Jaw that served the surrounding district from 1914 to 1941.

It was named after the first postmaster, Charles Leak. Mr. Leak was an Englishman who had served for years in the Imperial army, but received his discharge just prior to World War I. Coming to Canada in 1914, he proceeded west as far as Moose Jaw, where he filed on the SW of 35-13-26, west of the second meridian, as a homesteader and within a matter of months was successful in opening a rural post office at his farm.

In turn this post office was taken over by a neighbor, Walter Lavier in 1915 and then by another neighbor, Ernest Clegg in 1916.

The saddest story in the district concerned Mr. Clegg and his family. In the late fall of 1917, Mr. Clegg began to dig a well by hand and at twenty-seven feet struck not water but coal.

Surprised, but not too disappointed, he hauled out some of the new-found fuel, tried it in his stove and found it to be fairly good. He hauled out enough to spend a comfortable winter with his wife and ten-year-old son.

The following spring, after he had completed his field work, Mr. Clegg went down his "well" for further investigate his find. He was overcome with "black-damp" gas. In the frantic rescue attempts by his family, his wife and son died in the well with him. Neighbors discovered this triple tragedy days later.

With the untimely passing of the Ernest Clegg family, the Leakville post office was taken over by Jess Fullwater and his wife, who farmed the NE 27-13-26, west of the second meridian.

Mr. and Mrs. Fullwater found it impossible to carry on farming and also operate the post office, so in the spring of 1918 Leakville moved back to its former location on the Clegg farm which had been purchased by Walter Lavier. Mr. Lavier operated it until it closed out in 1941.

Mail came once a week by team from Baildon in the early years and in later years by team or car from Tilney.

This information came from Mr. and Mrs. A. I. Lavier, Calgary, Alberta.

LEASK

Leask is 60 miles north of Saskatoon. It has a population of 500. Leask was first settled in 1904. It was incorporated as a village in 1912 when the CNR line pushed through from Prince Albert to North Battleford. The village was named after Robert Leask, a homesteader on whose land the townsite was located.

LEBRET

Lebret is a village 53 miles northeast of Regina in the Qu'Appelle Valley. Metis settlers were the pioneers in the area and in 1884 an Indian residential school was founded at this point. The village was named Lebret by Senator Girard in honor of Father Lebret who was in charge of the mission in the early days. He was also the first postmaster of Lebret.

LEEVILLE

The hamlet was named after the family of H. Lee, a homesteader on whose land, 18-8-29-2, it was located. Almost everything moved to Assiniboia in 1912 and 1913.

LEGHORN

Leghorn is on a CPR line about halfway between Maple Creek and Swift Current. It was named for a seaport in the province of Tuscany in Italy.

LEIGH

Leigh was an inland post office (now closed) located at S6-T27-R10-W3, which puts it just east of the present town of Wiseton. The post office was named after a town in Scotland.

LEINAN

Leinan is the second last stop on a CPR branch line north of Swift Current that ends just short of the South Saskatchewan River at Stewart Valley. It was named for Axel Leinan, first postmaster and storekeeper, who set up business there in 1908. Some of the first settlers into the district were: Peter Mjolid, Eric Holverson, Evan Jorgenson, Morris Brandhaugen, Gilbert Johnson,

Mr. and Mrs. Phiefer, Mr. and Mrs. Schorak, Mr. and Mrs. Lindahl, all farmers.

LEIPZIG

Leipzig is a small town on a branch line of the CPR that runs south of Wilkie to Kelfield. The settlement is predominately German and they named the town in memory of one of the largest and most colorful cities of their homeland, Leipzig.

Early settlers included the following: Melchior Muller, Johannes Novokowsky, Joe Gartner, Alvis Stark, Vinzenz Schweda, Dominik Muller, Melchior Schermann, Wenzel Suchan, August Franke, Jakob Gerbinsky, Johannes Salewsky, Michael Huber, Johann Schmidt, Stephan Leidl, Georg Reininger, Simon Star and Henrich Nestman.

During the First World War Leipzig changed its name to Arperes. This was done to honor A. R. Peres, the manager of a syndicate from Chicago USA, that farmed twelve quarters of land called "The Seed Farm." Shortly after the war ended the name was changed back to Leipzig.

Melchior Muller describes how he handled a balky ox thus: "I was breaking on my homestead and it was hot. I stopped my team of oxen to rest and one of them lay down. I let him rest for awhile, then I slapped him a little and urged him to get up. He wouldn't budge. I talked nice to him but he just lay there and chewed his cud. I got thinking, what can I do? I took a small bundle of grass and laid it by his back. Then I lit it. The ox got up and off we went plowing. Once, later on, that ox tried the same trick with me and all I did was pick a bit of grass and lay it beside him and he didn't even give me a chance to light my match!"

LEITCHVILLE

Leitchville was an inland post office (now closed) which was located at S20-T9-R19-W3, just west of the present town of Wiseton. It was named by the first postmaster who added a "ville" to his name.

LEMBERG

The town of Lemberg is situated between Fort Qu'Appelle and the Manitoba border. It was incorporated into a village in 1905 and as a town two years later. It received its name after a city in Poland, the country from which many of the first settlers came. Lemberg has a number of distinctions, among them the fact that the late Rt. Hon. J. G. Gardiner taught school there. Other teachers at Lemberg active in politics have included G. H. Castledon, Yorkton M.P. and M. J. Haver of the Social Credit party.

LEMSFORD

Lemsford is located on the "Empress" line which links Swift Current and the town of Empress on the Alberta-Saskatchewan border. It is one of the province's heaviest grain growing areas. The hamlet was named after an RCMP constable who was among the first residents in the area.

LENEY

Leney, the "L" in a series of alphabetically-named stations on the CNR line from Saskatoon to Biggar, is situated between Kinley and Mead on the northeast quarter of section 30-35-11-W3. It was named in honor of a railway official.

Some of the early settlers were: Howat, Weir, Kay, Scharf, Smith, Macpherson, Downie, Carr, Sharon, Goodfellow, Underwood, Neale, Burrows, Hewitt, Allan, Hodgins, Langhorn, Mellish, Kees and Furber. Some of their descendants are still prominent in the district.

The first grain harvested was hauled to market in Saskatoon by horses or oxen. The coming of the railroad in 1908 and the building of elevators lightened labor for the community, as building material and supplies were shipped by rail instead of requiring a three-day trip to and from Saskatoon. Leney thrived and gradually grew into a village. It consisted of a Grand Trunk station, section houses, hardware store and post office, two general stores, four elevators, livery barn, restaurant, butcher shop, bakeshop, two lumber yards, a blacksmith shop, a school, a bank, a municipal office, a telephone office, a hotel, a town hall, a poolroom and barbershop, a flour mill, and a garage and implement business. There were not many residences as the majority of people lived in their place of business.

The winter months were brightened by visiting, house parties, card parties and quilting bees. Often there were storms, making it unsafe to travel as the trails would be blown full. No travellers were ever turned away at night or at mealtimes. The coming of the telephone provided a speedier exchange of news and business, and it was very helpful in times of sickness.

Time passed and many changes took place. Perdue, on the CPR line only a mile to the north grew into a bigger town at the expense of Leney. People moved, business places moved or were boarded up, until today Leney consists of just a handful of occupied residences.

LENS

Lens was a country post office south of present day Carragana. It opened in 1932 with Thomas Mawhinney as postmaster. Upon the retirement of her husband, Mrs. Thomas Mawhinney took over and was postmistress until the post office closed out in 1943.

In 1920 the scheme and plan for the proposed townsite of Lens was surveyed for the Soldier Settlement Board where the village of Prairie River is now situated, and was approved by the Minister of Municipal Affairs, Regina, Saskatchewan. It was an ambitious and progressive one, involving approximately 162 acres, and was designed to serve and provide trading and shipping facilities for those who took up land fifteen miles to the south, in the Porcupine Soldier Settlement. It was connected with the townsite by what was known as the Prairie River road — the road of many bends! The proposed scheme made provision for a hospital, school, library, church, hotel, parks, businesses, industrial and residential districts. However, for some undisclosed reason, or reasons, this townsite never became a reality.

LENVALE

Lenvale came into being in 1928 when the CPR line was built. Sage was the first name chosen, but it was shortly changed to Hanson when an attempt was made to move the Bagley post office to it, with H. O. Hanson as postmaster. However, the postal department objected to this because they had another office of this name. It was decided to name the siding in honor of Len Fleshberg who had originally homesteaded the land.

LEOFELD

When the Benedictines came to this area, seven miles southeast of the present town of Cudworth in 1903, Pope Leo XIII was on the see of Peter; the name Leo Feld (Leo's field) was given to the first settlement, which quickly set up a church and school. These were both named St. Boniface in memory of the great English Benedictine missionary of the 8th century.

A little village grew up around the church and school. A store and post office served the community with the first mail being brought in from Dana. Most of the early settlers were of German descent and three of the first families were: Arnoldi, Britz and Renneberg.

When the railway came through in 1918, Cudworth, seven miles to the northwest, developed as a town gradually the village of Leofeld disappeared, with the exception of the church which was preserved as an historic site. Holy Mass is still offered there on occasions, especially on June 7th, the feast of St. Boniface.

The people of the area now attend the church of St. Michael in Cudworth.

LEOFNARD

The GTP built north from Young to Prince Albert in 1911. Leofnard is on that line between the thriving towns of Cudworth to the south and Wakaw to the north. At its height Leofnard had three elevators and two stores. Oldtimers who arrived just at the turn of the century included: Henry Medernach; Johnny Leiffer; Henry Temple; Heinie Kamptman; John Kurtenbach; John Boychuk; Bill Swick; Henry Schmidt; Tony Heck; the Oleksyn brothers, Bill, Mike, Steve and Nick; the Kostenuiks and the Didows.

These early settlers came by train to Rosthern and then drove in. There is some question about the naming of Leofnard. It is thought by some that the Leo came from Leo Kurtenbach. This was proposed by his father, John, when Leo died at an early age. No one we contacted had any idea where the "fnard" came from.

The last store at Leofnard closed in the summer of 1968. The last proprietor, Johnny Leiffer, built a fine new home beside it and that's about all there is left except one elevator.

Of all the people who have left the district Orland Kurtenbach is probably the best known. He is captain of the Vancouver Canucks (National Hockey League).

LEOVILLE

In 1930 Leo Carpenter took out the first homestead in the district. Within five years a dozen other families joined him and the settlement was named Leoville in his honor.

These early settlers used to supplement their income by hunting and trapping and the best muskrat trapping was where the Catholic church now stands.

LEPINE

Lepine is in north-central Saskatchewan on a CNR line that runs from Saskatoon to Melfort. It is said to have been named after Ambroise Lepine, one of Louis Riel's lieutenants during the Red River Rebellion.

LEROSS

Leross is between Kelliher and Lestock. It was named after the paymaster whose name was Le Ross. It was incorporated as a village in 1909.

LEROY

Starting at Venn and running for miles in a northeast direction is a big boggy draw. In the early days a settlement developed at the N.E. end of this and was called Bog End. It was a descriptive and helpful name to early travellers who were forever getting stuck in it.

In 1919 the railway came north from Lanigan and named it Onwa. The residents objected to this and the name gave way to Leroy in remembrance of Private Jack Leroy, a local boy, who was killed in the First World War.

LESLIE

Leslie is between Elfros and Foam Lake. It was incorporated as a village in 1909 and named Leslie after Mr. John Leslie, comptroller for the CPR.

At one time Leslie had a bank, a doctor, a drugstore, a lumberyard, a hardware store, a blacksmith shop, a poolroom, a John Deere implement agency, an IHC agency, a railway station and agent, three grocery stores, two churches, a public school, a high school, a town hall, a hotel and a cafe.

By 1969 all that was left was a Co-op store, a Co-op bulk station, one church and the town hall. The children are all bussed to Foam Lake which is a growing town. This story is a familiar one; the larger places are getting larger and the smaller places are getting smaller. Speedier transportation and the mechanization of farming is changing the face of Saskatchewan.

Leslie, a predominately Scandinavian settlement, has been and is noted for the wonderful scholars they have turned out. It was due to the combination of a dedicated principal, Mr. Edvin Fowler, who taught there for many years and is now retired and still makes his home at Leslie, and the serious sensibleness that Scandinavians bring to any task. Many are the doctors, nurses, lawyers, teachers, engineers and businessmen from Leslie who bear such names as: Harold Halldorson, Norman Nordal, Judith Thorsteinson, Paul Goodmanson, and Kris, Jill, Helgi and Magnus Eyolfson.

LESTOCK

Lestock is on the main line between Saskatoon and Melville. It is named for John Lestock Reid who came from Bowman, Ontario to Winnipeg in 1870. He was employed by the dominion government as a land surveyor.

In the archives office of the University of Saskatchewan they have a map that he drew of the narrow river lots at Batoche.

During the rebellion of 1885 he was paymaster for the Midland Battalion. When he retired he went to live in Prince Albert.

LETT

Lett is the second grain point north on a CNR line that runs from Oban Junction to Battleford. The line was built by the GTR in 1912. The first settlers into the district were Mark and Jack Lightburn of the Naseby district. Their sod shack still stands on SW 32-37-16-W3. William and James Affleck came to Lett in 1906 and

Archie, James' son, is now the reeve of the municipality and still farms the original homestead. Other early settlers were: John Meikel, John Allan, David Gray and Peter McRorie.

All grain points on this line were put in at six-mile intervals regardless of where settlements or early post offices were located. In an early Waghorn's Guide of the 1920s Mr. Archie Affleck remembers reading that Lett and Salter were GTR officials.

LEWISTON

Lewiston post office, west of the present town of Imperial, opened in the early 1900's. It was named for its first postmaster, William Lewis.

The post office has long since closed out and residents of the district now get their mail at Imperial.

LEWVAN

Lew Van Ostrand of Iowa arrived in this district 50 miles southeast of Regina in 1902 and was instrumental in bringing in several other families. When the GTP arrived in 1911 they purchased the townsite from Mr. Ostrand and named it in his honor by combining the first two parts of his name. Among the early homesteaders who came to the district were the following: Marden, McLaughlin, Warnke, Rowe, Gough, Jacques, Kerr and Isham.

LIBERTY

In May, 1904, Ben Wolff, accompanied by his nephew, Charlie, came to Regina and Assiniboia from Liberty, New York. He bought a team of broncos, a lumber wagon and supplies in Regina and drove to Craik. This was the year of the big flood at Lumsden and the railroad bridge was washed away. A pontoon bridge was built and his outfit was the second one to cross on it. Joe Tannahill, driving a pair of small mules hitched to a buggy, was first. They drove to the Liberty district and camped in a tent all summer and put in a few acres of crop. The lumber for a house was hauled from Craik and this was built with sods laid around the outside walls for greater warmth. Mr. Wolff's family arrived in November. There were three other families in the district that winter — Mac Tannahills, Ed. Crumlys, Tom Zim-

mermans and the bachelor shacks of Bill Wolff, Frank Allen and Clay Cushing.

The preliminary survey of the CPR was put through on the west side of present day No. 2 highway. Then in the winter of 1906-07 a group of surveyors had their camp in Mr. Wolff's farmyard and spent many social evenings in his home, playing the piano and singing.

The honor of naming the townsite was given to Mr. Wolff and he chose Liberty because it had been his hometown in New York State. Wolff Valley School, near Liberty was named for Mr. Wolff.

LIDGETT

Lidgett was a rural post office in the Wood Mountain area. It opened on July 1, 1912, with Mr. J. E. Lidgett as postmaster. He was followed by Mr. N. G. Fagan and Mrs. Florence Lidgett. The office closed on May 11, 1937, when Mr. Andrew Condlin was postmaster.

LIEBENTHAL

Liebenthal is a settlement southeast of Leader. It is a predominately German district and many of the first settlers came from Liebenthal, Kansas, U.S.A. The name had come there from Germany and so Saskatchewan got it second-hand.

LIGHTWOODS

Lightwoods is a district four miles west of McKague and south of Tisdale. The name originated in the early 1900's from the lightly-wooded growth of poplar, spruce and willow in the vicinity. The name was suggested by George Prosser, one of the early English settlers.

LILAC

Lilac is on a branch line of the CNR that runs between Denholm and Prince Albert. It is a small place with only 13 people living there. It got its name from a lone lilac bush that the railway builders found growing alongside the right-of-way.

LILLE

Lille is the first stop on a CPR line south of Wartime that ends at Matador. It was named after the city of Lille in France.

LILLESTROM

Lillestrom is less than ten miles north of Old Wives' lake. Mr. Mort Wiltside, who now lives in British Columbia, settled in this area in 1914 and became postmaster the same year. The CPR put a line through this community in 1929; the last post office site was located approximately one-half mile from the Lillestrom section house. The last official mail before the post office closed came on January 15, 1960.

The name of Lillestrom came about in an interesting manner. It was named after one of the battles of World War I. The battle was fought at Lille, France. The strom was just added. Strom is French meaning stream.

There is another story as to how Lillestrom got its name. Mr. Bjorn G. Bolstad of Wayne, New Jersey, wrote to say that it is named for a town in Norway and that Lillestrom in Norwegian means little stream.

LILYDALE

Lilydale post office was located fourteen miles south of Maidstone across the Battle river. Settlers moved into the district in 1905 and a post office was opened with the name Huran.

In 1911 a school district was formed and one of the first settlers, Mr. Elyah Marshall, asked that it be named Lily in memory of his baby daughter, Lily, who had died in Ireland at the age of nine months.

The settlers agreed and added the "dale" to make a better sounding name; it was appropriate too, since there are plenty of hills and dales in the district.

Mr. Elsey operated the post office from 1913 to 1959 and then his daughter, Nellie, ran it until it closed in 1963.

LILY PLAIN

Nestled in a crook of the North Saskatchewan River 20 miles west of Prince Albert is the rural post office of Lily Plain. It got its name from the abundance of tiger lilies that used to grow in the clearings.

In 1900 the first settlers, Mr. and Mrs. Bishop and Dan Dufy, a bachelor, came into the district which now consists of one church — St. Luke's Anglican — a community hall, a one-roomed school —

now closed — and a post office in the home of Mrs. M. E. Wilkinson.

LIMERICK

The first homesteader in the district was Edward Loosing. He was an Irishman from Limerick, Ireland, and when the post office was established in his home, he called it Limerick after his home in the Old Land. The CPR built a branch line from Assiniboia to Shaunavon in 1913 and it came through Limerick.

It is interesting to note that as the village of Limerick gradually grew almost all of the streets were given Irish names: Galway, Shannon, Brian, Kerry, Patricia, Connaught and Killarney.

LINACRE

Linacre is the second last stop on a CPR line that comes in from Alberta and stops at Fox Valley. It is named for a place in the British Isles.

LINDEQUIST

One mile south of the lone Pool elevator at Lindequist, the first grain point west of Battleford on a CNR line that runs to Carruthers, is the homestead of Colin Greener. The railroad came in 1913 and Mr. Greener worked on a section of the grade for the Barnes brothers of the U.S.A. who used a steam shovel and mules. In 1914 he signed up and spent four years in France. In 1919 he returned to his home and has lived there continuously ever since.

Other oldtimers in the district were the Boultons; their descendants — Alex, Erwin and Kenneth — still reside nearby. The Pool elevator was built in 1927 and named Lindequist after the section foreman, Harry Lindequist. He was a particularly well-liked man and impressed the Pool officials who supervised the building of the elevator.

Asked what interesting incident has stood out in his memory, Mr. Greener puzzled for a minute and then said, "Anderson knocking the Liberals out of action!" He went on to describe the parade of cars between the towns (Battleford and North Battleford) on the night of the election which was led by Mr. R. B. (later Judge) Mills. They were celebrating the victory of Mr. Huston over Mr. Pickel and Mr. Edwards.

A query about the saddest incident brought a story where names are better left out. It centered around a shooting. Lindequist district was the centre of a number of ranches. The spring roundup was in full swing and the cook, a man, had trouble getting one cowboy up and mobile. This went on for some time and one morning the cook shoved and pulled a little too hard and the cowboy (a real cowboy, not the drugstore type) pulled a gun and shot the cook. Another late riser, the only witness to the tragedy, didn't wait to put on his boots but took off for Battleford in his stocking feet. He informed the "Mounties" and the culprit was caught, tried and sentenced to be hung. He escaped the gallows and was committed for life when he turned state's evidence on a particularly shrewd man in the district who had been making and selling home brew. The man was sentenced to five years at hard labour.

Mr. Colin Greener was eighty, when we talked to him in 1971, and as we left his home late that evening the rabbits were out feeding on his lawn. He told us of the havoc they had caused in his garden and he said, "As soon as you leave I'm going to commit murder on them and I don't want any witnesses around." However it was said with such a twinkle in his eyes that we felt the rabbits were safe enough.

LINKLATER
Linklater, on a CPR line in southeastern Saskatchewan, was named for J. Linklater, agent at Reston, Manitoba. Later he became agent at Arcola; Saskatchewan. He is now retired.

LINTLAW
Lintlaw is the second grain point southeast from Kelvington. Lintlaw was first the name of the school in 1909, then the post office in 1910 and finally the incorporated village in 1921. The name was suggested by John McChesney who farmed in the community. It is believed to be derived from two Scottish words Lint Law, meaning "a sloping field of flax."

LIPSETT
Lipsett is the first stop south of Melfort on a line to Humboldt. Tom Irvin arrived in this district in the 1890s and named it

Pleasant Valley. The post office is still Pleasant Valley. When the CNR steel came in 1912 the people wanted to call the station Pleasant Valley but there was a place by that name so they called it Lipsett in honor of Colonel John Lipsett, a local man, who had been a casualty in the Boer War.

LIPTON
Building a stretch of track west from Lemberg to Lipton in 1904 the CPR had a surveyor in charge by the name of Miles Patrick Cotton. Two miles west of Balcarres they put in a water tower and called it Cotton. Eight miles west of Balcarres they built a station and section house and called it Patrick. The next station, which is now Lipton, was named Miles by the CPR officials, but the little settlement that had started there in 1883 objected. Led by Joe Atkinson, Charlie Neil, Thomas Norris, John Redpath and others, a committee chose the name Lipton and they had their wishes granted. Lipton was chosen in honor of Sir Thomas Lipton, Scottish tea merchant and yachtman, who had recently (1903) lost his third try to win the America's Cup, which is the award given for the international championship of yachting.

Lipton (1850-1931) was a man to catch the imagination. He was born in Glasgow of Irish parents. They were poor and Lipton began to work at the age of 10 as an errand boy. His rise to be a successful business man was spectacular, but he had a lifelong interest in the poor. He left a fifth of his fortune "to the poor mothers of Glasgow and their children." Lipton is a proud name and it stood in the way of having three places in a row in Saskatchewan named for one man.

LISIEUX
Lisieux is on a CPR line straight south of Old Wives' lake and less than 20 miles from the international boundary. It was named after the parish of St. Theresa of Lisieux.

LITTLE BUFFALO
The story of the inland post office of Little Buffalo is closely related to the flag-station of Bazentin, which is on a CNR line between Medstead and Belbutte.

Prior to 1915 the area around Bazentin was settled and in 1915 it was organized into a Local Improvement District under the name of Carrollton. There was a Carrollton school one mile south of the Bazentin site. The post office then was known as Carrollton and it was situated across the road from the school at the farm home of William O'Carroll, its first postmaster. In 1918 the Carrollton post office was moved to the farm home off Rudolph McGreevy, one mile east of the Carrollton school, and he became the second postmaster. In 1927 the post office was again moved one-half mile south of its former site to the farm home of its third and last postmaster, William Stuart Simpson. At this time the Carrollton post office was asked to change its name because of mail getting frequently mixed with that of Carlton, Saskatchewan. Residents who lived south of the large lake of the area, Little Buffalo, suggested that name and it was accepted. Little Buffalo post office was closed out in 1949.

LITTLE WOODY

Little Woody is an inland post office fifteen miles southeast of Scout Lake. It takes its name from Wood Mountain to the west, a famous landmark dating from 1874 when in the fall the North-West Mounted Police purchased the International Boundary Commission Supply Depot at Wood Mountain. Its exact location is 24-4-29-W2 and Mr. William Forsyth was the first postmaster.

LIVELONG

The first settlement in this district was a Hudson's Bay post at the south end of Turtle lake. When trouble arose with the Northwesters everyone took refuge on Spruce Island. The post was eventually abandoned. The first homesteaders arrived in 1905 and O. E. Warner started a store on the site of the old post.

When the steel reached Turtleford to the west, homesteaders poured into the district and a post office and school opened up called Patch Grove so named by Charlie Colson and Charlie Nelson. Patch Grove school became the centre of social and community life until Mr. Warner built a summer resort and a large dance hall at the lake. In 1918 he built an inboard motor launch, "The Pioneer,"

complete with Model T engine. Another tourist attraction was his tame moose.

Mr. Warner took over the post office of Patch Grove from Mr. Reid and at the same time the name was changed to Livelong, suggested by Mrs. Frank Wilson who had come from a place called Livelong in the United States.

In 1927 the CPR built a branch line from Turtleford to Glaslyn and the post office gave its name to the new community.

LIZARD LAKE

Lizard Lake is an inland post office twenty-five miles north and east of Biggar. It may have been named because of an unusually large number of lizards found there. It could have been named because someone thought the lake was in the shape of a lizard. It could have been a transplanted English name since the tip of Cornwall is known as "The Lizard" and it is there that records of ships passing are kept and duly published in the newspapers including shipping news.

The Lizard Lake post office was actually situated on the south shores of Wilson lake while Lizard lake, from which the post office took its name, was to the south.

LLEWELLYN

Llewellyn was an inland post office set up in 1890 in William Hunter's home located on NE section of 4-38-4 west of the third meridian. Mr. Hunter was the first postmaster and also the Justice of the Peace for the district. The mail came by carrier from Batoche.

Attempts to determine the significance of the name or when the post office closed have been unsuccessful, but from Mary Pattison's book *Cory In Recall*, we know the names of some of the first patrons it served: The David Blackley family, Andrew Blackley, Frank Clark and Archie Brown.

LLOYDMINSTER

Anglican Reverend Isaac Barr wanted to bring Canada closer to the British crown by colonization and to do this he began in August, 1902, at fifty-five years of age, to promote his idea for a colony.

It was to be on the North Saskatchewan River and would have its own transport company, supply co-operative, agricultural college and embryo medicare plan.

Barr was far from an organized leader and his poor handling of the whole project led some to believe he might be a con man, however, history has not proved him so. His greatest weakness was that he lacked organizational ability and common sense.

On March 31, 1903, 2000 settlers arrived at Saint John, N.B., and were met by Barr. They had already suffered on the voyage from poor sanitation, inadequate accommodation and seasickness.

When they arrived, they were also met by wintery weather, poor accommodation (immigration sheds), and the prices they had to pay for supplies once they arrived in Saskatoon by train were sky-high because the little city was not prepared for such a strain on its provisions. They were sold barely-broken horses and many of their wagons were overturned by the untrained animals.

There were arguments over homesteads and jobs, because the new railway which would have supplied them with paying jobs had not even been built.

The settlers lost patience with Barr and his empty promises. They elected their chaplain, Reverend George Exton Lloyd, to be in charge of the party and forced Barr to sign over all control of the project. Barr even gave up control of his own homestead where he had hoped to build a town called Barrview.

There is now a marker about a mile north of Lloydminster at the site of the colonists' first camp. The town was named for their chaplain, Reverend George Exton Lloyd!

LOCKWOOD

Lockwood is on a CPR line running north from Regina to Lanigan. It was named for Mr. Lockwood, a district passenger agent when the line was being built in 1907. The same year Mr. McGee built a store which was the first business in Lockwood. The first preacher, Mr. Crossly, held services in the homes until a Presbyterian church was built in 1911 which the Methodists also used. Some of those who attended these services were: Percy Tate, Neil MacKenzie, Charles Campbell; John Gillis, Maxwell Ellis and Angus McKinnon.

There were also a considerable number of Germans in this settlement and among them were the following: Henry Herr, Frederick Meissner, John Schroab and Theodor Kuhm.

LOGANTON

Loganton was a rural post office and store less than six miles northwest of Delisle. It was opened in the home of Sandy Currie in 1904 before the GTP or the CNR had lines in the district. It did a booming business because of the large territory it serviced. Goods were freighted from Saskatoon and Bill Russell brought the mail out twice a week.

Sandy Currie had three brothers, Pete, Dave and Duncan, who operated a store in Saskatoon. One of their employees, Fleet Logan, was a great friend of the family. He took out a homestead in the district and Mr. Currie suggested the name Logan for the new post office. It was refused but a compromise was arrived at in the word Loganton.

Some of the early settlers who used the store and post office were: Jack Price, Jake Martin, Henry Gesy, John and Alex McKillican, John Shillington, W. A. Miller, M. B. Wood, I. N. Henderson, D. McKenzie, Henry Mohr, Fleet Logan, Ed Frey, George Little and Bill Helm.

LOG VALLEY

Janet Graham of Central Butte sent in the following information. "Log Valley is an inland post office that is now closed. The meeting to decide on a name for the post office was held in a log cabin where the Saskatchewan river breaks north of Morse. At that time there were a lot of old logs in the area of the river valley. One story has it that the name was suggested because of the logs.

"Another story is that the meeting was held in a log cabin built of logs from the valley. Today people in this district have to travel over thirty-five miles for their mail due to one post office after another being closed up."

LONE ROCK

In 1912 there were enough children in the area to warrant building a school and it was called Lone Rock because of a large stone by the school gate. Later a post office was petitioned for and in the 1920s when the CPR came through, post office, school and name moved to the village that grew up three miles north of the old school site.

One of the original settlers was a Barr Colonist. His son went two miles to the old Lone Rock School as a child and the school now stands on his lawn for sentimental reasons.

LONESOME BUTTE

This is an excerpt from a letter written by Mrs. Allis Ellis of Pilot Butte.

"The Lonesome Butte is a fairly high hill beside the West Poplar river, six miles north of the international boundary and some twenty miles south of Wood Mountain. It is the only hill for some miles around and so it stands out by itself on the "Poplar Flat" hence the name "Lonesome."

At one time there was a Lonesome Butte post office (1911) and a Lonesome Butte school. The mail was brought in once a week from Wood Mountain, with team and democrat in summer and with team and sleigh in winter. In 1931 the CPR ran a spur line west of Rock Glen to Killdeer. We then got our mail from Rock Glen and Killdeer twice a week. My husband was the postmaster for several years for which he received the magnificent sum of sixty dollars a year.

The post office closed out in 1956 and the school was not far behind.

I went to Lonesome Butte to teach in 1924 and there I met my husband, who was secretary of the school board. We were married in 1926 and I lived in the district until 1961."

LONE SPRUCE

Lone Spruce is a country post office 20 miles north of Shellbrook. The P.A. Lumber Company cut timber in this district before it was opened for homesteading in 1915.

When a post office was opened Mrs. Wendel suggested the name Lone Spruce because that was the view she had looking north from her kitchen window. The first settlers into the district were the Hansons and Hoopfers and they came in by ox cart.

LONGACRE

Longacre is on a CNR line a short distance northwest of the Elbow. The

name told how the settlers felt as they looked at their fields. The same feeling comes through again and again at Broadview, at Expanse, at Horizon, and at Broadacres.

LONGHOPE

Longhope is a locality south of Turtle lake 27-50-18-W3, which is near Glaslyn. It was named by the first settlers, who were English, for Longhope, their hometown in England. The post office is closed and all that remains is the name of a locality.

LONGLAKETON

Longlaketon was an inland post office of the early years. It was situated less than twenty miles northwest of Silton. It derived its name from nearby Long lake or Last Mountain lake.

LOOMIS

When Mr. Lavick homesteaded in the district in 1909, there were no fences, no roads, and only a few acres of cultivated land. It was a great wilderness. The closest railway was at Harlem, Montana, 55 miles to the south.

Many places in Saskatchewan have had a change of names but few can compare with Loomis. The first country post office was run by Louis Anderson and was called Rapdan. Then came Carris. Echo was the next name and finally when the CPR ran a line through from Notukeu to Val Marie in 1923 the townsite was called Loomis in honor of Harry Loomis, one of the early settlers.

One of the first NWMP offices was Louis Anderson's farm. They had a jail in the basement and an office upstairs. One of the first "trials" was between two neighbors, K. Tenkate and Stanley Horton. Mr. Tenkate had shot Mr. Horton's dog. Horton won the case. Mr. Tenkate was sentenced to a $30 fine or 30 days in jail. He had no money so his neighbor, T. G. Miller, paid the fine for him. Homesteaders were always ready to help each other.

LOON LAKE

Thirty miles north of St. Walburg is the village of Loon Lake. It is nestled in a beautiful woodland setting. One mile west of the village is the first of a circular chain of seven lakes named "Makwa Lakes." Makwa is the Cree Indian word for "loon" and the first and largest lake is named Loon lake after that typical northern bird whose lonely cry often echoes across the waters.

On the east corner of Upper Makwa, seven miles west of Loon Lake, is "Steele Narrows." It was here that Major Steele caught up with Big Bear's group of Indians as they retreated from the battle of Frenchman Butte during the war of 1885. Steele's scouts scattered them and thus enabled Big Bear's prisoners to escape. These were the last shots fired in the Saskatchewan Rebellion.

LOON RIVER

Loon River is an inland post office in north-central Saskatchewan on Loon river which flows into Loon lake. The first location of the post office was in the home of Mr. Gervais, NW¼ of Sec. 15-T59-R21-W3. It opened in 1930 and over the years it served a large territory; the present postmistress is Mrs. Frank Bodana on Section 25.

Some of the people who have used the post office over the years are: Joe Boulanger, Tom Helco, Mr. F. Starnes, George Dufrense, "Slim" Doering, Mr. Lantz and Ed Adrian.

LORADO

Lorado is one of a complex of mining towns centering on Cracking Stone Peninsula on the north shore of Lake Athabasca.

LOREBURN

The first station north of Elbow on the way to Outlook is Loreburn. It was named by CPR officials after Robert Reid, first Earl of Loreburn, a distinguished British parliamentarian and jurist.

Loreburn is an average Prairie village with 315 souls calling it home.

LORENZO

Lorenzo is an inland post office east of Mayfair. it is situated at 24-46-10-W3. The first postmaster, Leopold Talarski, moved there from Lorenzo, Idaho, and sent in the name in memory of his hometown. It was accepted.

LOST RIVER

Lost River is a country post office 12 miles west of Codette. In 1907 the first Lost River post office was opened in Bonar's store at the SW corner of 6-50-16-W2nd.

Lost River was named by an early mail carrier for a little creek that flowed all year round across the W½ of 31-49-16-W2nd down into this little Saskatchewan river valley and disappeared into porous ground in a soft maple bluff on the SW¼ of 6-50-16-W2nd.

LOUVAIN

Settlers began to move into this district, twenty miles northeast of Biggar, as early as 1908. Some of the first to arrive were Alfred P. Smith, Louis Dugan, Joe Fidget, George, Tom and Jack Hull, Arthur Friend, Frank Worthington, Emric, Cory and Walter Bulger, Jack Staples, Albert Buds, Bob Randal, Ernie Smith, Jack Lee and Harold Turner.

A school district was formed in 1916 and named Louvain for a decisive battle of the First World War, and later when a post office was established it also took Louvain for a name.

Jack Wilkinson was the first postmaster and he had it in his home. Mail was hauled out from Biggar once a week. Next the post office moved to the home of Bert Wells and it closed out under him in the 1940's.

LOVE

There are several versions of how Love got its name! The railway was put through in 1930. For a few years there was no station, only a siding, but there was the odd car of wheat loaded by shovel and many cars of wood were shipped out. Bill Aestrope, and his son John, set up a cordwood camp here. One of their crew fell in love with a girl who worked in the cookshack. Their love affair was a topic for discussion on many occasions. One of the crew, who considered himself a wit, called it the Siding of Love. It was a simple thing to change it to Love Siding which finally became the village of Love.

Another story is that Love was the name of a railway official connected with the first train over the line. This possibility is strengthened by the fact that in 1930 the chief of the CPR passenger bureau in Winnipeg was F. S. Love and there was James A. Love who was a CPR engineer in Winnipeg.

LOVERNA

Miss Gertrude Wilson of Sunset Lodge, Kindersley, Sask., contributed this information.

"In the early summer of 1911, the Grand Trunk Pacific Railway surveyed the route for their branch line from Biggar, Sask., to Hemaruka, Alta., and their stakes indicated that the new railway would pass directly across my father's farm. The GTP appointed W. K. McFarland, a homesteader in our district, as their representative. He requested that the new townsite be named Loverna after a married daughter, Mrs. Loverna George, who lived in the States. The request was granted.

Early in 1912 buildings were quickly put up on the townsite even before the ground was surveyed into lots and streets. My dad became the first postmaster and Bill Shepherd opened the store. Almost overnight a restaurant came into being. A Chinese laundry started. A pool room came next and then a lumber yard opened. With the opening of the post office in the fall of 1912 mail was hauled weekly, by team and wagon from Macklin, 60 miles to the north.

The railway grade was built in the summer of 1912 and the arrival of the steel the following year was an occasion for a celebration and dance. As we saw the smoke from the 'pioneer' engine as it followed the track-laying crew, we dropped our ironing or our bread-making or whatever we were doing and everybody trooped down the grade to meet it and we were given the opportunity to drive a spike before the project entered Alberta (Loverna is the last station on the Saskatchewan side.)

That night the homesteaders from near and far gathered in the pool hall and danced with joy, to the tunes of John Foss's fiddle. The lunch at midnight was doughnuts and coffee served by the few women who had come with their husbands to the homesteads.

In 50 years there have been many changes, many people; times have been good, sometimes bad. But there is nothing

that ever quite equalled the thrill of seeing a town born."

LUCKY LAKE

Lucky Lake is on a branch line from Dunblane to Beechy. It took its name from a lake five and a half miles north of the town. This lake was originally called Devil's lake. It was so named by the Indians because of a mysterious light that shone over it at night. No one was able to find out what caused this light. Then one day Jock Swansen, an early settler, had an experience that changed the name of the lake.

Jock had hobbled his oxen but the mosquitoes were so bad the oxen became frantic, broke their hobbles and ran away. They headed into the lake where Mr. Swansen was able to catch them. He was so glad that he said, "This isn't Devil's lake; this it Lucky Lake." And that's how the name came to be changed.

LUMSDEN

The original name of this place was "Happy Hollow." This was changed to Lumsden in 1890 to honor Hugh D. Lumsden, the supervising engineer for the Qu'Appelle, Long Lake and Saskatchewan Railway and Steamboat Company. The first train over this line from Regina arrived in Saskatoon on May 11, 1890.

LUMSDEN BEACH

Lumsden Beach is a popular summer resort near the southwest end of Last Mountain lake. It took its name from the nearby town of Lumsden which in turn had taken its name from Hugh D. Lumsden, the supervising engineer for the Qu'Appelle, Long Lake and Saskatchewan Railway and Steamboat Company when the line was built.

LURGAN

Lurgan is the first stop north of Tisdale on a CPR line that runs to Nipawin. It was named for Lurgan, a city near the south shore of Lough Neagh in Northern Ireland.

LUSELAND

Luseland derived its name from the Luse Land Development Company which was largely responsible for bringing settlers into the district. The head men in this company were John Luse and his son, Sam. Their headquarters were in St. Paul, Minnesota, but many of their settlers were drawn from Nebraska and Indiana. They came in great excursions to Scott which in 1908 was the end of the Grand Trunk Pacific Railway and from camps there they drove overland in cars and buggies to pick out homesteads.

LUXTON

Luxton is right next to Lampman in the southeast corner of the province, and like Lampman and many places nearby it is named for a writer. Luxton was named for William Fisher Luxton, Journalist, (1844-1907). He was born in Devonshire, England, and came to Canada with his parents in 1855, was educated at St. Thomas and at Lobo and became a teacher. In 1866, in partnership with G. W. (later Sir George) Ross, he established the Strathroy *Age*; was later editor of the Seaforth *Expositor* and the Goderich *Daily Home Journal*. On November 9, 1872, the first issue of the *Manitoba* (later *Winnipeg Free Press*) appeared with his name as editor.

LYDDEN

Lydden was the first name of the post office and townsite of what is now Duperow, just a short distance west of Biggar. Because of a mix-up in freight deliveries with the town of Glidden, the railway changed the name to Duperow. However, the post office continued to be called Lydden for a number of years but finally gave in and became known as Duperow, too. The post office is now closed and the residents get their mail from Biggar.

The name Lydden was suggested by Harry Hawkins to commemorate Lydden, England.

M

MACDOWALL

Macdowall is just south of Prince Albert. It was named for D. H. Macdowall, who at the time was a member of the firm of Moore and Macdowall, saw mill owners in Prince Albert. He was a member of Parliament for the old district of Saskatchewan, 1887-1896.

MACDONALD'S SIDING

MacDonald's Siding was two and one-half miles east of Orley on a CNR line that ran from Melfort to Hudson Bay. It was a saw-mill town that started in the 1920's and was operated by D. N. MacDonald. It had a post office named for him. At its height, the mill employed 200 men and they turned out, on an average, eight million board feet of lumber a year.

The operation closed down when Mr. MacDonald died shortly after receiving word that his son had been killed in World War II.

In its day MacDonald's Siding was a mail drop and deliveries were made to Mistatim and Orley by handcar (jigger) about once a month. Today nothing remains of the mill site.

MACKLIN

Early in 1906, T. D. McCallum trekked from Saskatoon to what is now known as Macklin. Two days after McCallum arrived Mr. W. Scott, who later became the first mayor of the town, arrived. James Hillis was the first school teacher. The original post office was a mile out of the town and a landmark in the town now is an old shack which was used as a trading center for Indians.

A few months after the arrival of Mr. McCallum the settlement took the name of Macklin, named after an executive of the Winnipeg Free Press, Harry Macklin, who was following the GTP railway construction at that time and reporting for his paper. The naming of the streets of Macklin follow this theme in that they are all named for famous newspapers of the day: Leader, Post, Empire, Herald, Telegraph, Tribune, and Times.

Macklin has survived a number of disasters, commencing with a miniature cyclone in 1909 which completely destroyed the hotel and damaged many othe buildings. There was no loss of life. A few years later fire wiped out an entire block of the town, including a drug store, bakery, and furniture store. Then in 1934 the school was razed and the same fall the Pool elevator went up in flames.

These setbacks were overcome and Macklin, 150 miles west of Saskatoon, and within a few miles of the Alberta border, is a prosperous town.

MACNUTT

MacNutt is the first grain point inside the Saskatchewan border on a CNR line that runs northwest to Canora.

It was named for Thomas MacNutt who was at one time the government farm instructor for British newcomers to the district. He represented his district in the provincial legislature at Regina and became speaker there. Later he went into federal politics and for a time was chairman of the Liberal caucus at Ottawa.

MACOUN

Macoun is named in honor of John Macoun. Working for the federal government about 1880 he visited many parts of the Prairies. He gathered botanical specimens and data regarding the climate, plants and birds. The West was just opening up and many unfounded stories of the country were abroad. Macoun corrected the early impressions of the West. His reports of the great possibilities for agriculture in the southern plains of the Prairies changed the proposed route of the CPR farther south.

MACRORIE

In the spring of 1912 Macrorie was the end of the steel for the Canadian Northern Railroad and a name was to be chosen. It boiled down to two prominent families in the district: the Kendalls and the McQuarries. The McQuarrie name was chosen and submitted but due to a spelling error it didn't come out that way.

MACWORTH

MacWorth is an inland post office less than ten miles northwest of Killdeer. It opened on January 1, 1918, with William S. Stait as postmaster. Postmasters to follow were Mr. Otto Degner, John Hindle, Dingman Korporal and Hazel Panko. It closed out in 1968 when Mrs. Janet Galloway was postmistress. MacWorth was named for two of the early settlers in the district, Mr. MacEachern and Mr. Worth.

MADGE LAKE

Madge Lake is situated in Duck Mountain Provincial Park near the Saskatchewan-Manitoba border. It was named for the wife of Mr. Charles Harvey who was a surveyor in the area around 1904. Madge Lake had been formerly called Island Lake, Clear Lake and Lake Kamsack.

MADISON

Madison is the second stop west of Eston. Originally it was called Noremac which is Cameron spelled backwards. This was in honor of a large clan of Camerons in the district. Settlement was slow. The name was changed to Madison in honor of James Madison fourth president (1809-1917) of the United States. It was hoped that this name would attract some Americans. It did. A large group came from Boston and their country school was named Bostonia. The only original Bostonians left in the district are the Annables. They grow a lot of wheat at Madison. The population of the town is only 105 but they have five big elevators which are kept very busy.

MAESHOWE

Maeshowe, a rural post office (now closed) was about seventeen miles southwest of Webb in southwestern Saskatchewan. The name is a contraction of Maes Howe and this commemorates an historic site on the Mainland of the Orkney Islands.

Maes Howe has been described as the most magnificent chambered tomb in Western Europe. It stands on gently sloping ground beside the main road from Kirkwall to Stromness.

From the outside it appears as a large grassy mound 115 feet in diameter and 24 feet high standing near the centre of a circular ditch and bank. Entrance to the heart of the mound is through a passage thirty-six feet long and four feet 6 inches high. Inside, there is a spacious chamber fifteen feet square. To the left and right and also opposite the entrance, burial cells open off the central chamber. All were empty when the tomb was excavated a century ago, and the reason for this is to be seen on the walls. Some time in the twelfth century, Vikings broke into the Howe and robbed it of a great treasure, or so they tell us in the runic inscriptions which they cut on the walls.

There are other places in Saskatchewan that take their name from the Orkneys. One is Orkney and the other is Orcadia.

MAIDSTONE

Excerpt from *Between The Rivers* a booklet published in 1955 by Maidstone and district:

"What a gala year 1905 was for us! With train service now assured from Saskatoon to Edmonton, a village was popping up and several people gathered at a picnic arranged for the purpose of selecting a name for the new center. However, it was found that CNR officials passing through had decided to name it Maidstone.

Saskatchewan became a province in September, 1905, so our address was no longer 'Siding 5, Northwest Territories,' but Maidstone, Sask.

It is thought to be named for Maidstone, a city southeast of London, England."

MAIN CENTRE

This little town, at the end of a branch line out of Mawer in south central Saskatchewan, is divided into two parts, Old and New Main Centre. Old Main Centre developed in the early days as a main trading center and hence its name. When the steel was extended from Mawer it missed Main Centre by a quarter of a mile. Many of the people did not move their homes and places of business to the location of the station and elevators. Therefore, two towns exist today, Old and New Main Centre.

MAIR

The branch line of the CNR from Maryfield to Carlyle was built in 1911 and has four grain points, all named for famous writers: Ryerson, Mair, Parkman and Service.

John Mair (1469-1550) was a Scottish scholarly writer; professor of philosophy and divinity, Glasgow (1518); professor of philosophy and logic, St. Andrews (1522), having Patrick Hamilton, George Buchanan, and perhaps John Knox as students.

Some Boer War veterans were the first to settle in the Mair district, Percy and Craig Skinner and Albert Banham. Mr. Thomas from England was next.

When the first post office was established in 1911, Henry Patten became the postmaster and he hauled the mail from Walpole.

MAGYAR

Magyar is an inland post office fifteen miles straight south of Touchwood. There's a lot of history, past and present tied up in that name.

Americans like to be called Americans and not Yankees. Magyars like to be called Magyars and not Hungarians. Charlemagne died in 814 and his Empire soon crumbled. Barbarian invasions threatened the civilized world. On the east, hordes of wild Slavs and of wilder Magyars broke across the frontiers. The Magyars spread out on the plains of what is now Hungary and staked their claim. They first had to fight for their lives in a "sea of Slavs." They then started northeast but the Saxon King Otto I crushed them in a horrible slaughter at the battle of Lechfeld.

Next came pressure from the Turks of the southwest. The Turks eventually conquered the country and the Magyar nobility fled to Austria. Next it was Austria's turn as the Turks laid siege to Vienna. Austria gradually beat them back and recovered Hungary. The Magyar nobility returned but had to fight Austria for "Home Rule" which was gained in 1867. From 1888 to 1914 many Magyars emigrated to the United States and Canada. The fundamental cause of early immigration to this continent was the oppressive feudal land system of Hungary in which the interests of the people who actually tilled the soil were forgotten. Between 1888 and 1910 large-scale emigration began when the normal distress was heightened by crop failure, cattle disease and the ravages of philoxera vastatrix in the vineyards.

Those who came to Saskatchewan settled at Esterhazy (that is a story in itself), Otthan, Kaposvar, Bekevar, Halmok, Saltcoats, Lestock, Colonsay and Plunkett to name just a few.

In general they have prospered in the land of their adoption — in many cases to a remarkable extent. In 1925, when Stockholm celebrated its silver jubilee, the Hon. James G. Gardiner, then premier of Saskatchewan, said, "The success which has marked the Hungarian settlement at Stockholm is indicative, not only of the ability of that race to flourish under conditions existing here, but is indicative also of the fact that they are amenable to the discipline which the laws of this British nation have imposed."

In late 1956 when rebellion in Hungary was suppressed by Russian intervention and many Hungarians sought refuge in Austria, the Canadian government instructed its immigration officers in Europe to give priority to the claims of those who wished to emigrate to Canada. Within three months more than 10,000 came to Canada and the movement reached 33,000 by mid-1957.

The first post office at Magyar was located at 28-25-15-W2, and the first postmaster was Thomas Beagle.

MAJOR

Major is on a CPR line that runs from Wilkie south and west to Lacombe, Alberta. This line reached Major in 1914. At that time the district was called Obrechia. This was the first year of the First World War and there was a strong military feeling abroad. This showed not only in the naming of Major but many other places in Saskatchewan: Wartime, Amiens, Somme, Cavel, and Leader. On this particular railway line Major is not the only name with a wartime connotation. We have Fusilier, the next town, and further on in Alberta the town of Veteran.

MAKWA

When the Canadian Northern Railway built a line from North Battleford to St. Walburg in 1912 the intention was to go on to the town of Loon Lake and then circle west to link up with a line from Alberta. Several miles of grade were laid but the line was never put in.

Right around the town of Loon Lake you find bunched together: North Makwa, South Makwa, Makwa River and several Makwa Lakes. Makwa is the Cree word meaning Loon. To hear this beautiful bird start a new day with his distinctive call is a thrill to all nature lovers. In the water he is so fast that he can catch a fish but on shore where he comes to nest he has more waddle than a duck.

MALMGREN

Malmgren was a grain point six miles northeast of Rosetown on a CPR line that ran from Rosetown to Perdue. The line was put through in 1927 and three elevators were built, in this order — Union Pacific, Western Grain, and Pool. Neil MacLeod of 818 Main Street in Rosetown bought grain there for Western Grain for years. Today everything is gone. Mr. MacLeod told us this story: the grain point was named by CPR officials for a Norwegian sea captain. He also told us of Jim White, one of the men who drew grain to him. He said that even after Jim had been in Canada for thirty years he spoke as though he had only been out from Scotland for three days.

Other early residents who patronized the hamlet were: Frances Alexander, Wilson Johnson, William Campbell, Stewart and Sam Mooney, Alex, Alfred and Bill Hutchin, William Webb, William Duncan, Richard, Emil and Walter Potratz, R. D, Bartlett, Jerry Griggs, Henry Frerichs, Freeman Bush, James Torry, Wes, Bert and Vern Evans, Mr. N. W. Hopkins, George Hansberg, Arthur Lord, Frank Ridgewell, Len and Lorne McKay, Jade and Jim Lang, Clarence McNally and Stanley Davis.

MANITOU BEACH

The North American Indian had a king-god who was called the Great Spirit. His name was Manitou, or Power and his presence was in all things. For centuries, Little Manitou lake, situated three miles north of Watrous, has been known to the Prairie Indian people as "the place of healing waters" and because of its attributed medicinal qualities, the Indians named the lake Manitou. Manitou Beach takes its name from the lake.

During the summer months the little beach community becomes a veritable hive of activity. Most people come to swim in the lake or bathe in the indoor swimming pool that has a special heated section for those exclusively interested in possible medicinal properties of the lake.

Camp Easter Seal, summer recreation spot for Saskatchewan's handicapped children and adults is located at Manitou Beach.

In 1962 the Wardley Brine Shrimp Company Limited established a small industry on the lake. Their unique salt water fishing operations provides brine shrimp for tropical fish food.

Some come to Manitou Beach for fun and dancing. They have the finest floor in the province there — cushioned on horsehair, tons of it. You couldn't build one like it today. There just aren't that many horses left!

MANKOTA

Many of the early settlers who poured into our province at the turn of the century came from the northern United States. In some cases they simply gave their new home the name of their old home and so we have in Saskatchewan a Cando, a Spiritwood, a Cavalier, and so on.

Mankota was named for the hometown of many of the early settlers in the district of Mankota, Minnesota. Mankota, Saskatchewan, is at the end of a CPR branch line that meanders west of Maxstone and roughly parallels the international boundary twenty-five miles to the south.

Mankota is ranching country and a unique feature of the town is a community-made cattle-sale arena. They raise some of the finest Hereford and Angus cattle in Saskatchewan and surrounding districts. Buyers come from Manitoba, Ontario and the U.S.A. to the sales. They sell about 6000 cattle a year. In 1971, sales totalled $2,000,000.

MANNERY

Mannery post office opened on September 15, 1911 and when the railway came to Frenchman Butte in 1928 the post office moved into the town.

The first postmaster had been Mr. J. A. Wild and he turned it over to John Markley.

MANOR

Manor is named in memory of Cannington Manor. In the 1880s in direct contrast to the humble homesteader who was coming in to seek his "promised land," a few enterprising capitalists raised money in eastern Canada and Britain and attempted to establish farming on a grandiose scale on the Prairies. One such romantic scheme was Cannington Manor. An Englishman of means, William Pierce, chose land 40 miles southwest of Moosomin. His intention was to build an ideal community, composed of well-to-do Englishmen, and establish a mode of life in the gracious English manner.

In spite of a good start in which a beautiful church, a community hall, stores, flour mills, two cheese factories, and a pork factory were built, it did not quite work out. The promised branch line became a reality in 1900, but it by-passed Cannington Manor and was constructed 10 miles away where the new community was called "Manor."

The ready money had made a prosperous community for awhile, but the dream of a romantic English colony disintegrated in the harsh reality of the Prairie climate. A few settlers stayed to become successful farmers but the majority moved away and Cannington Manor with its fine buildings was left desolate for over half a century. It is now a provincial historic site.

MANTARIO

The neighboring town of Alsask, right on the border, is derived by taking parts of the names of Alberta and Saskatchewan. Mantario followed the same system and took part of Manitoba and Ontario to form their name.

This was done, both, because of the example set by Alsask and because many of the original settlers in Mantario had emigrated from Manitoba and Ontario.

MAPLE CREEK

Maple creek rises in the Cypress Hills and flows north into Big Stick lake. The town of Maple Creek takes its name from the creek. Maple Creek came into being at freeze-up in 1882, when construction of the railroad halted a few miles east of the present townsite. Instead of returning East, a few of the construction crew decided to winter there. About 12 men made up the population of Maple Creek during the winter of 1882-83.

At the present time, generally speaking, the land north of Maple Creek is farm land, and to the south it is grazing land where large herds of cattle still roam.

Pioneers in Maple Creek still like to think back to the days when it was all ranch land and they like to call Maple Creek, "The Old Cow Town."

MARCELIN

The Indian name for the district was "Sequopa" which means a group of trees. In 1889 Antoine Marcelin arrived from Olga, North Dakota. Until 1902 he lived in the Muskeg Mission. He then moved to what is now Marcelin and bought up 1900 acres of land.

On September 4, 1906, a meeting took place in Victor Lalonde's house which resulted in a request for a school for the area. The first school board was composed of Antoine Marcelin, Mr. Manseau and Mr. L. LeHovillier. Reverend Father Ovide Lajeunesse acted as secretary. In 1907 the school was officially established and called Marcelin in honor of Antoine Marcelin.

When the Canadian Northern Railway arrived in 1912, Mr. Marcelin suggested that the village be called St. Albert but he was persuaded to let it be called Marcelin after him.

MARCHANTGROVE

Nestled in a beautiful grove of poplars ten miles north of Shellbrook is the inland post office of Marchantgrove. It is in the store of Mr. R. E. Acott, a retired line elevator agent.

In 1910 it was named for Henry Marchant, the first postmaster. Besides running his store and post office he taught school and put in his time on a homestead. Two of his daughters still live within a mile of the store. Other old-timers of this district are Don Carlson, Douglas Green, Delbert Denton and Ebert Bloom.

Originally the name was in two parts, Marchant and Grove, but the postal officials, in the interest of efficiency, shortened it to one word Marchantgrove.

MARCHWELL

The first homestead entry is what is now the Marchwell district was made in 1882 by Frank Petch, a horse rancher. A number of other settlers came in shortly after and formed what was known as the Wolverine settlement. This was before the railway came through and some came by steamboat on the Assiniboine river as far as Fort Ellice, or, after the main line of the CPR was built, to Moosomin, and then north for 50 miles.

In 1886, the Manitoba and Northwestern Railway reached the district. This railway was taken over by the CPR at the turn of the century. In 1902, a firm of bankers and merchants known as March Brothers and Wells, from Litchfield, Minnesota, bought up large tracts of land in the area and brought in settlers from the United States, mostly Scandinavians. In 1906 the CPR put a siding in this district and named it Marchwell, in honor of March Brothers and Wells.

MARENGO

Marengo is west of Kindersley. It was named by a pioneer for his home town in Illinois which in turn had been named for one of the famous battles of the Napoleonic Wars. On June 14, 1800 Napoleon caught up with the Austrian army under Baron Melas at the little hamlet of Marengo in northern Italy and in a day-long battle he defeated the Austrians and regained Italy. The battle was close and only the astute handling of Napoleon's heavy cavalry by Francois-Etienne Kellerman saved the day.

MARGO

Margo is between Invermay and Kuroki. The Railway (Great Northern) arrived in 1905. Some fifty families were in the district prior to that and they had to haul their supplies from Sheho, twenty miles to the south.

Margo was incorporated as a village on April 24, 1911 and grew steadily until the early 1950's. At that time the population was 350 and forty-eight business establishments served the immediate area and the surrounding district. They had two passenger trains running daily, except Sunday from the East in the morning and West in the evening.

By 1976 the population had dropped to 200. Only eight businesses remained. There were no passenger trains and the average size of farm rose from one-half section to two sections.

The village of Margo took its name

from Margo Lake and the lake, in turn, had been named to commemorate the tragic death of a young girl whose first name was Margot.

John Girand of the district has done considerable research into the origin of the name Margo, and the circumstances surrounding the girl's death. This led him to the Western Development Museum at Yorkton. In the library there he found a book which provided details about his uncle's (John Flaws Reid) experiences in the North-West Rebellion. A chapter in the book dealt with Bob Reid and his ranching venture near Margot Lake. As well, it related details about the death of the girl.

MARIETON AND MARIETON BEACH

Marieton is an inland post office less than twelve miles west of Long or Last Mountain lake in a line with Gibbs. Marieton Beach is on the shores of the lake.

William and James Tingery home-steaded first in the district. The post office opened November 1, 1884, in James' home and continued there until 1908. It was named in honor of Marie Gibbs, wife of a popular government land agent, who was responsible for bringing many other settlers to the district. A. Flavel took over the post office from Mr. Tingey and ran it until he retired. It was then taken over by his son, E. E. Flavel, who was there until it closed in 1942. Mr. Flavel then moved to California.

The first mail came in from Regina and was met by a driver from Strassburg (changed to Strasbourg during high feelings in World War I). They stayed overnight at Marieton and then the drivers made their return trips, 20 miles to Strasbourg and 50 to Regina, the following day. When the Regina-Saskatoon CNR line was built the mail came from Lumsden, then when the Kirkella-Lanigan CPR line was built in 1908 the mail came in from Bulyea. When in 1911 the Regina-Bulyea CPR line came through, the mail came in from Silton.

MARKINCH

Markinch is on a CPR line between Southey and Cupar thirty miles north of Regina. Paul Blaser and Tom Bradwell were the first settlers and they came in 1900. The railroad arrived in 1905. In 1906 they built the bridge over Loon creek and moved on west. The railway officials named the townsite for Markinch in Fifeshire, Scotland.

Markinch is a familiar name to many prairie people, particularly subscribers to the Western Producer. It was near Markinch that Tom Melville-Ness first settled when he immigrated to Saskatchewan in 1927. Because of the kinship he felt for Markinch, Saskatchewan and a village by that name not far from his birthplace in Kingskettle, Fifeshire, Scotland, he chose Mark Inch as a pen name for articles he wrote.

His personal little column *Prairie Wool* — gathered by Mark Inch delighted readers. Mr. Melville-Ness retired from the Western Producer in 1973 and in retirement was appointed registrar of the Saskatchewan Institute of Agrologists. He continued his *Prairie Wool* column in the Western Producer.

On December 19, 1976 Tom Melville-Ness died suddenly at his home in Saskatoon. He was 68.

He had been honored with a fellowship in the Agricultural Institute of Canada and had just been named a member of the Order of Canada, a public recognition of his lifetime of service to his fellow Canadians.

Markinch and all of Saskatchewan are proud to have had Tom Melville-Ness as a resident.

MARLIN

Marlin was a rural post office south and west of Glaslyn. It started in the home of Mr. Albert Hinz on SE 10-50-17-W3. He named it for an American rifle. Following Mr. Hinz several people had the post office and store and it moved about in the district. The last move put it out on highway 4, where the proprietor then was Bill Doeherty. The building was completely destroyed by fire in 1964 and was never rebuilt. There was a Marlin school in the area but it is closed and the children are bussed to Glaslyn. In the district and apart from the school there was a large "National Hall," the scene of some very lively dances as well as church services for the Ukrainian district it served. It is now closed.

Some of the oldtimers of the Marlin district were: Yarmack, Kury, Mack, Dmytryshyn, Hrycyna, Pawlyshyn, Zaychkowsky, Tarchuk, Burras, Shekeketka, Sofurn, Carlington, Fezulak, Pylypow, Kinish, Coller, Kozekewich, Chonkiw, Michnik, Lysycia, Maximchuk, Chippocks, Shondolla, Lewchuk, Showchuk, Dedur, Nesterok, Sawchuk, Harasym, Prokup, Bandurka, Maluk and Hawryliw.

MARNEAU LAKE

Marneau Lake was an inland post office east of Archerwill. It was established in the early 1900's and closed out when the CPR arrived in the 1920's and Archerwill developed as a town.

MARQUIS

Marquis is 25 miles north of Moose Jaw. When the CPR right-of-way came through in 1909 Mr. McFaden and Mr. Meagher each gave land for the townsite. However, they could not agree as to whose name should be used and while they were still in doubt and in disagreement, the CPR named it Marquis. This honored an important hybrid wheat developed by Charles Saunders in the early 1900s. It took him several years to get the type of grain he wanted. In 1907, there were only 23 pounds of the Marquis seed. The wheat was first distributed to farmers in 1909. Word of the new variety spread quickly. It was used extensively in the northern United States as well as Canada and in the year 1918 more than 300,000,000 bushels were produced. Marquis ranked as the outstanding spring wheat for 20 years.

MARRIOTT

In 1905 the Marriott post office started in the home of Marriott Douglas at 36-31-14-W3. Through the years it moved about a great deal and finally came to rest at the junction of number 4 highway and the grid road that connects Plenty to Tessier. It's exactly 18 miles south of Biggar and 18 miles north of Rosetown. Marriott is interesting in that the municipality, the grain point on the Rosetown to Perdue railway, and the location described above all have the same name.

Mr. Guran had a fine garage, general

store and post ofice complex there but he closed its doors in March of 1972 and it's all boarded up now. There is a small cluster of "open air" mail boxes there that are served by a rural route out of Rosetown. However, the community is far from dead. The Howard Powell Composite School which was opened in 1953 is located nearby. This school was designed to handle grades one to ten. In 1963-64 a gymnasium-auditorium was added. Enrolment dropped and it handled one to eight. Another drop came in 1972 when it was reduced to teaching one to six in two rooms. There were two beginners in the fall of 1972. This information was obtained from Mrs. Ruth Wiebe, right on the spot, in one of the two country schools hauled in and converted into teacherages.

A half a mile to the east is the Marriott municipal office which is painted right up to the minute and has secretary-treasurer Oren Taylor in attendance. He has written an extensive history of the district and has on display the gold-headed cane presented to Mr. Marriott Douglas when he left Galt, Ontario, to homestead in the New West.

One mile west on the grid is the Czechoslovakian Pioneers Memorial Hall. It's the best-kept and most-used center in the scattered community. Spacious and well-kept grounds surround it. An excellent ball field is close by, complete with concession stand. It's the home park of the "Marriott Blues" a crack men's fastball club, that plays in the Wheatbelt Fastball League.

MARRIOTT

Marriott is a hamlet 19 miles northeast of Rosetown on a CPR line that runs to Perdue. There used to be four elevators there, the Pioneer, UGG, Federal and Pool. The Pioneer burned down some years ago and was never replaced. The three remaining elevators are operated by Danny Sorenson for the UGG. Layton Angus used to have a post office and store but it's all gone and Layton now lives in Zealandia.

John McLeod, an early resident in the district, was responsible for the naming of Marriott. It was named for the municipality in which it resides — Marriott number 317.

The following were in the district in the early years: Gordon, Norman and Malcolm Douglas, Alec Carnegie, Jack and Ernie MacMillan, Jack Nash, Jack Johnson, Charlie Kerr, Sid and Walter Card, R. H. "Bob" Cowan, H. R. Powell, Mike Gawletz, Ted Scriebens and Harry Busby.

MARSDEN

The following information came from Clarence A. McInnes of Marsden who has resided in the district since 1906.

"The name of Marsden goes back to the year 1908. At that time the whole territory was known as Manitou, named for Manitou lake three miles to the south. In that year Alex Wright opened a post office on his farm, three-quarters of a mile north-east of our present townsite. Mrs. Wright named it after her birthplace of Marsden in Yorkshire, England."

When a branch line of the CPR came through from Wilkie to Lloydminster in November of 1923, the town took Marsden for its name.

MARSHALL

Marshall is the first place of any size on a CNR line that runs south and east from Lloydminster to North Battleford. The area surrounding the village was first settled in the spring of 1903 by members of the Barr Colony, a group of people brought to this country from England under the leadership of Rev. Barr and later Dr. Lloyd (who in time became Bishop of Saskatchewan, and after whom Lloydminster was named).

The Barr Colonists arrived in Saskatoon in March of 1903. Saskatoon at that time was the end of the railway line and the settlers travelled, by covered wagon and oxen, from that point to the areas in which they were locating. Some ended their journey at Battleford and others continued west.

The first settlement in the Marshall area consisted of a store (Hall & Scott), post office, blacksmith shop, and an Anglican church (St. Georges); the settlement was known by the name of Stringer, being located on the land of Lewis Stringer, one mile from the present townsite. When the townsite was formed and the Canadian Northern Railway came through in 1905, the railway relocated the village and changed the name from Stringer to Marshall. No one left knows anything about this significance of the name, Marshall. It is a very common surname and also a place name. You can find a Marshall in the following states: Arkansas, Illinois, Michigan, Minnesota, Missouri, North Carolina, North Dakota, Oklahoma, Texas and Virginia. This does not exhaust the list.

Prior to the coming of the railroad Battleford, 100 miles distant, was the nearest town and the railway terminated at Saskatoon. During the first few years many of the pioneers lived in dwellings made of sods. Lumber at that time was difficult to obtain and had to be hauled by wagon and oxen from Fort Pitt.

The settlers suffered many hardships during those early years, particularly during the first winter which began in early October and lasted until late May. Because of the unusually long winter there was a shortage of supplies. The inhabitants were not familiar with the ways of the climate of the country and therefore were not prepared for the long winter and gruelling times ahead. The story is told of one settler who, in need of supplies, walked the 12 miles to Lloydminster and back in extremely cold weather, pulling a hand sleigh, in hopes of being able to obtain a few staples, such as tea, sugar, flour, etc. All he was able to procure was a sack of flour which was shared with his neighbors.

The first settlers of the Marshall district were a hardy lot and many of them lived to a ripe old age. Many saw their dreams come true, reaped benefits from their early trials and struggles and saw the next generation firmly established.

MARTENSVILLE

Some years ago Isaac Martens and his son Dave began to sub-divide their farm land into smaller plots. At first these plots were sold as acreages but later they were again sub-divided into lots. According to law, streets were allowed. A hamlet was then incorporated and it had to have a name. The government asked permission from the Martens to allow their name to be used. This was granted and the little settlement just north of Saskatoon on Avenue A became known as Martensville.

MARYFIELD

There is not too much information as to the origin of the name of the village of Maryfield. Some believe it derived from the name of an English Manor, from which a family emigrated to this area. Others say there was a family of people who lived here in the 1880s whose surname was Maryfield. Still others say the first baby girl born here was Marion Fielding, thus the derivation of the name.

MARYSBURG

Marysburg was formerly called Dead Moose Lake. The lake is three miles west of the hamlet. In 1925 the name of Marysburg was officially adoped through the efforts of the parish priest at that time, Father Mathias Steger, OSB. Father Mathias did not appreciate the name of Dead Moose Lake and suggested that Marysburg would be more fitting for the community which would be related to the name of the local church, "Assumption of the Blessed Virgin Mary."

MARYVILLE

Maryville is a very special place on the riverbank four miles north of Sutherland near Saskatoon. The idea for its origin was conceived by Most Reverend Francis J. Klein, D.D., shortly after he established the Saskatoon Catholic Centre in 1960.

He bought the property — an old hunting lodge — and converted it into a summer residence for all Sisters in the Saskatoon Diocese.

Over the years a church, four cottages, a main lounge, swimming pool, basketball court, shrine and various service houses were built on this picturesque site.

It was named for Mary, mother of Jesus.

MASEFIELD

Masefield is in the southwest corner of the province on a CPR branch line that ends at Val Marie. Many writers and authors have been honored by having a Saskatchewan town named for them and this one was likely named for John Masefield, English poet, playwright and fiction writer. He ran away to sea at the age of 13 (1891); came back and settled near London and devoted himself to writing (1897). He was very successful and at one point in his career he was poet laureate.

MATADOR

Matador was named in honor of the Matador Land Cattle Company organized in 1882 with its home office in Trinidad, Colorado. It operated ranches in Texas, the Dakotas and Montana. Soon after the turn of the century it secured a lease on 140,000 acres in what was then the Northwest Territories. The south boundary of this lease was the South Saskatchewan river for 20 miles. The headquarters of the ranch was seven miles from Saskatchewan Landing. They ran 65,000 head of cattle and hundreds of horses. For various reasons the Matador abandoned the Canadian lease about 1921. Soon after this the Matador community pasture was organized to serve the purpose of supplying grazing for hundreds of farmers and ranchers within a radius of 50 miles. The most recent development in this district has been the establishment of the Beechy Co-operative Farm. This was set up in 1949 by a group of veterans of the Second World War.

MATCHEE

The CPR line north from Medstead to Meadow Lake runs through heavy bush. Matchee is on this line and is named for a well-known and highly respected Indian of the early days, Chief Matchee, of the Meadow Lake Indians.

MAWER

Mawer is between Central Butte and Darmody on a CNR line that runs north and west of Moose Jaw and ends at Riverhurst. From Mawer, a branch line runs west to Main Centre.

The Mawer district was settled in the years 1904-1910. One of the first homesteaders was Joseph Nouch, who filed on the SW quarter of S30-T21-R3, west of the third meridian, in 1904. Other early settlers were: Wilkie, Baldin, McIlroy, England, Carr, Watkins, Fuller, Selby, Munroe, McKee, Peterman, Grant, Gibbie, Van Averall, Willard, Gibson, Johnson, Murdock, Reid, Beck, Wendel and Clay.

Grain was hauled by horse or ox team to Mortlach until the CPR Outlook line was put through in 1908. The Grand Trunk came as far west as Mawer in 1913 and extended to Riverhurst in 1915.

Mr. Martin A. Moore is generally credited with naming the new town. According to some Mawer is a contraction of Martin Moore. Others have it that Mr. Moore named it after Bryn Mawr, in Pennsylvania. Another version, the most plausible of all, states that the village was named for Miss Mawer, stenographer in the Grand Trunk Pacific office in Winnipeg.

There have been so many changes since 1913 that it is difficult to give a coherent account of the village buildings as some have been built, some torn down, others moved in or out, some merged with others and some burned. All have different owners as not one of the original inhabitants remain.

MAXIM

In 1913, the CPR built a branch line northwest from Estevan that ended with Tribune, Maxim and Neptune. These towns flourished, particularly Tribune.

The first blow fell in 1926 when the CPR built another branch line that started six miles east of Tribune and ran west to Minton. Towns that sprang up along this line cut into the business of those to the north. Maxim was one of these and business dwindled so much over the years that in 1959 the CPR applied for, and got, permission to abandon the part of the line that included Tribune, Maxim and Neptune.

Because many of the early settlers had come in from South Dakota and Nebraska they chose Maxim in honor of Sir Hiram Steven Maxim (1840-1916) an American engineer and inventor of the Maxim gun. He later became a British subject.

MAXSTONE

Maxstone is 12 miles south of Assiniboia. The first settlers located there in 1907 but the railway (CPR) did not arrive until 1926. The district was named in 1913. Originally the settlers wanted to call it Stonehenge but that name was taken by a neighboring village to the west. Therefore, they settled for Maxstone in honor of their first postmaster, Alex Maxwell and they were able to incorporate stone from the name Stonehenge.

Maxstone was never very large — 50 people at most. The store closed in 1957 and the post office in 1965. The population is now down to 25.

MAXWELTON

Maxwelton was a rural post office in the Viceroy-Verwood district. It was established on July 1, 1912, and the first postmaster was George Steneley. The first homesteaders included a lot of Scottish people. The post office was named for Maxwelton House in Southern Uplands in Dumfries, Scotland. The office closed out on September 7, 1954.

"Maxwelton's braes are bonnie
Where early falls the dew,
'Twas there that Annie Laurie
Gave me her promise true."

It's hard to say whether the Scots were pining for the "Auld sod" or were happy about the new.

MAYBERRY

Mayberry is a rural post office located at 25-12-27-W2, which is 25 miles straight south of Moose Jaw. The postmaster is Donald Mayberry and that's how it got its name.

MAYFAIR

In 1909 Mr. William Clease moved from this district into Saskatoon and lived in the Mayfair district. He later moved back to this area and settled on a farm 21 miles north of Speers. When a school was built in the area he was instrumental in having it named "Mayfair." In 1928 when the CNR was built through to Medstead from Speers, a townsite was started four miles from the Mayfair school. The town was named for the school "Mayfair." Years later the old school was moved into Mayfair and now serves as the Roman Catholic church.

MAYMONT

The village of Maymont is about halfway between the cities of Saskatoon and North Battleford on highway #5.

It was named for May Montgomery, niece of Mr. McKenzie of McKenzie and Mann railway construction contractors, who built the line through the area in 1905.

Miss Montgomery had asked her uncle to name the village Montgomery but he said he couldn't because a town in Manitoba had that name. Therefore, he took her first name and the first syllable of her last name and combined them to form the name, Maymont.

Until 1930 when the CPR was built from Saskatoon to Baljennie, Maymont was the market town and shopping center for the settlers of Spinney Hill and Sonningdale districts. At first they crossed the river by boat, but in 1907 a ferry service was installed and this was used until the 1970's when a grand new bridge joined the south bank to the north. Along the north shore there is now a lovely park and many people come to relax and enjoy the pastoral view of the Eagle Hills with their wooded crests forming an uncommonly fine landscape.

MAYVIEW

Mayview is a relatively new area. Bruce Christy, Otto Gulzow and Fred Herzog arrived in 1928. In 1929, in the month of May, an Irishman by the name of Pat Brophy made application for a post office. He and Mr. Herzog were responsible for sending in the name of Mayview, which was selected. The significance is that it was May when they made their request and from Mayview you get a good view. There is no railway in the immediate area. The nearest one is the CNR at Holbein twenty-five miles to the south. North of it is Prince Albert National Park.

MAZENOD

Settlers began moving into this area well ahead of the surveyors and they located along the "Old Pole Trail", the old telegraph line, which ran from Moose Jaw to the N.W.M.P. outpost at Wood Mountain.

Mr. and Mrs. John Kelly were Mazenod's first villagers. Mr. Kelly ran the dray service from the CNR which came in 1913. Mrs. Kelly cooked and baked for the bachelors round about.

Father Louis Pierre Gravel, for whom Gravelbourg is named, was the parish priest for Mazenod until the building of a church in 1915. The lumber for this church was hauled from Mortlach. When the railway arrived in 1913 it was Father

Gravel who suggested that the village be called Mazenod after Bishop Charles Eugene de Mazenod of Marseille, France, who was the founder of the Oblate Fathers. The name was accepted. Three of the well known names from Mazenod in the area of government are the brothers Edward and Robert Walker who have both served as MLAs. Mrs. Louise Lucas was a farm housewife here when she first began to take an interest in the political life of Saskatchewan.

McARA

McAra is on a CPR line near Regina. When the line was built the grain point was named for James McAra, Mayor of Regina at the time.

McCALLUM

McCallum is on a CPR line near Regina. It was named for E. D. McCallum, Regina real estate magnate during the early years of the city.

McCORD

McCord is between Ferland and Glentworth on a CPR line in the south of the province. The first post office in the district was called Gravesburg after the postmaster, Mr. Graves. Then in 1920 the name was changed to Nully.

Jim McCord came West in 1916 and purchased land from George Chauvier who had come from Lemoge, France. Mr. Chauvier operated a small store on this land where McCord now stands. The post office at this time was four and one-half miles south and it was suggested that Mr. McCord try to get a post office at the store. Their efforts were successful and when the names were sent in McCord was the one picked by the postal officials.

Today, Winters McCord, a son, lives in McCord and is the caretaker of a fine four-room public school. This information was sent in by Donald Blake, a grade five student at McCord Public School.

McEACHERN

McEachern post office was opened in 1914 30 miles southeast of Mankota on NW33-1-8-W3. It was named for McEachern creek which, in turn, had been named for an early rancher in the district. The first postmaster, Joe A. Yates, had the office in his home. Others who looked after the post office as the years passed were: Mrs. Hagel, Mrs. Krane, John Brown and Clint Brown who was operating it when it closed out.

McEachern is good ranching country and some of the finest Hereford and Angus cattle in Saskatchewan are raised there. First families into the district included the following: Raush, Kowolofski, Fred Book, John Brumberger, Joe Yates, Gus Loewen, John Keller, the Millers and the Kohls.

McELHANNEY

McElhanney was an inland post office that was established in 1921 when a rural mail route was started from Prairie River. Knobby Clarke was the first mail carrier and his last call, seventeen miles to the south, was McElhanney. The first postmaster was G. B. McPherson and when he left the district in 1925 G. F. Johnston took it over and combined it with a general store on his farm.

It was Mr. Johnston who introduced Eli Hooper to McElhanney. Mr. Hooper had come to Prairie River in the first week of May, 1927 to look for a homestead. He was introduced to Garth Johnston who asked him, "Can you drive a car? I have one that was shipped in, in a box-car, and I can't take it and the team to McElhanney." Mr. Hooper agreed to drive the car, and taking a Mr. Best with him, he started out on the Prairie River Road. The road was a narrow grade, mostly travelled on by wagons, as there were very few cars in the district. The wagons left a deep rutted track and there were many mud holes which had been corduroyed with poles. Coming to a creek they found that the bridge had dropped about two feet. If they stopped they could be stuck in the mud, so Eli stepped on the gas. There was a sudden bump as the car jumped over the bridge, and Mr. Best's head went through the windshield. Mr. Best said, "Don't you know that I just came out of the hospital in Tisdale?" To which Mr. Hooper replied, "If we hit a few more holes like that you will likely be going right back there."

Mr. Hooper filed on a quarter section four miles southeast of McElhanney. He then returned to the prairie and married Clara Harris of Colonsay. It was not until March of 1928 that Eli returned to his homestead. He had been given another quarter section for soldier's grant, so that give him 320 acres of solid poplar forest. He did not have to travel far to get the wherewithall to build his log house.

After the house was built Mr. Hooper made another trip out and shipped in a carload of settler's effects. It took many trips to haul all the equipment out from Prairie River with a team and wagon. On May 24th Mrs. Hooper arrived at Prairie River. Her husband met her at the station and they started out for the homestead with a wagon load of equipment and poultry. Mrs. Hooper was thrilled with the new log house all chinked up with moss, and the beautiful trees all around. She was one of the first women in the settlement to live east of the McNab Creek.

McGEE

McGee is on a CNR line which runs from Rosetown to Kindersley. It was named for D'Arcy McGee, one of the most brilliant orators in Canadian parliamentary history. He entered politics as an Independent and represented Montreal West from 1858 until his untimely death from an assassin's bullet in 1868. He was a delegate to the Charlottetown and Quebec conferences and was an eloquent advocate of Canadian union. He was in a very real sense one of the Fathers of Confederation.

McGILL'S SIDING

McGill's Siding was less than a mile northwest of Adine which itself was a loading platform on a CNR line that ran southwest of Biggar to Dodsland. It was named for Archie McGill on whose land it was located. Besides Mr. McGill. J. J. Rogers, Alec MacLeod and Hugh McCready, were active in having the siding put in. It also had a flag station. Today it's all gone and the land is broken up and farmed.

McKAGUE

On May 10th, 1919 Herbert McKague, after whom the hamlet is named, drove south from Melfort with a herd of cattle and horses in search of free range. He came to a stop just short of Barrier river south of the present site of McKague. He had a family of six sons who helped him establish a large ranch.

When the CPR came through in the fall of 1923 it fired the early settlers with enthusiasm and in an effort to be in on the ground floor they began working knee deep in water to clear the main street and approach to the station. Ditches were dug and the water was drained off. Mr. Roberts was the first station agent. The first building was put up by Alphonse Dupas. A combined post office and store operated by Mr. Major was next. A Pool elevator was built and the first agent was Bert Baldwin. McKague was the name agreed upon and thus the hamlet started to grow.

McLAREN

McLaren, ten miles north of Maidstone, was a post office and store run by the McLaren family. It was just north and west of Pine Island in the North Saskatchewan River. This island was the site of a Federal Government archeology project in 1966. At that time they uncovered the remains of three early fur-trading posts.

McLEAN

Near Duck Lake on March 26, 1885, the first shots in the Saskatchewan Rebellion were fired. The North-West Mounted Police and volunteers from Fort Carlton, under Superintendent L. N. F. Crozier were turned back.

News of the victory sped across the prairies and Big Bear's discontented band at Frog Lake perpetrated the saddest incident of the war, the massacre at Frog Lake. Next they started down river to Fort Pitt. At that time Mr. McLean was in command of the Hudson's Bay Company post there. The small garrison of twenty-three men faced three hundred Indians. The story goes that when the Indians began attacking, Mr. McLean said he had never known one he was afraid of and he left the Fort unarmed to parley with them. He was advised that if he and his family would submit themselves as prisoners the police in the Fort would be allowed to leave. Thereafter the McLean family gave themselves up and Geoffrey Dickens, son of the novelist Charles Dickens, and his police were allowed to leave down river to Battleford. Fort Pitt was looted.

For weeks the McLeans, the women from Frog Lake, and William Beasdell Cameron remained as prisoners of the Indians, once being offered freedom if Amelia, daughter of Mr. McLean, consented to marry one of the chiefs. She would not and it was not until some time after the battle of Frenchman's Butte when Major Sam Steele's patrol caught Big Bear's band crossing the "Narrows" at Loon Lake that they were able to escape and make their way south to safety.

Mr. McLean later became inspector for the department of Indian Affairs. For some time Amelia was secretary to the Indian Commissioner at Winnipeg and later married Fred H. Paget, chief clerk of the Indian department there.

The town of McLean twenty-three miles east of Regina on the main line of the CPR is named for this courageous family.

McLEAN

Jim McLean opened his post office and store on his farm eight miles north of Adanac in 1905. His customers, some of whose descendants still live in the district, were: George, Bill and Clarence Imrie, Jim and Charlie Fawell, Henry and Angus Knuff, John Coad, John Lloyd, Bob Beaman and Amaziah Beeson.

The mail came in from Battleford by democrat. The post office and store did not last long after the railway was built. Jim closed it in 1909, sold the farm and moved down to Unity where he built a general store.

His son, Fred, was the first Rhodes Scholar turned out by the town and later he went on to a very successful career in medicine. Dr. McLean passed away in 1976 in Pincher Creek, Alberta.

This information came from Fred Housen, long-time resident of Unity.

McMAHON

A CPR line runs south of Swift Current and branches at Hak. One line goes to Tyson and the other to Meyronne. On the line going to Tyson, the first grain point is McMahon. It was named for Frank McMahon, a brakeman on the line. He now lives in Smith Falls, Ontario.

McMORRAN

McMorran is the end of a CPR branch line built north and then west of Rosetown in the early 1920's. It was named for a CPR employee, Roy McMorran, clerk in the Vancouver office. He was so honored because he had won the Military Medal during World War I.

McMorran was never a big place. The recent hearings that have been held before the Hall Commission have recorded that the line will likely be abandoned.

McTAGGART

McTaggart is the first grain point north of Weyburn on a CPR line that runs to Moose Jaw. It was named McTaggart for Ralph McTaggart, roadmaster, after the line was put in.

In 1898 the first settlers, Bob Pulfer, Billy Reynolds and Fred Bowdick arrived. During these early years McTaggart had two stores, a lumberyard, station, and all that went to make up a prairie town. Now it's down to four elevators and a combined Esso service station and confectionery run by Art Ward and a post office looked after by Mrs. Reaney.

MEACHAM

This little town is 40 miles east of Saskatoon. The population is about 200. It was named in honor of Mr. Meacham, one of the first settlers.

Another version states it was named for a Lord Meacham.

MEAD

Mead, on the CNR line west from Saskatoon, was only a siding. Keppel, on the CPR less than a quarter of a mile north, was the town. Mead had a flag station, a loading platform and a section house. The railway officials, following their alphabetical pattern (Juniata, Kinley, Leney, Mead, Neola) gave Mead its name; it had no local significance.

Some of the early settlers to load grain at this siding before an elevator was built at Keppel in 1910 were: Alvin Trapp; Alex Williamson; Frank Brown; the Croziers, Andrew, Jim, Walter, Bob and Tom; Claude Woodcock; Dave and George Towriss; Hugh Mainland; John Paul; Reg Martin; George Lawless; Roy Talbot; Dave, Bill and George Todd. Strings of empty box-cars would be "side-tracked" and left to be loaded. If you wanted to ship grain you had to get some into the car before someone else did. In good crop

years competition was keen for the cars. One time Roy Talbot threw a little sack of grain into a moving car through the open door. Another man on the other side was trying to jump into the car when the sack of grain hit him on the head and knocked him out of the car — so Talbot got the car!

MEADOW LAKE

Meadow Lake, Saskatchewan's most northerly town, traces its name to the early French traders, who knew it as Lac Des Prairies, the prairie land surrounded by forests.

The first settlement was a Hudson's Bay Company post established by Peter Fidler (1769-1822) on a tributary of the Beaver river that flows out of the north end of the lake. He was a fur-trader and surveyor who apprenticed to the company in 1788 and spent the rest of his life in its service in the Canadian Northwest.

The next settlers to move in were ranchers and they began coming in 1912. However, development was slow until the arrival of the ralroad in 1936. Meadow Lake had been incorporated as a village in 1928 but with the advent of the railway it became a town in 1936. Its growth has been steady ever since and it is best known now for its annual stampede, one of the most successful in Saskatchewan.

MEATH PARK

In 1929 the CNR started to grade for a railroad north from Prince Albert to Henribourg and then swung east to Nipawin. The first train did not run until 1932. Long before the railroad came to the district it was called Meath Park. Many of the early settlers came from England: Frank Calvert (first settler in the district), Albert Elwood, Bill Hollingshead, Sam Cousins, Levi Farnsworth, Smokey Simpson, Frank Ashdown and Elmer Jones. Other settlers came from Scotland: Lawrence McCauley, Neil McDermid, Jock McCorkindale, Tom Twert, Edwin McKay and Bill Davidson. There were also a number of Swedish names: Mobel Fladager, Reuben Halgeson, Stan and Peter Larson, Frank Johnson and Oral Keeting. Since the first school was called Surrey the name Meath Park likely came from England just as did Paddockwood and Forest Gate to the north.

The original settlement was three miles southeast of the present townsite and some did not move to the new railroad in 1929 so for a while there was an Old Meath Park and a New Meath Park. This did not facilitate mail delivery and Old Meath Park disappeared as a name and the site became known as "Janow Corners." There are still buildings there: a boarded-up school, a Polish Roman Catholic church, a few dwellings and the foundations of the first store in the district which was operated by Mr. Bearse.

W. J. 'Bill" Berezowsky, a former MLA for East Cumberland farms near Meath Park. Naturally, he is quite a booster of Meath Park and some of it has rubbed off on others. Mr. P. J. Kyle and his son, Murray, who run a combined post office and regional library, are not at all surprised with the recent number of starts in building sites in the town. In fact, their attitude seems to be that Prince Albert is just a suburb of Meath Park! That's the spirit that built the west and is still building in the northwest!

MEDSTEAD

Sylvester Perry opened the first post office in his home in 1910. He suggested the name Medford because he had come from Medford, Wisconsin. The postal authorities did not accept it because they thought the name would conflict with Melfort. They suggested a change to Medstead. It was agreed upon.

In 1916 R. A. Doidge opened a store three miles from the present townsite and the post office moved to the store. When the railway arrived in 1927 the post office moved again to the new town.

MEETING LAKE

Meeting Lake is an inland post office that takes its name from the lake on which it is located. There are two stories as to how Meeting lake got its name. Both of them are logical and both are interesting. In the twenties two beaches developed that were outstanding. Cottages were built and crowds swarmed there on holidays. Jack Peters had one of the beaches on the east end, in the pines. He also ran a fox farm and a sawmill. The other beach was operated by Mr. Aumack and his cottages were in the poplars with a lovely white sand beach. In the vicinity of Meeting lake the pines of the north meet the poplars of the parkland, hence the name Meeting lake.

The other story is that at the west end of the lake there was a huge circular pavilion that not only catered to regular dances with orchestras brought in from North Battleford but that was the center of a great agricultural fair so important in the early days. This fair drew entries from Rabbit Lake, Robinhood, Mullingar, Mayfair, Glenbush, Medstead, Belbutte, Spiritwood and Bapaume. It was a popular meeting place and hence the name Meeting Lake.

Meeting Lake is still popular as a summer resort.

MEETOOS

Meetoos is on the CPR line between Chitek Lake and Meadow Lake. This line for the most part runs through heavy timber and this accounts for the name Meetoos, which in Cree means The Place of Trees.

MEGAN

Megan was a postal district eight miles east of the town of Arborfield. It was named for Megan Lloyd George, daughter of the war time Prime Minister of Great Britain during the first World War.

The first postmaster was Herb Griffith and some of the people his post office served were: Tom Anderson, Harvey Scott, Jim Skinner, Duncan Livingstone, Jack Oliphant, Cyril Thomas, and Emil Strad.

These homesteaders had to haul their grain to Eldersley or Crooked River until the railroad came to Arborfield in 1930.

When the 1918 flu epidemic swept the prairies, Mr. and Mrs. Griffith fell ill. Their nearest neighbor was the Henry Cummins family, seven miles to the west. Fortunately Herb had a collie dog and he went to the Cummins home and made such a fuss that Henry hooked up his horses and drove over to see if anything was wrong at the Griffiths'. When he got there he found that Herb and his wife were so ill that neither one could get out of bed to get in wood and the fire had gone out. It was a close call.

There were many close calls in the

early days and some did not fare as well as Mr. and Mrs. Griffith — thanks to a faithful dog.

MELAVAL

Melaval is a hamlet 35-8-4-W3. The CPR named it for Melaval Kadry, a Syrian-American, whose homestead the CPR bought for a townsite in 1913. Some of the first homesteaders in the district were: John Cochran, John Donahue, James Murray, Ambrose and William Liddy, Elmer Smith, William Bydinham, Andrew Ramage, Richard Wannamaker, Henry Wheeler, Henry Grose, C. W. Johnson and others.

Melaval was a thriving hamlet in its day. At its height it had a population of 125 with 2 blacksmith shops, three garages, a hotel, a livery barn, two stores, three implement agencies, a restaurant, a drugstore, a butchershop, a school (with grades 1 to 8), a United Church, 6 elevators, a bank, a curling rink, a community hall, and 2 passenger trains a day. This has almost all dwindled away, with the present population at 55 or 60.

MELBA

Melba is the name of a siding on the CPR mainline 42 miles west of Moose Jaw. It was created in 1912 when the double track was laid west. It was first known as Walker being named for one of the train dispatchers on the line. A small station, complete with operator was set up at the siding. Because it was so close to Secretan no town ever developed. The next year the CPR made four-mile sections out of the single 10-mile stretches and this caused a section gang to be set up at Walker and a passing track was laid.

As for changing of the name there are several stories. Here is one: When the passing track was being laid the large work gang had a lady cook who was a very good singer. In the evenings it was common for all to gather for a sing-song. The boys nicknamed her "Madame Melba" for a well-known opera singer of that period. Visiting railway officials were often entertained and somehow the name Walker got changed to Melba.

MELFORT

At the approach of the steel to Melfort in 1904, Mrs. Reginald Beatty, the first lady settler in the district, was asked by the Canadian Northern officials of the day to name the new town. She chose the name of Melfort in memory of her family place in Argyle, Scotland.

MELVILLE

Melville, the smallest city in Saskatchewan, is a divisional point on the CNR. It was named in honor of Charles Melville Hays, who was at the time of the building of the townsite, the president of the Grand Trunk and Grand Trunk Pacific Railways. On April 14, 1912, he was one of the 1513 people who lost their lives in the sinking of the ill-fated Titanic.

MENDHAM

The train ride ended at Maple Creek for Jacob Heisler and George Alex Marshal. They bought a team and wagon and headed north over the "Battleford Trail." When they arrived at their locations, after 60 miles of travel, it was December in 1907. They did not go directly to their homesteads. Instead they sought temporary shelter in caves dug into the hills along the South Saskatchewan river and stayed there until March of 1908 when they came out and built log houses two miles west of the present location of Mendham. That year Glen Mitchell, John Jangula, John Antoni, Fred Sukut, and Jacob Gunther arrived and from then on the community grew.

This is how Mendham got its name. Charles Mendham, an employee of the CPR, enlisted in 1916 and went overseas. The CPR, as a mark of appreciation, called stations along their lines being built at that time after employees who had enlisted. The Leader southwest branch was just being completed and the first station was called Mendham.

MENNON

Mennon is 25 miles north of Saskatoon. The majority of the early settlers were Mennonites and they named the hamlet Mennon in honor of Menno Simons (1492-1559), the founder of this particular religious group. The sect was organized in 1525 at Zurich, Switzerland, and its beliefs are based on the teachings of the New Testament, especially those in the Sermon on the Mount. After centuries of migration through the Germanies and

Russia, during which they had periodically suffered civil disabilities and persecution, the Mennonites came to Manitoba in the 1870s and to this area in the late 1890s.

MEOTA

The community around the southwest end of Jackfish lake, 21 miles north of North Battleford, was almost completely homesteaded before the railway arrived. Mannix, Tait, Iverson, Robertson, Davis, Ball, Sutton, Gilliland and Wilkinson were some of the early settlers.

Joseph Dart, an independent merchant, had left Edmonton in 1904 with a single barge load of supplies and came down the North Saskatchewan (carefully following the HBC double markers in the channel to avoid sandbars) as far as the mouth of the Jackfish river. He contracted Moise Hall and Pete Jepson to freight his supplies north. They followed the Jackfish river taking the dismantled barge with them as loose lumber. Mr. Dart located on the west bank just a short distance downstream from the present railway bridge where the Fort Pitt trail forded the Jackfish river. His first store was a tent but this was later replaced by a substantial building.

When an application for a post office was made, Mr. Arthur Mannix, who lived on "Ten Point", was responsible for choosing an Indian name for the site. His suggestion of Meotate (meaning "good places to camp" or "it is good here") was shortened by postal officials to Meota. This post office was located in Dart's store. Mr. Dart did a good business, both with the local homesteaders and travellers over the trail.

Joe Iverson, a son of one of the early pioneers and still a resident of Meota, tells a story of how one of these weary, thirsty men stopped at Dart's store and the first thing he asked for was a drink of water. Mr. Dart, in his usual courteous manner, told him to help himself from the barrel outside. In a few minutes the man came back spluttering and when he was again able to talk said, "Mister, I've been so dry on these prairies at times that I've had to drink from an alkali slough, but this is the damndest water I've ever tasted!" In those days coal oil was shipped in wooden barrels and he had dipped from the wrong barrel.

When the railroad came from North Battleford in 1910, Mr. Dart moved to the townsite and brought his post office with him, thus giving the town its name. Mr. Dart's older son, John, and John's wife, Nannette, still operate the family store.

Today, on the hills which surround Jackfish lake, farm implements continue to turn up stone artifacts that date back thousands of years. In places artifacts and "chips" are numerous. These were the campsite of Stone Age men. Apparently they, too, found it a good place to camp.

The mixed train is largely a thing of the past. The one that used to operate through Meota is a good example. It started out from North Battleford and ran to St. Walburg, stayed there overnight and returned the next day. It carried everything: cream cans, barbed wire, mail and passengers. One car at the end of the train was reserved for them. The train stopped at every point along the way, with the result that many stories were inspired by the slow-paced journey.

One such story concerns a young couple who got on the train at Meota during the 1930's. There was a long stop there because Meota was a bustling little village at the time. They called at Cavalier. Then came Vawn and another long, long wait.

The young lady said to the conductor as he boarded, "I hope we get to Edam soon because I'm going to have a baby."

To which the conductor replied, "Lady if you are in that condition you shouldn't have gotten on this train."

"Mr. Conductor," said the lady, "when I got on this train I wasn't in this condition."

Today the North Battleford to St. Walburg line is still open. Millions of bushels of grain are brought out every year by box car but the station at Meota has been closed for years.

MERID

One hundred and ten degrees longitude is the meridian that forms the boundary line between Saskatchewan and Alberta. Merid is on a CNR railway between Alsask and Marengo, very close to this line. Merid is a contraction of the word meridian, hence the name.

MERLE

Merle is a country post office just off the east end of Barrier lake. The closest railroad towns are Bjorkdale on the CNR 16 miles to the north and McKague on the CPR 16 miles to the northwest.

The first settlers came into the district in 1911 and included the families of Fred, Ed, and William Ham, and J. Goldsworthy. The first post office was opened in 1932 and named Merle for Merle Trombley the first postmaster. The office closed in 1966 and the patrons now get their mail at either Bjorkdale or Archerwill.

MERRINGTON

Merrington was a rural post office and store which was established in 1910 four miles north of Kindersley by the late C. W. Baker.

With the coming of the railway and the start of the townsite of Kindersley, the Merrington post office closed out.

Descendants of Mr. Baker now operate a store in Kindersley.

MERRYFLAT

Merryflat is a country post office 35 miles south of Maple Creek. It is situated on a flat. The first settlers: Mose Pettyjohn, Bert Jones, George Kelly, Everett Parsonage and Ike Stirling were a sociable lot. In those days there was no radio, T.V., community hall or even a school house, that could be used as a central meeting place. But this did not deter the settlers. In turn, they used their homes and when they were a little cramped for dancing space they moved the furniture aside; sometimes they moved it outside. This district became known far and wide for its merry times. Hence, the name of the post office became Merryflat. When a school was built in 1915 they called it Merryflat, too. Today the closest railway is at Senate 17 miles to the south.

MERVIN

In 1912 the railroad started north from Edam where it had slowly crept from North Battleford. But long before it arrived at Mervin the place was established and named. Mervin was an important "stopping place" on the old trail that ran from Paynton across the river and up into the St. Walburg country. It was operated by Mr. and Mrs. Archie Gemmell and it was named for their son, Mervin, who now resides in Smith Falls, Ont.

Additional information about Mervin brings to light a "like-father-like-son" story. Mr. Douglas Hicks started teaching in the rural school of Wheatfield north of Perdue, then went overseas at the outbreak of World War I. When he returned he took up teaching and from being principal of King Street school in North Battleford, he went on to be school inspector of the Mervin district. North beyond the rails or roads he opened up dozens of little log schools in the 1920s and 1930s. From Mervin he moved on to be school superintendent in the Watrous area and stayed there until his retirement. He now resides in Victoria.

While at Mervin, a son, Douglas, was born in the Turtleford hospital, a town five miles to the north. Doug has followed in his father's footsteps by teaching at all levels before entering the Saskatoon public school system. He was appointed principal in 1961 and area superintendent in 1967. In 1970 he took leave of absence to work on his doctorate in Educational Administration at the University of Saskatchewan. Dr. Hicks is presently employed as administrative assistant to Dr. F. J. Gathercole, director of education, Saskatoon Public Board of Education.

MESKANAW

From The Western Producer of April 14, 1960:

"Mr. Traill was a Hudson's Bay Company officer. He served as post manager at Fort Pitt, Slave Lake, Vermilion, Fort St. James, and Carlton.

After Carlton he retired and decided to go into cattle ranching. An old Indian had told him of a good location south of Waterhen Lake, in the Kinistino district. He investigated this area, and finding it suitable, he located there on the bank of Yellow creek. Here in 1897 he erected buildings, put up hay, and purchased a herd of good cattle. His daughter, Maria, joined him as housekeeper and their home became the first stopping place for all newcomers to the district. Mr. Traill got along very well with the Indians, too, as the following story will testify. One day a large group dropped in to visit and it just happened that Mr. Traill was out of meat. He gave one of the Indians a gun and two shells (hand loaded) and asked him to get some ducks. In a short time he returned with 17. Meskanaw is the Cree word meaning 'trail' or 'road' and Meskanaw is named for Mr. Traill."

METINOTA

Metinota is a village on the south shore of Jackfish Lake. It was formed in the early 1900's by professional and businessmen of North Battleford and named for nearby Meota.

Lately, Saskatoon people moved in and now you have the cottage names: East, Berstrom and Thompson very prominent.

Metinota is a well-kept beach and the summer cottages compare favorably with any on the lake.

MEYRONNE

Meyronne is 40 miles west of Assiniboia. Settlers from France arrived in the district in 1908 and when a post office was opened in 1909 it was given the name Meyronne in honor of the charming little village of Meyronne, France.

MIDALE

Midale is named in honor of Mr. Ole Dale, who was the first settler to arrive in the district, and Dr. R. M. Mitchell, a pioneer doctor. They took the first two letters of Mitchell and the last name of Mr. Dale to make the name, Midale.

MIDDLE LAKE

Middle Lake is on a CPR line that runs from Lanigan to Prince Albert. It is named for nearby Middle Lake the smallest of three lakes in a line. Lenore Lake to the east is the largest. Basin Lake to the northwest is the next largest in size and Middle Lake is the smallest and in between them, hence the name, Middle Lake.

MIDNIGHT LAKE

This information is taken directly from a letter sent to us by Mr. R. Warwick of Midnight Lake.

"First of all, Midnight Lake is only a country store and post office situated on No. 4 highway about half a mile south of the lake, which can easily be located on any map about fifty miles north of North

Battleford. It used to be a mile north on the banks of the creek that ran from Midnight Lake to Stoney Lake. Midnight Lake is not a summer resort type of lake but a huge body of water surrounded by large hay flats. The post office is supposed to be closed shortly due to this so-called economy drive.

Naturally the post office was named after the lake. It was first located in a country store owned by John Hills, who later moved to Glaslyn when the railroad was built. Settlers started to move into the district about 1912. I came in 1919 after my discharge from the army in World War I.

The only sensible story I can offer for the origin of the name is that a survey party looking for a camping spot arrived at the lake at midnight and called the lake accordingly. It is definitely not of Indian origin because not having our method of telling time and no clocks or watches they had no such word in their language. The only way they can signify the white man's name in Cree is to call it Sleeping Lake which is what you should be doing at midnight. So in Cree it is Nee-pa-ta-o Sa-gi-ee-gan."

MIKADO

Mikado is the second stop northwest of Kamsack. At the time the railway line was built the Russo-Japanese War was being fought (1904-1905). Sympathy for the Japanese ran very high in Canada. The naming of Mikado was evidence of this. Other places in Saskatchewan named for people directly engaged in this war were: Fukushiama, Togo and Kuroki.

In choosing Mikado, which is the ancient title of the Emperor of Japan, and early settlers of Mikado paid the highest of honors to that country.

MILATY

Milaty is situated at Mile 80 on the Indian Head Subdivision. It was named for Mr. Milaty, a pioneer in the district, little else is known about it.

MILDEN

It was customary for the railroads or for some workman to give a name to a new town. The first one suggested for the town was Tisbest. The second was Jordanville and this was aimed at honoring an early settler by the name of Jordan.

Milden, the name eventually used, was a combination of the two names, Mills and Bryden. By taking the Mil from Mills and the den from Bryden they arrived at Milden. This was done to recognize the service that Mrs. Mills and Mrs. Bryden, wives of early settlers, had rendered in furnishing meals and home-made bread to many of the bachelor homesteaders.

The above information was supplied by G. W. Somerville of Milden.

MILDRED
Mildred is between Spiritwood and Amiens on a CNR line that runs from Medstead to Shellbrook. Before the railway came many settlers moved in about 1908 and among these were the following: Fred, Charlie and George LaFluer, and Jim Harper. The district was named Arluie.

When the railroad came in 1928 the name chosen for the townsite was Mildred. This was done to honor the postmaster's daughter, Mildred Howard, who died of TB in 1913.

MILE 62
The Hanson Lake Road or Highway 106 was started in 1957 at Smeaton and completed to Flin Flon, Manitoba a distance of 240 miles by 1962. It was named for Olaf Hanson, a long-time prospector in the district.

At Smeaton (once called Dorrit) the road starts at Mile 0. There were no post offices along the way and communication with the outside world was by two-way radio. However, in 1975, a post office was established at Mile 62 — the first along the road.

MILE 102
A great deal of thought went into the choosing of many of the place names in Saskatchewan. Consequently, some of our history is preserved in this manner. However, there are exceptions, and Mile 102, just outside of Melfort, is one. The railway officials gave it its name and in railway vernacular this means that it is 102 miles from the railway divisional point of Hudson Bay to the east.

MILESTONE
The Soo Line extension of the Canadian Pacific Railway was completed from North Portal to Pasqua Junction during the summer of 1893, and appeared on the first passenger time card under date of September 24th, of that year. As the construction of the railway progressed, section houses were erected at Macoun, Yellow Grass and Rouleau and station houses at Estevan, Weyburn and Milestone. Milestone was named in honour of C. W. Milestone, superintendent of the new Soo Line extension.

All that vast tract of open prairie through which the new railway had been constructed was called the South Regina Plains and was known back in the eighties and early nineties as the "Dry Belt." In fact the whole region south of Regina was set down in 1857-58 by Captain Palliser, as being included within the boundaries of the "Great American Desert."

This "Dry Belt" or "Great American Desert" turned out to be one of the best and most consistent wheat producing areas of the Prairies, dotted every seven or eight miles as far as the eye can see with the tall red sentinels of the plains — prairie elevators.

Sometimes a critical finger is pointed at these grain points in that they are all the same. There is, the comment says, nothing to attract attention to any one of them. Milestone has one variation, it has the DeLuxe cafe which advertises itself as "Canada's largest small restaurant — Seating capacity 10,000 (44 at a time)."

MILLETON
Milleton was an early post office northeast of Lashburn located at 4-51-23 W3. It is now closed and is served by a rural route out of Maidstone. We have not been able to establish how Milleton got its name.

MILLERDALE
Millerdale is on a CNR line from Dodsland to Coleville. Drive into it on highway 30 and you divide the place in two — on the railway side is a new Pool elevator, on the highway side is the home of Bert Radke, the agent. That's all there is to Millerdale except for the boarded-up general store of H. G. Deschner that closed in 1966.

Paul Miller lived 26 years in Germany, 26 years in the United States and by the time of his death in 1932 he had lived 26 years in Canada. In 1906 Paul came to Canada and homesteaded the SW quarter of section 6, later the site of Millerdale, which was named after him. Paul Miller was noted for his size and strength. Once he pulled his son-in-law Pete Doll, who weighed 180 pounds, hand-over-hand up in a bucket from the bottom of a 30-foot well they were cleaning. In threshing time if a bundle wagon pulled in too close to the belt of his threshing outfit, he simply put his back under it and heaved it over to where it should be.

Other early settlers in the Millerdale district besides Mr. Miller were: Pinchbeck, Gardiner and Murphy.

MILLY

Milly is five miles south of McCord. Today there is nothing but a cairn marking the site of Milly School. In the early days the Graves, an influential family, had the post office in their home and it was called Gravesbourg. The name lasted only one year because of continual trouble with mail destined for Gravelbourg. The name was changed to Milly to honor one of the daughters of Mr. Graves. The Milly post office did a lot of business in the early days because it was the only post office for a wide area, predating all the now established town post offices. When the CPR came through to Mankota they moved the post office but not the name. McCord was the name chosen for the new townsite and post office.

MINISTIK BEACH

Ministik Beach is the main beach on Madge Lake in Duck Mountain Provincial Park. It is located at 24-30-30 W1. Ministik in Cree means island. Hence, Ministik Beach means Island Beach.

MINNEHAHA

Minnehaha post office came into being in 1910. The first postmaster was Pete Jepson who operated a small store on N.E. 33-49-18-W3, about fifteen miles northeast of Edam. He used a log building across the road on E. Goodall's homestead S.W. 4-50-18-W3 to start with, and by 1910 when the post office was to open he had built a log building on his own land for the store and post office.

The district at that time was used for ranching, for the Jackfish Creek running

through the area provided plenty of water and natural pasture for cattle and horses. The noise of the water running over little rapids of stones could easily be heard for some distance, especially in evenings when all was still.

Joe Davis (a one-time teacher at Louisville School and who had filed on a homestead in the district) and Pete Jepsom gave the district the name "minnehaha", suggested to them by the sound of the running water. The name was taken from the poem "Hiawatha" and was the Indian word for "Laughing Waters".

The name still remains and is very much in the local news. The school (named after the post office) has been converted into a Co-op Hall and many rural activities take place there. It is the only rural school building in a large area still being used.

MINTON

Minton is the end of the steel on the CPR's Minton-Estevan line. It is one of Saskatchewan's youngest villages, being incorporated in 1951.

Minton was named after an early settler by the same name and like other towns in this southern portion of the province, many settlers came from eastern Canada and the United States.

In November of 1944, 65 miles southwest of San Pedro, California, the lookout of a U.S. patrol boat sighted a large balloon floating over the sea and dragging some kind of appendage in the water. It was secured, deflated and hauled aboard. The appendage seemed to contain parts of a radio transmitter, a couple of barometers and it was thought to be a harmless Japanese meteorological balloon. A few days later another of a slightly different type was recovered from the sea of Hawaii. The package had been damaged and most of the contents lost. Then, on January 12, 1945, at Minton, Saskatchewan, a complete undamaged balloon package was found. It had become entangled in a barbwire fence, the envelope had torn free and disappeared. It was the first Japanese fire balloon chandelier to be recovered intact in North America. It was intended that the balloons would float across the North Pacific on the west-to-east jet stream which was known to exist between six and eleven miles above the ocean.

The purposes of the balloons were to set fire to the forests of the west coast of North America and to demoralize the population with the high explosives which they carried.

The Japanese intended to launch 20,000 balloons. In the end they built 9,000 of which they actually used two-thirds. Two hundred and ninety-six were recovered in the States and Canada and their remains were identified by experts.

Not one fire was started by the incendiaries. Five children and one woman were killed in Oregon when they disturbed the balloon package, detonating the anti-personnel bomb, but these were the only reported casualties.

Failure of the fire balloon campaign is attributed to two things: self-imposed press censorship in North America and the weather. Winds aloft over the north Pacific blow strongly (a balloon could make the trip in 96 hours) and relatively steadily from the west during the winter and early spring. But at this time of year the forests are rain soaked on the coast and snow covered in the interior. Had the winds been favorable during the late summer and fall, incendiaries would have started forests fires which would have been impossible to control.

In every major war, some new offensive weapons are devised or clever modifications are made to current types. The Big Bertha gun of World War I and the Japanese fire balloon had much in common. Both were imaginative weapons, both were ingeniously contrived desperation machines used at the end of their respective wars and both failed in their purpose.

MISTATIM

Mistatim is the second stop east of Crooked River. The wide-ranging Cree Indians left some interesting souvenirs of the period when they hunted the bushlands and prairies of Saskatchewan. The place name, Mistatim, is one of these along with Chitek, Cabri, Meetoos and Meota.

There are two versions of how Mistatim was named. The first is that the dog was the only beast of burden of the Indians until the Spaniards introduced the horse to the natives of the American continent. Spanish horses throve on the plains of Mexico and were, from time to time, stolen by the Indians of the prairies west of the Mississippi, and so passed northward. The first horses were seen in southern Saskatchewan about 1730. In 1787 an old chief told David Thompson that when his band heard of them they could not make out what they were. They had heard that the Snake Indians to the south had them. On a Snake raid north a horse was killed by an arrow shot into its belly, but the Snake Indian that rode him got away. Many Indians went to see the dead horse and they admired it. He put them in mind of a stag without horns; and they did not know what name to give him. Since he was a slave to man, like the dog, he was named Big Dog (Mistatim).

The second version comes from old-timers in the district. An Indian hobbled his horse out for the night. Next morning he discovered the horse had broken the hobble and escaped. He searched and searched but never found him. When questioned about the missing animal the Indian replied, "The mist ate him." In other words, he couldn't find him in the fog.

Indians are superstitious and he actually thought his horse had been swallowed up by the mist.

Gradually local legend contracted "Mist ate him" into Mistatim and that is how the town got its name. Take your pick.

Today Mistatim is a solid little town with a population of close to 300. It has two elevators, Pool and Pioneer, two stores, a garage, a hotel and a sports complex that is unique.

Under one roof it has a hockey rink, community hall and curling rink all served by a common concession centre.

MISTAWASIS

Mistawasis was one of the most distinguished and progressive Indian chiefs of the northern Plains Crees. Mistawasis means Big Child. Poundmaker, another great Cree chief, gave Mistawasis the nickname The Iron Buffalo of the Plains. Thus he was well thought of by his peers. He was also well thought of by the white man. He was the first member of the northern tribes to be presented to Governor Morris, and the first to sign Treaty Number Six at Fort Carlton. He was one of four Cree chiefs selected to travel east to attend the dedication ceremonies at Joseph Brant Memorial in October of 1886. So impressed was he by what he saw in eastern Canada that he said he wished to learn all the white man knew, and when an inspection of reserves was carried out in 1888 his was found to be one of the most advanced, the residents there raising grain and cattle.

He was one of the first Indian chiefs of the West to embrace the Christian faith. He chose to be a Presbyterian and a minister out of Prince Albert serves his reserve today.

When Prince Albert was threatened during the Saskatchewan Rebellion in 1885 Mistawasis offered to bring his band to its defence. When the Rebellion was over the government presented him with a flag in token of his loyalty. He raised and lowered it on his reserve morning and evening until his death in 1903. He was over 100 years old and on the day of his death the flag was flown at half-mast.

MITCHELLTON

Mitchellton is just south of Old Wives' lake between Ardill and Galilee on a CNR line. Alonzo Mitchell came to the district in 1909 and settled about one mile west of where the eventual railway townsite was located. In 1910 he built a store and house and had a post office called Mitchellton. When the railway came he moved to the townsite and that's how it got its name. Mrs. Hart Herbert and Leon Mitchell were his children.

MOFFAT

About nine miles south of Wolsely, the traveller on the gravel road to Candiac will pass a well-kept cemetery to the east of the road. If he is alert he will also notice, a few hundred yards father down the road, a durable and unpretentious stone church with a small framed porch painted white and green. This is Moffat, the church which formed the nucleus for what was once a lively rural community.

The earliest point in time at which we could make an imaginary visit to Moffat and find the community developed would be the year 1887. At that time the district was a maze of trails leading mysteriously around the bluffs, some of these trails recently made by wagon wheels of homesteaders. The main roads were old buffalo trails which were noted by the surveyors in 1882. The long trail which took a southeasterly course through the centre of the district became known for many years as "The Old Moffat Trail." The Scottish settlers built their first kirk not far from this trail on land which had been purchased by a man named Dr. Moffat, of Motherwell, Scotland, and from this the community became known as Moffatville. However, when in 1886 Mr. Alexander Kindred began to operate a local post office in his house they found that it could not be registered as Moffatville because there was another post office by that name, so the church, the post office and the whole community shortened the name to Moffat. With the founding of the post office and the school in 1886, Moffat reached the status of a fully-developed community.

Moffat was quiet, religious and distinctly Victorian. From 1900 to 1930, it was in full bloom; fast-driving teams and then roads and automobiles accelerated social life, and sport and entertainments became more frequent. In 1906 the eastern area of Moffat was serviced by its own railroad, when the Wolseley-Reston line was built and the sidings of Adair and Deveron made Moffat more accessible than ever before. In 1911, the whole rural area was serviced by rural telephone systems.

The rural telephone systems are still operating, but almost everything else is gone. Not a schoolhouse stands in the whole community. In 1961 the Wolseley-Reston railroad discontinued service and the tracks were taken out, the depots and grain elevators carted away. But Moffat church is open. It joined the United Church in 1925, and is now known as St. Andrew's United Church, Moffat. When it held its eightieth anniversary service in June, 1964, two hundred people crowded in to join the present members in paying tribute to those who had founded the community. It is the last concrete landmark left between Wolseley and the Canadian National Railway to show that there was once a highly organized open-country neighborhood in the area. Like most rural communities, Moffat has gone a full cycle of development and decline, and now the focal points are shifting to the urban centers. Reluctantly, we must watch as this splendid pioneer community and others pass into history.

MOLANOSA

Molanosa is on highway number two on the way north from Waskesiu to La Ronge. It is close to the north end of Montreal Lake. It is the approximate geographical center of Saskatchewan. The name, Molanosa, was selected by local people who combined the first two letters of each of the words MOntreal LAke NOrthern SAskatchewan.

MOLEWOOD

Molewood was an inland post office forty miles northeast of North Battleford. The first settlers into the district were Claude and Norman Parkhouse from Plymouth, England. They came in 1911 and were soon followed by their parents, Florence and Edward Parkhouse and brothers Basil and Oscar and sister, Joyce. The next settlers into the district were Chris Blixrud, Philip Kunz, Shorty Peterson and Harry Strang.

In 1912 Mrs. Parkhouse and Claude opened a post office and named it Molewood after their farm home in Surrey, England. The mail was first hauled by Mr. Heno from Sandwith post office.

In 1919 a school district was formed and a school built and named Molewood (#4295). The first teacher was Miss Winnifred Green from Birmingham, England.

When the CNR built a railroad through from North Battleford to Medstead in 1927, Sandwith, eight miles to the east, became the trading and educational centre. Soon after Molewood post office and then the school closed.

A very sad story is associated with Molewood district. While digging a well by hand, a homesteader, Mr. Shepherd was buried alive when it caved in on him.

MONARCHVILLE

Monarchville is an inland post office 10 miles north of Biggar on number 4 highway. George Holt keeps the only business there, a combined service station, store and post office. The only other building is Monarch School which has been closed for years and the children are bussed to Biggar. The building is now used for a hall.

There is no special significance in the name of Monarch or Monarchville. It just follows a pattern of naming places for the royal family. Other examples are Imperial, Rex and Regina.

MONCHY

Monchy is a customs checkpoint on the international boundary ten miles south of Masefield on No. 4 highway.

H. G. Richards homesteaded in this area. At the outbreak of World War I he enlisted, and joined the British Imperial Army in Belgium. Lance-Corporal Richards was killed August 9, 1915 at Hooge, Belgium.

When the Monchy customs office was established in the 1950s Fred Richards, a brother of the deceased soldier, was invited to choose the name for it. He suggested Hooge. This was not acceptable to post office officials who in turn suggested Monchy, after a small village close to Hooge, Belgium.

This information comes from Fred Richards of Orkney, Saskatchewan.

MONDOU

Mondou is right on the edge of great ranching country on a spur line of the CPR that runs down from Wartime to Matador. The post office is closed now and people get their mail at Elrose to the north. The hamlet was named to honor a famous syndicate that operated a ranch run by a French-Canadian by the name of Mondou.

MONTA

Monta was a water tower 2 miles west of Baldwinton on a CPR line that runs northwest to "Lloyd." It was on the bank of Stringer lake which really was little more than a slough. No one ever lived there because the pump house was attended to by the section gang that operated out of Baldwinton. Engineers on the old steam engines used it only in an emergency claiming the water was "light" and not suitable for use. With the advent of diesel engines it became obsolete and was dismantled several years ago.

MONTMARTRE

Montmartre, Sask., has a name of noble origin. Its name signifies "Mount of Martyrs," and comes from Montmartre, Paris, France, a former Common on the outskirts of Paris, which acquired world fame as a place of national pilgrimage.

It was named by the first colonists who came to the district from France in the spring of 1893. Some of the families to arrive at that time were: Tremaudan, Berneau, Cariou, Fromheur and Mouchenotte.

The first CNR engine passed on October 22, 1907, and from April 14, 1908, there has been regular train service with Regina.

MONT NEBO

Mont Nebo is the third stop west of Shellbrook on a CNR line to Medstead. Mr. C. Cameron came to the district in the early 1900s and homesteaded on a hill 2 miles north of the present hamlet. This was on the old Fort Carleton to Green Lake trail. He set up a stopping place for travellers and opened a store.

Mr. Cameron was a very religious man and when he applied for a post office he turned to the Bible for a name and suggested Mont Nebo from Deuteronomy 32, verses 48-52. "And the Lord said unto Moses that very day:

"Ascend this mountain of the Abarim, Mount Nebo, which is in the land of Moab, opposite Jericho; and view the land of Canaan, which I give to the people of Israel for a possession; and die on the mountain which you ascend, as Aaron your brother died in Mount Hor, and was gathered unto his people: because you broke faith with me in the midst of the people of Israel at the waters of Meribathkadesh, in the wilderness of Zin; because you did not revere me as holy in the midst of the people of Israel. For you shall see the land before you; but you shall not go there, into the land which I give to all the people of Israel."

When the railroad came through the country post office moved to the rail site and gave it its name. Two sons of Mr. Cameron still farm in the district.

MONTREAL LAKE

The settlement at the intersection of Montreal Lake and Highway Two takes its name from the lake. With roads pushing further into northern Saskatchewan and with tourists becoming more aware of this vast area where the midsummer sky scarcely darkens above the spires of spruce fringing on the lakeshore, for twilight often lingers until dawn, Montreal Lake is becoming more and more attractive to summer visitors.

MOOSE JAW

There is a romantic version of the naming of Moose Jaw that goes like this:

A titled Lord from England was encamped on a small creek west of Regina in the early days engaged in a buffalo hunting expedition. One of the Red River carts in use by the party broke down and the Englishman repaired it with a moose's jaw bone. Amazed at the dexterity of the white man the Indians called the place Moose Jaw.

This version is pretty well discredited on the grounds that the nobleman cannot be identified; the name "Moose Jaw" appears in the Palliser (1857) and Settee (1861) journals before any titled travellers are known to have been in the area. Settee, an ordained Indian clergyman, calls it "Moose Jaw Bone" creek. The more generally accepted version now is that the name was applied by Indians and derived from the configuration of the creek.

MOOSE RANGE

Take the CNR northeast from Melfort to Carrot River and the second last stop is Moose Range. A few miles to the west is the post office of Elk Hill (now closed). Here, within a few miles, two of the most sought-after big game animals in Saskatchewan are honored.

The moose is the largest member of the deer family. He is not a pretty animal, in fact, he is ungainly, but his power, size and elusiveness place him high on the list of desirable game animals of not only Saskatchewan, but North America. Other places honor him too: Moose Jaw, and Moose Valley near Kipling.

MOOSE VALLEY

Moose Valley was a hamlet twelve miles south of Kipling and twenty-five miles from Moose Mountain Provincial

Park from which it took its name. Its exact location is 31-11-5-W2. The post office opened in 1911 and the first postmaster was W. F. Goddart. The late Joseph Bodnar was the postmaster there for 27 years. There was a store in connection with the post office in the 30s. Everyone loved to come to Moose Valley especially at the Christmas season. On a still night you could hear the sleighs and cutters and the bells on the horses for miles as they approached the hamlet. Young and old came; with no money and no cars the most convenient spot to meet one another was at the post office.

By 1940 mail delivery was twice weekly from Kipling. The post office was closed on October 30, 1954. The original log house that housed it still stands.

In the early years this district of rolly woody land had a considerable population of moose which accounts for the following names: Moose Mountain Provincial Park; Moose Mountain creek and Moose Valley rural post office.

MOOSOMIN
Archdeacon R. B. Horsefield states that Moosomin is the Cree word for "mooseberry" or high bush cranberry. It is also the name of an Indian chief of that period who later settled on a reserve near Battleford.

MORIN CREEK
Morin Creek is an inland post office forty-two miles straight north of Livelong. It was named for a family of Metis and some of their descendants still live there.

MORSE
Morse is in southwestern Saskatchewan between Ernfold and Herbert. This is a digest of a long letter that was received from Mrs. Edward Conn concerning the history of the town:

"First settlers arrived in 1904 with large numbers arriving from 1907 to 1909 inclusive.

By 1908 a hamlet was staked out and there were 50 inhabitants. By 1909 the population doubled. In 1910 Morse became a village. In 1912 it became a town with a population of 900.

Today, the population has dropped to between 500 and 600. 1975 was a good year with a large number (close to twenty) trailer homes set up.

Over the years Morse has had some disastrous fires. In 1910 the first major fire burned Steven's livery barn, the hotel, J. J. Ryans real estate office, the Bank of Commerce and the Imperial lumberyard. They were all rebuilt.

In 1912 a fire destroyed H. Scharf's bake shop and J. R. McKenzie's home. That was in the spring. In the fall a third fire levelled Fred Dohlman's butcher shop, the Imperial lumberyard (again), Trott and McDonald's feed lot and Steven's livery stable for a second time."

MORTLACH
Mortlach is between Caron and Parkbeg on the main line of the CPR just west of Moose Jaw. There are two versions as to how it got its name. One, English settlers claim it was named for a village in England. Two, Scottish people claim it was named for a place in Scotland. This seems to be the better of the two, since in Scotland in Banffshire there is a Dufftown which has a church dating back to the seventeenth century that is called the "Church of Morlach" in a parish of the same name. Also, Lord Strathcona, a principal figure in the CPR was born near Morlach Church.

Among the first settlers were Kaymis Michael and Sadook Daman. They home-steaded the land on which Mortlach now stands. Mrs. Sophie Daman still resides in the house built when they were married in 1910. The first house in the village was built by John Scott in 1905. It is still standing but is not occupied.

Other early settlers were Mr. and Mrs. George Hall, Mr. and Mrs. William Ashworth and Mrs. Margaret Lucas. The first meeting to form a school district was held on July 20, 1905, with 14 persons present. D. W. Hosie was installed as chairman and the other two members on the board were J. P. Dean and W. L. Hodgins. The first teacher was Miss Annie Ross and she also acted as secretary for the school board.

The first post office was opened in 1905 and the postmaster was Mr. Thomas Bradley. There is a range of hills just south of Mortlach and to the north there are flat grassy plains that stretch for a hundred miles. Down the middle of it runs Thunder creek. This location made it a very desirable pasture for buffalo. The Indians had camps all along the route using the hills as lookouts for buffalo and marauding Indians.

In the vicinity of Mortlach and Besant Park two middens have been found showing people had camped there for centuries.

The best known person in the town is Mr. Kenneth Harris Jones, known as "Casey." He came to Mortlach from London, England, in 1911 as a carpenter. As a boy in England he was very interested in archaeology. During the 30s when soil blew right down to the hard pan he started collecting Indian arrowheads, spear points and other artifacts. His collection was known far and wide and eventually he sold it to the Glenbow Foundation in Calgary. Mr. Jones also became an artist of note and his paintings now hang in the Parliament Buildings in Ottawa and Regina. His prairie scene of the midden at Besant as he pictured it years ago is particularly good.

MOSELEY

Moseley is the first grain point north of Humboldt on a CNR line that runs to Melfort and on in a northeasterly direction to end at Carrot River.

It was named for Moseley, Virginia, U.S.A., the hometown of some of the early settlers.

MOSSBANK

Mr. Robert Jolly of Kirkenbright, Scotland, homesteaded on the NW ¼ of 12-11-30 west of the 2nd in June of 1907. His brother, Alex, who actually located the land, filed on the quarter to the south. Seeing a need for a post office, Robert Jolly applied and the name Mossbank was chosen, a more euphonious word than his native "Mossegeil."

The post office was officially opened on September 15, 1909 on his farm.

In 1914 the CNR came close to this country post office and soon it moved in and gave the townsite its name.

MOSSY VALE

Mossy Vale, an inland post office (now closed), was situated ten miles northwest of Ravendale. Pete Ens was the first

postmaster and he suggested the name that was accepted by postal officials.

Moss, sometimes feet thick, on the ground under trees and this all had to be cleared or burned off before settlers could plant crops. Fires started in the summer sometimes burned all winter in the deep moss and it was a strange sight to see smoke coming up through the snow in December.

Ellis Hamilton, a trapper, was one of the earliest residents of the area. Later he married Miss Thelma Olson, one of the first teachers in Mossy Vale school, which had taken its name from the early post office.

MOZART

Mozart is between Wynyard and Elfros on a CPR main line that skirts the south end of Big Quill lake. It consists of two elevators, a covered curling rink, a Centennial hall, Co-op store, and a handful of well-kept homes. The garage burned down in the summer of 1970.

Mr. Thor Arnason, manager of the Co-op store in Mozart gave this account of how the town came to get its name:

"When it came to the naming of the village in the early 1900s the honour was given to Mrs. Lund, the wife of the station agent. She was a talented musician and very well thought of in the community. She not only named the village Mozart but the theme was carried out in the naming of the streets after the following great musicians: Wagner, Liszt and Chopin."

MUDIE LAKE

Mudie Lake is an inland post office near Pierceland from which it gets its mail. Mr. Mudie, an early settler, gave his name to the lake and the post office took its name from its proximity to the lake.

MUENSTER

Muenster is a town on the Dauphin-Saskatoon branch of the CNR, 84 miles east of Saskatoon. The Benedictine Fathers arrived at Muenster on the feast of the Ascension, May 21, 1903.

The locality was first called St. Peter's Colony. When the first store and a number of dwellings were erected, the name was changed to Muenster after the celebrated city of Muenster in Westphalia, Germany. Muenster (in Latin monasterium) really means monastery, a very appropriate name for the place where the Benedictines founded their first monastery in Canada.

MULLINGAR

Mullingar is N.E. of North Battleford on a branch line that runs from Speers to Medstead.

In the summer of 1906 in what is now the Mullingar country there were only two settlers, one was a family of five, a Mr. and Mrs. Kruger and their three small children, and a single man who had built a shack on the same township. During 1907 the whole country filled up.

When postal services were established the residents were asked to suggest a name. Their choice of Mullingar was to honor the place of origin of many of the residents, Mullingar, Ireland.

MUSCOW

Muscow is a grain point on a CNR line between Fort Qu'Appelle and Edgeley. It is a Cree word meaning hard, firm or strong.

MUSKEEGAN

Muskeegan was an inland post office southwest of Hudson Bay. It opened in 1934 with Alfred Bradley as the first postmaster.

In the fall of 1932 a meeting was held at the home of Alec Jordbro to organize a school district. A Board was elected, comprised of Bill Ducker (chairman), Matt McCabe and Al Truswell (secretary-treasurer). A "bee" was held and the logs cut and hewed two sides. The contract to build the school was let to Alec Jordbro, Duncan McDougal and Jack Forrest.

A name for the school district submitted to the Department of Education by Duncan McDougal was accepted. He chose the name Muskegon for that place in Michigan where as a young man he

had worked logging. However, in sending in the name the secretary misspelled it and so the school district of "Muskeegan" appeared on the records.

With the school in operation the assessing of land and collection of taxes became the responsibility of the local secretary, as well as to keep the school financed.

In the homesteading days of this community most people put up a shack of logs with no floor, and a pole roof, with hay and soil usually thrown up on top to hold the heat. Quite often there was just one window, but if a wife and children were involved it had to be a little more elaborate, possibly a lumber floor and roof. When horses became more plentiful in the area, people took out logs and hauled them to J. Forrest's on the river, where Mike Saufert, a Settlement farmer, brought his saw mill and cut the logs into lumber. Few people had cash to pay for the sawing so the toll was half the lumber.

MUSKIKI SPRINGS

Number 2 highway between Dana and the Bremen corner bends around the west shore of Muskiki lake. The railway was built along the east shore in 1912, and when in the 1920s a salt factory was built on the lake shore, it ran a spur line in to it. The name given to the siding was Muskiki Springs. These springs are fresh-water springs that feed the lake. They even bubble up in places off-shore! Archdeacon Horsefield indicated that the name was of Cree origin, meaning "medicine."

Muskiki lake developed into a summer resort and Leo Renneberg built wooden houses where you could get a hot salt bath. You could also — and this is amazing — get clear cool spring water. There were many other concessions at the lake.

The salt content of the lake is very high — higher than at Watrous. In August and September when natural evaporation is at its height it is not uncommon to see huge solid rafts of pinkish crystals floating on the surface of the lake and when the sun is just right, a pinkish glow is reflected in the white clouds overhead.

N

NADEAUVILLE

Nadeauville is a rural post office located at 5-16-21-W3, which is 33 miles south of Lancer in the middle of "The Great Sand Hills." The postmaster is Mr. J. B. Nadeau, hence the name. Nadeau is for Mr. Nadeau and ville is French for town.

NAICAM

In the 1920s the CPR began building north from Lanigan. Approximately 20 miles north of Watson the town of Naicam came into existence in 1921 and remained the end of the steel for several years. Then the line was completed on to Melfort. The railway contractors on the line were Naismith and Campbell. They took the first three letters from each name to form Naicam.

NASEBY

In the early 1900s the GTP branched north at Loverna Junction (just west of Biggar) and ran the Pleasant Hills line north to Battleford. Naseby was the first grain delivery point. It was named for the Battle of Naseby (just north of Oxford, England) fought in 1645 between the reorganized New Model Army under Oliver Cromwell and the forces of Charles I under Prince Rupert. Rupert commanded the right wing of the royalists, Cromwell the right wing of the parliamentarians. Both were victorious, but Cromwell, returning from the charge, attacked Rupert's horse in the flank and routed the royalist forces. The king was hopelessly defeated. The small armies that remained loyal to him in different parts of the country were soon scattered, and the war was over. Charles I was later executed.

The first settlers into this part of the country came directly from Scotland: the Allans, the Grays, the Smiths, the Aitkenheads and the Meikles. Later the Afflecks and Lightburns, also of Scottish descent, came from Ontario.

The late John F. Allan, of Battleford, who was a frequent commentator over CJNB North Battleford, came from that country and here in his own words were his feelings as a boy.

"I remember many things about the beginning of the old Scottish settlement which later became Naseby and Lett areas. It was the Swift Current Trail that was our highway. On our first trip in the early spring of 1906, it was a lonely road. I remember, my first trip out three years later, when I went to Battleford with my father. As we started to come down out of the Eagle Hills, I could see Battleford. As we got lower down into the plain off the hills the town seemed to disappear until we got in near the Battle river some six or seven hours later, due to the slow progress of our ox team. Battleford surely looked like the mecca of all Canada to me that day! I have seen much since that time but nothing so precious as that cherished memory, to me, a small boy who broke away from the sod shack for a day or two."

NASHLYN

Nashlyn is on a branch line of the CPR south of Consul. It got its name in a rather unique way. It was first called Rector by the railway officials. The people of the community disputed this and suggested it be changed to honor Isaac Stirling a properous rancher and prominent MLA in the district. Mr. Stirling, in a very gentlemanly gesture, declined the honor and suggested the name of Mrs. Helen Nash, a widow who had served the district as postmistress long before the influx of settlers that the railway brought. The CPR officials accepted the wishes of the community and the name Nashlyn was settled on.

NEEB

Three brothers John, Harry and Earl Neeb and Philip Eldred moved north from Bradwell to homestead in the district just as the CPR built from Prince Albert to Meadow Lake in 1931. They started the Neeb and Eldred store and when the post office was opened it took the name of Neeb in honor of the three brothers. Mr. Philip Eldred, one of the original partners, is the present postmaster.

This information came from Mrs. Philip Eldred of Chitek Lake.

NEELBY

Neelby elevator is three to four miles southwest of Kipling. At one time it had a store and post office. The name Neelby is of Scandinavian origin meaning "near town."

NEGUSVILLE

This was an inland post office located at S16-T35-R10-W3 just south of the present site of Kinley. It was named for the Harry Negus family. He kept the post office in his home and managed to look after it and do his farm work while wife, Nellie, went great distances to serve as midwife.

Often she would be absent from home for weeks at a time as was the case when she visited the Cruikshank home, the Mainland home and the E. Scharf home in the Tweedyside district to the west. In each case she delivered the pioneer women of baby boys without the aid of a doctor and stayed for a few days to get the mother oriented before moving on to help in the next home. She is fondly remembered by many families — some of these still reside in the district but many have spread from coast to coast.

She did not forget her "babies" either — after she and Harry had retired to Saskatoon she visited the hospitals regularly and, particularly during the 30s when it was financially impossible for someone to stay in Saskatoon or even to come in to visit regularly, she called to see anyone from her district and to report to the families concerned as to the progress of the patient.

NEIDPATH

Neidpath is located 40 miles southeast of Swift Current. In the 1920s men were asking for suggestions for a name for this new town. A lady who had emigrated to this area from Scotland suggested it be named after Neidpath Castle. There is a town in Scotland with this name also.

NEILBURG

Neilburg lies on a CPR line from Wilkie to LLoydminster and was a thriving hamlet before the branch line came through in 1923. It was named after the first post office in the district, which in turn had been named for Clifford O'Neil who kept it and a small store on his farm about a mile from the present village.

Lindsay E. Gibbons arrived in Neilburg on April 1, 1924. He had been assigned to take over the new UGG elevator. But Lindsay was much too active to be just an elevator agent and over the years he developed a farm, a multi-company implement agency, a Ford dealership, and a ball team — the Neilburg All-Stars. He really had to call them that because young men came to play for him from all over northwestern Saskatchewan. The All-Stars were famous — the team to beat. They first entered the Saskatoon Exhibition tournament in 1928 and won it in 1931, missed the next two years and then came up with four straight wins — in '34, '35, '36, '37, and again in 1939. After their four straight wins the Exhibition Board gave them the trophy outright. It is now in the possession of Pete Prediger of Saskatoon. Pete, who joined the team in the early 30s, married the daughter of a local merchant and, in turn, became a Neilburg fixture with his own store. When Lindsay went to the coast for a time in the 40s and 50s Pete carried the ball, and the Neilburg team, under his management, not only were contenders in their league but managed to win the Saskatoon Exhibition tournament in 1961. Over the years Pete has played in 28 Saskatoon Exhibition tournaments and was with the Neilburg team in seven of its eight victories.

Other players with the team over the years would include the following: the Silver brothers, Ron and Art; "Red" Oaks; Tommy McKenzie; Bill Frost; Al Weber; Tom Bessie; Al Flohr; Pete Ferrie; Arlo Harris; Don Conklin; Shorty Jackson; Pete Russell; Ron Wright; Walter Ellis; Lefty Arnold; Mel and Roy Ottem; and a host of others.

Sometimes a man has to die before anyone says any good of him — not so with the citizens of Neilburg. In 1971 they presented Lindsay Gibbons with a "day," the key to the town, etc. and a plaque which reads:

"Presented to L. E. Gibbons.

With our heartfelt thanks and appreciation for 45 years of dedicated service rendered in the fields of sports and community leadership in this area. From your Friends and Neighbors of the Neilburg District."

On June 8, 1972, North Battleford,

prior to a ball game between Unity and North Battleford held a "night" in tribute to Neilburg's "Mr. Baseball" to mark the end of Lindsay's active career in sports. At that time, with Eldon Elliott, sports director of CJNB acting as MC, presentations were made to Mr. Gibbons by the president of the League, the Beaver Baseball Club, Morris Campbell (an ardent baseball fan) and Ken Nelson. Each paid tribute to Lindsay's contribution to sports, especially baseball.

Here is a typical "Gibbons" idea which got the whole town and countryside in behind a project. The year — 1928, the need — a well for an open air hockey rink. They knew they could get water by digging 35 to 40 feet. Lindsay was not only able to persuade 40 men to dig, but had some fun too, when they put the numbers from one to forty in a hat and each man drew and the pledge was to dig the foot corresponding to his number. Water came in at 32 feet while Finlay Wilcox was digging and when he came out of the hole you could hear him all over town.

NEOLA

Neola is the first stop east of Biggar. It was named by the GTP who built the line and followed their pattern of naming towns in alphabetical order wherever possible. This stretch started at Juniata and went Kinley, Leney, Mead, and Neola. The significance of the name Neola is unknown.

Joe Lambert was one of the early settlers. He was a section foreman for the Grand Trunk Railway and in 1909 homesteaded on land adjacent to his section house. He also kept the post office at Neola for many years.

NEPTUNE

Neptune is the end of a branch line of the CPR that runs northwest from Estevan. The first post office was situated at 25-5-16-W2, and the first postmaster was William H. Stoven.

The name is a fanciful one. Neptune is a planet of our solar system which we can never see with the naked eye. The French astronomer Dominique Arago suggested the name Neptune, in honor of the sea god of Roman mythology.

NESS POST OFFICE

In 1909 the first post office in the Jackfish Lake area opened in a small log building. Mr. Moise L'Heureux was the postmaster and he had a small store with living quarters in the back. Perched on a high spot on the very edge of the northwest shore of the lake it still stands among the farm buildings now owned by George Bru. This post office served an area for ten miles around.

Moise L'Heureux had the contract to haul the mail from Battleford once a week at five dollars a trip. The country was sparsely settled. The Mounted Police had a station a half-mile west of the creek bridge with the first constable in charge being Dan Sullivan.

Following Mr. L'Heureux as postmaster were Tom Duhaime, George Ness (for whom the post office was named) and Charles Day.

It never really closed but was moved to Jackfish village a few miles to the north and west. This village grew up around a splendid Roman Catholic Church. The post office is there now in the store of Beulah and Roland Corbeil.

The old Ness post office building still stands by the lake with its turf roof turning green every spring but gone are the days when people came from "clear across the lake" in the winter to buy, visit and gossip which was all a part of "going for the mail."

NETHERHILL

Netherhill is on a CNR line west of Rosetown. The name is of Scottish origin and was brought to Canada by John Craig. In 1881 when toll bars were abolished in Scotland, Mr. Craig bought the house and land which for many years had been known as Netherhill Toll Bar, in order to use the land for a farmstead. He took down the old toll building and built a modern house in its place. This land was located close to Bieth, about 20 miles west of Glasgow, and lay in a shallow valley between two hills — hence the name. Its location compares with that of the village of Netherhill in Saskatchewan, which is also in a shallow valley with higher ground to the north, east and south.

In 1906 Mr. Craig came to Canada and homesteaded on land across a road allowance from the eventual site of the village. When the Goose Lake Line arrived in 1909, Mr. Craig was responsible for the designation of a name for the new village of Netherhill. Mr. Craig was the first secretary-treasurer of the surrounding municipality of Hillsburgh. He was the postmaster from 1908 to 1936 and a justice of the peace. His farm home is still occupied by his son, George.

A distinguished graduate of Netherhill is Dr. Balfour W. Currie, vice-president (Research), University of Saskatchewan, Saskatoon campus.

NEUANLOGE

Neuanloge is a small village four miles south of Hague. The name is German and means New Settlement. It is one of several places between Osler and Hague where Mennonite families settled in little villages and worked their land around these. Community life centred around the church, school and store. Some of the first families who arrived in the late eighteen nineties and early nineteen hundreds were: Peters, Janzen, Klassen, Ens and Wiens.

There is a story about those early days that bears repeating in a day when thermostats automatically control the heat in most homes. Several Neuanloge men left the village early in the morning to travel ten miles north and then east across the Saskatchewan river for some poplar wood for fuel. It was early spring before the river breakup. The trip there was without mishap and the cutting of trees was in full swing when, towards afternoon, they heard a distant rumbling noise. The river ice was going out!

They hurried their ox teams — as much as you can hurry an ox — back to the river. It was noticeable that already considerable water had accumulated on top of the ice. With an extra "whoop" the teams were driven out onto the ice; before they were halfway across, the oxen were ankle deep in water and men began to throw the wood off their sleighs to lighten the load. As they neared the west side of the river the water became belly deep and for the last few yards everyone — men and oxen — swam for their lives. They all made it.

This is a true experience taken from the historic records kept by Mr. Jake Friesen

of Hague. Think of this story when next you hear a slight "whirr" as your furnace cuts in.

NEUDORF

Neudorf is a village between Lemberg and Killaly on a CPR line that runs north of the Qu'Appelle Valley. The first settlers were predominately Austrian and at the suggestion of Mr. Wendel they named their village for the hometown of many of them, Neudorf, Austria.

NEUHORST

Neuhorst is a country store five miles northwest of Osler. The centre of activity at the present time is the store operated by John Loeppky. He used to have the post office but now, the area is on a rural route out of Saskatoon. There used to be a school also, but the children are now bussed into Osler.

The first settlers were of Russian descent and they named it Neuhorst which in English means a new grove of trees. This name aptly fits the parkland of Saskatchewan. In the late 1880s settlers coming into the district were let off the train wherever they wished to stop. They unloaded their livestock and other effects, set up tents and started their new life on the prairies.

Mr. and Mrs. Isasc Neudorf of 1211-8th Avenue North, Saskatoon, (now retired) were well acquainted with the beginnings of Neuhorst. Some of the earliest settlers were Isaac Loeppky, Abe and Peter Klassen, Abe Ens, Jacob and John Wiebe, David Reddekopp, Jacob Bergen and Henry Neustader. In 1922 this little settlement went through an exciting time. Many families became disturbed over two things. First, the scarcity of land for their sons, and second, the switch from German to English in the schools. Until that time their schools had been taught in German, now with instruction being in English they feared their children would lose the German language and culture.

After a wide search they settled on Mexico as the most promising location to make a new start and for the next twelve years a small but steady stream of emigrants left Neuhorst and district for homes there. They were, for the most part, very successful farmers, as Mennonites are wherever they go.

A success story of a family is found in Neuhorst. Mr. and Mrs. Aron Ens had four sons, Carl, Danny, Henry and Bill. The first three were on the "Osler Monarchs" coached by Spero Leakos of Saskatoon, when that team won the Saskatchewan Softball Championship in 1953. Bill was the ace pitcher for the Saskatoon Merchants team of the same time.

These boys moved into Saskatoon and the success of Danny, Henry and Bill in the used and new car field has been phenomenal.

Almost all members of that championship softball club of '53 have gone on to success in the business and professional world. Johny Braun and Pete Guenther became successful realtors, Alf Driedger and Al Friesen hold top teaching positions. Harold Milavsky is a chartered accountant. But best known of all are the Leakos brothers: Jim became a doctor and Spero, besides running a successful restaurant business, became regarded as Saskatoon's "Mr. Baseball."

NEVILLE

Neville is on a CPR branch line that was built southeast of Swift Current in 1911. It was named for one of the railway survey crew. Settlers who were in the area ahead of the railroad included the following: Whyte, Murphy, Little (who kept a stopping place), Benson, Froslee, Pearson, Esch, Payne, Bell, Bowles, Mitchell, McKenna, Noble, Cameron, Burton, Duncan and Allan.

NEW OTTAWA

New Ottawa started as an inland post office less than ten miles southeast of the present town of Speers.

It was in 1903 than Reverend John Grenfell of the Bell Street Church, Ottawa, toured this area. He went back to his flock with such glowing reports that it led to a migration of his parishioners to the West. They formed the nucleus of the "New Ottawa" settlement, taking up sixty-seven homesteads in all. Although some did not stay, many remained, among them: Baird, Stacey, Broadhead, Sarginson, Burgess, Thomas, Kerr, Bush, Webb, Curry, Hodgins, Neelin, Kinmond, Haryott, Radley and King.

In the same year Jack and Frank

Langley came from near Rosthern, Ed Moore and his family from Prince Albert and other early arrivals included W. G. Scott, Bob Woods and his son, Lloyd, Bill English, J. and A. Anderson, M. Brouseau, Wm. Bain, W. Cummings, R. Redhead, MacPherson and Dobkins.

The first store was in the Baird home. It was a real convenience to the people of the district. The first post office for the New Ottawa people was in the home of Henry King. In 1905 it was moved up to the Baird store for greater convenience, where the mail was brought in by team from Maymont.

R. J. Scott was one of the first mail carriers. He taught school at the Twin Lakes School near Radisson and would bring the in-coming mail when he came home for the weekend. When he went back to Twin Lakes on Monday, he took the out-going mail with him. His mail bag read "New Ottawa."

Many fine men have ministered to the spiritual needs of the district. Rev M. M. Culp was the first ordained man to take the charge. He performed the first wedding, uniting in marriage Fred Thomas and Sarah Hobden.

In the spring of 1913, the CNR built a railway from North Battleford to Prince Albert and Speers developed as the trading center and New Ottawa remained as a district.

NEWANLAGE

Newanlage is a Mennonite settlement four miles southwest of Hague. Mr. Krahn runs the store which serves the farmers around and the dozen families that live in the village. The name in English means new layout or new home.

NEWBY

The GTR built west from Battleford in the early 1900s on its way to Lloydminster. It stopped at Carruthers in 1913 and never built on. There is a junction on this line at Rosemound and the first grain point past it was called Newby for John Newby on whose land it was located. It had one elevator, a Pool.

Settlers who were into the district ahead of the rails besides Mr. Newby were: Jim Thompson, Jim and Frank Robinson, Jack Coulter, Calvin Dobey, Jim Ray, John Rutley, Bob Coulter and

Russell Parker. Mr. Newby opened a small grocery store in his log home; at that time it was the only store between Paynton to the north and Unity to the south. He freighted all his supplies from Paynton by ox team.

Today almost all of this is gone. In late July of 1971, Ellsworth Woodward hauled the last load of wheat to the elevator. When the elevator closed,Dave Crittall, the agent, took over the management of the Pool elevators at Tatsfield and Carruthers.

NEW HILLSDALE

This early post office was opened in the home of Archie Smith just south of the present site of Leney. The mail was brought to New Hillsdale from Saskatoon via the Eagle Creek post office.

Although New Hillsdale was only in existence from 1905 until 1909, when the Grand Trunk Pacific built west from Saskatoon to Leney, it played an important part in the lives of the pioneers. In this day of radio and television, it is hard for us to appreciate what mail day meant to the homesteader who, in many cases, was miles from his nearest neighbor. Getting the mail meant, not only hearing from loved ones far away, but a chance to visit with other pioneers who had come in to collect their mail.

NEW HOFFNUNG

New Hoffning is a small Mennonite village five miles north of Hague. The name in English means new Hope or Place of Hope. It was established in 1899 by the following families: David, John, Henry, Peter and Isaac Martens, Peter Pauls, Henry Harder, Bernhard Derksen, Henry Vogt, Andres Rudolph, John Giesbrecht and Peter Kasper.

NEW OSGOODE

Before the turn of the century, Hugh E. Jones of Carnarvon, Wales, a marine engineer by trade, felt the call of the West. After a brief stint of farming in Manitoba, he crossed the Carrot river on a pole bridge in 1905 and made a home for his family and a name for himself in New Osgoode.

New Osgoode is on a branch line of the CNR that runs north from Crooked River to Arborfield. The first church service was held in Mr. Jones' home. The first post office was in his house, too. It was named for Osgood, Ontario, the point of origin of many of the settlers in the district. Mrs. Howse, the first woman in the district, named the post office. The extra "E" in the name was a mistake in spelling by the postal officials.

Mr. Jones was a justice of the peace and he conducted trials in the front room of his house. His children, Violet and two younger boys, Ifan and Llewelyn, would be sent out to play if it was a nice day or if the weather was not nice they would be told to stay in the bedroom. They liked this better because they could listen at the door.

Later Mr. Jones became secretary of the municipality and still later served two terms (1917 to 1926) as Liberal MLA for the district in the William Martin administration.

When the CNR extended its branch line northeast to Arborfield in 1929 the Jones' home at New Osgoode became a "stopping place" for travellers. Meals were served at 25 cents each.

In the early 30s New Osgoode reached its peak with two elevators, two stores, a post office, a combined blacksmith shop and garage, and a combined poolroom and barbershop.

By 1969 it had dwindled to seven families and people did their business at either Zenon Park or Tisdale.

We are indebted to Mrs. Violet Franklin of Tisdale, a former postmistress at New Osgoode, for this information.

NIPAWIN

Nipawin takes its name from a height on the Saskatchewan River four miles upstream from the present townsite. The name means place where one stands. Commanding a wide view of plain and river, the Indians used to stand there and watch for people coming.

The place was also important because it was at a bend of the river where trail and canoe routes met and the Indians could be sure of meeting friends there no matter how they travelled.

NOBLESVILLE

Noblesville, an inland post office and store, was straight east of Archerwill. The first settlers into the area were from the

United States and they brought their name with them. Noblesville, Indiana, is just northeast of Indianapolis, the capital of the state.

NOKOMIS

This is taken from "The History of Nokomis" published in 1955:

"Mrs. Thomas Halstead is responsible for the naming of Nokomis. Before the railway arrived she made application for a post office in her sod house with the request that the name 'Nokomis' be chosen. She had selected the name Nokomis from Longfellow's poem 'Hiawatha,' because to her, newly arrived from England, the west represented the romantic domain of the Indians.

"Nokomis turned out to be at the junction of the old Grand Trunk Railway running east and west, and the CPR running north and south. The Grand Trunk officials had picked Blakemore for a name and the Canadian Pacific had chosen Blaikie. Neither prevailed. When the settlement started to grow at the junction the country post office of Nokomis was moved into the back of the Montgomery and Henry store, Mrs. Halstead continued as postmistress and the whole place became known as Nokomis."

NORA

Nora is between Rose Valley and Archerwill on a CPR line that runs from Wadena north to Nipawin.

Prior to this line being built in the middle 1920s, a settlement of Scandinavians (mainly from Minnesota) had homesteaded the area. An inland post office named Nora was operated by the McLeod family who had moved in from Outlook.

This post office had been named by the first postmaster for his daughter, Nora. Oscar Moe is one of the few residents left in the once bustling town.

When the steel came through the country post office moved into town and gave it its name.

At its height, Nora had two elevators (Pool and Searle), two grocery stores, two hardware stores, two schools, a community hall, a pool hall, a barber shop, a restaurant, a skating rink and a curling rink, plus many fine residences.

In the 1950's, Nora began to shrink and by 1977 only one Pool elevator operated by Mr. Carpenter and a handful of residences occupied by retired farmers remained. The schools are gone, the children bussed to Rose Valley or Archerwill.

Nora produced an outstanding citizen in Hugh Mattila. Islae Carol Johnson of North Battleford has written a book about him entitled "Mush On." It's a book for all ages and contains dozens of pictures of the North where Hugh Mattila trapped and hunted for years before finally settling down to homesteading near Nora.

In retirement, Mr. and Mrs. Mattila moved to Saskatoon where they continue to enjoy their children and particularly their grandchildren.

NORBURY

Norbury is a rural post office at 10-50-10-W3 which is six miles south of Spiritwood. The original postmaster was Mr. H. M. W. Norbury, hence the name. It's proximity to the good town of Spiritwood and good roads have made it obsolete. The office closed many years ago and only the name remains in the district.

NORDALE

Nordale is one of the newest place names in Saskatchewan. Originally Prince Albert grew up entirely on the south side of the river. In later years a settlement developed on the north side, particularly on the road to Shellbrook and on out as far as Buckland. Names for it in general use were North Prince Albert and Pine Hill.

In the summer of 1968 the Prince Albert city council ran a competition which offered a prize of twenty-five dollars for a new name. Here are six of the names sent in that were not used: Pine Ridge, Timberlain, Howard Heights, Misty Meadow, Cozy Corners and Pine Grove.

Nordale, the winner, was sent in by five-year-old Donna Forbister.

NORMANTON

This district was looked over as early as 1903 by some settlers driving out from Saskatoon, 50 miles to the east. The majority of these first homesteaders were from England. Mr. and Mrs. Albert Mellish, Mr. and Mrs. Furber, Mr. George Whitfield and Mr. William Sowter came to erect tents and soon after built more permanent accommodations.

Mail and all requisites for living and farming had to be transported from Saskatoon. Many obstacles were met on the way — including alkali sloughs and, particularly, Eagle creek which until May was almost impassable. Some settlers who attempted to cross the creek were forced to recover their possessions from the water. Their wagon boxes had been lifted off their running gears and floated downstream.

A post office (namely New Hillsdale) was established, six miles away at the residence of Archie Smith. All mail had to come from Saskatoon via Eagle Creek post office.

In 1907 the settlers decided to build a school. It was named Normanton after a town in Yorkshire, England, from which the first secretary, Mr. W. G. Heptinstall, had come.

About this time a post office was established at the home of Mrs. Hallett and it also took the name Normanton. The mail was then hauled from New Hillsdale. Mr. Sam Young started a small store in his house. Jack Courtney sold meat to the homesteaders and he later became the butcher for a "beef ring," which enabled the people of the community to have fresh beef each week during the summer. Once a season, each member of the ring put a beast in to be butchered, at the slaughter house on Mr. Courtney's farm. Every Friday a beast was butchered, cut up into shares of 20 lbs. each which the farmers could pick up on Saturday. In theory, by the end of the season each member should have gotten back the weight of the beast he had put into the ring. Every week members were supposed to get a roast and another different cut of meat — human nature being what it is — some people felt they should have steak all the time and so there were the usual number of complaints but, all in all, it worked out very well.

The store, the post office, the school and the church have all closed now, and only the district and one elevator bear the name of Normanton.

NORQUAY

Hugh Wylie named Norquay in 1907. This is taken from his long letter to me which tells how it happened.

"I happened to be reading a book 'The Making of the Great West' by Reverend A. G. MacBeth, a descendant of the early Selkirk settlers. A considerable portion of the book was devoted to the history of John Norquay.

"In 1870 at the age of 29 he was elected to the first legislative assembly of Manitoba. In 1878 he became premier of Manitoba. I greatly admired this man who had risen from humble beginnings and when the early settlers here asked me to suggest a name for our townsite I suggested Norquay. It was accepted."

NORRISHVILLE

Norrishville was an inland post office near Strongfield. Mr. W. H. Norrish was successful in getting the post office in 1910 and up to 1916 he operated it with mail brought in from Hawarden. Mr. A. Ernest Norrish, a son, was acting postmaster from November 1914 to November 1915. The office was later closed out due to good roads. The place was appropriately named because the Norrish family consisted of Mr. and Mrs. W. H. Norrish and seven sons, John, Alf, Charlie, Edwin, Norman, Ernest and Harold. There was one daughter, Mary. The Norrish "clan" held a Home-Coming Party on the third of July 1971.

NORTH BATTLEFORD

In 1905 when the Canadian Northern steel reached a point across the North Saskatchewan river from historic Battleford (the important town in the area at the time), the post office department called the place selected for the new settlement, North Battleford. It caused quite a furore at the time. The Battleford residents vigorously protested the ruling of the postal authorities, claiming that the adoption of "their" name for the new townsite would draw trade away from their community. In this they were proven correct. The infant townsite of North Battleford also protested. They wanted to be called Riverview. However, the postal department's decision stood.

By March 21, 1906, the population had reached 500 and North Battleford was incorporated as a village. Four months later the village became a town. Today it is a thriving city of over 12,000.

The highlight of sport in North Battleford goes back to 1931-32 when the "Beavers" won the Provincial Hockey Championship and went on to meet the "Winnipegs" in a two-game-total-goal series. The series was played in Winnipeg and the first game was tied 2-2, then North Battleford lost the second game 2-0. The Winnipegs went on to easily defeat Hamilton for the Dominion Championship and they handily won over all teams in the 1932 Olympic Games played at Lake Placid, New York.

Players on the Beaver team, managed by Bob Cruickshank and Jack Abbott, included the following: Lindsay Gibbons, George and Bob McIvor, Bill Hoffman, Les Whittles, Harold Picketts, Tony Hemmerling, Harry Hailwood, Elmer Piper and Bob Marion.

NORTH BIGGAR

North Biggar is on the main line of the CPR about a mile north of the divisional point of Biggar on the main line of the CNR. There are only two places of business, a Pool elevator and a station. Mr. Gilbert Nimmo runs the elevator and Mr. Glen Kruger runs the station. Goods come out from Saskatoon by CPR truck transport and Mr. Joe Tenant makes the deliveries to Biggar.

Actually no one lives in North Biggar. Mr. Nimmo lives in Biggar and Mr. Kruger lives in Saskatoon and commutes to his work by driving a little over sixty miles twice a day.

NORTHMINSTER

Northminster is the first grain point north on a CPR branch line that runs to Hillmond. It was named for being north of Lloydminster.

NORTH PORTAL
AND NORTHGATE

In the extreme southeast corner of Sask., two railroad lines, one from Moose Jaw and one from Regina, pass into the United States. Two towns, North Portal and Northgate make these "ports of entry." The north in each name signifies that they are on the north, or Canadian side of the international boundary. Portal

means gate, door or entrance and "gate" means gate. The railroad gave these towns their names.

NORTH ROSETOWN

North Rosetown is a mile north of Rosetown proper on a CPR line that comes down from Perdue. It consists of two huge elevators, the Pioneer and the Pool. This combined with the four large elevators in Rosetown on the CNR — the Pioneer, the Pool, the UGG and the Federal — gives Rosetown a reason to call itself "The Heart of the Wheat Belt." Other places may have six elevators on more but not on the scale of Rosetown. Many of Rosetown's elevators are so large that agents have "helpers" — an unheard of position in the average country point.

NORTH SASKATOON

This is a day and age of specialization and North Saskatoon Siding, a wire-fenced compound two miles north on Warman Road, is a good example. It has been put in to handle two specific products: cars and trucks. The CNR owns the property. Melchin Transport leases it from them and uses it as an unloading, loading and storage area. The CPR car transport uses the facility also. Trailer trucks handle 8 cars while tri-level rail carriers hold 15. A dealer never touches a car until it is delivered to his lot.

NORTHERN LIGHT

Northern Light was an early inland post office eight miles east and one mile north of the present town of Domremy. The first mail came from the railway at Duck Lake via Domremy by horses and buckboard once a week.

When a railway was built straight north from Young to Prince Albert in 1918 it passed within two miles of the post office. The little village of Domremy and the buildings were moved to the new townsite.

From then on the mail for Northern Light came by truck from Domremy. At that time Northern Light had a store, post office and several houses. The next step came when it was put on a rural route and the local post office closed. The store soon followed and today there is little left at Northern Light except the name, one of the most significant in Saskatchewan.

Few people can view without awe this glowing flickering light that at times lights up the whole sky. This must have influenced the residents, many newly arrived from France, to choose this as the name of their new home in North America.

This information came from Agnes Denis of Saskatoon whose grandfather was intrumental in establishing St. Denis, a hamlet twenty-five miles east of Saskatoon.

NORTHLAND

In the fall of 1908 the CPR built through to Elbow. Prior to that, mail had to be hauled from Davidson. About five miles southwest of the present town of Dunblane was the rural post office of Northland. The name had some connection with the North-West Territories which were formed shortly before the post office opened. With the coming of the railways and better means of communication and transportation, the post office was closed out and the people got their mail from Dunblane.

NORTHSIDE

In the early 1900s there was a Northside post office about sixteen miles north of Prince Albert. It was called Northside because it was north of Prince Albert. When the new highway came in and a branch went east to Henribourg the Northside post office was moved to the junction thirteen miles out and renamed Spruce Home. Later when a post office was opened at the junction of No. 2 highway north and a grid road east to Paddockwood, the name Northside reappeared as a post office in the store of Henry Lacount. The store and post office changed hands several times. The present post office is in the Lucky Dollar store of Ernest Wiberg and it serves about fifty families. The local school has closed and the children are bussed to Christopher Lake.

In 1962 the old curling rink became unsafe and the Northside Community Club built a new one. Curling for young and old is the center of social life in this farming community during the long winter months.

NORTHWAY

The Canadian Northern Railway built north from Dauphin, Manitoba, in the early 1900s, crossed over into Saskatchewan at Hudson Bay Junction and proceeded west through Melfort and Birch Hills. It turned north, crossed the South Saskatchewan river on the Fenton bridge and went north into Prince Albert. The CPR built north from Regina, crossed the GTP at Nokomis and then ran on to Lanigan.

It reached Northway district in 1929 and at Northway Junction it acquired "running rights" from the CNR and ran over the Fenton bridge and on into Prince Albert. Northway is two miles south and a mile east of Fenton. Northway consisted of a flag station, stockyards and a loading platform. Only the flag station remains and it houses a stove, a coal bin, a telephone and a shelf on which is kept the CNR log book. All CPR trains stop here and this is the entry from July 9, 1969:

"Train — CP no. 85; Unit number — 8117; Signals — nil; Engineer Kopella; Time of arrival — 8:40 a.m.; Time of departure — 8:50 a.m.; Conductor — Meissner." Between July 1st and July 9th the log book showed that seventeen trains had passed this point. CNR trains are not required to stop or log.

Northway is a contraction of part of the words Canadian NORTHern RailWAY and it designated that the railway turned north. No passengers are carried on these lines now but the following families were a few that used to "flag" the trains at this point: Hunter, Davis, Lavigne, Schaefer, Agnew, Brewster, Russell and Wait.

NOTTINGHAM

In 1913 the CPR built a branch line from Lauder, Manitoba to Alida, Saskatchewan. Nottingham is the second last stop on this line. It was named Nottingham by Sir Harry Brittain, an English author. Sir Harry played an important part in the organization of the Imperial Press Conferences of the day which worked for mutual understanding among the various countries of the British Empire. In recognition of his work the president of the CPR asked him to name the Saskatchewan stations on this line. For this site he chose Nottingham to honor Nottingham, England.

NOTUKEU

Notukeu is in the extreme southwest corner of the province where a branch line from the main line of the CPR runs back east to Val Marie. It is named for meandering Notukeu creek.

"Notukeu" is of Cree origin, meaning "old women" and hence has the same origin as Old wives lake into which the water of the creek eventually flows.

NUT MOUNTAIN

Nut Mountain is the second last grain point on a branch line of the CNR which runs from Sturgis to Kelvington. It's a descriptive name but is a little misleading. The nut part of the name comes from hazel nut bushes which grow in profusion on the slopes of the hills they call mountains. We haven't any real mountains in Saskatchewan (including Blackstrap Mountain), only hills which appear high in comparison with our general prairie landscape.

Vic Brown, elevator fire inspector working out of North Battleford, recalls a time when Nut Mountain was a humming little place. Today he says it's a ghost town with no future in sight.

Travelling widely in the province he finds this in many places, smaller places get smaller and smaller and some have already gone. The only mark left is the elevator or elevators serviced on certain days and at set hours by an agent who may live twenty miles away.

O

OAKSHELA

Oakshela is on the main line of the CPR and the second stop west of the divisional point of Broadview. It's an Indian word meaning "child".

OBAN

Travel the CNR main line west out of Biggar and the first stop is Oban Junction from which a branch line runs north to Battleford. Only an old Pool elevator, number 169, is at the spot. It is covered with dull grey metal siding and is so old that the name of the place is not painted on it.

By 1976 the elevator was closed and only Mr. and Mrs. J. Ratke and their two children, Randall and Carla, live in a converted store. Mr. Ratke farms extensively in the district.

Oban, Saskatchewan, was named for the lively seaside town of Oban in the highlands of Scotland.

Oban, Saskatchewan, also knew lively times. At its height it had a big station, a general store and garage, a blacksmith shop, a school and a pool hall, but most exciting of all, it had, for a year, the promise of a glauber salts extraction plant.

Water from Whiteshore Lake, a short distance to the west, was trenched and then pumped into lagoons where natural evaporation took out the bulk of the water. The residue was then put through a heated extractor.

However, this method proved so expensive that only a few car loads were produced before it shut down for good. While the plant was in production, dozens of men were employed and Oban was a lively little town.

Years later, on the shores of the same lake, Midwest Chemicals built a plant at Palo, the first station west of Oban, and they were successful in producing glauber salt there.

ODESSA

Pioneering settlers from the environs of Odessa, Russia, came to Saskatchewan just after the turn of the century and gave to this southern community they helped found, the same name as the historic city and district of the Old World.

The endeavors of these first citizens were commemorated by the present inhabitants of Odessa in 1954 when the area marked the 50th anniversary of the first settlers' arrival and the 40th anniversary of the founding of Holy Family Parish. Reverend Father Frank Gerein wrote a history of the parish and community to mark the occasion.

ODHILL

Odhill is in northern Manitoba but it deserves to be put with Saskatchewan place names because it was named for Mr. O. D. Hill of Melfort.

Mr. Hill began practicing law at Melfort in the fall of 1911. In 1916 Albert E. Cairns joined him as a partner and in 1927 James N. Gale joined the firm which continued to be known as "Hill, Cairns and Gale" until Mr. Hill's retirement from the firm in 1937.

Mr. Hill was very musical and contributed much to the social activities of the community. He served on the town council of Melfort for a number of years and was mayor in 1919-1920. He also served as a member of the board of the Lady Minto Hospital at Melfort and spent a term as its chairman.

Mr. Hill was very active in the work of promoting the completion of the Hudson Bay Railroad to Churchill and in recognition of his services a station on that line (between Wabowden and Thicket Portage) bears the name "Odhill."

OGEMA

The first settlers arrived in 1908 but it was not until 1911 that a post office was established with the name of Ogema. The pioneers had selected Omega, which is the Greek word for end, as at that time the settlement was the "end of the rail line." On making application for registration of the village name they were told by the authorities that there was another village with that name and two communities with the same name would not be allowed. The settlers then changed Omega to Ogema. This used the same letters. It is at the same time an Indian word meaning "big chief."

OGLE

A CPR line runs straight south of Assiniboia and the third grain point out is Ogle. This was wide open ranching country in the days before the railroad (which did not arrive until the middle 1920's) and one of the most famous ranches operated on English capital and was managed by Lord Ogle. The grain point was named for him.

OKLA

Okla is a small village on a branch line that runs from Sturgis to Kelvington. It was named by the Lock brothers who had emigrated from the U.S.A. They simply took the first four letters of their home state, Oklahoma.

OLD WIVES

Over 100 years ago a great fire swept across the Regina Plains, Qu'Appelle Valley and district. The buffalo, having no pasture, trekked west to the unburned grasslands. The Cree Indians of Qu'Appelle followed the disappearing buffalo westward. But by going west they were reaching Blackfoot country, the land of their enemies. However, the Crees were desperate and they followed the buffalo. They found great herds by a large lake, made camp and the hunting began. They soon secured all the meat they could hope to carry back to Qu'Appelle. Then the long straggling line of hunters, women, and children wound about the lake-side. Suddenly, someone saw men on horseback silhouetted against the sky. "Blackfoot!" The fearful truth was whispered along the straggling and slow-moving line of Crees.

The long cavalcade tried to hurry and close in for defence for they knew the Blackfoot were near. A party of Blackfoot horsemen appeared. They circled, galloped, shouted and shot arrows at the huddled Crees. The Crees fought back. Then suddenly the Blackfoot disappeared into the hills.

The Crees held council, one Cree had been killed and several wounded. The Crees knew the Blackfoot would return with reinforcements. How could the Crees, loaded with meat and encumbered with women and children, hope to outride the Blackfoot? An old Cree women went to the Chief and said, "We old women have counselled and made a plan. We are no longer of any use. This is our plan. Draw up the camp for defence. Do it in sight before the sun goes down. The Blackfoot will attack at dawn. We old women will keep the fires burning all night. Take the young women and children and by morning you will be far away."

The plan was carried out and all night long the old women heaped the camp fires with buffalo chips and the glow of the fires told the Blackfoot scouts, watching from the hills, that the camp was inhabited. When the Blackfoot charged in the morning at dawn, they found a few old women wrapped in blankets tending the fires. They were so angry at being tricked that they massacred the brave old mothers. The rest of the Cree hunting party got safely home to Qu'Appelle.

As the story spread this lake came to be known as Old Wives' lake. At the turn of the century the lake's name was changed to Johnstone lake, to honor Sir Frederick John W. Johnstone, a titled Englishman, who spent some time hunting in the district. However, due to repeated pressure from interested people, the original name, Old Wives' lake, was restored in 1953.

The village of Old Wives got its name because of its proximity to this famous lake.

O'MALLEY

O'Malley post office was named for Mike O'Malley, one of the first settlers in the district.

O'Malley post office opened on June 25, 1908 in the O'Hara home with Tom O'Hara as postmaster. It was located at 6-32-6. James McGowan was postmaster during 1910 and 1911 and by then the post office had moved to 12-32-7. That same year, Joe Walker took over the duties in the same location.

Sam Scissons became postmaster in 1925 and the office moved again to 1-32-7. Sam was followed by his son, Ed, in 1938.

Mrs. George Marchant became postmistress from 1952-55. Then the post office closed and the district was served by Gledhow post office until 1963. Since then both districts have been served by a rural route, R.R. 3 from Saskatoon.

ONION LAKE

Onion Lake is an inland village on the western edge of Seekaskootch Indian Reserve one hundred and thirty miles straight north of Lloydminster.

It started out in 1884 as a HBC trading post with Mr. Hart, Mr. Gingras and Mr. McDonald in charge. The name for the village came from Onion lake in the middle of the reserve; the lake in turn got its name from the profusion of wild onions that grew along its shores each spring. The Indians used the onions as a

sort of spring tonic after a winter of moose, deer and buffalo meat.

After the 1885 uprising the government agencies for Frog Lake and Makoo, in Alberta, were moved to Onion Lake and agent, Mann, looked after all three reserves. A detachment of NWMP was also posted there.

In 1894 Reverend John Matheson and his wife, Dr. Elizabeth Matheson, arrived and in the course of their long ministration built a residential school, a hospital and a fine Anglican church. In one corner of the church grounds they and two of their children lie buried. The church must have been an imposing sight in its day and even though it is empty now and the grounds overgrown with weeds, the sight of it stops you and makes you think.

ONWARD

The CPR built west from Kerrobert to Lacombe, Alberta in 1914. To signal the start of the line the first siding was called Onward.

On March 20, 1977 I received a letter from J. B. MacGregor of Brampton, Ontario. Mr. MacGregor spent the summer of 1924 and 1925 near Onward which consisted of one elevator, a disused boxcar for a station, and a general store and post office operated by a man whose first name was Stanley, but Mr. MacGregor cannot recall his last name. In July, 1972, Mr. and Mrs. MacGregor drove from Kerrobert to Superb in an attempt to locate Onward but could find no trace of it. There were some faint indications of the road that once crossed the railway from north to south.

ORCADIA

Orcadia is on a CPR line just a few miles northwest of Yorkton.

"An unpretentious little stone church halfway across Canada recently celebrated its 75th anniversary. With its bare undecorated doorway at one end, and the plain windows along the sides, you would hardly recognize it for a place of worship, but since 1963 Orkney Church has been an historic site scheduled by the provincial government.

It did not get its name by accident; it was given by the Orkney settlers who made their homes in the eighties and nineties of the last century in this rural municipality of Saskatchewan west and north of Yorkton. They called the district where they settled Orcadia. The tradition is that a number of the people who came there in the early 1880s were from Eday, and that the islands' steamer which they knew so well was the source of the name.

The first settlers were directed to Orcadia by the York Colonization Company which had its headquarters in York County in Ontario. One of the settlers, John Flaws Reid who was a Member of Parliament, 1917-1921, died in 1943. Other early settlers were Kelso Hunter and John Rousay.

It was a little while before the Orcadia pioneers were able to live a completely normal life. Western Canada was greatly disturbed by the Riel Rebellion of 1885, and for a while the women and children lived behind a stockade, while the 63 men of the district, formed a home guard.

In 1894 the settlers decided to replace their log meeting house with its turf roof. Stones were collected from the fields, local limestone was burnt to provide mortar, and one of the farmers who was also a stonemason built Orkney Church. Another tradesman, whose name was Rendall, did the woodwork, and the pulpit he made is still used today."

After the church came a school — built just across the road. After the school came the grain point on the CPR — Orcadia.

This whole account was taken from a newspaper clipping from the Orcadian, a newspaper published in Kirkwall, Orkney, Scotland, and graciously sent to us by Mrs. Mary E. R. Ronnie of Binscarth, Manitoba.

ORDALE

Ordale is a hamlet west of Shellbrook on a CNR line that runs to Medstead. It was first settled by Norwegians and Swedes who came in from 1900 to 1910. Some of the first settlers were: Gust Thompson, Gust Senum, Bertal Olson, Henry Elefson and Gust Lande.

The railway came in 1928 and accepted the name the settlers suggested. "Or" in Norwegian means tree and "dale" means dale or valley. It's a pretty name that describes the surroundings.

ORKNEY

Orkney is the second last stop on the CPR branch line that runs from Notukeu to Val Marie in the extreme southwest of the province. The name is tied to one of Saskatchewan's outstanding personalities, George Spence.

Born on an Orkney Island farm Spence came to Canada in 1900, when he was 21 years of age, and in turn dug for gold in the Klondike and then returned to take up a homestead in dry southwestern Saskatchewan, 100 miles from a railroad. It was a country of buckbrush, cactus, and antelope — and had some rattlesnakes, too. The first thing he did on the homestead was break two acres for trees. Next he packed in 200 young trees on his back from Swift Current. And to further astonish the neighbors, he planted fruit trees, plums, apples and cherries. He did have success and his dry land surprised everybody. He didn't let any water escape from his farm. He had a dugout reservoir to solve his stock watering problem, long before the idea was popularized.

When the CPR finally came through in 1923 it was Mr. Spence's brother-in-law who suggested that the townsite be named Orkney.

ORLEY

Orley, the second stop east of Crooked River on a CNR line that runs from Melfort to Hudson Bay started out as a saw-mill town, as so many of the points along the line did. Its first name was "Frederick's Siding" named for George Fredricks who, in partnership with Jim Randall, built the first mill. It burned down. A second mill was built and it, too, burned down. Then a planing mill was built. When it burned in 1942, timber operations closed.

At its height, this operation employed 250 people and turned out eight million board feet of lumber a year.

Mr. Frederick had a store and post office in connection with his homesteading and lumber interest. Orley was a busy little place. Another store was opened by D. E. Dertell.

When the railway began a search for a name shorter than Frederick's Siding, a meeting was held to discuss a name. Orley Collins, roadmaster for the railway, was present, and someone suggested that it be named for him. The suggestion was accepted and Frederick's Siding became Orley.

When the timber operations ended, Orley closed down and today all that remains is a few shacks and the foundations of the original mills overgrown with weeds. The post office, the last business in Orley, was taken over by Nora Randall and was housed in the front room of her home. This, too, was eventually closed out. Today, there is no one residing in the town. One of the last residents to move was Don Randall and he now lives in Mistatim, four miles to the east.

ORMEAUX

The first grain point northwest on the CPR line from Debden to Meadow Lake is Ormeaux. It was named for Adam Dollard des Ormeaux (1636-1660), soldier and native of France. He came to Canada in 1657 and was appointed commandant of the garrison at Ville-Marie (Montreal). In the spring of 1660 he led a party of sixteen Frenchmen up the Ottawa river to wage war on the Iroquois; and at the Long Sault he and his companions died, May 25, 1660, after defending for a week an improvised fort against many times their number.

Dollard in the south of the province is also named for this courageous Canadian. The first settlers into the Ormeaux-Pascal-Victoire area came from Quebec and listed among them were: Duret, Bonneau, Coudreault, Frenette, Beaulac and Brassard.

The Pool elevator closed at Ormeaux in 1967 and the grain is now trucked into Debden. The school (Ormeaux) closed in 1963. The senior students are bussed to Debden and the juniors attend Victoire, a Roman Catholic parish school a few miles to the southwest.

ORMISTON

The Ormiston post office was first opened in 1911. It was situated in the home of postmaster Brandenberger about seven miles southwest of the present site of Ormiston. It was named for "Dad" Ormiston, a colorful character of the early days.

In January, 1912, David Lamberton was made postmaster and the post office was moved into his dwelling in about the

same locality. In January, 1915, David Lamberton gave up this work and his son, William, took over. From 1915 to 1925 the post office was in William's farm home and mail was hauled twice weekly by team from Readlyn, 20 miles away.

In 1925 the CPR came to Ormiston and the town started to grow. Mr. Lamberton moved his building containing the post office into Ormiston and gave the townsite its name.

Ormiston grew steadily and due to the foresight of the town fathers of the twenties and thirties who urged people to plant trees (Manitoba maples, and elms), today the town appears as an oasis of trees on the baldheaded prairie.

Two factors have been at work in keeping Ormiston a healthy little town. One, in 1940 Fred Hall's farm just south of Ormiston was bought by the government as headquarters for the PFRA manager in this district. Tracts of land around Ormiston turned out to be too sandy for farming. The government bought up this land and converted it into a community pasture. This has led to a diversification from straight grain farming and it is a healthy financial development for the district.

Two, the sodium sulphate deposit known as Horseshoe Lake is located two and one-half miles southeast of Ormiston. Mining here has been going on since 1929. Ownership has changed over the years and at present is held by a group of pulp mills under the name of the Ormiston Mining and Smelting Co. Ltd. The finished product is used in the breaking-down process of wood pulp into paper.

ORMSIDE

The Ormside post office 10 miles north of Stenen opened in 1915 in the home of Mr. Harsh on section 28, township 35, range 3, west of the second meridian.

John McGerrigle was the man who was given the honor of naming the place. His original suggestion was Ormsby, the name of his former home in Quebec. However, the post office department refused it and a compomise was reached with Ormside.

Mr. E. L. Anderson of Oneco, Florida, who formerly lived near Ormside, relates a touching story of early days on the prairies.

"When we came to Saskatchewan in the autumn of 1906 'Big George' Anka, an Austrian, had for sheer necessity of survival left his young wife and baby, to go south to earn enough money in the harvest fields to keep them through the winter.

About the middle of November my father and I were hauling a load of poles for firewood and on passing George's house we stopped in to see how Mrs. Anka was getting on. As there was no answer to our knock on the door, father opened it and looked in. On the earth floor of the cabin was a year-old child who had cried itself to sleep. We went to the stable to look for the mother and then, coming up from a little poplar grove, dragging a pole came Mrs. Anka, she had run out of fire wood, but was asking help from no one. We unloaded our wood in the yard and, although she could speak no English, her grateful tears were thanks enough.

The first thing George Anka did when he arrived home was to come and thank us. I remember him as a big handsome man with a big black fur coat and a sweeping moustache."

OROLOW

Orolow is eleven miles south of Krydor. It was settled at the turn of the century by immigrants from the Western Ukraine: Swystun, Zerebeski, Shewchuk and Podiluk, to name a few of the earliest.

A school came first and they applied to have it named Ordiw for a village many of them had lived in before coming to Canada. Now, whether the man who filled out the application had a unique style of handwriting or whether the man doing the processing couldn't read very well no one knows, but the name came out Orolow. At least they had agreed on the first and last letters!

The original Orolow was a four-square kitty-corner arrangement with a school, a church, a post office and a store. The post office took its name from the school and the first postmaster was Joe Zamulinski. The first store was operated by Mike Chmele. The store was the first to go, then Joe Zamulinski built a piece on his post office as a store but that went too, and finally, a few years later, under Eli

Zamulinski, the post office closed.

This information came from Mr. Walter Podiluk, Director of Education for the Separate Schools of Saskatoon, a graduate of Orolow School.

OSAGE

The village of Osage is located on the NE ¼ sec. 33-T11-R12-W2 in the province of Saskatchewan. The section on which it is located was formerly owned by Mr. F. P. French of Osage, Iowa, U.S.A. When it was established that a townsite would be located on this land, a meeting of the settlers was called to decide on a name for the village. John McRae, an employee of a land company, had helped many homesteaders locate and he was well thought of in the district. Many wanted to call the village McRae. However, the CPR had other ideas and they named it Osage in honor of Mr. French's hometown of Osage, Iowa.

The village was incorporated in 1906 and in the election that followed L. J. Kelly was elected overseer. At that time there were no councillors, the overseer administered the affairs of the village, made the assessments, and collected the taxes under the supervision of the minister of municipal affairs.

In 1907, a debenture was sold and the money was used to build board sidewalks and make other improvements.

OSCAR LAKE

Oscar Lake is an inland post office about fifty miles east of Altican.

Oscar Lake was named for a man but, despite considerable correspondence, we have not been able to ascertain his last name or the significance of naming a lake for him.

OSLER

Osler is seventeen miles northeast of Saskatoon on a CNR line that runs to Prince Albert. It is named for Edmund Osler, of Osler, Hammond and Nanton, the railway contractor team that built the line in 1890. He is a brother to the famous doctor, Sir William Osler.

The railway builders proposed to call three townsites in a row for Osler, Hammond and Nanton but the Mennonite village of Hague was well established ahead of the steel and wouldn't hear of the name. The idea was dropped and we have Nanton showing up in Alberta but we can find no trace of Hammond in Canada.

Osler and many fine Mennonite villages about it have developed into one of the dairying districts that supply the city of Saskatoon.

OSTROVICH

Ostrovich is a small Mennonite village in the Osler-Warman area less than thirty miles northeast of Saskatoon. It was named for a Russian village from which many of the early residents emigrated in 1899.

OTTER LAKE

The little settlement on Otter Lake, just a few miles south of Otter Rapids where highway 102 crosses the mighty Churchill, is still called Missinipe. There are outfitters, a small hotel and pub there, a store, post office and camp ground.

Missinipe is a Cree word meaning "much" or "very big" water. This name was applied to the Churchill River system of which Otter Lake is a small part. Otter Lake from which the settlement took its name was a good source of fur. The otter, like the beaver, has two growths of fur. Its underfur is short, soft, and a whitish-gray in color. It was much sought after in the early days of the fur trade in Canada.

OTTHON

In 1894 a small group of Hungarians came to this district. They followed a land agent by the name of Kovatch and the following families settled in: Haydu, Brehozki and Steve Balint. They dug cellars and made roofs over them with sod and became cave dwellers until such time as they could build better houses. Many other settlers came and it developed into a village.

The GTP railway came in 1912 and Mr. Belint was ready for them. All over the place on fences, on buildings and on gate posts he stuck cards with the name Otthon on them. The strategy worked. The GTP called the village Otthon, which in Hungarian means "Our Home."

OUNGRE

There is a very interesting story behind the name of Oungre, it is probably the only name in Saskatchewan that was bought! As far back as 1906 settlers moved into the district and the post office of Byrne was established in the home of Mr. Byrne. The settlers were sure a railroad would be built within a few years. However, time dragged on and long hauls to Macoun, Westby, Ambrose and Estevan, were necessary until finally the CPR arrived in 1927. They got their little station built and on it painted the name Byrne.

The place boomed and soon a Dr. Brown came; a hospital followed; a butcher shop was built; a restaurant; a livery stable; and all the services needed in a new village. Everything was bustling and there was need of a community hall but the village fathers were short of money. Now in this area the Jewish Colonization Association had bought large tracts of farm land and had brought in many settlers. The members wished to honor their general manager, Dr. Louis Oungre and his brother, Edward, in some way for their efforts in establishing their community. They offered the people of Byrne $500 to help build a community hall if they would adopt Oungre for the name of the village. No one objected and so the new station sign was taken down and Oungre was put up.

OUTLOOK

In 1908 the CPR purchased the townsite from the original homesteader. The sale of lots took place on August 26. It was then a harvested wheat field with grain standing in the stooks. The auctioneer was T. C. Norris of Brandon, Man. he afterwards became premier of Manitoba. Many people who bought lots that day had already hauled in lumber from Hanley and on the following day the air was full of the sound of hammer and saw.

As to the naming of the town, two members of the CPR land development company were responsible for that. Previous to the purchase and sale described above they had stood on the east bank of the South Saskatchewan river and had looked up and down the wide river valley and across to the far horizon. The story is that one of them exclaimed, "What a wonderful outlook!" Hence the name Outlook.

OUTRAM

Outram is the second station west of Estevan on the line that goes to Tribune. It was named for Sir James Outram (1864-1925) clergyman, mountaineer. He was ordained a priest of the Church of England in 1890 but owing to ill health he retired in 1900 from active parochial work and turned to mountaineering in the Canadian Rockies. He was the first to climb some of the higher peaks, notably Mount Assiniboine. Mount Outram was named in his honor as well as the village of Outram.

OVENSTOWN

In 1907 Miss Maude Horseman, who had been teaching in New Brunswick, came west to join her parents on the homestead in the Scotstown district west of Unity. She had not been there long when they heard that a new school district, Ovenstown, had been formed. It was located halfway between present day Cloan and Rockhaven.

Seventeen-year-old Miss Horseman applied for the position of teacher and was subsequently hired. However, when she arrived to start teaching there was no sign of a school. It developed that the people of the district had rented a sod shack for a school room but she was there for a week before they got enough benches and a blackboard so school could start. She taught in the sod shack from February until July, 1908, when the new school was built. It was officially opened with a large picnic.

Dr. Robert Ovens had taken out a homestead in the district and when a post office was applied for his name was chosen and "town" added. Mrs. Trenamen ran the first post office and store.

When the railway came north from Wilkie to Cloan in 1911 the Ovenstown post office closed and the people got their mail from Cloan.

OXARAT

Twelve miles south of Vidora and just south of Cypress Hills is the rural post office of Oxarat. Grant MacEwen in his book, "Blazing The Old Cattle Trail," gives a very vivid description of the man for whom Oxarat is named.

In 1884 Michael Oxarat drove into Fort Calgary with a band of 200 Oregon and Montana horses. The man Oxarat was uncommon at any time or place and during the weeks that followed his arrival neither the peaceful citizens nor the Mounted Police could make up their minds if the lean and swarthy Frenchman was a gentleman or a horsethief.

He and helper, Charlie Thebo, drove that herd clear through to Brandon. It was a frontier first. There they found a ready market among the homesteaders who were only too glad to turn in their oxen.

Having sold his bronchos, Oxarat went back to Montana, got more horses and came back in the spring, this time to stock his new ranch in the Cypress Hills. His stock increased until he was the biggest producer of horses between Winnipeg and Medicine Hat. For the most part he used Morgan sires but he also bred thoroughbreds and for a number of years sent some of the fastest horses to race meets in the Territories and Manitoba.

OXBOW

Oxbow is one of the more interesting place names in Saskatchewan. It derives its name from Boscurvis (which is Latin for oxbow) a rural post office and school district named by Mrs. T. M. Baird, the first teacher, because of the oxbow on the Souris River in that district. Later Oxbow was adopted as a townsite on the railway directly north of Boscurvis.

Oxbow designates the shape of a wooden frame called a yoke by which two draft animals especially oxen are joined at the heads or necks for working together. The curves of winding rivers that have been cut off from the main stream are called oxbow lakes. The closest oxbow lake to Saskatoon is Pike lake.

P

PADDOCKWOOD

The honor of naming the place was given to Mrs. Pitts, the first woman settler in the district. The year was 1912, the occasion was the application for a post ofice. Mrs. Pitts requested that it be named Paddockwood after her birthplace, Paddockwood, Kent, England.

Paddockwood is the end of a branch line of the CNR built up from Prince Albert through Henribourg in 1924. A fieldstone cairn a mile west of the town, erected by the Paddockwood Homemakers Club in 1966 in co-operation with the Saskatchewan Department of Natural Resouces, tells a fascinating story.

During the last years of World War I (1917-1919) the British government began to develop through the Empire Settlement Plan a system to provide for the demobilization of their war economy. The major problem was the massive army — numbering several million men — that had been raised by conscription. With the reduction of military spending, there were likely to be fewer jobs in peacetime than during the war, yet the mass of soldiers had to be reintroduced into the labour force.

One of the solutions to this problem was to settle the demobilized men on crown land in the Dominions — Canada, Australia and South Africa. Soldier Settlement Bills were enacted to provide transportation to the free homestead for the man and his family and government credit was issued to establish him on his new farm. Between 1919 and 1930 about 20,000 people moved to, and settled in, Canada under this plan. Paddockwood was selected as one of the sites where this took place and dozens of returned men and their families moved into the district.

During the war, too, the Red Cross had set up an extensive organization. Their part in this plan is described by the inscription on the cairn which is as follows:

PADDOCKWOOD RED CROSS OUTPOST HOSPITAL

"Opened in October, 1920, the first Red Cross outpost hospital in the British Empire was established on this site. Following the first World War the Red Cross decided to allocate funds for the provision of hospital and nursing services in pioneer areas being settled by returned soldiers. Paddockwood was chosen as the first site, the community providing the building and the Red Cross furnishing the trained staff.

For almost three decades the hospital served the needs of the pioneer settlement providing emergency services at all hours. In July, 1949, the outpost was closed."

Today, nothing remains but the cairn. The hospital, a frame building, has been moved east into Paddockwood and is used for a dwelling and Mr. Nelson Genge farms the land.

PALMER

Palmer is between Gravelbourg and Mazenod, close to Old Wives' lake. Talmage and Beecher Palmer, from Freeland, P.E.I., filed on homesteads in 1907. They moved onto their property in 1908. They operated a small store which also included the post office named for them. This was three miles north of the present village site.

When the Canadian Northern arrived in the summer of 1913, Mr. T. H. Sutherland built the first shack store (12 x 16) and for a month he was the only inhabitant. The post office was then moved to the new village and gave its name to the town. At one time there was a bank, two general stores, a hardware, a pool hall, a restaurant, a drugstore, a blacksmith shop, three implement dealers, a dance hall, a garage and a lumberyard. Now there is only one store, a dance hall, a machine shop and a post office.

PALO

Palo is seventy-five miles northwest of Saskatoon on the main line of the CNR to Edmonton. The first settlers arrived in 1906 and included the following: John Glaister, Peter Hogg, George and Arthur Hall, Bill Struthers, Mace McIntosh, Bob and John Dixon, Don Campbell, Bill Shaw, Dick Williams, Sam Johnson, Dan Cole, Mike Friczycz, George Goddard, Bob Howarth, Jim Stewart, Billy Wilson and Oliver Wells.

Battleford to the north was the nearest railway and settlers came in with their oxen, tents and sometimes horses. The first winter was bitterly cold. Hay and wood had to be hauled from 35 miles away. Many trips were made. The men's lunch would be frozen and with nowhere to stop and warm up they would run around the sleigh to keep their feet from freezing. They put their frozen lunch in their mouths and waited for it to thaw.

The first child born in the district was Donald McIntosh. The first marriage was Bud Weaver and Nellie Goddard. The first minister was G. Gervan. He travelled around by horse and buggy and he had a tiny organ with him. The first doctor was Mr. Henderson who set up a practice in Landis. The closest newspaper was at Landis, first stop to the west. The editor was Mr. Bennett.

The name Palo is Spanish for stake or trees. In that there were no trees the conjecture was that the name was derived from stakes set out to mark the railway grade. Perhaps Spanish or Mexican laborers were working on the track.

Midwest Chemicals has a glauber salts extraction plant a few miles south of Palo. This is situated beside Whiteshore lake. The lake water is pumped into lagoons where natural evaporation takes out the bulk of the water. In the late fall and winter the white residue is stockpiled by frontend loaders and trucks. This is fed into a continuously turning gas-fired drum which is forty feet long and placed at a slant. The salt is fed in at one end and "tumbled" to the other where it comes out a greyish-white powder. There are a few small uses for the product but the bulk is used by the paper industry where it helps in the breaking down of pulp wood.

PAMBRUN

Pambrun is 40 miles south and east of Swift Current. It is named for Pierre Chrysologue Pambrun (1792-1841). He was born in L'Islet just below Quebec. In 1815 he entered the service of the Hudson's Bay Company and in 1816 he was taken prisoner by the bois-brules of the North West Company on the Qu'Appelle river. In 1821 he was stationed at Cumberland House and in 1824 he was transferred as a chief trader to the Pacific slope. Here he spent the remainder of his life. He died at Fort Walla Walla, in the Oregon Country, in 1841 as the result of injuries received when breaking a wild horse.

PANGMAN

Pangman, a village 60 miles straight south of Regina, incopoated in 1911, is named for Peter Pangman (1744-1819) whose name first appears in history on a fur-trading licence for the upper Mississippi in 1767. In 1774 he transferred his energies to the Saskatchewan; and he was engaged in the fur trade on the Saskatchewan almost continuously until 1790. In 1783 he joined Gregory, McLeod and Co.; and in 1787, when this firm was abandoned by the North West Company, he became a full partner in the North West Company. He retired from the fur trade in 1794; and in that year he purchased the seigniory of Lachenaie, in Lower Canada; and here he died on August 28, 1819.

PANTON

Panton is between Ranger and Penn on a CPR line that runs north from Medstead and ends at Meadow Lake. It was named for a prominent Battleford family. In the 1930's Jim, a son of Dr. Panton, made a name for himself in track and field. His specialty was the high jump.

PARADISE HILL

Paradise Hill has a colorful name with a history behind it. After a perilous and fruitless expedition to the Klondike before the turn of the century, the Beliveau brothers, Alphonse and Ernest, returned to the country they had explored 10 years previously, 100 miles northwest of Battleford. Setting eyes on what he thought was the most promising spot of the region, a plateau 12 by six miles snuggled in a bend of the North Saskatchewan river, Ernest exclaimed, "This is Paradise!" And thus "the hill" got its name.

He remained to ranch and later to farm. When municipality No. 501 was formed on Jan. 1, 1913, he suggested the name of Paradise Hill. It was accepted. When the railroad arrived in 1928 — a spur line from Spruce Lake to Frenchman Butte — the new townsite was officially christened Paradise Hill.

PARK BLUFF

Park Bluff was an inland post office five miles south and west of Robinhood. Its first postmaster was Ernest Webb, second postmaster was William H. Wood and the last one was Hubert W. Wood. It closed in 1931. The post offices were held in these postmasters' homes.

The Park Bluff school was opened in 1912 five miles south of Robinhood. It closed in 1921 with the remaining students going to nearby schools, Canyon and Robin. In 1932 the school re-opened, but closed again in 1964.

The first chairman of the Park Bluff school board was H. M. Coons, and the secretary was E. Webb.

The name Park Bluff was drawn out of a hat that included a number of suggestions contributed by the early settlers. The terrain of the land is park-like and bluffs are scattered here and there.

This information came from Mrs. W. J. Osler of Medstead.

PARKBEG

Parkbeg is on a CPR line which runs west from Moose Jaw to Swift Current. It was named after the village of Parkbeg near London, England.

PARKERVIEW

Parkerview is at the end of a branch line of the CNR that runs northwest of Yorkton. The first building took place in 1920. At that time, people had to travel 18 miles to the nearest town. There were no cars and the roads were very rough. One of the farmers, Frank Crowther, built a country store. In 1922 a second store was built by Paul Coates. When a post office was put in the little settlement became known as Crowtherview.

The railway arrived in 1928 and with it came a change of name, Parkerview. This was done to honor the Hon. James Mason Parker (1882-1960). Mr. Parker homesteaded in 1906 on the SW ¼ 26-14-W2, a few miles south of Leross. He served as councillor and later reeve of the R.M. No. 247 (Kelliher) for a number of years. In 1917 he was elected as an MLA for the Touchwood riding and held that post until 1938. From 1934 to 1938 he was the Speaker of the House.

PARKMAN

Parkman is on a branch line of the CNR that runs from Maryfield to Carlyle in the southeast of the province. It was named after Francis Parkman, a brilliant historian. The people of Canada owe a deep debt to Parkman for rescuing from the dusty tombs of the old French archives, and from Jesuit and Sulplician annals, the glowing and vivid history of the period when Canada was "Nouvelle France." Parkman was born in Boston in 1823 of a scholarly family. He was very delicate as a child but early showed a strong literary tendency. While still in his teens he determined to write a history of the last French war in America. As the project grew in his mind, he enlarged it to a history of the conflict between the British and French in North America. He gathered all the information obtainable on the subject, educated himself in woodcraft and became adept in the use of the rifle, paddle and snowshoe. After graduating from Harvard he travelled to the Western Plains where he spent a summer with the Sioux. He camped with them and hunted the buffalo, heard around their campfires of their wars and rumors of wars, and studied their character. Much of what he learned of these Indians aided him in his later portrayal of the Iroquois of Canada, a people of the same racial and linguistic stock. He embodied his experiences in a noble work the "Oregon Trail," which is unquestionably the best book on this subject ever written in America.

PARKSIDE

Parkside is seven miles by rail west of Shellbrook. When Mr. Waterhouse arrived in the district in April of 1903 it was unpopulated and unnamed. He called it Parkside, the name of his hometown in England.

When the CNR from Prince Albert to North Battleford came through in 1912 the townsite was bought from Mr. Evenson and named Willis. This site was three miles north of the original Waterhouse homestead. In time, the site was incorporated, and the incorporating officers disregarded the name of Willis and chose the name Parkside instead. Mrs. May Jackman (nee Waterhouse), who came to the district as a young girl, is still a resident there.

PARK VALLEY

Park Valley is ten miles north and east of Debden. It is very close to the southwest side of Prince Albert National Park, hence the name.

PARRY

Parry is between Dummer and Moreland on a CNR line southeast of Moose

Jaw. It was probably named to honour Sir William Edward Parry, 1790-1855, who made several voyages in search of the North-West Passage and published illuminating accounts of his adventures and discoveries.

Parry began to hum in 1911 with the arrival of the steel. Two stores went up. Due to a mistake by the railway, lumber intended for a station at Dummer was unloaded at Parry and the carpenters built a station there! Parry only had the station agent for a very short time but Dummer had one for many years. The first elevator to go up was the Saskatchewan Co-operative and this was followed in 1912 by the Reliance. A restaurant was opened by Charles Truke. Mr. Jorgison built a poolroom. The first lumberyard, Weyburn Security, was opened for business. Yes, 1911 was an exciting year for Parry.

PAS TRAIL

Pas Trail was a post office (now closed) twenty-five miles northeast of Nipawin. It was named for the old Pas Trail that trappers and lumbermen used to go from Nipawin to Cumberland House.

It was nicknamed the "tote trail" because most of the time it was necessary to backpack into the area.

One of the earliest settlers was the Larson family. Marion Larson taught in the rural school of Reno there for several years.

PASCAL

Pascal, a predominately French community, is the second grain point northwest on the CPR line from Debden to Meadow Lake. It was named for Rt. Reverend Albert Pascal, OMI, DD, first bishop of Prince Albert.

PASQUA

Pasqua is named in honor of an Indian chief of that name. Like his father, "The Fox," Pasqua was the chief of a band of Plain Cree Indians.

PASWEGIN

Paswegin is the first stop on the CNR west of Wadena. It is very close to the north shore of Little Quill lake which may account for its name, which in Cree means "boggy ground."

At the time when the CNR was being built through this part of the country the contractors, McKenzie and Mann, made a tour of inspection. They slowly pulled into the village in their parlor car and at the outskirts McKenzie noticed a construction worker repairing a switch. He turned to Mann and said, "That man's name is Wegin. Joe Wegin." Later as they pulled by the station Mann observed that there was no name on it, to which McKenzie replied, "Well, didn't we just pass Wegin?"

PATCH GROVE

When the steel reached Turtleford homesteaders poured in, a post office and a school opened up and was called Patch Grove. It was named by Charlie M. Nelson.

Patch Grove school became the centre of community life. Church services were held there by a minister who came out from Battleford. In the early 1900's he brought the mail and gave it out after the service.

In 1927 the CPR built a branch line from Turtleford to Glaslyn and Patch Grove post office moved into the town of Livelong and took that name.

PATHLOW

Pathlow is the second stop south on a CNR line from Melfort to Humboldt. It was named for a school and post office that were operating before the railway came. These had in turn been named by an early English settler who came from Pathlow, England.

PATRICK

The CPR built west from Lemberg to Lipton in 1904. The head surveyor on the line was Miles Patrick Cotton. Eight miles west of Balcarres they built a station and section house and named it Patrick.

PATTEE

Pattee was named for one of the staff of the GTR that built this line from Regina to Moose Jaw in 1912. The elevator was built in 1913. One of the first families to arrive consisted of Mr. and Mrs. Hugh Frew and their four girls and three boys. This was on December 23, 1882.

Others who soon followed were: John McRae, John McGilvery, Anthony Nevilles, Sam Purse, Jacob Silter, John McLean, and Ed Clarke and his brother, "Peg Leg."

The Cotton Wood creek runs northeast of Pattee down into Lumsden Valley and when the trial of Louis Riel was being held in Regina many visiting Indians camped along its banks.

PATUANAK

The rivers that flow into Lac La Loche start a chain of lakes and rivers that eventually join the great Churchill watershed. First they flow south through Peter Pond lake; they cross over at Buffalo Narrows to Churchill lake; they flow south into Lac Ile a la Crosse where they turn north to empty through a narrow strait at Patuanak into Shagwenaw lake. Patuanak in Cree means "at the rapids." The water never freezes there.

There is a Roman Catholic mission at Patuanak under Father Dufor which serves the Indian and Metis fishermen of the area. This is Father Dufor's headquarters and he has three other small missions in the area. His mode of travel is by boat in summer and ski-doo in winter. He "comes out" by way of Ile a la Crosse, forty-five miles to the southwest and from there he travels by car.

Communications are remarkably good throughout our North. In fact, in cases of sudden serious illness, accidents, criminal offences, forest fires, and any other emergencies, they can be swift — as swift as radio. The DNR, RCMP and private companies combine to give complete coverage. Ski or float-equipped planes together with helicopters take over when someone or something has to be lifted, in or out, in a hurry.

PAYNTON

Early retirement from the Northwest Mounted Police by three constables in 1888 meant the beginning of the settlement now called Paynton. The men, Paynter, McCready and Shields, homesteaded in the area and went on to establish themselves as prosperous farmers.

This area was settled with a rush when the Barr Colonists began coming in 1903. Two years later there were more than 200 people in the community and it was time for it to become an organized village.

In 1905 when it was incorporated the original name suggested was Paynterton. This was to honor two men. The first part was for Paynter and the "ton" was taken from the name of a prominent Barr Colonist, William Thornton. However the postal officials abbreviated it to its present form. Paynton is on the main highway from North Battleford to Lloydminster.

PEEBLES

When the Wolseley-Reston Line was built in 1907 it crossed the newly constructed CNR line at this point. The hamlet which sprang up at the junction was called Kaiser. When war broke out in 1914, anti-German feelings ran high, and the name was changed. A Scotsman by the name of George Axford was running the only store in the hamlet, and he suggested the name, Peebles, after his home in Scotland. There were other Scottish people in the district such as McFarlanes and the Parleys, and they made no objection to a Scottish name. Doug McFarlane is the MLA for this constituency.

PEERLESS

During the course of compiling this book we have written hundreds of letters and we've received hundreds of replies. Occasionally we get a letter that just has to be reprinted in its entirety because it catches the flavour of what we're trying to do — recapture a little of the romance of homesteading days and get down some historical facts before they are lost.

This is a letter written to Wendy Ens, a grade six student at Henry Kelsey, by Mrs. Francis Hankey of Goodsoil:

Goodsoil, Sask.,
January 5, 1970.

Dear Wendy:

Thank you for your interesting letter and especially for the part about yourself. We also have a girl your age who has very similar hobbies, interests and favorite subjects.

Now to get to your request, I wish I could help you more, but I have very little information as to the origin of the name of Peerless, Saskatchewan.

It was rumored that the storekeeper at that time was trying to get a post office at his place, and of course, he had to suggest a name. He thought hard. It so happened that a B.A. gasoline truck was driving by, and they sell an oil by the brand name of Peerless, and this was advertised on the truck in big letters, Well, there was the answer to the storekeeper's problem. Why not call that place "Peerless?" Other residents agreed that the name was fine, and so the name stuck.

Mind you, I don't know how much of this is fact, and how much is fiction, but I have asked several people and they all tell the same general story.

There is an elevator at Peerless. The building is still standing there, but it was bought by a private individual some years ago and he uses it just to store his crops. The Saskatchewan Wheat Pool had built it, and operated it for ten or twelve years, but closed it down because of the fact that the railway was never extended from either Meadow Lake or St. Walburg, and the grain still had to be hauled by trucks to either of these places.

There is one store, a cafe, the post office, school, community hall and six houses.

Goodsoil had been on the map long before Peerless came into being. There had been settlers at Goodsoil in the early 1920s. There was a store and post office opened up a few years later. In fact, this whole district had been called Goodsoil for many years and it was only after the different school districts were formed that there was any actual split. Also after this time, a bit of rivalry sprang up and it was probably due to this that the hamlet of Peerless came into being. They wished to be self-sufficient, so that they had a store, school and post office there. This seemed rather odd, because Goodsoil is only three and one-half miles north of Peerless, and Flat Valley (also a store and a post office which had been there for years) three and one-half miles south of it. However, this is what they wanted and this is what they got!

As far as human interest stories are concerned, there were many; humorous, sad ones, and interesting ones. There were dances and house parties in the homes every so often. Everyone went, including the children. Mass was held in some of the homes with Father Schultz being our first priest. He travelled with

horse and buggy or horse and cutter, but he visted the homes faithfully. This part of the country was practically solid bush in those days, with only trails for roads.

The settlers worked very hard. They had to for they had only the hand tools that they brought with them when they moved here. Most of their food was either grown, hunted or fished. People ate more fish, rabbits, prairie chickens, deer and moose than anyone cares to remember. To this day, wild meat is no delicacy to me — it reminds me of the hard times we had as children.

I do hope I have been of some help to you. You had addressed the letter to my husband, but he isn't too fond of writing, so he asked if I would answer you. I know I've rambled on and on but I guess one of my favorite subjects in school was composition, so that accounts for it.

Wishing you every success with your projects and a Happy New Year.

PEESANE

Peesane is the first stop east of Crooked River in the far northeast of the province. It is an Indian name meaning "nice home" or "nice house". This is what the Indians called the CNR station section house and tool sheds built there when the steel went through in 1905.

In the early years Peesane was a humming place with three saw mills run by Turnbull and Barnman, Pierce and Edworthy and one other mill.

It had three stores, a post office, pool room and barber shop, a station, and many other places of business.

When logging operations closed down the town went back. Today, even the station has been moved away.

PELICAN NARROWS

Pelican Narrows is a Hudson's Bay post on Pelican Lake that has operated continuously since 1874. It was first called Pelican Lake but the name was changed in 1876. The narrows referred to is the stretch of fast water joining Pelican Lake to Mirond Lake. Posts had been established and abandoned on this site by both the "Bay" and "Northwesters" before this time.

The first was a "Canadian house," (meaning one built by traders from Montreal), built as early as 1779, but according to Peter Fidler, the Hudson's Bay Company surveyor, it had already been demolished before he visited the site in 1792.

PELLY

Pelly takes its name from Fort Pelly, the former Hudson's Bay Company post, which was founded in 1824 and named after Sir John Pelly, governor of the company. The area was frequented by Indians and traders throughout the 19th century. In 1874 Fort Livingstone, also known as Swan River Barracks, the first headquarters of the NWMP was built nearby.

PENKILL

Penkill is the second last stop on a branch line of the CPR that runs south and west from Conquest to McMorran. The three men who founded the district of Penkill were Thomas Finlayson, Robert Shankland and Will McLean.

The settlers were not long in this lone land before their desire for a closer communication with their families became overwhelming. Application was made for the right to operate a post office. It was established in 1908 with Robert Shankland as postmaster. It was named for the family seat of the Boyds, Penkill Castle, Girvin on the Clyde, the estate where Robert Shankland had been born and had lived as a boy.

PENN

The country post office and store at Penn is on a rail line from Shellbrook to Meadow Lake. When this roadbed was built in 1932 all the gravel came from a pit just behind the present store.

Penn at that time had a very promising future as it was planned to make this a divisional point. A two story section house was built and the crews working on the track worked out of Penn.

Mr. Tripp opened the original store and submitted the name of Penn as his family had originally come from Pennsylvania. Some of the early settlers in the district were Dan Nakazney, John Sanderson, Albert Blair, and Tom Lavin.

Mr. Lavin homesteaded in what later turned out to be an Indian Reserve. He resisted all government efforts to buy him out or accept a different location and the farm is still in the Lavin family although completely surrounded by the reserve.

PENNANT

The first settlers into this district were the ranchers George and Henry Valentine. They came in 1901. The CPR came through in 1911 and Pennant boomed because it served the large district north of the river clear to Matador. In 1912 there were four lumber yards in a town of 300 people. In 1928 the CPR ran a spur line south to Verlo.

The naming of the town occurred when a surveyor found a pennant near the site. Later this theme was carried out in the naming of the streets and avenues of the town. So in Pennant besides the usual Railway, Saskatchewan and Prairie avenues you have Halyard, Ensign, Standard, and Banner streets.

PENSE

It was in the year 1881 that some awkward-looking oxen-pulled wagons rolled to a stop beside what is now known as Grand Coulee and eight men pitched their tents 100 yards north of where the TransCanada Highway crosses the coulee.

They were the first settlers of the Pense district; men who had travelled all the way from the end of the steel at Brandon, Manitoba, by ox-cart to get a new start in the far reaches of what was then part of the Northwest Territories. Among these eight hardy pioneers were Andrew Blair and Robert Mellis.

A year after these men pitched their camps the steel had reached Regina and passed through some distance to the west. It was in this year that the intriguing story of the naming of Pense took place.

A party of Canadian newspapermen, headed by Edward Baker Pense, president of the Canadian Press Association, was following the laying of the steel across the prairies. In the party were Mr. and Mrs. John King, parents of the late Rt. Hon. W. L. MacKenzie King, long-time prime minister of Canada.

The party continued to the end of the steel, some distance west of Grand Coulee, and there transferred to wagons to be taken to the site of the present village of Pense. Ties and rails were placed on the grade and the ladies of the party pounded at the spikes with sledgehammers. A bottle of champagne was poured on the ground and the location was named after Mr. Pense.

PENZANCE

Penzance is between Liberty and Hold-fast on a CPR line north out of Regina. The first settlers came in 1903 and included the following: Erlandosons, Larsons, Beers and McMillans. By 1904 the district was almost completely settled by people from the British Isles, Eastern Canada and the USA. They came as far as Craik on the old Grand Trunk Railway and then east across country to Penzance. In the early fall of 1911 the CPR put a rail line through which closely followed Last Mountain lake giving the settlers a much-needed means of transportation for their grain. The village of Penzance was started in the spring of 1912 and was incorporated as a village in the same summer. Two of the early English families, the Rayners and the Hunts were instrumental in having the new village named Penzance, for Penzance, England.

PERCIVAL

Percival is between Broadview and Whitewood on a CPR line in the southeast of the province. It is said to derive its name from members of a well-known English family who settled there in the early days. It was a member of this family, Spencer Percival, who while prime minister of Britain (1809-1812) was assassinated by a bankrupt broker, John Bellingham.

PERDUE

Perdue is a village 40 miles west of Saskatoon on the main line of the CPR. It was settled in 1908 with the coming of the railway and was named after Judge W. E. Perdue of Winnipeg.

There are many stories of Perdue and during the Second World War at least one person discovered that "Perdue" means "Lost" in French. Here is the story:

Many of the Free French, as boys who had escaped from France were called, were stationed at the Saskatoon RCAF station while training to become pilots. One radio operator for the air force tells of being at the controls at the air base in Saskatoon during the time the Free French were flying cross-country practice flights. One pilot, in the airship named Able-Baker, kept calling saying "Je suis Perdu." The operator kept answering, "Roger, I check your position as Perdue," but he kept on calling until another pilot, realizing that Able-Baker was actually saying, "I'm lost," came to the rescue and sorted out the situation so that Able-Baker was brought safely back to base.

A garden to the pioneers was a necessity—from it came much of the food that was to see them through the winter months. The late Hughie Mainland of Perdue loved to grow things and to work in his garden. "It fitted all moods," he said, "if you were happy, you hoed; if you were sad, you hoed; and if you were mad, YOU HOED LIKE HELL!"

A distinguished graduate of Perdue is Dr. John Egnatoff who at present (1972) is professor and head of the Department of Educational Administration at the University of Saskatchewan, Saskatoon Campus. He is also chairman of the Board of Education Saskatoon S.D. No. 13.

PERIGORD

The hamlet of Perigord is on a hillside some fifteen miles north of Kelvington on highway 38. The scene is dominated by the Church of St. Athanasius which crowns the peak of a high hill overlooking the countryside.

The first settlers were Metis who came, prior to 1909, from Lebret and the Touchwood Hills. They included the following families: Gaspard, Chartrand, Genaille, Galarneau and Campeau.

In 1910, more settlers came — Moise Rousseau, Napoleon Bachand, Ovide Marquette and Valmore Belanger. At this time the first post office was opened and called Perigord. The name is that of a province in France. More and more French families moved in: Bosse, Langlois, Pelletier, Lamoureux, Audette, Viens, Poirer, Dupont and dozens of others.

In the autumn of 1911 the first church was built under the direction of Father Gamache. It was situated on a site one mile north of the present hamlet.

PETAIGAN

Petaigan is a country post office, combined with a store and filling station on highway 123, eighteen miles south of Squaw Rapids Hydro Electric Dam.

The location of the post office has been moved three times in the past thirty years.

The original site was one-quarter mile east, and two miles south of the present location. It opened in the early thirties with the late Mr. William Ross as its first postmaster. It was named for the nearby Petaigan river which flowed north into Tobin lake. The name Petaigan is of Indian origin and means "a river being blocked at the upper part of its course by many beaver dams."

The Petaigan post office now carries the Petaigan name alone, because the river which gave it its name has been swallowed up by an enlarged Tobin Lake caused by water backing up from the Squaw Rapids Dam.

This information came from Mrs. P. V. Miller, assistant postmaster at Petaigan.

PETERSON

Peterson is between Meacham and Totzke on a north-south CNR line from Prince Albert to Watrous. Johnny Panchuk, who is a barber at 1028 Avenue L. South, Saskatoon, was born and raised there and he gave us this information.

Peterson was named for Alfred Peterson, an early settler, who lived north of town. At a spring on his land the CNR had a pumphouse and ran a water line 9 miles north to the Totzke water tower.

Johnny, as a 16-year-old boy, remembers being a straw monkey on a custom threshing outfit. Jackob Skari was the engineer, Tony Bobbin was the fireman and an Indian from St. Louis drew water. That just took care of the engine! The separator was a 44" Aultman-Taylor with a huge appetite. Twelve stook teams, two field pitchers and two spike pitchers completed the outfit. The men carried their own bedrolls and slept in what shelter they could find. Tony Bobbins' bed roll was the envy of all because it contained a thick feather tick. It kept him warm on the coldest of nights. When the outfit moved he would place his bed roll on the feeder of the separator. One day it happened! The engine backed into place, the belt was slung over the pulley, and the old Red River Special swallowed the bed roll. Feathers flew everywhere. Tony was thunderstruck! He crossed himself with both hands and exclaimed, "Jeesus Miah" which freely translated from the Polish means "Oh my, what shall I do now?"

PHEASANT FORKS

Pheasant Forks was an inland post office and store fourteen miles south of Goodeve. It was established by Mr. Koshlay in 1904 on his homestead. He not only ran the post office but hauled the mail from Goodeve.

PHIPPEN

Phippen is a small village just east of Unity. The railroad officials named it after Judge Frank Hedley Phippen of Winnipeg. The first post office in the district was Kingsview. This is about where Tako is now and not far from Killsquaw lake where Sifto Salt has a huge solution salt mine. The first mail carrier for Kingsview was Arthur Palmer and he and his black ponies made a weekly trip, Battleford to Kingsview, whatever the weather.

PIAPOT

Piapot is named in memory of an intrepid Indian. He was a Cree chief, one of three who refused, at first, to sign a treaty and go on a reserve. He continued to roam the Prairies. In an effort to embarrass the authorities whom he felt were responsible for the disappearance of the buffalo, the Indian's livelihood, Chief Pie-a-Pot pitched his camp across the right-of-way of the CPR near Maple Creek and brought construction to a halt. When the railroad builders asked him to move, he refused. His young braves raced about on ponies firing their guns in the air. The Mounted Police were called. Only two policemen could be sent, a sergeant and a constable. When they arrived, the chief still refused to move his tent. In fact, he refused to move from his tent. Then the sergeant told Pie-a-Pot he had 15 minutes in which to get his tent out of the way. Pie-a-Pot didn't move. When the time was up, the sergeant jumped off his horse, walked into Pie-a-Pot's tent and kicked out the main pole, and Pie-a-Pot was nearly caught by the collapse of his own house. The sergeant did the same to the next tent, and then he turned to the chief and his astonished braves, saying. "Now move and move quickly." They did.

PICHE

Piche was the name given to the first post office at what is now Bents, Saskatchewan. However when the railway came through in 1928 the settlers chose Bents for the name of the station and, when the post office moved in, it also took the name of Bents. Piche as a location on the map disappeared for a while but then reappeared as the name for a siding between Albertville and Meath Park in the northern part of the province.

PICKTHALL

Pickthall was a grain point on the CPR line that runs north and west from Rockglen to Mankota. It is between Scout Lake and Maxstone.

It was named for Marjorie Lowry Christie Pickthall (1883-1922), a Canadian author who was born in London and came to Canada in 1899. She was an author of verse and fiction, including "Wood Carver's Wife," and "Other Poems."

The Wheat Pool elevator was torn down in 1964 and little remains in the district but the name, Pickthall.

PIERCELAND

Pierceland is fifty miles northwest of St. Walburg. It was named for an early settler, Mr. Pierce.

PIKE LAKE

The curves of winding rivers that have been cut off from the main streams are called oxbow lakes. Pike lake about twenty miles up-river from Saskatoon is a good example of one. It is named Pike for the great northern pike, a sporting game fish. For years Pike lake was a favourite summer resort for many Saskatoon people. A store and post office, a golf course (more uphill than down) and dozens of cottages ringed the narrow little lake.

In 1963 the DNR took over and they established so many facilities, including a beach, that on week-ends thousands picnic and swim at the lake.

The Saskatoon public schools make excellent use of Pike Lake. Within easy walking distance is a nature trail, a sandy area and a bog area. Regular excursions are taken by Grade 6 pupils and more are planned for the future.

PIKES PEAK

The building of the Canadian Northern Railway in the early 1900s up from North Battleford to Lloydminster led to the opening of homesteads north of the "river." Many Americans came into this area and an inland post office was opened in the home of Mrs. L. Carson of 36-49-24-W3, to serve the community.

The name chosen, Pikes Peak, had already been famous in the United States. It is one of the best known of the Rocky Mountain peaks in Colorado. It is 14,110 feet high and is named for Lieutenant Zebulon Montgomery Pike, who tried unsuccessfully to scale it in 1806. Today the top can be reached on horseback or by a nine-mile cog railway. A 30-mile automobile highway leads to the top from Colorado Springs. The famous Pikes Peak Auto Race is held there every summer. The United States Weather Bureau maintains one of the biggest meteorological stations in the world on Pikes Peak.

The name applied to a post office and locality in Saskatchewan was intended to attract American homesteaders. The post office is closed out now and the residents get their mail at McLaren.

PILGER

The name Pilger was selected by Pius Mutter, when he became the first postmaster of this district in 1905. He chose Pilger, which in German means Pilgrim, because he thought it appropriate to describe the early settlers who had moved into this utter wilderness.

At that time the nearest railway was at Rosthern, 75 miles away, with nothing in between but an uncultivated and uninhabited region.

When the CPR came through in 1929 it adopted the name of the early post office.

PILOT BUTTE

Pilot Butte is the first grain point east of Regina on the main line of the CPR. It is named for one of three small flat-topped hills in the district. Used in the early days as a look-out, the hills gave a good view of the surrounding Regina Plains.

Mr. Andrew and Cambridge Martin and William Bettridge were the first settlers in the district. They came in 1884. Besides farming they started a red brick plant. Many of the present homes of the village are of red brick.

Pilot Butte reached its peak early in the 1900s when Interocean Manufacturing Ltd. built another brick plant. Besides the two brick plants there were two boarding houses, a hotel, two livery stables, a tannery, three elevators, a stockyard, a blacksmith shop, a poolroom and bowling alley, a jeweller, a butchershop, a lumberyard, a town hall, two churches, a section house and a station, and about 800 people.

Being so close to Regina had a detrimental effect on the village as the years passed and better roads and better cars took people to the city to shop.

PINEHOUSE LAKE

Pinehouse Lake post office is on Pinehouse lake east of Ile-a-la-Crosse. The lake and post office were previously named and shown on the maps as Snake Lake. On the 4th of November, 1954, at the request of the local inhabitants the name was changed.

PINKHAM

Pinkham is the second stop west of Kindersley on a CNR line that leaves Saskatchewan for Alberta at Alsask. The following is taken from a history of the district written in 1955:

"The trail from Battleford to Medicine Hat, commonly referred to by the pioneers as the 'Old Hat Trail', wound its way through the region and it was following this trail that the first settlers: O. B. Appleby and W. O. Taylor arrived at the present townsite in 1906. In 1910 the grade for the Canadian Northern Railway (Goose Lake Line) came west from Kindersley. At that time a house 16x16 built by Mr. E. Lomas was the only building in Pinkham. Mr. Lomas was appointed postmaster that year and his family joined him in 1911. He started a small store the next year. At first, a stage drawn by horses delivered the mail, later this was replaced by the mail car when passenger train service began.

The name, Pinkham, for the post office was suggested by Mr. Lomas and it honored Charles Pinkham, a local real estate dealer, who was a striking figure in his top buggy and team of black pacers. He favored a rusty black swallow-tailed coat, top hat and 'boiled shirt'."

PINKIE

Pinkie was the first grain point west of Regina on the main line of the CPR. It was established in 1882 and flourished for a time. It was named for Pinkie Cleugh in Scotland, a district in Northeast Midlothian. It was near the present city of Musselburgh and marked the site of a battle in 1547 in which an English army under the Duke of Somerset defeated the Scots.

Pinkie had a second distinction of historical interest. Up until the middle 1970's the Canadian dollar bill had a prairie scene on the back. That picture was of Pinkie, Saskatchewan.

This information came from CPR files and Professor Lowry Knight of Saskatoon.

Because of its proximity to Regina, Pinkie has been absorbed by that city and the elevator is gone.

PINTO

All that is left of Pinto today is the CPR depot and a few stark lone timbers and grassy holes to indicate this once bustling village. Pinto grew up amidst the spotted hills of red shale, green ground cedar, and grey clay banks of the Souris river, in southeastern Saskatchewan. It was these surroundings which prompted the name "Pinto," suggested by one of the ranchers in the district.

In the early days most of the people were ranchers. Some of the more prominent were: Harry and Joe Ballison, Harold Longney, Henry, George, Alex, Tom, and Robert Dunbar, Ross La Rou, Price, and McKay. The last three were rustlers and had to leave one night, cattle and all.

The CPR railway was built about 1896 and Pinto began its struggling existence. By 1910 there was one store, a boarding house, the post office run by William McAllister of Winnipeg, and about 20 houses. A large coal mine was operating at the townsite but the tipple burned down in 1910. Another mine, "Excellor," was opened a mile from Pinto and operated until 1920.

PIPESTONE

Pipestone is on the CPR in southeastern Saskatchewan. It was named for nearby Pipestone Creek which rises south of Oakshela and flows south and west into Manitoba where it joins the Souris.

PITMAN

Pitman is a hamlet consisting of three elevators and a post office. The CPR list of place names states it was named for Sir Isaac Pitman.

The people who live in this area do their trading in Rouleau which is seven miles to the east. The children attend school there, too.

PLAIN VIEW

Plain View is a post office northwest of Melville, 28-24-7-W2. It's an understandable name. When an early settler rested and looked out at the horizon there was likely a plain view in every direction. This same feeling gave us such Saskatchewan place names as Broadview, Horizon, Expanse, Broadacres, Longacre, Prairie View and others.

PLASSEY

Where the CPR crosses the CNR at a "diamond" near Young a number of small points are located: Plassey, Xena, Zangwill, Ancrum, Forslund and Renown. Even Young did not grow very much because the divisional point of Watrous on the CNR to the east became the big town.

Plassey is a siding on the CPR between Young and Renown. There used to be a section house, a bunkhouse, a station, as well as a Co-op elevator. Some of the first settlers in the district were: Mac Meagher, Allan Leslie, Dennis Sullivan, Alec Murray and Jack Davidson.

There's a lot of history in the name Plassey. In 1756, Robert Clive (1725-1774) was fighting the local Nabobs on one hand and France on the other for domination in India. While Clive was visiting England Surajah Dowlah attacked Calcutta and captured one hundred and forty-six British. These he imprisoned during a hot summer night in a room twenty feet square. In the morning only twenty-three of the prisoners, haggard and half-insane, emerged from the "Black Hole" of Calcutta. With three thousand troops about one thousand of whom were British, Clive at once sailed to the relief of Calcutta, and early the next year recaptured the city. Six months later, in 1757, at Plassey, just north of the city, he decisively defeated Surajah Dowlah. This battle of Plassey gave the British control of the rich and fertile province of Bengal and enormously extended their power and influence in the Far East.

PLATO

Plato is less than 20 miles east of Eston. The first settlers arrived in 1909 and included D. J. Maloney, James Topp, Richard Brust, Pat and George Ryan, and Arthur Maland.

The Canadian Northern Railway came in 1915 and the officials asked the settlers to submit names. The one sent in by Richard Burst was accepted. He chose Plato because he had come from Plato, Minnesota, U.S.A.

PLAYER

Player is on a CPR line in southeastern Saskatchewan. It was named for Fred Player, former yardmaster at Swift Current.

PLEASANT VALLEY

Pleasant Valley, just a few miles out of Melfort, was settled in 1892, centering around the homes of Samuel Spry, James McPherson, T. N. Irvine and James Cowell. They came, for the most part, from southern Ontario. Previously the area had been settled by Salteaux Indians as far back as 1884.

In 1915 a United church was built and served the community until its closing in 1959. The first store was built and owned by Charlie Stewart in 1914. It was some years later that he took over postal duties from Mr. Robertson. The first postmaster was Charlie Heath, followed by Mr. Shaw and then Mr. Robertson.

In 1945 James and Kay Stewart remodelled the post office and managed it until its closing in 1970. Now citizens are served by a green box which sits on the side of the road.

When the Saskatchewan Wheat Pool built a large elevator they named it Lipsett instead of Pleasant Valley because of a similar name in Ontario. However, the name Pleasant Valley lives on in the district.

PLEASANTDALE

Pleasantdale is between Lac Vert and Silver Park on a CPR line that runs from Melfort to Watson. In 1905 the first homesteaders moved in and settled on the even sections. A few of them were: Charlie Coyle, Wes Wilson, Bert Sheere and Mr. Hill.

Bert Sheere built a little log store and started the first post office. He was asked to submit three names. He sent in Windgap, Rosedale and Pleasantdale. Pleasantdale was the name chosen.

In 1910 the uneven numbered sections were thrown open for homesteading, and they were quickly picked up. When there was some grain to be sold it had to be hauled to Watson or Melfort. It was a two-day trip. If you hauled No. 2 wheat and the elevator agent only had room for No. 5, you had no choice; you had to take No. 5.

The first church was built in 1920. Around this time there were rumours of a railway coming in. It was a guess as to where to build a town. Business places started going up one and a half miles east of the present town. A Grain Growers store was built at Jim Strachen's. Two other stores were built and then the Bank of Hamilton, a real estate office, two garages, a confectionery, a boardinghouse, a hotel, a lumberyard, a livery barn and a post office. One-half mile north of the present town another town was started with a store, a garage, a shoe repair shop and a barber shop.

The CPR came to Pleasantdale on October 19, 1923. All the buildings from both towns were moved by large steam engines to the railroad and took the name of Pleasantdale.

PLENTY

Plenty is about halfway between Stranraer and Druid on a CPR line that runs from Rosetown to Macklin. In July of 1910, three enterprising young men, Charlie Richards, George Wilson and Sam Young, put up buildings on land a half-mile south of what is now the village of Plenty.

When the railway came through and the site of Plenty was definitely established, the McLeod brothers moved the buildings to the new site with their Case steam engine. These buildings formed the nucleus of the village.

The village is supposed to have been given the name of Plenty by one of the engineers who surveyed the railway line, because the only crops he saw after

leaving Rosetown were in the Plenty district.

Charlie Richards operated a general store. George Wilson operated a hardware, and the first post office was located there. Sam Young, a cook by trade, and Archie Peter McMillan, opened the first restaurant. Many a day Sam used over 100 pounds of flour to make bread, which bachelors for miles around came to buy. Some of his steady boarders included Bill McConnell, Jack and Dan McIntosh, Bill Sillars, Archie Fraser, Peter and Chris McMillan, and A. M. Percival.

The latter opened the Union Bank of November 6, 1910. He came down on "train days" from Rosetown; his "office" consisted of clearing off one of Mr. Young's tables. Then, with his suitcase full of money set beside him and with a gun on the table he was ready for business.

One of the better known first residents of the Plenty district is Mr. Linton Tooley. Born in Hitchin, Herefordshire, England, he came to Canada as a young man and settled at Plenty with his brother, Harold. Following a distinguished career in World War I he went to Saskatoon and in his spare time continued an interest he had had since a youth, the organization of scout troops. He worked wonders in the young city and his efforts were rewarded in 1956 when Saskatoon bestowed upon him its Citizen of the Year award. Scouting, too, recognized his contribution and in 1957 he received the "silver acorn" the second-highest award in scouting.

Plenty is holding its own today and with its splendid primary school, elementary school and North West Central High School it will likely continue to do so.

PLUNKETT

Plunkett is on the main line of the CPR east of Saskatoon. In 1908 the grade for this line went through and in 1909 the steel was laid. Some of the early settlers were: Haugrud, Clavelle,. Northgrave, Klastes, Viau, Batch, Hanson and Brecht. Several sources say that it was named for Viscount Horace Plunkett, a shareholder of the CPR.

POKROVKA

Doukhobor immigrants settled on a communal farm at Pokrovka across the river from Borden. About fifteen families settled there: Paul Kinakin and his son, Larry; George Antifave; Fred Boolnoff; brothers, Nick, George and Savel Kinakin; Fred Esavoloff; Wasel and Peter Osatchoff; Pete Chernkoff; Pete Sherstibotoff; Kuzma Tarasoff; George and Peter Popoff; and Alex Demoskoff.

Alex Demoskoff's son, John, born and raised in the "village", became a farmer near Environ and later opened a general store in the hamlet. Today, he's still in business and keeps a little livestock (sheep and pigs) in barns out behind the store.

John, when interviewed on Sunday morning, May 30, 1976, proved to be a busy man. Customers kept dropping in all morning and it was easy to see why he is called locally, "The Friendly Merchant".

POLLOCKS

Pollocks was the site of a lone elevator between Mehan and Ebenezer just north of Yorkton. It was named for Jack Pollock on whose land the grain point was established. The elevator was torn down in 1945 and all that remains is the name.

PONASS LAKE

Ponass Lake was an inland post office on the shore of Ponass Lake just west of Rose Valley. It opened in the early 1900's and closed in the 1920's when the CPR arrived on its way through from Wadena to Nipawin.

PONTEIX

Ponteix, originally known as Notre Dame d'Auvergne, was founded by a Roman Catholic missionary, Father Albert Royer. Notre Dame d'Auvergne was located a half-mile north of Notukeu creek and 1913 saw the opening of the newly constructed railway on the south side of the creek and this resulted in the surveying of the present townsite of "Ponteix" the name being in commemoration of Father Royer's home parish in France.

Incorporation as a village came in 1914 and since that time growth has been steady. One of the more important developments in recent years has been the construction by the PFRA of a dam on Notukeu creek near the village. This was completed in 1953 and led to the organization of the Ponteix water users association for irrigation of land west and east of the town as far north as Vanguard. It also provides a good domestic water supply for Ponteix.

PONTRILAS

The second stop south of Nipawin on the CPR is Pontrilas. The line was completed in 1924 and the settlers were asked to submit three names. Runciman, Turgan and Pontrilas were the three put forward and the one suggested by Mr. Robert Wall, Pontrilas, was chosen. Mr. Wall was a Welshman who lived two miles northeast of the village. Pontrilas has a namesake in Wales and it means Town of Three Lassies.

POPLAR GROVE

Poplar Grove is a locality southeast of Broadview at 4-14-2-W2. It's a descriptive name given by the early settlers. However, go back before the settlers and there were very few poplars on the prairies, particularly near Broadview.

Devastating prairie fires swept the country regularly and the only trees likely to survive were in or near water. As a matter of fact one tribe of Indians on the plains, the Blackfoot, derived their name from early settlers because in walking over the burnt black countryside following a fire their feet and legs became black.

POPLAR POINT

Poplar Point is a small promintory on the east shore of Cowan Lake approximately twenty-one miles northwest of the town of Big River.

The name goes back to the early 1900's when Cowan Lake was used as a transportation waterway for floating cut logs down to the Ladder Lake sawmill at Big River.

Occasionally the giant booms broke apart, spilling their contents which would pile up on the points. Hence the name Poplar Point.

The man who named it was a trapper and had a mink ranch as well. Today his original log cabin has been preserved and it is used for accommodation of guests who visit the fishing camp now located there.

Operated by Peter, Kathy and John Lomax, Poplar Point Resort is just one of dozens scattered over the clearwater lakes of Northern Saskatchewan. Northern Pike, perch and pickerel are the main game fish taken while along the shoreline beaver, otter, mink and muskrat abound.

The large spruce, poplar, birch and heavy bush surrounding the campsite make it a natural habitat for moose, bear and deer.

PORCUPINE PLAIN

This area in northeast Saskatchewan was thrown open for homesteading in 1919, right after the First World War. First choice was given to veterans. Two members of the survey gang, Robert Green and Roy Busteed, came back to settle here.

In 1929 the CNR ran a line south from Crooked River to Reserve. Richard Cooper named the townsite Porcupine but this name was refused because there was already a Porcupine in Ontario. However, it was decided to add "plain" to it.

PORTER

Porter is the second stop south of Battleford on a CNR line that comes up from the main line at Oban Junction. This line is now abandoned. It was named for Mr. A. S. Porter, an Englishman who headed an American land company named for him.

He got his start when the government closed out the Pheasant Rump Indian Reserve near Kisbey. After relocating some three hundred Assiniboine Indians they sold the land to the Porter Land Company for a dollar an acre. The Company turned this into a tidy thing by reselling it to settlers for anywhere from two to twenty dollars an acre. Mr. Porter reserved a substantial tract for his own which he named Warmley after his ancestral home in England. For a glimpse of his style of living read the story of Warmley.

PORTREEVE

Portreeve is between Lemsford and Lancer on a CPR line that skirts the Great Sand Hills to the north in the southwest-

ern part of Saskatchewan. The choice of name was decided by the drawing of a name from a hat by the CPR officials.

The name Portreeve was misleading to the settlers as the name would seem to indicate the presence of water nearby. The real meaning of the word is "A magistrate or mayor of a town or borough" and is of old Roman origin.

In 1909 the earliest known settlers came. This was before the railroads, and supplies had to be brought overland from Swift Current or Gull Lake. Part of the old Gull Lake Trail is still discernible in the Sandhills which are still virgin country south of the village.

Settlers who arrived in 1910 included the following: Cuthbert Gordon, Albert Nairn, Jim Wilson, Jack McMaster, Art Flumerfelt, George and Florrie Widdifield, and John Lindberg.

This information came from Mrs. J. B. Thomson of 132 Riel Crescent in Saskatoon, Saskatchewan.

POUNDMAKER

Poundmaker is just a lonely unused station on a branch line out of Battleford to Baldwinton that passes between the town of Cut Knife and the famous Cut Knife Hill.

In the 1870s when the Indians went on reserves, Chief Poundmaker was awarded land that included Cut Knife Hill. He was camped on the side of this hill when he was attacked by Colonel Otter and a detachment of troops from Fort Battleford, during the Northwest Rebellion of 1885. He defeated the troops. He did not let his braves pursue the retreating soldiers. After the fall of Batoche, Poundmaker sent word that he was prepared to come into Battleford and surrender. He did. Tried in Regina, he was sentenced to 4 years in Stony Mountain Penitentiary.

On his return to the reserve he was in very poor health. Before settling down he made a trip to his relatives, (he was part Blackfoot) in Alberta. He died there on July 4, 1886 and was buried at Blackfoot Crossing which is near Gleichen.

In 1967, as one of the many Centennial projects, his remains were brought back to Saskatchewan and interred on the top of Cut Knife Hill.

When the GTR came through in 1913 they named this point Rossman. Later it went by the name North Cut Knife and still later it was named Poundmaker. It never had an elevator — just a passing track, a siding and a station. The station has been taken away to some other point and there is a little left but the name — a proud one — Poundmaker.

POYSER
When the CPR and GTP left Saskatoon for Edmonton, they built very, very close together. At Cazalet the lines were a few feet apart — they used the same "cut." In fact, Cazalet's first name was Double Crossing. West of Biggar they spread out a bit but at Unity they came together again and just beyond Unity at Poyser Siding they crossed, the CPR swinging south and GTP going north. Poyser Siding is a grain loading point that was put in over 10 years after the main line had been built. It was named for Harold Poyser, a farmer on whose land it was located.

PRAIRIE RIVER
Prairie River is on a CNR line east from Tisdale to Hudson Bay. This line was put through in 1905. The following information on Prairie River is taken from "Gleanings from the Weeklies" from an article written by Walt Riddell for the Star-Phoenix of Thursday, March 4, 1971:

"Building mountains could become a fad in this province. The latest to boast a mountain is the little village of Prairie River, 25 miles west of Hudson Bay.

It was put there by the community and PFRA. In 1970, the PFRA assisted the local people in building a large dugout to store water for use in the community and the surrounding agricultural area.

As the dugout is located near the elementary school, the citizens reasoned that a hill had always been an attraction for youngsters and the earth from the dugout would form a good-sized hill. As a result, the 20,000 cubic yards of dirt taken from the dugout was used for a hill while at the same time the dug-out supplied water for the community's domestic needs and also supplemented the requirements of about 900 head of cattle owned by 40 district farmers."

PRAIRIE VIEW
Prairie View is a rural post office close to Rush lake. The first settlers came into this district with their oxen and little wooden trunks in 1909. David Ruf, who is retired now and lives in Swift Current, was one of the first. A railway never did reach the settlement and it was not until 1940 that the present rural post office was established. Two names were submitted, Prairie View and Muskrat Lake. The post office officials decided on the former.

PREECEVILLE
The town of Preeceville is situated along the north bank of the Assiniboine river in northeastern Saskatchewan. It was good ranching country and it was not until 1904 that homesteaders began to move in. The CNR arrived in 1912 and it derived its name from the Preece family.

Mrs. Preece fed the railroad crews as the track was being laid and her son, Fred, homesteaded the land on which the town stands.

PRELATE
The first settlers came to Prelate in 1903 and most of them came by way of Montgomery's Ferry which is still in operation 9 miles north on the South Saskatchewan river. Mr. N. Dollard came in 1907. Prelate was already named by that time. Prelate is the title of a high-ranking church official whether in the Church of England or the Roman Catholic Church. In this case, since the majority of the settlers were German Catholic, it was done to commemorate the Catholic Church.

To carry out the theme the streets and avenues of the town have been named as follows: streets — Canon, Dean, Bishop, Cardinal, Abbot and Prior; avenues — Cathedral, Minister and Abbey.

The first post office to serve the area was opened in 1912 and was housed three miles south of the present site of Prelate. When the CPR arrived in 1913 it was a blessing because prior to that the mail and supplies had to be hauled from Swift Current, seventy miles to the southeast.

PRENDERGAST
Prendergast is on a CPR line between Medstead and Meadow Lake. It is named for James Emile Pierre Prendergast (1858-1945) who in 1902 was a judge of the Supreme Court of the Northwest Territories. In 1905 he became a judge of the

Supreme Court of Saskatchewan. He later became chief justice of Manitoba.

PRIMATE
Primate is on a CPR line that runs from Kerrobert to Macklin. When the first homesteaders came to Saskatchewan and settled on the new land and built up a new town they had a feeling of being first. They weren't really, because the Indians were ahead of them. Nevertheless, they felt that way and the naming of Primate is a good example. The word primate comes from the Latin Primus, meaning first.

Primate is a hamlet between Macklin and Salvador on a line which came through in 1910. Many settlers were in ahead of that and some of these were: John McGugan, Robert Armstrong, Richard Bestock, Donald McLean, George and Tom O'Gorman, H. O. Johnston, Arthur Carscadden, G. N. Shaw, Jack Montgomery, Jack Argue, J. J. Campbell, George Wilson, Frank Hazelwood, C. F. Kilborn, Harry McKinnon and W. B. Kilborn.

The first postmaster and storekeeper was Mike Sheddy.

PRINCE
Benjamin and Alphonse Prince, brothers, were the first settlers in the Highgate district. They arrived from St. Gregoire, Quebec, in 1882. They were successful farmers.

Later they went into business in Battleford. Ben became mayor in 1898 and was made a senator in 1909. Prince was named in his honor.

PRINCE ALBERT
Prince Albert is a city on the North Saskatchewan river at the junction of numerous CNR and CPR lines, 87 miles north of Saskatoon.

The area was frequented by fur-traders from the late 18th century. In 1776, Peter Pond, explorer and fur-trader, built the first trading post on the north shore of the river just west of the present site of Prince Albert.

The next important development was the arrival of Reverend James Nisbet and a party of settlers who arrived in 1866 and established a Presbyterian mission around which a village grew. Reverend Nisbet named it Prince Albert as a tribute to the consort of Queen Victoria.

PRINHAM JUNCTION
Eleven miles north of North Battleford between the hamlets of Prince and Hamlin is Prinham Junction. The CNR branched out from here in the early 30s to run a line to Medstead; the CPR had "running rights" as far as Hatherleigh and then they built from there to Mayfair. Prinham was formed by combining part of the names of Prince and Hamlin.

In the early years Prinham Junction had a flag station. With so many trains going up and down the line people would get on a train in the morning and go to North Battleford for a day's shopping and then come back out at night on some other train.

The highlight of traffic on this line (besides the grain out and the coal in during the fall) came in the years 1928 to 1937 when the Beaver Hockey Club of North Battleford, under its manager, the late Jack Abbott, made several bids for Canadian hockey supremacy. Its rise to popularity climaxed in the latter years when the Beavers stormed their way to the Allan Cup finals only to be defeated by Sudbury in the fifth and deciding game of the final series held at Calgary.

One of those who well remembers the special trains that carried fans from the St. Walburg line and the Medstead line is Herb Chapman. He still lives and farms beside Prinham Junction. Others from this district who cheered Vic Miles, Eddie O'Keefe, Davy Duchak, Cam Burke, Harry Hailwood, Squee and George Allen, Joe Schwab and Elmer Piper as they battled for the Beavers were: Jim White, Bill and Bob Tebay, Bob Sheppard, Ed King and Leonard Lanegraff.

The lines west of the junction are up for abandonment. In fact, they took the rails up from Redfield to Mayfair years ago. The line to St. Walburg has only two trains a week and hasn't carried passengers for almost ten years.

PRONGUA
Mrs. A. Kallechy of Chitek Lake told me that her grandfather, Jeff Prongua, was employed as an Indian agent on the Sweet Grass Reserve 25 miles west of North Battleford in the 1800s. When the land around Cut Knife began to be homesteaded settlers found the drive from Battleford too long to complete in

one day. Mr. Prongua decided to move to a new location on the edge of the reserve and there he started a stopping place and a store. When the railway came through in the early 1900s they named the siding Prongua after its first resident, Jeff Prongua. When the Wheat Pool opened an elevator there he became its first agent.

PRUD'HOMME

Prud'homme is between Dana and Vonda on the main line of the Canadian Northern Railway which was built in the early 1900s.

Originally settlement had started as far back as 1897 by predominantly French immigrants. The first name of the community was Marcotte's Ranch. When the steel arrived in 1904 it was renamed Lally Siding. In 1906 it became Howell and stayed that way until 1922. That year it was renamed Prud'homme in honor of Joseph H. Prud'homme, Bishop of Prince Albert and Saskatoon.

Not many places in Saskatchewan or elsewhere can claim that many changes of name.

PRYOR'S BEACH

In 1928 Arthur Thomas Pryor bought nine acres of land from Mr. Hines and started Pryor's Beach, a summer resort, eight miles east of Liberty on the south side of "Big Arm" on Last Mountain Lake and he operated it until the early winter of 1942 when, unfortunately, he met his death by drowning when he fell through the ice while setting fish nets.

His brother, Bob, took over then and ran it until 1955 when he sold out to Bob McBride.

PUNNICHY

One story has it that Punnichy was the Indian name for Mr. Heuback, a redheaded trader and postmaster of the early days. Mr. Heuback was completely bald except for a ring of hair around his shining dome. To the Sioux Indians he was "chicken without feathers" or Punnichy.

PYM

Pym is on the old Goose Lake Line that the Canadian Northern built southwest of Saskatoon, and it is the last grain point before you reach Rosetown. It's just an elevator. It's a small name, too, but like other small places in Saskatchewan it commemorates a lot of history, in this case British history.

John Pym (1584-1643) was one of a group: Hampden, Holles, Hazelrigge, Strode and Lord Kimbolton (afterwards Earl of Manchester), who stood up to Charles I. Charles got into deep trouble trying to finance his overseas wars and ended up by plunging England into civil war. In the end he lost his head. John Pym died in bed on December 8, 1643, and a grateful England buried the great parliamentary leader in Westminster Abbey.

The Pool elevator at Pym five miles east of Rosetown closed its doors in the early 1970s and the Pool elevators at Rosetown handled the grain.

In 1974 the vacant elevator burned down. All that remains are the cement foundations and a pile of weeds.

Q

QUANTOCK

Many of our place names came from England. Quantock would probably come from the lovely Quantock Hills in West Somerset where one gets a beautiful mixture of wild hills, cultivated farmland and the Bristol Channel in the distance.

Quantock, in Saskatchewan, is the first stop west of Rockglen on a branch line of the CPR that ends at Killdeer. The post office was in the farm home of Harry Atkinson about four miles east of the present Quantock.

The mail came from Assiniboia to Joville (now Lisieux) then to Quantock and on to the Borderland post office run by Mrs. John Linthicum, later by Mrs. Peter Kay. Still later, Sam Linthicum took over as postmaster and ran it until the post office closed. Sam now lives in Rockglen.

QU'APPELLE

An ancient Indian legend tells how it got its name — an Indian brave travelling down the Qu'Appelle River Valley to his wedding heard his name called out. It was the voice of his sweetheart but she, he knew, was many suns away in camp. Puzzled the brave answered, "Who calls?" but only a spirit voice mimicked, "Who calls?" Troubled, the brave sped homeward, only to learn that his loved one had died. With her last breath she had called his name. Ever since, so the legend goes, the valley has been known as Qu'Appelle or Calling River Valley.

Qu'Appelle is the French way of saying "Who calls" and Qu'Appelle takes its name from this Indian legend.

QUILL LAKE

Quill Lake is on a CNR line that runs very close to the north end of the Quill lakes. It takes its name from these lakes.

This is one of the greatest breeding grounds for wild fowl in all the western country, and in the fall of the year sportsmen come from all over the continent to enjoy the fine shooting.

In the old days the quills of the wild geese or "outrades" as they were called by the French Canadian voyageurs, were traded in by the Indians at certain posts of the Hudson's Bay Company. For some years considerable consignments of these quills were shipped out of the country for use as pens.

Late in 1903, R. A. Gordon, one of the first men to acquire a homestead in the present Quill Lake area was appointed postmaster and suggested the name Quill Lake for the new office, to which the Department agreed. The location for the office was in a corner of Mr. Gordon's sod-roofed log cabin.

Prior to that date, mail for the settlers had come from Yorkton to Fishing Lake Post Office, Assiniboia, NWT, thirty miles east of the settlement, the Milligan family being in charge of the Fishing Lake Office. They sent the mail to the settlement at every opportunity by surveyors, railroad builders or settlers, whoever was coming to the settlement. Three weeks was the longest period without mail.

It is of interest that Milligans had come to the Fishing Lake Indian Reserve area many years before and Harry had freighted supplies to General Middleton's forces from Qu'Appelle to Duck Lake in 1885.

By midsummer 1904 a regular weekly mail service was established, with service being by team and democrat or sleigh, depending on the season. Harry Milligan was the mail carrier from Yorkton and he supplied other small offices along the way like Sheho, Foam Lake and Fishing Lake. Quill Lake was the last point on the route.

The mail arrived at Quill Lake on Sunday afternoons. This was a most convenient time for the settlers as, Mr. Gordon being the obliging postmaster he was, they could pick up their mail on the way home from the religious services which were conducted in the log school close to the post office.

After the railroad came through, the siding was first known by a number, then named Lally out of respect to a railway official. Mr. Gordon approached the Department to have the name changed to Quill Lake to correspond with the post office name. His suggestion was accepted.

The business people who were locating in the new hamlet objected to going a mile and a half to the post office and petitioned the Department to have the post office moved to town with Theodore Rasmusson as postmaster. The request was granted and in 1905 it was established in his hardware store.

QUINCY

Medona post office opened in 1905 on the N.E. quarter of 24-35-8, with Mrs. S. A. Coates as postmistress. Mail was hauled by Bill Russell from Saskatoon to Medona and on to Loganton further west.

Because of a similarity of name with Medora post office in Manitoba there was a considerable mix up in mail at times and the smaller post office, Medina, was asked to change its name. They chose Quincy because some of the settlers had emigrated from Quincy, Illinois, U.S.A.

The post office closed out in 1908 with the arrival of the railway (Goose Lake Line) in Delisle. Patrons served by the post office during its short life were: William Chambers, John Hewitt, Mike Bratlin, Jim Robertson, James William Chovin, James and Charles Smart and Joe Sutton.

QUINTON

Quinton is between Punnichy and Raymore on a CNR line southeast of Saskatoon. It was named after a railway engineer. The name was chosen by the railway company (disregarding an application by the residents of the district for another name) as they claimed that the first letters of the names of the different stations should be in alphabetical order.

R

RABBIT LAKE

The settlers that filled up this country trekked in from North Battleford after the Canadian Northern reached there in 1905. One of the first was Mr. C. Rowan who opened a store and post office three miles west of the present townsite.

Others who arrived about the same time were: George Cavey, Albert Smith, Fred Stannard, Walter and Louis Schlermann, Fred and Emil Kobernick, Wes Bell, John Seibert, Isaac Eisenberg (storekeeper), August "Gus" Hanson (creamery), John Aumack and "Dad" Wilkins.

One of the most famous people in this district was Dr. Storey. He was a dedicated country doctor whose services were available no matter what the weather. His son, Sandy, farmed the homestead that bordered the town.

Rabbit Lake was named for a small lake one and a half miles southwest of the townsite. The dry years of the thirties took their toll of the lake and it has seldom had water in it since. The lake received its name from the abundance of rabbits in the vicinity.

The settlers had a long time to wait for a railway — it was not until 1928 that the CNR put a branch line through from Speers to Medstead.

RADISSON

The name Radisson honors the famed early French explorer and fur trader, Pierre Radisson. This area in the elbow of the North Saskatchewan river was known in the early days as the Great Bend District. The first store and post office was south of the present townsite on the homestead of J. S. Goodrich. this settlement was called Goodrich, too, but when the Canadian Northern Railway came along they renamed it Radisson.

RADVILLE

Radville is a divisional point on the CNR southwest of Weyburn. Steel reached the point in 1910. The townsite was surveyed and building began. Just how rapid the growth was is indicated by the results of a census count in June, 1911, just two years after the original survey. Radville's population was 1300. However, 700 of these were railway construction workers who were engaged in building a roundhouse and yards.

The name of the community is an almost unrecognizable corruption of the name of the homesteader on whose land the townsite was located, Conrad Paquin. Founders called for suggestions on the name, got a large number which were duplicated in other parts of the country and decided to go along with the last syllable of Conrad, plus the ville to denote a settlement.

RAK

Rak is the first grain point north and west of Aberdeen on a CNR line that runs to Melfort. It is on land owned now by D. M. Bayda of 102-104th St. Saskatoon. Rak was named for a prominent early family of the district. Orest Rak still farms the homestead three miles east of the grain point and Rak school is on his land.

RALPH

Ralph is the first grain point on a CPR line that runs southeast of Weyburn to Estevan. The district was surveyed in 1892 but it was not until 1900 that John J. Borrowman, the first settler, took up a homestead. He was followed by: Frank Miller, Clem and Charles Cugnet, Ernest G. Stewart, A. J. Thieman, Jacob W. Westley, Leopold Weissinger, Charles Johnson, Stephen Willey, Herman Erickson and Jacob Fladager.

Being nine miles out from Weyburn Ralph developed into a lively little village. The first building to go up was a blacksmith shop owned by Charles Johnson. Charles Anderson built a warehouse for grain. In 1906, the Weyburn Security Company built a lumberyard. It was run by George Stewart. A post office was built in 1907 and it was run by Charles Cugnet. Mr. Dalgliesh built the first store and he eventually took over the post office.

Ralph was named after Ralph McTaggart, a railroad roadmaster on the line.

Improved communication by road and auto caught up with Ralph and the long all-day round-trip to Weyburn became a fifteen minute jaunt. Ralph gradually went downhill and the post office was closed in 1948. All that were left by 1970 were the elevators, because the surrounding area is a good grain growing district.

RANGER

Ranger is on a CPR line that runs northwest of Medstead to Meadow Lake. When this line went through in the early 30s there was a forest ranger's tower close to the site. Robert Orr of Cater was the ranger at the time and he was instrumental in the naming of the place.

RANGEVIEW

Rangeview is about ten miles south of Robsart. The post office has been closed for several years; it formerly got its mail from Vidora. Rangeview is in cattle range country and the name of the place is an accurate description. Ranches dotted this part of Saskatchewan and even American stock roamed it free of fences in the early years.

RAPID VIEW

Rapid View is 16 miles west of Meadow Lake on the Makwa river. The first settlers, the Bobier and Henderson brothers, J. J. Green and family, William Pura, and J. P. Schwartz, came in 1929. The best crossing of the river was at the rapids where it was reasonably shallow most of the time. Horses could walk over the stones pulling wagons piled high with settlers' supplies. There were no bridges or roads at that time. In 1932 a school district was formed and a post office was opened near this odd river ford. They all took the name Rapid View.

RATCLIFFE

In April, 1906, Mr. and Mrs. Ratcliffe and their three small sons, Ernest, Dick,

and Jim, left Balmagee, North Castle Douglas, Scotland, for western Canada. Their first stop was Moose Jaw. Mrs. Ratcliffe and the boys stayed in the Immigration House there while Mr. Ratcliffe went to Weyburn in search of land. He located in what is now the Ratcliffe district.

After he had built a sod house he sent for his family. All the furniture was homemade. Mrs. Ratcliffe papered the walls with the colored pages from an Eaton's catalogue. The pictures on the walls were cut from newspapers sent by relatives in the old country.

The first winter, they were reported frozen to death. Sergeant Let of the RNWMP came out from Estevan to investigate. He found them well. However, not so fortunate was a young man, Jim Cousins, homesteading on the next quarter to them. On a beautifully mild February morning he left their place to go to a nearby ranch for meat. A storm suddenly came up; he turned back but missed their buildings by only a few feet and was frozen to death.

In 1926 the CPR came through from Bromhead to Minton. It passed within three miles of the Ratcliffe farm and the post office which Mr. Ratcliffe had started in his home in 1908 moved in and gave the town its name

RATNER

Ratner is an inland post office eleven miles from the end of the steel at Gronlid. It got its name from an early pioneer, Harry Ratner, who opened a country store four miles from the present site. The first mail (1907) came from Star City. Three years later Mr. Ratner got the post office in his store. In 1969 Ratner had a Co-op store, a bulk oil distributing business, a ball diamond, a picnic area, a 2-sheet curling rink, a Lutheran Church and a post office in the Co-op store with mail delivery every day.

RAVENHEAD

The CPR build a short branch line east from Hatherleigh through Craigavon, Whitkow, Redfield, Green Canyon — crossed the CNR at Mayfair — and ended a short distance beyond at Ravenhead. This line did not work out and was abandoned as far back as Redfield by the mid 1940s and the rails were taken up.

The name Ravenhead had two sources. Raven came from the large number of ravens in the locality. The raven is a large cousin of the crow. The head part of the name came from the simple meaning of the word: to be found at the top or front.

RAVENSCRAG

Ravenscrag is less than ten miles from Cypress lake just south of Cypress Hills Provincial Park. Bald Butte in this park is 4175 feet above sea level and is the highest point of natural elevation in Saskatchewan. Early settlers mistook the eagles that nested in and near the park for ravens and this accounts for the name.

A similar mistake south of Lloydminster resulted in a place being called Buzzard. It may be that Albatross got its name in much the same way.

Eagles were common in the early days and have been sighted as late as 1967 at Baljennie by the late John F. Allen, a naturalist and historian, who retired and lived in Battleford for most of the 60s.

Ravenscrag was first called Point View and that was its name when Spencer Pearce filed on his homestead there in 1890. The railway came in 1914 and with it the change of name.

RAVENSDALE

Mr. and Mrs. Robert Martin and son, Dale (six months) squatted on land in this district in 1931. Mr. Martin got a job with the survey crew and when, in October of 1932, the land was opened for homesteading, he was one of the first to file.

In 1933 the McAfee brothers, J. P., Earl and Frank, moved into the district. J. P. was the one who had the greatest influence because he went out to gather names to petition for a post office. The country at that time was heavily timbered. There were no roads — only cut lines. There were no bridges. Mr. McAfee travelled on horseback over muskeg and forded creeks where the water was up to his saddle. He tells the story that on returning home one weary night only the ears of his horse were dry.

However, he succeeded in getting the required number of signators and applied for a post office. The name he submitted was Cumberland Trail. This was turned

down because there were other established names similar to it such as Pas Trail. Then he suggested the name Ravendale to commemorate the vast number of ravens and Dale Martin the first boy to come to the community. The name was accepted and Mr. J. P. McAfee got his post office which he set up in conjunction with a store. He was the postmaster for he next twenty-nine years.

The McAfees retired and now live in Saskatoon in the winter and return in the summer to the family farm near the hamlet of Ravensdale.

RAYMORE

Raymore is another in a long list of towns named in alphabetical order by the GTR from Winnipeg to Edmonton. Prior to the coming of the railroad in 1908 settlers received their mail from Kutawa on the old telegraph line from Fort Pelly to Clark's Crossing. Some of the earliest settlers were: Richard Watt, Headley and Charles Frost, Wilfred Jones and Archie McLean. The latter had the first store in Raymore. Other pioneer merchants were: Harold E. Martin, druggist; James Tate and Harry Golden, general merchants; Bill Kelly and Bill Moody, hotelkeepers. The first grain elevator was the "Scott" operated by Thomas M. Scott, the second was the National run by Sam L. Troskey. The post office was kept by Mr. McLean.

READLYN

Readlyn is a town between Verwood and Willows on a CPR line in the south of the province. The Dean homestead was the site of the first post office, Deanton (named after the Dean brothers, L. S., R. W., and E. S.). Mrs. R. W. Dean was the first woman in the district. She arrived with two sets of twins under four years of age. The post office was opened on March 3, 1908.

The first post office facilities consisted of a wash tub placed under the bed in the twelve by eighteen shack. When settlers came for their mail, the letters in the tub were sorted through until the proper one was found. This post office was also the drop-off point for mail to Winside and Leeville (now Assiniboia). Mr. R. W. Dean would ride horseback to these points delivering the mail to them. The mail was brought to Deanton post office on the Willow Bunch or Pole Trail by Mr. Mab Gaudry. In the summer he travelled by team but in winter he often used a dog sled when the snow was deep. He took the protection of the mail very seriously and always carried a knife and a rifle.

When the railroad came through in 1912 the Deanton post office came to town and the name was changed to Readlyn on May 1, 1913. The first part of the name honors an early settler, Mr. Read, and the second part indicates that the town was built in a valley or "Lynn".

The new village was incorporated on August 13, 1913 and soon became the trading centre for a larger area. All the settlers as far north as Marigold and Bliss Lake and from as far east as Creemore and Dryboro Lake hauled their grain to Readlyn and bought many of their supplies there.

Good years followed and by 1916 Readlyn had three grocery stores, two hardwares, two blacksmith shops, three machine agencies, two coal and wood yards, a pool hall and a church.

In the early twenties the town held its own but 1929 was the beginning of the end. The drought years and depression that followed caused some to lose everything, including heart. People simply picked up and left. The Second World War saw many young people enter the services — many never to return.

So, the business center dried up and today Readlyn has one store, a post office and one elevator.

The CP Rail service over the years had not helped either. First carrying passengers, then mail and finally express. Now they haul two trains a week — sodium sulphate from Ormiston and grain when box cars are available.

REDBERRY

Redberry got its name from Redberry Lake just south of town. It is six miles wide, twelve miles long, and 150 feet deep. The lake got its name from the profusion of raspberries (red berries) that grew along the shore.

RED CROSS

Red Cross is beyond the end of the steel north of St. Walburg. It is a district served by a general store. The first settler was a trapper, R. Stein. He came in 1910. During the First World War (1914-1918) Mr. Arnold built the present store. He was an American and he wished to remain neutral, so he flew a Red Cross flag above his premises. When it came time to add a post office the name Red Cross was suggested and accepted.

RED DEER HILL

Originally called Aaskana by the Indians, the name of this place was changed in 1883 to Red Deer Hill.

The transmitting tower for radio station CKBI, Prince Albert, is ten miles to the south of the city (clearly visible from No. 2 highway) right on top of Red Deer Hill. Deer Park district is at the south base of the hill.

The deer liked to congregate on the hill to take the sun but more important, to see. It's a big hill and as a hunter came up one side the deer could easily slip down the other. There were plenty of deer in the country as well as on the hill. These were white-tail "jumpers" that are now coming farther south each year as farms get larger and farmers get fewer, and as the absence of the prairie fires of the early years allows the growth of the parkland poplar areas which provide shelter for them.

There is a Pool elevator at Red Deer Hill, with Arthur Sukut as the agent. Raymond Pilon ran a store there for years but it closed at Christmas time in 1967. A few houses remain. The post office has moved out to the highway as part of a combined Texaco gas pump, store and machine shop operated by Mr. and Mrs. R. D. James.

Some of the earliest settlers in the district were George Joyce, Bob Tait, Tom Peterman, John McLaren Paul, John McArthur Paul, Bob Giles, Angus Morrison, Ed Paul, William Harmon and several families of McLeods.

George Joyce was the man who invented the modern automatic coupler for box cars; before that they used a crude pin affair like the king bolt on a wagon, which was very dangerous when it came to hooking moving cars together. His coupler came into common use on all railroads in Canada and the United States, but since he did not have his patent protected he did not profit from the invention.

Dr Lorne Paul of the University of Saskatchewan was raised in this district. His father, John M. (for McArthur) Paul, has a sign by his gate which reads "S.E.-4-46-27-2." By 1969 he had completed 27 years as councillor for Red Deer Municipality. If you're ever in the district drop in. You'll be welcome. John is a big man who talks easily and when he talks history comes alive.

RED EARTH

Red Earth is an inland post office and store on the Red Earth Indian Reserve forty-five miles northeast of Carrot River. The reserve serves 500 to 550 families of full-treaty Cree Indians. The present chief is John William Head, who at thirty is very young to be a chief. This position is not hereditary but is decided by a democratic vote by the band.

Mr. Clancy is the storekeeper and postmaster. He commutes to Carrot River every day, but the mail comes out only on Tuesdays. A heavy concentration of iron in the soil gives it a rusty-red color. Water flowing through this soil takes on a red tint. Therefore, in addition to a Red Earth post office and Red Earth Reserve we have nearby a Red Earth lake, and also a Red Earth creek which flows through the reserve and north to the Carrot river.

REDFIELD

Redfield is on a short branch line of the CPR which built east from Hatherleigh through Craigavon, Whitkow, Redfield, Green Canyon — crossed the CNR at Mayfair and ended a short distance further on at Ravenhead. This line did not work out and in the 1940s it was largely abandoned.

By the 1950s Redfield was the end of the line. The tracks had at one time carried on beyond that point. The only service provided by the railway was to haul grain out following the harvest. With this, Whitkow, which had developed into a good sized town was literally boarded up.

The first settlers into the Redfield area came from Redfield, South Dakota. The inland post office was named Redfield and when the railway arrived, the nearby post office gave its name to the grain point.

RED JACKET

Red Jacket, the first grain point west of Moosomin, commemorates one of the stopping places of the NWMP cavalcade on their trek west from Fort Dauphin (now Emerson, Manitoba) to Fort Macleod, Alberta, in the summer of 1874. One of the distinguishing features of the dress of the Force was the scarlet tunic, hence "red jacket." Over the years the town of Moosomin grew into the trading center and today Red Jacket is little more than a grain point.

RED PHEASANT

In the year 1878 Red Pheasant, an Indian chief, moved with his band onto a reserve about thirty miles south of Battleford and ten miles north of Cando. He gave his name to the reserve, the railway point with its one Searle elevator, and to the store and gas pumps on highway 4.

It was very close to Red Pheasant that Poundmaker on his reluctant way to Batoche in 1885 intercepted a caravan of teamsters freighting supplies from Swift Current to Battleford. He confiscated the lot without any bloodshed. A historical marker points out the spot.

The best known contemporary figure from this reserve is Allan Sapp. Picking up the rudiments of painting at the Indian residential school at Lebret, he showed a lot of natural talent. Under the sponsorship of Dr. Gonnar of North Battleford, Mr. Sapp blossomed out as a full-fledged artist in the 60s with showings at the Mendel Art Gallery in Saskatoon and a show in London, England.

REDVERS

Redvers is a village on the CPR Regina-Souris line, twelve miles from the Manitoba border. It was named after the famous English general, Sir Redvers Buller.

REFORD

Reford is between Cavell and Scott on the main line of the old GTP west of Biggar. Jacob Stang is the Pool elevator agent there, and that is all that is there! Reford almost became a big town. It was picked for the divisional point of the GTP but the railway was unable to strike water so essential to the old steamers, and they backed all the way to Biggar to get it, making it the new divisional point and making that 60-mile stretch from Saskatoon one of the shortest lengths between divisional points in western Canada.

The astonishing thing about Reford is that it wasn't named Wilkie. The names of the first tax roll read: George Lachner, George Howitson, John Rutherford, Joseph and Ernest Irwin, and then the rest were Wilkies — Charles, Alexander, John, W. R., James, W. F., and H. H. (Taxes in those days were $8.00 to the quarter. They were $50.00 in 1970.)

The GTP were responsible for the naming of the town. Designed but not destined to be an important townsite, Reford was given a proud name. Robert Reford (1831-1913) was an important merchant and capitalist. In 1870 he founded in Montreal a steamship agency business, the Robert Reford Company, which became the agent for the Donaldson Line to Glasgow, the Thompson Line to London, Hull and Newcastle, and other lines. He became president, not only of this company, but of a variety of other businesses; and before his death became one of the outstanding capitalists of Montreal. Some of his money and influence were behind the GTP, hence the name.

There were two elevators in Reford in the beginning, the Atlas and the Grain Growers. Two stores, one lumberyard, a Presbyterian church and a livery barn went up. Muchmore ran the store and Bob Smith had the livery barn.

When Reford's dreams of becoming a divisional point went by the board and when the CPR in its turn backed up from Adanac to Wilkie to find water, almost all of Reford businessmen moved to Wilkie. Wilkie, which became the divisional point on the CPR, was just six miles to the north of Reford.

In later years the CPR ran a branch line south to Kelfield. They crossed the main line at Reford and had to service the "diamond." Tom Stout was the resident caretaker.

Harry Griffiths has lived within sight of Reford all his life. In fact, he was a member of the first school board. Harry and his wife (the daughter of Tom Stout) have fond memories of Reford. One of the most vivid is that of the washout of the tracks in the spring of 1921. For a time the passenger train would come as far as Reford and then people and baggage would have to be transported over the temporary track by hand-car and put upon a waiting train on the other side. No sooner was that section of the track repaired than another section washed out at Tako, the second stop to the west. Passengers were then given a choice 1) to stay on the train 2) to go back to Scott and be put up in hotel and 3) to go via hand-car over the washout to Unity. It was days before the track was repaired, and in those times a lot of people depended on the trains for transportation.

REGINA

Regina, the capital city of Saskatchewan, was originally known as Pile of Bones Creek from a huge pile of bones near the old crossing below the present city. A profusion of whitened bones left by the Indians after their buffalo hunts dotted the prairie in all directions.

In 1882 when it was decided to move the capital of the Northwest Territories from Battleford to the south, Pile O'Bones was the site chosen. It is understandable that people began to think in terms of a new name.

The governor-general, the Marquis of Lorne, was asked to make the choice. As he was married to Princess Louise, he christened it Regina in honor of his wife's mother, Queen Victoria.

REGWAY

Regway is a port of entry on highway 6 straight south of Regina and opposite Port of Raymond on the American side.

An inquiry of a border guard as to how it got its name was not very revealing. He said, "I think they took part of the name Regina and added way to it."

After thinking it over, maybe Regway means literally that if you headed north, you are on the way to Regina.

REINFELD

Reinfeld is one of a nest of Mennonite villages between Osler and Hague just north and east of Saskatoon. Reinfeld is German and means clean field. It is only two miles north and east of Hague. At one time it was a fair sized village but now is down to one farmer and one empty house. The first families came into the district in 1897. Some of them were: Dycks, Friesens, Schmidts, Remples and Peters.

The Peters family built a "zimlin" style home before their new home was completed. Mr. Peters dug a 12x16 hole, three feet deep. The dirt was left at the edge. On this were erected logs for walls to a height of eight feet, then a pointed log roof was made and covered with sod. There is still a hollow in the old abandoned yard that marks this place 4 miles south of Hague and 600 yards east of the CPR tracks.

A variation of the zimlin house is one that is built into a bank with the protruding part shingled with sod. More than once a grazing cow has been known to almost deliver her milk right on the living room table.

Thatch became a popular roofing for the first frame houses. It was made from tall, full-length slough grass tied into wrist-thick bundles.

RELIANCE

Reliance is an inland post office fifteen miles southwest of Mankota. In the spring of 1910 Mr. Angus McMillan built the first shack in the Reklaw district. He hauled his lumber from Swift Current. In mid summer Mr. and Mrs. Sayers came West on their honeymoon. In 1913 Mr. Walker was appointed postmaster and the post office was named Reklaw which is Walker spelled backwards.

Mail became mixed up with Retlaw, Alberta, and the post office officials suggested a change of name. Reliance was the name chosen; it had no particular significance.

RENOWN

How Renown came to be selected for the small hamlet of that name is not clear. It is generally supposed that, like the GTR, the CPR which came through in 1910 was in the habit of naming places for minor officials or members of the construction crew. Thus many men who have long since been forgotten, are immortalized in Saskatchewan place names.

What is known for sure is that the first settler in the district was Charles Wilson, a genial rancher who, in 1904, established himself three miles south and one and

one-half miles west of the present site of Renown. From then on, until the influx that came with the railroad, settlers arrived steadily. Here are a few of them: William Reid, R. J. Gill, Andrew Dahlvong, Franz and Oscar Hedlin, Avery, Walter, Harold, and cousin John Reid, Art Hill, Eric Greaves, Robert Martin, Bill Evans.

There was a Chinese homesteader, Wackee De Que, who succeeded in getting clear title to his land. A minister, S. S. Westby, also proved up. So you see it takes men from all walks of life to start a community.

RESERVE

Reserve is at the junction of a CNR line built north from Sturgis. At Reserve one line goes north to Hudson Bay and the other line goes northwest to Crooked River. Reserve got its name from the railway because it's in a forest reserve.

RESOURCE

Resource is just south of Melfort. The siding and consequent hamlet of Resource, was named by the railway authorities due to the efforts and persistence of a local farmer by the name of Cobena Smith.

The siding is situated between Silver Park and Clemens which are eight miles apart. The railroad officials contended it was not necessary to place a siding between these two points. However, Mr. Smith was persistent and the officials had to admit he used every resource he could think of in his arguments. Finally they decided to give him his siding and they named it Resource.

REVENUE

Revenue is the third stop south of Wilkie on a CPR line that runs to Kerrobert. When the first settlers took up their homesteads there were no other homes but their sod houses. There was no town or railway and they had to go to Battleford to do their shopping. In 1906 Bill Delaney opened a post office and a grocery store which was called Pascal. In 1907 another post office which was called Meno was opened on Chamberlain's farm. The mail was brought from Battleford every two weeks. This post office was open until 1915, although after the railways were built to Scott and Wilkie residents of the district got their mail more often.

In 1912 the town was surveyed and preparations were made for building a railroad — the grade went in in 1911 and the steel was laid in 1912. The first trains ran in 1913 but before this, in January of 1913, the district officially was named Revenue. Why? When the CPR engineer surveyed the town he thought it would be a good district for "revenue" and Revenue it was called.

Some of the first settlers were: Brossart, Ell, Schann, Schmidt, Weber, Volk, Adams, Bertsch, Heidt, Hummel, Sahli, Senger, Halter, Welter, Weran, Zerr, Wolf, Usselman, Gerrin, Elder and Garnier.

In 1972 the Pool took over all elevators — five of them! Al Germshied is the agent and his helper is Dennis Elder. There's little left of Revenue as a town, just the post office in Joe Herle's house. The school children are bussed to Tramping Lake. There's one train a week but when "quota is on" the trainloads of grain are still shipped from this "revenue" point.

REWARD

Reward is sixteen miles southwest of Unity on a CNR line built to Bodo, Alberta. It was named by railway officials for Reward, a variety of wheat. Marquis wheat developed by Dr. (later Sir) Charles Saunders in 1903 was widely used in Western Canada. It was called the King of Wheats. However, it failed when stem rust invaded the Canadian wheat fields in 1916. The search was on for a rust-resistant wheat!

In 1923 Mr. L. H. Newman succeeded Sir Charles Saunders and developed two varieties, Reward and Garnet. Other varieties were developed at the Dominion Rust Research Laboratory at Winnipeg — Renown and Regent. Apex, developed at the University of Saskatchewan, also did well.

In 1931 when the CNR built southwest from Unity, Reward wheat was in general use and thus they named the third grain point on the line after it. Reward has proved to be good grain country. It has four elevators that are taxed to capacity with wheat from the rich farmlands that surround the town.

Holy Rosary Roman Catholic Church

two miles south of the present townsite was an early landmark and center of religious activity, dating from 1919. Berthold Imhoff's painting adorns the vaulted ceiling.

In May of 1932, after much planning and discussion with the priests of St. Joseph's Colony, Bishop Prud'homme asked that an annual pilgrimage in honor of the Blessed Virgin Mary be held in the Colony on July 16, the feast of Our Lady of Mount Carmel. Being central to the Colony, Holy Rosary Church was chosen as the site.

Early in the morning of July 16, 1932, the first pilgrims were on their way. They were greeted by the ringing of the bell as they gathered one-half mile south of the church and walked in procession to the Shrine, where they attended several Masses, followed by an outdoor polyphonic High Mass at 11:00 a.m. Father Schneider preached the first pilgrimage sermon. The climax of the day was a procession of the Blessed Sacrament and benediction at the Shrine, which ended with 3000 pilgrims singing "Holy God We Praise Thy Name."

The first shrine was a humble affair — a canopy of cloth shaded the altar and was adorned by a picture of Our Lady. In 1936 a wooden structure was built which served as the grotto until the present shrine was built in the summer of 1966. The church was closed in 1963 and a new Holy Rosary Church was built in Reward. The site and shrine are still used for annual pilgrimages.

REX

Rex L. Jones and Edward Greenstreet emigrated from Mansfield, Nottinghamshire, England, in 1905. They settled on adjoining quarters north of Lloydminster. They later had adjoining post offices named for them and, when the CPR ran a line north from Lloydminster to Hillmond in 1928, adjoining grain points were also given their names. The Rex post office opened on February 1, 1910, with George W,. Powers as postmaster. It operated until March 26, 1953.

Other early residents were: John Powers, Charlie Hughes, Moores, Stringers, Halpennies, Amphlets, Hepworths, Everests, Wilfred Waterhouse, William Nelson and George Simpson.

REYNAUD

Reynaud is 12 miles east of Wakaw on the CNR which is intersected at that point by a north-south CPR line from Humboldt to Prince Albert. Mrs. Helen Reynaud, granddaughter of the man for whom the townsite was named, is the postmistress. Her grandfather, a widower, came from France in 1897 with six children, the youngest four years old. They lived for two years at St. Louis before they homesteaded in the district that was later to bear his name.

RHEIN

Rhein is 20 miles northeast of Yorkton. Many of the settlers came from German villages along the Wolge river in Russia. The village was named by Emil Meugersing whose home town was Koln (Cologne), Germany on the Rhein (Rhine) river. He came to Rhein in 1905 and in partnership with Jacob Kinsel, was the founder of the Rhein Hardware Company.

RHEINFELD

Rheinfeld is a Mennonite village ten miles east of Wymark. Early settlers in the district were of German descent. Rheinfeld in English means Clear Field.

RHEINLAND

Rheinland is a Mennonite village four miles northeast of Osler on the CNR line from Saskatoon to Prince Albert. Rheinland is a German name that means Clear Land.

It never had a station, an elevator or even a loading platform. It consisted of a general store, first operated by Cornelius Driedger and then by Peter Dyck. It closed in 1964.

Mr. Isaac Neudorf of Saskatoon remembers attending school there, at which time he and the other 40 students took their lessons in German. He also recalls his father telling him that in the wintertime when the usual roads became blocked with snow the people of the district drove their horses and cutters on the railroad to Osler. It was always kept clear and the method worked well. One day during a blizzard when visibility was very poor and Abe Peters and Jakes Giesbrecht were driving along the track, they thought they heard a train. They

quickly jumped out and lifted their cutter off the tracks. They had just managed to get their horse clear when a train roared by. Yes, pioneering on the prairies was sometimes hazardous!

RHINELAND

Rhineland is a Mennonite village twelve miles southeast of Swift Current. The name is German and when translated into English it is Clear Land. The post office is listed as open, with mail coming in from Wymark. Mr. Peter Fehr's store there is closed and most of the shopping is now done on number 4 highway at Mr. Lizee's store opposite Springfeldt or else in Swift Current.

RHYL

Rhyl is between Asquith and North Kinley on the main line of the CPR a little over twenty miles west of Saskatoon. Because it was so close to Asquith it did not develop as a town. At its best it had a loading platform for grain and chutes for cattle, also a section man's house and a section man's residence. Today, it has a single tool shed and signal box. It still supplies a passing track that is usually lined from end to end with empty potash cars.

This is in sharp contrast to the bustling seacost town of Rhyl, Wales, for which it is named. If you wish to locate that place, look in the Blackpool area.

Marshall Mercer, Jack and George McKenzie and Jim Paisley were a few of the early settlers from around Rhyl who hauled their grain to Asquith. It was then served by four elevators, Linde (a private elevator), North Star, Western and Canada West, as well as a flour mill which was operated by Mr. McLean.

RICETON

Riceton is about twenty-one miles southeast of Regina. The GTP was completed in 1912 and the townsite was named for Mr. J. S. Rice who owned the land. The first elevator was built in 1913 and in all, four went up. Some of the first settlers were Johnston, Cane, Smith, Miller and Leach. At its height the village had several businesses including a bank, a livery barn, a cafe, a lumberyard and three stores. It was a thriving community. However, with the advent of the automobile and better roads and the proximity of the community to Regina, business dwindled away. By 1968, the population of the village was down to 128.

RICHARD

Richard is named in honor of Emile Richard, a pioneer rancher. In the late 1800s he moved into the district and built up a huge ranch of 400 horses and 1100 cattle. He supplied beef and horses to the NWMP Post at Battleford.

The NWMP maintained a post at his ranch. He prospered and built a great palatial red brick house that was a landmark in the district. The first mail service was quite simple; settlers from the surrounding district had their mail addressed care of Richard's Ranch, Northwest Territoties, Battleford; and the regular police patrol brought it out for them.

RICHARDSON

Richardson is the first stop on a CPR line that came into Regina from the southeast in 1904. It was named for Judge Richardson who presided at the trial of Louis Riel.

The earliest settler to arrive in the district was Hugh McLean from Ontario. He came in 1882 and was followed by Edward Weeks, Robert Rogers, Sidney Burgess, William Clancy, Andrew Shane, Joe McGill, R. H. Moore, and James Brooks—all from Ontario.

RICHLEA

Richlea is the first grain delivery point east of Eston on a CNR line. The post office was first called Pengam, named by the Edwards brothers for their home in Wales. It opened in 1910 but as the name was often confused with Pangman the postal department asked the community to consider a change of name. Richlea was created by combining "rich" for the soil with "lea" for the meadow-like prairies.

Tom and Richard Williams and William and Russell Pope, Percy Bateman and Fred McQuay were the first homesteaders, coming in 1906. In 1907 Alexander McKinnon, Benjamin Lewis, Frank Greensides and C. J. and A. M. Banting joined them.

The district continued to grow; a school was applied for and was opened June 30, 1914. Here is part of a letter written by Mrs. Mark McNichol who, as Miss Mae Bennett, was hired as the first teacher:

"Forty years ago, as the first teacher of Richlea School, I found conditions far different from what you experience today. The railroads hadn't reached Richlea yet, and the town consisted of one store and a small one-roomed house that had been moved in from a farm to serve as a school.

Even the trustees were new on the job. All correspondence had been from Brock and they failed to tell me that Richlea was 25 miles away and that I was supposed to go the rest of the journey with the mailman. As was quite usual in those days the train was late and the mailman could not wait, so there was no one to meet me. When I inquired around and found that I still had all that way to go and no way of getting there, I was ready to take the next train home. However, I learned that the minister was driving that way and he offered me a ride. When I finally arrived at the Dean home where I was to stay they gave me such a warm welcome that it made me forget the uncertainty I had had."

The district must have appealed to her for she married one of the men of the district, Mark McNichol.

RICHMOND STATION

Richmond Station is at the intersection of Forty-second Street and Warman Road. Either it is named for the Richmond Heights building development it adjoins or Richmond Heights is named for the Station. This is a moot question.

However, one thing is clear and that is the siginfance of the name. It is named for Richmond-on-Thames, England, the site west of London where Henry VIII had Sir Thomas Moore put on trial. This was an odd case in which the King impeached a man who had been his Lord Chancellor. Sir Thomas disagreed with Henry's wish to set aside his wife, Catherine of Aragon. Frustrated and impatient, Henry had Sir Thomas beheaded.

At Richmond Station, Saskatoon, there are waiting room facilities where people may entrain or detrain. From here a branch line runs downtown to service the industrial areas. Train crews work out of this point and it not uncommon to see twenty cars park beside the building.

258

RICHMOUND

A spur line of the CPR goes from Leader and ends at Fox Valley, Saskatchewan; Richmound is between Horsham and Linacre on this line. Early settlers filed on homesteads in 1910. The first was Charlie Wilde and family from Baldur, Manitoba; then the Stadolkas, Porters and Coveys from the USA; and many others of German, Scandinavian, Polish, Scotch, Irish and English origin.

The municipality of Enterprise No. 172, was organized in 1913 with L. J. Freeman as the first secretary-treasurer (he held that post until 1946) and Charlie Wilde as the first reeve.

The first post office was established in 1911, 3 miles west of the present village, with Charlie Wilde as postmaster. He also had a small general store in his house. The Oasis School (now Richmound School District 780) was built in 1912, with Miss Enid Gibbard as the first teacher. The school is still on the same site but it has 14 teachers now and buses bring pupils in from many other school districts.

The name was given to the district by Mrs. Charlie Wilde, because of the rich soil and the slightly rolling land making a mound here and there.

In the early days mail and provisions were brought by wagon and sleigh from Maple Creek, a distance of 50 miles southwest, a two-day trip each way. Wheat was also hauled in this manner. A stopping place, now Golden Prairie, called colloquially The Halfway House, was the farmstead of Sal Preston. Their house and stable were always open to travellers, whether the occupants were there or not.

Later, bridges were built over Bitter lake and the town of Forres, now Hatton, sprang up. Settlers were able to make the trip to Forres and back in two days. In cold weather the men often had to walk halfway to keep warm. Sometimes a blizzard would come up and visibility would be reduced to nil, so the men would have to let the horses find the way home. There were only trails to follow.

Most of the wheat hauling was done with so called four-horse teams in tandem as seen on TV Westerns. The RCMP patrolled the area from Maple Creek on horseback to check for rustling of cattle or shooting of wild game out of season, also to check on health and other problems of the settlers.

RIDGEDALE

Ridgedale is on a branch line of the CNR that runs from Melfort to the end of the steel at Carrot River. One of the first families into the district was John Garton and his son Alfred. The Gartons left England on the 29th of May, 1906, on the steamship Lake Manitoba, and made only brief stops until they reached the Ridgedale district. Many other settlers followed: Jack Grant, Harry Rowswell, Joe Smith, Frank and Gus Hess, Charley and Bert Perry and Fred Humphrey.

It was customary in England to give one's farm a name and Harry Roswell called his Ridgeway because of the ridges, dales and small creeks that abounded. When Jack Grant applied for the first post office he suggested the name Ridgedale and it was accepted. This post office was in his home, three and one-half miles southwest of the present townsite. When the CNR arrived in 1921 officials had the name Ealing all ready for the town, but by petition of the local people it was changed to Ridgedale.

Mr. Alfred Garton of 1145 Avenue L S. in Saskatoon tells a sad story of the early days:

Mr. Garroway, the teacher at Ridgedale School, made arrangements with Fred Humphrey to get a ride into Tisdale on a Saturday. He agreed to be at a certain place at a certain time and he said to Mr. Humphrey that if he wasn't there Mr. Humphrey was to go on without him. It was winter and it was cold. Mr. Garroway did not show up at the agreed time and Mr. Humphrey went on without him. Mr. Garroway did come along but too late and the tracks in the snow told the story. He wandered and got lost. This happened on a Saturday and it was the following Thursday before they found his frozen body half bent over a barbed-wired fence.

RIDPATH

Ridpath is 7 miles west of Rosetown. It was named for John Clark Ridpath (1840-1900). He was an American historian born in Putnam county, Indiana, who wrote popular histories and historical

259

textbooks, including "A Popular History of the United States of America" (1876).

Being so close to the vital trading center of Rosetown, Ridpath never consisted of more than two elevators. Its name reminds us of the many other places in Saskatchewan named for authors.

RIVERHURST

A GTP line built in 1916 northwest from Moose Jaw ends just short of the South Saskatchewan at Riverhurst. Riverhurst was named at a special meeting of settlers in July 1915. Before the coming of the railway there were two rural post offices in the area. Riverside and Boldenhurst. They took the "river" from Riverside and the "hurst" from Boldenhurst to make Riverhurst.

One of the settlers was Dr. J. E. Kitely. He and his wife arrived in 1914. Dr. Kitely served a large area around Riverhurst. He retired in 1945 and now lives in Vancouver.

RIVERSIDE

Riverside was an early rural post office near the present town of Riverhurst. Its first mail came all the way from Davidson and later from Elbow when the CPR reached there in 1908.

When the GTP built northwest from Moose Jaw in 1916 and established Riverhurst, Riverview post office was closed and gave up part of its name to the new town. This also closed another post office in the area, Boldenhurst, and it, too, gave up part of its name to form Riverhurst.

RIVERVIEW

The first post office in the Elbow area was Riverview, two and a half miles north of the present town and so named because of its view of the South Saskatchewan River.

It was established prior to 1905 and served a large district. Mail was hauled from Davidson. When the CPR came through in 1908 to Elbow this post office moved into the town.

ROAN MINE

Roan Mine post office is closed now. It was located in Roan Mine Coulee west of Minton. At one time it had a good general store and served the farmers south of Hardy and Ceylon. Mail was transported from Minton by horses and sleigh in winter and horses and democrat in summer. It was named for the Roan Coal Mine nearby.

ROBINHOOD

Robinhood is on a CNR line between Glaslyn and Medstead. It was first called Robin. The school in the district was also called Robin but residents living there now cannot agree as to whether the school or the townsite came first. Either way the name Robin caused a mix-up in mail with Roblin, Manitoba, and being the smaller place, Robin was asked to change its name. The residents didn't like the idea of a complete change and they suggested to the postal authorities that "hood" be added to Robin. Their request was granted.

It is believed that the idea for the "hood" came from the huge Robinhood Flour signs which were very numerous in the early days. It was not uncommon for the company to paint the entire side of a merchant's store with such a sign. One of these signs is still visible on the McDonald and Binns store (closed in 1967) at Prince, Saskatchewan. It was only one of dozens and dozens of these signs throughout Saskatchewan.

ROBSART

It was not until 1910 that the big migration got under way into the semi-arid area lying to the south and west of Moose Jaw. The CPR purchased a quarter section of land from Chris Peterson and gave it the name Robsart. This was selected from the heroine of Scott's "Kenilworth," Annie Robsart.

Mr. Peterson was one of the first settlers to move in. He came with his family and household effects to Maple Creek. There he bought three oxen, one of which was a large black ox named Diamond. When an ox was no longer able to work it was butchered; it made very durable beef. In the fall of 1912 Mr. Peterson decided to take his family to Medicine Hat for the winter, to find work for himself and at the same time, send his children to school. He sold three of his oxen to another settler, but old Diamond had outlived his days of usefulness as a work ox, and Mr. Peterson decided to turn him into beef.

Now, one large ox made too much beef for one family, so he proceeded to sell the surplus throughout the community. No one could buy much, but almost everyone bought some. That was one time when the whole community was in agreement — some beef is tough! For several years afterwards when a housewife got some beef that she could hardly boil tender, she was sure it must be a piece of "Old Diamond."

ROCANVILLE

Rocanville is a village in the S.E. of the province only 10 miles from the Manitoba border and just north of Moosomin. It is named for the first postmaster of the district, A. H. Rocan Bastien.

ROCHE PERCEE

Roche Percee is close to Estevan in the heart of the soft coal or lignite district. Many of the villagers are employed in strip mining.

Roche Percee was first called Pierced Rock by the Indians who roamed the Souris River Valley in which the village is situated. In the valley there is an outcropping of sandstone rock that takes the forms of giant lizards and dinosaurs. Among these is long rock much higher than the rest and it has a hole right through it.

Hence, the name, Pierced Rock or Roche Percee, from which the village took its name.

ROCK POINT

Rock Point was an inland post office, store and gas station southwest of Bratton. It was on a rocky promontory on the edge of what were known locally as the "Finland Hills" which stretched south almost to Beechy. These hills were so named because many of the early settlers came from Finland.

ROCKFORD

Rockford is an inland post office situated on NW¼-10-37-7-W2. It got its mail via Endeavour. Miss Anna Johnson was the first postmistress and she chose the name because of the rocky place where they forded the Assiniboine river.

ROCKGLEN

Rockglen is a town 100 miles south of Moose Jaw. It is situated in a picturesque valley and gets its name from the large rocks on the surrounding hills. Although it is only a small community, it has one of the most active ski clubs in Saskatchewan, and has had for years.

Rockglen has a unique wildlife wonder one and one-half miles south of town in a heavily wooded draw that runs down to a valley. Over 100 blue herons nest in this valley. They nest in the trees and fly five miles east to Fife lake to feed. You can stand on top of the draw and look right down into their nests.

ROCKHAVEN

Rockhaven is the third stop northwest on a CPR branch line from Wilkie to Lloydminster. There are two stories as to how it got its name.

One states that not far from the village is a huge high rock that weighs hundreds of tons. It is almost as large as Mistaseni (which now lies at the bottom of Lake Diefenbaker). This rock is almost hidden by trees now but in the early days prairie fires kept the country clear of trees and this rock was a land mark to travellers, especially those returning from their trip to Battleford along the old Sounding Lake Trail. When they could see the rock far off on the prairie they knew they were almost home. Hence, the name Rockhaven became associated with the district around the rock.

The other story is that the name had nothing to do with the rock. The story goes that this was originally part of the Swathmore district and that with the arrival of the steel in 1911 two of the Rorke brothers started a business at the new townsite and that Clayton Rorke and his brother-in-law, Charles Metcalfe, were instrumental in having the railway officials accept the name Rockhaven after the community of the same name that they had come from in Ontario.

There may be a dispute about the origin of the name but no one will dispute the following. In the late 20s a local Rockhaven hockey team that could hold its own with North Battleford featured Bill Hoffman, the McIvor brothers, George and Bob, and Lindsay Gibbons of Neilburg. These players were invited to play with North Battleford Beavers and they formed the backbone of the Beaver team which won the provincial championship in 1931-32.

RODDICK

Roddick is a siding between Duck Lake and Macdowall. It was very close to this spot that the first shots in the Rebellion of 1885 were fired. It was named to honor Dr. Thomas George Roddick (1846-1923), Canadian physician. Dr. Roddick was deputy surgeon-general in the Rebellion and established the field hospital in the small settlement of Saskatoon to care for the injured from Duck Lake, Fish Creek and Batoche. In later years as a Conservative member of the Dominion House of Commons (1896-1904) he introduced the Roddick Bill, to establish a central national registration and uniform standards for all licensed medical practitioners throughout Canada, and was instrumental in securing its passage (1902) as the Canadian Medical Act.

RODERICKVILLE

In 1912 the rural school of Roderickville was built and named for Roderick McKenzie, a bachelor, who donated a large bell which was rung by a rope.

In the early 1930's, the CNR built a branch line west from Avonlea to Swift Current. It passed near the school and the grain point on the line between Neidpath and Burnham became Roderickville. Jack Ferguson was the first farmer to ship a carload of grain.

The 1959-60 Pool map showed it had one elevator. The 1969-70 Pool map showed neither elevator or name. By 1971, the whole line was abandoned and by 1976 the rails and ties had been taken up and the line was totally abandoned.

This information came from Mrs. Lorna Ward of Swift Current. She added, Roderickville was of special interest to me because my father, Mr. J. Allan Watt, homesteaded there at the age of 18. I was one of three daughters who attended Roderickville School for several years via horse and buggy and cutter. The school was destroyed in 1961 and the bell was sent to a mission school in Africa.

ROKEBY

Rokeby is the second stop east of Yorkton. It was named for R. T. Rokeby, a railway official stationed in Winnipeg at the time the Manitoba and Northwestern Railway built the line into Yorkton in 1886.

ROMANCE

Romance is on a branch line of the CPR that runs northeast of Lanigan to Watson. There's a lot tied up with this name besides love, etc. The origin of the word was French where "un roman" meant a novel. The modern connotation of this word is an exciting adventurous story.

Nothing could be more exciting than opening up a wilderness for settlement whether this be done by railroad or by those who came before the railroads or even roads. The writer of these lines has aptly expressed this thought:
There are homesteads which have seen deeds
That battle fields with all their pomp
Have little to compare with.
Life's great play may, if it has an actor great enough
Be well performed upon a humble stage.

RONCOTT

For years Bengough was the end of a branch line west of Radville. In 1924 when the CNR extended the line to Willow Bunch, Harvester, seven miles west, was the first elevator siding built. The name was later changed to Roncott to honor RONald PresCOTT, a young man of the district who lost his life in World War I.

ROSCOMMON

Roscommon is the first grain point on a CPR line south of Gull Lake. It was in all probability named for Roscommon Castle in the town of Roscommon, in the county of Roscommon, Ireland.

ROSEFIELD

Rosefield is an inland post office about 20 miles southeast of Masefield from which it gets its mail. Early settlers were impressed with the flora of the prairies and in some cases like Briercrest, Tiger Hills and Crocus they named their places for flowers.

Bounty wanted to encompass all flora and suggested Botany for their name. Rosefield appears in another place in Saskatchewan. Rosenhof, an inland post office 12 miles southeast of Swift Current is a German name meaning garden of roses.

ROSEMAE

In 1908 Rosemae, which got its name by reversing the name of the first post-mistress, Mae Rose Switzer, was situated on section 35-25-3-3. Mr. C. Martinson had the contract to haul mail from David-son to Rosemae and Riverview. In 1910 Mr. W. S. Hewitt took the contract to haul the mail from Riverview to Rosemae and the post office was moved to his home on 34-25-3-3 where it remained until 1961 when it was closed since only three families remained in the district. A son and grandson carried on after Mr. Hewitt passed away in 1938.

When the railway came through in 1910 mail was brought from Elbow, a distance of fifteen miles. The Hewitt's kept a store in their house until the 1950's when most people had cars and went to town. One of the many conveniences they provided was taking the local cream cans to and from the station.

In 1906 a school was built a mile south of Rosemae. It was called "Washburn" No. 1612, until 1920 when it was changed to Rosemae.

Besides the Hewitt family some of the early settlers were: Switzers, Johnson, Barlow, Wilkes, and Smith.

Rosemae post office may be gone but the soils department of Saskatchewan has seen fit to remember it by naming a type of soil "Rosemae Clay Loam".

ROSEMOUND

All that is left at Rosemound is a signal house and the junction. From here the CPR has "running rights" over the CNR to Battleford. This GTP line which was built in 1911 was racing the CPR north-west from Wilkie to see who would get to Lloydminster first. The GTP lost and after it left Rosemound going northwest it built to Newby, Tatsfield and stopped at Car-ruthers. The line is one of the first that will be abandoned because it never was of much use in the best of times. The name Rosemound started out as a school district on the banks of historic Cut Knife creek. The school was on a mound or knoll and there was an abundance of wild roses, hence, Rosemound.

It has been sixteen years since the elevator burned down at Rosemound and all that's left at the junction is a signal house.

ROSENGART

Rosengart is a Mennonite village northwest of Hague. Settlement started in 1899. The name in English means Rose Garden. David Derksen was one of the first homesteaders. Not at first, but now the inhabitants have painted their homes to match the beautiful colors in their flower beds. Rose Garden is well named.

ROSENHOF

Rosenhof is a Mennonite village eleven miles southeast of Swift Current. The first settlers came in there in the early 1900s — well before the railway. Mrs. Cornelius Wieler, as the oldest person in the village in 1970 well remembered the early days in unpainted houses with barns attached. The barn was always larger than the house.

The village used to have a store but it is closed now. Rosenhof when translated into English means a yard full of roses or flowers.

ROSE PLAINS

Rose Plains, a station on the CNR just north of Regina, was so called from the profusion of wild roses that were growing there when the first settlers took up land in 1882. It was in this neighborhood that the late Hon. G. W. Brown, at one time lieutenant-governor of the province, commenced his career as a homesteader.

John Isaac of Calgary writes as fol-lows:

"My father homesteaded in the district in 1902. At that time there were only two other settlers, Robert Neuby and Thomas Hartley. When the post office of Rose Plains was opened in 1904, Robert Neuby was the mail carrier. He hauled it from Redvers on the Arcola branch of the CPR.

My father froze to death on November 30, 1904, while bringing home a load of wood from the Moose Mountains. He left a young family of 6—the youngest was two weeks old. We were destitute. How-ever, our neighbors pitched in and helped us to 'prove up.' Thanks to that wonder-ful spirit we were able to struggle through a period when there was little money and few conveniences."

ROSERAY

Roseray is on a CPR branch line that runs south from Pennant to Verlo. Settlers filled up this district almost twenty years before the railway came. Among them were: Reg Hurrell, Bill and Russell McLean, Joe Cushing, Tony and Peter Dahl, and Bill Dempsey. These settlers, some of whom came in as early as 1909, had to go to Webb over twenty miles to the south for their mail.

In 1911 Oscar Simard applied for a post office and was accepted. The name chosen from the three he sent in was Roseroy, his mother's maiden name. However, when the post office kit arrived it was misspelled as Roseray. In spite of a mild protest the name stood. When the railway arrived in 1928 the rural post office moved to the townsite and gave it its name. Four grain elevators were speedily built and it has remained a good grain point ever since.

ROSETOWN

Rosetown is situated on the CNR, Saskatoon-Calgary line. It is 72 miles southwest of Saskatoon.

The first settlers arrived there in 1904-1905 and named the town after James Rose, one of the pioneer settlers.

It was incorporated as a village in 1909 and a town in 1911.

It was common practice to place a lamp or lantern in a window at night because it was so easy to get lost at any time on the prairie and particularly so in stormy winter weather.

An anxious wife, setting a kerosene lamp in a window after dark to help guide her husband home from a trip to a neighbors for a load of oats, remarked that she hoped he would not get lost. "Oh Mommy," said her four year-old, "Daddy didn't go to get lost, he went to get oats!"

In 1976, Cargill Grain Company opened its first high-throughput inland grain elevator just outside Rosetown.

ROSE VALLEY

Rose Valley is on a CPR line that runs from Tisdale to Wadena. Here is a town that got its name from a Grain Growers Association! Mr. Marten Nelson was the man who made the actual motion at the meeting. Next came the post office. We don't know the year, just that it was called Rose Valley. When the CPR came through in 1924 they accepted the name for their townsite.

ROSSALL

Rossall was originally an inland post office fifteen miles east and a mile and a half north of North Battleford. It was opened in 1911 in the home of George Belmont on NW¼ of 14-44-14-W3. The Belmonts came from Vermont, USA, and named it for their native village there.

The post office moved about the Whitewood Lake area quite frequently: in 1914 Mrs. Fred Sharpe got it; in 1920 Fred Smith; in 1923 Mr. Al Halliday. When rural delivery started in 1926, the Rossall post office made its last move to the home of Mr. and Mrs. Bert Wedlake on the Forest Hall road. This lasted until R. R. No. 2 was started out of North Battleford.

We were indebted to Mr. Jim Sharpe of 9019-16th Avenue of North Battleford for this information.

ROSSDUFF

The inland post office of Rossduff was located sixteen miles south of the present town of Dinsmore.

The post office and store (now closed) were housed in a separate building which has since been moved into Dinsmore. It proved to be the start of a fine outdoor museum with other buildings being added over the years. Willis Clark is in charge of this growing project.

As a boy of five, Ernie Hedger, son of Harry, remembers going to the store for candy and the post office for mail. Mr. McRobbie was one of the first postmasters and probably was responsible for the name which is definitely of Scottish origin.

Descendents of Drayton Thompson still farm in the district and a son, Roy, looks after the community pasture as well.

This information came from Mr. and Mrs. Ernie Hedger of 1310 Colony Street, Saskatoon.

ROSTOFF

Rostoff, an inland post office, was named for Michael Rostoff. It was west of Lucky Lake in what became known later as the King George area. It was established well before the CNR built through in 1922. But, with the coming of the railway which went on to end at Beechy, it closed out.

ROSTHERN

It is alleged that when the railway was built from Regina to Prince Albert in the late 1880s, a man by the name of Ross was drowned in the creek which flows through the town of Rosthern. The stopping place on the railway, at this point, was called Ross-terne which later became Rosthern. "Terne" is old English for tarn, meaning a "pool."

A similar story to the above has this added: "A story which appears to have a louder ring of authenticity to it claims the name originally was "Rose thorn" and not "Rosthern." The story has it that the name was derived from the numerous rosebushes which flourished in the area when the first settlers arrived here, and that later it was changed to "Rosthern" quite by accident—through a spelling error.

Enquiries have been made at the Provincial Archives in Regina and at the CNR head offices, all to no avail. There are no records on the name and its origin. It appears on the topographical survey sheet 1894, as "Rosthern," and was officially adopted for the post office in 1897.

ROULEAU

Rouleau is a town 30 miles southeast of Moose Jaw. It was named for C. B. Rouleau, judge and member of the Northwest Territories Council of the 1880s. He was the resident stipendiary magistrate of Battleford, who presided at the trial of the eight Indians following the Saskatchewan Rebellion. They were convicted and hung inside the Fort Battleford stockade on November 27, 1885. The most notorious of the eight was Wandering Spirit who on April 2, 1885, shot Thomas Trueman Quinn, Indian agent, during the Frog Lake massacre.

ROWATT

Rowatt, the first grain point south of Regina where the railway crosses the number six highway, came into being in 1911 with the building of the Grand Trunk Pacific, later named the Canadian National Railway.

The first elevator, the Security, was built in 1912 and was followed later by the Paterson and the Pool.

The settlement was named after a Superintendent from head office of the railway who was sent in to oversee the project. The land the GTP bought to build Rowatt on was owned by S. H. Jones who had moved there in 1898. Mr. Jones purchased the land from T. C. Craigie who had homesteaded it just after the Riel Rebellion.

The first family to live in the station was T. O'Conner's, and the last to live there was David Hughes. It has since been moved.

Around 1900 a Colony was formed four miles northeast of Rowatt by immigrants from Austria and Hungary. There were sixteen homes in the Colony. They later settled around the district.

In 1906 the first school board of South Regina S.D. #1518 was formed. Serving on it were T. C. Craigie, Charles Jackson, and S. H. Jones.

In 1908 the South Regina Telephone Co. was formed by Mr. Monney, W. Elliott, J. Elliott, T. C. Craigie, John Duncan, Chas. Jackson and S. H. Jones. Mr. Jones also served on the first council of Sherwood Municipality #159 when it was formed in 1912.

A store was built at Rowatt in 1932 by Lloyd Wallace who also ran a service station and the post office. J. M. Metz took over the post office in 1945. It closed in 1969. The filling station is now operated by D. Powell.

A Catholic Church was built in Rowatt, as well as homes for the elevator men. All of these but one are now housed in Regina. There is one other home owned by P. Lalonde.

The district still has many farms run by sons and grandsons of the original families.

We are indebted to Mrs. Marjorie Bell (nee Jones) of Regina for this information. As a small girl, Mrs. Bell grew up in Rowatt.

ROYER

Royer is the first grain point north of Meyronne on a CPR line that runs down from Swift Current. It was named for

Father Royer, a Catholic priest who had a large church and parish in the district well before the railway arrived.

ROZILEE

Rozilee was an inland post office ten miles north and east of Shellbrook. Grace Shaw of Prince Albert remembers the naming of it. The settlers wanted to call it Rose because of the profusion of wild roses. The post office turned thumbs down on the name as there was a post office nearby with the name Wild Rose. So, they settled for Rozilee.

RUBY LAKE

Ruby Lake is the first stop north of Hudson Bay on the CNR line that runs to The Pas in Manitoba. It was named "Ruby" because of the clear water in a lake nearby.

RUDDELL

Ruddell is the third stop south of North Battleford on the way to Saskatoon. In 1903 Jack White arrived in the district and homesteaded two miles west of the present townsite. The next year saw quite an influx of settlers: the Turnbull brothers, the Robinson brothers, and Mr. McCann, to mention just a few. One settler came in pushing a wheelbarrow loaded with all his possessions. He came all the way from Saskatoon! The Turnbulls drove a team and wagon to Saskatoon for lumber to build their house. Before a post office was established the settlers walked to North Battleford for mail.

The village was first named Lucerne but with the coming of the Canadian Northern Railway in 1905 it was changed to Ruddell and no one seems to know why.

The first settler, Jack White, had two sons. One still farms the home place.

During the years 1967-77 the town of Ruddell went steadily downhill. First the station closed and then one by one the businesses in the town boarded up until in 1976 a unique sign appeared on the highway: "RUDDELL 1 MILE NO SERVICES". However, the Pool elevator, post office and church were still in operation until the second week in February, 1977. At that time, Wiebe Movers of Saskatoon trucked the 39,000 bushel elevator by

road one mile north to the farm of P. Martynes and Son.

This farm, twenty-five quarters and sixty head of cattle is run by Art, son of Peter Martynes, his wife, Ida, sons, Konrad and Markus, daughter, Natasha and one hired man. In the driveway of their farm home is its name "Fazenda Montanai". Fazenda is Spanish meaning farm and Montanai is the name of the village in Crimea from which Peter Martynes emigrated to Canada.

RUDY

In the early 1900's Rudy Nystuen opened an inland post office (which he named for himself) and a store six miles north of the present site of Outlook. Three miles further north was the Rudy Ferry.

With the coming of the CPR in 1908, which bridged the South Saskatchewan, post office, store and ferry closed and the thriving town of Outlook took over.

RUFUS

Rufus is on the main line of the CPR west of Regina between Grand Coulee and Pense. It hasn't had an elevator for over twenty years, but the name lives on in the district.

Rufus mean "Red".

There are several versions as to how it got its name but the one that seems logical is that it was named for Red Fife Wheat which Charles Saunders crossed (after years of research) with Hard Red Calcutta to develop Marquis, a rust-resistant variety so important to the economy of Western Canada.

RUNCIMAN

Runciman is on a CPR line that runs north of Tisdale to Nipawin. It was named by railway officials for Walter Runciman (1870-1949), an English politician, who served his country well and was rewarded by being created a viscount in 1937.

Runciman is a small place which centers around a Pool elevator and Ed Fisher's general store and post office.

RUNNYMEDE

The first settler in the district was Mr. Moriarty who came in 1883. Some of those who followed were: Joseph

Schindler, A. MacDonald, Mr. Carmecut and John Olshewski, Mr. Johnson, the first postmaster, was instrumental in having the village named Runnymede for Runnymede, England.

There's a lot of history in this name. Runnymede is an English meadow on the south bank of the River Thames, about 36 miles southwest of London. On June 15, 1214, on this meadow, the barons of England forced King John to sign the Magna Carta, which limited the powers of the king.

RUSH LAKE

Rush Lake is on a CPR line that runs from Moose Jaw to Swift Current. The townsite took its name from a nearby lake that always produced a large crop of bull rushes.

There were large ranches in this district before the coming of the rails or the homesteaders. Prominent among them were the following: the Z, the 76 and the Turkey Track.

Homesteaders came in and made their mark but during the depression many of them left. In recent years a limited amount of irrigation has produced good hay crops, and dairying and beef feed lots are doing well.

RUTAN

Rutan is a grain point between Meacham and Young on a CNR line out of Prince Albert. Train service is supplied only as far as Meacham now. The line from there on is being taken up and used to supply potash mines in the area. Therefore, it will not be long until the elevator at Rutan is moved or dismantled. This is regrettable because Rutan commemorates an important name in Saskatchewan business and politics.

William Winfield Rutan was the son of Andrew Jackson Rutan and Anne Jane Rutan. His parents moved from Eastern Canada to the United States, settling in Minnesota in 1885. Here his father, a doctor by profession, served in the first legislative assembly of the state. William was born March 28, 1865, at Le Suer, Minnesota. He arrived at Melfort during the winter of 1901. He became one of Melfort's first merchants when, in partnership with C. B. Jameson, they started business on the site of the present Star

Store, corner of Main and Burrows. They operated a hardware business and tin shop and were the agents for McCormick farm implements.

From 1908 to 1911 Mr. Rutan served the Liberal interests as federal Member of Parliament for the Prince Albert constituency.

Mr. Rutan, while being interviewed by newspaper reporters in 1902, was asked why a man of his experience had selected this district as a home. He replied, "In all the one-crop countries I am familiar with, that is, states that largely depend on one crop, the loss of that crop brings business to a standstill. Therefore, in selecting a point for a permanent home and the establishment of a new business, a mixed farming district was essential. In my opinion this part of Saskatchewan was the best suited for that purpose, I had ever seen."

His success as a businessman in the district proved the wisdom of his choice. On his retirement Mr. Rutan moved into Prince Albert and later he moved to the west coast.

The above information was gathered prior to 1973. On Friday, January 14, 1977, the Saskatchewan Wheat Pool announced that the 33,000 bushel elevator at Rutan would be moved to Floral to replace the elevator there that was destroyed by fire in September of 1976.

The elevator will be moved, upgraded with new equipment and provided with a 94,000 bushel crib annex. The elevator is to be given a 4,500 bushel-per-hour trackside leg and a 4,500 bushel-per-hour overhead shipping scale.

To be included in the installation are an attached office, an attached farm supplies warehouse and a ten-horsepower dust collection unit. The work is expected to be completed by the end of June, 1977.

RUTHILDA

Ruthilda is named after Ruth and Hilda Goodwin, daughters of Mr. and Mrs. A. D. Goodwin, early settlers who lived a few miles north and east of the present village.

In the late 20s and the early 30s Ruthilda had three elevator agents who were all good ball players: Kitch Moore, Gordon Ferguson and Morrie Morrison. These plus the Edwards brothers, Archie and Earl, of Traynor formed the nucleus of an outstanding ball club that featured at times some of the following: Tom Bessie of Biggar, Slim Baker of Handel, Don Conklin of Rutland, and Bill Dunbar of Kinley.

They were good enough to hold their own against the Texas Colored Giants and the Kansas City Monarchs, first of many colored teams to tour Western Canada. The quality of ball was "Triple A" or better, and it might be said that colored teams who toured later were not in that class at all.

RUTLAND

The first settlers in Rutland were English and they named it for their home country in England. Bounded by Leicestershire on the west and north, Lincolnshire on the east and Northamptonshire on the south, Rutland is England's smallest county. Oakham is the largest market town and Uppingham is its educational center.

The three neighboring towns of Senlac, Evesham, and Rutland commemorate English battles: Senlac (or Hastings) 1066; Evesham, during the Baron's war, 1265; and Rutland, during the War of the Roses, 1470.

RYERSON

Ryerson is in the southeast corner of the province on a CNR branch line from Carlyle to Maryfield. It commemorates the name of Dr. Egerton Ryerson, a man whose life was a shining example for others to follow. From boyhood days he showed a strength of character and depth of feeling beyond his years. He was born in 1803 of Loyalist stock. He was soon a sturdy lad, and from his earliest years was an energetic worker on his father's farm.

At the close of the American War in 1815, when he was only twelve years old, he became deeply religious. He was a Methodist and quite early he decided to enter the Methodist ministry. He was instrumental in the building of Victoria College and became its first principal.

In 1844 he was appointed superintendent of public schools in Upper Canada, and is truly the father of the Ontario public school system.

In 1848 he established the Journal of Education and for twenty-eight years continued to edit it. When he retired to private life in 1876 he did not remain idle. He wrote the "History of the Loyalists of America and their Times" and this was followed by "Story of My Life." Dr. Ryerson died on February 19, 1882.

S

SAINT FRONT

Saint Front is an inland post office north of Quill Lake. The first settlers of the district arrived in 1911. They were Emile Gillard, Florien Mantes and Joseph Barset, all from France. They had to chop down trees and clear a way for tents in which they lived until they could build log houses for themselves and a log barn for their cattle. At first they got their mail at Quill Lake, a distance of twenty-five miles. This was a great inconvenience and in 1912 the settlers gathered and made application for a post office. Mr. Mantes submitted the name Saint Front, in honor of his birthplace in France. It was granted. The first postmaster was Mr. Florien Mantes. He brought the mail on horseback from Crevier, eight miles south of Saint Front. The Crevier post office does

not exist any more. The population of Saint Front is 109.

Saint Front was sent in the second century by the church in Rome to be the apostle of Perigord and Bordelais in France. His feast day is October 25.

ST. ALDWYN

St. Aldwyn is north of Swift Current on a CPR branch line that runs to Stewart Valley. It was likely named for St. Aldwyn, England, a little place in the Cotswold country of Gloucestershire and from which Lord Aldwyn takes his title.

ST. ALPHEGE

St. Alphege is a grain point on the main line of the CPR seven miles east of Wilkie. Being so close to the divisional point of Wilkie it never developed beyond a grain point.

There is a tragic story of how Saint Alphege became a saint. Saint Alphege (Aelfheah; Elphege), when a young man entered the monastery of Deerhurst in Gloucestershire, England. He rose in the church ranks to Bishop of Canterbury. During this period England was suffering severely from the ravages of the Danes. Joining forces in 1011 with the rebel Earl Edric, they marched into Kent and laid seige to Canterbury; the leading citizens urged Saint Alphege to seek safety in flight. This he absolutely refused to do. In the terrible massacre of men, women and children that followed, he was captured trying to protect his people. They put him in a dungeon and demanded three thousand gold crowns for his ransom. When it was not raised he was taken to Greenwich and barbarously put to death.

His body was recovered and buried in St. Paul's in London, but was transferred to Canterbury with great honor by the Danish King Canute in 1023.

That Saint Alphege did not actually die for the faith was pointed out by one of his successors, Lanfrance, to Saint Anselm, but the latter replied that in his opinion to die for justice was tantamount to martyrdom. In contemporary times his feast day is observed in the dioceses of Westminster, Clifton, Portsmouth and Southwark.

So another of our small places in Saskatchewan has a name with a lot of history behind it.

A visit to St. Alphege in the fall of 1976 revealed that the Searle elevator was gone. It had been closed in 1966 and in 1974 it was torn down and sold for lumber.

All that remains of the site along the railway are a few piles of scrap lumber overgrown with weeds and the oil heater that once warmed the elevator office.

ST. BENEDICT

In the early 1900s in the southern part of Illinois, near Wetaug not far from Cairo and St. Louis, a small struggling Benedictine Priory named Cluny, made an important decision. They decided that Cluny had no future in its present site; the land was productive enough, but the climate was unhealthy, due to the many marshes in the vicinity and malaria seized practically every member of the community. Many places were scouted.

In May, 1903, the Benedictines of Cluny Priory came to Canada and established at Muenster, a new monastery in the heart of Saskatchewan!

Their influence spread. St. Benedict is named in honor of this Order.

The story of the saint for whom St. Benedict was named is an interesting one:

"Saint Benedict (Joseph Labre) was born in France in 1748. He received a good education under the care of his pious parents and a priest of Amettes, the place of his birth. In his twelfth year he began to learn Latin under the care of his uncle, a priest, and for four years he applied himself to this and other studies with pleasure. However, as he grew older he changed and was in turn a Trappist, a Carthusian and a Cistercian. None of these ways of life satisfied him and he led the life of a pilgrim. Finally he was taken into a house of charity and died there on April 16, 1783."

ST. BOSWELLS

St. Boswells was the name Mr. Turnbull and Mr. Kennedy, two early settlers in the district, chose for the first post office which was opened in 1910. It honored their hometown of St. Boswells in Dumfrieshire, Scotland. The post office gave its name to the townsite.

ST. BRIEUX

In 1904 Father Le Floch brought a boatload of Breton farm families, on the St. Malo, to take up homesteads east of the French-speaking Duck Lake area. The name chosen for the settlement was St. Brieuc, after their home in Brittany, but through a mistake at Ottawa, the spelling used for the post office was St. Brieux.

ST. CYR LAKE

St. Cyr Lake is an inland post office 20 miles northeast of Meadow Lake on highway 55. It takes its name from St. Cyr lake a few miles to the north which drains into the Beaver river system. A stretch of steep rounded hills goes through the area and shows up again south of Meadow Lake at Cabana. These were formed by glacial till left by a receding ice age.

269

At one time St. Cyr Lake was an important trading center with two stores — one operated by J. J. Russell — a church, an excellent hall and a fine curling rink. The hall and curling rink were set in a spacious sports ground about a quarter of a mile north of the store. The church sat in between. Some of the earliest settlers were the Fillions: Charles, Victor and Carl.

Saint Cyr died in 304 A.D. The story goes as follows: To avoid persecution, Julitte left Iconium with her three-year-old son, Cyr, and sought refuge at Tarse. Discovered, she was tortured and as she was repeating with her son, "I am a Christian," the infuriated judge took the child and broke his head against the pavement. Both are patrons of Nevers and their particular feast day in France is June 16.

ST. DENIS

St. Denis is a hamlet twenty-five miles east of Saskatoon and just one mile north of number 5 highway. It has a Catholic church, a school, a teacher's residence, a general store, a post office, a confectionery and a garage. Several houses complete the hamlet.

There never has been a railway near the place, which is served by truck transports. The name St. Denis came from the church in 1908.

Saint Denis (third century A.D.) is the patron saint of France. Saint Gregory of Tours reported that Denis was sent to preach the gospel in Gaul during the reign of Emperor Decius (249-251). He became bishop of Paris, and died a martyr. His feast day is October 9.

ST. GREGOR

St. Gregor is the first stop east of Muenster. It was named for the parish of St. Gregory. This parish was founded by Prior Bruno Doerfler on January 17, 1907, a day on which the thermometer registered 36 degrees below zero. It was the only parish personally founded by Prior Bruno. The parish in turn, had been named for St. Gregory (590-604) the first of 16 popes of the Roman Catholic Church to take the name Gregory. Saint Gregory I, called The Great, was born of noble family. He became vitally interested in religious matters. When he came

into possession of his family's fortune, he devoted it to the founding of monasteries. Gregory was especially interested in missionary activity. St. Gregor is a result of that type of work.

ST. HIPPOLYTE

Four miles west of Vawn is the district of St. Hippolyte, a settlement of predominately French Roman Catholics who named their settlement for St. Hippolyte du Fort, France. They arrived there in the early 1900s. By 1906 they had a small church with Father Jullian as spiritual leader. The settlement grew around the church. Mr. Plante and Mr. Poulin opened stores and at its height St. Hippolyte had a school, a butcher shop, and a hall operated by Mr. Nadeau. Other early residents included the following: Pousseau, De La Salle and Rousseau.

In 1908 they built a fine big church with lumber shipped from Duck Lake via Delmas. When the CNR built up from North Battleford to St. Walburg in 1910 everyone was sure it would go through St. Hippolyte, but it didn't. It missed the settlement by two miles.

Mr. Poulin moved his store to Vawn but the others did not budge. For years they tried to get the railroad to build a spur line in to them. At election times their prospects looked bright. They were a solid Liberal block—the only three Conservative votes in the district were those of Fred and Stan Boyd and Ben Hillier—and with a sympathetic government at Regina it seemed only a matter of time until they would get what they wanted. However, the railway remained firm. The line was not built.

St. Hippolyte carried on a spirited rivalry with Vawn for years and it was not until the 60s that the church was moved to "town." Business and the school followed and there are only a few vacant houses and foundations left at St. Hippolyte.

This information came from Mr. Billy Boyd, long-time resident of the Vyner school district, who now makes his home in Meota.

St. Hippolyte was named for Saint Hippolytus. He was baptized by Saint Lawrence, and suffered martyrdom at Rome under the Emperor Valerian in 258 A.D. He was tormented in numerous ways, scourged, and then, tied by the feet to a team of horses, he was cruelly dragged over thistles and thorns until he died.

ST. ISIDORE de BELLEVUE

In 1902 Father P. E. Myre arrived and built a church close by and opened another post office a few miles south of Garonne. Father Myre found the view from Minnitinas Hill so beautiful he named it Bellevue which in French means "Beautiful View." He later added St. Isidore as the Patron Saint so that it would not get mixed up with other places called Bellevue.

In 1964 the municipality, as a centennial project, began to develop Minnitinas Hill into a winter resort area complete with ski jump and lodge.

Today, the hamlet has a church, post office, two stores, one cafe, a garage, a curling rink and a central school, accommodating 230 students. It is not on a railway or highway but is seven miles from Domremy which is on No. 2 highway between Saskatoon and Prince Albert.

Saint Isidore was born in Madrid, Spain, in the latter half of the twelfth century. For the greater part of his life he was employed as a laborer on a farm outside the city. Many marvellous happenings accompanied his life-long work in the fields and continued long after his holy death. He was favored with celestial visions and it is said the angels sometimes helped him in his work in the fields. Saint Isidore was canonized in 1662. In 1947, he was proclaimed the patron of the National Rural Life Conference in the United States.

ST. JULIEN

Draw a straight line from Rosthern to Wakaw. Halfway along it is country post office of St. Julien. Draw a line three miles northeast of Ypres in Belgium and you are at the village of St. Julien. It was there on the morning of the 24th of April, 1915, that the first gas attack was launched on the Western Front. As the greenish-yellow cloud rolled in across No Man's Land, Canadians, who held that section of the front, donned their makeshift respirators—cotton bandoliers wetted and tied over nose and mouth—and

fought on, St. Julien fell but farther back the British and Canadians' dogged defence at Ypres ended the "Race to the Sea."

The war of movement was over and parallel lines of trenches stretching in a zigzag pattern for 400 miles from the Swiss mountains to the North Sea became the habitation of millions of men for nearly four years.

St. Julien, Sask., is named for the battle that took place at the historic little village of St. Julien in Belgium.

A distinguished graduate of St. Julien is Mr. M. J. "Mike" Kindrachuk, currently employed by the Saskatoon Public Board of Education as superintendent of elementary schools.

ST. LAURENT

In 1870 many Metis moved from the Red River valley near Winnipeg, where they were being pressed by settlement, to the South Saskatchewan river valley south of Prince Albert. That was the start of "La Petite Ville" (The Little Town). They sent a messenger to the existing Roman Catholic mission at Ile-a-la-Crosse to request a priest. In 1871, Bishop Grandin of Saint Albert assigned Father Alexis Andre O.M.I. to serve the spiritual needs of the growing Metis community. Father Andre constructed his mission on the west bank of the Saskatchewan river five miles north of Batoche to serve Metis, Indians and white settlers. He named his tiny settlement St. Laurent, in remembrance of his brother who had been named after that particular saint.

The first collection of rude huts quickly grew and a modest log church was erected in 1874, a dormitory and residential school in 1875, and a convent in 1883. Although in the heart of the area in which the Saskatchewan Rebellion of 1885 took place, the St. Laurent mission was not harmed. Because of their opposition to his revolt, Louis Riel had the Fathers imprisoned. As peace returned to the Saskatchewan the mission re-opened. But because of rapid immigration, the subsequent displacement of the Metis and the growth of large urban centers like Prince Albert and Saskatoon, with their own dioceses, St. Laurent has never again enjoyed the pre-eminence as a spiritual center it had in its first decade.

Today it is the beautiful rustic site of Our Lady of Lourdes Shrine. It's a silent site for most of the year but during pilgrimage time it serves it purpose by bringing the people closer to God. Less than a mile north along the river bank is the great buffalo pit of Gabriel Dumont's time. It is silent the year 'round. Tall, tall trees have grown up from the bottom of the deep ravine and only the occasional call of a crow or the chattering of a squirrel breaks the silence.

This information comes from "Saint-Laurent de Grandin" by Le R. P. Jules le Chevallier O.M.I. loaned to us by Fred Anderson of Duck Lake.

Saint Laurent died in 258 AD. In 257, though St. Laurent was still a young man, Pope Sixtus II ordained and appointed him as one of the seven deacons of the Roman Church. Summoned by the Prefect of Rome to surrender the treasury of the church, he distributed it to the poor. As tradition has it, he was roasted alive on a red-hot gridiron over a slow fire. He was made a patron of shopmen, cooks, firemen; was invoked against burns, conflagrations, lumbago; and was implored over spoliated churches.

ST. LOUIS

Although it has a population of only 500 there's a lot of history wrapped up in the settlement of St. Louis, 20 miles south of Prince Albert where the CNR bridge, built in 1914, crosses the South Saskatchewan. This site is close to the intersection of two early trails. One came from Fort a la Corne, crossed this coulee, and ran to Batoche where it joined the old hunting trail which followed the right branch of the South Saskatchewan to the Elbow. This route was first used by the founders of Fort a la Corne in 1753. After the Hudson's Bay Company built near the same site in 1850 the route carried all the overland traffic between the Metis settlement on the South Branch and this point. The other trail was a branch of the main "Saskatchewan" trail which traversed the plains between Fort Garry and Edmonton. It left the main trail near Humboldt and ran north to Prince Albert. Between 1887 and 1898 it crossed the river at St. Louis right where the railway bridge now stands, at what was known as McKenzie's

Crossing. Norman McKenzie, a former captain, ran the ferry.

The first group of settlers came from St. Boniface, Manitoba, in 1882 and settled less than two miles downstream where they built a mission, a school and a sawmill. The following were in the party: Boucher, Boyer, Bremner, Gingras, Caron, Trottier, Grugon, Richard, Chatlain, Joubert, Thoisnier and Trouillard.

Jean Baptiste Boucher was the leader and it became known as Boucher's Settlement. The first post office was named Boucher. When the railway came through from Watrous via Young to Prince Albert in 1914 the settlement moved upriver two miles to its present site. Father Le Eugene Le Coq was instrumental in having the place named in honour of the patron saint of the parish St. Louis. Saint Louis was an early king of France, who fought in the crusades and was made a saint for his efforts.

St. Louis, Missouri, is also named for him and a statue of him is in Forest Park there entitled "Saint Louis the Crusader."

ST. MARGUERITE

St. Marguerite was a Roman Catholic church built in 1915, just south of the town of Paradise Hill on the N.E. of 18-53-22 W3 on ten acres of land. For years it was the center of a thriving community. However, when the railway came through, Paradise Hill was the town. The church was moved in and all that remains today is an overgrown cemetery.

One of the stones that remain reads: Ici Repose Le Corps de Clarisse E. Royer. Espouse, de Albert Prince Née le 15 Août 1859. Dècédée le 18 Juillet 1915.

One other stone, that of Madame N. Blanger shows that the cemetery was used as late as 1928. However, the majority of the people buried in the cemetery have been exhumed and moved into the cemetery at Paradise Hill.

ST. MEINRAD

St. Meinrad was an inland post office situated on Section 15-41-26-W2. It was named for the local parish priest, Father Meinrad, who had the Leofeld Parish.

Mail was hauled out from Dana. At first there was only the post office and a small store. In 1908, the Roman Catholic Church of St. Leo was built. Then a separate school was added and the first teacher was John Medernack.

In 1912 the railway came through and Cudworth, five miles away, became the trading centre. St. Meinrad post office closed soon after, the church remained until the 1960's when it, too, closed.

ST. VICTOR

St. Victor, incorporated as a village on July 1, 1964, is south of Montague Lake fifteen miles southeast of Assiniboine. The first post office was opened under the name of Mullrany on September 1, 1911, and the first postmaster was Mr. M. J. Mulligan.

In April of 1914 Father Victor Rahard was installed as the first parish priest. He served until 1918. In 1914 the name of the post office was changed to St. Victor. This was done to honour Father Victor Rahard who had been named after Saint Victor. This saint was pope from 189 to 199, the first of three popes of the Roman Catholic Church by that name.

It is interesting to note, too, that in 1914, the year the name of the village was changed to St. Victor, all boys born were named Victor and one baby girl was given the name Victorine.

St. Victor is the home office of the Family Life Assurance Company, which was incorporated by a special act of the Parliament of Canada on December 21, 1963. In a period of declining numbers of small villages, St. Victor has held its own and its population is just over the one hundred mark.

An article in the Monday, November 15, 1976 issue of the *Star-Phoenix* of Saskatoon read *"Saskatchewan Town for Sale* Family Life Assurance Ltd. is moving out of this small community of about 110 and, as a result, most of St. Victor is up for sale.

St. Victor, about 170 miles southwest of Regina, is a company town. There are no grain elevators and no railway or bus service. The only store is company-owned and open only when the Family Life staff is off work.

For sale are eight company-owned houses, eight privately-owned houses, the store building and an 8,400 square-foot office building.

Mike Blondeau, who has been vice-president and general manager of the firm for the last one and one-half years, said the shareholders of the company have decided to enlarge the company and move to a place where the present staff of 35 can be enlarged to 200.

Where they will go is anybody's guess. Meanwhile, does anyone want to buy a town?"

ST. WALBURG

The railway up from North Battleford reached St. Walburg in 1921 and stopped. It had been planned to have it run further north and then turn west to join up with a line in Alberta. The old grade is still visible part way to Loon Lake.

Three years before the steel reached St. Walburg, Mr. and Mrs. R. Musch homesteaded in the district three miles southeast of the present townsite. They had a small store in their home. When the railway came in they moved into the town and opened the first store there.

The CNR gave the people the choice of a name for their district and St. Walburg was named for an English nun who died in 779. She was made a saint for her untiring work with the German people. However, many local residents contend that there was a definite reason for picking this particular sant—and it was because they wanted to honor Mrs. Walburga Musch. From 1909 to 1912 she had established a reputation as an untiring community and church worker in the district. She still resides in St. Walburg. It is significant that the story did not come from her but from her legion of friends, one of whom is Mrs. Walter Podiluk of 14 McAskill Crescent, Saskatoon, who lived and worked in St. Walburg for years.

SAGEHILL

Sagehill is a post office situated at the Canadian Forces Base, Dana, located in the heart of the prairie wheat belt approximately fifty miles east of Saskatoon and sixty-six miles south of Prince Albert. The site, geographically named "Sagehill", was constructed in 1962 atop the largest hill in the area, the domed towers survey the endless acres of rich farmland and grain elevators associated with Saskatchewan.

C.F.B. Dana is a component of NORAD, the organization responsible for aerospace surveillance and air defence of North America, and the 24th NORAD Region at Great Falls, Montana, exercises operational control of the unit. Overall Command is exercised by Air Command Headquarters at Winnipeg, with operational matters being reported through Air Defence Group HQ at North Bay, Ontario.

SALTBURN

Saltburn is the second last stop on a CNR branch line running from Eston to White Bear. The early post office was situated at 21-23-16-W3 and has since been closed. The first postmaster was Mr. M. Lindsay and he named it for his home at Saltburn by the Sea, England. When the railway came through they took the name from the post office.

SALTCOATS

Originally Saltcoats was named Stirling. It received this name from the Allan Brothers of Stirling, Scotland. They were the founders of the Allan Steamship Lines and organizers of immigration parties coming from Stirling, Scotland to Canada. The district was first settled in 1888.

Later it was found there were two Stirlings in Canada. The other one was in Ontario. This led to a little mix-up in mail and through the influence of the Allan Brothers the name Stirling was changed to Saltcoats which was the name of a large seaside center in Scotland not far from their home of Stirling.

SALTER

Salter is the third grain point north on a CNR line that runs from Oban Junction to Battleford. The line was built by the GTR in 1912. Salter has two Pool elevators and the agent, Mike Monchuk, runs them both as well as caring for the one at Lett, first grain point to the south.

First settlers into the district included: John Munroe, John Hume, Jock Lane, Alec Kunoff, Jock McLeod, Roy Cunningham and Dave Paisley.

Mr. Archie Affleck, reeve of the municipality, (1971), remembers reading in an early Waghorn's Guide of the 1920s that Lett and Salter were GTR officials.

SALT LAKE

Salt Lake, an inland post office, 13 miles northeast of Denzil and 24 miles southwest of Unity was closed on July 30, 1966. It took its name from Salt lake nearby. In the summer much of this little lake would dry up and such a quantity of pure salt lay on the ground that in the early 20s a company built a small factory and began to gather it commercially. However, being 12 miles from the nearest railroad made it an unprofitable venture and it closed up in 1923.

SALVADOR

The village of Salvador had its beginning on September 5, 1910. It is midway between Kerrobert and Macklin on a CPR line out of Moose Jaw. In April of 1911, the first train pulled in. Mr. Bob Winters was the agent. The station had been named Salvador in honour of an early Spanish explorer, who is said to have discovered this continent. This may be true in that there is a country of Salvador in Central America.

By 1913 three elevators were up and in operation: the McLaughlin, the Co-operative and the Federal. Later, the Alberta Pacific was built. Situated in one of the best grain growing districts of Saskatchewan, it was not long before these elevators were handling over a million bushels of grain a year. Some other Salvador firsts were: general store—Fletcher and Clarke; post office—Mr. J. Michon; lumberyard and hardware—Ross and Kippen of Unity; hotel (40-room)—Norman Fletcher; poolroom and barbershop—Mr. A. Taylor; livery barn—Mr. U. A. DeBoice. The first school was built in 1911 and the first teacher was Miss A. M. MacDonald.

Salvador was a sports-minded town. For years its annual sports day was one of the best for miles around. They were one of the first small centers in northern Saskatchewan to sponsor an exhibition ball game with the touring "House of David," a bewhiskered baseball team from the States, that one year featured Grover Cleveland "Pete" Alexander, ex-Big League pitcher. Another year they had "Babe" Didrikson Zaharias (1914-1956) pitch the first three innings for them. She was tremendous athlete and with the club she had behind her very few prairie ball players got to first base.

SANCTUARY

Sanctuary is on a rail line south of Wartime between Mondou and Tuberose. The rail end is at Matador. Settlers came into the area long before the railway. Some of the earliest were: the Smiths, Bassets, Atkinsons and the Jones brothers.

The steel was laid in 1922-23. A nearby quarter secion of land and lake had been set aside as a bird sanctuary by the residents and that's how the town of Sanctuary got its name.

The town has faded during recent years due to better roads, faster cars and the threat of railway abandonment. However, many are still hanging on. The main center of business is the Pioneer Co-op store.

SANDGREN

In building a railway grade sections were let out to earth moving contractors. Sandgren, fifteen miles south of Kindersley, owes its name to Mr. Sandgren, the contractor who built the railway grade.

In 1969 it consisted of one Pool elevator and one Pool agent's house. Population was 2, Mr. and Mrs. J. B. Houston.

SANDWITH

Sandwith is on a CNR line between North Battleford and Medstead. The early settlers in the district called it Hyde Park in memory of Hyde Park Square in London, England. The local school is still named Hyde Park. When it came time to name the post office the name Sandwith was sent in by Martin Dodd to honor a very kind neighbor, Jack Sandwith. This name was accepted.

SANDY BAY

From part of a long and interesting letter by Andrew McKinley of Sandy Bay:

"The small lake we are on here is an inlet from the Churchill river. Our village runs parallel with the lake shore for about a mile. As to how we got our name, I smile every time I think of it, as I don't think I ever saw such a sea of mud as this place can be when it rains. It's real sticky gumbo! However, at the far end of the village, by the Churchill river, there is a bay with nice sand. That's where we got our name.

Now right across a short stretch of the lake to the southwest there is Island Falls. It is an island on the Churchill river in the midst of a fall. Hence, its name Island Falls. There, on the island is the Churchill River Power Company which supplies electric power to Flin Flon and the Hudson Bay Mining and Smelting Company. We get our power from there, too."

SANDY LAKE

Sandy Lake settlement is on the northwest corner of Gwillim lake in the northern part of Saskatchewan. It was so named because of the lovely sandy bottom of Gwillim lake. The Gwillim river enters this lake at the north end and continues out through the south end to drain into the Churchill river system.

SANFORD DENE

In 1912 the inland post office (now closed) of Sanford Dene was established near the present town of Hazlet. One of the earliest pioneers in the district was A. J. Schmidt, who came from the United States.

SASKATCHEWAN LANDING

The Old Swift Current-Battleford Trail crossed the South Saskatchewan river at Saskatchewan Landing about 30 miles northwest of Swift Current. There is a creamish-yellow field stone and cement two-storey building on the south bank that still marks the spot. Besides it there is a historic marker which reads:

GOODWIN HOUSE

"Built about 1900 of stones gathered from the surrounding hills this house was the residence of the Frank Goodwin family who settled here in 1898. It served as a stopping place in the period 1904-1914, and housed the Royal North West Mounted Police detachment, 1905-1914."

A ferry was used to cross the river until a bridge started in 1949 was completed in May of 1951. After an ice jam carried away the main spans in the spring of 1952, reconstruction was completed before the spring break-up in 1953. Provision was made in the original design for conversion to a higher-level bridge, and this work was carried out in 1965-66.

In the early days John K. Austring (now a prosperous blueberry farmer of Pitt Meadows, British Columbia) worked as a young man on the Ed Tulley ranch 12 miles east of the Landing. He remembers driving into Goodwin House for mail, groceries and the "makings." He also recalls hiring out to the manager of the Matador Ranch, when every spring they used to ship 2000 head of two-year-old steers from Texas to Waldeck and then drive them across the river to pasture on the open range. He remembers being one of two men in a row boat on each side of the herd as the steers were forced to swim the spring flood. He also remembers the inevitable loss of steers caused by the "milling" of the herd as the first animals were forced into the water. Each year, in the fall, the Matador took 2000 steers back over the river but water was so low by then that there were no problems and horses rode the "point." He remembers the winter of '06-'07 when snow lay so deep on the level that cattle could not paw down to the grass and they were forced back, by starvation to the coulees along the river bank where they ate the brush and willows right down to the roots. Thousands died.

His brother, Ole, still farms in the district and gets his mail at Stewart Valley.

SASKATOON

John N. Lake, leader of the Temperance Colony which established Saskatoon, gave it its name. Lake's diary of Saturday, August 19, 1882 reads: "Camped at 2 p.m. Minnetonka is the name of our camping place, the finest we have every had. Sect. 29, Twp. 36, R. 5." The following day, a Sunday, Lake conducted Saskatoon's first religious service: "Preached at 11 a.m. to 10 persons, 4 of whom came 3 miles on foot. Text: Heb. 11: 12-13th." The service was held on the top of a high bank that now marks the Nutana section of the city and it was at this service that Mr. Lake christened the new settlement, Saskatoon.

Where did he get the name? The story is told that one of the Indian chain bearers in the survey party brought Mr.

Lake a handful of native berries that grew in abundance along the river bank. The bearer called them saskatoons. Mr. Lake chose this as the name of the settlement he was founding.

SAXBY

Saxby is named after a small hamlet in the Eastern Township of Quebec, Saxby's Corners. At this place there was a small store operated by a man named William Saxby, who had originally come from England. The name Saxby was among a number submitted to the Department at Ottawa in 1907 for the Saskatchewan post office by Mr. Ward K. Savage and it was duly authorized. Mr. Savage was postmaster for many years.

SCENTGRASS

Scentgrass is on a CNR line north of North Battleford on the way to Medstead. It is named for the lake of the same name in the district. The lake in turn received its name from a sweet vernal grass found in the vicinity which has a special scent when cut for hay and which is regarded as attractive to stock although not necessarily of high feeding value. Just as all the rabbits in Saskatchewan are not at Rabbit lake so all the sweet or scentgrass is not at Scentgrass. Of areas in the northern United States within the "Great Plains" each has its own Sweetgrass or Scentgrass place name, showing the plant to be widespread on the plains.

SCEPTRE

Sceptre is on the CPR Empress line in southwestern Saskatchewan. The railway named the townsite and whereas a sceptre is a rod or staff carried by a ruler it has no other significance to the people of the district.

In 1909 the first settlers began arriving by way of Swift Current, Maple Creek and Kindersley. By 1911 some of the best land had been taken up. Most of the settlers arrived by oxen-drawn wagons.

In 1911 Mr. Ivy and Mr. Blezard opened the first post office and store. Mr. A. Shields built the first house. The Alberta Pacific built the first elevator with Mr. B. Steele as agent. The first garage was run by J. Shields and D. Stair. A curling rink and restaurant were added to the town. In 1912 Green and Baldridge built the first hotel. It had a dining room with beautiful murals on the walls. All this was complemented by a spacious bar.

Football and baseball were the favorite summer sports and Sceptre fielded some very good teams as late as the thirties.

SCHLORENDARP

Schlorendarp is a small Mennonite village of five families eight miles northwest of Osler. It is a quaint name that can be translated as Slipper Village. Another translation would come out as quiet or peaceful village.

SCHOENFELD

Schoenfeld is a Mennonite village 4 miles southeast of Wymark. In English Schoenfeld means Beautiful Field. Abe Friesen's store is closed, the children are bussed to Swift Current. First families who came in about 1904 included the following: Epp, Friesen, Froese, Ens and Letkeman.

SCHOENWEISE

Schoenweise is a Mennonite village in the Osler-Hague area northeast of Saskatoon. Schoenweise is a German word which translates into English as Beautiful Meadow.

SCLANDERS

Sclanders is a grain shipping point between Viscount and Plunkett on the main line of the CPR east of Saskatoon. It was named for F. MacLure Sclanders who arrived in Saskatoon in 1908 and became commissioner of the Board of Trade. Mr. Sclanders was president of the St. Andrew's Society in addition to being active in many other local organizations. He is best remembered for his work with the Saskatoon Home Reunion Association whose objective was to bring out to homesteaders in Canada, the families, or parts of families, that had of necessity been left behind in the "old land."

SCOTSGUARD

Scotsguard is 18 miles northeast of Shaunavon. It was first called Notukeu but when the railroad came in 1913 they had to change it because another town had that name. The name chosen was Scotsguard and this was suggested by Ed Smith, the first station agent, who had been a Scots Guard in his youth. Scotsguard was a booming little town in the early days and by 1925 had a population of 350. However, with centralization it has dwindled to less than sixty.

SCOTT

With the advent of the railway in 1908, Scott became an enterprising town. Named in honor of the treasurer of the Grand Trunk Pacific Railway, Frank Scott, of Montreal, it was incorporated as a village in 1909 and as a town in 1910. On the main line of the Transcontinental, it attracted an influx of settlers through the Luse Land Development Company, which ran excursions from St. Paul, Minnesota, to Scott, bringing in 100 prospective buyers at a time, and taking them around the country in six two cylinder Reo cars, democrats and buggies.

SCOUT LAKE

Scout Lake is about 20 miles south of Assiniboia. In the early days this was good ranching country with a lot of open range. The first name in the district was Scout Hill a few miles west of the present townsite. This high hill was so named by men who used it for scouting stock, particularly bands of wild horses.

Eventually a little lake east of the hill came to be called Scout lake. The first post office in the district was established in 1910 on Mr. Fenwick's farm very close to the hill. Prior to this mail was received at Elm Springs 15 miles to the west. When the CPR built south from Assiniboia in 1925 it passed close to the east side of Scout lake which gave its name to the new townsite. The present population is 55.

SCRIP

Many soldiers from Canada took part in the Boer War (1899-1902). At its conclusion many received "scrip land" in western Canada in recognition of their services. One of these was Ben Dixon who settled north of Little Quill lake. He acquired the post office in the district and named it in honor of the type of land grant he had.

The correct terminology was "scrip" but "script" was the popular mispronunciation of the term but the post office was called Scrip. The closest railroad to Scrip is at Clair, 14 miles to the south.

SECRETAN
Secretan is on the main line of the CPR forty-two miles west of Moose Jaw. This line was built in the 1880s well ahead of the settlers, who came in the 1890s. Two of the first to arrive were Mr. W. P. Wheeler and Mr. Jack Byers.

The first merchant and postmaster was Mr. Jenkins. In 1914 Mr. and Mrs. Burnside built a new store and post office which is still in use.

For miles before it reaches the grain point the grade is not steep but it climbs steadily. Mr. John H. Secretan, the civil engineer who laid out the grade said, "Every locomotive engineer who works this line will curse such a grade and so they may as well curse me." That is why he was instrumental in having the townsite named for himself.

This information comes from Mr. Ken W. Clark of Winnipeg.

SEDLEY
Sedley is on a CPR line that, from a mile southeast of Regina, runs diagonally across the sections to Stoughton, 88 miles away, without a bend. It was named by Dr. R. J. Blanchard in 1906 to honor his brother, Sedley Blanchard, a Winnipeg lawyer who died of typhoid on March 7, 1886. Dr. Blanchard had been a prime mover in organizing the Winnipeg General Hospital.

SELKIRK
Selkirk was an early post office southeast of Paradise Hill. Charles Morgan operated a small store in conjunction with it, but the store and post office have long since closed.

The name Selkirk is a historic one and honors the Earl of Selkirk who settled 800 immigrants from the highlands of Scotland in Prince Edward Island in 1803 and about a hundred in 1811 in Red River Valley (now Manitoba and Minnesota).

SEMANS
This is another in the alphabetical sequence of names that ranged all the way from Winnipeg to Edmonton on the old GTP. Semans is between Tate and Raymore. It was the maiden name of the

bride of one of the railway officials. It has no significance to the town.

Two oldtimers, Mrs. McCallum and Mrs. A. J. Shetler, sent in this information. Semans has a population of 385 and is far enough away from big centers that it is holding its own.

SENATE
Senate is in the extreme southwest corner of the province. Senate was free land—no one filed on the site, so in 1913 the CPR started the townsite, sold lots and had the land surveyed and registered by January 20, 1914.

The CPR selected the name, Senate, and also named the streets and avenues of the town after senators of the day: Roy, Prince, Lougheed, Ross, etc.

George Shepherd, curator of the Western Development Museum in Saskatoon, and his mother and father, were among the first settlers to enter the district. They arrived in May of 1913.

SENATOR
Halfway between Davis and Fenton on the railroad southeast of Prince Albert that goes through Lanigan and on to Regina there used to be the flag station of Senator. This was put in a few years after the railroad was built, and was due to the efforts of the early settlers of the district and the influence of Senator T. O. Davis. It was named for him. It consisted of a small flag station, stockyards and loading platform. Everything is gone—absolutely everything—and in 1968 even the land, the railway right-of-way, was put up for bid.

Many men and their families used this station—Hugh Ross, Earl Yont, Jack Baird, Bert Leask, Bert Brewster, Tom Agnew, Ernie Isbister, Forbes Stevens, Bert Cox, Dick Setexy and Guy Mack, to name just a few. This is an amazing district in one respect, ninety per cent of the original homesteaders are either on their farms or those farms are being worked by their descendants. As Mrs. Ross said, "There has been very little change in the people of this district."

Yes, they have good gridroads now, better machinery, better houses and better cars but there has been no great change in the community or the spirit of the people. When fire destroyed a home in the district some time ago the neighbors pitched in and radio station CKBI in Prince Albert helped, too; soon they had to send the news over the air, "Please don't bring any more money, or goods, we have enough." That's hard to beat for a true story and it answers the question that so often comes into older people's minds, "Has the spirit of compassion and simple genuine hospitality, so evident in the early days, gone with these hurry, hurry times?" No, that spirit hasn't disappeared; people may not have the same opportunities they once had to display it, but when it's needed it's still there.

SENLAC
Senlac is on the CPR main line west of Unity. The first settlers arrived in the district in 1905 and among them were the following families: Albert Norton, Bill Ried, and Frank Newman. When the steel arrived in 1909 the settlers, many of them English, suggested the name of Senlac to remind them of their homeland. It was accepted. Senlac Hill is to a Briton what Queenston Heights is to a Canadian. William of Normandy landed at Pevensey, west of Hastings, September 29, 1066. Fifteen days later, on October 14, he defeated and killed King Harold II of England on Sussex Downs at Senlac Hill.

SERATH
Serath is eighteen miles straight north of Southey on West Loon Creek. It was an inland post office of the early days and mail was hauled either from Southey to the south or Raymore about the same distance to the north.

However, it is still the center of a Wheat Pool committee, even though there are no longer any Pool facilities there.

The name is a rare one and despite considerable digging no clues as to the significance of the name, Serath have been uncovered.

SERGENT
Sergent is on a CPR line between Chitek Lake and Meadow Lake. It was named for Leon Sergent, the first storekeeper in Meadow Lake. He is now retired and lives there.

SERVICE
Service is the first grain point northeast of Carlyle on a CNR branch line to Maryfield. It is named in honour of Robert Service, who has achieved considerable repute from his Canadian verse dealing chiefly with life in the Yukon during the stirring days of the Gold Rush.

He was first in the employ of the Canadian Bank of Commerce at Victoria, BC, and then served at Vancouver and Kamloops. He was afterwards moved to Whitehorse in the Yukon Territory and it was while there that he commenced to produce his verses of the northland, which achieved an immediate popularity. He published several volumes of verse and also did some journalistic work. His chief prose "The Trail of 98," did not meet with the same response accorded to his verses.

During the First World War he drove an ambulance for two years. It is apparent that Service had been a close student of the works of Rudyard Kipling.

SEWARD
Louie Lloyd writes from his home in Abbotsford, BC, to tell how Webb got its name. Back at the time the CPR was being built across the Prairies there was an influential railway official working on the line whose name was Beverley Seward Webb. Whether they were named in his honour or whether he had them named for himself we do not know, but the first three stops west of Swift Current are Beverley, Seward and Webb.

SHACKLETON
On the CPR's "Empress" line with connections into Swift Current, the village of Shackleton, population 125, probably is carrying around more history than centers 10 and 20 times its size. A directory of its streets would see listed such famed Arctic and Antarctic explorers as Perry, Scott, Amundsen, Oates, Franklin, and Nassen. These men were very much in the news about the time the village was organized, and the history-making expeditions they headed were commemorated in the naming of the community's streets.

Sir Ernest Henry Shackleton (1874-1922), for whom the village is named, was a junior officer on an Antarctic expedition with Robert F. Scott, in 1901. In 1907 he sailed in command of the Nimrod which reached a point 97 miles from the South Pole and which sent parties to the summit of Mt. Erebus and to the South Magnetic Pole. On another trip in 1914 his ship the Endurance was crushed in the ice and he made a trip of 800 miles with five companions to the north coast of South Georgia to get help. He died at South Georgia while on a third expedition. He is the author of two books, "Heart of Antarctic" and "South", which give accounts of his expeditions.

SHAMROCK

How the name Shamrock was arrived at has several connotations, all of which may have had some bearings on the final selection. It is recalled by some that one of the preliminary meetings was held in Erinvale School, on the 17th of March, and during the course of the meeting one of those present chose to replenish his chew of tobacco, and observed the shamrock-like emblem on the plug; . . . Shamrock apparently was the natural derivative of all those factors. It was applied to the rural municipality established in 1912 and to the village incorporated in 1924.

SHAND

Shand is the first grain point southeast of Estevan on a CPR line that runs to North Portal and on into the U.S.A. It was named after P. D. Shand, one time chief clerk to the superintendent at Moose Jaw.

SHAND CREEK

Shand Creek was an inland post office northwest of Somme. It opened in 1927 with J. F. McLean as postmaster. The office was named Shand Creek, a tributary of Deer River which empties into Red Deer Lake in Manitoba. The creek had been named for Mr. J. Shand who came to the area in 1925 to become one of the original settlers.

Arthur Rowan (1928-47) followed Mr. McLean as postmaster and he, in turn, was followed by J. T. Rowan who operated the post office until it closed out in 1951. People from Shand Creek now get their mail at Somme.

SHAUNAVON

Shaunavon is a town on the CPR at a junction of highways 13 and 37, 70 miles southwest of Swift Current. It was incorporated as a village in 1913 and as a town in 1914.

Shaunavon serves a prosperous mixed-farming area, and is the seat of a judicial district. It has a hospital, a rural municipal office, and a weekly newspaper, Standard.

Shaunavon combines the names of two great figures of the CPR, Shaughnessy and Van Horne.

The above story came direct from the Provincial Archives in Regina. The story below comes from Mrs. Robin Faber of Shaunavon, dated July 9, 1972. It reads in part: "I have done a thorough research on this name for the Historical Folklore Society. . . . Shaunavon was not named after Shaughnessy and Van Horne . . . Mr. F. G. Horsey, a pioneer businessman of this town, was the CPR townsite representative in 1913 and he assured me that he was *personally* in the Calgary office when a wire came through from Lord Shaughnessy declining the honor of having the town named after him, but suggested they name it Shaunavon after an area about his home in the old country, which they did. . . . Commonly and carelessly pronounced Shaun a vun in this day and age . . . its proper pronunciation is Shaun-avon. This information confirms the origin which I grew up knowing and always resenting the "Van" Horne theory. If the latter was correct why is the spelling 'von'?" The lady has a valid point.

SHEHO

Sam Wunder was the first into the area. In 1890 he came to the Canadian plains from Aberdeen, North Dakota. The original Wunder homestead was located six miles west of the present townsite.

Today Mr. Wunder's son, Harry, who came to the homestead with his parents, still resides on the family farm, living in the original dwelling built by his father. The pioneers who followed Sam Wunder came as far as Yorkton by train and then journeyed with horses the remaining 58 miles west to the virgin homesteading country.

The community's first store was built

by a Yorkton business man, Levi Beck. Unlike a large number of Saskatchewan centers, Sheho does not owe its name to the expediency of naming a railway station. The tiny settlement had been known as Sheho before the railway came and the general district was referred to as Sheho, the Indian word for prairie chicken, long before the first settlers themselves arrived.

SHELL LAKE
Shell Lake is fifty miles west of Prince Albert on Highway 3. The area was surveyed in 1910. The first settlers, Mr. and Mrs. Robert Schwartz and their sons, Richard and Alfred, came in 1911. Richard still lives in Shell Lake.

In 1912 Mr. John J. Morrow drove through the district looking for a homestead. He writes that the years 1911 to 1914 saw an influx of settlers, most of whom were single. In 1913 the R.M. of Shell Lake was formed taking its name from the lake about twelve miles from the present townsite. The Shell Lake school district was formed the same year.

Many of the homesteaders enlisted during 1914-18 and when they returned they took up farming under the Soldier's Settlement Board. The railroad came through in 1927 and the townsite was established at a point about two miles east of what had previously been the center of the district. This required quite a change in the pattern of road development. Prior to the railroad, quite a little hamlet had developed near the school and post office. A community hall had been built, a municipal office and a site for the annual agricultural fair was set aside. All these things had to be moved to the new townsite.

A great tragedy occurred in the Shell Lake district when a man, who had just been released from the mental hospital, murdered the Peterson family. The greatest achievement for the town would be the development of Memorial Lake Regional Park.

Mr. Morrow writes "Our village, though not rapidly expanding, is a viable community with a very attractive regional park, part of which is within the village limits. We have a splendid ice arena, a new curling rink, a ten room school with a fine gymnasium, several churches, and a very good hotel plus other amenities common to small western towns."

SHELLBROOK
It was in the fall of 1909 that Art Lake, a local farmer, was forced to move sufficient stooks of wheat to allow room for the excavations and start of construction of two hotels, thus marking the start of Shellbrook. However, it wasn't until 1910 that things started booming. It was in that year that the CNR reached the district linking it with Prince Albert to the east. With the new railroad line in operation, settlers flocked into the district. By 1912 the population had climbed to 300 and the village had been named for the Shell brook which flows into the Shell river two miles to the north.

SHIPMAN
Shipman is between Foxford and Smeaton on a CPR line that runs from Prince Albert to Nipawin. It was named for Dr. Shipman of Montreal who had a financial interest in the line.

SILTON
Silton is near the south end of Last Mountain lake. When the CPR came through in 1911 the townsite took the name Silton from a rural post office kept by Mrs. C. Benjafield in her farm home, and which was named for the old Benjafield family home in England. The post office was then moved into C. C. Whitehead's store and the first mail was given out in the new town on September 15, 1911.

In 1935 when times were very hard, Silton and district decided they needed a curling rink. Money was scarce so they planned to make the structure of bales of hay. A baler was borrowed and farmers got busy with mowers and in three days 600 bales were ready. There were many willing hands and the rink was soon built. An old box car was borrowed from the CPR and put at one end of the rink where it served as gallery and lunch room. The rink was wired and the lighting was good. There were two sheets of ice. Enthusiasm ran high and everybody curled and had a marvelous time. But alas, the life of the rink was short. In the spring of 1937 a citizen doing a clean-up job around the rink had the misfortune of the fire getting away from him and the rink went up in smoke, but the curling rocks were saved. Plans were then made for a rink made of lumber and in due time it was constructed.

SILVER GROVE

These are excerpts from a five-page letter received from Mrs. A. Vockeroth, Thornhill, Ontario.

"In 1903 when Saskatchewan was still a Territory my parents, Mr. and Mrs. Ernest Müller, emigrated from Germany to what became the Silver Grove community. I was five years old at the time. Our nearest post office was Wingard across the North Saskatchewan almost 20 miles away.

As our district filled up their need for a post office grew and in 1905 permission was granted and the Silver Grove post office opened in the home of Mr. and Mrs. George McKay. Later it was operated by Mr. and Mrs. Conrad Riffer.

The name Silver Grove was chosen at a public meeting. It commemorates the decorative silver-leafed shrub commonly known as silver willow.

In 1906 a rural school was built and named Silver Grove.

Post office and school have been closed for years but the name Silver Grove lives on in the community."

SILVER PARK

Silver Park is south of Melfort on a CPR line to Watson. Wilbert MacAlister was the first man into the district and he named it Silver Park for the white poplars that grew in abundance. When the sun struck them just right they sparkled like silver.

Mr. MacAlister came in from Prince Albert, 75 miles to the northeast, in 1903 and lived in a dugout for the first few years. His original homestead was less than two miles from the site of the present hamlet. The dugout he lived in was "filled in" in 1968.

Dave, a brother of Wilbert, had the first post office in his house. That was in 1906. The grade for the railroad came through in 1923 and the first trains ran in 1924.

SILVER SPRAY SUMMER RESORT

Silver Spray Summer Resort was established on the east shore of Manitou Lake four miles south of Neilburg by Mr. and Mrs. Add Robinson and their son, Lyle, in the middle thirties.

At its height, ball tournaments were held on the school grounds of East Manitou Rural School nearby and they were followed by a dance at night in the Silver Spray Pavilion, one of the best dance halls for miles around.

As the resort grew, many residents from Neilburg built cottages along the lake front: Fred Magdalinski, Jack Dell and Pete Prediger. Pete was installed in the Saskatchewan Sports Hall of Fame in 1975 for his contribution to the community in baseball and hockey.

The name Silver Spray commemorates two things. Silver, for the silver sheen on the wolf willow and spray for the storms that swept the lake.

Today, there is little left of Silver Spray. With the coming of improved roads, cars and prosperity, Neilburg residents have headed north to the fishing lakes that dot our province like Turtle, Lac des Iles and LaRonge.

SILVER STREAM

Silver Stream is to the east of Leacross and was named by an early settler as a result of his first sight of the Leather river at sunrise.

SIMMIE

Simmie is the end of a branch line of the CPR that runs south from Swift Current. With the exception of a few early ranches no one came into this district until 1906. Bill Ballentine, Joe, Bud and Albert DeLong filed on the first homesteads. In 1908, Angus McCarty, Jack Davidson, Albert and Finley Hoy, P. Anderson, D. Bannerman, G. H. Morstad and O. Larkin arrived. This was the beginning of a great influx of settlers and it continued until 1916.

Those coming to homestead usually left the main line of the CPR at Swift Current or Gull Lake and made the trek out to their claims by team and wagon. This was a slow and arduous journey and such places as Atkinson's ranch, John Simmie's and A. DeLong's became regular stopping-over places for the new settlers. At the site of the present town of Simmie, the homestead shacks of John Simmie and his son, Archie, and George Stephenson are still visible.

SIMPSON

Simpson was named after the Canadian businessman, administrator and explorer, Sir George Simpson (1792-1860). He was a native of Scotland who came to Canada originally as a superintendent of the Hudson's Bay Company. He later gained fame in other fields leading the first overland expedition to circle the globe (1841-1842).

The district was first settled in 1904 and among the first to arrive were the pioneer families of Bill Grieve, William Cole and E. C. Howie.

SINCLAIR

Sinclair is on a CPR line in southeastern Saskatchewan. It is named for Peter Sinclair, an early settler.

SINNETT

The post office, Sinnett, was named to honor Reverend J. C. Sinnett, a chaplain in the South African War, and founder of the "Irish" colony in this district. Eventually it was settled by many nationalities, some of whom drove in from Prince Albert in 1905. When the rails reached Humboldt the settlers came in from there. By 1907 the CPR reached Lanigan and then that became the big supply town. Grain was delivered there until the CPR built from Lanigan to Melfort. Sinnett is the first station northeast of Lanigan on the Melfort line.

Some of the early settlers were: John Tallon, John Laverty, Allen McEachern, Mike, Harold and George Hayes, Simon Sullivan, Pat Slattery, Ed Sinnett, Lawrence Dunn, A. Fenske and John Koverinski. Of all the early settlers only Allen McEachern remains on the original homestead.

SINTALUTA

The word Sintaluta is an Assiniboine Indian word meaning "the end of the fox's tail." About five miles southwest of the townsite is a valley. In the early days, this valley was inhabited by many red foxes. The valley was known as Red Fox Valley; the district known as Red Fox school. In the spring a stream flowed from the valley and was known as Red Fox creek. This creek wound its way across the Prairie and eventually emptied into a big slough about one half mile south and east of the townsite. Thus, the Red Fox creek ended at the slough and hence "the end of the fox's tail."

It was at Sintaluta in 1906 that farmers, under the leadership of E. A. Partridge organized the United Grain Growers Grain Company.

SISLEY

This is the story of Laura Sisley. She was the daughter of a London banker and on his death she inherited a small fortune. At the time she was directing a boys' club at a Church of England in the heart of London.

When the Barr colonists were organizing to come to Canada, Miss Sisley thought it would be a good opportunity for some of her boys to join them. About twelve of these underprivileged young men came out with her. She paid all expenses.

Her basic idea was to start a small colony of her own, and so she had her boys settle in a block east of Lloydminster and north of Lashburn.

Miss Sisley's generosity soon became a byword. This characteristic, coupled with the considerable expense of bringing her boys to Canada and establishing them here, placed a severe drain on her financial resources. The first winter several left to seek work in Saskatoon and in the bush north of Prince Albert.

Only three returned in the spring to the Sisley colony: Tommy Simpkins, for whom Miss Sisley first kept house, George Edwards, and Benjamin Flight.

To eke out a living, Miss Sisley gave music lessons to the children of the new settlers and operated the first post office in the area. It was known as the Sisley post office.

Wherever the need for aid was greatest in those pioneering days, there was Miss Sisley with wise counsel and a helping hand. She traversed the prairie trails by oxen for countless miles on her errands of mercy.

Later she kept house for George Edwards and when he married she kept house for Benjamin Flight.

When she died October 2, 1920, all Lashburn mourned her passing. In her memory they erected a baptismal font in All Saints Church.

This information came from Mrs. Joe

McLean of Lloydminster, daughter of George Edwards.

SISTER BUTTE

Sister Butte was the name of a country school twelve miles south of the most southerly railway in the Glentworth area. It was about eighteen miles from the U.S. border. It was one of the earliest schools organized and its number was 643. The post office took the name of the school.

The name itself came from a landmark — two buttes rising on the horizon and visible from the north for thirty miles. However, from any other direction one would scarcely notice them since the surrounding area is a high tableland and the buttes are located right at the north edge of the "bench" as it is commonly known.

Today, the landmark is all that remains. The post office closed down fifteen years ago and the school was torn down and converted into a house in Glentworth.

SKULL CREEK

Skull Creek is an inland post office southeast of Maple Creek. It is located at 4-11-22-W3. James Mann was the first postmaster and he named it for the place he had come from in Colorado.

SLED LAKE

The following information came from Reverend Maurice Lafrance O.M.I., St. Jude's Parish, Green Lake.

Sled Lake is a small permanent settlement on the southwest shore of Sled Lake. The lake was named by its first residents, Mr. and Mrs. Baptiste Mirasty. Baptiste as a young married man moved from Ile-a-la-Crosse down the Beaver River and when navigation became impossible he took a short cut across the muskeg. When asked how he moved his canoes to Sled Lake he replied that he Sled (slid) them across. He named the lake, lived there for many years and raised 15 children.

Sled Lake turned out to be a good fishing lake and wonderful hunting and trapping area. It soon became a stopping place for the fish freighters who were bringing their loads out to the railhead at Big River.

In the 1940's a small saw mill was built but it soon closed. People lived in peace and isolation. Gradually a road was built to Dore Lake and to Sled Lake and tourists came in numbers. Narcisse Mirasty (13th child of Baptiste) built three cabins for their convenience.

Soon a store and filling station will be built by George Lafleur. He has also contracted for the bussing of school children to Dore Lake, a distance of twenty miles.

Sled Lake has a total population of thirty-four. These come from nine families all of Metis extraction: Anderson, McKay, Roy (two), Lafleur (two), Regon, Fleury and Quintal.

SMALES

Mr. Smales came from Scotland as a young man and commenced working for the Grand Trunk Railway. Years later he became a section foreman for the CNR at Kenaston. During this time a hamlet grew up between Kenaston and Bladworth which was named Smales in his honor.

SMEATON

Smeaton is a village on the CPR 50 miles northeast of Prince Albert. The railway arrived in 1930 and named it after Senator R. Smeaton White.

SMILEY

Smiley is the second stop west of Coleville on the Biggar-Loverna CNR line. It was named for Ernest Everett Smiley (1877-1956). He was born in Pettis County, Missouri and came to Saskatoon, Saskatchewan in 1905.

In 1906 he filed on a homestead in the Smiley area and by the time the railway came through in 1913 considerable settlement had taken place in the area. One of the original houses of that period is still standing in the village. The lumber for it was hauled overland from North Battleford.

In the early 1950s oil and gas were discovered at Smiley in commercial quantities and it is now part of an extensive "field" that centers on Coleville.

SMITHBURG

Smithburg consisted of an inland post office, store, dance hall and school (Lothian), situated on Section 7-29-28-W2. Mail came out from Davidson.

A disastrous fire destroyed the post office and store in the late 1940's and they were never rebuilt.

The name Smithburg was for the Smith family on whose land it had been built.

SMITHVILLE

Smithville is six miles west of Saskatoon on highway 14. The first settler was Mr. J. J. Conn, who came in May of 1883. He participated in the rebellion of 1885 as a freighter, and for this service was given the choice of a second homestead. He filed on 160 acres six miles northwest of the little white church that stands on 33rd Street.

After the rebellion Mr. and Mrs. Henry Smith and their four sons located on land almost adjoining. It was from this family that the community got its name. All buildings were made of logs and these were hauled from Moon lake. The men would leave between 4 and 5 o'clock in the morning and cut and trim their load and be home after dark. The woodcutters would hang their lunch pail on the harness on the back of the horse, then cover it with a blanket which would also cover the horse so that the warmth from the horse would keep the lunch from freezing.

Mr. Jones owned the first threshing machine, which was run by a horse-power sweep. A man stood on top of the machine and drove the eight horses round and round. They changed horses often. The machine was hand fed and the straw was kept away with a team and bucking pole. The grain was bagged.

The new 22nd St. highway passes right by the Smithville cemetery, in that cemetery can be seen the names of a few of the other oldtimers who made up the district besides Henry, Albert and Clement Smith: Elmer and George Freethy, Clark and William Graham, Francis Wood, Robert Gillis, John Hatton, Harry Dodds, Thomas Arthur, Perry Bird, Benjamin Budgeman, David and Alexander MacTavish, William Partridge, John Dalgleish and John Kellington.

SMOKING TENT

The second point east of Hudson Bay on the CNR is Smoking Tent. It commemorates a religious observance of the Indian.

Traditionally, the Indian believed in the Great Spirits of Good and Evil, both of which influences manifested themselves in mundane affairs, and which appeared to be in continual conflict, with varying success on each side. He had a hazy idea of a future existence in a Heaven after his own mind, where all men good and bad would live again under better conditions. But, what we call Heaven and the future life were not uppermost in the Indian's mind. The present was too close at hand, too pressing, to be relegated to any second place; also, advantages that were definite, even if only temporal, and that could be appreciated by experience, far outweighed and completely over-shadowed the dubious delights of a future existence. So, when the Indian prayed, he prayed for something in this world, not in the next; that would take care of itself.

He reverenced the Supreme Being as the Source of Life. He prayed to the Thunder Bird as the Arbiter of Life and Death; and he prayed to his Familiar — if he had one. Vows of various kinds were made to these Deities and were mostly kept. In honour of and to propitiate the Thunder Bird, was celebrated the annual Sun Dance, which was the greatest public religious ceremony of the Indians. He had others: The Open End Tent, The Vigil, The Scalp Dance, The Math-Tah-Hit-Too-Win (passing off something to each other) and The Smoking Tent.

The most serious of all the Indian observances, in fact the one conducted without any foolery or skylarking of the younger and lighter-minded of the community, was the Smoking Tent. Only the serious and mature were allowed to participate, and only males. It was an annual observance — in the early fall — and, strange to say, was not a dance. In another way, too, it differed in that no drum was used, the rattle taking its place. However, it had similarities to the other religious observances in that there was singing, pipe smoking, and finally, feasting. The ceremony was basically one of oblation. The best in food that the community could afford was thrown on the fire as an offering, and the pipe was turned in every direction possible, for the use of all possible spirits, as each person had his own particular guardian and guide.

Thus, the name Smoking Tent has an interesting background.

SMOKY BURN

Smoky Burn is in the Carrot River country. It was the result of a forest fire that struck in 1937 and burned out a spot three miles square. Fired again in 1942 the "Burn" was left entirely flat. Settlers began to move in in 1946 and smoke from their clean-up operations hung in the forest clearing for months. The size of the burn did not change for 4 or 5 years but farms have now pushed the forest back and the boundaries of the original burn are no longer discernible.

SMUTS

Smuts is between Rak and Alvena on a CNR line from Saskatoon northeast to Melfort. It was named for Jan Christian Smuts (1870-1950), a South African soldier and statesman. He practiced law at Capetown and Johannesburg, then was Boer leader in the Boer War (1899-1902). After the war he was largely instrumental in effecting the Union of South Africa. During World War I he was the man who led South African troops into battle in support of Britain. He became prime minister of the Union of South Africa (1919-1924). He was made field marshall in 1941.

SNIPE LAKE

Snipe Lake is the first stop west of Eston. The hamlet takes its name from a small lake a few miles to the north. The lake was named, like many others in Saskatchewan, for one species, in this case a snipe, of the myriads of waterfowl that covered every lake in the early days. The person who actually named this lake was Mrs. Alex Orr. There is a small population of only 18 persons at Snipe Lake. At one time there were many more.

SNOWDEN

Bob English, the first settler at Snowden, came originally from Quebec in 1927 with the idea of settling in southern Saskatchewan. But conditions didn't suit him there and he trekked north to a spot 65 miles northeast of Prince Albert. That spot today is the hamlet of Snowden.

The scenery was pleasing to his eye. The stately pine trees, tamarack and spruce were appealing. He soon learned that they were not only scenic, they also provided shelter for herds of elk and moose. The creeks teemed with fish, and he decided to homestead, although it seemed that no one else had as yet discovered the spot.

Not long after Bob English had located, Harry Snowden arrived and the two became fast friends and decided to homestead together. Money was scarce so Harry Snowden took the job of operating the ferry across the Saskatchewan river at Nipawin. All went well until one day the ferry broke loose from its mooring, and Harry Snowden was carried away with the swift-flowing waters, never to be seen again.

Bob English was instrumental in having the hamlet of Snowden named in memory of his friend.

SOKAL

This inland post office which is between Wakaw and Prince Albert was located at 18-43-27-W2. Philip Manczur was the first postmaster and he named it after his hometown Sokal, Russia. The post office is closed now and the residents get their mail from Wakaw.

SOMME

Somme is on a CNR line between Crooked River and Reserve. This name commemorates one of the most famous parts of the Western Front of the First World War. It was in northern France and took its name from the Somme river.

It was on this front from July to November of 1916 that the British launched an attack to relieve Verdun in the south. Casualties from this single sustained battle totalled 1,380,000 — more people than now live in Saskatchewan.

SONNINGDALE

Alfred Storer homesteaded here in 1882. It was not until 1907 that enough people arrived to petition for a post office. It was operated by George Thurston and the name was Sunningdale. This name was chosen to honor the country estate of the Prince of Wales.

In June of 1927 a branch line of the CPR north from Asquith to Baljennie arrived at the townsite. The railway officials agreed to the name Sunningdale but due to a mix-up in the ensuing registration, a "u" became an "o" and the result was the name Sonningdale.

SOUNDING LAKE

In the early days there was a well-defined trail from Battleford southwest to Sounding lake just over the line in Alberta. The Blackfoot name for the lake was Oghta-kway.

The legend that was told is that an eagle with a snake in its claws flew out of the lake making a rumbling noise like thunder.

There may be something to this. Ospreys, who are fish hawks, and a little smaller than an eagle, would dive from a great height and go well below the water to catch fish. The explosion could be caused by the powerful strokes of the wings as they sprayed water in all directions as the bird came up. The snake in the claws was probably a long, thin "jack" which all of us have caught or seen at one time or another.

SOURIS RIVER

Souris River is halfway between Frobisher and Northgate on a CNR line that leaves the province at the latter point. It takes its name from the Souris river which flows through it. Souris is French for mouse, and after this river crosses into American Territory it is called the Mouse river.

SOURIS VALLEY

Souris Valley is the first point southeast of Radville on the CNR. It took its name from the nearby Souris river. Souris is French for mouse. In the year 1903, Jean Baptiste Martin, then a British Columbia mining cook, decided that farming was for him. So, on returning to St. Leon, Manitoba, where his family was living at the time, he stopped over at Weyburn. There, at the land office, he filed on a homestead for himself, one for Theodore Labossiere, one for his father and another for his brother, William. The next year they moved out and built. In the

spring of 1907 the Bourassa school was built named for Lindorph Bourassa. In the same year a Roman Catholic church was built and Father Nadeau from Quebec was installed as priest.

Louis Massonier, an immigrant from France, opened a store. It was at this time the community took on the name Souris Valley and residents obtained a post office with the mail being hauled out from Weyburn.

In 1910 the railway came through. It was the first railway south of Weyburn to the American border. When the railway was being surveyed, the engineer in charge had hard words with the storekeeper (who at this time had great prestige in the community) which resulted in the engineer changing the direction of the roadbed, from due west to northwest, by-passing Souris Valley by three miles. A station was built and to this point everything was moved except the church, which still remains on its original site today.

Due to a lack of available water at the new site (a good supply of water was essential for the big steamers) everything was again moved, this time to Radville, which developed as the divisional point. The lone elevator left at Souris Valley was dismantled in the 1930s.

SOUTHALL

The CPR ran a very short stub line from Bromhead north and west to Tribune. The only other grain point is Southall. It was possibly named for Southall in Middlesex, England, which is now more or less a part of the London conurbation.

SOUTH ALLAN

South Allan is a settlement 9 miles south and 2 miles west of Allan from which it takes its name. The story revolves around the farm of Fred Smith which comprised 27 quarters of land.

In 1952 when it came time to sell, twelve men: Nels Jensen, Tony Glow, Bill Wilkinson, Hollis Walker, Dave Murray, Herman Boon, Lewis Koshinsky, Hugh Goetting, Norman Nelson, Pat Trew, Warren Benedict and Ivan Nicholson formed a Co-op and bought the farm. Most of these men came from surrounding territory where they owned land.

South Allan developed into a lively community with a post office and store, a school that taught grades one to twelve, a curling rink, a United Church and a community hall called Lost River after the municipality it was in.

The farm operated this way until 1963 when it was taken over by five of the men. Now that number is down to four: Bill Wilkinson, Lewis Koshinsky, Herman Boon and Nels Jensen. They live in the original settlement but they do not farm or operate co-operatively. The store and post office are gone and residents are on R.R. No. 1.

A considerable community spirit survives as they call themselves the "Happy Gang." They curl and enjoy socials in a recently renovated hall; they have a snow plow club to keep them in touch with the outside world in the long winter and to keep the roads open to bus their children to school in Allan. Until 1970 they had a grades one to six school in the community.

SOUTH ELBOW

South Elbow is no longer in existence. It never was a town but it was a station on the CNR between Central Butte and Dunblane on a line built in 1925-26. It was at a point where a traffic bridge crossed the South Saskatchewan river. Originally it had two houses, the station and the section foreman's house. It was named by the CNR for the town of Elbow which is on the brow of the river-valley hill overlooking South Elbow.

Since the completion of the South Saskatchewan River Project the whole area has been covered by Lake Diefenbaker.

SOUTHEND

Southend is at the south end of Reindeer lake. It consists of a post office in a Hudson's Bay store that serves an Indian reserve of 200 people.

SOUTHEY

Southey is a village 30 miles north of Regina. Mr. Chandler, an early resident, named the town after Robert Southey, an English poet.

Some, but not all, of the streets in the village are named for poets: Burns, Frost, Byron, Cowper and Browning. The main street is named Keats.

A distinguished graduate of Southey is Dr. Olaf Rostad, who is currently employed by the Saskatoon Public Board of Education as area superintendent of elementary schools.

SOUTH FORK

The first South Fork post office in the district was opened in 1905 at the Billie Axton ranch, one mile northwest of the present townsite. When the CPR came in 1914 this post office was moved into the village store and operated by O. P. Cole

South Fork was so named because it is near the south fork of Swift Current creek which flows nearby.

SOUTH HOLLYWOOD

South Hollywood was an early inland post office twelve miles northeast of Nipawin. The first postmaster was Bert Cavanaugh, a farmer, and he had a separate building on his land for the office.

Later a rural school was built and took the name of the post office. We have not been able to establish the significance of the name but it is interesting to think of not only a Hollywood, but South Hollywood in Saskatchewan!

SOUTH MAKWA

On May 16, 1926 Hugh E. Ellis opened the post office of Makwa, a position he held until September 26, 1943. On February 15, 1939, due to the forming of a site two miles south where a Roman Catholic church was situated, Mr. John E. Melling opened a South Makwa post office.

Thus to avoid confusion Makwa's post office was changed February 15, 1939 to North Makwa. This post office closed November 1, 1957 and once again Makwa was just Makwa, ten miles east of Loon Lake on the highway leading to Meadow Lake.

SOUTHMINSTER

The Barr Colonists arrived at Lloydminster in 1903-1904. A number of them settled on land about six miles southeast of Lloydminster and called their community Southminster. Some of those early settlers were Foote, Cooper, Whitebread, Rowles, Bottomley and Buckmaster. The latter had the first mail route and he used his home as a post office.

By 1910 there were enough children to warrant a school. In 1926 the CPR built out through Southminster and a Pool elevator was built. The Ladies' Club of Southminster was organized in 1941 and it's an active organization using the school (now closed, with the children bussed to Lloydminster) for parties, showers, etc. A curling rink was built in 1950.

This community is in the famous Lloydminster oil field and it is music to hear the engines throb night and day as the giant grasshopper pumps bring the "black gold" to the surface.

SOUTHVIEW

Southview is a rural post ofice in the Wood Mountain area. It opened on July 1, 1912, with Mr. David Mayne as postmaster. He was followed by Mrs. Malton Pearce and it closed on June 30, 1944, with Mr. William A. Wetherall as postmaster.

SOVEREIGN

Sovereign is on a CPR line that runs from Milden to Rosetown. It's another in a group of names honouring royalty. Others would be Regina, Prince Albert, Imperial and Victoria Plains in Saskatchewan and Coronation and Court in Alberta.

First settlers into this district were: Harry McIntyre, William John McIntosh, Billy Orr, Billy Saunders, Bob Timer, William Isley, Jim Elliott and R. K. "Rod" McFadyen. Mrs. McFadyen now lives at 129 9th St. E. in Saskatoon and here is her description of how homesteaders made their Christmas trees.

"We took a bare poplar tree and covered the branches with cotton batting which were in turn sprinkled with tinsel and then hung with strings of bright paper chains, popped corn and ornaments obtained from Eatons. There were also bright boxes from the same source which we filled with mixed candies. Small real candles were clamped on to the branches to light up the whole effect. They were dangerous but beautiful. It was a very happy celebration of Christmas in a new land and there never was another one quite its equal."

SPALDING

Saskatchewan and Spalding came into being in the same year, 1905. Spalding has had two locations, the earlier one from 1905 to 1920, being two miles northeast of the present townsite.

The first homesteaders were George Elliott, Norman Morrison and J. W. Hutchison. Mr. Hutchison opened the first store and post office in 1906 and the name Spalding was chosen for Mrs. Hutchison's birthplace, Spalding, England.

When the CPR put a line through from Melfort to Watson in 1921, "Old Spalding" which was quite a sizeable community moved to the tracks. In olden days Spalding was a center of soccer and it is interesting to note that in 1911, on the occasion of a visit of Sir Wilfrid Laurier, a soccer team from Spalding played a team from Humboldt for the entertainment of the honorable visitor.

SPAYER

Spayer was an early inland post office that opened on the N.W. quarter of 34-30-26-West of the third meridian and drew its mail from Maple Creek, far to the south. It served a thriving community for years.

When the CPR built the "Empress Line" northwest from Swift Current in 1913, the mail for Spayer then came from Leader, ten miles to the north.

Two of the earliest settlers in the district were Heinrich Adam Wenzel and his wife, Maria. They had emigrated from Russia to North Dakota where they farmed for two years before moving to Canada in 1909.

The heart of the early community was St. John's Lutheran Church built in 1911, and a parochial school which taught grades I to XII. When the consolidation of schools came in Saskatchewan, the students were bussed to Leader. The school closed and the once thriving community faded.

Today, as you travel south on highway 21, you pass right through the heart of the community. All that remains is part of the school (now used as a community centre) and the graveyard which adjoins it.

Across the highway is a red elevator with bold white markings "Wenzel Seed Cleaning". It marks the farm home of Mr.

and Mrs. Leonard Wenzel and son. Mr. Wenzel is a grandson of Henrich and Maria Wenzel. The elevator was moved in from Lemsford in 1971.

This account of the inland post office of Spayer is typical of the changing face of Saskatchewan.

SPEERS

Taken from the North Battleford News-Optimist of October 19, 1965.

"On July 31, 1913, an open air picnic was held about where Main Street is now. It saw the dedication ceremony when the name 'Speers' became official, honoring Mr. C. W. Speers, a Government Immigration Officer."

The most exciting sporting event over the years would have to be the winning of the Canadian high school curling championship by Speers in 1962. The team was as follows: Skip — Mike Lukowich, Third — Eddie Lukowich, Second — Doug McLeod, Lead — Dave Moore, Coach — Percy Moore. The Lukowich brothers became school teachers and went on to curl together for years.

SPINNEY HILL

Spinney Hill is the second last stop on a branch line north from Asquith to Baljennie.

In 1903 Peter Niven, a Scottish immigrant, filed on a homestead that is now Spinney Hill. In 1904 he trekked in by ox team from Prince Albert. In Scotland all farms are named. Mr. Niven called his Glenside. Later a local improvement district and a school district were formed, both called Glenside. However, when the residents of Glenside applied for a post office they were told that name had already been chosen. Mr. Pearson, the secretary who had immigrated from England, then submitted Spinney Hill and it was accepted. In his part of England, what we call a bluff or small grove of trees was called a spinney. The land around Spinney Hill is rolly and bluffy. Hence, the name Spinney Hill fits quite well.

Spinney Hill never had an elevator, just a loading platform. Eventually a gravel highway connected Asquith with Battleford and it ran four miles west of the Spinney Hill grain point.

A post office and small store on the highway served the community for years.

Then came the bridge over the river to Maymont and the tremendous development of highway 376. This continued on past Spinney Hill and on into Battleford. In 1975 the Pool elevators closed at Baljennie. Even before this, in the early 1970's, people began to shop elsewhere and Spinney Hill store and post office closed. Now there is just a boarded-up building with twenty green mail boxes sitting outside — eleven of which are used, but this is surrounded by beautiful evergreens and lilac bushes — testimonies of the industry of the early homesteaders.

Farms in the vicinity are large and cattle raising is big business.

SPIRITWOOD

The first post office in the district was opened in 1912 in what was then known as the Norbury district on the Norbury family farm. The first postmaster was Rupert Dumond, an American, who named the hamlet after his hometown in North Dakota.

SPOONER

Spooner post office is twenty-five miles north of Star City. It was named for the first postmaster, Mr. Spooner. The post office has been closed for years but the name is still used in the district.

SPRINGFELDT

Springfeldt is 12 miles south and one mile east on number 4 highway out of Swift Current. It is a small Mennonite village. There are 10 houses and a population of 38. Right between the farms of David Wall and Jim Martens is a large fresh water spring which gives the village its name — in English it means "spring field."

Mr. David Wall was born right beside the spring which is roughly an acre in size. The dike to hold it is built of stones and earth with a small spillway. There is eight to ten feet of water in it. When it overflows in the spring it simply soaks into the ground before it goes very far. There are other springs up and down the draw but that is the only one that amounts to anything.

The village used to be predominately Walls but now it's Wiebes: Corny, John, Corny again, Peter and Jake. Gilbert

Braun, Bill Schlamp and John Knelson round out the families.

Mr. Wall has a huge book 15" x 10" and five inches thick which is written in German and is called The Martyr's Mirror. It is the story of the persecution of Mennonites through Holland, the Germanies and finally Russia. They left Russia for the United States, Canada, Mexico, Bolivia and Honduras. The book is 227 years old and has a leather-over-wood cover and metal braces on the corners.

SPRINGSIDE

Springside is a village on the CPR 16 miles northwest of Yorkton. It was named after the many springs of excellent water throughout the district. These were of great help to the early settlers, particularly the ranchers.

SPRING VALLEY

Mr. E. J. Reimann submitted the name Spring Valley for a town which is situated about 35 miles from Moose Jaw on the branch line to Gravelbourg.

In 1913 Mr. Reimann moved, with his family of nine, from Browns Valley, Minnesota to homestead in this district. He found a spring on his farm and combined that with the "Valley" from Browns Valley to form the name of the town. Mr. Reimann later had the I.H.C. implement agency in Spring Valley.

A bachelor, Arnold Park, moved from Browns Valley at the same time as the Reimann family. The next year he sent back to Minnesota for his girlfriend to join him and they were married in Moose Jaw.

SPRINGWATER

The first known settler in the district was D. C. McMillan, who walked in from Saskatoon in 1905, built a sod shack on the north side of Lake Ens, and despite his 70 years of age, helped other settlers to locate their homesteads and get started.

Springwater was the name of the first post office in the district and was operated by John McConnel. He named it for the many fresh-water springs in a coulee on his property. In 1911 Mr. McConnel moved the post office to the village and this was one year before the GTR pushed a branch line southwest from Biggar to Loverna. Springwater is the third stop out of Biggar and when the railway arrived it adopted the name of Springwater from the post office.

SPRUCE BLUFF

Spruce Bluff, an inland post office, opened the 16th of January in 1910 and closed August 31st, 1920. The postmasters during its short life were: Harry Spice, William Trask and Julia Johnston.

The name was a common one since spruce trees were everywhere. Harry Spice hauled the first mail from Mervin.

Some of the patrons of the post office were: Johnson, Ellis, Shaver, Bleakney, Nasby, Gillend, Funk, Bell and Meyers.

SPRUCE HOME

Spruce Home is a rural post office on No. 2 highway north of Prince Albert. It was opened in 1907 by Olaf Granum. He was asked to name it and he suggested Granum. It was refused because there was already a Granum in Alberta. Then he translated Granum from his native Norwegian into English and it came out Spruce Home. The name was accepted.

SPRUCE LAKE

The CN steel started northwest from North Battleford in 1910 where it was to hook up with the railway at Grand Centre, Alberta. This line was slowly built in sections. First it reached Edam in 1912 and then Turtleford about 1914 where it stopped for years. The next move was on to Cleeves, then Spruce Lake and it finally reached St. Walburg in 1921 where it stopped completely.

During each prolonged stop along the way the town at the end of the steel would boom and one of the biggest booms was at Spruce Lake.

Spruce Lake, prior to the arrival of the steel, carried the name of Alamark in honour of Mr. A. L. McKee, an early homesteader in the district. At its height in the early 20's Spruce Lake had four elevators — Home Grain, North Star, Reliance and National. It also had many other businesses which included the following: four general stores, two cafes, a hotel, a livery stable, a harness shop, a bank (The Standard), a municipal office, a shoe repair shop, a market garden, an

Imperial Oil agency, a pool hall and barber shop, a school, an Anglican church, a garage, and for two years a newspaper, The Spruce Lake Times, edited by Tom Collins who has now retired to the west coast.

Spruce Lake literally serviced the North. Then when the steel moved on to St. Walburg in 1921 it became the large trading centre and Spruce Lake dwindled over the years until today there is only one elevator (The Pool), and a handful of businesses.

SPY HILL

Spy Hill is the second station inside Saskatchewan on the main line of the CNR that runs through Melville.

There are three legends as to how it got its name:

1. That the Hill, which was named Spy Hill long before the village came into existence, was called Spy Hill because the Indians used to use it to "spy" out the surrounding land and watch for enemies approaching from the Qu'appelle Valley and other nearby points. When the village was settled around 1881, it took its name from the historic hill.

2. The hill itself is the setting of a famous Indian Legend. A revengeful wife who had deserted her tribe, succeeded in her determination to massacre them. Then discovering that her husband, the Chief — The Wolverine — alone had escaped, sought him out on Spy Hill and there stabbed him to death.

3. A legend tells of a band of Cree Indians who made camp near the hill. A Sioux Indian was sent to see if he could make off with some of the Cree ponies, but he fell asleep and was discovered by one of the Crees. The Cree picked up a stone and killed the Sioux, exclaiming "Kappa gammaho" which means "I have killed a spy." Since the custom was not to bury enemy dead, the Sioux's body was elevated to the top of the hill, the grass cut from beneath him, and the body left for the birds and animals to devour. Ever afterwards the hill and district was known as "Kappa gammaho" or Spy Hill.

SQUAW RAPIDS

Squaw Rapids is an important place now. In 1963 the first units at the Squaw Rapids Hydro-Electric Generating Station, 46 miles northeast of Nipawin on the main Saskatchewan river went into operation. Squaw Rapids, the first hydro plant on the provincial system, is the first of a series of projects to harness the energy potential of the Saskatchewan river. Within the near future a series of power plants will convert the Saskatchewan river into a chain of lakes, each with a dam and power-generating station.

There are many possibilities as to how Squaw Rapids got its name. One, it was a place where it was necessary to portage. The Indians were noted for letting their women do the heavy work and so they may have named it for that reason. Two, maybe a boat load of squaws shot the rapids. Three, and most likely, a squaw or squaws went through the rapids and did not survive. In any case it is an interesting name.

STALWART

Stalwart is between Liberty and Imperial on a CPR line that runs parallel with Last Mountain Lake. This line was built in 1910 at a time when many settlers came from Britain. Stalwart was a large British Battleship. The British are a proud people and one of the things they were proud of then was their navy.

A search of CPR files of the Saskatoon Division shows that not only Stalwart but Liberty, Imperial and Renown were named for battleships. However, in the case of the latter three towns, there are other versions of how they got their name.

STANDARD HILL

Ten miles north of Maidstone is the locality of Standard Hill. Originally this was a Scandanavian settlement and descendants of the first families still farm there: Johnstons, Gerbigs, Skulruds.

At one time there was a school, a post office and a store — all named Standard Hill.

In the 1960's, Silver Lake Regional Park was established and it became the home of the Standard Hill Lakers, a baseball team that has, over the years, made a name for itself. Competing in a league that includes the North Battleford Beavers, Neilburg Monarchs, Wilkie Outlaws, Mervin Flyers, Rabbit Lake

Merchants and others, they won the league championship in 1976.

STANLEY MISSION

The Stanley Mission settlement on the Churchill River centers around Holy Trinity Church, the oldest church in the Saskatchewan Anglican Diocese.

Although the mission was established in 1846, the actual building of the church took place between the years 1853-60. Lumber and logs used in the construction were all whip sawn near the site. The hinges, locks and other hardware, as well as the stained glass windows, were brought from England through Hudson Bay, and transported from there up the waterways and overland by a long and difficult journey. Reverend Robert Hunt and his wife were chiefly responsible for the building of the church and invested their personal savings in its erection. They came out from England in 1850 and after a couple of years at Lac la Ronge, arrived at the Indian settlement on the Churchill River called by its Cree name Omachewa-isp'imewin (various spellings), or "The Uphill Shootingplace." The Hunts called their mission Stanley after Mrs. Hunt's home in England, Stanley Park.

Today Stanley has a population of 658, 99 percent of whom are Cree Indians. The supplies for the settlement came in by winter tractor train from La Ronge. Fox, mink, fisher, squirrel, otter, lynx, beaver and muskrat are caught in the area.

STARBLANKET

Starblanket was a rural post office located at 2-51-7-W3, which is on the Sandy Lake Indian Reserve north of Mont Nebo. It is the name of a former Indian chief, Star Blanket, but the post office officials in the interest of efficiency spell it Starblanket. The office has been closed for some time.

STAR CITY

Star City is 13 miles east of Melfort. It was named after a pioneer resident, Mr. W. Starkey, who settled in the district in 1899.

STEEL DALE

Steel Dale was an inland post office northwest of Beechy. It opened in the early 1900's and closed when the CNR reached Beechy in 1922.

STEEP CREEK

Steep Creek is an inland post office thirty miles east of the city of Prince Albert lying between the forks of the North and South Saskatchewan rivers. It got its name from a nearby creek. Everyone who crossed that body of water with horses and oxen had trouble coming down to the water and even more trouble getting back up the bank.

The first settler in this area was Jake Bead. In 1876 he travelled down the North Saskatchewan and built a log cabin at the "Forks".

The Steep Creek post office was opened in 1913 with Mrs. Annie Cozens as postmistress. Mr. Berkech, who was eighty-nine years old in 1970, came to the district in 1907 and filed on a homestead. His son, William, still farms the place in summer but spends the winters in Prince Albert.

Steep Creek is very close to La Colle Falls, an ill-fated hydro-electric project that was backed by Prince Albert money. It kept the city in debt for years and years, and only recently has that debt been paid off.

The only simultaneous triple hanging in Canada occurred in the open courtyard of the old Prince Albert jail on October 17, 1919. The series of events which led to the hanging of Dr. Joseph Gervais, Jean Baptiste and Victor Carmel included such widely separated incidents as draft dodging, whiskey making, rustling, arson and automobile theft.

The three men caused one of Western Canada's largest manhunts when they eluded a posse of soldiers in the Steep Creek area, twenty-five miles east of Prince Albert.

Eventually they were caught and convicted for killing a sheriff's bailiff and an RCMP officer, terrorizing people in the Prince Albert area during the week of November 15, 1918.

Oldtimers still talk about the Steep Creek murders, a bizarre and tragic event.

STEINBACH

Steinbach is a Mennonite village in the Hague area. It was named for Steinbach,

Manitoba. This, too, was originally a Mennonite village. Many of the inhabitants of the whole Hague district came originally from Steinbach, Morden and Gretna, Manitoba. The first to arrive in Steinbach, Saskatchewan, were Abram and Gerhard Sawatzky who came in somewhere between 1900 and 1905. Many families followed.

Characteristic of most Mennonite villages was their "one street," with houses and barns spaced out evenly on both sides and left for large yards and gardens. Usually, a church, a school and a store were established. Oftentimes, the church and school were in the same large yard, some even had a connecting covered-in-corridor. The church and school were for the most part plain buildings. The store inevitably had a "sit down space" around the heating unit. Mennonites love to visit and this was an ideal spot.

The name Steinbach is of German origin and means Stone Creek.

STELCAM

Stelcam is the second grain point on a CPR line that runs southeast of Moose Jaw through to North Portal and on into the U.S.A. It was named after "Stella Campbell" wife of the superintendent E. W. Duval.

STENEN

The Stenen district was first occupied with traders, ranchers, and squatters. Tetlock, Bagnall, Seebach, Stevenson, and Riddle were some of them. The first homesteaders arrived in 1902 and Mr. Wilson was the first to file a claim. In 1906 Mr. John Stenen, his wife, and seven children, came up from North Dakota and homesteaded where the town now stands. When the railroad arrived in 1911 Mr. Stenen donated enough land for a townsite on condition that the town bear his name. Railroad officials agreed to this. Mr. Stenen lived in the community until 1923 and then he moved to California.

STEPPES

Steppes is the first stop east of Carlyle. Steppe is the Russian word for plain. The steppes of Russia stretch throughout the Ukraine, eastward to the Caspian Sea, and to the Alti Mountains in Central Asia. These are great stretches of level grassy land with few or no trees.

The Great Central Plains of North America stretch up into Saskatchewan and are much like the Russian steppes.

STEWART VALLEY

Stewart Valley is at the end of the steel on a branch line north of Swift Current. For many years this area was known as "The Landing." In 1888 the NWMP established a post here.

The first rancher to make his home in this region was Jim Smart in 1888. In 1891 he operated a ferry across the South Saskatchewan. In 1906 R. B. Stewart and family of Hastings, Ont., took up land in this district and it became known as "The Stewart Settlement." The name changed to Stewart Valley when the CPR came in 1928.

STOCKDILL

Stockdill is the second stop south of Rosetown on the CPR. It was named for C. E. Stockdill, Assistant to the Vice-President at the time the line was built. This information came from CPR files.

STOCKHOLM

Stockholm is on a CPR line between Esterhazy and Dubuc. Six miles south of Stockholm along No. 9 highway, stands a small stone cairn commemorating the beginnings of the Augustana Lutheran Church. Looking east from the cairn, you will see the church about a mile distant, crouching on a hill, its broad shoulders outspread.

The Augustana Lutheran Church is built of brick and all of its windows are of stained glass. The large north window depicts "The Good Shepherd," the south one, "Christ Knocking at the Door." When one learns that this church was built around 1918, when the surrounding countryside was largely unbroken bushland, one marvels at the courage and faith of the early pioneers.

Who were these pioneers? Back in the 1880s settlers came from Sweden seeking new homes and opportunities. Times were hard in the Old Country, free homesteads beckoned. So they came and named their settlement New Stockholm and here they built their log houses, cleared the brush with axes, broke the land with oxen, broadcast seed by hand and harvested with a scythe. Such was the beginning of the first and largest Swedish colony in Canada. Some of these early pioneers were the Johanson family, two Olson families, Miss Britta Severtson and the Alexander Stenberg family.

Those of Lutheran faith formed the earliest Canadian Augustana congregation in 1889 and a small log church was built. That church was the site of the Canada Conference in 1913. The present structure was commenced in 1918 — and has served steadily ever since.

The railroad arrived in 1903, until that time the mail had been brought from Whitewood on foot. The hamlet was named Stockholm by Mr. Alex Stenberg.

STONE

Stone is an inland post office at 10-10-21-W3, which is fifteen miles straight south of Tompkins. The first postmaster was Mr. P. Fernquist. The office moved about a bit and is now located at 10-16-21 W3. It was named for F. V. Stone, assistant to the President of the CPR with headquarters in Montreal.

STONEHENGE

The Craddock family, the first pioneers of the district, originated from Stonehenge, England. They named the hamlet.

Stonehenge, the huge circle of standing stones on Salisbury Plain, Wiltshire, England, was first mentioned historically in the 9th century A.D. Legend and history have been busy ever since about the stones and their significance.

STONY BEACH

The hamlet of Stony Beach is about halfway between Regina and Moose Jaw. It derived its name from a small lake three miles to the northwest. This little lake is spring fed and very stony and would never make a beach, yet the area was called Stony Beach before the turn of the century, when a post office was set up in the farm home of George Doan, in 1901.

Settlers who came in the 1890s, were: Love, Doan, Young, Hagerty, Poyser and Taylor.

STONY NARROWS

Stony Narrows settlement is where Brustad river enters into the south end of Cree lake 57°14' - 107°04'. It is so named because of the high granite gneiss cliffs that occur on both sides of the narrows.

STONY RAPIDS

Stony Rapids settlement is on the north side of the narrowest part of Fond-du-Lac river which joins Black lake to Lake Athabasca. It was so named from the great number of stones and boulders which are encountered when running these rapids.

Stony Rapids was settled by trappers in the early 1920s. The settlement was built because that was as far as the barges could go with supplies before they'd hit "white water." Two of the earliest names in the settlement were Robillard and Mercredi.

The post office was established on June 12, 1937.

STORNOWAY

Stornoway is 18 miles east and six miles north of Yorkton. The CNR, on its way from Russell, Manitoba, to Canora, Saskatchewan, reached Stornoway in the winter of 1911. The railway bought a quarter section of cleared land from Mr. Barns and put in a switch track enabling the train, and all the cars, to be turned around so that they could return to Russell loaded with goods from the village area.

Building boomed with two general stores, an elevator, a livery barn, a lumberyard, and a hardware, going up. Before his store was built, W. Weeks of Weeks General Store unloaded his goods on the open prairie and sold from there. The most exciting building to go up was a 20-room hotel complete with poolroom and bar. Mr. Runo, the proprietor, sold three glasses of beer (at that time a glass had a quart capacity) for 25 cents. His establishment added life to the town. The closest post office to this temporary railhead was Barvas and it was operated by Murdo McIver. When a name was sought for this new townsite it was he who suggested Stornoway in honor of his hometown of Stornoway, Scotland.

STORTHOAKS

In 1913 in the extreme southern corner of the province the CPR built a branch line from Manitoba into Saskatchewan that ended with Storthoaks, Nottingham and Alida. The president of the CPR wished to honor Sir Harry Brittain an English author, who had played an important part in the organization of the Imperial Press Conferences of the day which worked for mutual understanding among the various countries of the British Empire. So he asked Sir Harry Brittain to name some stations on this new railway line. Sir Harry suggested that the terminus be called Alida, in honor of his wife, Lady Alida. He suggested the name Nottingham, but we can't find out why. Storthoaks was suggested because that was the name of his estate in Yorkshire. He wished it to be spelled Storth Oaks but this was not granted and it's all one word. Storth means strong. People from Storthoaks and Alida have visited Sir Harry at his home in England.

STOUGHTON

Like many other villages in Saskatchewan there is some doubt about the naming of Stoughton. Some say it was named for the chief dispatcher of the CPR in Montreal, while others say it was named for the conductor of the first train that came through the village. In one thing they agreed, the railway named the town. Still another version is that it honors John Stoughton Dennis, a former surveyor-general of Dominion lands and deputy minister of the interior.

The CPR from a mile southeast of Regina runs diagonally across the sections to Stoughton, 88 miles away, without a bend. It is the longest straight line of rail in the world.

STOVE CREEK

Stove Creek drains Stove Lake into the Assiniboine River on Section 30-37-7 W2. Stove Lake was named for an incident that happened to a couple of forest timber surveyors who, in attempting to cross the lake by canoe, upset and lost their camp stove.

The creek took its name from the lake and the district that grew up along the creek did the same. In 1926 Stove Creek school was built. At that time residents got their mail from Rockford, an inland post office on the N.W. quarter 10-37-7-W2. Rockford got its mail from Endeavor. However, the Rockford post office moved about so much that Stove Creek farmers sometimes had to travel almost twenty miles through the bush to get to it. In 1927 they applied for, and got, a post office of their own. Joe Stadnik was the first postmaster and Tony Stadnik hauled the mail from Lintlaw once a week. Some of the patrons served were Joe Delowski, Harry Galbraith, Pete Barran, H. E. Tanner, Ed Beatty and August Siverreen.

This information came from Mr. G. H. Galbraith who came to the district as a lad of eighteen in 1917. Today, he is the Reeve of the Municipality of Hazel Dell which takes in Stove Creek.

STOWLEA

Stowlea post office near Paradise Hill opened in 1913 in the home of Jim Badgley on N.E. 13-54-22 West of the 3rd. He kept it until he went overseas in 1915. It was taken over by Robert Kidd who was postmaster for 35 years. The office changed hands twice after that; Grace Malden followed Mr. Kidd and finally it closed out in March of 1953 in the home of Mrs. Susan McGowan. It had been named Stowlea by Mr. Badgley for a town, Stow, in the Southern Uplands of Scotland.

In July of 1935 a cyclone struck and hail as big as golf balls fell. Granaries were wrecked and scattered. A big hip-roof barn was lifted up and dropped on some cattle taking shelter beside it.

Another tragic story occurred in 1940 when a man used an axe to kill two of his bachelor neighbours and then shot himself.

STRANRAER

Stranraer, a seaside resort on the west coast of Scotland, gave its name to the typical prairie town of Stranraer which lies midway between Plenty and Herschel. Besides being famous for its black gumbo soil Stranraer is in good goose country. In the autumn, the early homesteaders used to hunt geese in a unique way. It was found that if one drove an ox toward the geese it didn't bother them at all and it was possible to get close enough for a shot. One man used his milk cow to hunt geese. Perhaps some of our hunters today could adopt this method, which is better than taking pot shots at cows in mistake for wild game.

There was a fair sprinkling of Scottish names in a list of the oldtimers and this, no doubt, accounted for the name. Some of these first settlers included the following: Emma McEachern, Fredrick Thomas, George Walker, James and Archie MacDonald, John Patterson, George Galbraith, Laney Hough, Duncan and John McFarlane, Robert and Thomas Coulter, and Duncan McLellan, to name just a few.

STRASBOURG

Originally Strasbourg was settled by German immigrants and named after Strasbourg, Germany.

STRATHALLEN

Strathallen is the second last stop on a CPR branch line that runs south to Killdeer. Fred Paul, now of Rockglen, was an early rancher in the district. In fact he was born and raised there. The first store and post office was opened on April 4, 1932. Mrs. Frances Mason was the first postmistress and she was followed by Henry William Hugh Pierce, then Mrs. Edna Margaret Gillies, and on December 9, 1953, it was taken over by Mrs. Mabel Nina McKee. The Strathallen post office closed in 1968.

Mr. Mason was responsible for naming the village and he chose to call it Strathallen for his hometown in England.

STREHLOW

Strehlow elevator still stands; the second grain point south of Saskatoon on a CNR line to Regina. It's between Haultain (now demolished) and Dundurn.

Jack Briggs, the present agent at Grasswood, bought grain at Strehlow in 1939-40. People who drew to him were Adolph Wolfe, Harold Ducie, and Johnny and Duncan Bethune.

Strehlow was named for one of the early settlers, Hugo Strehlow, who lived three miles north of the site. By far the most famous resident of the district was Charles August Palmer. He broke from Jesse James' robber band in the late 1800s and fled to Canada where he buried himself on a homestead in the bush near Strehlow. He brought his son, Earl, with him and they built a substantial sod house with no windows and a thick plank door over which a bell was suspended that rang at the slightest movement. The only light inside the house came from empty clear-glass whiskey bottles carefully imbedded in the roof. The house had no floor and only poplar poles for a bunk-bed.

Reinholdt Tamke of 322 Avenue D S., Saskatoon, one of the early ranchers in the district, remembers that once while out searching for stray cattle he had occasion to visit Mr. Palmer. Mr. Tamke carried a ten-gauge Winchester pump gun and on seeing this Mr. Palmer went back into the house and brought out an identical model which had several notches in the stock. He said that he hadn't thought up to then that there was another gun like his in Canada.

Mr. Tamke was a little sceptical of the stories Mr. Palmer told but upon retirement he had occasion to travel and visit in the States. It was then that he found out that Mr. Palmer had been telling the truth all along. In fact, when compared to the American version, Palmer had been modest.

The reason for his fortress-like shack was that he had a price on his head and he was afraid that Canadian authorities would take him back to the States. His fears were ungrounded and he lived to ranch horses and cattle in the area until in 1916 he died in bed at the age of 96.

Mr. Jack Briggs remembers him as having the most piercing eyes he had ever encountered. As Mr. Briggs put it in his own words, "He didn't look right through you; he looked inside of you."

STRONG

Strong is two abutted and boarded-up Pool elevators halfway between Hanley and Kenaston. They were open until 1966 and the agent lived there. The elevators are now used for storing grain on a long-term basis.

Arthur "Dewey" Nystuen, a retired Hanley merchant, sent in the information on how Strong got its name. It was named for James Strong, the Hanley station agent of the early 1900s. Mr. Strong had, besides his regular duties, land interests south of town. He was instrumental in having a siding put right on his land. Three elevators, the State in 1913, the Central in 1914, and the Saskatchewan Co-op in 1924 were built there. One elevator burned down and the Pool took over the other two.

Mr. Strong was a very talented musician and as Hanley's bandmaster had one of the finest bands for miles around. They gave regular concerts in the Hanley Opera House.

Some of the men who first drew grain to Strong were: Elmer Sira, Elmer and Jack Catoon, Delmer Torgeson, Ernie Epp, Gib Zudinch, Floyd Haight, Carman and Max Anderson, and Arthur Begstresser.

STRONGFIELD

The village of Strongfield is on a line between Outlook and Elbow. The first man into the district was George Armstrong, a homestead locator and real estate promoter. This was in 1903.

The townsite was originally called Conan but because of a conflict of names with another point on the CPR, the name was changed to Langevin.

When the CPR came through in 1908 it was decided to use the last part of Mr. Armstrong's name, add the word field and call the village Strongfield.

Some of the first settlers here to load wheat "over the platform" in 1908 were: Armstrong, Alton, Kennedy, Wilcox, Norrish, Damon, Taylor, MacPherson, Strand, Ledingham, and McKee.

STRONG PINE

Strong Pine is an inland post office a few miles north of the North Saskatchewan river and very close to the forks. It is two miles north of the ill-fated La Colle Falls, a hydro-electric project that went bankrupt in such a way that it left the city of Prince Albert in debt for years and years.

Theofil Capustin, the first settler, came into the district in 1905. The land was not surveyed and so he squatted until the survey came through. He opened a post office and grocery store in 1915 and chose the name Strong Pine. The name certainly is suitable, even today. When you're at Strong Pine you're in the pines.

STRUAN

Struan is between Arelee and Sonningdale on a CPR line built northwest from Asquith to Baljennie in 1927.

Mr. and Mrs. Peters opened the first post office in their homestead home in 1915 one and one-half miles west and one-half mile south of the present village. The mail was hauled in from Perdue.

Mrs. Peters named the post office, Struan, for her home village in Scotland.

When the railway came through in 1927, the country post office moved into Struan and gave it its name. The post office was taken over at that time by Mr. and Mrs. Franklin Lyons and housed in Bailey's store.

In 1940 Tom Bailey took over and ran the post office until it was closed and placed on a rural route.

I am indebted to Geof Barrington, long-time resident of Sonningdale, now retired and living in Saskatoon, for this information.

STUMP LAKE

Primrose is a very large, deep lake straddling the Saskatchewan-Alberta border at 55° latitude. Stump lake is small and shallow (five miles long and one-half mile wide) a short distance south of it.

In 1911 a logging camp was established a mile east of the lake to take out the excellent stand of marketable timber. The lake was named by the lumberjacks because of the numerous huge white stumps — some 30 feet high standing in this body of water, bearing to the fact that it had once been dry land.

In 1918 a forest fire swept through the locality, wiping out the camp and much of the timber.

In the winter of 1919-20, the land was surveyed. Albert Bloom was the first to move into the district. He arrived from Polwarth in August of 1919.

The land was opened for homesteading in 1923 and from then until 1927 many families moved in.

Mr. Bloom applied for a post office in 1927. His request was granted and he named it Stump Lake. In 1929, Everet Bloom started a small store in conjunction with the post office. He and his family operated it until 1937 when he sold the store to Harvey Lahmeier. Mr. Bloom continued to operate the post office until 1945.

Harvey Lahmeier married Mr. Bloom's daughter, Mary, and they built the present Stump Lake store and operated it and the post office until 1977, when they sold out to Alfred Svendsen. Mr. Bloom had given forty years of service to the district.

This information came from Edgar Duvall of Stump Lake.

STURDEE

Sturdee is a few miles east of Yorkton. It takes its name from Admiral Sturdee of the British Navy who, early in the First World War, won a dramatic victory against the German Pacific squadron off the Falkland Islands. Before the declaration of the war, the Germans had a squadron of considerable strength in Pacific waters. The ostensible reason was the troubles in Mexico. Shortly before the declaration of war the squadron departed for an unknown destination. When it was finally sighted off the Falkland Islands in October the British ships closed in and despite inferior armament they sank the entire squadron with the exception of the light cruiser Dresden.

STURGEON VALLEY

Sturgeon Valley is an inland post office four miles from the southwest end of Sturgeon lake. It is operated by Leo Harris and consists of a combined post office and store with a Royalite gas pump. It serves the nearby Sturgeon Lake Indian Reserve (population 600) where John Charles is the chief.

There is a considerable farming community to the north. Sturgeon Valley takes its name from nearby Sturgeon lake. This lake is drained south by Sturgeon river which joins the Shell and they empty into the North Saskatchewan. It is not uncommon for sturgeon to go up this river in the spring to spawn in the lake.

The first settlers in this rugged part of the country were Orrin and Wesley Cowles who arrived in 1916. They were ranchers. The second year they borrowed enough money to buy two carloads of young feeder steers and sold them in 1920 for an average of $31.12 apiece, at the first auction sale in the new stockyards in Prince Albert. In 1918 Charlie Cowles, a brother, bought a truck — the first in the district. It was a Maxwell with solid hard rubber tires so it wasn't much easier to ride in than a wagon. When it got on sandy roads the wheels would spin so Charlie always carried horse blankets to put under them to give him a grip. The truck's top speed was 20 miles an hour. Considering the hard tires and the roads of that time it was fast enough.

STURGIS

L. Andrew Olson walked into the district in April of 1903. He was the first settler. After building a little home and working up a little land he brought his family out from Sweden in 1905.

Andrew Soderlund was another pioneer who walked into the new district. Homesteading in the area before there was a town at all, he hauled his grain by oxen to Canora, 26 miles to the south.

Prior to the railroad being built through the settlement in 1912, a trading center grew up named after its post office, Stanhope. However, when the steel arrived it did not run anywhere near the post office location. The post office was then moved to the railway line and the community that developed around it was named Sturgis after a place called Sturgis, South Dakota, which was the home town of the new postmaster, F. Brooks.

SUCCESS

W. B. Jones of Success contributed this information:

"My father bought the half section upon which Success now stands, from the CPR in 1905. At that time the odd-numbered sections in most townships, with the exception of 11 and 29, were owned by the CPR for a distance of some 20 odd miles on each side of the main line.

The Swift Current, Saskatchewan, to Empress, Alberta branch line was started in the fall of 1911. Before construction started representatives from the railway chose the locations along the railway survey and bought the land required for townsites. In the case of Success the whole section was bought with the idea of developing a demonstration farm.

At the time of the sale my father was living in South Dakota so the agent was sent there to deal with him. After considerable difficulty and many telegrams to the CPR office, the transaction was finally made and the agent wired back one word, 'Success'."

SUMMERBERRY

The name began with the Indians of the early days as they always timed their visits to this area with berrypicking time. To the north is the Qu'Appelle valley with its many adjoining coulees. These are favorite berry-picking spots as the saskatoons, chokecherries, cranberries, pincherries and raspberries all grow in abundance in good seasons. So the place of the summer berries became Summerberry.

Summerberry is a small village one mile north of the Trans-Canada Highway Number One between the towns of Wolseley and Grenfell. The village is very pretty in the summer with its trees and a creek and a dam. The main line of the CPR with its three elevators and annexes forms the northern edge of the village.

The large stone school which was built in 1907 and given the number 33 closed in September, 1966. At one time it held 85 pupils but the remaining few are bussed to Wolseley eight miles to the west. The population of the village has dropped to 60 but among them are names dating back to the early settlers: Laidlaw, McQuoid, McCowan, King, Linnell, Waugh, Fleming, Smith, Scobie, McMain, Lewis and Bowering.

SUMMER COVE

Summer Cove is a country post office south of McCord. The first postmaster was Ferdinand Morisette whose son, Walter, now holds the job. Mr. Morisette chose the name Somerset but it was refused so he just chose Summer Cove because it was close to Somerset in sound.

An account of how this family got to the district is worth recording:

"Mr. and Mrs. Morisette with their seven children, Alfred, Joseph, Angeline, Agnes, Eva, Maude, and Walter, came by train from Wisconsin, U.S.A. to Mortlach and then started south 120 miles by wagon through a roadless country. It took them two weeks to arrive at their destination by following the banks of Wood river. Only one house broke the monoto-

ny of the landscape from Gravelbourg south."

SUMNER

In 1882 a number of English settlers homesteaded in a block just north of Esterhazy and a little south of Zeneta. One of these, James Sumner, located on SW 4-20-1 W2 and acquired a post office which he kept in his home. He named it Sumner. The first mail was hauled in from Whitewood to the south on the main line of the CPR.

The post office closed out in 1907 when the Grand Trunk Pacific was built west. The village of Zeneta on this line became the trading center.

This information came from Richard A. Nevard of Fort San, Saskatchewan.

SUNNY GLEN

When the CNR built southwest from Unity in 1930 headed for Castor, Alberta (they got as far as Bodo), the second grain point on the line, about twelve miles out, was Sunny Glen. The name came from a country school less than two miles to the east. Jim White, Joe Davis, Earl Ross, Jim Coutts, John Sherwood, Jim Horsman, Sebastian Stabbler, John Bretzer, Lawrence Keller, George Metcalf and Bert Tibbel were some of those who first delivered grain to the Searle and Federal elevators there. Frank Chegwin was one of the first buyers. The railroad was very welcome because it saved the farmers the long haul to Unity with triple deck grain tanks pulled by four-horse teams.

This is one of the railway lines that has been proposed for abandonment. Trains do not have a regular run on it now, they only come down the line when there's wheat to haul out.

SUNKIST

Sunkist was an inland post office east of Demaine. The first mail was hauled by Mr. Tuplin from Davidson, across the river. It was a long haul.

The name came from an orange as popular today as it was then. The post office closed out when the CNR came through in the early 1920's and the town of Demaine developed.

SUNNYVALE

Sunnyvale was a rural post office in the Viceroy-Verwood district that opened on

September 10, 1910, with Mr. M. H. Jordan as postmaster. He chose a very pretty name that described its location in a sunny vale. A railroad, better roads and cars caused it to be very short-lived. The office closed on April 4, 1912.

SUPERB
Superb, the second station west of Kerrobert on a CPR line running to Lacombe, Alberta, owes its name to a chance remark by Nellie McClung. This popular Canadian novelist and champion of women's rights was travelling through this part of Saskatchewan in the summer of 1913. That was a dry year and the prairie was parched brown so when she came to the heavy gumbo soil of this area where the grass was still green she exclaimed, "Superb, an oasis in the desert!"

This remark remained in the minds of the settlers and when the rails came through the following year and Ashley Walker moved his nearby country post office into the townsite, Superb was chosen as the name.

SUPREME
Supreme is on a branch line of the CPR that runs east from Notukeu to Val Marie. It is a station south of Cypress Lake at 28-2-26-W3. Supreme is more than a name, it's a feeling. A feeling the land-hungry homesteader (160 acres for 10 dollars!) had as he proudly looked at his farm. This feeling comes out in other prairie towns: Superb, Fortune and Success.

SURBITON
This district was first known as Hall's Crossing named for Charlie Hall, the first settler to arrive in the district. This was in 1904. Other early families in the district were Abrook, Law, Smith, Davy and Hopkins. William F. Hopkins farmed near the present townsite and when the railroad came through in 1913 his wife had the honor of naming the town Surbiton for her hometown, Surbiton, a suburb of London, England.

SURPRISE
Surprise is eighteen miles west of Golden Prairie near the Saskatchewan-Alberta border. Many of the early settlers were of German extraction and came up from North and South Dakota at the turn of the century. Their forefathers had emigrated to the USA from Bessarabia.

The first post office was opened in a converted granary in the farmyard of Mr. and Mrs. Bill Schneider. Mrs. Schneider was postmistress. Her son, Melbert, took over from her and the office was closed in the 1950's.

There was also a rural school four miles north of the post office. It also took the name of Surprise and has long since been closed.

The derivation of the name Surprise came about in this way. The Federal Government turned out glowing brochures of homesteading possibilities in Western Canada and distributed them in Ontario, Europe and the northern United States. When people arrived in the southwest corner of Saskatchewan they coined the expression: "Surprise! Surprise! not a tree in the country." It is possible that Surprise got its name in this way.

This information came from Mr. and Mrs. Jim McNeill of Saskatoon. Mrs. McNeill grew up in Surprise and vividly remembers that as a very young girl she was often sent to get the mail. She remembers Mrs. Schneider as a tall stately lady.

SUTHERLAND
Sutherland, which in 1956 amalgamated with Saskatoon, was named for William Charles Sutherland. He was a graduate in law from the University of Manitoba. He came to Saskatoon in 1903 and was elected to the legislature in 1905. He was speaker of the legislative assembly from 1908 to 1912. He also operated a large wheat farm near Sutherland.

SWAN PLAIN
Swan Plain is an inland post office near Norquay, 26-36-1-W2. It takes its name from the Swan river. This river was discovered by La Verendrye and was named Riviere des Cygnes by him probably because of the number of swans in the vicinity. In the trade returns from Fort Pelly Post, swan skins appear in considerable numbers.

SWANSON
The earliest records of this district, which is 12 miles south of Delisle, show

that Abraham Swanson, Bud Smith, Jack Jennison, Bill Nesbitt, Mr. Gray, Mr. Jay, Mr. Moen Sr., Henry Johnson, T. Girvan and Bert Wood were some of the early homesteaders who arrived between 1905 and 1908.

Mr. Abe Swanson was the first postmaster and mail had to be hauled from Hanley, crossing the South Saskatchewan river at Rudy ferry southeast of Swanson. The ferry was operated by Mr. Gibson until 1911 when Mr. Nichols took over.

The first storekeepers were Jelmar and Ernest Warner and the first blacksmith was Jens Larson. Mr. Larson's blacksmith shop was demolished by a cyclone in 1910 and after that he did the blacksmithing at his farm.

The GTP came through in 1911-12. It was later taken over by the CNR. The town used to be comprised of a bank, 2 grocery and dry goods stores, a Chinese laundry, a hotel, an implement store, 2 lumberyards, a livery stable, a pool hall, a hardware store with a dance hall upstairs, an Anglican church and 3 elevators. Dr. Chapman was the doctor.

Swanson is an excellent mixed-farming district but with better roads and methods of travel it is shrinking fast. They now have a hall; a Pool elevator; a store, post office and service station combined; a Catholic church; a Lutheran church and about 15 homes close in.

Abraham Swanson, for whom the town was named, came to farm in the district in 1905. He eventually had 6,400 acres under cultivation using a Rumely steamer and a 14-bottom plow.

SWARTHMORE

Swarthmore, the town that never was. The story of Swarthmore district began in Heathcote, Ontario, early in the century, when William Ira Moore, an active leader in the Society of Friends, discussed with other members of the sect the idea of establishing a meeting in Western Canada. Members of the Society were already settling in various parts of the West. It was hoped to bring them together in a single area.

In 1903, Mr. Moore and several other Friends, after driving over the area, were able to get consent of the government to a six-months option on townships 41 and 42, ranges 21 and 22 west of the third meridian. This was called The Friend's Colony. Several families of Friends moved in. The first Quakers to reach the district were Walter and David Armitage of Newmarket, Ontario, and Amaziah Beeson and his son, Ed, from Indiana. They arrived June 17, 1904, having driven their oxen from Saskatoon.

To Friends the natural name for the colony was Swarthmore. Swarthmore Hall in Yorkshire, England, was the home of Judge Fell and his wife, Margaret, who was one of the earliest members of the Society of Friends. After the judge's death, Mrs. Fell married George Fox, the founder of the sect, and Swarthmore Hall became the center from which spread the Society.

In high hope that the expected railway (CPR) would be laid through the colony William "Billy" Brockelbank had W. H. Sing survey thirty-five acres of lots on the NW¼-33-41-20. These he sold in Ontario at $10 a piece. A list of the owners, mostly non-resident, is shown in the first tax roll of Swarthmore School, dated August 21, 1906, and still extant. The school was built one and one-half miles east of the proposed townsite.

Actually, the first building was a modest church put up with lumber hauled out from Battleford. Walter Armitage was the minister. The second building to go up was a general store and post office operated by Amaziah and Ellen Beeson. Art Palmer, a man who had lost both legs, drew the mail from Battleford. He also went as far south as Kingsview (now Tako).

The railway did not come; it followed the GTR all the way from Saskatoon west to Unity as close as three-in-a-bed resulting in one of the worst cases of railway duplication in Canada. Only after they passed Unity (Swarthmore is about 18 miles north and east) and crossed did the two lines branch out and really serve the best interests of the country.

The Quaker colony was not able to fill its commitments in filling up the land and homesteads had to be thrown open to others. In fact, by 1915, the United Church had taken over and a fine church stands there today.

In the 20s Swarthmore got a second chance when the CPR built northwest of Wilkie to Lloydminster but again it was bypassed—this time ten miles to the north.

Nevertheless, Swarthmore developed into a fine farming district and over the years hundreds of thousands of bushels of wheat have been grown and hauled out to the railways at Adanac, Rockhaven and Cut Knife.

Today there still remains that thirty-five or so acres of townsite. It's now covered with thick prairie wool, as thick as the government and legal red tape that surrounds it and prevents it from being turned into grassland.

Too, there remains the ruts of the old Sounding Lake Trail that ran southwest of Battleford to Sounding Lake in Alberta. Mrs. Walter Haight (nee Verla Armitage) of 145 - 3rd Avenue East, Unity, can show you where they are.

Her husband, Walter, mayor of Unity and semi-retired farmer and businessman, was one of the originals of the Swarthmore district. He likes to tell in his quiet way the story of Jock McTavish, a Presbyterian, who after attending his first Quaker service and finding out that they never passed the collection plate became an instant, ardent, and long-time follower of the Faith.

SWEETGRASS

Sweetgrass is a bare loading platform on the Sweetgrass Indian Reserve fifteen miles west of Battleford. It's on a CNR branch line that ends at Carruthers. The railway point takes its name from the reserve.

This reserve was named for a famous Cree Indian chief of the mid-19th century who was the leading spokesman in the treaty negotiations at Fort Pitt in 1876, and the first signatory of that treaty, No. 6. While he died early in 1877, his band later (1880) selected the reserve named for him west of Battleford, and a grandson of the same name was chief a few years later. The chief's name is said to have been given to him when in his youth he made a lone-trip into Blackfoot country, killed one of the enemy and captured over forty horses. When he returned to the Cree camp he held up a tuft of grass dipped in the blood of his victim, and the whole camp took up the cry, "Sweet Grass," the name by which he became known (Wee-kas-koo-kee-sey-yin).

The present population of the reserve is close to 500 and the chief is Joe Weenie.

SWIFT CURRENT

For centuries the only men to camp beside Swift Current creek were roving bands of Indians. By the 1860s white men, who made their living trading with the Indians, were regularly travelling beside the creek, which flows down from the Cypress Hills and winds across the Prairies for 100 miles, eventually emptying into the South Saskatchewan river. Travellers found it confusing that the creek and river bore the same name, Saskatchewan, so they called the smaller stream Swift Current, the English derivation of "Saskatchewan," which means swift flowing. The city of Swift Current is situated on this creek and takes its name from it.

SWINBOURNE

In the early 1900s the CPR and the GTP literally built side-by-side all the way west of Saskatoon to Unity. Just a few miles beyond that point they crossed and the first grain point on the CPR beyond Unity was Buccleugh. Buccleugh was only a loading platform where you drove up, took the heavy metal grain scoop, humped your back and went to it loading the car directly. Mechanical grain augers had not been heard of!

Grain in those days was hauled out during the winter and farmers west of Buccleugh, particularly in the Scotstown District, found hauling grain a long cold day. Led by Harry Routledge, Bill Cutts, Joe Casey and Jack McLean they petitioned the CPR for a closer loading point. In 1927 they got it at Swinbourne about halfway between Buccleugh and Unity. Four elevators popped up—the Federal, the Pool, the National and one other—and they were soon doing a land-office business. The Stewart brothers Cec and Jimmy, and Hughie Gibson were some of the early grain buyers. Mr. and Mrs. Whittaker opened a small restaurant where teamsters could have a hot meal. Swinbourne was humming and several small businesses located there.

The railroad offered to call the place

Routledge but Mr. Routledge declined. CPR officials then named it for Lord Swinburne (1837-1909), a noted English poet. It came out officially with an extra "o" and no one knows why.

Today, all that is left are two Pool elevators, number 978 and 702. They are full of grain and boarded up. Not another building stands and only crumbly cement foundations overgrown with weeds mark the spot.

SYBOUTS

Sybouts is the name of a small post office in the Big Muddy region of Saskatchewan. It was named after J. P. Sybouts, a man of Dutch extraction, who was one of the earliest settlers. There are extensive sodium sulphate deposits in the vicinity.

SYLVANIA

Sylvania is the second stop south of Tisdale on a CPR line to Wadena. It has a population of 180 with three elevators, a garage, a poolroom, a hotel, two stores, a post office, a modern school built in 1965, and a new closed-in skating rink built also in 1965.

The first settler to come to this district was M. J. W. Bayliff. He arrived in 1903 and the following were not far behind: Ratcliffes, McMurdos, Playfords, Jacksons, Buxtons, Boyds and Fergusons. The settlement was known as Whitecoat and this was the name given to the first school built in 1908. The first post office was opened in the residence of Mr. William Ratcliffe in 1907 and he was instrumental in choosing the name Sylvania, which is Latin for "beautifully wooded country." The name fits this little village in the parklands of Saskatchewan

T

TABLELAND

Tableland is the first stop west of Estevan on a branch line of the CPR to Minton. This is just another in a long list of Saskatchewan place names that reflect the feeling of the early settlers as they looked out on the wide wide prairie. Names like Broadview, Longacre, Broadacres, La Plaine, Viewfield, Expanse and Horizon have something in common with Tableland. There is even a Flat Valley in Saskatchewan.

TAGAGWA

Tagagwa is the first stop west of Weyburn on a line of the CPR that runs through Axford and on to Wallace where it branches. Tagagwa is a Cree name for "Flat Land". Certainly, in this part of Saskatchewan, the name is most descriptive.

TAKO

The district surrounding Tako was settled in 1904. Mrs. Roy King operated the first post office in her home on a rise of land two miles east of the present site of Tako. Because of the wonderful view she had from her farm home she named

her post office Kingsview. Some of the early settlers were: Jimmy Dickson, Alec Taylor, Frank Krips, Johnny Grant, Bill Dempster, Tom Gauley, Joe Savard, and Tommy Lloyd.

When the railway came through in early 1900 the officials were following the practice of naming the places alphabetically. The people of the district wanted to keep the name Kingsview but the railway officials overruled them. When the post office moved to the townsite Mrs. Aked, the first postmistress, suggested the name Tako. She had made it up using the "T" from Alec Taylor, the "A" from her own name, the "K" from Frank Krips, and the "O" from Allard Olson. (Mr. Olson really resided at Phippen but as he was an oldtime fiddler who played for dances around the country he was well-known in the district). When a school was built in the town it was called Kingsview to compensate for the loss of the name.

The first store was operated by Tom Gauley, then Fred Davis had it for many years and in June of 1967 Mrs. Russell Bowrun, the last proprietor, closed it for good. A faded Davis' store sign still hangs above the door.

The two remaining residents in Tako, Mr. and Mrs. John Domony, have lived there for 15 years. He operates the Pool elevator and she teaches school at Unity.

In 1939 King George VI and Queen Elizabeth made a cross-Canada tour. At most of the larger places such as Unity and Biggar they made a brief appearance on the rear platform of their royal train, however the king requested that the train make an unscheduled stop in order that everyone could get out and have a stretch. The train stopped at Tako and much to the surprise and delight of the few people present who had merely gathered to watch the train go by, the royal couple walked among them shaking hands. Old-timers still talk about the thrill it gave them and all agree that this was the historical highlight of the district of Tako.

A visit to Tako revealed the following: the elevator is closed — has been for over four years — Mr. and Mrs. Domony have moved to Unity and their house in Tako has been taken over by Mr. and Mrs. Grant Davidson. The school and the old hall are gone. When they were dismantled the lumber was used to build a fine new Four Square Memorial Hall which houses a very active club from the following communities: Crooked Valley, Local Centre, Queenston and Tako.

Mr. and Mrs. Jack Stephenson, who operate a large farm nearby, supplied much of this information.

Early in 1977 the Tako Pool elevator was successfully transported by highway from its original site to Muddy Lake Farms Company Limited. Moving of the 38,000 bushel elevator the distance of 15 miles came off without a hitch. Wiebe Movers of Saskatoon have so far successfully moved more than 100 elevators.

TALLMAN

Tallman is hamlet near Redberry lake on a CNR line that runs from North Battleford to Prince Albert. In 1907 Don Parent, a Frenchman, homesteaded on the land where Tallman is situated. He was tall, well over six feet, and slim which made him appear even taller. His nickname was "Tallman."

The railroad was built in 1912 but Tallman grew slowly — it wasn't until 1925 that they got a post office. Today it

consists of two grain elevators, and one general store combined with a post office. Population? Nine.

TALLPINES

Tallpines is between Reserve and Usherville on a CNR line that runs north of Sturgis to Hudson Bay. The word is very descriptive of the locality because by this time a traveller has left the prairie and parkland of the south behind and is into the pines, the tall pines of the north.

TALMAGE

Talmage is on the CNR main line between Worcester and Brough. A line from Talmage goes southwest through Weyburn and on to Radville. It was named for Mr. Lewis Tallmadge who came from New York State in 1904, and purchased some land including what is now the townsite. In 1910 surveyors came and staked out a railway and the steel was laid in 1911. When the railway officials bought the land from Mr. Tallmadge they agreed to name the point after him. When the name came out it had only one "l" and the "d" had been dropped. However, it was never changed.

Talmage has met the fate of many small towns, in 1965-66 alone it lost: a station agent, a post office, a store, and a consolidated school which included eight rural schools. We received this information from Mrs. M. Tallmadge, wife of a descendent of the family, for whom the town was named.

TANGLEFLAGS

Early settlements on the prairies had a tendency to be "one of a kind": the French at Gravelbourg, the English at Evesham, the Ukrainians at Dnieper, the Germans at Leipzig, the Irish at Shamrock, the Scottish at McTaggart and so on. Their names reflected their nationalities. However, when the area around Tangleflags was thrown open for homesteading people of many ethnic groups arrived. When it came time to pick a name for this inland post office several groups were vocal and a compromise was reached on a name that is one of the most colorful and interesting in Saskatchewan.

Where is Tangleflags? It's northeast of

Lloydminster in line with Frenchman Butte but on the south side of the river.

The first postmaster was Henry Beavington who hauled the mail from Hewitt's Landing. Some of the early homesteaders were Walter and Earl Chapman (1906), Amundruds (1907), Charley Despard, Bellingtons, Beavingtons, Jack and Tom Harbin, Matt Smiles, Jack Hickman, Charlie and Billy Hobbs, Guy and Ceddie Copper, Joe Makin, Bill Cosh and Sid Simons.

TANKA

Tanka was simply a water tower between Milden and Gaines on a main line of the CPR. A plentiful supply of good water was essential to the huge steam engines that pulled out trains years ago. Hence Tanka, a water tower that piped spring water for over three miles, came into being. It was so close to Milden that it never developed, even as a grain point.

TANNAHILL

Tannahill, a siding just east of Maple Creek, was named for Robert Tannahill (1774-1810), Scottish song writer and author of such favorite songs as "Gloomy Winter's Noo Awa' ", "Jessie The Flower Of Dunblane" and "The Braes O' Gleniffer".

TANTALLON

Tantallon was named for Tantallon Castle in Scotland, the homeland of the famous Douglas family of the district. At the age of 12 James Moffat Douglas came to Canada with his family and settled near Cranbray, Upper Canada. He was educated at the University of Toronto, Knox College, and Princeton Theology Seminary. Ordained a Presbyterian minister in 1867 he served in Ontario, India, Manitoba and finally at Moosomin, Saskatchewan.

On his retirement from the active ministry in 1893 he devoted himself to farming at Tantallon. He entered politics and became a leading spokesman for the Patrons of Industry, the first important agrarian protest movement on the Prairies and in 1896 he was elected to the House of Commons for Assiniboia East. He played an important part in presenting the case of the farmers against the CPR and the elevator companies. Their protest led to the establishment of the first federal Royal Commission on the grain trade in 1899 and the passage of the Manitoba Grain Act in 1900. Douglas was re-elected in 1900 and appointed to the Senate in 1906. He was buried in Tantallon on August 19, 1920.

TARNOPOL

Tarnopol is a predominantly Polish and Ukrainian settlement 30 miles southwest of Melfort. In 1907 five Polish families came to the district. They were: Anton, Tom and George Stocki, Andrew Lisniowski and Marcin Zembik. They came from the province of Tarnopol in Poland and were responsible for naming the townsite. In 1939 the part of Poland that includes Tarnopol was taken over by Soviet Russia and it now forms part of the Ukraine.

TATE

Tate is a small town just east of Watrous. The first settler to file a homestead in the district was Richard Kells. This was in 1904. The settlers who followed were mainly of Scottish descent. They had a habit of saying Ta te instead of good-bye. When they settled in Saskatchewan it was Ta te to their homeland and they took Tate as the name of the new home. This story came from Andrew King, the oldest living member of the community

The Saskatchewan Archives has information that the name was chosen by railway officials, following the alphabetical pattern of names on the line, and that it honors D'Arcy Tate, then solicitor for the Grand Trunk Pacific Railway Company.

TATSFIELD

Tatsfield is the second last grain point on a CNR branch line that runs from Battleford to Carruthers. Before the steel arrived in 1913 there was a well-established name in the district, Wardenville. This was named to honour Sandy and Jimmy Warden. Sandy was a well-liked jack-of-all-trades who at one time had been the Indian Agent on the Poundmaker and Little Pine reserves.

A post office and store run by Mr. William Murphy and a school built in 1911 were also named Wardenville.

However when the GT Railway built the line they chose to honour one of their officials and they named the point Tatsfield. The Wardenville post office moved into the townsite and took the name Tatsfield. The first store was operated by Mrs. Robinson in the office of the Scottish Co-op elevator.

Eventually a store was built and this in conjunction with the post office was operated by several people, one being Bob McInnis of Cut Knife. The last to have the store was Mr. Fawell and he closed out in the 50s.

TAYLORSIDE

If you draw one line west of Melfort and another south of Beatty, their point of intersection will be very close to Taylorside. At one time it had a post office, a store, and all the services needed in an early farming community. John Taylor (1843-1928) was an unusual man in that he pioneered three times. In June of 1873 he emigrated from England to Muskoka, Ontario, one hundred and fifty-three miles north of Toronto. His family followed the next year. He farmed two hundred acres of dense bush. It was a period of great struggle and hardship to hew a home out of the forest; no roads; miles away from the nearest town and over one hundred miles from the railroad.

In 1886, again came the call to move and he located in New Ontario, where he pioneered for five years. Then the lure of the West caught his fancy and in 1891, he went in for his third spell of developing land in a new area, settling in what is now known as Taylorside, where he continued to farm until 1917.

Mr. Taylor was once asked by a reporter "What kind of recreation did you have in those days?" He thought for a few moments on that and with a twinkle in his eye he replied, "Well, it wasn't a big problem with us and only three or four days a year were set aside for it. If you were British it was the 24th of May, Canadians used the first of July, Americans the fourth, and Orangemen the 12th. You see, by the time we had grubbed trees or picked roots all day, struggled with oxen or horses half-crazed with flies and mosquitoes, milked the cows after supper and then fixed fence or hoed in the garden until it was dark, we weren't looking for recreation — we were looking for bed!"

TAYLORTON

High on a man-made hill less than fifteen miles south of Estevan on highway 39 is a gear, suitably plaqued to tell a little of the history of coal mining in Saskatchewan. The gear once formed part of a machine that operated in the district, now dwarfed by the machines of the 70s. Center of the activity was the town of Taylorton now abandoned but still visible a mile to the north. A single tall brick chimney is the only thing left standing but sturdy cement foundations are all about in the undergrowth now grazed by cattle.

The name, Taylorton, came from John Taylor who gained control of the Souris Valley coal mine in 1900.

Souris lignite coal is either burned raw or as briquets. Right now trainloads of char are sent out in sealed potash cars to be further processed in the United States. The Boundary Dam electric generating plant just west of Estevan and clearly visible is a user of lignite coal from its own mine where a huge dragline scoops out thirty-three yards of dirt at a bite. This machine is called "Big Max." These deposits make Saskatchewan the largest producer of lignite coal in Canada.

TESSIER

In 1904 Dr. Wilfred Onesime Tessier took up a homestead on N.E. 36-32-11 W 3rd along the Old Bone Trail. He opened an office in his home and later two stores were built across the road from his home. One was run by the Shatilla Brothers and the other by R. J. Davis.

When a post office was acquired by Alex Shatilla it was named Tessier to honor the doctor. When the railway extended west from Saskatoon to Rosetown in the early 1900's it was nicknamed "The Goose Lake Line" because of its proximity to Goose Lake. The rail line was built a few miles north of the original Tessier and the post office moved to the new townsite and gave it its name.

Growth was rapid and by 1914 there were six elevators to handle the grain: British American, Canadian Consolidated, Saskatchewan Co-operative, Will

Grant and the two operated by The Goose Lake Grain Company. At that time there were over thirty-five businesses besides a school and two churches in Tessier. Dozens of fine residences completed the town.

Today Tessier is down to two elevators, the Pioneer and the Pool. Two businesses remain, a general store and a garage, both of which are operated by the Johnson family, Blondel, Vivian and sons.

The school is gone and the students are bussed to nearby Harris. What has happened to Tessier has been repeated in dozens of towns in Saskatchewan. However, Tessier is not dead or dying. Many fine residences remain. One is owned by Gilbert and Mrs. Hanson who came from Nebraska in 1908 and farmed in the district until their retirement.

When you next visit Tessier, call on Vivian Johnson and you will see on the post office wall a portrait of Dr. Tessier.

TETLOCK

Tetlock was the first post office established in the Canora district in 1891. The postmaster was James Tetlock and later Jack Tetlock. It was situated two miles south of Burgis on the White Sand river. In 1904 Jack Tetlock moved to Canora and the Tetlock post office closed.

THACKERAY

Thackeray is the first grain point on a CPR branch line that runs north from Wilkie to Lloydminster. In the south and southwest of the province it was common practice to name a town after a writer, and over a dozen places derived their names this way. The practice was less common in the northwest, so Thackeray is an exception. The late John Allan of Battleford lived in this district for a time and he heard that it was named for William Makepeace Thackeray (1881-1863) who was one of the greatest British novelists of the Victorian Age.

William Thackeray and Charles Dickens were the outstanding novelists of their time. While Dickens wrote of the lower classes and the social abuses that kept them in want and misery, Thackeray described and satirized the snobbishness of the upper classes. He hated sham and pretense, and ridiculed society's worship of wealth and rank. Vanity Fair, Thackeray's greatest novel, deals with the rise of a scheming woman, Becky Sharp.

THAXTED

Thaxted is the first grain point north of Melfort on a CPR branch line that ends at Gronlid. It likely was named by someone who had fond memories of Thaxted, North Sussex, England.

THEODORE

The town of Theodore was named after Theodore Seeman, a cattle rancher who lived two miles west of the present town.

At one time it was called New Denmark. Theodore is 29 miles west and north of Yorkton on Number 14 highway. You can find it on any map.

THE TWO RIVERS

The Reindeer river connects Reindeer lake to the Churchill river. On Reindeer river less than 20 miles north of the Churchill river is the settlement of The Two Rivers 55°-45'-103°09'. The name was adopted by the Canadian Permanent Committee on Geographical Names on September 6th, 1956. At this point two rivers flow into Reindeer river. Of one nothing is known but the other is Trapp creek, named after the World War II casualty Pilot Officer Byron A. Trapp.

THRASHER

Thrasher is a siding 12 miles south of Rosetown on a branch line of the CPR that runs from Milden to Matador. It was named for John Thrasher, a trainman who won the Military Cross in the First World War.

THUNDERCHILD

Thunderchild is a post office on the Thunderchild Indian Reservation. Chief Thunderchild — Pee-yas-seew-awasis in the language of the Cree — was one of the Chiefs who signed the Northwest Territories Treaty with Lieutenant-Governor Alexander Morris at Fort Pitt in 1876.

After signing the treaty, he and his band settled between the rivers west of Fort Battleford near the village of Delmas. In 1908 the reservation was changed to its present location near the town of Turtleford.

THUNDER CREEK

Thunder Creek is a locality west of Chaplin. The name was derived from the way the thunder used to echo and re-echo down a deep valley which had steep sides cut out by glacial streams of long ago.

TICHFIELD AND TICHFIELD JUNCTION

Lions, named for a local man, was a village on a CNR line between Macrorie and Dunblane. The first settlers came in 1902. Soon there was a store, several houses, a service station and three elevators.

When the CNR ran a spur line to Beechy the village of Lions was one mile from the actual junction. The towns-people of Lions did not move to the junction. A small village grew up at Tichfield Junction, named for a small village in England. Through the years a store, post office, station and school were built at Tichfield Junction. The villages grew closer together and finally Lions changed its name to Tichfield.

From 1920 to 1945 Tichfield was quite an active community because of the railway junction so close by. One early settler, Mr. Carl Samuelson, tells of getting a group of his friends together and after getting permission from the train crew, boarding the engine and heading for the dances at Dunblane, five miles away. They would take turns at shovelling coal into the burner of the engine to keep the steam up while the others would be dancing. After the dance, they would come on the return trip to Tichfield. They also made many four-mile trips to Macrorie with their cars on the railway tracks when the roads were impassable.

By 1970 there was nothing left at the Junction and only three elevators and three houses (one not used) remained at Tichfield.

TIEFENGRUND

In the early 1890's a German Mennonite community began to develop eight miles northeast of the present village of Laird. They named it Tiefengrund which means "deep ground".

The first mail came from Rosthern, a community larger than Saskatoon at that time. A post office was next established at Fort Carlton and when that burned down during the North-West Rebellion, a post office was set up in Pete Neufeld's home at Tiefengrund and named for the community. Cornelius Regier was the first postmaster and the office opened in 1897. It closed out in 1906 forcing local residents to go to Laird for their mail.

The first community building was the school. People attended church at nearby Eigenheim. The first school teacher was John G. Diefenbaker's father, George. John and Elmer attended the school. The second teacher was David Toews, who taught until 1903.

Elder Peter Regier organized the Rosenort Mennonite Church and they built across the road from Tiefengrund school in 1910. Reverend Abram Friesen was the first minister and today his grandson, Robert is carrying on in his footsteps.

This information came from Mr. and Mrs. Frank Harder of Saskatoon.

TIGER HILLS

There are hills at Tiger Hills — plenty of them. One mile south of the elevator is a very high hill from which you can see Jumping lake far to the south. In the early days tiger lilies carpeted every natural clearing. This beautiful flower, once so common throughout Saskatchewan, became our floral emblem. The first settlement in this district was in ahead of the railroad (CPR) and the district was named Tiger Hills by the following oldtimers: Alvin Olson, Alfred Thinglested, Henry Hanson, Lawson Wilson, Mr. Leland, Mr. Sutcliffe, Usher B. Ayles and Oliver Braaten. Tiger Hills is predominantly a Scandinavian community.

In discussing a name some people suggested Tiger Lily Hills but others thought it too cumbersome. They settled for Tiger Hills, one of the nicest place names in Saskatchewan. The people of the district are nice, too, as attested to by Hugh John McKenzie "Buckshot" Ross, who taught there from 1933 to 1940 and now farms south of Davis. Mr. Ross said he well remembered his first day as a teacher. It was in the square Tiger Hills red-brick school No. 1516 that sits on a plain two miles east of the elevator. On his first day 58 children showed up. He sent the older students out to play while he sorted out the younger ones. It seemed that everyone wanted to go to school! However, when he had finished fifty-two were left, grades one to ten and he started in. He taught there for six years with an average enrolment of fifty-five and then he joined the RCAF as a mechanic. He served in many points in Canada and rose to the position of an inspector of planes being built for the government. On discharge he went back to the home farm near Senator siding. He is still highly thought of in the Tiger Hills district and one has only to mention the name, Hugh Ross, to get a conversation going.

Tiger Hills, unlike many other small communities in Saskatchewan, was never much of a place for size. It was small and what there was of it was scattered. Mr. Alvin Olson's blacksmith shop was a quarter of a mile west of the elevator. Mr. Braaten opened a store beside Mr. Olson's blacksmith shop and when Usher B. Ayles took over he moved it a little farther west to the highway. It is now closed. The school was two miles east of the elevator and stands all alone. It is now used as a community center and is well kept. The Pool elevator is open for grain two days a week and the buyer is Mr. Glen McCallman. He spends the other three days buying for the Pool at Fenton. This is beautiful country with a symbolic Saskatchewan name, Tiger Hills.

TINY

Tiny is the first grain delivery point west of Canora on a CNR line. It may have been named for a township in Simcoe County, Ontario, organized in 1822. The township was named after one of Lady Sarah Maitland's three pet dogs: Flos, Tay and Tiny.

Lady Sarah was the wife of Peregrine Maitland, Lieutenant-governor of Upper Canada, 1818-1828.

At one time the hamlet of Tiny had a station, a church, a couple of stores, a garage and three elevators. About all that's left are the elevators.

TISDALE

At one time this community was known as "Doghide" after the Doghide creek which flows nearby. When the CNR came through the name was changed to Tisdale in honor of a railway official, F. W. Tisdale. It was incorporated

as a village in 1905 and as a town in 1920.

TITANIC

Titanic is an inland post office half-way between Carlton and the Wingard ferry.

In 1908 officials of the White Star Steamship Company announced that they would eclipse all previous records in shipbuilding with a vessel of staggering dimensions. The Titanic resulted. If you stood her on end she was 882½ feet high; the largest building in the world at that time was the Woolworth Building in New York at 750 feet. She was considered unsinkable. So much so, that she did not carry near enough lie boats for the 2500 passengers she could accommodate.

On Wednesday, April 10th, 1912, she sailed out of Southampton, England, at noon on her maiden voyage bound for New York. She was out to set a record and in spite of several warnings of an ice field ahead she did not let up in speed.

She struck a huge iceberg on the night of April 14-15, and sank within a few hours carrying many to their death. The British inquiry reported 1490, the British Board of Trade 1503, and the U.S.A. 1517. Three things we know for sure: 1) Charles Melville Hays, president of the Grand Trunk Pacific Railways, was numbered among the heroic men who willingly stood back to make room for women and children in the life boats. (Melville, Saskatchewan, is named for him.) 2) The Carpathia caught the SOS and raced 58 miles to the rescue. It picked up 705 survivors at dawn. 3) Besides giving a name to an inland post office in Saskatchewan she gave a new word to the English language, titanic. When you speak of anything being titanic it means it's really big.

In 1970 newspapers carried accounts of plans to try to salvage the great ship.

TOGO

The first settlers began to arrive in this district at the time of the Russo-Japanese War of 1904-1905. The town of Togo was named for Admiral Togo who was at that time gaining fame. It was he who led the Japanese Fleet in a startling victory at the Battle of Tsushima.

Events leading up to it were spectacular. Japan broke off diplomatic relations with Russia on February 6, 1904. On February 8, Vice-Admiral Heichachiro Togo's fleet attacked Russian ships at Port Arthur and Vladivostok. They bottled up the remaining ships by mining the harbor entrances. Ships that escaped were defeated in the Battle of the Sea of Japan.

Then the Russians ordered the Baltic Fleet, under Admiral Zinovi Rojestvensky, to sail to the Far East. This 28-ship fleet steamed all the way from the Baltic Sea around Africa, across the Indian Ocean, and into the Korean Strait. But there the Japanese Fleet under the command of Vice-Admiral Togo nearly annihilated it in the Battle of Tsushima.

TOMPKINS

Tompkins is fifty miles southwest of Swift Current on the main line of the CPR. It was named after a railroad contractor, Thomas Tompkins of Brockville, Ontario.

In the January 5th, 1977 issue of the *Gull Lake Advance*, a picture was reproduced which showed a passenger train beside the new station on December 13, 1912. At that time there were 750 people in Tompkins according to John Batter, a resident of the district for a long time. Today, February, 1977, there are about 300 residents.

The first man into the district was Bill Horsborough. He came in 1903 and set up as a squatter in the Great Sand Hills about twenty-five miles north of the present town. The second settlers of note were the Dimmocks. They chose a site fourteen miles south and established a ranch. Bernard Dimmock, a son, still operates it.

The townsite was built on the homestead of Matt Casey. From 1907 until 1912 a converted boxcar served as a station and freight shed.

The homestead boom came in 1910-12 and tapered off until it closed out in 1920. By 1915 there were seven elevators in operation. By 1976 five of them were still standing.

In 1967 a full train load (fifty-two cars) of sheep were loaded to be shipped to the East.

The last station agent to serve at Tompkins was Murray Tremka. He completed his duties in 1968 and two years

later the building was torn down for lumber.

Every town produces at least one character and Tompkins was no exception. It had Bill Wells. Bill arrived with his dad from Idaho in 1912. In 1922, at the age of fourteen, he was driving a six-horse team on a stage coach from Burns Landing to Smithers on twisting mountain roads in British Columbia. When he was 17 he was separator man on a large threshing outfit in Northern Alberta. He broke broncos at a set price per head for ranchers around Pincher Creek. He joined the rodeo circuit and last held the job of constable on the one-man Tompkins police force. He died with his boots on at 11:00 p.m. on the main street of Tompkins one peaceful evening in 1970. His heart failed him.

This information came from Henry C. Poegal who, with his father, Christopher, came to Tompkins in 1929.

TONKIN

Tonkin is less than 10 miles east of Yorkton. It was named for Mr. Tonkin who lost his life in World War I. The CNR came in 1915.

The following is a list of firsts for Tonkin. In 1915 two elevators were built, the Bawlff with Mr. C. Walker as agent and the Gibson Grain Company with Mr. Peaker as agent. In 1916, the United Church was built and it's still in use. In 1926, Mr. Callender opened the first store and post office. In 1928, the Pool built an elevator with Stan Callender as agent. In 1954, the Co-op store was opened. In 1948, the curling rink was built. In 1951, John Brigidear built his welding shop. In 1965 the store was sold and moved to Gerald.

In 1966 Tonkin had a population of 32. It had one elevator (the Pool), one welding shop, one garage and a post office.

TORCH RIVER

Torch River is a farming district with a Co-op store, a Baptist Church, a community hall, and until recently, a school. The students are now bussed into Nipawin.

The earliest settlers in the district and the tribe of Alex Daniels' from the Fort a la Corne reserve got along very well. Every spring the Indians would call at the settlements along the Torch river and pick up hides. For every two hides they collected they would return one tanned hide.

Torch River takes its name from the Torch river which rises in Candle lake and flows southeast until it empties into the North Saskatchewan.

TORQUAY

Torquay came into being in 1913 when the CPR ran a branch line from Estevan to Neptune. One of the railway officials on tasting the well water on the townsite exclaimed that it reminded him of Torquay, England and so they named the town Torquay

Mrs. S. Johnson, postmistress at Torquay, says that she often gets letters directed to Torquay, England, and a few years ago a couple from England called at Torquay because of its name. They found little similarity because Torquay, Saskatchewan, is out on the dry Prairies and Torquay, England, is a famous seaside resort on the south shore of England near Plymouth.

TOTNES

Totnes is the third last stop on a CPR branch line to McMorran. When the railroad was being built in 1923 the road boss asked Mrs. John Riddalls what she would like to name the station. She suggested Totnes because she had lived near a village by that name in Devonshire, England.

TOTZKE

In 1905 the Canadian Northern built through from Humboldt to Warman and in 1911 they built west out of Watrous and north from Young to Prince Albert. Totzke was the junction of these lines. Dana, a mile to the west on the main line, became the town and Totzke remained small.

In 1967 the train from Prince Albert came only as far south as Meacham and the Totzke station closed. The balance of the rails have been taken up to form spur lines into the potash mines at Allan and Rutan.

Totzke is named for Albert Frederick Totzke, MLA for Vonda, 1908-1917, MP for Humboldt, 1925-1935. He was a druggist at Vonda at the time. Some of the earliest settlers in the district were the

following: Yuzwenko, Wawryk, Markewich, Misura, Kyba, Deptuck, Slywka, Chilliak, Sopotyk, Bodnar, Evanishen, Matieshen, Popovitch, Komarnicki, Dushenko, Maruk, Chyliak, Leskow, Luczak, Sluchinski, Miciopa, Megyesi, Lesyshen, Sluchinska, Pirozuk, Galgan, Skarra and Kowalski.

TOUCHWOOD

Touchwood gots its name from the dry pithy wood of dead poplar trees of the district. The Indians gave it its name because when they went to light a fire they just had to touch it with a spark from a flint.

Another interesting thing was that it burned with little or no smoke. One Indian woman from the File Hills Reserve says that in the early days they would often make a long trip to get a load of this pithy wood for their camp fires. Then, when there was any hostility, their enemy could not see any smoke and consequently would not know where they were camping.

TOUCHWOOD SIDING

Touchwood Siding is the first stop east of Punnichy. The Grand Trunk Pacific arrived there in 1908. There is quite a territory known as Touchwood. The rolling hills were known as the north and south Touchwoods.

TRAILL BAY

Following World War II several lakes, bays and rivers in Northern Saskatchewan were named for members of the armed forces who lost their lives in services.

Traill Bay on the north shore of Trade Lake, just east of Stanley Mission, was named for Wesley Arthur Roger Traill.

Wesley Traill was born June 12, 1924 at Kingsland, Saskatchewan and was educated at St. Louis and in 1937 moved to Prince Albert. Upon graduation from Collegiate there, he enlisted in the Prince Albert Volunteers. He was eighteen years old.

Posted overseas, Wesley Traill (L86777) served two years and was cut down by a sniper's bullet while acting as a stretcher bearer in Belgium on October 24, 1944. He is buried near Antwerp, Holland. His grave has been visited by relatives and friends.

TRAMPING LAKE

Tramping Lake is a grain point on a CPR line between Wilkie and Kerrobert. It takes its name from nearby Tramping lake. The Tramping Lake came from two sources, Cree and English. The Cree word translated into English meant Thundering Hooves. The English called it Tramping Lake because of the well-tramped buffalo trails that led to it from all directions.

Mrs. Kauffman of St. Alphage remembers, as a girl of fourteen, trekking overland in 1906 with her family from Battleford to their homestead near Tramping lake. She said the buffalo trails down to the water were wide, numerous and up to 14 inches deep. It was very difficult to cross or drive with them and not tip your wagon. She said there were a hundred gophers and a pair of badgers on every knoll. Buffalo bones (complete skeletons) were strewn everywhere.

Poundmaker, a great Cree chief, and his band made a practice of wintering at the southern tip of the lake. Nearby there were fresh water springs, wood for fuel; in winter deer sheltered in its coulees and in spring there was a plentiful supply of fish. Today Tramping Lake is an educational center, surrounded by a good grain growing district and, in addition, it has a fine regional park on the lake nearby.

TRAYNOR

Traynor is on the main line of the CPR between Biggar and Wilkie. R. A. Stewart of Colby, Kansas, came to the district in 1906. The steel did not arrive until 1908 and Mr. Stewart recalls a visit to Saskatoon whereby he travelled over the new grade on horseback. He met the steel gang at Perdue. On one of his other visits to Saskatoon he recalls seeing the wreck of the Steamship "Medicine Hat" on the 19th Street bridge.

When the railway arrived they named the town Traynor in honor of one of their officials. This same official, while visiting the town, noticed they had spelled his name "or" instead of "er". He had the sign changed on the station house. However it's hard to change things once they are set and Traynor is back to "or" today. Following the arrival of the railway in 1908 Traynor developed into a thriving little town with two elevators, three stores, one hotel, a livery barn, blacksmith shop, bank, school, churches, and all the facilities needed to support a farming community.

In the early days the settlers of our province worked hard and played hard. During the short summer season between seeding and harvest small prairie towns had a continuous round of combined agricultural fairs and sports days that ended with a big dance in the community hall. They became a vital part of the entertainment life on the prairies. They generated a local pride and activity that is hard to describe. Each town had a baseball club and it was every boy's dream to "make the team". Competition was so keen and plentiful that baseball players on the prairie developed to the point where some were invited to try out with the Big Leagues in the States. Archie Edwards of Traynor was one of these.

In 1928 he was invited to the Boston Braves and Chicago Cubs training camps. He was offered a triple A contract but preferred to return to Saskatchewan where he played with Ruthilda.

Now there are only two residents who were among the original settlers, Russell Buglass and Jim Shaw. What has happened to Traynor has been repeated over and over throughout Saskatchewan. First the railway cut back its services, then the station and eventually the elevators closed. Businesses folded. The main store and post office which Billy Edwards had run changed hands many times but held on under its last owners, Clark and Ann Wirachowsky until 1971. When they closed it they moved the post office to the front room of their home. On May 31, 1976 it too closed — the last place of business in Traynor. Now, residents travel to Landis, six miles southwest on the main line of the CNR for even their mail.

There are only a handful of families left with a total population of twenty out of what Mr. Buglass described as once a "bright little town".

TREELON

Treelon is fifteen miles straight south of Climax on highway 37. It is a port of entry and was named after the lone tree that stood on the banks of Lone Tree lake. It was the only tree in the country. Much indignation was felt by the natives one morning in the summer of 1913 when it was found that someone, who apparently needed a log, had chopped the tree down.

An excellent little booklet "Climax Before and After" was compiled in 1955 by A. H. Stevens and published by the Climax Board of Trade. On the very last page there is a picture of the famous "Lone Tree."

TREGARVA

The name Tregarva has been familiar to early settlers since 1882 but the origin of the word has become lost in obscurity. Some say the name is Irish, others contend that it comes from a town in Wales. Still others claim it is an Indian name meaning "barren of trees," and finally, some believe the name was bestowed upon the community by the federal government. Information received from the post office authorities discloses that records of that date are not available. Some pioneer settlers must have been responsible for the name Tregarva, for it was associated with the district as early as 1882 and adopted by the first post office established in the Petrie home.

When visiting is not a possibility, the next best thing is mail and so it was with Mr. J. E. Petrie (SW¼-S34-T19-R20-W3) who offered to keep the post office in his home, already bulging with seven children. The first post office was opened there on February 1, 1885, and remained there for 28 years. The mail was brought from Craven once a week by Mr. Hoskins on horseback and later by Mr. Reuben Taggart. Much money was sent by mail in those days. Payments for carloads of wheat came by registered letter.

The Bulyea branch of the CPR was gradually making an appearance. The CPR found the present site of the hamlet a convenient spot to build a "Y" on the track for trains about to enter the valley enroute to Craven.

At its height Tregarva had the following: a post office, a store, three elevators, a Co-op store, a small hotel, a Massey-Harris implement agency, a lumberyard, a blacksmith shop (the first "Village Smithee" was Jock McNally). From a very small station built in 1914 Tregarva progressed to a larger one with Mr. Brown as

agent. Earlier, one just flagged the train at the elevators.

By 1970 practically all of this had disappeared except the elevators and a few houses. The district is permanently established but the hamlet is faltering. However, one might dream of the foreseeable future and of Tregarva becoming a select suburb and shopping centre of Regina, which has only to extend about ten miles in the right direction to make this a reality.

TREWDALE

Trewdale, on a C.P.R. line in southern Saskatchewan, is named after postmaster Trew who ran an early post office in the vicinity. This information came from the CPR files.

TRIBUNE

In 1906 Gerhart Voechting came to Tribune as a 17-year-old lad and filed on SW 13-4-14-W2. Today, his son Harold farms two miles from the homestead on which he was born. Two generations of Voechtings have given a lifetime of service to their community.

In 1913 the CPR built a branch line northwest from Estevan and it ended with Tribune, Maxim and Neptune. The name Tribune was given to the townsite by the CPR officials and the story goes it was in recognition of the extensive and favourable coverage given to the building of the new line by the Winnipeg Tribune, a popular paper of the time.

A few of those who were in before the railway besides Gerhart Voechting were: George and Henry Kurtz, Ed Schefte, Minor Slager, Mike Kramer, George Pepper, John Stainbrook and Cecil Cull.

The years that followed the building of the railroad were busy ones and the most prosperous for the town. Although the population rarely exceeded 300 the decade 1916 to 1926 saw Tribune reach its peak. Blessed with a large trading area, particularly to the south, five general stores opened in the town. Two lumberyards, a branch of the Weyburn Security Bank, a newspaper (The Tribune Star), three garages, a blacksmith shop, two livery barns, a billiard hall and barbershop, a liquor store, one hotel, two cafes and two churches completed the little town.

In 1926 the first blow fell when the CPR built another branch line that started about six miles east of Tribune and went west to Minton. Towns that sprang up along this line cut into Tribune's business. In fact, some of Tribune's merchants moved to the new townsites along the line.

In 1959 the CPR applied for and got permission to abandon the line between Tribune and Neptune. The town has steadily dwindled since 1926 and now the population is down to 135.

Grain is still king at Tribune. In 1970 it had a specified delivery acreage of 78,000 acres and there were 145 permit holders.

TROSSACHS

Trossachs is situated 18 miles west of Weyburn on the old Wood Mountain Trail. Years before the country was settled this was used as a camping site by Indians and settlers because it had the largest grove of trees for miles around. It was named by a CPR employee because it reminded him of his hometown of Trossachs in Scotland.

Trossachs is a magnificent wooded valley in Perth County, Scotland. Sir Walter Scott (1771-1832) made the valley famous in his poem, "The Lady of the Lake" and his novel "Rob Roy." Trossachs lies between Loch (Lake) Katrine and Loch Achray. Since Walter Scott's time man has improved on this district by making a little chain of four lakes. They are all connected and a small excursion steamer runs regularly through them.

TRUAX

Truax is the first station south of Avonlea. It was built on land which had been homesteaded by a family by the name of Schuetts.

The Schuetts had come from Ontario and when the railway came through in 1911 they were instrumental in having the station named Truax in honor of a member of the Ontario Provincial Legislature, George Truax.

TUBEROSE

Tuberose is the third last point on a CPR line that extends south from Milden to Matador. Mrs. Charles Davenport, one of the early settlers, was given the opportunity to name the place and she chose Tuberose, a name derived from a flower popular in her native Minnesota, USA.

Many places in Saskatchewan are named for native flowers. Wild Rose, Rose Valley and Briercrest commemorate our lovely prairie rose. The province's floral emblem is remembered with Lily Plain and Tiger Hills. Willows and Willowbunch recall the clumps of tough native shrubs that lined most water courses. The settlers at Bounty were so taken with the carpet of prairie flowers that their suggested name for the townsite was Botany.

TUFFNELL

Tuffnell is the last stop on a branch line of the CPR east from Lanigan to Goudie. Sam Wunder (1889) and Albert Hair (1891) were the first settlers into the district. They got their groceries and mail from Sheho. In 1906 Mr. and Mrs. Charles Woodhead started a store in the district and in 1908 the railway came through. The townsite was named by the railway for John Tuffnell, a director of the Manitoba and North Western Railroad.

TUGASKE

The village owes its name to the Indian word, Tugaske, which means "flat land" but the popular and more apt translation is "good land."

J. Cooper and W. Wilson were the first settlers to arrive. The year was 1904.

The CPR pushed north from Moose Jaw and arrived in 1907. The first station agent was Tom Kelleger, an Irishman.

Today, Tugaske is on highway No. 42, nine miles from the Qu'Appelle Dam.

TULLIS

In the fall of 1905, a group of land seekers left southern Manitoba. One of the group, John S. Tullis, filed on NW quarter 18-24-7-W3 for himself, and the other three quarters of section 18 for his three sons, Jim, Dave and Melville, by proxy. He also filed for his brother William, in Ontario.

They went back to Manitoba and next spring brought out supplies and equipment and started their homestead duties. Their nearest railway point was Davidson, sixty miles away, and their post office was Riverview, two miles north of Elbow.

In 1906 at a meeting to discuss the establishment of a post office and supply store, it was moved that J. S. Tullis have the post office and that it be named Tullisville. Permission was granted to open the post office on January 8, 1907. Jim and Dave Tullis had the contract to haul mail from Davidson.

In the fall of 1908, the steel of the CPR went through Elbow, mail was hauled to this center rather than Davidson, reducing the distance considerably.

At about this time more post offices were established in the area and mail was distributed from Tullisville to Lucky Lake, Greenbrier, Northland and Rossduff.

At a meeting in March 1909, J. S. Tullis was chosen as a delegate to take a petition for a railway to the proper authorities. This he presented to Premier Scott. A railroad was finally laid as far as Dunblane in 1913 or 1914 and mail was then dispatched from there.

In 1919 the steel went through Birsay and to Tullisville. It arrived at Lucky Lake on December 24th. At the suggestion of the CN engineer, McKenzie, the name of Tullisville was changed to Tullis.

Fred Smith built a store and post office in 1919 and later was a grain buyer. J. S. L. Tullis had an implement agency and eventually became a grain buyer. A. E. Cunningham had a garage, A. R. Inkster was the local blacksmith and Dave Tullis hauled freight. In 1921, there were thirty farmers in the district.

Gumbo Flat School was built three-quarters of a mile from the village, being more central for children attending school.

Mrs. Edith Hvidston was the postmistress when the store closed in 1964.

At present, the Pool Elevator and the Co-op bulk oil station are operating.

This information came from Mrs. J. H. Cannon (Nee Ellen Tullis).

TULSA

This post office opened about 1914 on N.E. 13-55-22 W3. The first and only postmaster was Dr. Puckett who had come to the area from Tulsa, Oklahoma. The remains of the post office can be seen near the present Loon Lake highway. One of Dr. Puckett's sons died and the family

all left the district in 1920 and the post office was closed.

TUNSTALL

Tunstall is tucked away in the southwest corner of the province. It's the only grain point on a short CPR branch line that runs north from Hatton to the end of the line at Golden Prairie. It was possibly named for Tunstall, Suffolk, England. However, the name Tunstall is also to be found in the counties of Kent, Lancashire, Norfolk, Staffordshire and the East and North Ridings of Yorkshire. Someone from any of these counties could have been responsible for its origin.

It is also possible that it commemorates the famous Bishop Tunstall who supported the Tudor monarchs.

TURNOR LAKE

Turnor Lake settlement is named after the lake of the same name. The name was proposed by Guy Houghton Blanchat, D.L.S., B.C.L.S., in 1918 after Philip Turnor.

Philip Turnor was born in England in 1752. He was engaged by the Hudson's Bay Company in 1778 as a surveyor, the first man to be engaged in this capacity by the company.

Accompanied by his brother, John, he travelled throughout Rupert's Land surveying the company's establishments. He supervised the building of Fredrick House in 1785 and stayed there until 1787. In the autumn of 1787 he returned to England, drafting maps of the country through which he travelled. He returned to Canada in 1789 and was stationed at Cumberland House. He instructed David Thompson and Peter Fidler in surveying, 1790-92. In 1792 he made a journey to Lake Athabasca and returned to England.

The map of North America published in 1795 embodies the results of Turnor's surveys. All subsequent maps of the interior of Canada were based on his work. He died in London early in the 1800s.

TURTLEFORD

From the North Battleford News-Optimist of December 10, 1965:

"A ford is a place where a stream or river can be crossed easily. Usually the banks are wide, the water is shallow, and the bottom is firm. John Bloom, an American and Frank Webb, a Briton, met at such a place on the Turtle river in 1907 and decided to settle down. Using their oxen to break ground they began farming and during the next few years many more people settled near them."

TUXFORD

The CPR began to talk of a line through from Moose Jaw to Outlook in the early 1900s. When Brigadier General G. S. Tuxford, then a homesteader in the district, heard that CPR officials were in Moose Jaw planning to lay out the line, he journeyed there. He met the officials, drove them to his farm and with great hospitality, diplomacy, and a couple of days of good goose hunting, managed to convince them that this district had a great future in growing grain. So that is how Tuxford got its name.

TWAIN

Twain is between Rush Lake and Herbert on a main line of the CPR in southwestern Saskatchewan. There is a possibility that it was named to honor Mark Twain whose writings were very popular at the turn of the century. Many towns in Saskatchewan were named for authors. Twain in Scottish means two. There is a Twain, California, and settlers from there may have been responsible for the name.

TWAY

Tway is between Reynaud and Crystal Springs on a CPR line that runs north of Humboldt to Prince Albert. It may have taken its name from Tweed, Scotland. In 1160 the name was spelled Tweda. It is derived, probably, from Twy, "to check or bound" in reference to the characteristics of the river. Too, it may have been twa which is two in Scottish.

TWEEDSMUIR

Nestled in the pines eight miles northwest of Christopher lake is the little store and post office of Tweedsmuir. The first post office in the district was half a mile east of the present location and was called Emma Lake.

When Emma lake developed as a popular summer resort it also opened a post office called Emma Lake and during the summer there was a bit of confusion in mail deliveries and so the original Emma Lake post office considered changing its name. At about this time Canada's Prime Minister William Lyon Mackenzie King (1874-1950) took the governor general of Canada, Lord Tweedsmuir, formerly John Buchan (1875-1940), on a motor trip to his showplace, Prince Albert National Park. They spent some time at Waskesiu. As the post office was being moved to its present location in Bob Hamilton's home at that time it was decided to ask that it be named Tweedsmuir. The name was accepted. Mr. and Mrs. E. Selander run the present combined store and post office.

TWIN LAKES

In 1913 the Twin Lakes post office opened just east of Hillmond in the home of William Noble. His son, George, was the mail carrier who brought the mail from Lashburn. George Noble had come to Canada from England in 1910 and worked on farms in the Lashburn and Marshall areas for two years before taking out his homestead near Hillmond. When his parents, Mr. and Mrs. W. H. Noble, their two sons, Harry and Hartley, and their two daughters, Amy and Florence, decided to join George in Canada in 1912, they left England just ahead of the Titanic. Harry Noble says that they were in the same floe of ice as the Titanic went down in, but being a slower boat and not trying to break any records like the Titanic was, they went 250 miles out of their course to get around the ice. They were 13 days crossing and when they landed at St. Johns they heard that the Titanic had sunk.

TWIN VALLEY

Twin Valley was an inland post office five miles east of Scout lake. Its exact location is 30-4-29-W2. The first settler in the district was Mr. Oscar Field, and he became the first postmaster.

Twin Valley was named because of two valleys meeting in the district. One from the southwest with the Wood river running through it; the other joining it from the southeast with a creek flowing through the village of Glentworth. The creek joins the Wood river at the north end of the Twin Valley district.

The post office was used until the railroad came through in 1928, after which the village of Glentworth took over.

TYNER

Tyner is on a branch line south from Eston that ends at White Bear. The first homesteaders in this district came from South Dakota in 1906. Mr. Burns kept the first post office and he called it Tyner in honor of a neighbor, Harry Tyner. The first mail was brought in from Swift Current, 75 miles to the south, by buckboard drawn by horses or mules. George and Fred Walen came in 1906 by way of Dakota but they were originally from Norway. The story is told that in the spring of 1907 with the horses all busy breaking the prairie, George walked to Swift Current and carried back a sack of flour, a plowshare, and a carton of "snoose."

There was another story that hadn't such a happy ending. Mr. John Paulson walked to Elrose and back in the winter of 1914 and froze his toes quite badly. After much suffering he cut them off himself with hoof clippers. They healed well.

The CNR came to Tyner in 1925 and three elevators were built.

TYSON

Tyson is at a "diamond". There, a CPR line from Moose Jaw to Hak crosses a CNR line that runs from Swift Current to Avonlea. Tyson was named for an early pioneer family. Descendants still live in the area.

TYVAN

Tyvan is about halfway between Regina and Stoughton on a main line of the CPR. The name Tyvan was given to the townsite by railroad officials. They combined the first letters of "Tyler" and "Van Horne," names prominent in the railway building of the day. Mr. J. Stewart Houston, one of the earliest settlers, arrived in 1905.

U

UNA

Una was the first post office in the Bengough-Viceroy district. It opened on March 2, 1908. It was operated in the sod house of Mrs. Stover, who named it for her daughter, Una. The post office closed on April 14, 1914.

Homesteaders of Scandinavian origin came into this district as a block from Hannaford and Wallum, North Dakota. They had an established band in their hometown and they brought their instruments with them. Johnny Rosvold built a large sod house and that was where they practiced once or twice a week. Members of the band were: Charles Rosvold (leader), O. E. Mossing, Henry Heiberg, Elmer Troxel, Arthur Rosvold, Johnny Rosvold, Henry Rustad, M. H. Hagen, Arthur Broughton, Oscar Nelson, Henry Stromme, Bernard Mossing, Ole Alm, Carl Mossing, Walter Seibert, Emil Monson, Louie Alm, Olaf Bakke and Emil Mossing.

This Una Band became known far and wide and had many engagements. First, at the 4th of July celebration at Lang in 1907 and 1908; at Willow Bunch in 1909; at Forward in 1910; at Weyburn in 1914; at Bengough, Viceroy, Pangman and Ogema in 1911 and 1912; at Regina Exhibition in 1915 and 1918; at Regina and Saskatoon Grain Growers Convention and at Milestone in 1918.

They also played at Whitetail and Flaxville in Montana.

UNION JACK

Union Jack is the name emblazoned on the lone elevator at this rail siding, and the farmers in the surrounding area are proud of it. But the name was not chosen without controversy.

It was back in the 1920s when the CNR line from Weyburn to Radville was built that it all started. The railway company wanted to name the siding Verendrye, after the man who was supposed to have been the first white man to see the Rocky Mountains. Local residents objected when it was discovered that Verendrye had not seen the Rockies, but instead the Black Hills of South Dakota. Local folk and the railway officials finally decided to use "a patriotic name."

What was more patriotic, in the days long before the great flag debate, than the name of the undisputed flag — the Union Jack?

UNITY

Unity, 120 miles west of Saskatoon on the main CNR line, was named for Unity, Wisconsin, U.S.A., the home of some of the early settlers in the district.

The drilling of exploratory wells for oil in 1946 led to three important discoveries — potash, natural gas and salt. The first attempt at potash mining in Canada was made at Vera, seventeen miles west of Unity. It was unsuccessful. However, the discovery of natural gas in commercial quantities at End Lake just south of Unity and the success of a Sifto Salt Plant a mile east of Unity have been instrumental in Unity's steady growth.

The history of Unity is closely tied to that of the late H. P. "Percy" Moffatt. He was born on the 25th of March in 1887 in Cumberland, Ontario, twenty miles east of Ottawa. As a tall thin seventeen year old he arrived in March of 1904 in Regina at the same time as a spring blizzard and his first job was shovelling snow at twenty cents an hour. It was hard work but he was glad to get it. He went back east and came west again in 1906 and came as far south as the present site of the Sifto Salt Company. He worked briefly for a Mr. Routledge who had seven other men and seventy-five oxen. They broke some of the first prairie around Unity. Over the years and along the way at Lauder, Manitoba and Winnipeg, Mr. Moffatt had picked up the carpentry trade and he landed in Unity in 1914 as the manager of the Beaver Lumber Company. He was a tireless worker and gave much of his time to community work. In 1919 he was the last overseer of the village of Unity and on November 1, 1919, when it was incorporated as a town, Percy Moffatt was its first mayor; the rest of the town council were Messrs. D. J. Kennedy, J. H. Jones, J. M. McLean, Dr. J.

A. Routledge, T. L. Malcolm and L. C. Brockaway.

Later Mr. Moffatt moved to Vermilion as manager of the Beaver Lumber Company there. On his retirement in 1958 he moved back to Unity and into the Unimac, a home for senior citizens shared equally by Unity and Macklin.

Percy was an ardent sport, especially in curling and his "runners" were something to behold. He, Earl "Lock" Lockridge and William "Bill" Dempster were the best of their time and it was nip and tuck when they met, no matter what rink was in front of them. Mr. Moffatt passed away on July 27, 1971.

Unity, a good town in a good district, is one of the growing centers in Saskatchewan. It now has a population of 2700 and steady construction is evident.

Unity in the 1930's had possibly one of the best rail passenger services in Canada. On the main line of the CNR it had two trains a day, east and west. At North Unity, a mile or so away, the CPR ran a passenger train east early in the morning and it returned at night.

Then, when the first diesels came out the CN put on a "skunk". This train ran in the middle of the day. It had three coaches, so heavy was the travel on the line.

The "skunk" has long since departed from the line through Unity. Now the CPR has discontinud passenger service. The CN runs two passenger trains daily and has trouble filling them.

Perhaps you are wondering where the nickname "skunk" came from. Well, if you have ever been downwind from one you would know.

Two "skunks," now known as railliners, still operate daily out of Saskatoon. One goes to Regina and the other to Prince Albert. They consist of a single unit and they can really move.

UNWIN

Unwin is just south of Lloydminster. In 1924 the CPR started laying steel in the area and in 1925 they built the bridge over the Battle river. A bridge inspector, George Unwin, came through to check the work. The village was subsequently named for him. Mr. Page built the first store and opened the first post office. One of the earliest settlers was Mr.

Pritchett, a Barr Colonist, who came out from England in 1904. He is 85 years old and still resides in the village.

URANIUM CITY

Saskatchewan today is among the major uranium-producing areas of the world, a most important source of the vital raw material from which the world forges its modern weapons. Even more important and significant, uranium at some future date will play a vital role in the peaceful use of atomic energy.

Uranium City, near the north shore of Lake Athabasca, takes its name from the mineral, uranium, which was discovered there in the 1950s. Uranium City has passed its boom stage and is a sound community of 1000 residents. For four months in the summer heavy equipment and supplies are brought in by barge on the Athabasca route from the end of the steel at Waterways, Alberta.

Goldfields is a ghost town close to Uranium City. Settlement began with the discovery of gold in 1934 and the development of the property by the Consolidated Mining and Smelting Company. Labor shortages and a run of low grade ore led to the abandonment of mining operations in 1950. Most of the buildings have been moved to Uranium City.

URBAN

Urban is a railway "Y" four miles west of Asquith on the main line of the CPR. A branch line goes north from the "Y" and ends at Baljennie. It used to have a little house that served as a station. The trains stopped there and travellers could get aboard. George Martin, Dave Caswell, Herb Girdler and Jock McFadden are a few of the early settlers who used this service. All trace of buildings has gone by now (1973).

UREN

Uren, a town five miles east of Chaplin on the main line of the CPR was first called Cook's Siding in 1906-07. It was named for Jim Cook, station agent at Chaplin at the time. The first section foreman was Jack Huddemaker. One of the first settlers was Jim Candler who homesteaded a mile north. His grandson, Marvin, still farms the home place.

The CPR later changed the name to Uren to honor Mr. Uren, a clerk in the Moose Jaw Superintendent's office. This man later became a CPR superintendent in Vancouver.

Robert A. Skeldon sent in this information and he still lives near the town. The most exciting thing he remembers was as a lad attending school in 1913 when a prairie fire swept the country. It burned everything from Log Valley near the South Saskatchewan river to Caron near Moose Jaw. When it swept past the school the only thing that saved the building was the fact that the playground, which surrounded it, was packed down by children's play and acted as a fireguard.

The town at one time had two elevators, two stores, a blacksmith shop, boarding house, livery barn, pool hall, post office and church. They are all gone now and Uren is a ghost town.

V

VALEPORT

Valeport is at the south end of Last Mountain lake. The following account came from Senator Arthur Maurice Pearson of Ottawa:

"In 1903-04 my father headed the William Pearson and Company Limited. It was a Land Colonization Company. There was little transportation in Saskatchewan in those days and this company decided to put some settlers on what is now known as Last Mountain lake. Their port called Hyman was at the foot of the lake, some two miles northwest of Valeport. In 1906-07 the government at Ottawa decided to put in a canal from the town of Craven, using part of the Qu'Appelle river which ran through the marsh at the foot of the lake and then in a straight line out into the lake running towards Lumsden Beach on the west side of the lake across the Port Hyman. This made it possible for the company to build their lumber and coal yards further down the lake. They bought a homestead from Arthur Harbour and proceeded to build their lumberyard and dock for their boats and barges.

It just happened that this port was at the foot of a vale running down into the marsh and, consequently, the place got its name Valeport, which was chosen by William Pearson and Company Limited."

VALJEAN

The hamlet of Valjean is very close to Lake Chaplin. The CPR put the railway through and named Valjean for Mademoiselle Valjean, one of the secretaries of the railway officials in charge of constructing the line.

On the other hand, it may have been named for Jean Valjean, the famous hero of Victor Hugo's "Les Miserables."

VALLEY CENTRE

The following settlers came into the district in the early 1900s: Britten, Crawley, Nash, Noble, Trapp, Sharman, Cocking, Lahy, Vleck, Wardrop, Christensen, Lorentson, Wilkinson, and Ardell.

In 1911 a petition was made for a post office. William Murphy was the first postmaster. Hugh Moncrief was responsible for the name chosen. He submitted Valley Centre because to him it appeared to be in the centre of a valley. In 1928 the CPR built a branch line from Rosetown to Perdue. It came within a mile of the Valley Centre post office and the railway officials adopted the name for their station.

VALLEY PARK

Valley Park, an inland post office, six miles south of Pike Lake, opened June 1, 1928 on the SW of 27-33-6 W3 with Mrs. Leona Mason as postmistress. She kept a small store in conjunction with it.

Mrs. Mason was followed by her daughter, Sophie, and then Mrs. Alice Dahlen took over on July 20, 1943. She held it until it closed out on July 4, 1963.

Mail was brought out by truck from Saskatoon via Pike Lake to Valley Park and then on south to Gledhow and O'Malley. The first mail carrier was

Thomas Campbell and he was followed by Ed Scissons, who had a store and post office at O'Malley.

In 1963 the Valley Park post office closed out and since then the families have had their mail delivered by a rural route.

Valley Park post office was named by Andy Schram, an early settler, because it was in the valley of the South Saskatchewan River in a parkland setting.

Mrs. Alice Dahlen of Saskatoon recalled some of the stirring incidents of the history of Valley Park. These centered around three floods.

Ample warning was given to residents of Valley Park. When the ice jammed up at Riverhurst downstream residents of Valley Park were alerted.

In spite of all these warnings three disastrous floods took place. During one of these Mr. Kay's barn was swept away and never seen again.

People who lived five or six miles back from the river had their land and homes flooded. No lives were lost but some livestock was.

Since the installation of the Gardiner Dam downstream, the danger of flooding has passed and all that is left of Valley Park is the name.

VAL MARIE

Father Passaplan, a missionary priest from Swift Current, came in 1910 with the first homesteaders: Louis Denniel, Francois Pinel and Leon Pinel.

The vast expanse of treeless land surrounded by high hills suggested a valley. Father Passaplan therefore fittingly called the district Val Marie in honor of the Virgin Mary.

VALOR

Valor is seven miles west of Assiniboia. At one time it was a hamlet that included the following: a store, livery barn, lumberyard, poolroom, school and Chinese cafe. All this is gone and it's down now to a population of five. The Paterson, Pool and Federal grain companies are still in business because it's a good grain growing district.

Early settlers included: Knor, Seal, Mitchel, Sam Marshall, George Matchett, John Kellar, Adams, Scheweiller, Sinclair, Albert Shaw, Howard and Albert McGirr,

Henry Hodgins, Batty and Harry Horton.

The name Valor was given to the hamlet by CPR officials.

VALPARAISO

Valparaiso is a large coastal city in Chile. It is also a small town east of Melfort, Sask. Valparaiso is a Spanish word meaning "Valley of Paradise." The late George E. Green, the first postmaster, suggested the name of Beaver Forks but the post office department turned it down because there were other places in Canada with that name. His second suggestion was Valparaiso and it was accepted. The first mail came in by coach from Melfort.

VANCE

Vance is an elevator six miles east of Biggar on the CPR. The first post office was operated in a small store in the home of Mr. Lawrence. Early settlers in the district included: Batt, Johnstone, McIntosh, and Mann. The place name recalls a tragic story. The original survey called for a line 23 miles north of Biggar, to run near Lizard lake. Mr. Vance, a civil engineer, was surveying the line in the dead of winter. Mr. McNair, a local resident, was driving him with team and sleigh. After dinner one day they struck a stretch of very rough country and split up. Mr. Vance took to snowshoes to go right through it and Mr. McNair drove around to meet him on the other side. Mr. Vance did not make it and the next day they found his frozen body.

VANGUARD

When the CPR built south of Swift Current in 1912, Vanguard was for a time the end of the steel. Vanguard means the front part, particularly of an army. In this case they selected the word as a name for the townsite because it was the front end of a railway that hoped to build on south. However, it was not until 1931 that the railroad was extended south to join the main line at Meyronne.

VANSCOY

Vanscoy is 20 miles southwest of Saskatoon. The name was derived from one of the earliest homesteaders, a bachelor, Vern Vanscoy. The name originally was

Dutch and the spelling was Van Scoy but for a long time it has been spelled as one word.

Other early settlers who came to the district in 1901 included J. W. Chovin, Jim Robertson, Bill Chambers, Cleve Mathews, Bill Davidson and A. A. Ashley.

In 1965 they started drilling for potash between Vanscoy and Delisle. In 1969 Cominco successfully brought in a mine and Vanscoy and Delisle have benefited greatly from it. Too, people employed in Saskatoon have started to build homes there and, from a dwindling village of a few years back, Vanscoy is now steadily growing.

VANSTONE

Vanstone is a short distance west of Yorkton on a branch line of the CNR that ends at Parkerview. It was named after a prominent merchant at Yorkton, Harry Vanstone.

VANTAGE

Before the CPR pushed a line north from Assiniboia in 1914 the people had to travel a long way for supplies. The new railroad proved such an advantage that they dropped the "ad" and called their townsite, Vantage.

The earliest homesteaders included Mr. and Mrs. Bert Thompson, Mr. and Mrs. Schubert, Mr. and Mrs. O. Sanderson, Mr. and Mrs. Kuntz, Mr. and Mrs. W. H. Rowe, and Mr. and Mrs. W. Wilson.

VAWN

Thirty miles north of North Battleford is the village of Vawn. It was named in honor of four of its original homesteaders. "V" was for Louis Vallier. "A" was for Oscar Anderson. "W" was for William Kruger and "N" was for Mr. Nadeau.

VEILLARDVILLE

Veillardville community is six miles west of the town of Hudson Bay, Saskatchewan. The post office (now closed) was named for Mr. Louis Veillard. In April of 1908, at the age of eighteen, Mr. Veillard immigrated to Canada from his native France. He spent the first two years at St. Claude, Manitoba, and in 1910 came to Greenbush (8 miles west of

Veillardville) to work for a lumber company. The next year he was called back to France for his compulsory military service and he spent the next two years in North Africa as a mail dispatcher — on a camel of all things!

On February 10, 1914, he returned to France and married Angele Nicollet from his hometown of Chateauneuf, Savoie. They came back to Greenbush in the spring of 1914 and he returned to his old job in the lumber mill. In the fall of 1914 when war was declared, he returned to serve in the French army and was made a commissioned officer. He was gassed at Vimy Ridge and subsequently discharged. In 1917 he returned to homestead at the present site of Veillardville.

In 1920 he started a sawmill of his own. In 1925 he opened a grocery store and obtained a post office. William Quinn, a successful farmer, and he were close friends, and homesteaded together. One time in later years Mr. Quinn was asked why the community was not called Quinnville instead of Veillardville. His answer was this, "Mr. Veillardville actually arrived first, you see, he was riding in the front seat of the democrat and I was in the back.!"

VENN
In 1906 the GTR built through Venn, the first stop east of Watrous. Most of the towns and villages along this stretch of track were named alphabetically by the railway officials. At Venn they needed a "V" so they named it for Harry Venn, the foreman of the railway construction crew at the time.

VERA
The Grand Trunk Pacific employed the device of naming stations in alphabetical order. One such series in northwestern Saskatchewan ends with Vera, Winter, Yonker and Zumbro. Winter was named for Mr. O. Winter, the contractor building a section of the GTP railway in that area. Vera was Mr. Winter's daughter.

The first attempt at potash mining in Canada was made at Unity in the 1950s. The mine site was one mile east of Vera, but almost all the business for the company was done at Unity, fourteen miles away across the "valley". The following was taken from the Unity Herald of June 12, 1968.

"Work crews are cleaning up at the Continental Potash Corporation Mine site near Vera. The project has been inactive since 1961 when sinking the shaft met a major setback. It 'blew' at the 1732 foot level and filled with water. L and M Construction of Calgary has the contract for tearing down the tipple, filling the hole (a twelve-foot shaft) with gravel to the 1570 foot level and laying a 20-foot layer of cement atop the gravel. All buildings and equipment that are not sold are to be demolished. The Vera potash project was begun in the late 1940s by the Continental Potash Corporation Limited and its parent company, Bata Petroleum. At one point a total of 45 men were employed and housed in bunkhouses at the site.

The capping of the shaft writes finis to a mining operation (where the digging was by hand) that has been off and on for twenty years and fostered the speculation of bringing a boom to this area. It didn't but it was the forerunner of the multimillion dollar potash industry now flourishing elsewhere in Saskatchewan."

VERENDRYE
Verendrye is the first grain point south of Kindersley on a stub line of the CNR that runs to Glidden. It was named for a famous French family of explorers, the La Verendryes. By the 1730s French fur traders controlled most of the fur trade immediately north of Lake Superior and were eager to press further west.

In 1731 Pierre La Verendrye set out with fifty men, including three of his sons. Travelling straight westward they passed the Great Lakes and reached the great plains beyond. In their travels they erected forts on Lake of the Woods (1732), Lake Winnipeg (1734) and Assiniboine river (1738). Then they pushed westward to the upper Missouri, the Black Hills region (1742), and thus they became the discoverers of Manitoba, the Dakotas, western Minnesota and perhaps part of Montana and western Canada.

A fitting memorial to these great traders and explorers can be seen at Verendrye, North Dakota, in the form of a large globe on a granite base.

VERIGIN

Verigin is just west of Kamsack. It was named for Peter Verigin, the spiritual leader of some 8000 Doukhobors, who came to Canada from Russia in 1899.

VERLO

Verlo was a post office and store until the railway came into Pennant in 1929. At this time Verlo was known locally as S S Lake school district, named after a lake shaped like two S's, situated near the town.

After the railway site was established, the town took its name from the nearby post office. Firsts in Verlo were: store, Mr. and Mrs. Dave Tisdale; marriage, Mr. and Mrs. Chris Hanson; first baby born, Bertha Hanson in March of 1912.

Verlo still has four elevators, but no store or post office. Only about three families live there now.

VERULAM

Verulam is the first grain point northeast of Kerrobert on a CPR line that runs to Wilkie. It consists of one Pool elevator. It was given its name by railway officials and it is probably named for a township in Victoria county, Ontario. The township was named for James Walter Grimston (1775-1845), Earl of Verulam, brother-in-law of Lord Liverpool, premier of Great Britain, 1812-1827. The title is taken from Verulam in Hertfordshire, the ancient capital of Britain.

VERWOOD

The place name Verwood recalls a tragic story. The first pioneers, Mr. and Mrs. Edward Wood and their eight children, entered the district in 1906. Vera was a six-year-old daughter in the family. One day in July during the haying season she tried to help an older sister make tea for the haymakers. While stuffing a handful of hay into the stove to make the kettle boil, her dress was set on fire. She ran to her father. In her flight she inhaled the fateful flames and she died as a result of the burns. Three days later they laid her to rest in a secluded part of the homestead in a homemade coffin. Her folded hands held a bouquet of prairie flowers picked by her brothers and sisters. There was no minister present. Later he came and held a service over the lonely grave.

When the CPR pushed through the area in 1912 the settlers suggested that the townsite be named for Vera Wood. The officials agreed and the "a" was dropped from her name and that is the origin of the name of Verwood.

VESPER

Vesper is the second last stop on a short CPR branch line south of Swift Current that runs from Dunelm to Simmie. The track was laid in 1931 and two elevators were built on the townsite in 1932.

The name was chosen at a community meeting at the schoolhouse, when everyone voted on several names submitted. The first postmaster was Charles Grout. Some of the first homesteaders who came in 1906 were: Moses Bissell, Harold Ailsby, Frank Ferguson, Nap Blanchard, Jim and Will Dancy, Jim and Bill Paul, the Lindsays, the Ebergs, the Newtons, the Iversons and the Carlsons.

VIBANK

When the Canadian Northern Railway reached Vibank the settlers could not agree on a name. Some wanted to call it Alsace and others wanted to call it St. Paul. To settle the dispute the railway officials called it Vibank and no one seems to know why.

VICEROY

The Canadian Pacific Railway built the line from Weyburn to Forward in 1910, and then on to Viceroy in 1911. The line was completed to Assiniboia in 1912.

Viceroy got its name from the title "Viceroy of India", as the streets are named after men who held that position: Connaught, Cromer, Lansdowne, Dufferin, Curzon and Minto.

The village was incorporated on April 1, 1912, and the first council consisted of T. G. Ross, Mr. Pearson and E. R. White. T. E. Bailey, the bank manager, was appointed as secretary-treasurer.

The first post office was established on May 1, 1912, and the postmaster was Dr. J. B. Patterson. The growth of the village remained static during the 1920s and the times were moderately prosperous. The end of the 20s and the 30s were times of hardship and scarcity.

One bright spot in this period was the Twin Vees. This baseball team, made up of boys from Verwood and Viceroy, won the Saskatchewan Junior Baseball Championship in 1931. Some of the team members from Viceroy were: Isaac and Jake Asbell, Amos O'Neil, Roddy Boll, John Robstad, and Sam Asbell as bat boy. John Probe, principal of Verwood School, was the coach and manager.

VICTOIRE

Victoire is an inland post office west of Debden centered around the Roman Catholic parish church of "Our Lady of Victoire." In fact that's what the residents wanted to call their post office but the postal officials shortened it to Victoire. It is an educational as well as a religious centre in that junior grades are bussed in from Ormeaux and Pascal to a convent there. There is a store and a few retired farmers from the district have built their homes close to the church. All in all it's a fine little community.

VICTORIA PLAINS

T. C. Stebbing came out from England in 1880 and journeyed from Winnipeg to Edmonton by oxcart train. The following spring he came south and met the CPR surveyors where Regina is now. He squatted on what turned out to be the quarter section where the station stands. He had to take another quarter one and one-half miles to the east. Stacey Stebbing was born on this homestead in 1887. In 1900 the family moved to the Victoria Plains district. This name had been established years before in honor of Queen Victoria.

When the CNR built a road through from Melville to Regina in 1912 the officials called the station Mulcahey. The settlers were up in arms. They got up a petition asking to have the place renamed Victoria Plains. The request was granted.

VIDORA

Vidora is on a CPR line between Robsart and Consul in the extreme southwest corner of the province. When the railroad was being built the engineers and surveyors stayed for a time at the farm of G. McKinnon. Two young girls lived there, Mr. McKinnon's daughter, Dora, and her friend, Vada Curtis, whose nickname was Vi. The townsite was named by combining the first names of these two young girls. This combination is found in at least two other towns in Saskatchewan, Ruthilda and Baljennie.

The CPR states that it was a contraction of Vivian and Dorothy, the names of the wife and daughter of J. M. MacArthur, a railway superintendent.

Like many other Saskatchewan towns Vidora experienced a disastrous fire. In February of 1924, the original Burnett store, the post office, the Eagle Cafe operated by Harry Dan and Soo Wing, the poolroom and the community hall were levelled. Much of the town was rebuilt but in the years that followed improved roads did not make Vidora a trading center. It is now a quiet hamlet of 20 people.

VIEWFAIR

Viewfair is an inland post office (now closed) about twenty miles south of Dodsland. The following information is from the diary of Manley Shaver.

"March 8, 1908 — We went to see the post office inspector in Saskatoon. I agreed to draw the mail from Mirror, Alberta, to our office once a week for $75 per year for four years.

May 3, 1908 — Just one year tonight since we arrived here. There is considerable difference now. Am beginning to like it fine. We now have the post office and call it Viewfair. We were sworn in last week."

Here are comments made about her childhood by Mrs. Violet Stillson, a daughter of Mr. and Mrs. Shaver.

- Whenever Dad went to Saskatoon, or to any town, we could hardly wait for his return as he always brought us candies and goodies.

- Whenever Dad was away, Mother kept a light burning in the window as a guide.

- Gophers were a problem. The municipality paid us a penny a tail and many of our hours were spent snaring, trapping and drowning them. Sometimes we were even allowed to poison them.

325

VIEWFIELD

Viewfield was a grain point and hamlet that developed on a Grand Trunk Railway line between Benson and Huntoon in southeastern Saskatchewan.

The first settlers arrived before the steel came in in 1908. They were a mixed lot departing from various points such as Ontario, the United States and Europe.

They named their village, Viewfield, as so many others did in Saskatchewan, with a feeling for their surroundings. This great expanse of land with a high blue sky where you could see for miles, influenced their choice of name. Broadview, Kingsview (now Tako), Riverview and Waterview received their names under similar circumstances.

The Pool map of 1977 was the first to show that the elevator at Viewfield was closed. Elevators at Huntoon and Benson on either side are still open.

VIGILANT

In the vicinity of Wood Mountain was an inland post office, Vigilant, which opened on November 1, 1916, with Fred Rookledge as postmaster. It closed on December 4, 1926, under its second postmaster, Mr. Fred Tucker.

VIOLA

The railroad, GTP, was laid down through this community in 1907 and a four-car loading platform served the grain shipping needs until an elevator was constructed in 1924 by the Co-op Elevator Company.

The land on which the elevator and siding are located was donated by Eric R. Johnson, who was the owner and first farmer of the property. The siding was named for Mrs. Viola Johnson. The point never developed farther than a grain shipping outlet since the town of Nokomis, located 3 miles to the east, served the other needs of the community.

Mr. Johnson and a few other settlers homesteaded in the area in 1905 and the first sod was turned in 1906. Some of the first settlers were: A. A. Stalder, G. H. Hummel, H. McGinnes, D. Duer, E. Litwin, J. Rathgen and W. J. Johnson.

VISCOUNT

Viscount and the nearby village of Plunkett were named for Viscount Plunkett (1764-1854), renowned Irish lawyer, judge and orator, who was elevated to the peerage.

In 1908, the CPR line was graded through Viscount. The steel for this line, originally known as the Pleasant Hills branch, was laid in 1909 and the station was built the same year.

The earliest pioneers were: the Koob brothers, Theodore Dieno, Mike Berg, F. C. Leyh and Thor and Jergen Ask.

VOGEL

Vogel is the first stop east of Tyson on a CPR line that comes down from Moose Jaw. It was named for Mr. Vogel, a Canadian Pacific Land Agent of the early years.

VONDA

British journalist Cy Warman (1855-1914) who in later years made his home in Canada, followed the contractors, McKenzie and Mann while the Canadian Northern Railway was being built through this part of the country. He became very good friends of both partners who, out of their friendship for him, named a townsite for him (Warman) and one for his daughter, Vonda.

W

WADENA

Taken from the Saskatoon Star-Phoenix of November 2, 1961:

"The town established its roots in 1905 when the CNR arrived. The first homestead families had come from Wadena, Minnesota; and the Tolen family asked that the station be called "Wadena." The post office department granted their request.

WAITVILLE

Just off the east end of Jumping lake is the hamlet of Waitville. It was named for

Finley Wait who, in 1907, opened the first post office in the district in his log house one mile east of the present site. His son, Clarence Benjamin Wait, took over from him and later it was operated by a niece, Mrs. E. A. Tennyson. The post office then changed hands and locations several times until Bert Bolton took it over in 1949. It's now in his home beside the railway a few hundred yards west of a lone Searle elevator.

The elevator was put up in 1930 and led a struggling existence. It closed in 1962, all the grain was moved out of it in 1966, and today even the building is gone.

Waitville's only store, operated by Mrs. Hubert Hannah, closed at Christmas, 1967, and the closest stores now are at Birch Hills (10 miles to the north) and Crystal Springs (6 miles to the south). The school has closed and the building has been moved to Crystal Springs for a teacherage.

How Jumping lake got its name is an interesting story. Years ago an ice jam on the South Saskatchewan caused the river to jump its banks and flood much of the lowlands between Hoey and Waitville. It filled the existing lake to its brim.

Six years ago the Department of Natural Resources stocked the lake with pickerel fingerlings. They are a nice size now and even though they do not "bite" too well owing to so much natural food in the water, the conservation officers assure the local residents that it will only be a matter of time until they clear out the food and then there will be good angling. Meanwhile, the best way to get the pickerel is by net but that's illegal!

Ernest Wait, a grandson of Finley, farms a mile south of Fenton and it was he and his wife who enabled us to get this information.

WAKAW

Wakaw is a town on the Watrous - Prince Albert CNR line. Wakaw is the Cree word for "crooked" and was first applied to the neighboring lake. It was incorporated as a village in 1911 and as a town in 1953. It's a handy word to spell. It comes out the same whether you spell it backwards or forwards.

When John G. Diefenbaker first set up a law practice it was in Wakaw. His former office has been set up just as it was when he used it. During the latter part of the late Ross Thatcher's Liberal administration the house on Mr. Diefenbaker's homestead farm at Borden was moved to Regina and beautifully set up as a separate museum on the grounds of the Legislative Buildings. More is planned for him by way of a special separate library to house his papers at the University of Saskatchewan, Saskatoon Campus. We and our children will long remember this man — the only Saskatchewan-born prime minister of Canada.

WALDECK

Waldeck is a village eleven miles east of Swift Current on the main line of the CPR. Two of the first homesteaders were the late Reverend Klass Peters and Mr. Abraham. They came from Westphalia, Germany, in 1902, and were followed by many of their friends of the Mennonite Christian Faith.

In 1907 Reverend Peters became the first overseer of the village and it was he who suggested the name Waldeck which is German in origin and means "wooded corner". Likely he was thinking of the bunches of willows and trees that grew along the banks of the nearby Swift Current creek when he chose the name because these were in sharp contrast to the miles and miles of surrounding treeless prairie.

WALDHEIM

About 36 miles north of Saskatoon lies the little village of Waldheim. Mr. and Mrs. D. Neufeld, a young couple seeking a homestead, found a beautiful forest. They liked the place and cleared some land for themselves in 1885. Other people soon joined them and it wasn't long before a hamlet was formed. Now came the railway and the people were busy thinking of a name. Since the people were German speaking, the site was given a German name. In German "wald" means "forest" and "heim" means "home." Connecting the two it became Waldheim (Home in the forest).

WALDRON

Waldron is two stations east of Melville. It was named for Sir Alfred Waldron Smithers, who was chairman of the

Grand Trunk Pacific Railway at the time.

WALDVILLE

Waldville was a rural post office near Climax. The first postmaster was Tom Waldie who named it after himself. Mr. Waldie sold out to Alfred Gryde and the business was later taken over by John E. Gryde. Waldville, by reason of the store and post office, became a district. John Gryde carried everything from a keg of nails to material for the babies' diapers. Many a farmer had to thank John Gryde for supplying them with groceries when there was no money to pay for them.

WALLACE

Wallace is a booking station at the junction of the Canadian Pacific Railway lines to Assiniboia and Cardross. It has been called the smallest station in the world and although it is very small it does have a telephone. In the days of passenger service residents of the surrounding area used to catch the passenger train at this tiny station.

Wallace was named after Edward Wallace, who was the roadmaster of the Assiniboia line for years and was employed in that capacity when the spur line to Cardross was built. A long-time resident of Weyburn, he passed away on January 2, 1967.

WALLARD

Take three points of Ponteix, Mankota and Val Marie deep in the southeast part of the province and draw a triangle. In the center is Wallard. It has no railroad. It never has had.

It is a small country post office named for Mr. Waller, the first postmaster, and George Card the very first pioneer. Walter Knox, who still lives here was one of the first pioneers and he came to the district in 1910 at the age of 15. At that time the nearest town was Swift Current and all supplies had to be hauled in with horses or oxen — a distance of 80 miles.

WALPOLE

Walpole, northeast of Carlyle, is named for Sir Robert Walpole (1676-1745), English stateman. He was prime minister and chancellor of the exchequer (1715-1717). He strove to establish sound

finance at home and is said to have laid the foundations of free trade.

WANISKA

Waniska was an inland post office during the early years of Saskatchewan. It was nestled in a little "dobbie" house in a muddy coulee south of Bengough. It was operated by a lignite miner's wife and it was a boon to early settlers.

The mail driver augmented his income by carrying everything from passengers to cream cans on his regular run; by team and sleigh in winter and democrat in summer.

The first post office still stands even though it has been closed for several years. The name Waniska is of Indian origin but the meaning or significance is not clear.

WAPASHOE

Wapashoe obtained its name from an Indian who during the eighties camped in the vicinity of the place, gathering buffalo bones, which at the time strewed the prairies. There were a number of fine springs in the vicinity, and it became a favorite camping place of the roundup outfits during the days of the open range. The place gradually became known by the name of the Indian who was invariably camped there.

WAPELLA

Wapella is about halfway between Moosomin and Whitewood on a CPR line in southeastern Saskatchewan. The first group to settle there came in the 1880s. They were a group of Scottish "crofters" from the Highlands off the coast of Scotland. They were financed by Lady Cathcart.

They settled along the Pipestone creek south of the present townsite. Wapella is an Indian word meaning "water under ground." It was no problem throughout the district to get a good well at a shallow level.

The crofters were a "clanny" lot and many of them never lost their "burr." In fact, Gaelic, at times, is still spoken in the district. The group had a factor or leader, John MacDermid. In fact the whole settlement was full of "Macs." Right across the road from MacDermid lived John MacQueen and south of him and kitty-corner to MacDermid lived Malcolm MacDonald. MacDermid was a man who took things on the easy side. His farm was very ordinary. MacQueen, on the other hand, was industrious. Year after year he made improvements to his place until it was a model farm. He was very prosperous and being Scottish retained most of it. MacQueen passed away. Soon after MacDonald had occasion to visit MacDermid and in the course of their conversation asked, "How much did MacQueen leave?" MacDermid replied, "He left it all."

Bill Story of Saskatoon, a well-known radio broadcaster, gentleman farmer and raconteur without peer, was born and raised at Wapella. He recalls that the families of the Scottish settlement were large and there was a continual doubling of given names. To designate the person you were talking about it was necessary to use nicknames such as Long John, Little John, Stuttering John, Black Jack and Polite Alec. This practice was not confined to men and Bill distinctly remembers that, as a boy, upon seeing a huge lady that filled the seat of the buggy drive into the yard, he ran into the house and shouted to his mother, "Fat Flora is here!"

WARDENVILLE

Wardenville was an inland post office two miles northeast of the present site of Tatsfield. The post office was named for Sandy and Jimmy Warden. Sandy was a jack-of-all-trades and served for a time as Indian Agent on the Poundmaker and Little Pine reserves. The first postmaster was Mr. William Murphy. When the steel came through in 1913 and the post office moved to the townsite it was given the name Tatsfield.

When a school was built in 1911 it was named Wardenville. The first teacher was Miss Helen White and the last was Jack Cook in 1958. The children are now bussed to Cut Knife.

One of the distinguished graduates of the Wardenville school is Mr. Ray McInnis, the principal of the new composite high school in North Battleford.

WARMAN

On October 22, 1890 the extension of the Qu'Appelle, Long Lake and Sas-

katchewan Railway was completed from Regina to Prince Albert. In 1905 the Canadian Northern Railway by-passed Saskatoon — fifteen miles to the south — and created a "diamond" at Warman. Diamond was the first name given to the townsite.

At that time Saskatoon had only one railroad and its success under CPR stewardship was something less than spectacular. In eleven years only three homestead entries were made along a 120-mile stretch between Lumsden and Dundurn.

There was a promise of the Kirkella-Wetaskiwin branch of the CPR. However, the original Grand Trunk Pacific survey went through Hanley.

It began to look as though the "Diamond" now called Warman by the Canadian Northern officials for Cy Warman, British journalist who followed the contractors when they were building the Canadian Northern Railway and who in later years made his home in Canada, would become the city. However, it was not to be. Its lack of water facilities, which still continues, caused the CNR to run a spur line into Saskatoon and establish headquarters there. By 1913 many buildings had been moved from Warman to Saskatoon and thus ended Warman's hopes of being a big railway center.

WARMAN JUNCTION

Warman Junction, just north of Saskatoon, is used to connect the old Canadian Northern with the old Grand Trunk Pacific Railway (now both CNR) lines. It was named for Cy Warman, British journalist, who followed the contractors when they were building the old Canadian Northern Railway which had missed the little village of Saskatoon by crossing the South Saskatchewan fifteen miles to the north.

WARMLEY

Warmley used to be a townsite, post office and school district. Today it exists as just the name of a district. The school children are transported by bus to the town of Kisbey. The school, built in 1905, still stands and is used as a community center.

Warmley is located ten miles north of Kisbey, in the more westerly end of the Moose Mountains. Prior to 1902 this area was the Pheasant Rump Indian Reserve with approximately 300 Assiniboine Indians living on it. The Indian agent, Mr. C. Lawford, was also the first white man to live in this area.

In 1902 the government removed the Indians to other reservations, and opened this area for settlement by selling it to the Porter Land Company for $1.00 an acre. The land company in turn sold it to the settlers for from $2 to $10 per acre. The Porter Land Co. was an American company although their land agent, A. S. Porter, was an Englishman. Porter had dreams of making an English estate in this new land, similar to those in the old country. He laid out a townsite and named it Warmley after his ancestral home in England. At the townsite was a post office, blacksmith shop, school and cemetery, as well as his 17-room house, 2 large barns and accompanying buildings. Mr. Porter brought his family out from England and for a few years lived in this style. He is reported to have driven around his estate in a fringed-topped surrey with a liveried footman, to check on the land and men at work. During one winter when the Porters were away to California, the house was destroyed by fire. Although the Porters returned, they didn't stay, thus ending the Porter dream.

The post office was moved from the townsite to the home of Fred Whiteside, who also became the postmaster and mail carrier, bringing the mail from Kisbey. The Warmley post office continued to serve the community until 1961 with Richard Hourd as the last postmaster.

Among the first settlers to the Warmley district were Fred Stenders, James Maitland and William Swartz. The Warmley school was built in 1905 and the first teacher was James G. Gardiner, later to become premier of Saskatchewan and then minister of agriculture for the Dominion.

WARTIME

In the fall of 1913 the railway was in as far as Elrose. The road bed was graded on through in 1914 and a few buildings were put up. That was the year the First World War started so the town was named Wartime. It is not known if the Canadian Northern Railway named it or if the people of the district sent in the name.

WASECA

Waseca is between Lashburn and Maidstone on a CNR line from North Battleford to Lloydminster. The Canadian Northern built this line in 1905; prior to that early settlers had to go to Battleford for supplies, usually about twice a year, a distance by trail of around 70 miles. The supplies had been freighted to Battleford by horses or oxen. By the time Mr. W. H. Snell arrived in Waseca in 1911 it had been named by early homesteaders and it consisted of a general store run by Mike Donovan, a hardware and machinery agency run by H. Rhode, a lumberyard and post office run by William Goodridge, a restaurant run by Mr. Cox and an Anglican church sponsored by people in England.

Waseca is Cree and means Hill of Swan. It is named after a hill south of the village where swan heads were found in large numbers.

WASKESIU

Wa-Waskesiu in Cree means "red deer." From this Cree word, after dropping the first syllable, Waskesiu got its name; first the lake, then the river, and finally the townsite. We, in Saskatchewan, associate Waskesiu with Prince Albert National Park one of the finest in Canada. There are no railways in the vicinity. The nearest is the CNR in Prince Albert, 64 miles to the south. Waskesiu is almost the geographic center of Saskatchewan.

WATERVIEW

Waterview was an inland post office about eighteen miles northwest of Nipawin. Tom Robertson was the first mail carrier, followed by his son, Pete. The first post office was in the home of Mr. Lewis.

WATROUS

Some believe the town of Watrous got its name from the following story:

A small town was started on the main line between Saskatoon and Melville, about three miles south of Manitou lake. One of the biggest problems facing the early settlers was water. Although a number of wells had been dug there was always a shortage and so it was that when someone new came their first request was "Please water us." It then became known as the "water us town." As the months went by "Water us," became Watrous and so this was the name of this small town. Today Watrous gets its water from wells, one about eight miles and one about five miles from the town.

Actually Watrous was named after Frank Watrous Morse, vice-president and general manager of the Grand Trunk Pacific Railway at the time. The adoption of his middle name could be explained by the prior existence of the town of Morse.

WATSON
The district was settled in 1902 and the railway station was named after Senator Robert Watson of Manitoba, owner of the townsite.

WAUCHOPE
The CPR reached Wauchope in 1901 while the Boer War was still in progress and the townsite was named for a distinguished campaigner in that struggle, General W. Wauchope.

WAWOTA
Wawota is a village on the Reston-Wolseley line of the CPR 130 miles southeast of Regina. Kenosee and Carlyle lakes in Moose Mountain Provincial Park are only a few miles south. According to Dan Kennedy, noted Indian author of the neighboring Assiniboine Reserve, Wawota means "Lots of snow" or "deep snow".

WEBB
Louie Lloyd writes from his home in Abbotsford, B.C., to tell how Webb got its name.

"Back at the time the CPR was being built through the Prairies there was an influential railway official whose full name was Beverley Seward Webb. The first three stops on the line west of Swift Current are Beverley, Seward and Webb. This, we believe, is a record not repeated in any other part of Saskatchewan. Some are close to it as at Patrick and Cotton, Viscount and Plunkett, Albertville and Henribourg and D'Arcy and McGee."

WEEKES
The village of Weekes was nothing but dense north Saskatchewan bush when the CNR built its line from Crooked River east to Reserve Junction through the district in 1928. Weekes was one of several hamlets which sprang into existence that year in forest clearings.

The hamlet was named after A. S. Weekes, a land surveyor.

Jack Palphenier opened a store in 1934. He sold out to Mike Siery in 1936. It was the demand for lumber which developed after the Second World War which did much to speed the development of Weekes.

The largest lumber processing plant in the province is situated only 13 miles from Weekes. It is operated by The Pas Lumber Company and is the source of income for a large number of farmers in the adjacent area who supplement their crop earnings by cutting and selling timber which stands on portions of their holdings.

WEIRDALE
Weirdale is 38 miles northeast of Prince Albert on a CPR line to Nipawin that was built 1929-1931. The village of Weirdale was named after the Hon. Robert Weir who was, at that time, Member of Parliament for the district, and federal Minister of Agriculture.

This was timber country when it was first opened up but now they have cleared the way for many good farms.

WELBY
Welby is on the main line of the old GTP in the southeast part of the province. When the school district No. 1710 was formed in the community in 1907 it was called Pleasant Plains. The name was changed to Welby when the steel arrived in 1909. The post office and townsite were named Welby after Rt. Hon. Lord Welby, G.C.B., London, England, who was a director of the GTP Railway.

WELDON
Weldon is a short distance S.E. of Prince Albert. It was named for the son of an early settler, Weldon Ellis.

WELWYN
Welwyn is near the Manitoba border east of Whitewood. Mr. J. Wake was the

first settler in the district and when he opened a post office he named it for Welwyn Garden City, in Herefordshire, England. When the CPR came through in 1902 the post office gave its name to the village which was incorporated in 1907.

Other early settlers included the following: John C. Robinson, John Fisher and J. Melaney, who all arrived by ox cart. A stage route was started in 1883 between Moosomin and Birtle and this served the community for a time. When the CPR came through in the early 1900s Charlie Dumville built the first store. In 1905 he sold out to Seth Fleury. The first car load of grain was loaded from ground level by Tom Byrne.

Other well-known settlers included the following: Harper, Ireton, Ironside, McLellan, Morton, Parker, Santer, Swanson, Stewart and Wilson.

WENAUS

The Wenaus district between Verwood and Viceroy was first settled in 1910-1911. The first homesteaders were A. Pense, Carl Nelson, Severt Loseth, Abel Nelson, Albert Westgard, Ingebright Nelson, Nick Johnson, Aylmer Zumstein, W. E. Spicer, N. Ormstown, B. Cramer and George Hale. The first postmaster was J. E. Wenaus who had it in his home and gave it his name.

The pioneers suffered many hardships, some of which were lack of money, drought, sickness, blizzards, prairie fires and lack of fuel for heating their homes in winter.

One specific misfortune in this area was a prairie fire that started near Viceroy. Some farms were saved by the use of backfire and fireguards but the homestead of August Lidberg was struck by tragedy. The fire burned most of the cattle, horses and poultry, and killed both Mr. August Lidberg and his daughter Ella. Art Lidberg, the one son, got caught in a seed drill while trying to escape the fire and was badly burned before he managed to break loose and save his life by running into a slough. He was so badly burned that he carried scars for the rest of his life.

No account of Wenaus homesteading days would be complete without reference to a blithe, colorful woman who meant so much in the lives of others, Beret Duzan.

In those days when there was no doctor within miles and no telephone, she was often called on as a midwife. People came from far and near to fetch her and she always left her work and stayed until things were under control, or if nearby made daily visits to bathe the baby and see that all was well, despite the fact that she had a large family of her own. Even after the arrival of a doctor at Verwood and Winside, she was called to assist.

Before the turn of the century Jean Louis Legare had part of his ranch on the north shore of Willow Bunch lake. This included what was later to become the Landscape district. Legare had his winter ranch building in a large coulee with a heavy spring, on the shore of the lake about three miles southwest of Landscape.

After he lost all his stock in the hard winter of 1906-07 he let his lease go back to the province and the area was opened up for homesteading in 1909. There was a rush of homesteaders and the following, mostly single men, came: Ross, McKenzie, Davidson, Smith, McMillan, Reverend J. Horrocks, Reverend McLean, Reverend E. Brown, Buchanan, Bradley, Wenaus, Connaughty, Banks, Neff, McDowell, Macklin, Fletcher, Roose, Mickelson, Reddick, Watson, Olson, Robstad, Evers, Johnson, Juggins, Atkinson, Lees, Nickelsen, Iverson, Hawkins, Swayze, Harrison, Sutherland, Taylor, Carr, Schultz, Nicol and Murnson.

By 1912 the area was fully homesteaded and the railway was being built from Viceroy west. The Wenaus brothers, John and Axel, started a store and machinery agency. The post office was part of the store and Mr. Macklin was the postmaster.

Then on August 1, 1913, at the request of Dominion post office officials the name of Wenaus post office was changed to Landscape. There was a story that Wenaus conflicted with another name and the smaller place was asked to make the change. There is no special significance to the name of Landscape.

WEST BEND

In 1928 the CPR started to build a line south from Foam Lake to Bulyea. They built only 27 miles of track and stopped at Wishart. West Bend is half way from Foam Lake to Wishart and received its name from the way the track was laid out. The track came south from Foam Lake for 12 miles and then took a big bend to the west for 14 miles to Wishart. Hence, the name West Bend.

WESTERHAM

Westerham is between Estuary and Leader. It was possibly named for Westerham in Kent, England, made famous as the residence of the late Sir Winston Churchill.

WESTHAZEL

Originally spelled West Hazel this inland post office was near Turtleford. It is now closed. It was named by Finley MacDonald who settled in the district in 1906. He came from Manitoba, from a place called Hazel, and just tacked on the West.

Early settlers included Edward (Ted) Carriss and family; Mrs. C. Mackenzie, a widow with a son, Fred: James Hill and George Milligan. In 1907, Jim Underwood, Charlie Rush, Bill Clay and Hamish Lowry arrived. Malcolm Chisholm and his son Earle came in 1907 and the rest of the family followed in 1910.

WESTHOPE

Westhope was a rural post office established on the Harvey farm in the early years of the century near Macrorie. It was operated by the family until 1911, when with the coming of the Canadian Northern Railway the post office was moved to town and took the name Macrorie.

Westhope is a significant name. Thousands of people came from many parts of the world to Western Canada in the early 1900's. For ten dollars they could buy sixty acres of land where they hoped to establish themselves in a way not possible in their homeland.

WEST PLAINS

West Plains, developed in the early 1900's, was an inland post office, store and school ten miles north of Senate.

Some of the first settlers were Mr. and Mrs. William John Shepherd and their family. One member of the Shepherd family, George Fredrick, became known across Canada as an historian and author.

Mr. Shepherd was born in Canterbury, England, on March 20, 1890. He and his father emigrated to Canada in 1908 and were followed a year later by his mother, sister and five brothers. After establishing the eldest son on a homestead near Stalwart, the others moved in 1913 to the Cypress Hills, between Maple Creek and Senate. The Shepherd Brothers' farm became a focal point for the community since it included Mother's general store and the West Plains post office. George drew the mail.

Mr. George Shepherd became Secretary-Treasurer of West Plains School and married the school teacher, Miss Irene Eleanor Thompson. They raised two children, Eleanor and Gordon.

Farming and raising a family did not consume all of Mr. Shepherd's energy, so he began a writing career with a prize winning essay on dry land farming. His writings expanded from agriculture as he became the local authority on the history of the Cypress Hills. He talked to old-timers of the area and explored the hills and valleys, searching for clues to some early trading post or massacre site, or Fort Walsh, whose later reconstruction owed much to his early initiatives.

In 1950 Mr. and Mrs. Shepherd retired from farming and moved to Saskatoon where they opened a boarding house for university students. In 1953 he accepted a position as curator of the Western Development Museum. He worked long and diligently to establish the museum concept in the eyes of the visitors and the community.

The Saskatoon period was the most productive in his writing career, highlighted by the appearance of his two books, *West of Yesterday* and *Brave Heritage*. The former was an account of homestead days; the latter a series of stories, rearranged in book form, that are substantially the same as when published in the Western Producer, Saskatoon Star-Phoenix, Canadian Cattlemen, Farm and Ranch Review, Family Herald and the Mounted Police Quarterly.

Mr. Shepherd received many honors. In 1974 he was awarded an honorary doctorate of laws by the University of Saskatchewan. The George Shepherd Library at the Museum was founded in his honor and contains much of his own collection.

In October, 1977, Dr. Shepherd discontinued full time work at the Museum and moved from his Colony Street home to Porteous Lodge. He passed away there on February 19, 1978. His funeral service was held on Main Street in the Western Development Museum on February 22nd. A legion of friends from all walks of life attended.

With Dr. George Shepherd's passing, another chapter closes on one of those who experienced firsthand the opening up and development of our province.

WEST POPLAR

West Poplar is a customs point on the international boundary less than ten miles south of Killdeer, the end of a CPR line out of Rockglen. West Poplar takes its name from being on the west branch of the Poplar river.

WEYAKWIN

The following information was received from Valerie Harlton who, as an employee of the Department of Northern Saskatchewan Extension Services at La Ronge, is the editor of a monthly publication, Denosa.

"Weyakwin is the Cree word for 'swearing place'. The community was established when thirty-five families from Molanosa, on the north shore of Montreal Lake, relocated in an area by highway 2 where it crosses the Weyakwin river. As I have heard the story, the river crossing proved to be a difficult one, which caused travellers "to do a lot of swearing".

Weyakwin is about ninety miles north of Prince Albert and has a population of approximately 240 non-Treaty and forty-five Treaty Indians.

Chairman of the community's Local Advisory Council is Christian Nelson. Christian and his family were one of the original families that re-established at the site."

WEYBURN

There are two stories as to how Weyburn got its name. There is a romantic version and, of course, a practical one.

Most people prefer the romantic ver-sion. It concerns a party of thirsty Scots working their way west on a hot summer day. One of their number on seeing the Souris river for the first time was heard to exclaim: "Wee Burn" and hence, Weyburn came into being.

Other people, not so romantically inclined, insist the city got its name from a railway construction contractor who worked on laying the steel. This version has merit in that it was a common practice in those days for the railroad to name stations for their officials, employees, and friends.

WHEATFIELD

Wheatfield, ten miles north of Perdue, has one of the simplest and most descriptive place names in Saskatchewan. The history of Wheatfield began in 1903 when Mr. and Mrs. Andrew Fischer and their two children built their sod shack. Soon, other settlers came and by 1905 Wheatfield district claimed a population of some 40 families.

By 1905 Wheatfield had sufficient families to apply for a post office. Mr. A. A. Ashley was appointed to the position of postmaster at a yearly salary of $25 and the post office was located at his house, situated on the southeast corner of the northeast quarter of section 28. The post office is still standing and the quarter section now belongs to Mr. Clarence Bloomquist.

The community which received the mail at the Wheatfield post office comprised a large area. Mr. Ashley distributed mail across Eagle creek to the Caswells and Cowleys, and south to Kinley; west to Tramping Lake; north to Lizard Lake and the Russian settlements. Before a post office was established at Perdue, the residents of that district also got their mail at "Wheatfields" as they called it.

WHEATSTONE

Wheatstone is a grain delivery point on a branch line of the CPR running northwest from Weyburn and ending at Cardross. All that's left of a once bustling little village is the elevator. The agent lives in the next stop west, Ormiston. A huge CPR gravel pit at Wheatstone made it the headquarters of railway officials for some years. It's a good wheat farming area in spite of the stones. Hence, the name given to it by the CPR.

The story is told of Mr. Costea Daniel, one of the first settlers (1912), that when Mr. Elie Ritsco, another early settler, visited the community looking for land he found Mr. Daniel sitting dejectedly outside his "soddy" — and this just following a heavy rain. By way of explanation Mr. Daniel said to Mr. Ritsco, "I'd invite you in except that it's raining inside and will be for the next two days."

WHELAN

Whelan is fifteen miles straight west of Loon Lake. The post office and store are operated by Mrs. Pearl Neilly. She sells groceries, gas, dry goods and hardware.

WHITE BEAR

White Bear takes its name from White Bear lake 20 miles to the north and east. This lake had been named by the Indians long before any settlers moved into the district. It is reported that they had seen a white bear on the south shore of the lake. This is quite possible and it was likely a silver-tipped grizzly in just the right light. Then, too, it could have been an albino. Grizzly bears were very common on the plains in the early days as they followed and preyed on the buffalo herds. Henry Kelsey, in his dairy of 1690 makes mention of them. Once in self defence he had to kill two in one day which led to his Indian nickname of Miss-to-ashish which in English means "Little Giant."

WHITEBEECH

Whitebeech is a post office situated at 17-35-30-WPN. John Geddes was the first postmaster. It is thought that he mistook the local birch trees which shone white in the sun for beech trees and so sent in the name Whitebeech for his new post office.

WHITE CITY

Eleven miles east of Regina on number one highway is the new building development of White City. It consists of over 30 new houses — all on lots of considerable size. There is no significance to the name. There is a White City, a suburb of London, England, but it is thought that developers at White City in Saskatchewan just chose a nice sounding name to attract business.

There is only one local service, a fine

post office operated by Mr. Ramm. Deliveries of bread and milk are made from Regina three days a week. The children are bussed to Balgonie, six miles east.

There is an old one-room country school in the middle of the development and it was drawn in to give a meeting place for the ladies of the community. It looks out of place among the new houses.

The reason for the prosperous-looking post office is that a few hundred yards east is the factory that makes the famous "Dad's Cookies."

WHITE FOX

The village of White Fox is 86 miles east of Prince Albert. It is named for the White Fox river which flows through the district. The first settlers were Swedish and they began to arrive in 1915. One of the first pioneers was George King, who built and operated the first ferry to cross the Saskatchewan river just south of what later became the community of White Fox.

Veterans of the First World War who settled on the half-sections which represented their soldier grants, swelled the farming population in the early 20s.

In the early years, until 1921, Tisdale was the closest railway point to White Fox district. In 1921 a line was built north from Melfort as far as Ridgedale, cutting the haul to steel to 30 miles. The CPR extended its line north from Tisdale to Nipawin in 1925, leaving White Fox 10 miles from a railway.

In 1928 the CPR and the government built a combined railway and highway bridge over the Saskatchewan and in 1929-30 the railway came into the White Fox country.

WHITEPOOL

Whitepool is a single Pool elevator on a CNR line that runs from Dodsland to Coleville. The agent's house stands empty. He lives in Dodsland and comes out to buy at Whitepool on certain days; he spends the rest of the time buying at Hood, a grain point east of Dodsland.

Bernard Doll's farm is less than a mile from the elevator and he is responsible for the following story. In 1927, a partially dismantled elevator was brought in from another grain point and rebuilt. The

335

primer coat of paint on it was wnite and people referred to it as the "White Pool." When it came time for a name, Whitepool was chosen in spite of the fact that the elevator had by this time been painted the standard red.

WHITE STAR

Just off the highway about six miles north of Prince Albert you will find the lone Pool elevator No. 865. It is about all that remains of a once thriving community called White Star.

At the turn of the century this district was predominately French. Some of the early settlers were Calvez, Guedo, Cartier, Lempereur, Logodin, Delhomeaux and Lahayes. When they decided to start a school a group of homesteaders met at the home of Mr. Calvez to decide on a name. Many were mentioned but when Victor Calvez' daughter, Marie, seeing a white star on a baking powder tin suggested White Star for a name it was accepted. Later the post office, which was kept in the Calvez farm home, also took the name White Star.

In the late 1890s Brother Corbeil started a Roman Catholic orphanage near the present site of White Star. One of the groups of orphans that were raised there was a dozen boys from England. Since, when a boy reached the age of 18, Brother Corbeil filed on a homestead for him, an English element grew in the district. Each boy was given a quarter section of land, a team of horses and the few other necessities needed to start his homestead. The orphanage farm also had a saw mill which cut lumber for homestead buildings. Bill Chester, one of these English orphans, married Marie Calvez (the girl who originally named White Star) and lived in the district until his retirement to Prince Albert.

Over 50 years ago the orphanage was moved near the penitentiary in Prince Albert and is now known as St. Patricks.

The first mailman was Sam Monette and during the first few years he carried the mail on his back while he walked the 15 miles from Prince Albert to Albertville. He ate his meals at the Lahayes stopping place.

In 1895 Herman Lahayes had homesteaded near Melfort but in 1908 he moved to a new homestead at White Star. His son, Frank, who still lives on the original homestead, says things have changed in White Star — the school closed about five years ago and the children are bussed to Spruce Home; the station house was sold to Mr. Letwin and is now on his farm; the post office and St. Georges Catholic Church closed in 1965. In fact Mr. Lahayes says the residents of the district used to meet and visit for an hour before church and stay to visit for an hour after church. Now that they must go to Prince Albert for the service they hurry in, attend church and hurry home, and if they pass a car going 60 miles an hour they wave — in case he's a neighbor.

WHITEWOOD

Whitewood is on the main line of the CPR just south of the booming potash center of Esterhazy. It was named for a bluff of white poplars to which it is adjacent. This is a very ordinary name but there was nothing ordinary about "the French Counts of St. Hubert" and their efforts to establish a bit of France on the Prairies.

The first of the European gentlemen of means to arrive was Dr. Rudolph Meyer, a cultured French-speaking German. Whitewood was already functioning as a supply center when he arrived in 1884. Others who arrived about the same time were: M le Comte de Roffignac, M le Comte de Jumilhac, and M. le Comte de Soras. Several of them lived in Whitewood, others on their ranches. They built houses not on the scale of some in Cannington, but imposing for the time, imported whole families to work for them, land workers, gardeners, grooms, house servants and craftsmen. They imported expensive foods, wines, confectionery and all the various luxuries to which they had been accustomed. They dealt extensively in the town and the cash they put in circulation helped to put the whole district on its feet.

Thoroughbred horses and purebred dogs were brought from France, as well as the finest accessories of riding and driving equipment. They rode and drove a great deal.

The Counts and their families attended Race Days at Cannington. They went in coach and four or a three-in-hand with a coachman and footman in livery, tall hats with cockades, white gloves and all.

The Frenchmen's agricultural and industrial efforts are legend. They tried cattle ranching but losses were heavy due to severe winters. They tried sheep. There was a scheme to raise horses as remounts for the French army. All ventures were unsuccessful and Dr. Meyer gave up in 1889 and returned to France for good.

The Compte de Roffignac, described as a versatile, irrepressible enthusiast took over the leadership and after raising money from friends in France started a brushmaking factory which soon folded up. An attempt to make Graycoe cheese failed in one year, chicory was grown and put on the market for some time. But the most ambitious scheme of all, sugar beet, did not even get to the point of being manufactured into sugar.

The last of the Counts departed just before the First World War leaving no single member of their families. Much of their land was bought up by their own men. Of these, the many descendants have spread far and wide. The Counts did not, as they hoped, found a profitable replica of Old France, but they brought out the finest import a new country can have — men and women who endured hardship to establish permanent homes of good living.

WHITKOW

Thirty miles northeast of North Battleford is the town of Whitkow. It is on a CPR branch line that once ran up through Mayfair but the rails have been taken up from Redfield on and no regular train service has been provided for years.

Mr. and Mrs. Grosjean of France came to Duck Lake to homestead in 1892. They moved to the Whitkow area in 1906 and became its first settlers. In 1931 the CPR arrived and put up a townsite on NE 6-46-13-W3, which they named Belgian Flats. Prior to this a post office had been established some miles away, named Whitkow at the suggestion of Michael Kozlowski after his hometown in Poland. When this post office moved to the town the name was changed to Whitkow.

WIDEVIEW

This is a complete letter from Mrs. Kohl of Mankota:

"Wideview is located 15 miles southwest of Mankota on the wide open prairie of Section 4-4-9-W3. You could see for miles and miles. The post office was in my parents' home, my mother, Mrs. J. W. Hefner named it. She operated it for eleven years in a downstairs room of our house. Mother served meals to almost everyone who came to get mail. The mail came once a week by team and democrat from Kincaid 30 miles away. The NWMP patrolled the country in the early days. Our place was a regular stopping place for them.

In 1917 a Wideview one-roomed school number 3911 was built. Miss Mary Shepherd, a seventeen-year-old girl, was the first teacher. She had 35 students in 8 grades. All the bachelors waited anxiously for new teachers.

In 1926 my mother got tired of the post office (she got 52 cents a day to run it). It then moved four miles east to the home of Mrs. Syd Hook. Later Mrs. Mike Merrett had it and the last postmaster was George Hieser, all had them in their homes or ranch houses. Wideview is good ranching country and we raise fine Hereford and Angus cattle in the district. They are now sold in the sale arena at Mankota. The school is closed now and the children are bussed to Mankota. Some use is made of the building as a community hall and church.

First families into the district included the following: Mr. and Mrs. J. W. Hefner, Mr. and Mrs. Charles Kretlow, the Carlin family, the Andersons, the Bates brothers, Joe Hazelwood, Bill and Rose Highshaw, the Longpre family, Mr. and Mrs. Andy Blum and Mr. and Mrs. Ole Viker.

The Grain Growers were one of the first organizations in the district. They used to put on an annual rodeo a half mile north of our post office and home. At the rodeo there was a booth and many kids got their first ice cream cones there. At night there would be a "Bowery Dance" and sometimes they got very rough. Drunken cowboys fought at the drop of a hat. I remember one time of a cowboy biting another man's ear off.

A great deal of rustling went on in the early days and missing cattle were usually not discovered until round-up time. They were very difficult to trace in spite of their brands."

WILBERT

In 1903 F. J. Scully with his sons Joe and Miah, Bill Dodds (later an MLA from 1917 to 1929), Harvey Wimmer, Horace Dunn, and Tom and Steve Slack took up homesteads in the district. In 1904 Max Hume broke the first land on Mr. Scully's farm. In 1905 J. Doupe opened a country store on NE 16-43-32-W3 about 3 miles southeast of the present townsite. When he made application for a name "Lamont" was suggested in honor of Norman Lamont, a prominent man in the district. Postal officials refused because a town in Alberta already had that name and they suggested "Wilbert." The settlers accepted this even though the name had no significance in the district. James Roe hauled the first mail from Paynton.

The CPR had built through from Wilkie to Cut Knife in 1911 and when in 1923 they started to build on northwest to Lloydminster the first grain point was called Path. This greatly displeased the settlers who not only had a post office, Wilbert, but had built Wilbert school in 1910. James Roe drove about the country with a horse and buggy and had a petition signed to have the name Path changed to Wilbert. He was successful and the post office and store moved in to the townsite. The store has changed hands over the years; Shields, Reas, Twetens, Makares, and today (1973) it is operated by Mr. and Mrs. H. Wood and family.

WILCOX

The Soo Line was put through here by the CPR in 1893. The first settlers came in 1901 and included the following: Hunt, Davis, Smith, Burton, Seward, St. John, Greesen, Scherbel, Sandberg, Tarkelson, Konieczenz, Christie and Schultz. At first the trains did not stop at Wilcox and instead took the settlers' things as far as Milestone, which was a regular stop. From there the goods were transported by wagon to Wilcox, which was at that time merely a mile post — No. 39.

A deal was made in Moose Jaw that if the settlers would name their town Wilcox (after a CPR employee, Albert "Bert" Wilcox) the trains would be stopped there in the future, some spikes pulled and the rails pushed out onto the prairie, and the settlers' cars shunted off from the end of the train. This was agreed and the

method worked successfully. Wilcox was born.

Later Mr. Wilcox joined the staff of the CNR and rose to the position of assistant-general manager.

The next event of importance occurred in 1927 when Father Murray was assigned to the parish of Wilcox. The rest of the story is general knowledge: How Father Murray established, on the bald-headed prairie, Notre Dame of Canada. How, in the heart of the depression, he built a high school and college. Any boy or girl lucky enough to be admitted could get a sound education. A candidate didn't have to be a Catholic or a genius, but had to convince Father Murray that he or she truly wanted to make something of his or her life. And all this happened in a small unused furniture factory that became a classroom; a church basement that was turned into a kitchen; a rectory that became a boys' dormitory; a bank that, after it folded up financially, was taken over as a library (it's still the best building on campus), and on and on.

Many came, boys mostly — when they found they could pay their way, not in cash, but in coal, meat, vegetables, eggs or not at all. Youngsters that wouldn't have had a chance otherwise graduated and made their mark in the world. In the field of education, Frank Germann; in politics, Hon. Cy MacDonald, minister of welfare, and a former teacher in the college; in the business world, Max Bell; the list is endless.

Perhaps, Notre Dame of Canada will best be remembered in the sports world. Their "Hounds", complete with "dog house," took on anyone — anywhere. Nick and Don Metz, Garth Boesch, Gus and Bill Kyle, Chuck McCullough and Jack McLeod were all "power houses" in the world of hockey alone.

Then there was their war record. In World War II it is estimated that 1000 students took part. Their loss is recorded in stained glass under the window of St. Augustine: "In memory of 67 Notre Dame Hounds who gave their life for the City of God."

Father — Monsignor now — is hunched and white haired at 80. It must give him a tremendous feeling of accomplishment as he views the many fine brick buildings that have replaced the threshing outfit bunk cars. Besides his friends, strangers once they heard of his work or came to visit the campus contributed liberally to his dreams. One of the most notable of these contributors was the American novelist Rex Beach who left a legacy of $100,000 to the College.

If Father Murray were given one chance to convey one thought to a person, young or old, it would likely be this, "Every human life is insignificant unless you yourself make it great." This was the basis of the motto he gave his students, "Luctor et emergo" — Struggle and Come Through. That's what Father did.

WILD ROSE

Wild Rose is just a tiny country post office northwest of Prince Albert which you pass on the way to Sturgeon Lake. When it opened early in this century the country was heavy bush and in the clearings wild roses grew in profusion. Hence, the name Wild Rose. In 1966 the Wild Rose 4-H Homecraft Club, under the direction of Mrs. Helen Marquis, won a provincial radio competition using the subject, "Origin of place-names in Saskatchewan."

WILKIE

In 1905 the first settlers entered the district and C. J. Logan established a general store immediately north and a little east of the present townsite and it became known as Glen Logan. Mr. Logan's stock was hauled in from Battleford and North Battleford by the local settlers. When the CPR came through in 1909 it named the town Adanac.

Water was difficult to find at Wilkie, two stations farther west, which had been selected as the divisional point. When a plentiful supply of water was found at Adanac the CPR officials just switched names: Adanac became Wilkie, and what was to be Wilkie became Adanac.

Wilkie was named in honor of D. R. Wilkie, of Toronto, president of the Imperial Bank of Canada, and one of the backers of the CPR.

WILLMAR

Willmar is on a branch line of the CNR that runs from Lampman to Carlyle in the extreme southeast of the province. In 1900 Thomas Larkin, his two brothers, Martin and Gus, and his son, Edwin, took up homesteads in the district. They were influential in having it named for Willmar, Minnesota, USA, the place from which they had emigrated.

Between 1900 and 1905 the following families took up homesteads: Hays, Haddow, Mills and Willocks. The first post office was in the home of Mr. Willocks.

WILLOWBROOK

Willowbrook is on a short branch line of the CNR that ends at Parkerview. It derives its name from the fact that the first store, which by the way served also as a post office, was erected on the bank of a brook or small creek. This brook with its banks covered with pretty low-growing willows drained south and east into the Whitesands river which in turn flowed into the Assiniboine system.

An historic marker just outside the town gives the success story of Charles Avery Dunning, third premier of Saskatchewan.

WILLOW BUNCH

One of the oldest communities in the province, Willow Bunch, some 80 miles south of Regina, is steeped in history.

It was founded in the early 1870s by one of three groups of Metis who decided to leave their native Manitoba when it became a province in 1870. The group, made up of some 30 families, journeyed west to Big Muddy Valley and settled at the present site. The settlement was named Willow Bunch because of the predominance of willow bluffs in the area. The district was heavily wooded, with creeks, springs, lakes and, above all, an abundance of buffalo.

It was here that Sitting Bull moved his tribe north over the Canadian border following the massacre of General Custer's soldiers at the Little Big Horn. It was here that Jean Louis Legare, merchant trader, and trusted adviser of Sitting Bull was able to persuade him to accept the American government's offer of amnesty.

By 1879 the settlement had become permanently established. The records of the church reveal the name of Edouard Beaupre, born and baptized on January 9, 1881. Edouard, the eldest of 20 children born to Mr. and Mrs. Gaspard Beaupre, later became known as the Willow Bunch Giant, grew up to become the tallest man in the world before he reached his 20th birthday. He was eight feet two inches tall and weighed 396 pounds. He was a good cowboy but he had to give it up because his feet trailed on the ground — even from the back of a tall horse. Edouard then joined a travelling exhibition and toured Canada and the United States with the famous Canadian strong-man, Louis Cyre.

WILLOW CREEK

Willow Creek is a customs and immigration checkpoint in the extreme southwest corner of the province. It's south of the sparsely settled Cypress Hills on the Canadian side of the border and about forty miles north of Havre, Montana.

The prairies roll away to the horizon on every side. Only farmers, ranchers, and once in a long while, the stray tourist brave the mud and gravel road linking Saskatchewan with Montana. Mr. Jiggs White is the Canadian customs and immigration officer.

Willow Creek takes its name from Willow creek, a tributary of Lodge creek, which flows south into the great Missouri system. Also there is a Willow Creek, Montana, just a mile or so over the boundary line.

WILLOWFIELD

Jim was only two years old in 1910 when his parents, Mr. and Mrs. Dennis Shatko, came to homestead in the Willowfield district ten miles northeast of Cando, Saskatchewan.

When enough settlers arrived they applied for a post office. Wilfred Daunnais the first postmaster, set up postal service in his home on Section 18-40-14, west of the third meridian. In conjunction with it he operated a small store. He named the post office Willowfield because of its proximity to a large slough around which willows grew in abundance. This, plus the arable land surrounding it, gave him the idea for Willowfield.

The first mail came out from Maymont and Jack Cook, the carrier, made stops at Baljennie, Willowfield and Lizard Lake.

Mr. Daunnais ran a stampede each summer during the early years. Beside the local participants he brought in talent from as far away as Alberta. Usually they went on to take part in the Lizard Lake stampede while they were in Saskatchewan.

Some of the people served by the Willowfield post office were: Middletons, McConnells, J. R. Thompson, the Brennickis, Walter Purkis, Bert McClocklin, the Crows, Pritchards, Ouellettes, Amiotts, Trottiers, Desmalles, Whitfords, and George and Tom Swinley.

A school was built in 1939 and it also took the name Willowfield. Its opening enrolment was thirty-eight pupils.

Mr. Daunnais passed away in 1928 and his son, Charles, continued to operate the post office until he enlisted in the armed services in 1941 at which time the post office closed.

Mr. and Mrs. Jim Shatko provided me with this information and Mr. Shatko added that at one time they had quite a large lake close by known as "Flirting Lake". It was so named when the McConnel's daughter and Cook's son were seen walking beside the lake holding hands. "Just flirtin" was the remark of an oldtimer and so it became "Flirting Lake".

WILLOW RIDGE

Willow Ridge post office opened on November 15, 1915 on the S.E. 26-54-22 W3. It closed on March 31, 1920. The name is self-evident and the postmaster during its short life was Mr. H. Bullen.

WILLOWS

Willows is the first stop east of Assiniboia. It is on a CPR line that almost touches the south end of Lake of the Rivers in south-central Saskatchewan.

The first settlers, the Clark brothers, arrived in 1907 and the district was almost full by 1910. Mr. William Lewis had a country store in the district and when the CPR came through in the spring of 1913, he moved his store to the townsite. By leaving out a letter "l" in Will and an "i" in Lowis you get Willows, hence the name.

The Willows district became famous for its fine pottery clay and during the winter of 1913-1914 some twenty teams were employed in hauling clay to the railroad.

WILLOWVALE

Willowvale was an inland post office southwest of Assiniboia. Its exact location was 9-2-2-W3. It opened on November 1, 1913, with Mr. S. J. McKee as postmaster. He was followed by Mr. Albert E. McKee, Lucius J. Bobster, Mrs. Clara Bobster, and under Mrs. Mae McKee the post office closed on September 18, 1946.

WILSON LAKE

Wilson Lake was an inland post office some 30 miles north and east of Biggar. The settlers in this area were scattered through quite dense bush and as Mr. C. G. Rofe, who homesteaded in the district in 1910, said, "At one time our nearest neighbor lived 18 miles from us." Mr. Coffman had the post office. There was also a Wilson Lake school.

During the 1930s when most small lakes dried up Wilson lake became quite a resort area. People from miles around came to the large sports day held there and many families from Biggar and the surrounding districts had cottages along its shores.

During this time, too, much of the bush was cut and farmers drove as much as thirty or forty miles to buy a wagon-load of poplar poles which were taken home and cut up for firewood. The trip for this wood sometimes took two or three days under what would appear to be very rough conditions yet many of the teenage boys were delighted to be given the chance 'to go to the bush for fuel.' No doubt there would be more chance of adventure on the trail than at home milking the cows.

WIMMER

Wimmer is between Watson and Quill Lake. It bears the name of the first Benedictine Abbot in North America, and the founder of that order in the United States, Rt. Rev. Archabbot Boniface Wimmer, O.S.B.

WINDTHORST

In 1909 the CPR put in the Reston, Manitoba, to Wolseley, Saskatchewan, line very close to the CNR. Windthorst was one of the thriving towns on the line. Such prosperity didn't last; in 1962, the rails were finally taken up completely and sizeable places like Windthorst, Ken-

nedy, Wawota and Walpole found themselves without a railroad. However, roads are so good now that these communities have managed to hang on.

The majority of early settlers in this district were German Catholics and when the town was formed they named it after Ludwig Windthorst one of the organizers and leaders of the Centralist Party in Germany. Windthorst was an able opponent of Count Bismark.

WINGARD

Wingard is the site of one of the few ferries in operation on the North Saskatchewan. There is a post office, a store, an Anglican church, a hall and, until 1965, a school. There is no railroad, the nearest one being the end of the steel at Carlton.

The first settler into the district was Nels Peterson, a carpenter from Denmark who came in 1882. He named it Weingarten which is Danish for Wine Garden. Later, when a considerable group of English settlers moved in, notably Captain William Craig, the name was anglicized to Wingard.

Mr. Peterson built the first ferry in 1895. Previously an old boat or scow had been the means of crossing the river. He received a three-year contract from the government and this agreement is still in the hands of the Peterson family at Wingard. They still farm the land on which their grandfather settled 90 years ago.

Saskatonians who prefer a quiet drive to Waskesiu know the shortest way to the park is via Wingard. They were startled therefore in June, 1966, when near Waldheim they saw a freshly painted sign "To Marcelin Ferry." However, such a fuss was kicked up that the department of highways soon took down their brand new sign and, in this case at least, they shelved their new policy of naming ferries for the nearest "big town."

WINRO

Winro is between Qu'Appelle and Indian Head on the main line of the CPR. When the siding was being built, the men noticed hay in the field placed in what is known as "windrows". The word was abbreviated or letters deleted to read "Winro."

WINSIDE

Mr. and Mrs. Elmer Lapp were a young couple who came west and took up a homestead in 1907 on SW 23-7-26-W2. They built a sod shack and lived in it for two and one-half years. In this building they operated the post office which opened on April 1, 1909. It was named for Mr. Lapp's wife, Winifred. The mail was hauled from Moose Jaw to Willow Bunch and Wood Mountain over the Pole Trail by Mr. Mab Gaudrie. The Winside mail was left at the Denton post office. Here is was picked up by Mr. Lapp or delivered by Mr. Dean, operator of the Denton post office.

The earliest settlers in the district included the following: E. Lapp, R. Stevenson, R. J. Linton, W. Hartness, R. Harrison, S. Atchison, T. Tonberg, E. Palm, C. David, W. Davidson, P. R. Mallory, G. Greenwood, D. Colliette, A. Graham, M. Leibrand, F. Hendrickson, A. Johnson, H. Strasburg, R. J. Bain, I. Wilhelm, J. Howson, D. Williams, R. Boughton, J. Stoves, J. D. Donnell, W. Ernest, J. Lowry, R. Bywroth, Ed Trill, R. Coburn, Art Tarry, R. S. Beckett, C. A. Burnton, W. B. McBride and Ivor Iverson.

Many of the homesteaders were bachelors. Sooner or later most of them had to try their hand at making bread. Mr. Hartness says however it wasn't always successful. On one occasion he made a large batch of bread and tried to make it rise in a cook shack. He worked it over several times and got no results. Finally he threw the whole batch out into the yard. When the warm sun hit it it raised to tremendous proportions and his neighbor, Mr. Mallory, thought he had started to grow some super type of mushroom.

WINTER

Winter is on the main line of the CNR west of Unity. It was named for Mr. O. Winter, the contractor building a section of the GTP railway in that area.

WINTHORPE

Winthorpe is a small rural community fifteen miles south of Foam Lake. At the center of the district is an abandoned Anglican church. It was built in 1912 by a small group of those likeable English people who migrated to the prairies early in this century. Not content to live without a church, as soon as house-building and barn-raising was done, they set about to build one.

Logs were found, hauled and trimmed, and a church building 20 feet wide and 26 feet long was completed. It served as a church, community hall and school for almost three decades. Here is a list of some of the early families: Sentence, Mawer, Harvey, Hallam, Montgomery, Monagham and Martin.

In 1919 the congregation improved the building by sheathing the outside walls with drop siding. And, because they liked the sound of a church bell, they added a belfry and bell topped it with a cross. To commemorate the occasion they placed a marble plaque on an outside wall. It reads:

To the Glory of God

This tablet is placed here to commemorate the siding of the exterior walls of this church as a memorial to Pte. David Woodbury Harvey, who fell in action at Vimy Ridge, France, on the 11th of April 1917, and who was donor of the site upon which the church stands.

As the years passed and the region became settled the number of Anglicans in the district dwindled. Some died, others moved away. Opinions of oldtimers in the district vary somewhat but it appears that the church building has not been used for any purpose since 1939 or 1940. Since poplars have grown up around the building a passing motorist would likely not even notice it. The door is gone now but, because of the density of the tree growth, rain does not blow in on the six-inch maple flooring. Oddly enough, after 30 years of neglect the floor does not sag or squeak and no windows are broken. A pulpit still stands at one end of the building. Hidden and protected by the poplars the church building now stands abandoned, musty with memories of other, better days.

WINTON

Winton is an inland post office southeast of Prince Albert. It is located at 18-48-23-W2. Mrs. Olivia Hunt was the first postmistress and she named it for her hometown, Winton, Minnesota.

WISETON

The steel reached this district in 1913. A townsite was laid out and duly named

342

Sharp in honor of Walter Sharp from whom the land had been purchased.

The name didn't last long. In the same year it was changed to Wiseton to honor Sir Frederic Wise, an influential Englishman, who made a trip across the Prairies with officials of the railway company.

WISHART

Wishart is the end of the steel of a 27 mile long branch line of the CPR south and west from Foam Lake. It was named for Robert Wishart one of the early homesteaders in the district.

WITCHEKAN

Witchekan, an inland post office (now closed), was just off the northeast corner of Witchekan Lake. The Indians named this lake long before white men came to the country. In the very early years it went dry and all the fish in it died leaving a very strong smell. In Cree Witchekan means "Stinking."

The first settlers into the area were ranchers and great hay meadows surrounded the lake. When the CNR built east from Medstead to Shellbrook in 1928, the town of Spiritwood grew up just south of Witchekan Lake.

WIWA HILL

Wiwa Hill was an early inland post office which opened in the home of S. G. James on 18-13-5-W2. The post office is closed now and the residents of the locality get their mail at Shamrock.

Wiwa is a Cree word which means when literally translated "his wife." We were not able to find the significance of this in connection with the name of the post office.

WOLFE

Wolfe is on the main line of the CPR about halfway between Wilkie and North Biggar. No one lives permanently in Wolfe any more. Cliff Lindgren, the Pool agent at Traynor, comes up and buys grain one day a week. Across the tracks Doug Graham, who lives in Cando, has fixed up the elevator agent's house to be used in spring and harvest. His machinery stretches out along the right-of-way and he farms 1300 acres in the district. The school, closed since 1961, and one section house are all that is left of a once-thriving community.

In 1905 Russell and Jim Palmer homesteaded the land adjoining the present elevator site. Russell Palmer remembers that the first post office in the district was named Crocus and it was run by Ruby Cushing who brought the mail from Battleford.

Other oldtimers in the district were: Herbert W. Walker, George Henry Wilders, James McMaster, Alfred Newman, Jim Whitting, Tom Wright, Sidney Bingham, Neil Jillsett and Van Every.

When the railway arrived in 1908 the officials named the townsite Wolfe, in honor of Major-General James Wolfe (1727-1759) who commanded the English expedition against Quebec in 1759. He successfully scaled the heights to the Plains of Abraham and routed the French under Montcalm, thus completing the British conquest of North America. Both he and Montclam fell mortally wounded on the field.

The streets and avenues of Wolfe bear the following names: Railway Avenue is there, as in most prairie towns, and there is one other, St. Alphege, named for the grain point between Wolfe and Wilkie. The other five are Carleton, Dorchester, Colborne, Elgin and Amherst—which takes in an imposing amount of Canadian history.

Money was tight in homestead times and when it was discovered that Willie McTavish, a grade one student in Crocus School, needed glasses it was of some concern to the family. Glasses and case were procured and when the mother next saw the teacher she cautioned her to help Willie to take good care of his glasses and to be sure he took them off and put them in the case when he wasn't looking at anything.

WOLLASTON LAKE POST

Wollaston Lake is a settlement midway on the east shore of the large lake of the same name in northeastern Saskatchewan. It was likely named for a township in Hastings county, in Ontario, which was set up in 1837. It in turn was named for Dr. William Hyde Wollaston (1766-1828), a celebrated chemist of London. He added to Daltons' atom theory, and was honoured with the presidency of the Royal Society.

WOLSELEY

In November, 1869, Louis Riel and his followers seized Fort Garry and set up a "provisional government." The Red River Rebellion was born. It was short lived. On the 24th of August 1870 Colonel Garnet J. Wolseley led an armed force from Eastern Canada into Winnipeg to quell the disturbance. Not a shot was fired. Riel had fled to the United States. Wolseley is named in honor of Colonel G. J. Wolseley—later Sir Garnet J. Wolseley.

WOLVERINE

Wolverine is a grain point of two elevators on the CPR between Plunkett and Guernsey. It is named for Wolverine lake, a long narrow lake to the north that stretches almost to Humboldt and which is drained by Wolverine creek into Humboldt lake just south of Muenster. The Carlton Trail crossed Wolverine creek on its way west from Fort Garry to Edmonton.

The following excerpt from an article which appeared in the Esterhazy "Observer" on September 2, 1948, gives the story behind the naming of Wolverine creek:

"Although thousands of people cross this creek each year, few indeed know that its name is derived from an Indian legend steeped in romance and tragedy.

Long ago, according to this legend, there lived a Cree warrior named the Wolverine, whose lot it was to suffer the extreme misfortune both in love and in war. As with many others of his sex, a woman brought about his undoing. What were his shortcomings as a husband is not known, but we are told that the affections of his squaw were stolen by a brave of the Assiniboine tribe and that she deserted her own people and joined the band to which her lover belonged.

It is not unusual for deserters to feel a more intense hatred for former associates than do their natural enemies. If bad blood had existed between the two tribes previously, it may have been fanned to white heat by the renegade squaw.

Possibly at her instigation, the Assiniboines attacked the little band of Crees in the vicinity of what is now Spy Hill. All were massacred except the Wolverine, who, though wounded, escaped and crawled to the top of the hill. But he was to have no respite from the fury of the vengeful squaw; she trailed the luckless Wolverine to his resting place and killed him in his sleep.

Before the survey, the scene of the tragedy was called Wolverine Hill or Butte a Carajar by the Indians and halfbreeds. A large slough near the hill is still known as Wolverine Slough. Hind's map of 1857-58 designated the present Deerhorn creek as Wolverine creek, while our present Wolverine creek was called Big Valley creek. In the surveyors' reports of 1884, the creek nearest Spy Hill is called both the Red Deer Horn and the Wolverine, and the creek north of what is now Marchwell is referred to as Smith's creek, although it was known to the settlers of that time as Wolverine and the early settlement was called by the same name.

It seems highly probable that among the early freighters, traders and buffalo hunters the names of the two neighboring creeks were often confused and the term Wolverine applied loosely to both, until finally Deerhorn became the accepted name of the one while Wolverine remained the local name of the other. Undoubtedly all the applications of the name were derived from the Wolverine legend.

Forgotten is the name of the murderous squaw and forgotten is that of her Assiniboine lover, but the memory of the Wolverine is as enduring as the green hills above the creek which bears his name."

WOOD MOUNTAIN

The town of Wood Mountain got its name from a low range of hills that runs along the south central boundary of the province. The name was first given to the old NWMP post four miles south of the present town. This post had a stirring story in Saskatchewan's history.

In the fall of 1874, the North West Mounted Police purchased the International Boundary Commission Supply Depot at Wood Mountain. That winter, a number of sick animals were left there in charge of two constables, the rest of the force returned to Fort Livingstone.

When Fort Walsh was established in May, 1875, the detachment was removed and the rude log structures were used as an occasional stopping place for police patrols. When Sitting Bull and the Sioux under his command or influence crossed the boundary following the Battle of the Little Big Horn, the NWMP established an important detachment at Wood Mountain. From the fall of 1876 until 1881 this post was at the center of an amazing saga which saw a handful of men control the proud and powerful Sioux Nation.

From 1882 until the closing of the post in 1918, the Wood Mountain Detachment handled important duties of border patrol, stock inspection, the aiding of new settlers in the area as well as normal police duties. Throughout most of this period, the detachment based here patrolled an area stretching halfway across the province along the International Boundary.

In 1928 the CPR ran a branch line west from Maxstone to Mankota and it passed four miles north of this old post. The town that grew up by the tracks took its name from the old NWMP Post, Wood Mountain.

The first post office in Wood Mountain opened on August 8, 1894, with Mr. J. H. Thomson as postmaster. It had ten postmasters before the office was closed out by Mrs. Millie Nicholson on July 31, 1964.

WOOD RIVER

Wood River was an inland post office south of Lafleche on the Wood river which flows north into Old Wives' lake. It took its name from the Wood river which in turn took its name from Wood Mountain.

WOODROW

In December, 1908, the land in this area was opened for homestead filing. Squatters who were here in '06 and '07 were given the first opportunity to file. When the CPR was built in 1913 the officials had chosen "Weedy" as the name for the townsite. This was an unhappy selection as far as the citizens of the community were concerned. They resisted. The residents, predominately former Americans, chose to honor Woodrow Wilson, who was the newly elected president of the United States. They submitted the name Woodrow and it was accepted.

WORCESTER

Worcester is a small place just outside of Weyburn. The Grand Trunk road bed was laid in 1910 and the rails came in 1912. Previous to that the mail was hauled by team from Fillmore to the home of Mr. Sproat. He named the post office "Rainton" after a town in Ontario.

Due to confusion of two names Rainton and Paynton, the post office department asked Rainton to change its name. It is now Worcester named so by two gentlemen of the district who came from Worcester, England.

WORDSWORTH

The railroad officials gave Wordsworth its name. William Wordsworth (1770-1850) was one of the great British poets of the romantic era. He is not the only author of note to be so honored by having a Saskatchewan town named for him. In fact, within a very short distance of Wordsworth towns are named for the following authors: Archibald Lampman, Robert Browning, Thomas Carlyle, Robert Service, William Cowper, and Edgerton Ryerson.

WROXTON

Wroxton is located on a CNR line less than twenty-five miles east of Yorkton. It was first settled by Scottish immigrants and M. A. Matheson, a former postmaster, named the townsite. It is an English name and probably honors Wroxton, England, a large market-town southeast of Birmingham in Warwickshire.

Some of the first settlers who came into the district in the 1880's were: Nick Kostenuk, George Pringle, Ab MacDonald, George Lane, Harry Mapleton, Jim Muffet and the Jacob brothers. They ranched and delivered their cattle to the railhead at Saltcoats.

The first school was built in the district in 1905 and named Scotland. The first railway was the Canadian Northern built in 1908-10. It went west from Calder, through Wroxton and on to Stornoway. The branch line from Wroxton to Yorkton was built in 1913-14. Business places sprang up because of the passenger and freight trains along the line. The first station was built in 1913 and the first agent was Jack Robinson.

Wroxton's first car was a Gray Dort owned by William McGillivray. The first post office in the district was opened at Starleigh in 1910, four miles west of Wroxton. Later it was moved close to Scotland School and in 1911 it was moved into Wroxton by the postmaster, Mr. Matheson and renamed Wroxton.

In 1970 the population of the village was 125. There were four elevators, three grocery stores, a liquor store, one cafe, a municipal office, one shoe shop, a hall, and a combined curling rink and skating rink and a school. The school had 42 pupils. There were three teachers and eight grades. All this information came from Arlene Kostenuik, a grade eight pupil at Wroxton.

WYATT

Wyatt is the first grain point south of Swift Current on a branch line of the CPR that runs to Simmie. It was named after a 14th century English merchant. This information came from CPR files.

WYCOLLAR

This post office located at 29-43-35-W3 was in a store owned by Hartley Walton. He named it Wycollar after his home in Lancashire, England. Mr. Robert Graham hauled the mail from Lashburn by team once a week. Early homesteaders were: Joe and Bill Kessell, Sandy McMillan, Mr. and Mrs. Jas. McKague and family, Arthur Rose, the McIntyre family, Dave Rogers and Max Campbell.

Max Campbell remained in the district and in 1945 and again in 1953 was elected to the federal government.

WYMARK

Wymark is fifteen miles south and one mile east of Swift Current. It has one of the most interesting names in all of Saskatchewan. When the CPR built southeast of Swift Current in 1911 the first survey went right into Springfeldt. This Mennonite village didn't want it so the railway was put in a mile north and a townsite developed about a mile or so

northeast of the village. At first a "Y" was put in for trains to turn around and then when the line was extended it branched off in a "Y" at Hak to go to Tyson to the east and Meyronne to the southeast. Hence, the railroad men gave it the name Wymark.

Wymark developed into a very fine town with three elevators and many modern buildings. Lately (1972) it has dropped back a bit due to improved communications and its proximity to the thriving little center of Swift Current. There has even been talk of closing some of the elevators. However, it has many fine spacious homes and it is not likely to "dry up" as many other towns and villages in Saskatchewan have done over the past decade.

WYNOT

Wynot is an inland post office ten miles north of Lestock. It was named in 1909 by the late G. M. Atkinson who was MLA for Touchwood 1908-1917.

The first Wynot post office was in the home of Sidney Brown. In succession Mr. F. Powel had it, then Mr. D. F. McRae and now Mrs. Charles Howitt. Among the earliest settlers were the following: Walter Fee, Gavin Strong, Reverend Gilbert Cook, James McInnes, James Neeby and Charles Perry.

WYNYARD

The first settlers began to come to Wynyard in the year 1903. In 1909 the first train went through Wynyard. The first railroad agent was W. H. McNalley, who came from Sheho, Sask., in 1909. The railroad was CPR.

The name "Wynyard" was given the town by a CPR official, F. W. Peters, who asked his wife to suggest a name. She chose that of her family who resided in England.

Miss Anna Munro was the first school teacher. She taught from 1909 to 1912.

The first settlers were Icelandic people and the first overseer was S. A. Sigfusson.

X

XENA

The Grand Trunk Pacific, as map-readers have observed, employed the

device of naming stations on its main line in alphabetical order. Consequently, letters of the alphabet were used several

346

times, between Winnipeg and Edmonton, as the initial letter of the station, but "X" was used only once. This was at Xena, a village 56 miles southeast of Saskatoon, between the towns of Watrous and Young. We do not know the significance of the word Xena.

Y

YANKEE BEND

Yankee Bend is a settlement 32 miles north of Lloydminster and right across the river from Frenchman Butte. The name originated because many of the early settlers were Americans. Some of the more prominent were: Frank, Bert, Ralph and Floyd Howard; Ben Mudge; Bob and Ken Hougham; Earl, Ray and Barney Shars; S. Sidwell; W. W. Campbell; Mr. Hackrot and Mr. Flanders.

As other settlers came in they frowned on the name Yankee Bend and it was decided to call the school North Bend. Their mail came from Lloydminster first and later came from the hamlet of Greenstreet which is 12 miles south of the "Bend."

The year of 1910 was known as "Rabbit Winter." Livestock was scarce and not to be slaughtered for meat, but the prolific jack rabbits were healthy and freely used to supplement the other game which was plentiful. The rabbits were stewed, roasted, and made into rich rabbit pie. All these dishes were delicious — if you were hungry. Frank Howard tells of hauling grain out to Turtleford that winter. He cheered himself along the cold trail with the thought of a thick juicy steak for supper, a rare treat after months of rabbit diet.

He seated himself in the warm cafe and beamed as the Chinese proprietor came to call out the menu: "Labbit Steak, Labbit Loast, and Labbit Pie. . . ." offered his host!

YARBO

Yarbo is between Cutarm and Zeneta on a CNR line southeast of Melville. In the 1920's Yarbo was a lively little place with two grain elevators (Pool and National), a general store, post office, station and all other facilities that went to make up a prairie community.

The 1930's took their toll and Yarbo faded until the 1960's when potash was successfully mined in the area.

Mrs. Elmer Iverson (nee Milne) of Agincourt, Ontario, writes that on a recent visit to her home town it was hard to recognize the place any more. New roads had been built, houses had sprung up almost overnight and farms had changed hands.

Yarbo is not the only local town to feel the results of the potash boom, Esterhazy, Gerald and Churchbridge are growing. Esterhazy, with a population of 4,000 is the largest and is well on its way to becoming a city.

YELLOW CREEK

Yellow Creek takes its name from the nearby Yellow creek which flows north into Waterhen lake. Three of the first settlers to come in 1914 were John Nowak, Mike Romanow and Julian Borsa.

YELLOW GRASS

When the CPR surveyors came to the town late in the fall of 1885 the frost had hit the grass. The townsite was low and the grass was high and late in the evening when looking into the setting sun the foreman of the crew exclaimed to his men, "Look at the yellow grass!" The name stuck. Most of the other towns on the "Soo Line" are named for officials of the CPR, but not this one.

YEOMAN

Yeoman is on a CPR line about ten miles straight west of Weyburn. Originally yeoman meant a young man who was an attendant or manservant in a royal or noble household. However, the meaning that fits the name used in Saskatchewan is that of a yeoman as a freeholder of a class below the gentry, who worked his own land.

Land, "ten dollars for 160 acres," was the lure that brought thousands of immigrants from every walk of life to the prairies. To work your own land was a wonderful feeling; hard to convey to urban dwellers.

YONKER
Yonker is the first station west of Winter. Mr. W. O. Winter was the contractor building a section of the GTP railway in that area. Mr. Winter named Yonker for a sentimental reason. It was the maiden name of his mother.

Early settlers who came in 1907 included William Robinson, Malcolm Mack, John Murray, Thomas Morrison, John Parker, and John and George Pagett. They were soon joined by Mr. and Mrs. Jesse Strum, Bob, Dick and Ed Cammidge, Mr. and Mrs. Thomas Meagher and family, and Albert Dustow.

There was no store or post office until the following year and mail and supplies were brought from Lashburn which was 30 miles away.

The steel came in 1908 and the first store was opened that fall by Tommy Holmes.

YORKTON
The small town of York City, Assiniboia, Northwest Territories, was established in 1882 on the banks of a tributary of the Whitesand river about three miles northeast of the present site of the city of Yorkton. It was established by the York Farmers' Colonization Company as a trading center for the settlers of the York Colony. It retained that name until the postal authorities established the first post office in 1884 and named it Yorkton.

YOUNG
Young, "The Diamond of the Prairie," is the second stop west of Watrous on the CNR. It certainly had hopes of becoming a city — a "Hub City." The CPR had built a line from Regina north to Colonsay and Young was the "diamond" where it crossed the main east-west line of the GTP. The CNR later built north from Young to Prince Albert. There was also a proposed CNR line from Young to Yorkton on the east and Zealandia on the west. In addition there was a proposed GTP line from Young to Swift Current. Early hopes did not materialize and the divisional point went to Watrous. Even though there were an unusually large number of railroads serving Young it did not grow as anticipated.

Young started out big in farming, too, with the Middleton Farm putting 8640 acres into crop. It's still a good grain point with four elevators in operation.

Young, put in alphabetical order, honors Mr. F. G. Young, a real estate agent of the village who also handled insurance and loans.

YOUNG'S SIDING
Young's Siding is a short distance north of Yorkton on a CNR line to Canora. It received its name because the land for it was bought from John Young.

Z

ZANGWILL
Zangwill, six miles north of Young on a CPR line that ran from Regina to Colonsay, had a great start. It had a water tower, a station, a section house, a post office and store, and was served by three passenger trains a day. All this has gone and except for the railway right-of-way it is now farm land.

Mr. Arthur Todd of 707 9th Street, Saskatoon, was one of the first into the district. He arrived in 1906. He walked to his homestead from Hanley — about 40 miles. Others who soon followed included the following: John Larsen, Joe Broughten, Bill Boneham, Frank Molner, J. I. Cross, Charlie Bishop, Donald and Jim McVee, George Gale and Tom Moffatt.

Mr. Todd drove oxen for years and his first four were named Bright, Buck, Tom and Dart. The mosquitoes were awful in the early days and he used to see his black ox, Buck, just grey with them. Small wonder then that they sometimes took the equivalent of an unscheduled "coffee break" and dragged plowman and all into a convenient slough. Mr. Todd had this happen to him and I asked him how he got them out. "Well," he said, "I just carried a big strap and when I felt they had had enough I vigorously strapped them and we'd all come out and go back to work!" In the evenings smudges had to be made to make life bearable for man and beast. It took four oxen to a single furrow because the virgin prairie (especially if it was dry) was tough turf to turn. It took Mr. Todd four years to break 90 acres.

The most exciting development in the last few years has been the Zelma Reservoir in a chain of little lakes to service the potash mines in the area.

ZEALANDIA
When it came time for Zealandia to be named it was found that the railway officials had already selected Brock. The residents of the district disputed this. They suggested that the old timers of the district should be given a chance to submit names. Many did so and Mr. Inglebrett's suggestion of Zealandia was chosen. He had proposed this name in memory of New Zealand, his homeland.

ZEHNER
On the CNR line northwest from Regina to Melville the second stop is Zehner. We don't know how it got its name but we do know it is the birthplace of John Vernon, born Adolphus Raymondus Vernon Agopsowicz, a son of early Polish immigrants to the district.

In centennial year CBC-TV's top-rated program, after hockey, was "Wojeck". In it John Vernon played the part of Steve Wojeck, in a series about the underside of life as a big-city coroner sees it.

ZELMA
The towns along the Grand Trunk line were named in alphabetical order, and a name starting with "Z" had been chosen for the village. Local authorities disagree on how the name Zelma came to be selected. Some say it was drawn out of thin air; others say that Dr. Edgar suggested Zelma because that was the name of his sister-in-law (Mrs. Charlie Thode of Saskatoon). Whatever the explanation, the name was assigned to the site and with the completion of the railway in the fall of 1908, the village of Zelma began to take form.

ZENETA
Zeneta is between Yarbo and Atwater on a railway built by the old GTP. The name has no significance. It was just placed in alphabetical order in the interests of railway efficiency.

The line came through in 1907. Section 22 on which Zeneta stands had four homesteaders: Jack Lilly, Charlie Stack, Peter Fitzsimmons and Donald Mike. The railway bought them out for $2400. Other homesteaders at that time were Steve, Oliver and Arthur Pask, Pete Warmer, Howard Spence and Jim Baldwin.

At the start Zeneta was quite an important place. A good-sized station was built, stockyards were erected, a post office was established, two grocery stores opened, and several grain elevators were built. In other words all the things an average pairie town needed to service a community were there.

Zeneta had one thing extra. An American company bought up several sections of land north of the town and ranched. A large main ranch house was built with a smaller bunk house for the men. It was called the Polar Star Ranch.

There was little left in Zeneta by 1970, just the elevators, a store and post office combined and a handful of dwellings.

ZENON PARK
The first postmaster was Mr. Zenon Chamberland whose homestead was at what is now known as Four Corners. On Mr. Chamberland's land there was a small park or recreation ground where the people of the district gathered on Sunday afternoons and other holidays. With the granting of a post office, it was necessary to have an official name for the new district. Raymond Courteau and Zenon Chamberland journeyed to New Osgoode, the nearest post office, to fill in the necessary papers, and at the suggestion of Mrs. Sam Cook, at that time postmistress at New Osgoode, the name Zenon Park was submitted and later accepted.

ZUMBRO
Zumbro is on a CPR line just south of Manito lake and the second last stop before the railway enters Alberta.

The name has no significance. It is just the last of a long line of alphabetical names that start at Reford, over fifty miles to the southeast.

It's in rough, hilly, sandy country and

the grain point never consisted of more than a loading platform and a small station house.

When the line was put through in 1908, Mr. W. O. Winter was the contractor building a section of the GTP railway in that area. It is reputed that he called it Zumbro for his dog.